Reference Guide to Pascal Statements

Statement	Example of Use
program heading	`program GUIDE (INPUT, OUTPUT, INFILE, OUTFILE);`
comment	`{This section shows examples of Pascal statements.}` `(* Comments are ignored by Pascal. *)`

constant declaration
  integer
  character
  string
  real
	`const`
	`    STRINGSIZE = 20;`
	`    BLANK = ' ';`
	`    SCHOOL = 'TEMPLE UNIVERSITY';`
	`    DEANSLIST = 3.5;   PROBATION = 1.0;`

type declaration
  enumerated
  subrange
  string
  pointer
  record
 	
  array
  file
  set
	`type`
	`    COLLEGE = (BUSINESS, ARTS, EDUCATION, GENERAL);`
	`    STUDENTRANGE = 1..100;`
	`    STRING = packed array [1..STRINGSIZE] of CHAR;`
	`    CLASSPOINTER = ^STUDENT;`
	`    STUDENT = record`
	`        NAME : STRING;`
	`        GPA : REAL;`
	`        INCOLLEGE : COLLEGE;`
	`        NEXTSTU : CLASSPOINTER`
	`    end;  {STUDENT}`
	`    MAJORARRAY = array [STUDENTRANGE] of COLLEGE;`
	`    STUFILE = file of STUDENT;`
	`    GRADESET = set of 'A'..'Z';`

variable declaration
  record
  set
  text file
  file
  pointer
  array
  character
  integer
	`var`
	`    CURSTU : STUDENT;`
	`    GRADES : GRADESET;`
	`    INFILE : TEXT;`
	`    OUTFILE : STUFILE;`
	`    CLASSLIST : CLASSPOINTER;`
	`    MAJOR : MAJORARRAY;`
	`    NEXTCH : CHAR;`
	`    I, COUNTPROBATION : INTEGER;`

declaring function
  with BOOLEAN
  result
	`function MEMBER (NEXTCH : CHAR;`
	`                  TESTSET : GRADESET) : BOOLEAN;`
	`{Returns TRUE if NEXTCH is a member of TESTSET.}`

assignment (BOOLEAN)
set membership
	`begin {MEMBER}`
	`    MEMBER := NEXTCH in TESTSET  {Is NEXTCH in set?}`
	`end;  {MEMBER}`

(continued on last page)

Problem Solving and Structured Programming in Pascal

SECOND EDITION

Problem Solving and Structured Programming in Pascal

SECOND EDITION

ELLIOT B. KOFFMAN
Temple University

ADDISON-WESLEY PUBLISHING COMPANY, INC.
Reading, Massachusetts • Menlo Park, California •
Don Mills, Ontario • Wokingham, England • Amsterdam •
Sydney • Singapore • Tokyo • Mexico City • Bogotá •
Santiago • San Juan

This book is in the Addison-Wesley Series in Computer Science

James T. DeWolf, Sponsoring Editor

Hugh Crawford, Manufacturing Supervisor
Robert Forget, Art Editor
Fran Palmer Fulton, Production Editor
Karen M. Guardino, Production Manager
Richard Hannus, Hannus Design Associates, Cover Design
Maureen Langer, Text Designer

Library of Congress Cataloging in Publication Data

Koffman, Elliot B.
    Problem solving and structured programming in
Pascal.

    Includes index.
    1. Pascal (Computer program language)   2. Structured
programming.   I.   Title.
QA76.73.P2K63   1985   001.64'24   84-16811
ISBN 0-201-11736-3

Turbo Pascal™ is a trademark of Borland International, Inc.

Reprinted with corrections June, 1986

EFGHIJ-DO-89876

To my family—Caryn, Richard, Deborah, and Robin Koffman, for their constant love and understanding.

To my parents—Edward and Leah Koffman, for all that they have given me.

Preface

There have been many changes in the way the first course in Computer Science is taught since the first edition of this book was published in 1981. During the past two years I have been the chairman of the ACM Task Force that has been studying these changes with an eye towards updating the description of the recommended first course for Computer Science majors (CS1).[1] Parallel with this effort, the Educational Testing Service (ETS) published a set of guidelines for an Advanced Placement course in Computer Science.[2] The text has been completely revised and reorganized to conform to both of these guidelines.

This text can be used in any introductory programming course that emphasizes a careful, disciplined approach to programming in Pascal. Since the Advanced Placement course is a full year course, this text covers more material than would normally be completed in one semester. The additional material on searching and sorting algorithms (Chapter 9) and dynamic data structures (Chapter 10) are optional advanced topics in CS1 and would normally be deferred until CS2.

As in the first edition, the primary goal of this text is to illustrate and teach problem solving through the stepwise development of algorithms. To facilitate this, procedures are introduced much earlier in this edition. There are also several large case studies throughout the text that integrate

---

[1] Koffman, E., Miller, P., and Wardle, C. Recommended Curriculum for CS1, 1984. Communications ACM 27, 10 (Oct., 1984), 998-1001.

[2] Advanced Placement Program of the College Board, Advanced Placement Course Description: Computer Science, Educational Testing Service, Princeton, NJ, 1983.

topics and illustrate their application in a substantial programming problem with multiple procedures. Many new examples and programming assignment projects are provided.

Some of the important features of this new edition are:

Early introduction of procedures: Procedures without parameters are introduced in Chapter 2 and are used for self-contained operations that require no global variable access (no side-effects). Procedure parameters are discussed in Chapter 3. Early coverage of procedures will enable students to practice the top-down approach from the beginning and to become more adept at program modularization.

Interactive programming: The emphasis is on modern technology and interactive programming. The majority of examples are written as interactive programs; however, students are shown early how to convert these programs to run in a batch environment. There are some batch-oriented examples as well.

New chapter on recursion: There is a new chapter on recursion that provides many examples of recursive procedures and functions. Additional algorithms for searching and sorting arrays are also provided in this chapter.

Arrays: Single and multidimensional arrays are covered in one chapter instead of in two as in the first edition. Similarly, all material on records is covered in a single chapter.

New expanded case studies: There are a number of new, larger case studies within the text. The solutions to the case studies are all carefully developed. System structure charts are used to represent the flow of control and data between modules in a program system.

Spiral approach: A spiral approach is used to preview topics such as the `if` statement, `for` statement, and input/output. Features are introduced as needed rather than overwhelming a student by providing all the details at once.

Pedagogical aids:
- Self-check Exercises are provided at the end of most sections. Solutions to selected exercises are provided at the end of the text.
- Each chapter ends with a Chapter Review section that includes a summary, a table of new Pascal statements, and review questions.
- *Boxed material*: Syntax display boxes are used to describe the syntax of each new Pascal statement as it is introduced, while Program Style boxes discuss the importance of good programming style.
- *Error warnings*: Each chapter ends with a discussion geared toward helping students prevent and correct common programming errors. Several sections discuss debugging techniques.
- *Program comments*: All programs are carefully commented. Loop invariants and assertions are shown for some loops. For easy identification, the first and last line of each procedure or program is in blue type.

New design: The page layout is larger providing more white space and the overall tone is more user-friendly. The book has been completely re-designed with an eye towards making it easier for students to find figures, examples, programs, and special display boxes. A second color is used both to improve the appearance of the text and to clarify illustrations.

Pascal dialects: ANSI standard Pascal is covered in the text. Common extensions are described in appendixes on ISO standard Pascal, UCSD Pascal and Turbo Pascal.

Reference appendixes: There are also appendixes covering Pascal language elements, syntax diagrams, character codes, and error messages.

Complete instructor's manual: An Instructor's Manual provides a discussion of how to teach the concepts in each chapter. Sample test questions will be included as well as answers to all exercises, chapter review questions, and the Programming Projects found at the end of each chapter.

Transparency masters: A set of 131 transparency masters illustrating important concepts is available upon request.

Acknowledgments

Many people participated in the development of this text. The principal reviewers were most essential in finding errors and suggesting improvements. They include: William Eccles, University of South Carolina; Frank Friedman, Temple University; David Hannay, Union College; Helen Holzbaur, Temple University; Abraham Kandel, Florida State University; Raymond Kirsch, LaSalle College; David Moffat, North Carolina State University; Tom Nelson, North Carolina State University; Richard Rinewalt, University of Texas at Arlington; Paul Ross, Millersville University of Pennsylvania; Chris Speth, Western Kentucky University; Caroline Wardle, Boston University; Charles C. Weems, Jr., University of Massachusetts at Amherst; and Brad Wilson, Western Kentucky University. I am grateful to all of them for their considerable efforts.

Towards the beginning of this project, several faculty and members of the Addison-Wesley sales and marketing staffs participated in focus groups to discuss the first programming course in Pascal. These discussions were helpful in providing direction to the text and clarifying its organization. The faculty are: Linda Ottenstein, Michigan Tech University; David Neusse, University of Wisconsin at Eau Claire; Richard Rinewalt, University of Texas at Arlington; Ruth Barton, Michigan State University; and Howard Edelman, West Chester State University.

Finally, a number of faculty reviewed and commented on preliminary sections of the text. These faculty include: Gideon Frieder, University of Michigan; Gary Ford, University of Colorado; Abraham Kandel, Florida State University; Paul Hanna, Florida State University; M. Main, University of Colorado; Kent Wooldridge, California State University at Chico; Richard St. Andre, Central Michigan University; C. E. Wolf, Iowa State University; Angela Wu, American University; Yure Gurevich, University of

Michigan; Amir Foroudi, State University of New York at Fredonia; Morris Rang, II, Western Illinois University; Peggy R. Ayres, Linn-Benton Community College; Muhammed H. Chaudhary, Millersville University of Pennsylvania; Stanley Thomas, Wake Forest University; R. J. Del Zoppo, Jamestown Community College; David Rosenlof, Sacramento City College; George Beekman, Oregon State University; George Witter, Western Washington State University; J. M. Adams, New Mexico State University; John Lushbough, University of South Dakota; Dave Valentine, State University of New York at Potsdam; Dennis Martin, State University of New York at Brockport; Chris J. Dovolis, University of Minnesota; Barbara Smith-Thomas, University of North Carolina at Greensboro; Barent Johnson, University of Wisconsin at Oshkosh; Carl Wehner, University of Northern Iowa; Aboalfazl Salimi, Embry-Riddle University; Larry Wilson, Old Dominion University; Cary Laxer, Rose-Hulman Institute of Technology; J. Mailen Kootsey, Duke University; Jerry Waxman, City University of New York at Queens; Bruce J. Klein, Grand Valley State College; Eris Pas, Duke University; Gove Effinger, Bates College; Krishna Moorthy, Framingham State College; Brian Johnson, University of New Hampshire; and John Goda, Georgia Institute of Technology.

There were also many people involved with the actual production of the text. From Addison-Wesley, James DeWolf was the sponsoring editor and recruited reviewers, provided input and suggestions during the writing stage, and coordinated with the production staff. Bill Gruener also was the publisher with overall responsibility for the text. Karen Guardino was the production manager and saw to it that the book was able to meet a very tight production schedule. Maureen Langer refined the design of the text. In Philadelphia, Fran Palmer Fulton served as the Production Editor and coordinated and supervised the typesetting of the manuscript. I am grateful to all of them for their involvement and extra efforts to get this book published on schedule.

Philadelphia, PA   E.B.K.
December 1984

Contents

1   Introduction to Computers and Programming   1

1.1	Electronic Computers Then and Now	2
1.2	Components of a Computer	3
1.3	Problem Solving and Programming	6
1.4	Programming Languages	7
1.5	Processing a High-level Language Program	9
1.6	Introduction to Pascal	11
1.7	General Form of a Pascal Program	22
1.8	Using the Computer	26
1.9	Formatting Program Output	29
1.10	Introduction to Data Types	34
1.11	Common Programming Errors	36
1.12	Chapter Review	39

2   Problem Solving   45

2.1	Representing and Refining Algorithms	46
2.2	Using Procedures for Subproblems	52
2.3	Decision Steps in Algorithms	59
2.4	Tracing a Program or Algorithm	67
2.5	Problem Solving Strategies	69

2.6	Repetition in Programs	72
2.7	Generalizing a Solution	79
2.8	Repeating a Program Body	83
2.9	Debugging and Testing Programs	87
2.10	Common Programming Errors	88
2.11	Chapter Review	89

3   Control Statements   95

3.1	Syntax Diagrams	96
3.2	The if Statement Revisited	97
3.3	The while Statement	104
3.4	Procedure Parameters	111
3.5	Adding Data Flow Information to Structure Charts	128
3.6	Nested Procedures and Scope of Identifiers	132
3.7	Case Studies	136
3.8	Debugging a Program System	150
3.9	Common Programming Errors	151
3.10	Chapter Review	152

4   Simple Data Types   159

4.1	Constant Declarations	160
4.2	Numeric Data Types—REAL and INTEGER	161
4.3	Functions in Arithmetic Expressions	169
4.4	BOOLEAN Variables, Expressions, and Operators	175
4.5	Character Variables and Functions	180
4.6	Introduction to Programmer-defined Data Types	188
4.7	Input/Output Revisited	193
4.8	Case Study	201
4.9	Common Programming Errors	206
4.10	Chapter Review	207

5   More Control Statements   217

5.1	The case Statement	218
5.2	Set Values in Decisions	221
5.3	The General for Statement	223

5.4 The repeat Statement 225
5.5 Nested Loops 229
5.6 User-defined Functions 234
5.7 Case Studies 240
5.8 Common Programming Errors 251
5.9 Chapter Review 252

6   Arrays   263

6.1 Declaring and Referencing Arrays 264
6.2 Arrays with Integer Subscripts 266
6.3 Case Study 270
6.4 Manipulating Entire Arrays 276
6.5 Reading Part of an Array 282
6.6 General Arrays 283
6.7 Character Strings 288
6.8 Multidimensional Arrays 295
6.9 Case Study 302
6.10 Common Programming Errors 313
6.11 Chapter Review 313

7   Records   325

7.1 Declaring a Record 326
7.2 Manipulating Individual Fields of a Record 328
7.3 Manipulating an Entire Record 331
7.4 Arrays of Records 334
7.5 Case Study 335
7.6 Searching an Array 342
7.7 Sorting an Array 344
7.8 General Data Structures 348
7.9 Record Variants 352
7.10 Manipulating Strings Stored in Records 357
7.11 Common Programming Errors 363
7.12 Chapter Review 364

8 Sets and Files 371

8.1 Set Data Type and Set Operators 372
8.2 RESET, REWRITE, and the File Position Pointer 379
8.3 TEXT Files 381
8.4 Case Studies 385
8.5 User-defined File Types 396
8.6 Case Study—File Merge 401
8.7 Case Study—Data Base Inquiry 405
8.8 File Buffer Variable 411
8.9 Common Programming Errors 416
8.10 Chapter Review 417

9 Recursion, Searching, and Sorting 425

9.1 The Nature of Recursion 426
9.2 Recursive Procedures 432
9.3 Recursive Functions 439
9.4 Binary Search of an Array 449
9.5 Searching by Hashing 453
9.6 Additional Sorting Algorithms 457
9.7 Case Study—The Quicksort Algorithm 462
9.8 Common Programming Errors 467
9.9 Chapter Review 468

10 Pointer Variables and Dynamic Data Structures 475

10.1 The NEW Statement and Pointer Variables 476
10.2 Understanding Dynamic Allocation 480
10.3 Introduction to Linked Lists 481
10.4 Manipulating Linked Lists Using Pointer Variables 483
10.5 Case Study—Maintaining a Linked List 487
10.6 Stacks and Queues 500
10.7 Multiple-linked Lists and Trees 506
10.8 Case Study—Maintaining a Binary Search Tree 511
10.9 Common Programming Errors 518
10.10 Chapter Review 519

A   Appendix A: Reserved Words, Standard Identifiers, Operators, Functions, and Procedures   Ap-1

B   Appendix B: Additions and Extensions to Pascal   Ap-5

     B.1 Additional Features of ANSI/IEEE Pascal

     B.2 ISO Pascal

     B.3 UCSD Pascal

     B.4 TURBO Pascal

C   Appendix C: Pascal Syntax Diagrams   Ap-19

D   Appendix D: Character Sets   Ap-29

E   Appendix E: Error Number Summary   Ap-31

Answers to Selected Exercises   Ans-1

Index   I-1

Introduction to Computers and Programming

1.1 Electronic Computers Then and Now

1.2 Components of a Computer

1.3 Problem Solving and Programming

1.4 Programming Languages

1.5 Processing a High-level Language Program

1.6 Introduction to Pascal

1.7 General Form of a Pascal Program

1.8 Using the Computer

1.9 Formatting Program Output

1.10 Introduction to Data Types

1.11 Common Programming Errors

1.12 Chapter Review

This chapter introduces computers and computer programming. It begins with a brief history of computers and describes the major components of a computer including memory, central processor, input devices, and output devices. The chapter discusses how information is represented in a computer and how it is manipulated.

The major categories of programming languages are introduced. Simple computer operations are described along with some short programs that demonstrate these operations. There is a brief introduction to the Pascal programming language focusing on statements for reading and displaying information and for performing simple computations.

Also described are the steps involved in creating a Pascal program and the roles performed by various programs that are part of a computer system. These programs include the operating system, compiler, editor, and loader.

1.1 Electronic Computers Then and Now

It is difficult to live in today's society without having had some contact with computers. Computers are used to provide instructional material in some schools, print transcripts, send out bills, reserve airline and concert tickets, play games, and even help authors write books.

However, it wasn't always this way. Just a short time ago, computers were fairly mysterious devices that only a small percentage of our population knew much about. Computer "know-how" turned around when advances in *solid-state electronics* led to drastic cuts in the size and costs of electronic computers. Today, a personal computer (see color insert, Fig. 1.1) which costs less than $3000 and sits on a desk, has as much computational power as one that 10 years ago would have cost more than $100,000 and would fill a 9 by 12 ft room. This price reduction is even more remarkable when we consider the effects of inflation over the last decade.

If we take the literal definition for *computer* as a device for counting or computing, then the abacus might be considered the first computer. However, the first electronic digital computer was designed in the late 1930s by Dr. John Atanasoff at Iowa State University. Atanasoff designed his computer to perform mathematical computations for graduate students.

The first large-scale, general-purpose electronic digital computer, called the ENIAC, was built in 1946 at the University of Pennsylvania. Its design was funded by the U. S. Army, and it was used for computing ballistics tables, for weather prediction, and for atomic energy calculations. The ENIAC weighed 30 tons and occupied a 30 by 50 ft space (see color insert, Fig. 1.2).

Although we are often led to believe otherwise, computers cannot think! They are basically devices for performing computations at incredible speeds (more than one million operations per second) and with great accuracy. However, in order to accomplish anything useful, a computer must be *programmed* or given a sequence of explicit instructions (the *program*) to carry out.

To program the ENIAC it was necessary to connect hundreds of wires and arrange thousands of switches in a certain way. In 1946, Dr. John von Neumann of Princeton University proposed the concept of a *stored program computer*. The instructions of a program would be stored in computer memory rather than be set by wires and switches. Since the contents of computer memory can be easily changed, it would not be nearly as difficult to reprogram this computer to perform different tasks as it was to reprogram the ENIAC. Von Neumann's design is the basis of the digital computer as we know it today.

Components of a Computer

Despite large variation in cost, size, and capabilities, modern computers are remarkably similar in a number of ways. Basically, a computer consists of the five components shown in Fig. 1.3 (see color insert). The arrows connecting the components show the direction of information flow.

All information that is to be processed by a computer must first be entered into the computer *memory* via an *input device*. The information in memory is manipulated by the *central processor* and the results of this manipulation are stored in memory. Information in memory can be displayed through an *output device*. A *secondary storage device* is often used for storing large quantities of information in a semipermanent form. These components and their interaction are described in more detail in the following sections.

Computer Memory

Computer memory is used for information storage. All types of information—numbers, names, lists, and even pictures—may be represented and stored in a computer memory.

The memory of a computer may be pictured as an ordered sequence of storage locations called *memory cells*. In order to be able to store and *retrieve* (access) information, there must be some way to identify the individual memory cells. To accomplish this, each memory cell has associated with it a unique *address* that indicates its relative position in memory. Figure 1.4 shows a computer memory consisting of 1000 memory cells with addresses 0 through 999. Some large-scale computers have memories consisting of millions of individual cells.

The information stored in a memory cell is called the *contents* of a memory cell. Every memory cell always contains some information although we may have no idea what that information is. Whenever new information is placed in a memory cell, any information already there is destroyed and cannot be retrieved. In Fig. 1.4, the contents of memory cell 3 is the number −26, and the contents of memory cell 4 is the letter H.

Central Processor Unit

The *central processor unit* (CPU) performs the actual processing or manipulation of information stored in memory. The CPU can retrieve information from memory. (This information may be either data or instructions for manipulating data.) It can also store the results of these manipulations back in memory for later use.

The *control unit* within the CPU coordinates all activities of the computer. It determines which operations should be carried out and in what order; the control unit then transmits coordinating control signals to the computer components.

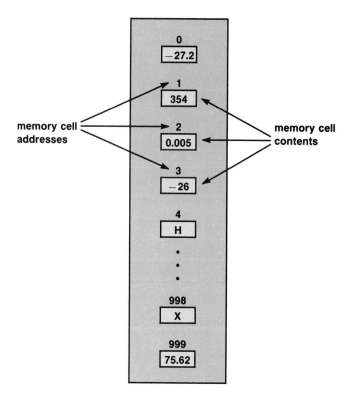

Fig. 1.4 A Computer Memory with 1000 Cells

Also found within the CPU is the *arithmetic-logic unit* (ALU). The ALU consists of electronic circuitry to perform a variety of arithmetic operations, including addition, subtraction, multiplication, and division. These arithmetic operations are performed on data that are stored in memory; the computational results are then saved in memory. The speed with which the ALU can perform each arithmetic operation is about a millionth of a second. The ALU also consists of electronic circuitry to compare information and to make decisions based on the results of the comparison.

Input and Output Devices

The manipulative capability of the computer would be of little use to us if we were unable to communicate with the computer. Specifically, we must be able to enter data for a computation into memory. Later, the computational results that are stored in memory can be displayed.

Most of you will be using a *computer terminal* (see color insert, Fig. 1.5) as both an input and output device. A terminal consists of a *keyboard* (used for entering information) and a *monitor* (used for displaying information). A terminal keyboard is similar to a typewriter keyboard except that it has some extra keys for performing special functions. A monitor is similar to a television or video screen.

Some terminals are equipped with *graphics capability* (see color insert, Fig. 1.6), which enables the output to be displayed as a two-dimensional graph or picture, not just as rows of letters and numbers. With some graphics devices, the user can communicate with the computer by moving an electronic pointer using a *joystick* or a *mouse*.

The only problem with using a monitor as an output device is that there is no written record of the computation. Once the image disappears from the monitor screen it is lost. If you want *hard-copy output*, then you have to send your computational results to an output device called a *printer* or use a hard-copy terminal (see color insert, Fig. 1.7).

A *card reader* is sometimes used as an input device. A card reader reads punch cards that have been prepared using a *keypunch*. Pressing a symbol on the keypunch keyboard causes a particular configuration of holes to be punched on a punch card. A card reader interprets these configurations of holes and sends the information to the computer.

Secondary Storage Device

There is another category of device, called a secondary storage device, that is found on most computer systems. These devices are used to provide additional data storage capability. Examples of secondary storage devices are *magnetic tape and disk drives* with their associated magnetic tapes or disks (see color insert, Fig. 1.8). Large quantities of information may be saved on a tape or disk.

The memory described in the computer memory section is often called *main memory* to distinguish it from *secondary memory* (tapes or disks). Main memory is much faster and more expensive than secondary memory. Also, most computers can have only limited quantities of it. Consequently, often it is necessary to add one or more secondary storage devices in order to expand the computer system's data storage capacity.

Information stored in secondary memory is organized into aggregates called *files*. Results generated by the computer may be saved as *data files* in secondary memory. Most of the programs that you write will be saved as *program files* in secondary memory. Any file may be transferred easily from secondary memory to main memory for further processing.

A typical computer system, including memory, a central processor, terminals, and tape and disk drives, is pictured in Fig. 1.9 (see color insert). In the remainder of this text, we will see how to use this *hardware* by writing *software* (computer programs) for specifying different kinds of data manipulation.

Self-check Exercises for Section 1.2

1. What are the contents of memory cells 0 and 999 in Fig. 1.4? What memory cells contain the letter X and the fraction 0.005?
2. Explain the purpose of the arithmetic-logic unit, memory, central processor, and the disk drive and disk? What input and output device will be used with your computer?

1.3 Problem Solving and Programming

We mentioned earlier that a computer cannot think; therefore, in order to get it to do any useful work, a computer must be provided with a *program* that is a list of instructions. Programming a computer is a lot more involved than simply writing a list of instructions. Problem solving is an important component of programming. Before we can write the program to solve a problem, we must consider carefully all aspects of the problem and then organize its solution.

Like most programming students, you will probably spend a great deal of time initially in the computer laboratory entering your programs. You will spend more time later removing the errors or *bugs* that inevitably will be present in your programs.

It is tempting to rush to the computer laboratory and start entering your program as soon as you have some idea of how to write it. You should resist this temptation and instead think carefully about the problem and its solution before writing any program statements. When you have a solution in mind, you should plan it out on paper and modify it if necessary before writing the program.

Once the program is written on paper, you should *desk check* your solution by "executing" it much as the computer would. You should carefully determine the result of each program statement using sample data that are easy to manipulate (e.g. small whole numbers). You should compare these results with what would be expected and make any necessary corrections to the program when the results are incorrect. Only then should you go to the computer laboratory and start to enter the program. Experience has shown that a few extra minutes spent evaluating the proposed solution in this way often saves hours of frustration later. The process you should follow is shown in Fig. 1.10.

In this text, we will stress a methodology for problem solving that we have found useful in helping students to learn to program. We will teach a technique called *structured programming* that should enable you to write programs that are relatively easy to read and understand and that contain fewer initial errors.

Most students have very strong positive or negative feelings about programming; very few students are ambivalent. Some of the reasons that programming can be less than enjoyable are the following:

1. You are learning a new language with its own *syntax* or rules of grammar.
2. You must carefully plan out what actions you would like performed and their sequence.
3. You must be explicit and accurate in describing what you wish done.
4. You must implement your solution in an existing programming language. What seems simple to write in English may require considerable effort to specify in a programming language.
5. You must carefully enter all program instructions and all data since

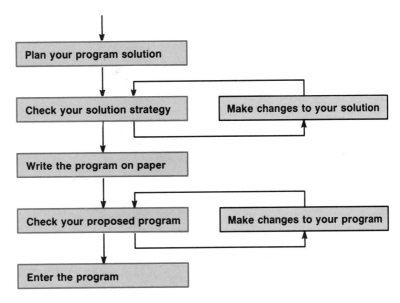

Fig. 1.10 Programming Strategy

each instruction must correspond exactly with the syntax of the programming language. Omitting a comma can cause your program to fail.

6. You will be dealing with equipment that occasionally malfunctions and sometimes is not accessible when you want to use it.

7. When you make a mistake (and you will make lots of mistakes) it is often difficult to determine what is wrong so that you can fix it.

This list is not intended to scare you, but to alert you to some of the problems that you may encounter. If you are careful, patient, and plan ahead you can avoid some of these problems. Planning ahead includes scheduling your time so that you can make use of the computer laboratory during hours when it is less busy.

1.4 Programming Languages

Languages used for writing computer programs are called *programming languages*. There are many different programming languages, which fall into one of three broad categories: machine, assembly, or high-level languages.

High-level languages are most often used by *programmers* (program writers). One reason for the popularity of high-level languages is that they are much easier to use than machine and assembly languages. Another reason is that a high-level language program is *portable*. This means that it can be executed without modification on many different types of computers. An assembly language or machine-language program, on the other hand, may only execute on one type of computer.

Some common high-level languages are BASIC, FORTRAN, COBOL, and Pascal. Each of these high-level languages has a *language standard* that describes the form and meaning of all its statements. Generally there are additional features available on a particular computer that are not part of the standard. A program will be portable only when the programmer is careful to use those features that are part of the standard.

One of the most important features of high-level languages is that they allow us to write program statements that resemble English. We can reference data that are stored in memory using descriptive names (e.g. NAME, RATE) rather than numeric memory cell addresses. We can also describe operations that we would like performed using familiar symbols. For example, in several high-level languages the statement

```
Z := X + Y
```

means add X to Y and store the result in Z.

We can also use descriptive names to reference data in *assembly language*; however, we must specify the operations to be performed on the data more explicitly. The high-level language statement above might be written as

```
LOAD  X
ADD   Y
STORE Z
```

in an assembly language.

Machine language is the native tongue of a computer. Each machine language instruction is a *binary string* (string of 0's and 1's) that specifies an operation and the memory cells involved in the operation. The assembly language statements above might be written as

```
0010 0000 0000 0100
0100 0000 0000 0101
0011 0000 0000 0110
```

in a machine language. Obviously, what is easiest for a computer to understand is most difficult for a person and vice versa.

A computer can execute only programs that are in machine language. Consequently, a high-level language program must first be translated into machine language using a special program called a *compiler*. The machine language program must then be loaded into computer memory by the *loader* program before it can be executed. This process is illustrated in Fig. 1.11 and described in more detail in the next section.

Self-check Exercises for Section 1.4

1. Explain the role of a compiler and loader.
2. What do you think the high-level language statements below mean?

```
X := A + B + C        X := Y / Z        D := C - B + A
```

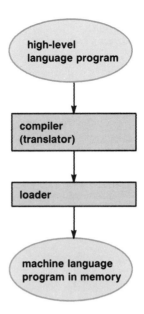

Fig. 1.11 Translating a high-level language program

Processing a High-level Language Program

Before it can be processed, a high-level language program must be entered at the terminal. The program will be stored on disk as a file called the *source file* (see Fig. 1.12).

Once the source file is saved, it must be translated into machine language. A compiler processes the source file and attempts to translate each statement into machine language.

One or more statements in the source file may contain a *syntax error*. This means that these statements do not correspond exactly to the syntax of the high-level language. In this case, the compiler will cause some error messages to be displayed.

At this point, you can make changes to your source file and have the compiler process it again. If there are no more errors, the compiler will create an *object file*, which is your program translated into machine language. The object file can then be stored in main memory by the *loader program* and then executed. Both the compiler and loader programs are part of your computer system. This process is shown in Fig. 1.12.

Executing a Program

In order to execute a program, the computer control unit must examine each program instruction in memory and send out the command signals required to carry out the instruction. Normally, the instructions are executed in sequence; however, as we will see later it is possible to have the con-

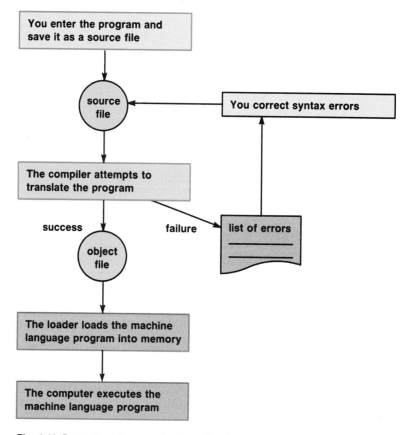

Fig. 1.12 Preparing a Program for Execution

trol unit skip over some instructions or execute some instructions more than once.

During execution, data may be entered into memory and manipulated in some specified way. Then, the result of this data manipulation will be displayed.

Figure 1.13 shows the effect of executing a payroll program stored in memory. The first step of the program requires entering data into memory that describe the employee. In step 2, the employee data are manipulated by the central processor and the results of computations are stored in memory. In the final step, the computational results may be displayed as payroll reports or employee payroll checks. An example of a program that does this is provided later in the chapter.

Self-check Exercises for Section 1.5

1. What is the difference between the source file and object file? Which do you create and which does the compiler create? Which one is processed by the loader?
2. What is a syntax error and in which file would a syntax error be found?

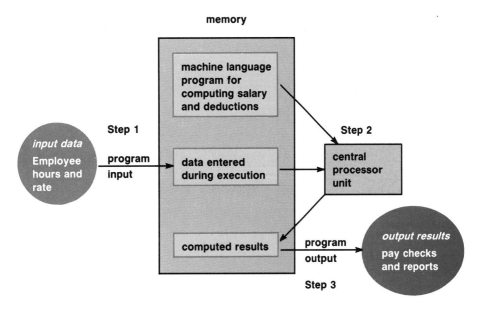

Fig. 1.13 Flow of Information during Program Execution

Introduction to Pascal

Pascal was developed in 1971 by Professor Nicklaus Wirth of Zurich, Switzerland. It is currently one of the most widely used languages for teaching programming. Its popularity is due to the fact that its syntax is relatively easy to learn. Also, Pascal facilitates writing *structured programs* —programs that are relatively easy to read, understand, and maintain (keep in good working order).

There are two similar standards for Pascal. This textbook will cover features of the language that are included in the 1983 ANSI/IEEE (American National Standards Institute/Institute for Electrical and Electronics Engineers) Standard. Features of this standard not discussed in the text are described in Appendix B1. Other features that are included in the ISO International Standard (but not in the ANSI/IEEE Standard) are described in Appendix B2. Finally, additional features that are often available but are not in either standard are described in Appendixes B3 and B4.

The rest of this chapter will provide a brief introduction to Pascal. Statements for reading data, performing simple computations, and displaying results will be described.

Two Sample Programs

Before beginning our study of Pascal, we will examine two short programs. Don't worry about understanding the details of these programs yet; it will all be explained later.

```
program HELLO (INPUT, OUTPUT);

var
    LETTER1, LETTER2, LETTER3 : CHAR;

begin
    WRITELN ('Enter a 3 letter nickname and press return.');
    READLN (LETTER1, LETTER2, LETTER3);
    WRITELN ('Hello ', LETTER1, LETTER2, LETTER3, '.');
    WRITELN ('We hope you enjoy studying Pascal!')
end.

Enter a 3 letter nickname and press return.
Bob
Hello Bob.
We hope you enjoy studying Pascal!
```

Fig. 1.14 Printing a Welcoming Message

Example 1.1

Figure 1.14 contains a Pascal program followed by a sample execution of that program. For easy identification, the program name and last line are in blue; the information entered by the program user also is in blue in the sample execution.

The program statement starting with var identifies the names of three memory cells (LETTER1, LETTER2, LETTER3) that will be used to store each letter of the nickname. Each program statement starting with WRITELN cause a line of output to be displayed during program execution. The first WRITELN statement generates the first line of the sample output, which asks the program user to enter three letters.

The program statement

```
READLN (LETTER1, LETTER2, LETTER3);
```

reads the three letters Bob (entered by the program user) into the three memory cells listed (one letter per cell). The next statement

```
WRITELN ('Hello ', LETTER1, LETTER2, LETTER3, '.');
```

displays these letters after the message *string* 'Hello '. The string '.' causes a period to be printed after the third letter.

Example 1.2

The program in Fig. 1.15 converts inches to centimeters. The number of inches to be converted is read into the memory cell INCHES by the statement

```
READLN (INCHES);
```

The statement

```
CENT := CENTPERINCH * INCHES;
```

```
program INCHTOCENT (INPUT, OUTPUT);

const
    CENTPERINCH = 2.54;

var
    INCHES, CENT : REAL;

begin
    WRITELN ('Enter a length in inches.');
    READLN (INCHES);
    CENT := CENTPERINCH * INCHES;
    WRITELN ('That equals ', CENT, ' centimeters.')
end.

Enter a length in inches.
30.0
That equals        7.620000E+01 centimeters.
```

Fig. 1.15 Converting Inches to Centimeters

computes the equivalent length in centimeters by multiplying the length in inches by 2.54 (the number of centimeters per inch); the product is stored in memory cell CENT.

The statement

```
WRITELN ('That equals ', CENT, ' centimeters.')
```

displays a message string, the value of CENT, and a second message string. The value of CENT is printed in Pascal scientific notation as 7.620000E+01. This is equivalent to 7.62 × 10 or 76.2 as will be explained later.

One of the nicest things about Pascal is that it lets us write program statements that resemble English. At this point, you probably can read and understand the sample programs, even though you may not know how to write your own programs. The following sections provide a detailed explanation of the Pascal statements seen so far.

Reserved Words and Standard Identifiers

Each of the statements in the programs in Fig 1.15 satisfies the Pascal syntax for that statement type. If the program statements that you enter do not follow this syntax, they may not be translated.

Each Pascal statement contains a number of different elements: reserved words, standard identifiers, special symbols, and names for data and programs. The *reserved words* have special meaning in Pascal and cannot be used for other purposes.

Reserved words in Figs. 1.14 and 1.15
```
program, const, var, begin, end
```

The *standard identifiers* also have special meaning but they can be used by the programmer for other purposes (not recommended).

Standard identifiers in Figs. 1.14 and 1.15
```
READLN, WRITELN, REAL, CHAR, INPUT, OUTPUT
```

There are also some symbols (e.g. =, *, :=) that have special meaning. Appendix A contains a complete list of reserved words, standard identifiers, and special symbols.

What is the difference between reserved words and standard identifiers? Although it is illegal to use a reserved word for the name of a data item, it is legal to use a standard identifier. However, if you do this, then Pascal no longer associates any special meaning with that identifier. For example, you could decide to use READLN as the name of a data item, but then you would not be able to use READLN to read a data value. Obviously, this would be a pretty silly thing to do, and we don't recommend it.

Besides standard identifiers, the programs in Figs. 1.14 and 1.15 contain other identifiers that are used as the names of programs or data. The form of these identifiers is described in the next section.

Other identifiers in Figs. 1.14 and 1.15
```
HELLO, LETTER1, LETTER2, LETTER3, INCHES,
CENT, CENTPERINCH, INCHTOCENT
```

PROGRAM STYLE

Use of uppercase, lowercase, and computer type

Throughout the text, issues of good programming style will be discussed in displays such as this one. Programming style displays will provide guidelines for improving the appearance and readability of programs. Most programs will be examined or studied by someone else. A program that follows some consistent style conventions will be easier to read and understand than one that is sloppy or inconsistent. Although these conventions make it easier for humans to understand programs, they have no affect whatsoever on the computer.

Reserved words will always appear in lowercase in programs; all other identifiers will appear in uppercase. We recommend that you follow this convention in your programs so that it will be easy to distinguish reserved words from other identifiers. Some Pascal compilers do not allow lowercase characters in Pascal statements. If this is true for your compiler, you will have to use uppercase for reserved words as well.

If both uppercase and lowercase are allowed, the compiler will not differentiate between them in reserved words or identifiers. This means that you can write the reserved word const as CONST or the special identifier READLN as Readln. However, const and READLN would be preferred according to our convention.

Within the text body, reserved words appear in a computer type font, making them easily recognizable.

Fig. 1.1 IBM personal computer

Fig. 1.2 The ENIAC computer (Photo courtesy of Sperry Corporation.)

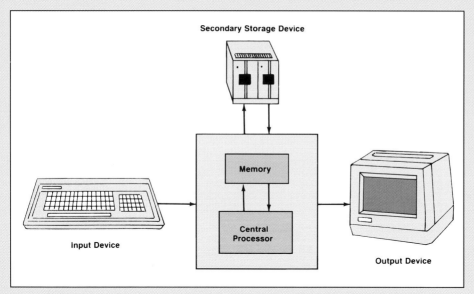

Fig. 1.3 Components of a computer (From Koffman and Friedman, *Problem Solving in Structured BASIC-PLUS and VAX-11 BASIC*, © 1984, Addison-Wesley.)

Fig. 1.5 A computer terminal

Fig. 1.6 Macintosh computer with mouse (Courtesy of Apple Computer, Inc.)

Fig. 1.7 A printing terminal (© Digital Equipment Corp. All rights reserved. Reprinted with permission.)

Fig. 1.8 Inserting a floppy disk in a disk drive (© Digital Equipment Corp. All rights reserved. Reprinted with permission.)

Fig. 1.9 VAX-11/780 computer system (© Digital Equipment Corp. All rights reserved. Reprinted with permission.)

Declaring Identifiers

How do we tell Pascal what identifiers will be used in a program? One way is the program heading

```
program HELLO (INPUT, OUTPUT);
```

which specifies the name (HELLO) of the program. INPUT and OUTPUT are standard identifiers; they indicate that data will be read into the program from an input data file (INPUT) and that output values will be written to an output data file (OUTPUT). The data file INPUT may consist of information entered at the terminal keyboard; information written to file OUTPUT may be displayed on the video screen.

Another way to tell Pascal the names of identifiers is through *declarations*. The *constant declaration*

```
const
    CENTPERINCH = 2.54;
```

specifies that the identifier CENTPERINCH will be used as the name of the constant 2.54.

Identifiers declared in a constant declaration are called *constants*. Only data values that never change (e.g. the number of centimeters per inch is always 2.54) should be associated with an identifier that is a constant. It is illegal to attempt to change the value of a constant in a Pascal program.

The *variable declaration*

```
var
    LETTER1, LETTER2, LETTER3 : CHAR;
```

in Fig. 1.14 gives the names of three identifiers that will be used to reference data items that are individual characters. The variable declaration

```
var
    INCHES, CENT : REAL;
```

in Fig. 1.15 gives the names of two identifiers that will be used to reference data items that are real numbers (e.g. 30.0, 562.57).

Identifiers declared in a variable declaration are called *variables*. Variables are used in a program for storing input data items and computational results. The standard identifiers (REAL, CHAR) used in the variable declaration tell Pascal what type of data will be stored in the variable. The *data types* REAL and CHAR will be discussed in more detail in Section 1.10.

You have quite a bit of freedom in selecting *identifiers* that are used to name your programs or data. The syntactic rules are:

1. An identifier must always begin with a letter.
2. An identifier must consist of letters or digits only.

You cannot use an identifier that is a reserved word in Pascal to name your data. Some valid and invalid identifiers are listed below.

valid identifiers
    LETTER1, LETTER2, INCHES, CENT, CENTPERINCH, HELLO

invalid identifiers
    1LETTER, CONST, var, TWO*FOUR, Joe's

Although the syntactic rules above do not place a limit on the length of an identifier, some compilers recognize only the first eight characters in an identifier. These compilers will consider the identifiers CONSONANT1 and CONSONANT2 to be the same identifier (CONSONAN); consequently, these identifiers could not be declared together in a program translated by such a compiler.

Some compilers include the underscore character in the list of characters specified in syntactic rule 2. On these compilers, the multi-word identifier INCHTOCENT could be written more clearly as INCH_TO_CENT; however, this is not valid in standard Pascal.

Every identifier used in a Pascal program must be either declared or predefined (reserved words and standard identifiers). The category of each identifier used in Examples 1.1 and 1.2 is shown in Table 1.1.

Table 1.1 Category of Identifiers in Examples 1.1 and 1.2

Reserved Words	Standard Identifiers	Identifiers
program, var, const, begin, end	INPUT, OUTPUT, CHAR, REAL, READLN, WRITELN	HELLO, LETTER1, LETTER2, LETTER3, INCHTOCENT, CENTPERINCH, INCHES, CENT

The features introduced in this section are summarized in the displays below. Each display describes the Pascal syntax and then provides an interpretation of the statement. Each of the elements in italics is described in the interpretation section.

PROGRAM STATEMENT

    program *prog-name* (INPUT, OUTPUT);

Interpretation: The name of the program is indicated by *prog-name*. The input data will be read from data file INPUT; the output results will be written to data file OUTPUT.

PROGRAM STYLE

Choosing identifier names

It is very important to pick meaningful names for identifiers as this will make it easier to understand their use in a program. For example, the identifier SALARY would be a good name for a variable used to store a person's salary; the identifiers S and BAGEL would be bad choices.

There is no restriction on the length of an identifier. However, it is hard to form meaningful names using fewer than three letters. On the other hand, if an identifier is too long, it becomes difficult to type correctly each time it appears in a program. A reasonable rule of thumb is to use names that are between three and ten characters in length.

If you mistype an identifier, the compiler will usually detect this as a syntax error. Sometimes mistyped identifiers wind up looking like other identifiers. For this reason, it is best to avoid picking names that are very similar to each other. Also, names that are almost the same can cause quite a bit of confusion.

Assignment Statements

One of the main functions of a computer is to perform arithmetic computations. In this section, we will see how to specify computations using the *assignment statement*.

The assignment statement

```
CENT := CENTPERINCH * INCHES;
```

in Fig. 1.16 is used to assign a value to the variable CENT. In this case, CENT is being assigned the result of the multiplication (* means multiply) of the constant CENTPERINCH by the variable INCHES. Valid information must be stored in both CENTPERINCH and INCHES before the assignment statement is executed. As shown in Fig. 1.16, only the value of CENT is affected by the assignment statement; CENTPERINCH and INCHES retain their original values.

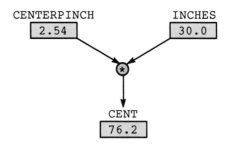

Fig. 1.16 Effect of CENT := CENTPERINCH * INCHES;

The symbol := is the *assignment operator* in Pascal and should be read as "becomes" or "takes the value of" rather than "equals". The : and = must be adjacent characters (no intervening space). The general form of the assignment statement is shown in the next display.

ASSIGNMENT STATEMENT

result := *expression*

Interpretation: The variable specified by *result* is assigned the value of *expression*. The previous value of *result* is destroyed. The expression can be a single variable, a single constant, or involve variables, constants, and the arithmetic operators listed in Table 1.2.

Table 1.2 Some Arithmetic Operators

Arithmetic Operator	Meaning
+	addition
−	subtraction
*	multiplication
/	division

Example 1.3 In Pascal, it is alright to write assignment statements of the form

```
SUM := SUM + ITEM
```

where the variable SUM is used on both sides of the assignment operator. This is obviously not an algebraic equation, but it illustrates something that is often done in programming. This statement instructs the computer to add the current value of the variable SUM to the value of ITEM; the result is saved temporarily and then stored back into SUM. The previous value of SUM is destroyed in the process as illustrated in Fig. 1.17; however, the value of ITEM is unchanged.

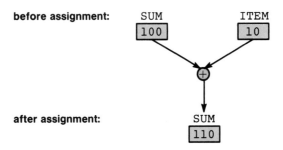

Fig. 1.17 Effect of SUM := SUM + ITEM

Example 1.4 Assignment statements can also be written with an expression part that consists of a single variable or value. The statement

```
NEWX := X
```

instructs the computer to *copy* the value of X into NEWX. The statement

```
NEWX := -X
```

instructs the computer to get the value of X, *negate* this value, and store the result in NEWX (e.g. If X is 3.5, NEWX is −3.5). Neither of the assignment statements above changes the value of X.

The READLN Statement

Information cannot be manipulated by a computer unless it is first stored in main memory. There are three ways to place a data value in memory: associate it with a constant, assign it to a variable, or read it into memory. The first two approaches can be followed only when the value to be stored will be the same every time the program is run. If we wish to be able to store different information each time, then it must be read in as the program is executing.

The READLN statement

```
READLN (INCHES);
```

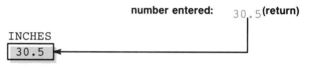

number entered: 30.5 **(return)**

INCHES

```
30.5
```

Fig. 1.18 Effect of READLN (INCHES);

is used in Fig. 1.15 to read a real number into the variable INCHES. This statement causes the number entered at the terminal to be stored in the variable INCHES. After typing a number, the program user should press the key labeled *return* or *enter*. The effect of this READLN statement is shown in Fig. 1.18.

The program in Fig. 1.14 reads a person's nickname. Each person using the program may have a different nickname so three letters are read in using the READLN statement

```
READLN (LETTER1, LETTER2, LETTER3);
```

This statement causes data entered at the terminal to be stored in each of the three variables listed above. Since these variables are type CHAR, one character will be stored in each variable. Fig. 1.19 shows the effect of this statement when the letters Bob are entered.

It is interesting to note that the four input characters in Fig. 1.18 comprise a single data value, the number 30.5 which is stored in the variable INCHES (type REAL). In Fig. 1.19, each input character represents a separate data value and is stored in a different variable (type CHAR).

The number of characters read by a READLN statement depends on the type of the variable in which the data will be stored. Only one character is read for a type CHAR variable; for a type REAL variable, Pascal continues to read characters until a character that cannot be part of a number is reached (e.g. a blank or a letter) or the return key is pressed.

How do we know when to enter the input data and what data to enter? Your program should print a prompting message (as explained in the next section) to inform the program user what data should be entered and when. The *cursor* (a moving place marker) indicates the position on the screen of the next character to be displayed. As each character is entered, the cursor advances to the next screen position.

Fig. 1.19 Effect of READLN (LETTER1, LETTER2, LETTER3)

letters entered: Bob **(return)**

LETTER1

```
B
```

LETTER2

```
o
```

LETTER3

```
b
```

The WRITELN Statement

In order to see the results of a program execution we must have some way of specifying what variable values should be displayed. In Fig. 1.15, the statement

```
WRITELN ('That equals ', CENT, ' centimeters.')
```

causes the line

```
That equals          7.620000E+01 centimeters.
```

to be displayed. There are actually three separate items printed: the string `'That equals '`, the value of the variable CENT, and the string `' centimeters.'`. A *string* is a sequence of characters enclosed in single quotes or apostrophes. When a WRITELN statement is executed, the characters enclosed in quotes are printed but not the quotes.

The number in the output line above is 76.2 expressed in *Pascal scientific notation*. In normal scientific notation, 7.62×10^1 means multiply 7.62 by 10 or move the decimal point right one digit. Since superscripts cannot be entered or displayed at the terminal, the letter E is used in Pascal to indicate scientific notation.

In Fig. 1.14, the statement

```
WRITELN ('Hello ', LETTER1, LETTER2, LETTER3, '.');
```

causes the line

```
Hello Bob.
```

to be printed. In this case, three variable values are printed between the strings `'Hello '` and `'.'`.

Finally, the statements

```
WRITELN ('Enter a 3 letter nickname and press return.');
WRITELN ('Enter a length in inches.');
```

are both used to display *prompts* or *prompting messages* in Figs. 1.14 and 1.15, respectively. A prompting message is a string that is displayed just before a READLN statement is executed to prompt the program user to enter data. The prompt may describe the format of the data expected. It is very important to precede each READLN statement with a WRITELN that prints a prompt; otherwise, the program user may have no idea that the program has stopped executing or what data to enter.

THE WRITELN STATEMENT

WRITELN (*output-list*)

Interpretation: The value of each variable or constant is printed in the order in which it appears in *output-list*. A string is printed without the quotes. The cursor advances to the start of the next line after the entire output line is displayed.

Self-check Exercises for Section 1.6

1. Indicate which of the identifiers below are Pascal reserved words, standard identifiers, identifiers, or invalid identifiers.

   ```
   END READLN BILL PROGRAM SUE'S RATE OPERATE START
   BEGIN CONST XYZ123 123XYZ THISISALONGONE Y=Z
   ```

2. Correct the syntax errors in the program below and rewrite it so that it follows our style conventions. What does each statement of your corrected program do? What is printed?

   ```
   program SMALL (INPUT, output) VAR X, Y, X , real:
   BEGIN 15.0 = Y; Z:= -Y + 3.5; Y + z =: x;
   writeln (x; Y; z) end;
   ```

3. Change the WRITELN statement in the program above so that the line

   ```
   The value of X is _____ pounds.
   ```

   is printed to display the value assigned to variable X.

1.7 General Form of a Pascal Program

In the preceding sections, we described six kinds of Pascal statements: the program statement, constant declaration, variable declaration, assignment, READLN, and WRITELN. They will appear in most of the programs that you write.

Example 1.5   A new program is shown in Fig. 1.20. This program computes an employee's gross pay and net pay using the algebraic formulas

gross pay = hours worked × hourly rate
net pay = gross pay − tax amount

These formulas are written as the Pascal assignment statements

```
GROSS := HOURS * RATE;
NET := GROSS - TAX;
```

in the payroll program shown in Fig. 1.20. New values of HOURS and RATE are read each time the program is executed; a constant TAX of $25.00 is always deducted.

```
program PAYROLL (INPUT, OUTPUT);

const
    TAX = 25.00;

var
    HOURS, RATE, GROSS, NET : REAL;

begin
    WRITELN ('Enter hours worked');       READLN (HOURS);
    WRITELN ('Enter hourly rate');        READLN (RATE);
    GROSS := HOURS * RATE;
    NET := GROSS - TAX;
    WRITELN ('Gross pay is $', GROSS);
    WRITELN ('Net pay is $', NET)
end.

Enter hours worked
15
Enter hourly rate
3.35
Gross pay is $          5.025000E+01
Net pay is $           2.525000E+01
```

Fig. 1.20 Payroll Program

This program first reads the data representing hours worked and hourly rate and then computes gross pay as their product. Next, it computes net pay by deducting a constant tax amount of 25.00. Finally, it displays the computed values of gross pay and net pay.

Semicolons, Begin, and End

In addition to the statements discussed so far, this program contains the reserved words begin and end and also punctuation in the form of semicolons and a period. Each Pascal program consists of a *declaration part* and a *program body*. The declaration part is used to describe the identifiers referenced in the program; the program body is used to specify the data manipulation. The reserved word `begin` is used to mark the beginning of the program body; the reserved word `end` marks the end of the program body and is always the last line in a Pascal program. Note that the last `end` is always followed by a period.

Semicolons are used to separate Pascal statements. Consequently, a semicolon always is inserted between statements in a program. A semicolon is not used after the reserved word `begin` nor before the reserved word `end` because they are not statements.

As shown in Fig. 1.20, it is possible to write a Pascal statement on more than one line. Both the variable declaration and constant declaration statements start on one line and finish on the next. A statement may be spread over two lines providing it is not split in the middle of an identifier, a reserved word, a number, or a string.

Also, it is possible to write more than one statement per line. We have combined a `WRITELN` statement that displays a prompt with the `READLN` statement that enters the data. A semicolon separates this pair of statements.

PROGRAM STYLE

Use of blank space

The consistent and careful use of blank spaces can significantly enhance the style of a program. A blank space is required between words in a program (e.g. between `program` and `PAYROLL` in the `program` statement).

Extra blanks between words and symbols are ignored by the compiler and may be inserted as desired to improve the style and appearance of a program. As shown in Fig. 1.20, we will always leave a blank space after a comma and before and after operators such as `*`, `-`, `:=`. Also, we will indent each statement in the program body. We will also write the reserved words `const`, `var`, `begin`, and `end` by themselves on a line so that they stand out. Finally, we will use blank lines between sections of the program.

All of these measures are taken for the sole purpose of improving the style and hence the clarity of the program. They have no effect whatever on the meaning of the program as far as the computer is concerned; however, they can make it easier for humans to read and understand the program.

Be careful not to insert blank spaces where they do not belong. For example, there cannot be a space between the characters `:` and `=` that comprise the assignment operator `:=`. Also, the identifier `TAXRATE` cannot be written as `TAX RATE`.

Programs in Memory

It would be worthwhile to pause for a moment and take a look at the payroll program in memory. Fig. 1.21 shows the payroll program loaded in memory and the program data area before execution of the program body. The question mark in memory cells HOURS, RATE, GROSS, and NET indicates that these variables are *undefined* (value unknown) before program execution begins. During program execution, the data values 40.0 and 4.50 are read into the variables HOURS and RATE, respectively. After the assignment statements shown earlier are used to compute values for GROSS and NET, all variables are defined as shown in Fig. 1.21b.

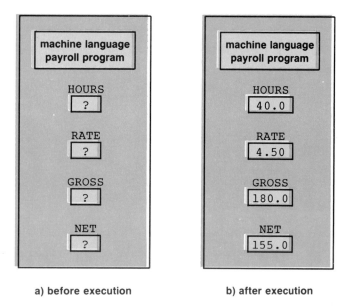

a) before execution   b) after execution

Fig. 1.21 Memory before and after Execution of a Program

Program Declaration Part and Program Body

We can summarize what we have learned about Pascal programs by examining the general form of a Pascal program as shown in Fig. 1.22. Every identifier used in a program must be declared exactly once in the *declaration part* of a program unless it is a reserved word or standard identifier. The reserved words const and var may appear at most once and in the order shown. All constant declarations come after const and all variable declarations after var. More than one *constant* may be declared, and there may be more than one *variable-list*.

The *program body* (including begin and end) follows the declaration part. Semicolons must be inserted between program statements; a period is required after end.

```
program prog-name (INPUT, OUTPUT);

const
    constant = value;
              .
              .
              .
    constant = value;

var
    variable-list : type;
                  .
                  .
                  .
    variable-list : type;

begin
    program statement;
                    .
                    .
                    .
    program statement
end.
```

Fig. 1.22 General Form of a Program

1.8 Using the Computer

After a program is written, it must be entered at the terminal. We talked about the process of translating and executing a program in Section 1.5 (see Fig. 1.12). The mechanics of doing this differ on each computer system; we will describe the general process in this section.

Interactive Mode and Batch Mode

There are two basic modes of computer operation: *batch* and *interactive*. The programs that we have written so far are intended to be run in interactive mode. In this mode, the program user can interact with the program and enter data while the program is executing.

Interactive mode is most common today and is normally used on a personal computer or a larger *timeshared* computer. Timeshared computers are often used in universities for instructional purposes. In this environment, many users are connected by terminals to one central computer, and all users share the central facilities.

In batch mode, all data must be supplied beforehand as the program user cannot interact with the program while it is executing. A computer system that only uses punch cards as its input medium must operate in batch mode. Batch mode is an option on most timeshared or personal computers.

If you use batch mode, then you must prepare a batch data file before executing your program. On a timeshared or personal computer, a batch data file is created and saved in the same way as a program file. This will be discussed shortly.

Since a batch mode program cannot interact with its user, it makes no sense to provide prompts. Each READLN statement reads data items from a previously prepared data file. Since there is no record of the data that are read, a WRITELN statement is used after (instead of before) each READLN statement to *echo print* the data values just read into memory.

The payroll program is rewritten as a batch program in Fig. 1.23. The file INPUT is associated with a batch data file instead of the keyboard. The first four statements in the program body are used to read and echo print the data. The statement

```
READLN (HOURS);
```

reads the value of HOURS from the first line of the batch data file; the next statement

```
WRITELN (' Hours worked are ', HOURS);
```

echo prints the value read into HOURS.

Each of the WRITELN statements in Fig. 1.23 begins with a string whose first character is a blank that is not printed. The reason for this is that batch programs often use a printer as an output device instead of a video screen. Some printers remove the first character from every output line and use it to determine the line spacing between this line and the one previously printed. Blank characters at the beginning of every line would result in single-spaced program output.

Fig. 1.23 Payroll Program as a Batch Program

```
program PAYROLL (INPUT, OUTPUT);

const
    TAX = 25.00;

var
    HOURS, RATE, GROSS, NET : REAL;

begin
    READLN (HOURS);
    WRITELN (' Hours worked are ', HOURS);
    READLN (RATE);
    WRITELN (' Hourly rate is ', RATE);
    GROSS := HOURS * RATE;
    NET := GROSS - TAX;
    WRITELN (' Gross pay is $', GROSS);
    WRITELN (' Net pay is $', NET)
end.
```

```
Hours worked are          1.500000E+01
Hourly rate is            3.350000E+00
Gross pay is $            5.025000E+01
Net pay is $            2.525000E+01
```

Operating System

Regardless of what mode of computing or kind of computer you are using, it will be necessary to interact with a supervisory program within the computer called the *operating system*. In large timeshared computers, it is the responsibility of the operating system to allocate the central resources among many users. Some operating system tasks are:

1. Validating user identification and account number
2. Making the editor, compiler, or loader available
3. Allocating memory and processor time
4. Providing input and output facilities
5. Retrieving needed files
6. Saving new files that are created

Even in smaller personal computers, the operating system still must perform tasks 2 through 6 above.

Each computer has its own special *control language* for communicating with its operating system. We cannot really provide the details here, but we will discuss the general process next. Your instructor will provide the specific commands for your system.

Creating a Program or Data File

In order to use an interactive system, it is first necessary to "boot up" a personal computer or "log on" to a timeshared computer. Once you have accomplished one of these tasks, you can begin to create your program.

In most cases, you will use a special program called an *editor* to enter your Pascal program. An editor is a program that is used to create and modify program and data files. After accessing the editor, you can begin to start to enter a new Pascal program. Once your program is entered, you must save the program as a permanent file on disk. The steps followed to create and save a program file are:

1. Log onto a timeshared computer or boot up a personal computer.
2. Get the editor program.
3. Indicate that you are creating a new file and specify its name.
4. Enter each line of your program.
5. Save your program as a permanent file in secondary memory.

Once your program is created and you are satisfied that each line is entered correctly, you can attempt to compile, load, and execute it. On some systems it will be necessary to give three separate commands to get this to happen; on other systems one command, such as RUN, will initiate this sequence of three operations.

In any event, if your program contains syntax errors, it will be necessary to *edit it* to eliminate the syntax errors. To accomplish this you will have to access the editor again, retrieve your program file, make the necessary changes to the Pascal program, save the modified program file, and attempt to recompile. The steps used to correct and reexecute a program file are:

1. Get the editor program.
2. Access your program file.
3. Correct the statements with syntax errors.
4. Save your edited program file.
5. Compile, load, and execute the new program file.

1.9 Formatting Program Output

In the sample program output shown so far, all real numbers were printed in Pascal scientific notation. Consequently, we had little control over the appearance or format of each output line. In this section we will learn how to specify the format of an output item.

Formatting Integer Values

It is fairly easy to *format* program output in Pascal and to control the exact form of each output line. This is illustrated in the next example for an *integer value*. An integer value in Pascal is a number without a decimal point.

Example 1.6   The program in Fig. 1.24 determines the value of a small collection of coins (nickels and pennies only). The variables are declared to be type INTEGER since it is impossible to have 2.5 coins. Only integer values can be stored in type INTEGER variables. The assignment statement

```
CENTS := 5 * NICKELS + PENNIES;
```

Fig. 1.24 Formatting an Integer Value

```
program COUNTCOINS (INPUT, OUTPUT);

var
    NICKELS, PENNIES, COINS, CENTS : INTEGER;

begin
    WRITE ('How many nickels do you have? ');    READLN (NICKELS);
    WRITE ('How many pennies do you have? ');    READLN (PENNIES);
    COINS := NICKELS + PENNIES;
    CENTS := 5 * NICKELS + PENNIES;
    WRITELN ('You have ', COINS :2, ' coins.');
    WRITELN ('Their value is ', CENTS :3, ' cents.')
end.

How many nickels do you have? 3
How many pennies do you have? 2
You have  5 coins.
Their value is  17 cents.
```

computes the value in cents of the collection of coins in the obvious way. The statement

```
WRITELN ('You have ', COINS :2, ' coins.')
```

causes an integer value to be printed between the two strings. The symbols :2 after the variable COINS specify that the value of COINS (8) should be displayed in two print positions. If a single digit is printed, it will be printed *right justified* or in the second position with a blank in the first position. In the output shown, there are two spaces before the digit 8 and one space after. Note the use of the space character at the end of the first string and the beginning of the second string in the WRITELN statement above. Why do you think these spaces are needed?

The program body in Fig. 1.24 begins with two WRITE statements that display prompts. The WRITE statement is described in the next section.

Table 1.3 shows how two integer values are printed using different format specifications. The character □ represents a blank character. The last table line shows that the width specification may be a variable (or expression) that has an integer value.

Table 1.3 Printing Integer Values Using Formats

Value	Format	Printed Output
234	:4	□234
234	:5	□□234
234	:6	□□□234
-234	:4	-234
-234	:5	□-234
-234	:6	□□-234
234	:LEN	□□□234 (if the value of LEN is 6)

The WRITE Statement

If you run the program in Fig. 1.24, you will see that the cursor remains positioned on the same line as the ? after each prompt is displayed. This is because the word WRITE is used instead of WRITELN in the statements that print the prompting messages. Whenever WRITE is used the cursor remains positioned after the last character printed (a space in Fig. 1.24); whenever WRITELN is used the cursor advances to the next line after the output is displayed. (On some compilers, it may not be possible to use READLN immediately after WRITE. If this is true for your compiler, then you should continue to use WRITELN instead of WRITE.)

The three statements

```
WRITE ('You have ');
WRITE (COINS :2);
WRITELN (' coins.')
```

would cause the same line of output to be displayed as the statement

```
WRITELN ('You have ', COINS :2, ' coins.')
```

WRITE STATEMENT

WRITE (*output-list*)

Interpretation: The value of each variable or constant in the *output-list* is printed. Any string in the *output-list* is printed without the quotes. The cursor does not advance to the next line after the output is displayed.

Formatting Real Values

The use of formats with real values will be illustrated next.

Example 1.7 The program in Fig. 1.25 computes the average speed traveled on a trip and also the gas mileage obtained. It uses the two formulas

$$\text{speed} = \text{distance} / \text{time}$$
$$\text{mileage} = \text{distance} / \text{gallons}$$

The input data consist of the trip distance and time and the number of gallons of gasoline used.

Fig. 1.25 Formatting Real Values

```
program TRIP (INPUT, OUTPUT);

var
     SPEED, TIME, DISTANCE, MILEAGE, GALLONS : REAL;

begin
     WRITE ('Enter distance in miles: ');    READLN (DISTANCE);
     WRITE ('Enter time of trip in hours: ');    READLN (TIME);
     SPEED := DISTANCE / TIME;
     WRITELN ('Average speed in MPH was ', SPEED :5:1);
     WRITELN;

     WRITE ('Enter gallons used: ');    READLN (GALLONS);
     MILEAGE := DISTANCE / GALLONS;
     WRITELN ('Miles per gallon was ', MILEAGE :5:1)
end.

Enter distance in miles: 100
Enter time of trip in hours: 1.5
Average speed in MPH was 66.7

Enter gallons used: 25
Miles per gallon was 4.0
```

The two WRITELN statements

```
WRITELN ('Average speed in MPH was ', SPEED :5:1);
WRITELN ('Miles per gallon was ', MILEAGE :5:1)
```

each display a string followed by a real number. The symbols :5:1 specify that the real number should be displayed in 5 print positions (*field width* of 5) and that there should be 1 digit after the decimal point. The output value would be rounded to one decimal place before being printed; the decimal point accounts for one position in the field width.

The output line printed by the first WRITELN statement above would have the form

```
Average speed = XXX.X
```

where the symbols XXX.X indicate the format of the real number (three digits, a decimal point, and a digit). The decimal point always would be positioned where indicated. A value less than or equal to 99.9 would have extra blanks preceding the first digit; a value greater than 999.9 could not fit in the field. You should always specify a field width that is adequate for whatever number might be printed; if you are not sure, then make it too big rather than too small. (If the field width is too small, most compilers will expand it automatically so that the number can be printed.) If the number can be negative, don't forget to leave a space for the minus sign.

Table 1.4 shows some real values printed using different format specifications. As shown in the table, it is possible to use a format specification of the form :*n* where *n* is an integer expression. In this case, the real value is printed in scientific notation using a total of *n* print positions.

Table 1.4 Printing Real Values Using Formats

Value	Format	Printed Output
3.14159	:5:2	□3.14
3.14159	:5:1	□□3.1
3.14159	:5:3	3.142
3.14159	:8:5	□3.14159
3.15159	:9	□□3.1E+00
−0.0006	:9	□−6.0E−04
−0.0006	:8:5	−0.00060
−0.0006	:8:3	□□−0.001

The WRITELN Statement without an Output List

In Fig. 1.25, the WRITELN statement without an output list

```
WRITELN;
```

causes the blank line in the middle of the program output. Execution of a WRITELN always causes the cursor to be advanced to the next line. If nothing was printed on the current line, a blank line will appear in the program output.

WRITELN STATEMENT (without an output list)

WRITELN

Interpretation: Execution of a WRITELN statement advances the cursor to the first column of the next line.

Formatting Strings

A string value is always printed right justified in its field. This means that blanks will precede a string if the field in which it is printed is bigger than the string. If a string contains more characters than the field in which it is printed, then only part of the string will be printed; the number of characters printed is the same as the field width. These points are illustrated in Table 1.5.

Table 1.5 Printing String Values Using Formats

String	Format	Printed Output
'*'	:1	*
'*'	:2	□*
'*'	:3	□□*
'ACES'	:1	A
'ACES'	:2	AC
'ACES'	:3	ACE
'ACES'	:4	ACES
'ACES'	:5	□ACES

Self-check Exercises for Section 1.9

1. Write a program that prints a diagonal line of five asterisks (i.e, the first line should have an asterisk in column 1, the second line an asterisk in column 2, etc.).
2. Extend the program in Fig. 1.24 to handle dimes and quarters too. You will have to change the format in the last WRITELN statement.
3. Show how the value -15.564 (stored in X) would be printed using the formats:

$$\text{X } :8:4, \text{ X } :8:3, \text{ X } :8:2, \text{ X } :8:1, \text{ X } :8:0, \text{ X } :8$$

1.10 Introduction to Data Types

A major reason for the popularity of Pascal is the fact that it is relatively easy to manipulate many different kinds of information in Pascal. So far in this chapter, we have written programs that manipulate numeric data and character data. We will review the properties of these *standard data types* next.

Two types of numeric data were manipulated: REAL and INTEGER. We used the arithmetic operators +, −, *, / and the assignment operator := to manipulate these data. In addition to the operators listed above, the integer arithmetic operators div and mod can be used with type INTEGER data. These operators will be described later; the Pascal operators are listed in Appendix A.

The basic distinction between these two data types is that real variables may be used to store data containing a decimal point and a fractional part, whereas integer variables can store only a whole number. For this reason, integer variables are more limited in their use; they are often used to represent a count of items (e.g. a count of coins).

A real number in Pascal is represented as a string of digits containing a decimal point. There must be at least one digit before and one digit after the decimal point.

A real number may also be written in Pascal scientific notation. In scientific notation, a real number begins with an integer or real value followed by the letter E and an integer (possibly preceded by a sign). Examples of valid and invalid real numbers are shown in Table 1.6.

Table 1.6 Valid and Invalid Real Numbers

Valid Real Numbers		Invalid Real Numbers	
3.14159		150.	(no digit after .)
−0.005		−.12345	(no digit before .)
+12345.0		.16	(no digit before .)
−15E−04	(value of −0.0015)	−15.E−03	(−15. invalid real)
−2.345E2	(value of −234.5)	12E.3	(.3 invalid integer)
1.2E+6	(value of 1200000)	.123E3	(.123 invalid real)
1.15E−3	(value of 0.00115)		

As shown by the last valid number above, 1.15E−3 means the same as 1.15×10^{-3} where the *exponent* −3 causes the decimal point to be moved left 3 digits. A positive exponent causes the decimal point to be moved to the right; the + sign may be omitted when the exponent is positive.

The standard identifier MAXINT is a constant that represents the value of the largest integer that can be manipulated in each Pascal system. Use the statement

```
WRITELN (MAXINT)
```

in a program to find out what this value is on your computer.

The third standard data type is type CHAR. We have already seen (Example 1.1) that type CHAR variables can be used to store any single character value. Character data are always enclosed in single quotes (e.g. 'A') when written in a Pascal statement; however, quotes are not used when character data are entered at a terminal. When a READLN statement is used to read character data into a type CHAR variable, the next character entered at the terminal is stored in that variable. The space or blank character is entered by pressing the space bar; it is written as ' ' in a program.

Example 1.8   The program in Fig. 1.26 reads three characters and prints them in reverse order and enclosed in asterisks. Each character entered at the terminal is stored in a variable of type CHAR; the character value '*' is associated with the constant BORDER.

The WRITELN statement

```
WRITELN (BORDER, THIRD, SECOND, FIRST, BORDER)
```

prints five character values. As shown in the program output, each character value is printed in a single print position. The order in which the characters are displayed is the reverse of the order in which they are read. The second character read in the sample run of Fig. 1.26 is a blank.

```
program REVERSE (INPUT, OUTPUT);

const
    BORDER = '*';

var
    FIRST, SECOND, THIRD : CHAR;

begin
    WRITE ('Enter 3 characters: ');
    READLN (FIRST, SECOND, THIRD);
    WRITELN (BORDER, THIRD, SECOND, FIRST, BORDER)
end.

Enter 3 characters: E K
*K E*
```

Fig. 1.26 Program for Example 1.8

In Fig. 1.26, the string 'Enter 3 characters: ' appears in a WRITE statement. Strings are used as prompts and to clarify program output. Strings cannot be stored in type CHAR variables. We will see how to process strings in Chapter 6.

The fourth standard data type is type BOOLEAN (named after the mathematician George Boole). There are only two values associated with this data type, TRUE and FALSE. We will see examples of *Boolean expressions* (expressions that evaluate to TRUE or FALSE) in the next chapter.

Self-check Exercises for Section 1.10

1. Identify the data type of each value below. Indicate those that are invalid.

```
'XYZ'   '*'   $25.123   15.   -999   .123   'x'   "x"   '9'   '-5'
```

 ## 1.11 Common Programming Errors

One of the first things you will discover in writing programs is that a program very rarely runs correctly the first time that it is submitted. Murphy's Law, "If something can go wrong it will," seems to be written with the computer programmer or programming student in mind. In fact, errors are so common that they have their own special name (*bugs*) and the process of correcting them is called *debugging a program*. To alert you to potential problems, we will provide a section on common errors at the end of each chapter.

When an error is detected, an error message will be printed indicating that you have made a mistake and what the cause of the error might be. Unfortunately, error messages are often difficult to interpret and are sometimes misleading. However, as you gain some experience you will become more proficient at understanding them.

There are two basis categories of errors that occur: syntax errors and run-time or execution errors. Syntax errors are detected by the compiler as it attempts to translate your program. If a statement has a syntax error, then it cannot be translated and your program will not be executed.

Run-time errors are detected by the computer during execution of a program. A run-time error occurs as a result of directing the computer to perform an illegal operation such as dividing a number by zero or reading nonexistent or invalid data. When a run-time error occurs, your program will stop execution and a diagnostic message will be printed that indicates the line where the error occurred. Sometimes, the current values of all variables will be printed as well.

Syntax Errors

Figure 1.27 shows a *compiler listing* of the payroll program with each line numbered. The program contains the following syntax errors.

- missing semicolon after the program statement (line 1)
- use of : instead of = in the constant declaration (line 4)

```
  1 program PAYROLL (INPUT, OUTPUT)
  2
  3 const
*****      ^14
  4     TAX : 25.0;
*****          ^16,50
  5
  6 var
  7     HOURS, RATE, GROSS : REAL;
  8
  9 begin
 10     WRITELN ('Enter hours worked');    READLN (HOURS);
 11     WRITELN ('Enter hourly rate')      READLN (RATE);
*****                                               ^6
 12     HOURS * RATE := GROSS;
*****            ^59
 13     NET := GROSS -TAX;
*****        ^104
 14     WRITELN ('Gross pay is $', GROSS);
 15     WRITELN ('Net pay is $', NET)
*****                                   ^104
 16 end.


  6: ILLEGAL SYMBOL
 14: ';' EXPECTED
 16: '=' EXPECTED
 50: ERROR IN CONSTANT
 59: ERROR IN VARIABLE
104: IDENTIFIER NOT DECLARED
```

Fig. 1.27 Compiler Listing of a Program with Syntax Errors

- missing semicolon after the WRITELN statement (line 11)
- assignment statement with transposed variable and expression (line 12)
- missing declaration for variable NET (lines 13 and 15)

The compiler's error messages are shown after the program and look nothing like the ones above. When a syntax error is detected, the compiler prints a line starting with five asterisks, a carat symbol (^), and a list of numbers. The carat points to the position in the preceding line where the error was detected. Each number is a preassigned code for the error; the relevant codes and their meaning are listed following the program.

As an example of how this works, the first error is detected after the symbol const is processed by the compiler. At this point the compiler recognizes that a semicolon is missing (after the program statement) and indicates this by printing error code 14 (";" expected). In this case, the position of the carat is misleading as the compiler could not detect the error until it started to process the constant declaration. There is also a missing semicolon in line 11; however, this time the compiler prints error code 6 (illegal symbol) after processing READLN.

Two error codes are printed after line 4 to indicate an incorrect symbol (: instead of =). The transposed assignment statement in line 12 is printed as error code 59 (error in variable); the compiler is looking for the variable in the assignment statement and detects an error when it reaches the asterisk. Finally, the missing declaration for variable NET is printed as error code 104 (identifier not declared) after lines 13 and 15. (See Appendix E for error numbers.)

Syntax errors are often caused by the improper use of apostrophes as *string delimiters*. Make sure that you always use a single quote or apostrophe to begin and end a string; double quotes are not allowed.

Another common syntax error is a missing or extra apostrophe in a string. If the apostrophe at the end is missing, the compiler will assume that whatever follows is part of the string. A string must begin and end on the same line.

The string below contains an extra apostrophe.

```
WRITELN ('Enter Joe's nickname: ');
```

The compiler will assume that the apostrophe used to indicate possession (Joe's) is terminating the string. This string must be entered as

```
WRITELN ('Enter Joe''s nickname: ');
```

where two consecutive apostrophes inside a string indicate possession.

Run-time Errors

Figure 1.28 shows an example of a run-time error. The program compiles successfully, but the variable X is not defined before the assignment statement

```
Z := X + Y;
```

Fig. 1.28 Compiler listing of a Program with a Run-time Error

```
1    program ERRORS (INPUT, OUTPUT);
2
3    var
4        X, Y, Z : REAL;
5
6    begin
7        Y := 5.0;
8        Z := X + Y;
9        WRITELN (X, Y, Z)
10   end.
```

```
Program terminated at line 8 in program ERRORS
Undefined variable in expression
```

```
                          --- ERRORS ---

X = UNDEF                                    Y = 5.000000E+00
Z = UNDEF
```

is executed. The error messages shown after the program listing indicate the cause of the error ("undefined variable"), the location (line 8), and the values of all variables in program ERRORS at the time of the error (X and Z are undefined).

As we indicated earlier, debugging a program can be very time-consuming. The best approach is to plan your programs carefully and desk check them beforehand to eliminate bugs before they occur. If you are not sure of the syntax for a particular statement, look it up in the text or in the glossary provided inside the covers. If you follow this approach, you will be much better off in the long run.

1.12 Chapter Review

Summary

The basic components of a computer were introduced. They are main and secondary memory, the central processor, and the input and output devices. A summary of important facts about computers that you should remember follows.

1. A memory cell is never empty, but its initial contents may be meaningless to your program.
2. The current contents of a memory cell are destroyed whenever new information is placed in that cell (via an assignment or READLN statement).
3. Programs must first be placed in the memory of the computer before they can be executed.
4. Data may not be manipulated by the computer without first being stored in memory.
5. A computer cannot think for itself; it must be instructed to perform a task in a precise and unambiguous manner, using a programming language.
6. Programming a computer can be fun—if you are patient, organized, and careful.

You also saw how to use the Pascal programming language to perform some very fundamental operations. You learned how to instruct the computer to read information into memory, perform some simple computations, and print the results of the computation. All of this was done using symbols (punctuation marks, variable names, and special operators such as *, −, and +) that are familiar, easy to remember, and easy to use. You do not have to know very much about your computer in order to understand and use Pascal.

In the remainder of the text we will introduce more features of the Pascal language and provide rules for using these features. You must remember throughout that, unlike the rules of English, the rules of Pascal are precise and allow no exceptions. The compiler will be unable to translate

Pascal instructions that violate these rules. Remember to declare every identifier used as a variable or constant and to separate program statements with semicolons.

New Pascal Statements

The new Pascal statements introduced in this chapter are described in Table 1.7.

Table 1.7 Summary of New Pascal Statements

Statement	Effect
Program heading `program PAYROLL (INPUT, OUTPUT);`	Identifies `PAYROLL` as the name of the program and `INPUT` and `OUTPUT` as names of data files.

Constant declaration
`const`
`    TAX = 25.00;`
`    STAR = '*';`
	Associates the constant, `TAX`, with the real value `25.00` and the constant `STAR` with the type `CHAR` value `'*'`.

Variable declaration
`var`
`    X, Y, Z : REAL;`
`    ME, IT : INTEGER;`
	Allocates memory cells named `X`, `Y`, and `Z` for storage of real numbers and `ME` and `IT` for storage of integers.

Assignment statement `DISTANCE := SPEED * TIME`	Assigns the product of `SPEED` and `TIME` as the value of `DISTANCE`.
READLN statement `READLN (HOURS, RATE)`	Enters data into the variables `HOURS` and `RATE`.
WRITE statement `WRITE ('NET = ', NET :8:2)`	Displays the string `'NET = '` followed by the value of `NET` printed in a field of eight columns and rounded to two decimal places.
WRITELN statement `WRITELN (X, Y)`	Prints the values of `X` and `Y` and advances the cursor to the next line.

Review Questions

1. List at least three types of information stored in a computer.
2. List two functions of the CPU.
3. List two input/output devices and two secondary storage devices.
4. A computer can think.   T   F
5. List the three categories of programming languages.
6. Give three advantages of programming in a high-level language such as Pascal.
7. What two processes are needed to transform a high-level language program to a machine-language program ready for execution?
8. What are four characteristics of a structured program?
9. Check the variables below that are syntactically correct.

```
Income  ____        TWO FOLD  ____
1time   ____        c3po      ____
CONST   ____        INCOME    ____
TOM'S   ____
```

10. What is illegal about the statements below?

```
const PI = 3.14159;

var C, R : REAL;

begin
    PI := C / (2 * R * R)
```

11. What computer action is required by the statement below?

```
var CELL1 : REAL;
```

12. Write a program to read a five character name and print the name out backwards.
13. If the average size of a family is 2.8 and this value is stored in the variable FAMILYSIZE, provide the Pascal statement to display this fact in a readable way (leave the cursor on the same line).
14. List the four standard data types of Pascal.

Programming Projects

1. Write a program to convert a measurement in inches to centimeters and meters.

2. Write a program to convert a measurement in meters to inches and yards.

3. Write a program to convert a temperature in degrees Fahrenheit to degrees Celsius.

4. Write a program to read three data items into variables X, Y, and Z, and find and print their product and sum.

5. Write a program to read in the weight (in pounds) of an object, and compute and print its weight in kilograms and grams. (Hint: one pound is equal to 0.453592 kilograms or 453.59237 grams.)

6. Eight track stars entered the mile race at the Penn Relays. Write a program that will read in the race time in minutes (MINUTES) and seconds (SECONDS) for each of these runners, and compute and print the speed in feet per second (FPS) and in meters per second (MPS). (Hints: There are 5280 feet in one mile and one kilometer equals 3282 feet.) Test your program on each of the times below.

Minutes	Seconds
3	52.83
3	59.83
4	00.03
4	16.22

7. Write a program that prints your initials in large block letters. (Hint: Use a 6 × 6 grid for each letter and print six strings. Each string should consist of a row of *'s interspersed with blanks.)

8. You are planning to rent a car to drive from Boston to Philadelphia. You want to be certain that you can make the trip on one tankful of gas. Write a program to read in the miles-per-gallon (MPG) and tank size (TANKSIZE) in gallons for a particular rent-a-car, and print out the distance that can be traveled on one tank. Test your program for the following data:

Miles-per gallon	Tank size (gallons)
10.0	15.0
40.5	20.0
22.5	12.0
10.0	9.0

9. A cyclist coasting on a level road slows from a speed of 10 miles/hr. to 2.5 miles/hr. in one minute. Write a computer program that calculates the cyclist's constant rate of acceleration and determines how long it will take the cyclist to come to rest, given an initial speed of 10 miles/hr. (Hint: Use the equation

$$a = \frac{V_f - V_i}{t}$$

where a is acceleration, t is time interval, v_i is initial velocity, and v_f is the final velocity.)

10. Write a program that reads the user's first and middle initials and then the first six letters of the user's last name. Blank characters should be entered if the user's last name has fewer than six letters. The user's name should then be displayed on the next line in the form last name first, space, first initial, space, and middle initial.

11. The diagram below shows two airline routes from Philadelphia to Dallas. Read each distance shown into a type INTEGER variable and then find the distance from Philadelphia to Dallas for each route.

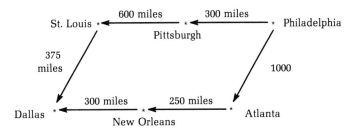

12. If a human heart beats on the average of once a second for 78 years, how many times does the heart beat in a life-time? (Use 365.25 for days in a year. Rerun your program for a heart-rate of 75 beats per minute.

13. In shopping for a new house, several factors must be considered. In this problem the initial cost of the house, estimated annual fuel costs, and annual tax rate are available. Write a program that will determine the total cost after a five year period for each set of house data below. You should be able to inspect your program output to determine the "best buy".

Initial house cost	Annual fuel cost	Tax rate per $1000
$67,000	$2,300	0.025
$62,000	$2,500	0.025
$75,000	$1,850	0.020

To calculate the house cost, add the initial cost to the fuel cost for five years, then add the taxes for five years. Taxes for one year are computed by multiplying the tax rate by the initial cost.

2

Problem Solving

2.1 Representing and Refining Algorithms
2.2 Using Procedures for Subproblems
2.3 Decision Steps in Algorithms
2.4 Tracing a Program or Algorithm
2.5 Problem Solving Strategies
2.6 Repetition in Programs
2.7 Generalizing a Solution
2.8 Repeating a Program Body
2.9 Debugging and Testing Programs
2.10 Common Programming Errors
2.11 Chapter Review

This chapter will focus on strategies for problem solving. The ability to solve problems is an essential component of programming. Problem solving strategies such as divide and conquer, stepwise refinement, solution by analogy, and solution by generalization will be illustrated.

We will see how to represent the list of steps in a solution strategy as an algorithm and how to implement an algorithm as a program. We will discuss how to hand-simulate or trace the execution of an algorithm or program to verify that it is correct.

The division of a problem into smaller subproblems will be discussed. A structure chart will be used to show the relationships between program modules that solve these subproblems. Also, the use of Pascal procedures to implement separate program modules will be introduced.

The necessity for decision steps and repetition in a problem solution will be demonstrated. Relational operators will be used to describe conditions that evaluate to true or false. The `if` statement will be introduced as a way to specify decisions in a program; the `for` statement will be introduced as a way to specify repetition.

2.1 Representing and Refining Algorithms

Divide and Conquer

One of the most fundamental methods of problem solving is to break a large problem into several smaller *subproblems*. This enables us to solve a large problem one step at a time, rather than to provide the entire solution at once. This technique is often called *divide and conquer*.

As an example, let us assume it is the year 2000 and we have a household robot (named Robbie) to help with some simple chores. We would like Robbie to serve us breakfast. Unfortunately Robbie is an early production model, and in order for Robbie to perform even the simplest task, we must provide the robot with a detailed list of instructions.

Robbie Serving Breakfast

Problem: Robbie is at point R (for Robbie) in Fig. 2.1. We want Robbie to retrieve our favorite box of cereal (point C) and bring it to the table (point T) in the next room. The position of these points and an additional point D (described later) is shown in Fig. 2.1.

Discussion: We can accomplish our goal by having Robbie perform the four steps listed below.

1. Move from point R to point C.
2. Retrieve the cereal box at point C.
3. Move from point C to point T.
4. Place the cereal box on the table at point T.

Solving these four subproblems will give us the solution to the original problem stated earlier.

Fig. 2.1 Robbie Serving Breakfast

We can attack each of these subproblems independently. In order to solve any of these problems we must have an idea of the basic operations that Robbie can perform. We will assume that Robbie can rotate or turn to face any direction, move straight ahead, and grasp and release specified objects. Given this information, subproblems 2 and 4 are basic operations, provided Robbie is in the correct position. First we will concentrate on moving Robbie (subproblems 1 and 3).

In solving the first subproblem

1. Move from point R to point C.

we must allow for the fact that Robbie can move only in one direction at a time, and that direction is straight ahead. Consequently, the steps required to solve subproblem 1 are:

1.1 Turn to face point C.
1.2 Move from point R to point C.

Step 3 may be solved in a similar way. However, since Robbie cannot walk through walls, the steps for solving subproblem 3 might be:

3.1 Turn to face the doorway (point D) between the rooms.
3.2 Move from point C to point D.
3.3 Turn to face point T.
3.4 Move from point D to point T.

To summarize the events so far, we divided the original problem of getting Robbie to bring our breakfast cereal to the table into four subproblems, all of which can be solved independently. Two of these subproblems were broken up into even smaller subproblems.

The complete list of steps required to solve our problem is shown below. This list of steps is called an *algorithm*. The process of adding detail to a solution algorithm (e.g., rewriting step 1 as steps 1.1 and 1.2) is called *stepwise refinement*.

Algorithm

1. Move from point R to point C.
   1.1 Turn to face point C.
   1.2 Move from point R to point C.
2. Retrieve the cereal box at point C.
3. Move from point C to point T.
   3.1 Turn to face the doorway (point D) between the rooms.
   3.2 Move from point C to point D.
   3.3 Turn to face point T.
   3.4 Move from point D to point T.
4. Place the cereal box on the table at point T.

Algorithms in Everyday Life

Algorithms are not unique to the study of robots or computer programming. You have probably been using algorithms to solve problems without being aware of it.

Changing a
Flat Tire

Problem: You are driving a car with two friends and suddenly get a flat tire. Fortunately, there is a spare tire and jack in the trunk.

Discussion: After pulling over to the side of the road, you might decide to subdivide the problem of changing a tire into the subproblems below.

Algorithm

1. Jack up the car.
2. Loosen the lug nuts from the flat tire and remove it.
3. Get the spare tire, place it on the wheel, and tighten the lug nuts.
4. Lower the car.
5. Secure the jack and flat tire in the trunk.

Since these steps are relatively independent, you might decide to assign subproblem 1 to friend A, subproblem 2 to friend B, subproblem 3 to yourself, etc. If friend A has used a jack before, then the whole process should proceed very smoothly; however, if friend A does not know how to use a jack it might be necessary to refine step 1 further.

Step 1
refinement

1.1 Place the jack under the car near the tire that is flat.
1.2 Insert the jack handle in the jack.
1.3 Place a block of wood under the car to keep it from rolling.
1.4 Jack up the car until there is enough room for the spare tire.

Step 1.3 requires a bit of decision making on your friend's part. The actual placement of the block of wood depends on whether the car is facing uphill or downhill, as described next.

Step 1.3
refinement

1.3.1 If the car is facing uphill then place the block of wood in back of a tire that is not flat; if the car is facing downhill, then place the block of wood in front of a tire that is not flat.

Finally, step 1.4 involves a repetitive action: moving the jack handle until there is sufficient room to put on the spare tire. Often, people stop when the car is high enough to remove the flat tire, forgetting that an inflated tire requires more room. It may take a few attempts to complete step 1.4.

Step 1.4
refinement

1.4.1 Move the jack handle repeatedly until the car is high enough off the ground that the spare tire can be put on the wheel.

Throughout the rest of this chapter (and book), we will discuss computer problem solving. Pertinent concepts from this section include:

- Dividing a problem into subproblems
- Solving each subproblem separately
- Assigning separate subproblems to independent program modules
- Refining an algorithm step to provide solution detail
- Decision making in an algorithm step
- Repetition of an algorithm step

Understanding the Problem

An important skill in human communication is the ability to listen carefully. Often, we are too busy thinking of what our response will be to really
hear what the other person is saying. This can lead to a lack of understanding between the speaker and listener.

Many of us suffer from a similar difficulty when we attempt to solve
problems that are either presented verbally or in writing. We do not pay
close enough attention to the problem statement to determine what really
is being asked; consequently, we are either unable to solve the stated
problem, or our problem solution is incorrect because it solves the wrong
problem.

This text is concerned with improving your problem solving skills, and
will present hints and techniques for problem solving. It is most important
that you analyze a problem statement carefully before attempting to solve
it. You should read each problem statement two or three times if necessary. The first time that you read a problem you should get a general idea
of what is being asked. The second time that you read it you should try to
answer the questions:

- What information should the solution provide?
- What data do I have to work with?

The answer to the first question will tell you the desired results or the
problem outputs. The answer to the second question will tell you what
data are provided or the *problem inputs*. It may be helpful to underline the
phrases in the problem statement that identify the inputs and outputs. Inputs are in blue and outputs in gray in the problem statement that follows.

Finding the Sum and Average of Two Numbers

Problem: Read in two numbers and find and print their sum and average.

Discussion: After identifying the problem inputs and outputs, we must
determine the amount and type of memory required to store these data.
Clearly, two memory cells are required for the input data and two memory
cells are required for the output information. We must also choose meaningful variable names for these cells which will hold type REAL data. We
will summarize these decisions as shown below.

PROBLEM INPUTS

the first number (NUM1 : REAL)
the second number (NUM2 : REAL)

PROBLEM OUTPUTS

the sum of the 2 numbers (SUM : REAL)
the average of the 2 numbers (AVERAGE : REAL)

Once the problem inputs and outputs are known, the steps necessary to solve the problem should be listed. It is very important that you pay close attention to the order of the steps. The algorithm follows.

Algorithm

1. Read the values of NUM1 and NUM2.
2. Find the sum (SUM) of NUM1 and NUM2.
3. Find the average (AVERAGE) of NUM1 and NUM2.
4. Print the values of SUM and AVERAGE.

Next, we should refine any steps whose solution is not immediately obvious. All of you know how to find the average of two numbers, but to further illustrate the refinement process, the refinement of step 3 is listed next.

Step 3 refinement

3.1 Divide SUM by 2 and store this value in AVERAGE.

The next step is to implement the algorithm as a program. This is done by first writing the declaration section of the program using the problem input and output descriptions; then the algorithm steps should be written in Pascal. If an algorithm step is refined, then the refinement is implemented instead. Consequently, we should implement algorithm steps 1, 2, 3.1, and 4 in the body of the program. The Pascal program is shown in Fig. 2.2.

Fig. 2.2 Finding the Sum and Average of Two Numbers

```
program FINDSUMAVE  (INPUT, OUTPUT);

{Finds and prints the sum and average of two numbers.}

var
    NUM1, NUM2,                    {two input numbers}
    SUM,                           {sum of NUM1, NUM2}
    AVERAGE    : REAL;             {average of NUM1, NUM2}

begin
    {Read the values of NUM1 and NUM2}
    WRITE ('First number? ');    READLN (NUM1);
    WRITE ('Second number? ');   READLN (NUM2);

    {Find the sum of NUM1, NUM2}
    SUM := NUM1 + NUM2;

    {Find the average of NUM1, NUM2}
    AVERAGE := SUM / 2;

    {Print the values of SUM and AVERAGE}
    WRITELN ('Their sum is ', SUM :8:2);
    WRITELN ('Their average is ', AVERAGE :8:2)
end.

First number? 10.5
Second number? 11.5
Their sum is     22.00
Their average is    11.00
```

The program in Fig. 2.2 contains some English phrases enclosed in curly braces { }. These phrases, called *comments*, are used to make the program easier to understand by describing the purpose of the program (see the comment under the `program` statement), the use of identifiers (see the comments in the variable declaration statement), and the purpose of each program step (see the comments in the program body). Comments are considered part of the *documentation* of a program as they help others read and follow the program; however, they are ignored by the compiler and are not translated into machine language.

As shown in Fig. 2.2, a comment can appear by itself on a program line, at the end of a line after a statement, or be embedded in a statement. The comment at the end of the line below

```
var
    NUM1, NUM2,                          {two input numbers}
```

is embedded within the variable declaration statement that is continued following the comment. The syntax and use of comments are described in the next displays.

COMMENT

```
{ this is a comment }
or (* this is a comment *)
```

Interpretation: The left curly brace {indicates the start of a comment; the right curly brace } indicates the end of a comment. Comments are listed with the program, but are otherwise ignored by the Pascal compiler.

Note: On some Pascal systems, the characters (* and *) must be used to indicate the start and end of a comment, respectively.

PROGRAM STYLE

Using comments

Comments are used to make a program more readable by describing the purpose of the program and by describing the use of each identifier. Comments are used within the program body to describe the purpose of each section of the program. There will generally be one comment in the program body for each major algorithm step.

A comment within the program body should describe what the step does rather than simply restate the step in English. For example, the comment

```
{Find the average of NUM1, NUM2}
AVERAGE := SUM / 2;
```

is more descriptive and, hence, preferable to

```
{Divide SUM by 2 and store the result in AVERAGE}
AVERAGE := SUM / 2;
```

Self-check Exercises for Section 2.1

1. Describe the problem inputs and outputs and algorithm for computing the sum and average of four numbers.
2. Describe the problem inputs and outputs and algorithm for the following problem: Compute the discounted price for an item given the list price and the percentage of the discount.

2.2 Using Procedures for Subproblems

The Structure Chart

As we mentioned earlier, one of the most fundamental ideas in problem solving is dividing a problem into subproblems and solving each subproblem independently of the others. In the simple problem just analyzed this was not a difficult task. Only one subproblem required refinement and that was not extensive. In many situations, one or more subproblems may require significant refinement as shown next.

Mother's Day Message Problem

Problem: Mother's Day is coming and you would like to do something special for your mother. Write a Pascal program to print the message "HI MOM" in large capital letters.

Discussion: There is more than one way to interpret this problem. We could simply print "HI MOM" as it appears on this line, but that would not be too impressive. It would be nicer to use large block letters as shown in Fig. 2.3. Since program output tends to run from the top of the screen downward, it is easier and more interesting to print the letters in a vertical column rather than across the screen.

Algorithm

1. Print the word "HI" in block letters.
2. Print three blank lines.
3. Print the word "MOM" in block letters.

The obvious refinements for each step are shown next.

Step 1 refinement

1.1 Print the letter "H".
1.2 Print the letter "I".

Step 3 refinement

3.1 Print the letter "M".
3.2 Print the letter "O".
3.3 Print the letter "M".

Fig. 2.3 Mother's Day Message

We can illustrate what we have done so far by using a diagram to show the algorithm subproblems and their interdependencies. This diagram, called a *structure chart*, is shown in Fig. 2.4.

As we trace down this diagram, we go from a more abstract problem to a more detailed subproblem. The original problem is shown at the top, or level 0, of the structure chart. Each of the major subproblems is shown at level 1. The different subproblems resulting from the refinement of each level 1 step are shown at level 2 and are connected to their respective level 1 subproblem. The right side of this diagram shows that the subproblem *Print "MOM"* is dependent on the solutions to the subproblems *Print "M"* and *Print "O"*. Since the subproblem *Print 3 blank lines* is not refined further, there are no level 2 subproblems connected to it.

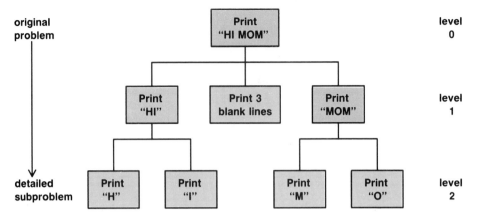

original problem

detailed subproblem

level 0

level 1

level 2

Fig. 2.4 Structure Chart for Mother's Day Message

The purpose of the structure chart is to show the structural relationship between the subproblems. The algorithm (not the structure chart) shows the order in which each step must be carried out to solve the problem.

Procedure Declaration

It is desirable to implement each of the subproblems shown at level 2 in Fig. 2.4 as a separate module. In this way we can concentrate on the design of each individual module without distraction. This can be done in Pascal by using a *procedure*.

The procedure PRINTM is shown in Fig. 2.5. A *procedure declaration* begins with a *procedure heading* which consists of the word procedure followed by the procedure name (an identifier).

procedure PRINTM;

A comment describing the purpose of the procedure will come next, followed by the *procedure body*. The procedure body always starts with

Fig. 2.5 Procedure PRINTM

```
procedure PRINTM;

{Prints the block letter "M".}

begin {PRINTM}
    WRITELN ('*        *');
    WRITELN ('**      **');
    WRITELN ('* *    * *');
    WRITELN ('*  **    *');
    WRITELN ('*        *');
    WRITELN ('*        *');
    WRITELN ('*        *');
    WRITELN
end;   {PRINTM}
```

begin and ends with end. In Fig. 2.5, the procedure body contains the seven WRITELN statements needed to print the block letter "M" followed by the WRITELN statement needed to print a blank line.

In this text, the begin and end that bracket a procedure body will always be followed by a comment that identifies the procedure name; the comment is added for clarity and is not required by Pascal. The semicolon following end is required.

The declaration of procedure PRINTM must appear in the declaration part of any program that uses it. The procedure declaration indicates that the identifier PRINTM is the name of a procedure and provides the list of statements that comprise PRINTM. Procedure declarations always follow the variable declarations in a program.

Procedure (Call) Statement

When procedure PRINTM is referenced in a program, the procedure body is executed and the block letter "M" is printed. The *procedure (call) statement*

        PRINTM

may be used to reference or *call* this procedure; i.e. to make it execute.

Figure 2.6 shows the body of the Mother's Day program, assuming that each subproblem at level 2 in Fig. 2.4 is implemented as a separate procedure. The program body (called the *main program*) implements the algorithm described earlier. Algorithm steps 1.1, 1.2, 3.1, 3.2, and 3.3 are implemented as procedure (call) statements; algorithm step 2 is a sequence of WRITELN statements.

Besides the WRITELN statements, there are five procedure (call) statements in the main program shown in Fig. 2.6. Procedure (call) statement PRINTM appears twice because the letter "M" must be printed twice. The comment {MOTHER} follows the begin and end that bracket the main program body.

Fig. 2.6 Main Program Body for the Mother's Day Problem

```
begin {MOTHER}
    {Print the word "HI"}
    PRINTH;
    PRINTI;

    {Print three blank lines}
    WRITELN;
    WRITELN;
    WRITELN;

    {Print the word "MOM"}
    PRINTM;
    PRINTO;
    PRINTM
end.  {MOTHER}
```

The procedure (call) statement is used to call a procedure into execution. Pascal requires that each procedure called by the main program be declared in the declaration part of the program (before the program body). The relative order of the individual procedures is irrelevant in this problem. The program so far is shown in Fig. 2.7; the remaining procedure declarations are left as an exercise.

```
program MOTHER (OUTPUT);

{Prints a mother's day welcoming message.}

procedure PRINTM;

{Prints the block letter "M".}

begin {PRINTM}
    WRITELN ('*        *');
    WRITELN ('**      **');
    WRITELN ('* *    * *');
    WRITELN ('*  **    *');
    WRITELN ('*        *');
    WRITELN ('*        *');
    WRITELN ('*        *');
    WRITELN
end; {PRINTM}

procedure PRINTH;

{Prints the block letter "H".}

begin {PRINTH}
    {body of procedure PRINTH goes here}
end; {PRINTH}

procedure PRINTI;

{Prints the block letter "I".}

begin {PRINTI}
    {body of procedure PRINTI goes here}
end; {PRINTI}

procedure PRINTO;

{Prints the block letter "O".}

begin
    {body of procedure PRINTO goes here}
end; {PRINTO}

begin {MOTHER}
    {Print the word "HI"}
    PRINTH;
    PRINTI;

    {Print three blank lines}
```

```
      WRITELN;
      WRITELN;
      WRITELN;

      {Print the word "MOM"}
      PRINTM;
      PRINTO;
      PRINTM
end. {MOTHER}
```

Fig. 2.7 Partially Completed Mother's Day Program

Note that it was not necessary to include file INPUT in the program statement of Fig. 2.7. This is because there were no input data to be read by the program.

A convenient aspect of the use of procedures in Pascal is that it allows us to delay the detailed implementation of a complicated subproblem until later (procedures PRINTH, PRINTI, PRINTO are not yet written). This is, in fact, what we are trying to do when we divide a problem into subproblems and add details of the solution through stepwise refinement. The use of procedures also enables us to implement our program in logically independent sections in the same way that we develop the solution algorithm.

Another advantage is that procedures may be executed more than once. For example, procedure PRINTM is called twice in Fig. 2.7. Each time PRINTM is called the list of eight WRITELN statements shown in Fig. 2.5 would be executed and the letter "M" would be printed. If we were not using procedures, these WRITELN statements would have to be listed twice in the program body.

Finally, once a procedure is written and tested, it may be used in other programs. For example, the procedures discussed here could be used to write programs that print the messages "OH HIM" or "HI HO." It would be very easy to write these programs.

Each procedure declaration may contain declarations for its own constants, variables, and even for other procedures. These identifiers are considered *local* to the procedure and can only be referenced within the procedure (more on this later). The displays that follow summarize the new statements introduced in this section.

PROCEDURE DECLARATION

procedure *pname*;

local-declaration-section

begin {*pname*}
    procedure-body
end; {*pname*}

Interpretation: The procedure *pname* is declared. Any identifiers that are declared in the *local-declaration-section* are defined only during

---

the execution of the procedure and can only be referenced within the procedure. The *procedure body* describes the data manipulation to be performed by the procedure.

PROCEDURE (CALL) STATEMENT

pname

Interpretation: The procedure (call) statement initiates the execution of procedure *pname*.

PROGRAM STYLE

Use of comments and color in a program with procedures

Several comments are included in Fig. 2.7. Each procedure begins with a comment that describes its purpose. The `begin` and `end` that bracket each procedure body and the main program body are followed by a comment identifying that procedure or program. The first and last line of each procedure declaration is in blue type. This is also to help you locate each procedure in the program listing.

Relative Order of Procedures and the Main Program

In the Mother's Day Message Problem, the main program body was written as a sequence of procedure (call) statements before the details of all procedures were specified. The next step would be to provide the missing procedure declarations. We will use this technique to write Pascal programs for most problems in the text.

When we actually pull the separate procedures and main program together into a cohesive unit (the final program), the procedures must be listed in the declaration part of the program directly following any variable declarations. Thus the procedure declarations will be listed before the main program body. The reason for this is that Pascal requires that every identifier be declared before it can be referenced.

When the program is run, the first statement in the program body is the first statement executed. When a procedure (call) statement is reached, control is passed to the procedure that is referenced. Any memory that may be needed for the procedure's local data will be allocated, and the first statement in the procedure body will be executed. After the last statement in the procedure body is executed, control is *returned* to the main program and the next statement after the procedure (call) statement will be executed. Any memory that was allocated to the procedure will be released to be reallocated for other purposes.

The sequence of execution of the Mother's Day program is illustrated in Fig. 2.8. The first statement in the main program body

```
PRINTH;
```

is executed first and calls procedure `PRINTH` into execution. After each of the `WRITELN` statements in `PRINTH` is executed, control is returned to the next statement in the main program body

```
PRINTI;
```

The above procedure (call) statement would, of course, call procedure `PRINTI` into execution.

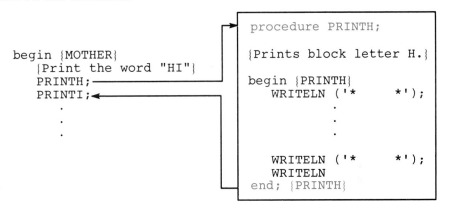

```
begin {MOTHER}                      procedure PRINTH;
    {Print the word "HI"}
    PRINTH;                         {Prints block letter H.}
    PRINTI;
      .                             begin {PRINTH}
      .                                 WRITELN ('*        *');
      .                                   .
                                          .
                                          .

                                        WRITELN ('*        *');
                                        WRITELN
                                    end; {PRINTH}
```

Fig 2.8 Flow of Control Between Main Program and Procedure

Self-check Exercises for Section 2.2

1. Provide procedures `PRINTH`, `PRINTI`, and `PRINTO` for the Mother's Day Problem.
2. Write a program to print "HI HO" in block letters. Provide a structure chart for this problem.

2.3 Decision Steps in Algorithms

In all the algorithms illustrated, each algorithm step is executed exactly once in the order in which it appears. Often we are faced with situations in which we must provide alternative steps that may or may not be executed, depending on the input data. For example, in the simple payroll problem discussed in Chapter 1, a tax of $25 was deducted regardless of the employee's salary. It would be more accurate to base the amount deducted on the employee's gross salary.

Conditions and Relational Operators

An example of a decision step is illustrated in the step below:

> If gross salary exceeds $100 deduct a tax of $25;
> otherwise, deduct no tax.

The refinement of this step should show that there are two alternative courses of action: either deduct a tax or do not deduct a tax. In order to determine what to do, a payroll clerk might ask the question "Is gross salary greater than $100?"; the clerk would perform one action (deduct tax) if the answer is "Yes" and the other action (deduct no tax) if the answer is "No."

We can describe the payroll clerk's decision process using the *decision step* below.

> if gross salary is greater than $100 then
>   Deduct a tax of $25
> else
>   Deduct no tax

This decision step is written in *pseudocode*, a mixture of English and Pascal. We will use pseudocode to represent algorithms.

This decision step specifies that either the action "Deduct a tax of $25" or the action "Deduct no tax" will take place, but not both. The evaluation of the *condition* "gross salary is greater than $100" determines which action will take place. A condition is a *Boolean expression*, which is an expression that evaluates to either true or false. If the condition value is true, then the task following the word then is executed; if the condition value is false, then the task following the word else is executed instead.

We can rewrite the condition "gross salary is greater than $100" in Pascal as GROSS > 100 where the symbol > means greater than. Most conditions that we use will have one of the forms

variable relational operator variable
variable relational operator constant

where the *relational operators* are the familiar symbols < (less than), <= (less than or equal), > (greater than), >= (greater than or equal), = (equal), and <> (not equal).

Example 2.1   The relational operators and some sample conditions are shown in Table 2.1. Each condition is evaluated assuming the variable values below.

X	POWER	MAXPOW	Y	ITEM	MINITEM	MOMORDAD	NUM	SENTINEL
0	1024	1024	7	1.5	-999.0	'M'	999	999

Table 2.1 Pascal Relational Operators and Sample Conditions

Operator	Condition	Meaning	Value
<=	X <= 0	X less than or equal to 0	true
<	POWER < MAXPOW	POWER less than MAXPOW	false
>=	X >= Y	X greater than or equal to Y	false
>	ITEM > MINITEM	ITEM greater than MINITEM	true
=	MOMORDAD = 'M'	MOMORDAD equal to 'M'	true
<>	NUM <> SENTINEL	NUM not equal to SENTINEL	false

Using a Decision Step in a Problem Solution

The problem that follows requires the use of a decision step in its solution.

Modified Payroll Problem

Problem: Modify the simple payroll program to deduct a $25 tax only if an employee earns more than $100 and deduct no tax otherwise.

Discussion: We will analyze this problem using the tools developed so far in this chapter. First, we list the data requirements and the algorithm.

PROBLEM CONSTANTS

maximum salary without a tax deduction (TAXBRACKET = 100.00)
amount of tax deducted (TAX = 25.00)

PROBLEM INPUTS

hours worked (HOURS : REAL)
hourly rate (RATE : REAL)

PROBLEM OUTPUTS

gross pay (GROSS : REAL)
net pay (NET : REAL)

Algorithm

1. Enter hours worked and hourly rate.
2. Compute gross salary.
3. Compute net salary.
4. Print gross salary and net salary.

As shown previously, problem constants have the same values for each run of the program as distinguished from problem inputs whose values may vary. Each constant value is associated with an identifier (TAX and TAXBRACKET above). The reason for this will be discussed after the program is completed.

The structure chart for this algorithm is shown in Fig. 2.9; the complete program is shown in Fig. 2.10. The refinement of algorithm step 3 follows.

Step 3 refinement

3.1 if GROSS > TAXBRACKET then
        Deduct a tax of $25
     else
        Deduct no tax

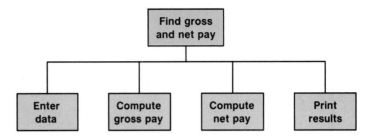

Fig. 2.9 Structure Chart for Modified Payroll Problem

Fig. 2.10 Program for Modified Payroll Problem

```
program MODPAY (INPUT, OUTPUT);

{Computes and prints gross pay and net pay given an hourly
 rate and number of hours worked. Deducts a tax of $25 if gross
 salary exceeds $100; otherwise, deducts no tax.              }

const
    TAXBRACKET = 100.00;      {maximum salary for no deduction}
    TAX = 25.00;              {tax amount}

var
    HOURS, RATE,             {hours worked, hourly rate}
    GROSS, NET : REAL;       {gross pay, net pay}

begin {MODPAY}
    {Enter HOURS and RATE}
    WRITE ('Hours worked? ');  READLN (HOURS);
    WRITE ('Hourly rate? ');   READLN (RATE);

    {Compute gross salary}
    GROSS := HOURS * RATE;

    {Compute net salary}
    if GROSS > TAXBRACKET then
       NET := GROSS - TAX        {Deduct a tax amount}
    else
       NET := GROSS;             {Deduct no tax}

    {Print GROSS and NET}
    WRITELN ('Gross salary is $', GROSS :8:2);
    WRITELN ('Net salary is $', NET :8:2)
end. {MODPAY}

Hours worked? 40
Hourly rate? 5.00
Gross salary is $ 200.00
Net salary is $ 175.00
```

In Fig. 2.10, the Pascal `if` statement

```
if GROSS > TAXBRACKET then
    NET := GROSS - TAX                {deduct a tax amount}
else
    NET := GROSS;                     {deduct no tax}
```

is used to implement the decision step (step 3) shown earlier. The comments on the right are embedded in the `if` statement. The next section will provide more examples of the `if` statement.

PROGRAM STYLE

Use of constants

The constants TAX and TAXBRACKET appear in the preceding `if` statement and in Fig. 2.10. We could just as easily have inserted the constant values directly in the `if` statement and written

```
if GROSS > 100.00 then
    NET := GROSS - 25.00
else
    NET := GROSS;
```

There are two advantages to using constants. First, the original `if` statement is easier to understand because it uses the names TAX and TAXBRACKET, which are descriptive, rather than numbers, which have no intrinsic meaning. Second, a program written with constants is much easier to modify than one that is not. If we wish to use different constant values in Fig. 2.10, we need to change only the constant declaration statement. If the constant values were inserted directly in the `if` statement as shown above, then we would have to change the `if` statement and any other statements that manipulate the constant values.

More if Statement Examples

The `if` statement in Fig. 2.10 has two alternatives, but only one will be executed for a given value of GROSS. An `if` statement can also have a single alternative that is executed only when the condition is true, as shown next.

Example 2.2 The `if` statement below has one alternative which is executed only when X is not equal to zero. It causes PRODUCT to be multiplied by X; the new value is saved in PRODUCT. If X is equal to zero, the multiplication is not performed.

```
{Multiply PRODUCT by a nonzero X only}
if X <> 0 then
    PRODUCT := PRODUCT * X
```

Example 2.3   The `if` statement below has two alternatives. It will call either procedure PRINTMOM or PRINTDAD depending on the character stored in variable MOMORDAD.

```
if MOMORDAD = 'M' then
    PRINTMOM
else
    PRINTDAD
```

The `if` statement below is identical to the one above except that a semicolon appears after PRINTMOM. A syntax error would be detected when the compiler reaches the word `else` because the semicolon terminates the `if` statement and the next statement cannot begin with the word `else`. This error is called a *dangling else*.

```
if MOMORDAD = 'M' then
    PRINTMOM;
else                                    {error -- dangling else}
    PRINTDAD
```

In the next `if` statement, a semicolon also appears after PRINTMOM. In this case, the semicolon separates the `if` statement from the procedure (call) statement PRINTDAD that follows it.

```
if MOMORDAD = 'M' then
    PRINTMOM;
PRINTDAD
```

The `if` statement above has one alternative; procedure PRINTMOM will be called only when MOMORDAD has the value `'M'`. Regardless of whether or not PRINTMOM is called, procedure PRINTDAD will always be called.

The next problem illustrates the use of `if` statements with one and two alternatives.

Finding the First Letter

Problem: Read three letters and find and print the one that comes first in the alphabet.

Discussion: From our prior experience with conditions and decision steps, we know how to compare two items at a time to see which one is smaller using the relational operator <. In Pascal, we can also use this operator to determine whether one letter precedes another in the alphabet. For example, the condition `'A' < 'F'` is true because A precedes F in the alphabet. The problem inputs and outputs are listed next followed by the algorithm.

three letters (CH1, CH2, CH3 : CHAR)

the alphabetically first letter (ALPHAFIRST : CHAR)

Algorithm

1. Read three letters into CH1, CH2, and CH3.
2. Save the alphabetically first of CH1, CH2, and CH3 in ALPHAFIRST.
3. Print the alphabetically first letter.

Step 2 can be performed by first comparing CH1 and CH2 and saving the alphabetically first letter in ALPHAFIRST; this result can then be compared to CH3. The refinement of step 2 follows.

Step 2 refinement

2.1 Save the alphabetically first of CH1 and CH2 in ALPHAFIRST.
2.2 Save the alphabetically first of CH3 and ALPHAFIRST in ALPHA-FIRST.

The structure chart corresponding to the algorithm is drawn in Fig. 2.11; the program is shown in Fig. 2.12.

In Fig. 2.12, the if statement with two alternatives saves either CH1 or CH2 in ALPHAFIRST. The if statement with one alternative stores CH3 in ALPHAFIRST if CH3 precedes the value already in ALPHAFIRST.

In the next chapter, we will see that if statements with several (more than two) alternatives are also possible in Pascal. The forms of the if statement we will use are summarized in the displays that follow.

Fig. 2.11 Structure Chart for Finding Alphabetically First Letter

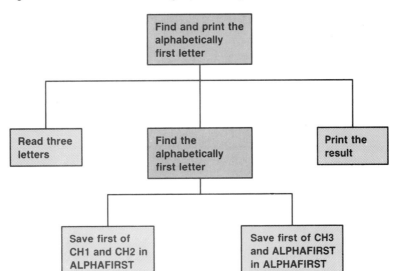

```
program FIRSTLETTER (INPUT, OUTPUT);

{Finds and prints the alphabetically first letter.}

var
    CH1, CH2, CH3,                      {three letters read}
    ALPHAFIRST : CHAR;                  {alphabetically first letter}

begin {FIRSTLETTER}
    {Read three letters}
    WRITE ('Enter any three letters: ');
    READLN (CH1, CH2, CH3);

    {Store the alphabetically first of CH1 and CH2 in ALPHAFIRST}
    if CH1 < CH2 then
        ALPHAFIRST := CH1              {CH1 comes before CH2}
    else
        ALPHAFIRST := CH2;            {CH2 comes before CH1}

    {Store the alphabetically first of CH3 and ALPHAFIRST}
    if CH3 < ALPHAFIRST then
        ALPHAFIRST := CH3;           {CH3 comes before ALPHAFIRST}

    {Print result}
    WRITELN (ALPHAFIRST, ' is the first letter alphabetically')
end. {FIRSTLETTER}

Enter any three letters: EBK
B is the first letter alphabetically
```

Fig. 2.12 Finding the Alphabetically First Letter

IF STATEMENT (two alternatives)

```
if condition then
    statement_T
else
    statement_F
```

Interpretation: If the *condition* evaluates to true, then *statement*$_T$ is executed and *statement*$_F$ is skipped; otherwise, *statement*$_T$ is skipped and *statement*$_F$ is executed.

IF STATEMENT (one alternative)

```
if condition then
    statement_T
```

Interpretation: If the *condition* evaluates to true, then *statement*$_T$ is executed; otherwise, it is skipped.

Structuring the `if` *statement*

In all the `if` statement examples, *statement*$_T$ and *statement*$_F$ are indented. If the word `else` appears, it is entered on a separate line and aligned under the word `if`. The structure of the `if` statement makes its meaning apparent. Again, this is done solely to improve program readability; the structure used makes no difference to the compiler.

Self-check Exercises for Section 2.3

1. Modify the structure chart and program in the First Letter Problem to find the alphabetically last of three letters.
2. Modify the structure chart and program in the First Letter Problem to find the first of four letters.
3. Write Pascal statements to carry out the steps below.
   a) If ITEM is nonzero, then multiply PRODUCT by ITEM and save the result in PRODUCT; otherwise, skip the multiplication. In either case, print the value of PRODUCT.
   b) Store the absolute difference of X and Y in Z, where the absolute difference is X − Y or Y − X, whichever is positive.
   c) If X is zero then add 1 to ZEROCOUNT; otherwise, if X is negative, add X to MINUSSUM; otherwise, if X is positive, add X to PLUSSUM.

2.4 Tracing a Program or Algorithm

A critical step in the design of an algorithm or program is to verify that it is correct before extensive time is spent entering or debugging it. Often a few extra minutes spent in verifying the correctness of an algorithm will save hours of testing time later.

One important technique is a hand trace or desk check of an algorithm or program. This consists of a careful, step-by-step simulation on paper of how the algorithm or program would be executed by the computer. The results of the simulation should show the effect of each step as it is executed on data that are relatively easy to manipulate by hand.

Table 2.2 shows a trace of the program in Fig. 2.12 for the data string THE. Each program step is listed at the left in order of its execution. If a program step changes the value of a variable, then the new value is shown; the effect of each step is described at the far right. For example, the table shows that the statement

```
READLN (CH1, CH2, CH3);
```

stores the letters T, H, and E in the variables CH1, CH2, and CH3.

Table 2.2 Trace of Program in Fig. 2.12

Program Statement	CH1	CH2	CH3	ALPHAFIRST	Effect
	?	?	?	?	
WRITE ('Enter three. . .')					Prints a prompt
READLN (CH1, CH2, CH3)	T	H	E		Reads the data
if CH1 < CH2 then					Is `'T'` < `'H'` ? – value is false
ALPHAFIRST := CH2				H	`'H'` is first so far
if CH3 < ALPHAFIRST. . .					Is `'E'` < `'H'` ? – value is true
ALPHAFIRST := CH3				E	`'E'` is first
WRITELN (ALPHAFIRST. . .					Prints E is the first letter. . .

The trace in Table 2.2 clearly shows that the alphabetically first letter, E, of the input string is stored in ALPHAFIRST and printed. In order to verify that the program is correct it would be necessary to select other data which cause the two conditions to evaluate to different combinations of their values. Since there are two conditions and each has two possible values (true or false), there are 2×2 or 4 different combinations that should be tried. (What are they?) An exhaustive (complete) desk check of the program would show that it works for all of these combinations.

Besides the four cases discussed above, you should verify that the program works correctly for unusual data. For example, what would happen if all three letters or a pair of letters were the same? Would the program still provide the correct result? To complete the desk check, it would be necessary to show that the program does indeed handle these special situations properly.

In tracing each case, you must be very careful to execute the program exactly as it would be executed by the computer. It is very easy to carry out the operations that you expect to be performed without explicitly testing each condition and tracing each program step. A trace that is performed in this way is of little value.

Self-check Exercises for Section 2.4

1. Provide sample data and traces for the remaining three cases of the alphabetically first letter problem. Also, test the case where all three letters are the same. What is the value of the conditions in this case?
2. Trace the program in Fig. 2.10 when HOURS is 30.0 and RATE is 5.00. Perform the trace when HOURS is 20.0 and RATE is 3.00.

2.5 Problem Solving Strategies

Often what appears to be a new problem will turn out to be a variation of one that you already solved. Consequently, an important skill in problem solving is the ability to recognize that a problem is similar to one solved earlier. As you progress through the course you will start to build up a *library* of programs and procedures. Whenever possible, you should try to adapt or reuse parts of a program that have been shown to work correctly.

Extending a Problem Solution

An experienced programmer usually writes programs that can be easily changed or modified to fit other situations. One of the reasons for this is the fact that programmers (and program users) often wish to make slight improvements to a program after having used it. If the original program is designed carefully from the beginning, the programmer will be able to accommodate changing specifications with a minimum of effort. It may be possible to modify one or two small procedures rather than rewrite the entire program.

Computing Overtime Pay

Problem: We wish to modify the payroll program so that employees who work more than 40 hours a week are paid double for all overtime hours.

Discussion: This problem is an extension of the Modified Payroll Problem solved earlier (see Fig. 2.10). Overtime pay must be added for those employees who are eligible. We can solve this problem by adding a new step (step 2A) after step 2 in the original algorithm. The data requirements are listed below followed by the new algorithm and the refinement for step 2A.

PROBLEM CONSTANTS

maximum salary for no tax deduction (TAXBRACKET = 100.00)
amount of tax deducted (TAX = 25.00)
maximum hours without overtime pay (MAXHOURS = 40.0)

PROBLEM INPUTS

hours worked (HOURS : REAL)
hourly rate (RATE : REAL)

PROBLEM OUTPUTS

gross pay (GROSS : REAL)
net pay (NET : REAL)

1. Enter hours worked and hourly rate.
2. Compute gross salary.

2A. Add overtime pay to gross salary.
3. Compute net salary.
4. Print gross salary and net salary.

Step 2A
refinement

2A.1 if HOURS > MAXHOURS then
   Add overtime pay to GROSS

As shown below, the `if` statement that implements step 2A should follow the statement in Fig. 2.10 used to compute gross salary.

```
GROSS := HOURS * RATE;

{Add overtime pay to GROSS}
if HOURS > MAXHOURS then
    GROSS := GROSS + ((HOURS - MAXHOURS) * RATE);
```

The assignment statement involves three arithmetic operators: +, −, *. We will talk more about how Pascal evaluates arithmetic expressions with multiple operators in Chapter 4, but for the time being it is sufficient to know that the parentheses cause the operators above to be evaluated in the order: − first, * next, and + last. Consequently, the overtime hours (HOURS − MAXHOURS) will be multiplied by RATE and added to the value of GROSS computed in algorithm step 2; the result will be the new value of GROSS.

Solution by Analogy

Sometimes a new problem is simply an old one presented in a new guise. You should try to determine whether you have solved a similar problem before and, if so, adapt the earlier solution. This requires a careful reading of the problem statement in order to detect similar requirements that may be worded differently.

Computing
Insurance
Dividends

Problem: Each year an insurance company sends out dividend checks to its policyholders. The dividend amount is a fixed percentage (4.5%) of the insurance premium paid in. If there were no claims made by the policyholder, the dividend rate for that policy is increased by 0.5%. Write a program to compute dividends.

Discussion: This problem is quite similar to the payroll problem just completed. The dividend amount may be determined by first computing the basic dividend and then adding the bonus dividend when applicable. This is analogous to first computing gross pay and then adding in overtime pay when earned. The data requirements and algorithm are shown next; the structure chart is drawn in Fig. 2.13.

the fixed dividend rate of 4.5% (FIXEDRATE = 0.045)
the bonus dividend rate of 0.5% (BONUSRATE = 0.005)

premium amount (PREMIUM : REAL)
number of claims (CLAIMS : REAL)

dividend amount (DIVIDEND : REAL)

Algorithm

1. Enter premium amount and number of claims.
2. Compute basic dividend.
3. Add bonus dividend to basic dividend.
4. Print total dividend.

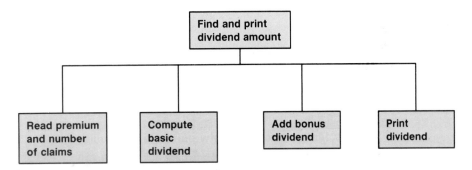

Fig. 2.13 Structure Chart for Insurance Dividend Problem

The refinement of step 3 above is similar to the refinement of step 2A in the payroll problem just completed. This refinement is shown next. The complete program is shown in Fig. 2.14.

Step 3 refinement

3.1   if CLAIMS = 0 then
       Add bonus dividend to DIVIDEND

In Fig. 2.14, 4.5% is written as the decimal fraction 0.045 and 0.5% is written as the decimal fraction 0.005. Since there is no % operator, decimal fractions are required in Pascal. All real numbers must begin with a digit; therefore, the zero in front of the decimal point is always required for a real value less than 1.0.

Fig. 2.14 Insurance Company Dividend Program

```
program COMPDIVIDEND (INPUT, OUTPUT);

{Finds and prints the insurance dividend.}
```

```
const
    FIXEDRATE = 0.045;        {basic dividend rate}
    BONUSRATE = 0.005;        {bonus dividend rate}

var
    PREMIUM,                  {premium amount}
    CLAIMS,                   {number of claims}
    DIVIDEND : REAL;          {dividend amount}

begin {COMPDIVIDEND}
    {Enter PREMIUM and CLAIMS}
    WRITE ('Premium amount: $');    READLN (PREMIUM);
    WRITE ('Number of claims: ');   READLN (CLAIMS);

    {Compute basic dividend}
    DIVIDEND := PREMIUM * FIXEDRATE;

    {Add any bonus dividend}
    if CLAIMS = 0 then
        DIVIDEND := DIVIDEND + (PREMIUM * BONUSRATE);   { Add bonus}

    {Print total dividend}
    WRITELN ('Total dividend is $', DIVIDEND :8:2)
end. {COMPDIVIDEND}

Premium amount: $1200
Number of claims: 0
Total dividend is $  60.00
```

Self-check Exercises for Section 2.5

1. Provide the complete program for Overtime Pay Problem.
2. Rewrite the algorithm for the modified payroll problem so that the computation of gross salary is performed in one step rather than in two (i.e. combine steps 2 and 2A). Use an if statement with two alternatives.
3. In Fig. 2.14, combine the two steps that compute DIVIDEND into one step using an if statement with two alternatives.

2.6 Repetition in Programs

Just as the ability to make decisions is a very important programming tool, so is the ability to specify that a group of operations is to be repeated. For example, if there are six employees in a company, then we might like to carry out the gross pay and net pay computations shown in Fig. 2.10 six times. We can express this in pseudo code as shown on p. 73.

Pascal provides three control statements for specifying repetition. We will examine one of these in the next section. The others will be introduced in Chapters 3 and 5.

for each employee do
  Read hours worked and hourly rate
  Compute gross salary
  Compute net salary
  Print gross pay and net pay

The for Statement

The for statement can be used to specify some forms of repetition quite easily as shown in the next examples.

Example 2.4 The statements below have the same effect.

```
{Print three blank lines}        {Print three blank lines}
WRITELN;                         for LINE := 1 to 3 do
WRITELN;                             WRITELN;
WRITELN;
```

If LINE is declared as an integer variable, the for statement above causes the WRITELN operation to be performed three times.

Example 2.5 Procedure PRINTI for the Mother's Day Problem (see Fig. 2.7) can be written using the for statement as shown in Fig. 2.15. This procedure prints 7 lines that contain asterisks in columns 4 and 5.

```
procedure PRINTI;

{Prints the block letter 'I'.}

var
    NEXTLINE : INTEGER;  {Loop control variable - from 1 to 7}

begin {PRINTI}
    for NEXTLINE := 1 to 7 do
        WRITELN ('**' :5);
    WRITELN
end; {PRINTI}
```

Fig. 2.15 Procedure PRINTI

The for statement is used to implement *counting loops* or loops where the exact number of loop repetitions required may be specified as a variable or constant value. In Examples 2.4 and 2.5, the number of repetitions required were 3 and 7, respectively.

The for statement in Fig. 2.15 specifies that the variable NEXTLINE should take on each of the values in the range 1 to 7 during successive loop repetitions. This means that the value of NEXTLINE is 1 during the first loop repetition, 2 during the second loop repetition, and 7 during the last loop repetition.

NEXTLINE is called the *loop control variable* as its value controls the loop repetition. The loop control variable is intialized to 1 when the for statement is first reached; after each execution of the loop body, the loop control variable is incremented by 1 and tested to see whether loop repetition should continue.

The loop control variable may also be referenced in the loop body, but its value cannot be changed. The next example shows a for statement whose loop control variable is referenced in the loop body.

Example 2.6   The program in Fig. 2.16 uses a for statement to print a diagonal line of integers. During each repetition of the loop, the statement

```
WRITELN (COLUMN :COLUMN)
```

causes the value of the loop control variable (an integer from 1 to 5) to be printed. The value of the loop control variable COLUMN also determines the position of the integer in each output line. Recall from Chapter 1 that a variable may be used to indicate an output field width and that an integer value is always printed right justified in its field. A trace of this program is shown in Table 2.3.

```
program DRAWDIAGONAL  (OUTPUT);

{Draws a diagonal line of integers.}
  const
     SIZE = 5;                {number of integers printed}

  var
     COLUMN : INTEGER;  {loop control variable}

  begin {DRAWDIAGONAL}
     {Print 5 integers}
     for COLUMN := 1 to SIZE do
        WRITELN (COLUMN :COLUMN)
  end. {DRAWDIAGONAL}

1
 2
  3
   4
    5
```

Fig. 2.16 Program to Draw a Diagonal

The trace in Table 2.3 shows that the loop control variable COLUMN is initialized to 1 when the for statement is reached. The for statement causes the WRITELN statement to be repeated. Before each repetition, COLUMN is incremented by one and tested to see whether its value is still less than or equal to SIZE (5). If the test result is true, then the WRITELN is executed again and the next value of COLUMN is printed. COLUMN is

Table 2.3 Trace of Program in Fig. 2.16

Statement	COLUMN	Effect
	?	
`for COLUMN := 1 to SIZE do`	1	Initialize COLUMN to 1
`WRITELN (COLUMN :COLUMN)`		Print 1 in column 1
Increment and test COLUMN	2	2 < = 5 is true —
`WRITELN (COLUMN :COLUMN)`		Print 2 in column 2
Increment and test COLUMN	3	3 < = 5 is true —
`WRITELN (COLUMN :COLUMN)`		Print 3 in column 3
Increment and test COLUMN	4	4 < = 5 is true —
`WRITELN (COLUMN :COLUMN)`		Print 4 in column 4
Increment and test COLUMN	5	5 < = 5 is true —
`WRITELN (COLUMN :COLUMN)`		Print 5 in column 5
Increment and test COLUMN	?	Exit loop

equal to 5 during the last loop repetition. After this repetition, the loop is exited and the value of COLUMN is considered undefined (indicated by the ? in the last table line). This means that COLUMN cannot be referenced again until it is given a new value.

COUNTING LOOPS

> `for` *counter* `:= 1 to` *repetitions* `do`
> *statement*

Interpretation: The number of times *statement* is executed is determined by the value of *repetitions*. The value of the loop control variable *counter* is set to 1 before the first execution of *statement*; *counter* is incremented by 1 after each execution of *statement*. The variable *counter* must be type INTEGER; *repetitions* may be a type INTEGER variable, INTEGER constant, or expression with an INTEGER value.

Note: If the value of *repetitions* is less than 1, *statement* will not be executed. The value of *counter* cannot be changed within *statement*.

PROGRAM STYLE

Loop control variables as local variables

In Fig. 2.15, the loop control variable NEXTLINE is declared in procedure PRINTI. Identifiers declared within a procedure are called *local identifiers*. All loop control variables used in a procedure must be declared as local variables.

Accumulating a Sum

We can use a counting loop to accumulate the sum of a collection of data values as shown in the next problem.

Sum and Average of Integers

Problem: Write a program that finds the sum and average of all integers from 1 to N.

Discussion: In order to solve this problem, it will be necessary to find some way to form the sum of the first N integers. The data requirements and algorithm follow.

PROBLEM INPUTS

the last integer in the sum (N : INTEGER)

PROBLEM OUTPUTS

the sum of integers from 1 to N (SUM : INTEGER)
the average of the integers from 1 to N (AVERAGE : REAL)

Algorithm

1. Read the last integer (N).
2. Find the sum (SUM) of all the integers from 1 to N inclusive.
3. Find the average (AVERAGE) of the integers from 1 to N.
4. Print the sum and average.

Step 2 is the only step needing refinement. One possible refinement is shown next.

Step 2 refinement

2.1　Add 1 to SUM
2.2　Add 2 to SUM
2.3　Add 3 to SUM
　　　　·
　　　　·
　　　　·
2.N　Add N to SUM

For a large value of N, it would be rather time-consuming to write this list of N steps. We would also have to know the value of N before writing this list; consequently, the program would not be general as it would only work for one value of N.

Since these steps are all quite similar, we can represent each of them with the general step 2.i below.

2.i　Add i to SUM

This general step must be executed for all values of i from 1 to N, inclusive. This suggests the use of a counting loop with I as the loop control variable.

Step 2
refinement

2.1 for each integer I from 1 to N do
Add I to SUM

The variable I will take on the successive values 1, 2, 3, . . . , N. Each time the loop is repeated, the current value of I must be added to SUM. The description of I follows.

loop control variable — represents each integer from 1 to N
(I : INTEGER)

The complete program is shown in Fig. 2.17. The statements

```
SUM := 0;              {initialize SUM to zero}
for I := 1 to N do
   SUM := SUM + I;      {add next integer to SUM}
```

are used to perform step 2. In order to ensure that the final sum is correct, the value of SUM must be *initialized* to zero before the first addition operation. The for statement causes the assignment statement

```
SUM := SUM + I
```

to be repeated N times. Each time, the current value of I is added to the sum being accumulated and the result is saved back in SUM. This is illustrated below for the first two loop repetitions.

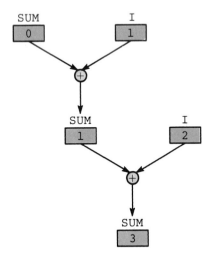

```
program SUMINTEGERS (INPUT, OUTPUT);

{Finds and prints the sum and average of all integers from 1 to N.}
```

```
var
    N,                  {the last integer to be added to the sum}
    SUM,                {the sum being accumulated}
    I : INTEGER;        {the next integer to be added to the sum}
    AVERAGE : REAL;     {the average of the numbers}

begin {SUMINTEGERS}
    {Read the last integer (N)}
    WRITE ('Enter the last integer in the sum: '); READLN (N);

    {Find the sum (SUM) of all the integers from 1 to N inclusive}
    SUM := 0;           {Initialize SUM to zero}
    for I := 1 to N do
        SUM := SUM + I;   {Add the next integer to SUM}

    {Find the average (AVERAGE) of N integers}
    AVERAGE := SUM / N;

    {Print the sum and average}
    WRITELN ('The sum is ', SUM :5);
    WRITELN ('The average is ', AVERAGE :5:2)
end. {SUMINTEGERS}

Enter the last integer in the sum: 6
The sum is      21
The average is  3.50
```

Fig. 2.17 Program for Sum and Average of Integers from 1 to N

A trace of the program for a data value of 3 is shown in Table 2.4. The trace verifies that the program performs as desired since the final value stored in SUM is 6 (1+2+3). The value of the loop control variable I becomes undefined after it reaches the value of N (3 in this case). As shown in the table, the statement

```
SUM := SUM + I
```

is executed exactly three times.

Self-check Exercises for Section 2.6

1. There is generally more than one way to solve a problem. It so happens that the formula

$$\frac{N(N+1)}{2}$$

may be used to compute the sum of the integers from 1 to N inclusive.

Write a program that compares the results of both methods and prints an appropriate message indicating whether or not the results are the same.

2. Write a program that finds the product of the integers from 1 to N inclusive. Test this program with values of N that are less than eight.

Table 2.4 Trace of Program in Fig. 2.17

Statement	N	I	SUM	AVE	Effect
	?	?	?	?	
WRITE ('Enter the. . .					Print a prompt
READLN (N)	3				Read 3 into N
SUM := 0			0		Initialize SUM
for I := 1 to N do		1			Initialize I to 1
SUM := SUM + I			1		Add 1 to SUM
Increment and test I		2			2 < = 3 is true
SUM := SUM + I			3		Add 2 to SUM
Increment and test I		3			3 < = 3 is true
SUM := SUM + I			6		Add 3 to SUM
Increment and test I		?			Exit loop
AVERAGE := SUM / N				2	AVERAGE is 6 / 3
WRITELN ('The sum. . .					Print the sum, 6
WRITELN ('The average. . .					Print the average, 2

2.7 Generalizing a Solution

After finishing a program, someone will often ask a "What if?" question. The person asking the question usually wants to know whether the program would still work if some of the restrictions implied by the problem statement were removed. If the answer is "No," then you may have to modify the program to make it work. You will be much better off if you try to anticipate these questions in advance and make your programs as general as possible right from the start. Sometimes this can be accomplished as easily as changing a program constant to a problem input.

One question that comes to mind for the last problem is: What if we wanted to sum a list of any numbers, not just the first N integers; would the program still work? Clearly, the answer to this question is "No." However, it would not be too difficult to modify the program to solve this more general problem.

General Sum and Average Problem

Problem: Write a program that finds and prints the sum and average of a list of numbers.

Discussion: In order to add any list of numbers, a new variable would be needed to store each item to be summed. The numbers must be provided as input data. The new data requirements and algorithm follow.

PROBLEM INPUTS

number of items to be summed (NUMITEMS : INTEGER)
each data value to be summed (ITEM : REAL)

PROBLEM OUTPUTS

sum of the N data items (SUM : REAL)
average of the N data items (AVERAGE : REAL)

Algorithm

1. Read in the number (NUMITEMS) of items to be summed.
2. Read each data item and add it to the sum.
3. Find the average of the data.
4. Print the sum and average.

This algorithm is nearly identical to the previous one. The only step that is significantly different is step 2, which is refined below.

Step 2 refinement

2.1 Initialize SUM to 0.
2.2 for each data item do
   Read the data item into ITEM and add ITEM to SUM.

In this refinement, the variable ITEM is used to store each number to be summed. After each number is read into ITEM, it will be added to SUM. If there are more data items, the loop will be repeated and the next data item will replace the last one in ITEM.

The number of data items is read into NUMITEMS. This value determines the number of loop repetitions that are required. A loop control variable is needed to count the data items as they are processed and ensure that all data are summed.

ADDITIONAL VARIABLES

loop control variable—the number of data items added so far
(COUNT : INTEGER)

The general program to find the sum and average of a list of data items is shown in Fig. 2.18.

```
program SUMITEMS (INPUT, OUTPUT);

{Finds and prints the sum and average of a list of data items.}

var
    NUMITEMS,          {the number of data items to be summed}
    COUNT : INTEGER;   {count of items added so far}
    ITEM,              {the next data item to be summed}
    SUM,               {the sum being accumulated}
    AVERAGE : REAL;    {the average of the data}

begin {SUMITEMS}
    {Read the number of data items to be summed}
    WRITE ('Number of items to be summed? '); READLN (NUMITEMS);

    {Find the sum (SUM) of NUMITEMS data items}
    SUM := 0;                                {initialize SUM to zero}
    for COUNT := 1 to NUMITEMS do
        begin
            WRITE ('Next item to be summed? ');
            READLN (ITEM);                   {read next data item}
            SUM := SUM + ITEM                {add the next data item}
        end; {for COUNT}

    {Find the average of the data}
    AVERAGE := SUM / NUMITEMS;

    {Print the final value of SUM and AVERAGE}
    WRITELN ('The sum is ', SUM :8:2);
    WRITELN ('The average is ', AVERAGE :8:2)
end. {SUMITEMS}


Number of items in the sum? 3
Next item to be summed? 4.5
Next item to be summed? 6.5
Next item to be summed? 7.0
The sum is  18.00
The average is  6.00
```

Fig. 2.18 Program to Sum a List of Data Items

PROGRAM STYLE

Defensive programming

The programs in Fig. 2.17 and 2.18 both have the same flaw: the division operation in the assignment statement

```
        AVERAGE := SUM / N;
or      AVERAGE := SUM / NUMITEMS;
```

cannot be performed if the divisor is zero. Instead, the computer will print an error message such as "division by zero" and program execution will stop.

You are correct if you are thinking that no reasonable person would enter a data value of zero for N or NUMITEMS, but program users often do not know what is reasonable and what is not. Therefore, experienced programmers often practice "defensive programming" to ensure that a program operates properly even for invalid data.

In Fig. 2.18, it would be safer to compute AVERAGE using the `if` statement below

```
if NUMITEMS = 0 then
    WRITELN ('Invalid data value (0) for NUMITEMS')
else
    AVERAGE := SUM / NUMITEMS ;
```

The program causes its own error message to be displayed when NUMITEMS is invalid; the program computes the value of AVERAGE only when NUMITEMS is valid. In either case, program execution will continue. This is preferable to having the computer stop the program because of an error.

Compound Statement

In the `for` statement

```
for COUNT := 1 to NUMITEMS do
    begin
        WRITE ('Next item to be summed? ');
        READLN (ITEM);        {Read next data item}
        SUM := SUM + ITEM     {Add the next data item}
    end; {for COUNT}
```

the `begin` and `end` are used to bracket three statements (WRITE, READLN, assignment) as one *compound statement* that forms the *loop body*. All three statements are executed each time the loop is repeated. The brackets were not needed before since the loop body was always a single statement. Whenever a loop body consists of more than one statement, a compound statement must be used as shown above.

A compound statement can be used with an `if` statement as well. Examples of this are found in Chapter 3.

PROGRAM STYLE

Use of semicolons

Semicolons are used to separate the individual statements in the compound statement shown above. Semicolons should not be used before or after begin or before end since the reserved words begin and end are not statements. This is consistent with our prior usage of semicolons. The semicolon after the end (end; {for COUNT}) separates the for statement from the assignment statement

```
AVERAGE := SUM / NUMITEMS;
```

that follows it in Fig. 2.18.

PROGRAM STYLE

Comment after end

The reserved word end appears twice in Fig. 2.18. The first end is followed by a comment (end; {for COUNT}) which indicates that it is used to mark the end of the for statement with loop control variable COUNT. This comment enhances the clarity and readability of the program. We recommend that you follow this practice as there will often be many occurrences of the word end in a program. Commenting in this way makes it easier to associate each end with its corresponding begin.

Self-check Exercises for Section 2.7

1. Write a general program to find the product of a list of data items. Ignore any data values of 0.

2.8 Repeating a Program Body

When we began the discussion of repetition in programs, we mentioned that we would like to be able to execute the payroll program for several employees in a single run. We will see how to do this next.

Processing Several Employees

Problem: Modify the payroll program to compute gross pay and net pay for a group of employees.

Discussion: The number of employees must be provided as input data along with the hourly rate and hours worked by each employee. The same set of variables will be used to hold the data and computational results for each employee. The computations will be performed in the same way as before. The new data requirements and algorithm follow.

maximum salary for no tax deduction (TAXBRACKET = 100.0)
amount of tax deducted (TAX = 25.00)
maximum hours without overtime pay (MAXHOURS = 40.0)

number of employees (NUMEMP : INTEGER)
hours worked by each employee (HOURS : REAL)
hourly rate for each employee (RATE : REAL)

gross pay (GROSS : REAL)
net pay (NET : REAL)

Algorithm

1. Enter the number of employees (NUMEMP).
2. for each employee do
   Enter payroll data and compute and print gross and net pay.

An additional variable is needed to count the number of employees processed and control the for loop in step 2.

loop control variable—counts the employees that are processed
(COUNTEMP : INTEGER)

The structure chart is shown in Fig. 2.19. The structure chart for the subproblem "find gross and net pay" was drawn in Fig. 2.9.

The declaration section of the program in Fig. 2.20 contains a large procedure (MODPAY) which is based on the payroll program in Fig. 2.10. The main program body consists of statements to read in NUMEMP (number of employees) and a for statement which repeatedly calls procedure

Fig. 2.19 Structure Chart for Multiple Employee Problem

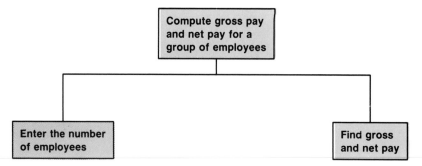

```
program MULTIPAY (INPUT, OUTPUT);

{Finds and prints gross pay and net pay for a group of employees.}

var
    NUMEMP,                     {total number of employees}
    COUNTEMP : INTEGER;         {loop control variable - count
                                 of employees processed        }


procedure MODPAY;

{Computes and prints gross pay and net pay given an hourly rate
 and number of hours worked. Deducts a tax of $25 if gross salary
 exceeds $100; otherwise, deducts no tax.                        }

const
    TAXBRACKET = 100.00;    {maximum salary for no deduction}
    TAX = 25.00;            {tax amount}

var
    HOURS, RATE,            {hours worked, hourly rate}
    GROSS, NET : REAL       {gross pay, net pay}


begin {MODPAY}
    {Enter HOURS and RATE}
    WRITE ('Hours worked? ');    READLN (HOURS);
    WRITE ('Hourly rate? ');     READLN (RATE);

    {Compute gross salary}
    GROSS := HOURS * RATE;

    {Compute net salary}
    if GROSS > TAXBRACKET then
      NET := GROSS - TAX          {deduct a tax amount}
    else
      NET := GROSS;               {deduct no tax}

    {Print GROSS and NET}
    WRITELN ('Gross salary is $', GROSS :8:2);
    WRITELN ('Net salary is $', NET :8:2)
end; {MODPAY}


begin {MULTIPAY}
    {Enter total number of employees}
    WRITE ('How many employees? ');  READLN (NUMEMP);

    {Compute gross pay and net pay for NUMEMP employees}
    for COUNTEMP := 1 to NUMEMP do
       begin
          MODPAY;            {process next employee}
          WRITELN
       end {for COUNTEMP}
end. {MULTIPAY}
```

```
How many employees? 2
Hours worked? 25
Hourly rate? 3.50
Gross salary is $  87.50
Net salary is $  87.50

Hours worked? 40
Hourly rate? 4.80
Gross salary is $  192.00
Net salary is $  167.00
```

Fig. 2.20 Multiple Employee Payroll Program

MODPAY. Each execution of MODPAY causes the payroll computations to be performed for a different employee.

The only identifiers declared in the main program are NUMEMP, COUNTEMP, and MODPAY. All other identifiers are declared as local identifiers in procedure MODPAY since they are manipulated only within the procedure.

Procedure MODPAY contains exactly the same declaration section and body as program MODPAY in Fig. 2.10. The only difference is that MODPAY is now written as a procedure instead of a program; consequently, its first line begins with the word procedure instead of program and its last line is end; {MODPAY} instead of end. {MODPAY}.

The ability to convert an entire program into a procedure is a very powerful programming tool. This capability enables us to reuse old programs as procedures in the solution of new problems. In this way, we can create new solutions from old ones.

Similarity between Procedures and Programs

The problem just completed points out the similarity between a procedure and a program. Both have a declaration part that begins with a heading (program . . . or procedure . . .); the declaration part is followed by a body (begin . . . end. or begin . . . end;). The declaration part describes the identifiers that can be referenced in the body; the body performs the data manipulation.

Although many procedures may be declared in a program, there can be only one program body. The program body always follows the last procedure declaration (if any) and is terminated by end and a period.

Procedure bodies and program bodies are translated into machine language and are saved in different sections of memory. When program execution begins, control is transferred to the memory address of the first statement of the main program body. When a procedure (call) statement is executed, control is transferred to the memory address of the first statement of that procedure body. After the procedure is done, control is transferred back to the statement in the main program body that follows the procedure (call) statement.

In the next chapter, we will see that a procedure, like a program, can call other procedures. Also, we will see how to pass information between procedures and between procedures and the main program. All of these capabilities increase the utility of procedures.

2.9 Debugging and Testing Programs

In Section 1.11, we described the general categories of error messages that you are likely to see: syntax errors and run-time errors. It is also possible for a program to execute without generating any error messages, but still produce incorrect results. Sometimes the cause of a run-time error or the origin of incorrect results is apparent and the error can easily be fixed. However, very often the error is not obvious and may require considerable effort to locate.

The first step in attempting to find a hidden error is to try to determine what part of the program is generating incorrect results. Then insert extra WRITELN statements in your program to provide a trace of its execution. For example, if the summation loop in Fig. 2.18 is not computing the correct sum, you might want to insert an extra diagnostic WRITELN as shown by the last line in the loop below.

```
for COUNT := 1 to NUMITEMS do
    begin
        WRITE ('Next item to be summed? ');
        READLN (ITEM);
        SUM := SUM + ITEM;
        WRITELN ('SUM = ', SUM, 'COUNT = ', COUNT)
    end; {for COUNT}
```

The extra WRITELN statement will display each partial sum that is accumulated and the current value of COUNT. Be careful when inserting extra diagnostic print statements as they can be a source of syntax errors or additional run-time errors. In this case, a semicolon also needed to be inserted after the assignment statement in the loop body. Sometimes it will be necessary to add a begin ... end pair if a single statement inside an if or while statement becomes a compound statement when a diagnostic WRITELN is added.

Once it appears that you have located the error, you will want to take out the extra diagnostic statements. As a temporary measure, it is sometimes advisable to make these diagnostic statements comments by enclosing them in curly braces. If errors crop up again in later testing, it is easier to remove the braces than retype the diagnostic statements.

Testing a Program

After all errors have been corrected and the program appears to execute as expected, the program should be tested thoroughly to make sure that it works. In Section 2.4, we discussed tracing an algorithm and suggested that enough sets of test data be provided to ensure that all possible paths are traced. The same statement is true for the completed program. Make enough test runs to verify that the program works properly for representative samples of all possible data combinations.

2.10 Common Programming Errors

When using comments, you must be very careful to insert each left and right curly brace where required. If the left (opening) brace is missing, then the compiler will not recognize the beginning of the comment and will attempt to process the comment as a Pascal statement. This should cause a syntax error. If the right brace is missing, the comment will simply be extended to include all program statements that follow it. The comment will not be terminated until the right curly brace at the end of the next comment is reached. If there are no more comments, then the rest of the program will be included in the comment and a syntax error such as "incomplete program" will be printed.

Remember that all identifiers in Pascal must be declared before they can be referenced. Consequently, the main program body must come at the end of a program, following the procedure declarations.

Make sure to use semicolons only at the end of a statement. If a statement is written over several lines, the semicolon may be placed at the end of the last line only. The semicolon in the `if` statement below will cause the syntax error "illegal symbol" when `else` is reached.

```
if X >= 0.0 then
    WRITELN (X :8, ' is positive or zero');
else
    WRITELN (X :8, ' is negative')
```

Don't forget to bracket a compound statement with `begin` and `end`. It is not sufficient to indent the compound statement, as the compiler ignores the indentation. Consequently, only the WRITELN statement is repeated in the program fragment below.

```
SUM := 0;
for COUNT := 1 to 10 do
    WRITELN (COUNT);
    SUM := SUM + COUNT;
WRITELN (SUM)
```

The assignment statement

```
SUM := SUM + COUNT;
```

will be executed after the loop is exited. However, since the loop control variable is undefined after loop exit, a run-time error will occur.

In the first part of this chapter we outlined a method for solving problems on the computer. This method stressed six points:

1. Understand the problem.
2. Identify the input and output data for the problem as well as other relevant data.
3. Formulate a precise statement of the problem.
4. Develop a list of steps for solving the problem (an algorithm).
5. Refine the algorithm.
6. Implement the algorithm in Pascal.

We showed how to divide a problem into subproblems and how to use a structure chart to show the relationship between the subproblems. The procedure was introduced as a means of implementing subproblems as separate program modules.

Several guidelines for using program comments were discussed. Well-placed and carefully worded comments, and a structure chart, can provide all of the documentation necessary for a program.

In the remainder of the chapter, we discussed the representation of the various steps in an algorithm and illustrated the stepwise refinement of algorithms. We used pseudocode to represent the loops and decision steps of an algorithm. We showed how to implement decisions in Pascal using the `if` statement and repetition using the `for` statement.

Algorithm and program traces are used to verify that an algorithm or program is correct. Errors in logic can be discovered by carefully tracing an algorithm or program. Tracing an algorithm or program before entering the program in the computer will save you time in the long run.

New Pascal Statements in Chapter 2

The new Pascal statements introduced in this chapter are described in Table 2.5 on page 90.

Review Questions

1. Briefly describe the steps to be taken to derive an algorithm for a given problem.
2. The diagram that shows the algorithm steps and their interdependencies is called a _____.
3. What are three advantages of using procedures?
4. Where in the final program is the main program body found and why?
5. When is a procedure executed and where must it appear in the main program?
6. A decision in Pascal is actually an evaluation of a(n) _____ expression.

Table 2.5 Summary of New Pascal Statements

Statement	Effect

Comment

```
{This is a comment}
(* So is this! *)
```

Comments document the use of variables and statements in a program. They are ignored by the compiler.

Procedure declaration

```
procedure DISPLAY;

{Prints 3 lines of 3 asterisks.}

const
    STAR = '*';

begin {DISPLAY}
    WRITELN (STAR, STAR, STAR);
    WRITELN (STAR, STAR, STAR);
    WRITELN (STAR, STAR, STAR)
end;   {DISPLAY}
```

Procedure DISPLAY is declared and may be called to print three lines of asterisks. The local constant STAR is defined only when DISPLAY is executing.

Procedure (call) statement

```
DISPLAY
```

Calls procedure DISPLAY and causes it to begin execution. The call must follow the declaration of DISPLAY.

`if` *statement (with one alternative)*

```
if X <> 0.0 then
    PRODUCT := PRODUCT * X
```

Multiplies PRODUCT by X only if X is nonzero.

`if` *statement (with two alternatives)*

```
if X >= 0.0 then
    WRITELN (X, ' is positive')
else
    WRITELN (X, ' is negative')
```

If X is greater than or equal to 0.0, the message ' is positive' is printed; otherwise, the message ' is negative' is printed.

`for` *statement*

```
for NUMSTARS := 1 to 25 do
    WRITE ('*')
```

Prints a row of 25 asterisks.

7. List the six relational operators discussed in this chapter.
8. What should be done by the programmer after the algorithm is written but before the program is entered (typed) into the computer?
9. Trace the following program fragment and indicate which procedure will be called if a data value of 27.34 is entered.

```
WRITE ('Enter a temperature: ');   READLN (TEMP);
if TEMP > 32 then
    NOTFREEZING
else
    ICEFORMING
```

10. Write the appropriate `if` statement to compute GROSSPAY given that the hourly rate is stored in the variable RATE and the total hours worked is stored in the variable HOURS. Pay time and a half for more than 40 hours worked.

11. Write a loop that reads in HOURS and RATE and prints out GROSSPAY as defined in questions 10 for 22 employees.

12. Modify the loop for question 11 to accumulate the sum of gross pay for all employees.

13. Provide a separate procedure called GRPAY that solves questions 11 and 12.

Programming Projects

1.   a) Write a program to print the message "XXOXOX" in block letters.
     b) Modify your program so that any six letter message consisting of X's and O's will be printed in block letter form. The message to be printed should be entered and displayed one character at a time.

2.   a) Write a program to simulate a state police radar gun. The program should read an automobile speed and print the message "speeding" if the speed exceeds 55 mph.
     b) Modify your program so that ten speeds are handled in a single run. Also, print a count of the number of speeding automobiles.

3.   Write a program that computes the product of a collection of 15 data values. Your program should ignore zero values.

4.   Compute and print a table showing the first 15 powers of 2.

5.   A program is needed that will read a character value and a number. Depending upon what is read, certain information will be printed. The character should be either an S or a T. If an S is read and the number is 100.50, the program will print

                    Send money! I need $100.50

     If a T is read instead of S, the program will print

                    The temperature last night was 100.50 degrees

6.   Write a program that reads in 20 values and prints the number of values that are positive (greater than or equal to zero) and the number that are negative. Also print `'more positive'` or `'more negative'` based on the result.

7.   Write an algorithm to compute the factorial, N!, of a single arbitrary integer

N. ($N! = N \times (N - 1) \times \ldots 2 \times 1$). Your program should read and print the value of N and print N! when done.

8. *Continuation of Project 6 in Chapter 1* Modify the program to handle several times in a single run. The number of data pairs should be the first problem input. Also, print a count of runners who break the four minute mile.

9. *Continuation of Project 8 in Chapter 1* Modify the program to handle all data in a single run. Print `'Out of gas'` or `'All the way'` as each pair of data items is processed. Assume that the trip distance is 300 miles.

10. a) If N contains an integer, then we can compute X^N for any X, simply by initializing a variable to 1 and multiplying it by X a total of N times. Write a program to read in a value of X and a value of N, and compute X^N via repeated multiplications. Check your program for

$$
\begin{array}{ll}
X = 6.0 & N = 4 \\
X = 2.5 & N = 6 \\
X = -8.0 & N = 5
\end{array}
$$

b) Modify your program to handle positive or negative values of N. Hint: X^{-3} is equal to $1/X^3$.

11. Given the bank balance in your checking account for the past month and all the transactions for the current month, write an algorithm to compute and print your checking account balance at the end of the current month. You may assume that the total number of transactions for the current month is known ahead of time. (Hint: Your first data item should be your checking account balance at the end of last month. The second item should be the number of transactions for the current month. All subsequent items should be the amount of a transaction.)

12. Write a program to compute gross and net pay for several employees. First, read in the number of employees and then the hourly rate and then the number of hours for each employee. Any hours exceeding 40 are to be paid time-and-a-half. Net pay is 65% of gross pay.

13. Write a program that reads in three numbers and finds and prints the smallest and largest number.

14. Write a program that prints a table showing classroom number, maximum size, number of seats available, and a message indicating whether the class is filled or not. Before reading any data, call a procedure to print some table headings indicating what the output represents. In an interactive program, the headings should be printed to the right of the screen so that they are not confused with the input data. Call another procedure repeatedly to read and process the data for each classroom. Use the following classroom

Room	Capacity	Enrollment
426	25	25
327	18	14
420	20	15
317	100	90

Sample output might begin:

Room number	Maximum size	Number enrolled	Remaining seats	Filled?
426	25	25	0	Yes
327	18	14	4	No

15. Write a program that will determine the additional state tax owed by an employee. The state charges a 4% tax on net income. Net income is determined by subtracting a $500 allowance for each dependent from gross income. Your program will read gross income, number of dependents, and tax amount already deducted. It will then compute the actual tax owed and print the difference between tax owed and tax deducted followed by the message ' SEND CHECK' or ' REFUND' depending on whether this difference is positive or negative.

16. Write a program that will help you determine the maximum number of traffic lights that can be purchased for $50,000. Assume that the purchase cost of each light is $5000 and the installation cost is $1000. Each light uses 420 kilowatt-hours of electricity a year and kilowatts are charged at $0.047 per kilowatt-hour. Enter a guess as to how many lights can be purchased and keep rerunning the program until the best answer is printed.

17. The New Telephone Company has the following rate structure for long-distance calls:
1) Any call started after 6:00 P.M. (1800 hours) gets a 50% discount.
2) Any call started after 8:00 A.M. (0800 hours) is charged full price.
3) All calls are subject to a 4% Federal tax.
4) The regular rate for a call is $0.40 per minute.
5) Any call longer than 60 minutes receives a 15% discount on its cost (after any other discount is taken but before tax is added).

Write a program that processes several calls by reading the start time for each call based on a 24-hour clock and the length of each call. The gross cost (before any discounts or tax) should be printed followed by the net cost (after discounts are deducted and tax is added). Use a procedure to print a table heading and a procedure to read and process each call.

Control Statements

3.1 Syntax Diagrams

3.2 The if Statement Revisited

3.3 The while Statement

3.4 Procedure Parameters

3.5 Adding Data Flow Information to Structure Charts

3.6 Nested Procedures and Scope of Identifiers

3.7 Case Studies

3.8 Debugging a Program System

3.9 Common Programming Errors

3.10 Chapter Review

The control statements of a programming language enable the programmer to control the sequence and frequency of execution of segments of a program. Control statements are used to call procedures into execution and implement decisions and loops in programs. The control statements introduced so far are: the procedure statement, the if statement, and the for statement.

Syntax diagrams will be discussed as a means of specifying the syntax of a Pascal statement, including control statements. An examination of the syntax diagram for the if statement will show how to write if statements with several (more than two) alternatives.

A new looping statement, the while statement, will be introduced. The repetition of a while loop is controled by a condition; the loop is repeated as long as (while) this condition is true.

There will be further discussion of procedures, and procedure parameters will be used for communication of information between procedures. The structure chart will be used to show the required data flow between procedures. Two large case studies will be implemented that use nested procedures in their solution.

3.1 Syntax Diagrams

Before discussing control statements, we will show how to describe the syntax of any Pascal language feature using a *syntax diagram*. The syntax diagram below describes a Pascal *identifier*. This syntax diagram references two other syntactical elements of Pascal: *letter* (A–Z, a–z) and *digit* (0–9). Recall that an identifier is a sequence of letters and digits starting with a letter.

Syntax Diagram for Identifier

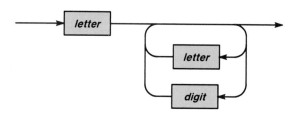

In order to use a syntax diagram, you must trace through the diagram following the arrows. You should start at the arrow tail on the left and finish at the arrowhead on the right.

The shortest path through this diagram is from left to right passing through the top box labeled *letter*. This means that a Pascal identifier may be any single letter (e.g. A, B, c, z).

There are many other paths through this diagram. Instead of exiting at the right after passing through the top box labeled *letter*, it is possible to follow either path leading down and to the left. These paths go through a box labeled *digit* or another box labeled *letter*. If the diagram is then exited, the identifier formed will consist of two characters (e.g. it, ME, R2, D2).

Since there is a closed cycle or loop in the diagram, the lower box labled *letter* and the box labeled *digit* may be passed through several times before exiting the diagram. Each time, a symbol from the box (*letter* or *digit*) passed through should be added to the identifier being formed. Some identifiers formed this way are: A, ABC, or A23b4cd5. It is impossible to trace a path that establishes 123 or 12ABC as valid identifiers.

You can use syntax diagrams to verify that a program statement is correct before you enter it. If a syntax error occurs during debugging, you can refer to the appropriate syntax diagram to determine the correct form of the element that is incorrect. Appendix C contains all Pascal syntax diagrams.

Self-check Exercises for Section 3.1

1. Which syntax diagrams in Appendix C would be used to verify that the statement below was syntactically correct? The identifier N would be classified as what kind of syntactic element? Answer the same question for the identifiers I and SUM.

```
for I := 1 to N do
    SUM := SUM + I
```

3.2 The if Statement Revisited

The syntax diagram for an `if` statement shown below

if Statement

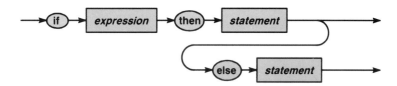

references the Pascal elements *expression* and *statement*. If the syntactic form of any of these is uncertain then the appropriate diagram should be consulted (see Appendix C).

The reserved words (`if`, `then`, `else`) are enclosed in ovals rather than boxes. When you pass through one of these ovals, the word inside should be inserted in the `if` statement being formed.

An `if` statement is completed by exiting at either of the arrowheads at the far right of the diagram. If the top path is followed, the `if` statement will consist of only one alternative (following `then`); there will be no `else` part. If the path leading down and to the left (through `else`) is followed instead, the `if` statement will consist of two alternatives.

The *statement* following the word `then` or `else` may be a single executable statement or a compound statement surrounded by a `begin` . . . `end` bracket. Some of the statements that may be used are assignment statements, procedure statements (including READLN or WRITELN statements), for statements, or other `if` statements.

More if Statement Examples

Example 3.1 The `if` statement below may be used to compute the discounted price of an item. It first determines the discount by multiplying the item price and the discount rate (a fraction); next, it deducts the discount. The compound statement is not executed when the discount rate is zero.

```
if discrate <> 0.0 then
    begin
        discount := price * discrate;  {Compute discount amount}
        price := price - discount      {Deduct discount from price}
    end {if}
```

Example 3.2 The `if` statement in Fig. 3.1 orders the values in X and Y so that the smaller number will be in X and the larger number will be in Y. If the two numbers are already in the proper order, the compound statement will not be executed.

```
if X > Y then
    begin {switch X and Y}
        TEMP := X;        {Store old X in TEMP}
        X := Y;           {Store old Y in X}
        Y := TEMP         {Store old X in Y}
    end {X > Y}
```

Fig. 3.1 If Statement to Order X and Y

The variables X, Y, and TEMP should all be the same type. Although the values of X and Y are being switched, an additional variable, TEMP, is needed for storage of a copy of one of these values. The need for TEMP is illustrated in the trace in Table 3.1, assuming X and Y have original values of 12.5 and 5.0, respectively.

Table 3.1 Trace of if Statement to Order X and Y

Statement Part	X	Y	TEMP	Effect
	12.5	5.0	?	
if X > Y then				12.5 > 5.0 — true
TEMP := X;			12.5	Store old X in TEMP
X := Y;	5.0			Store old Y in X
Y := TEMP		12.5		Store old X in Y

Example 3.3 The `if` statement below may be used to process a positive transaction amount (`TRANSAMOUNT`) that represents a check (`TRANSTYPE` is `'C'`) or a deposit. In either case, an appropriate message is printed and the account balance (`BALANCE`) is updated. Both the true and false statements are compound statements.

```
if TRANSTYPE = 'C' then
    begin {check}
        WRITE ('Check for $', TRANSAMOUNT);
        BALANCE := BALANCE - TRANSAMOUNT        {Deduct check amount}
    end {check}
else
    begin {deposit}
        WRITE ('Deposit of $', TRANSAMOUNT);
        BALANCE := BALANCE + TRANSAMOUNT        {Add deposit amount}
    end {deposit}
```

The two semicolons in the if statement above are used to separate the individual statements in each alternative. A common error would be to insert a semicolon after the first end (end; {check}). This would cause the if statement to be terminated prematurely, and the else would be "dangling." The error message "unexpected symbol" would probably be printed when the compiler tried to translate the rest of the if statement (beginning with else).

Example 3.4   The if statement below is a better way to find and print the average value of a list of items given their sum (see Fig. 2.18). Since the true task is a single statement only, it is not surrounded by a begin, end bracket.

```
if NUMITEMS = 0 then
    WRITELN ('Invalid number of items - average undefined')
else
    begin {NUMITEMS <> 0}
        AVERAGE := SUM / NUMITEMS;                {Compute average}
        WRITELN ('Average is ', AVERAGE :8:2)
    end {NUMITEMS <> 0}
```

In the event NUMITEMS is zero, the division is not performed and a message is printed instead. If the division were attempted in this case, an execution error would result and the error diagnostic "division by zero" would be printed by Pascal. Rather than have an execution error occur, it is much better to have your program test for this possible error and print its own diagnostic.

PROGRAM STYLE

Writing if statements with compound true or false statements

Each if statement in this section contains at least one compound statement surrounded by a begin—end bracket. Each compound statement is indented. The purpose of the indentation is to improve our ability to read and understand the if statement; indentation is ignored by the Pascal compiler.

The comment after each end helps to associate the end with its corresponding begin. The comments are not required either, but are included to improve program readability.

Semicolons are required between the individual statements within a compound statement. Semicolons should not be used before or after the reserved words then, else, begin, or end; however, a semicolon will be needed after the last end if another statement follows the if statement.

Nested if Statements

Until now, we used if statements to implement decisions involving two alternatives. In this section, we will see how the if statement can be used to implement decisions involving several alternatives.

A *nested* if statement occurs when the true or false statement of an if statement is itself an if statement. A *nested* if statement can be used to implement decisions with several alternatives as shown in the next examples.

Example 3.5 The nested if statement below has three alternatives. It causes one of three variables (NUMPOS, NUMNEG, or NUMZERO) to be increased by one depending on whether X is greater than zero, less than zero, or equal to zero, respectively.

```
{increment NUMPOS, NUMNEG, or NUMZERO based on X}
if X > 0 then
   NUMPOS := NUMPOS + 1
else
   if X < 0 then
      NUMNEG := NUMNEG + 1
   else {X = 0}
      NUMZERO := NUMZERO + 1
```

The execution of this if statement proceeds as follows: the first condition (X > 0) is tested; if it is true, NUMPOS is incremented and the rest of the if statement is skipped. If the first condition is false, the second condition (X < 0) is tested; if it is true, NUMNEG is incremented; otherwise, NUMZERO is incremented. It is important to realize that the second condition is tested only when the first condition is false. A trace of this statement for X = −7 is shown in Table 3.2.

Table 3.2 Trace of if Statement in Example 3.5 for X = −7

Statement Part	Effect
if X > 0 then	−7 > 0 — false
else if X < 0 then	−7 < 0 — true
NUMNEG := NUMNEG + 1	Add 1 to NUMNEG

Nested `if` statements may become quite complex. If there are more than three alternatives and indentation is not done consistently, it may be difficult to determine the `if` to which a given `else` belongs. (In Pascal, this is always the closest `if` without an `else`.) We find it easier to write the nested `if` statement in Example 3.5 as the *multiple alternative decision* below.

```
{increment NUMPOS, NUMNEG, or NUMZERO based on X}
if X > 0 then
    NUMPOS := NUMPOS + 1
else if X < 0 then
    NUMNEG := NUMNEG + 1
else {X = 0}
    NUMZERO := NUMZERO + 1
```

In this format, the word `else` and the next condition appear on the same line. All the words `else` align, and each *dependent statement* is indented under the condition that controls its execution. The general form is shown next.

```
if condition₁ then
    statement₁
else if condition₂ then
    statement₂
        .
        .
        .
else if conditionₙ then
    statementₙ
else
    statementₑ
```

The conditions in a multiple alternative decision are evaluated in sequence. If a condition is false, the statement following it is skipped and the next condition is tested. If a condition is true, the statement following it is executed and the rest of the multiple alternative decision is skipped. If all conditions are false, then *statement*$_e$ following the last `else` is executed.

Very often the conditions in a multiple alternative decision are not *mutually exclusive*. This means that it may be possible for more than one condition to be true for a given data value. If this is the case, then the order of the conditions becomes very important because only the statement following the first true condition will be executed.

Example 3.6   The table below describes the assignment of grades based on an exam score.

Exam Score	Grade Assigned
90 and above	A
80–89	B
70–79	C
60–69	D
below 60	F

The multiple alternative decision below prints the letter grade assigned according to this table. The last three conditions are true for an exam score of 85; however, a grade of B is assigned because the first true condition is SCORE > = 80.

```
{correct grade assignment}
if SCORE >= 90 then
   WRITE ('A')
else if SCORE >= 80 then
   WRITE ('B')
else if SCORE >= 70 then
   WRITE ('C')
else if SCORE >= 60 then
   WRITE ('D')
else
   WRITE ('F')
```

It would be wrong to write the decision as shown next. All passing exam scores (60 or above) would be incorrectly categorized as a grade of D because the first condition would be true and the rest would be skipped.

```
{incorrect grade assignment}
if SCORE >= 60 then
   WRITE ('D')
else if SCORE >= 70 then
   WRITE ('C')
else if SCORE >= 80 then
   WRITE ('B')
else if SCORE >= 90 then
   WRITE ('A')
else
   WRITE ('F')
```

Example 3.7   A nested if statement may be used to implement a *decision table* that describes several alternatives. Each line of Table 3.3 indicates a salary range and a base tax amount and tax percentage for that range. Given a salary amount, the tax is calculated by adding the *Base Tax* for that salary range, and the product of the *Percentage of Excess* and the amount of salary over the minimum salary for that range. For example, the second line of the table specifies that the tax due on a salary of $2000.00 is $225.00 plus 16% of the excess salary over $1500.00 (i.e. 16% of $500.00). Therefore, the total tax due is $225.00 plus $80.00 or $305.00.

Table 3.3 Tax Table for Example 3.7

Range	Salary	Base Tax	Percentage of Excess
1	0.00 – 1499.99	0.00	15%
2	1500.00 – 2999.99	225.00	16%
3	3000.00 – 4999.99	465.00	18%
4	5000.00 – 7999.99	825.00	20%
5	8000.00 – 14999.99	1425.00	25%

The if statement in Fig. 3.2 implements the tax table. If the value of SALARY is within the table range (0 to 14999.99), exactly one of the statements assigning a value to TAX will be executed. A trace of the if statement for SALARY = $2000.000 is shown in Table 3.4. The value assigned to TAX is $305.00 as desired.

```
if SALARY < 0.0 then
   WRITELN ('Error! Negative salary $', SALARY :10:2)
else if SALARY < 1500.00 then                          {first range}
   TAX := 0.15 * SALARY
else if SALARY < 3000.00 then                          {second range}
   TAX := (SALARY - 1500.00) * 0.16 + 225.00
else if SALARY < 5000.00 then                          {third range}
   TAX := (SALARY - 3000.00) * 0.18 + 465.00
else if SALARY < 8000.00 then                          {fourth range}
   TAX := (SALARY - 5000.00) * 0.20 + 825.00
else if SALARY < 15000.00 then                         {fifth range}
   TAX := (SALARY - 8000.00) * 0.25 + 1425.00
else
   WRITELN ('Error! Too large salary $', SALARY :10:2)
```

Fig. 3.2 If Statement for Table 3.3

Table 3.4 Trace of if Statement in Fig. 3.3 for SALARY = $2000.00

Statement Part	SALARY	TAX	Effect
	2000.00	?	
if SALARY < 0.0			2000.0 < 0.0 – false
else if SALARY < 1500.00			2000.0 < 1500.0 – false
else if SALARY < 3000.00			2000.0 < 3000.0 – true
TAX := (SALARY - 1500.00)			Evaluates to 500.00
* 0.16			Evaluates to 80.00
+ 225.00		305.00	Evaluates to 305.00

Self-check Exercises for Section 3.2

1. What would be the effect of omitting the first begin in the if statement of Example 3.3? What error messages do you think would be printed as the compiler tried to translate the rest of the if statement?
2. Write an if statement that assigns the larger of X and Y to LARGER and the smaller to SMALLER. Your statement should print 'X LARGER' or 'Y LARGER' depending on the situation.
3. Trace the execution of the nested if statement in Fig. 3.2 when SALARY is 13500.00.
4. What would be the effect of reversing the order of the first 2 conditions in the if statement of Fig. 3.2?
5. Rewrite the if statement for Example 3.6 using only the relational operator < in all conditions.
6. Implement the decision table below using a nested if statement. Assume that the grade point average is within the range 0.0 through 4.0.

Grade Point Average	Transcript Message
0.0 – 0.99	Failed semester—registration suspended
1.0 – 1.99	On probation for next semester
3.0 – 3.49	Deans list for semester
3.5 – 4.0	Highest honors for semester

3.3 The while Statement

In all the loops used so far, the exact number of loop repetitions required could be determined before the start of loop execution. We used the for statement to implement these counting loops.

In many programming situations, the exact number of loop repetitions cannot be determined before loop execution begins. It may depend on some aspect of the data which is not known beforehand, but usually can be stated by a condition. For example, we may wish to continue writing checks as long as our bank balance is positive. Pascal provides additional looping statements (while and repeat) to implement *conditional loops*. The while statement is discussed below; the repeat statement is discussed in Chapter 5.

Example 3.8   The while loop in Fig. 3.3 could be used to find the sum of the first N integers. The loop body is the compound statement (begin . . . end {while}) and is repeated as long as (while) the value of NEXTINT is less than or equal to N. In the loop body, each value of NEXTINT (starting with 1) is added to SUM and NEXTINT is incremented by 1. Loop execution stops when NEXTINT is equal to N + 1. The equivalent for loop is provided for comparison.

```
        while Loop                          for Loop
SUM := 0;                           SUM := 0;
NEXTINT := 1;                       for NEXTINT := 1 to N do
while NEXTINT <= N do                    SUM := SUM + NEXTINT
    begin
        SUM := SUM + NEXTINT;
        NEXTINT := NEXTINT + 1
    end {while}
```

Fig. 3.3 while and for Statements to Sum N Integers

The most obvious difference between the loops in Fig. 3.3 is that the while statement is much longer. This illustrates that the while statement should not be used to implement a counting loop; the for statement is easier to write and more efficient.

NEXTINT is the loop control variable for both loops in Fig. 3.3. The main reason for the extra length of the while loop involves the manner in which the loop control variable NEXTINT is manipulated:

- NEXTINT is set to an initial value of 1 (NEXTINT := 1)
- NEXTINT is tested before each loop repetition (NEXTINT <= N)
- NEXTINT is updated during each loop repetition (NEXTINT := NEXTINT + 1)

Although these three steps are implicit in the for statement, they must be specified explicitly when the while statement is used. If the loop control variable is not initialized properly before the while statement is reached, the loop repetition test will be meaningless. If the loop control variable is not updated, the loop repetition test will always be true and the loop will not be exited (*infinite loop*). The while statement is described in the next display.

WHILE STATEMENT

while *condition* do
    statement

Interpretation: The *condition* is tested and if it is true, the *statement* is executed and the *condition* is retested. The *statement* is repeated as long as (while) the *condition* is true. When the *condition* is tested and found to be false, the while loop is exited and the next program statement is executed.

Notes: If the *condition* evaluates to false the first time it is tested, the *statement* will not be executed.

Example 3.9   The while statement below could be used in Fig. 2.18 to ensure that a positive value is read into NUMITEMS. The loop body is repeated as long as the value of NUMITEMS is less than or equal to zero. The loop body will not be executed at all if the first value read is positive.

```
WRITE ('Number of items to be summed? ');
READLN (NUMITEMS);
while NUMITEMS <= 0 do
   begin
      WRITE ('Number not positive - try again: ');
      READLN (NUMITEMS)
   end {while}
```

The interaction that would result for the data values −3, 0, 7 is shown next.

```
Number of items to be summed? -3
Number not positive - try again: 0
Number not positive - try again: 7
```

In this example the READLN statement appears twice, before the while statement and at the end of the loop body. The first READLN (called a *priming read*) reads the first data value (−3); the second READLN statement would read any additional values of NUMITEMS (0 and 7). The priming read initializes the loop control variable and is needed whenever the value of the loop control variable is an input data item.

Example 3.10   The program in Fig. 3.4 prints each power, POWER, of an input integer N that is less than 1000 (MAXPOWER). The while loop is exited when the value of NEXTPOWER is greater than or equal to 1000. The assignment statement

```
NEXTPOWER := 1; {Initialize NEXTPOWER to the zero power}
```

initializes NEXTPOWER to the zero power. The loop repetition condition

```
NEXTPOWER < MAXPOWER
```

ensures that loop exit will occur at the proper time.

```
program POWERS (INPUT, OUTPUT);

{Prints all powers of N less than 1000.}
```

```
const
   MAXPOWER = 1000;                               {the largest possible power}

var
   N,                                  {number whose powers are printed}
   NEXTPOWER : INTEGER;                           {the next power of N}

begin {POWERS}
   WRITELN ('This program prints all powers < 1000 of an integer.');
   WRITELN ('Enter an integer: ');
   READLN (N);
   WRITELN;

   NEXTPOWER := 1;                {Initialize NEXTPOWER to the zero power}
   {Print each power of N less than MAXPOWER}
   while NEXTPOWER < MAXPOWER do
      begin
         WRITE (NEXTPOWER :4);
         NEXTPOWER := NEXTPOWER * N                    {Get next power of N}
      end  {while}
end.   {POWERS}

This program prints all powers < 1000 of an integer.
Enter an integer: 2
1  2  4  8  16  32  64  128  256  512
```

Fig. 3.4 Program POWERS

Within the loop body, the statement

```
NEXTPOWER := NEXTPOWER * N            {Get next power of N}
```

computes the next power of N by multiplying the previous power by N. If the new value is less than MAXPOWER, the loop is repeated printing the current value of NEXTPOWER and computing the next one.

In the sample run shown, the last value printed is 512; however, the last value assigned to NEXTPOWER in the loop body is 1024. Since 1024 is greater than 1000, the loop repetition test fails the next time it is evaluated, and the loop is exited.

It is important to realize that the loop is not exited at the exact instant that NEXTPOWER is assigned the value 1024. If there were more statements following the assignment statement in the loop body, they would be executed. Loop exit does not occur until the loop repetition test is reevaluated at the top of the loop.

Non-unit Loop Control Increments

A for statement can be used to specify a loop in which the loop control variable increases by 1 after each execution of the loop body. In situations where the change in the loop control variable is different from 1, a while statement may be used.

Example 3.11   The program in Fig. 3.5 prints a table of equivalent Celsius and Fahrenheit temperatures. The Celsius temperatures range from −10 degrees to 30 degrees in increments of 5 degrees. Within the loop, the equivalent Fahrenheit temperature is computed and printed, and the Celsius temperature is incremented by 5 degrees (CELSTEP).

```
program TEMPTABLE (OUTPUT);

{Prints a table of Celsius and Fahrenheit equivalents.}

const
   MINCEL  = -10;              {minimum Celsius temperature}
   MAXCEL  =  30;              {maximum Celsius temperature}
   CELSTEP =   5;              {increment between Celsius values}

var
   CELSIUS : INTEGER;          {Celsius temperature}
   FAHREN : REAL;              {Fahrenheit temperature}

begin
   {Print a table of Celsius and Fahrenheit temperatures}
   PAGE;                                    {start a new output page}
   WRITELN ('Celsius' :10, 'Fahrenheit' :15);          {print heading}
   CELSIUS := MINCEL;                          {initialize Celsius}
   while CELSIUS <= MAXCEL do
      begin
         FAHREN := (1.8 * CELSIUS) + 32;       {compute Fahrenheit temp}
         WRITELN (CELSIUS :10, FAHREN :15:1);
         CELSIUS := CELSIUS + CELSTEP          {get next Celsius value}
      end {while}
end. {TEMPTABLE}
```

```
Celsius        Fahrenheit
   -10             14.0
    -5             23.0
     0             32.0
     5             41.0
    10             50.0
    15             59.0
    20             68.0
    25             77.0
    30             86.0
```

Fig. 3.5 Printing a Temperature Conversion Table

PROGRAM STYLE

Printing a table

If the output device is a printer, the statements

```
      PAGE;                                {start a new output page}
      WRITELN ('Celsius' :10, 'Fahrenheit' :15);
                                           {print heading}
```

should cause two strings to be printed at the top of the next output page. (The statement PAGE may have no effect on a video screen.) The two strings serve as the table heading. In the WRITELN statement, the number following each colon specifies a field width. Since a string is printed *right justified* in its field, the last s in 'Celsius' is printed in column 10 and the t in 'Fahrenheit' is printed in column 25 (10 + 15).

The statement

```
WRITELN (CELSIUS :10, FAHREN :15:1);
```

is used in the loop to print a table consisting of two columns of numbers. Since field widths of 10 and 15 are used here also, the rightmost digit of each number will be aligned under the rightmost letter of its respective column heading.

Using a Sentinel Value

Very often we do not know exactly how many data items there will be when a program begins execution. In a batch or interactive program, this may be because there are too many data items to count them beforehand (e.g. a stack of exam scores for a very large class). In an interactive program, the number of data items provided may depend on how the computation proceeds.

There are two ways to handle this situation. After processing a data item, the program could ask whether there were any more data. The user would enter YES or NO and the program would either continue its processing (YES) or terminate (NO). A second approach would be to instruct the user to enter a unique data value when done. The program would test each data item and terminate when this *sentinel value* is read.

Example 3.12   The program in Fig. 3.6 finds the product of a collection of data values. It stops reading data when a value of zero is entered.

```
program MULTIPLY (INPUT, OUTPUT);

{Finds the product of all nonzero data items -- stops at first 0.}

const
    SENTINEL = 0;              {sentinel value}

var
    ITEM,                      {each data item}
    PRODUCT : REAL;            {product of all nonzero data}

begin {MULTIPLY}
    PRODUCT := 1;                                  {initialize PRODUCT}

    {Multiply PRODUCT by each nonzero data item}
    WRITE ('Enter first number or 0 to stop: ');
    READLN (ITEM);                                 {read first item}
```

```
    while ITEM <> SENTINEL do
        begin
            PRODUCT := PRODUCT * ITEM;            {compute next product}
            WRITE ('Next number or 0: ');
            READLN (ITEM)                          {read next item}
        end; {while}
    WRITELN ('The product is ', PRODUCT :8:2)       {print result}
end.  {MULTIPLY}

Enter first number or 0 to stop: 10
Next number or 0: 12
Next number or 0: 22
Next number or 0: 0
The product is 2640.00
```

Fig. 3.6 Program to Multiply Nonzero Data

The program in Fig. 3.6 illustrates the proper use of a sentinel value. In order to determine whether or not data entry is complete, each data item must be compared to the value stored in SENTINEL (0). In order for this test to make sense in the beginning, the first number must be read before the while statement is reached. The last step in the while statement must read the next number so that it can be tested to determine whether or not the loop body should be repeated. This general pattern is illustrated below.

> Read first data item
> while current data item is not the sentinel value do
>   Process current data item
>   Read the next data item

Remember, proper use of a sentinel value requires that the read appear twice: before the while statement (the priming read) and at the end of the loop body (the loop control variable update).

Self-check Exercises for Section 3.3

1. What values would be printed if the order of the statements in the loop body of Fig. 3.4 were reversed?
2. Modify the program in Fig. 3.4 to print both the power and its value. For the example shown, the table printed by POWERS should begin

POWER	VALUE
0	1
1	2
2	4
3	8

3. Write a procedure that prints the cumulative product of all numbers entered as long as that product is less than a specified maximum. Your procedure should ignore zero data values.

4. Use a `for` statement to implement the loop in Fig. 3.5. You will have to introduce a new variable for loop control.

3.4 Procedure Parameters

Until now, there was no communication of data between procedures or between procedures and the main program. Only data that were stored locally were manipulated by a procedure. This restriction has limited the usefulness of procedures.

This section will introduce a very important concept in programming, the use of procedure parameters. We will see that parameters provide a convenient way to pass information between a main program and a procedure. Parameters also make procedures more versatile as they enable a procedure to manipulate different sets of data.

Parameter Lists

We can make an analogy between a carefully designed program that uses procedures and a stereo system. Each component of a stereo system— tape deck, tuner, amplifier, turntable, speakers—is an independent device that performs a specific function. There may be similar electronic parts inside the tuner and amplifier, but each component uses its own internal circuitry to perform its required function.

Information in the form of electronic signals is passed back and forth between these components over wires. If you look at the rear of a stereo amplifier, you will find that some plugs are marked as *inputs* and others are marked as *outputs*. This means that the wires attached to the plugs marked *inputs* carry electronic signals into the amplifier where they are processed. (These signals may come from a tape deck, tuner, or turntable). New electronic signals are generated. These signals come out of the amplifier from the plugs marked as *outputs* and go to the speakers or back to the tape deck for recording.

Currently, we know how to design the separate modules (procedures) of a programming system, but we have no way to pass data between them. In this section, we will learn how to use *parameter lists* to specify the inputs and outputs of a module.

Simple Sorting Problem

Problem: Write a program that reads any three numbers into the variables NUM1, NUM2, NUM3 and rearranges the data so that the smallest number is stored in NUM1, the next smaller number in NUM2, and the largest number in NUM3.

Discussion: This is a special case of a *sorting problem*: rearranging a collection of data items so that the values are either in increasing or decreasing order. Since there are only three items to be sorted, we will solve this special case now; the general sorting problem is a bit more complicated and will be considered later. The problem inputs and outputs are described below.

Three numbers (NUM1, NUM2, NUM3 : REAL)

The three numbers stored in increasing order in NUM1, NUM2, NUM3

Algorithm

1. Read the three numbers into NUM1, NUM2, and NUM3
2. Place the smallest number in NUM1, the next smaller in NUM2, and the largest number in NUM3
3. Print NUM1, NUM2, and NUM3

We can think of the three variables NUM1, NUM2, NUM3 as representing a list of consecutive storage cells. To perform step 2, we can compare pairs of numbers, always moving the smaller number in the pair closer to the front of the list (NUM1) and the larger number closer to the end of the list (NUM3). It should take three comparisons to sort the numbers in the list; one possible sequence of comparisons is shown next.

Step 2 refinement

2.1 Compare NUM1 and NUM2 and store the smaller number in NUM1 and the larger number in NUM2
2.2 Compare NUM1 and NUM3 and store the smaller number in NUM1 and the larger number in NUM3
2.3 Compare NUM2 and NUM3 and store the smaller number in NUM2 and the larger number in NUM3

Table 3.5 traces this refinement for the input sequence: 8, 10, 6. The final order is correct.

Table 3.5 Trace of Steps 1 and 2 for Input Data: 8, 10, 6

Algorithm Step	NUM1	NUM2	NUM3	Effect
1	8	10	6	Read the data
2.1				NUM1, NUM2 are in order
2.2	6		8	Switch NUM1 and NUM3
2.3		8	10	Switch NUM2 and NUM3

The structure chart for this algorithm is shown in Fig. 3.7. Since steps 2.1, 2.2, and 2.3 perform the same operation on different data, it would be a waste of time and effort to write a different procedure for each step. We would like to be able to write one general procedure to order any pair of numbers. This procedure is shown in Fig. 3.8.

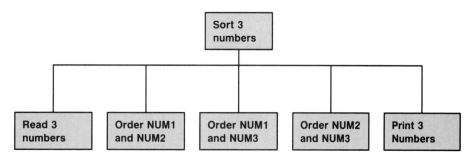

Fig. 3.7 Structure Chart for Simple Sorting Problem.

```
procedure ORDER (var X, Y : REAL);

{Orders a pair of numbers represented by X and Y so that the smaller
 number is in X and the larger number is in Y.                      }

var
    TEMP : REAL;                            {copy of number originally in X}

begin {ORDER}
    if X > Y then
        begin {Switch the values of X and Y}
            TEMP := X;          {Store old X in TEMP}
            X := Y;             {Store old Y in X}
            Y := TEMP           {Store old X in Y}
        end  {X > Y}
end;  {ORDER}
```

Fig. 3.8 Procedure ORDER

The body of procedure ORDER consists of the if statement from Fig. 3.1. The procedure heading contains a *formal parameter list* enclosed in parentheses.

```
(var X, Y : REAL)
```

A formal parameter list resembles a variable declaration statement. It identifies the *formal parameters* (X and Y) that will be used within the procedure in place of the variable names; the actual variables to be manipulated are determined when the procedure is called. We can think of X and Y as generic names for the procedure data; the specific names will be supplied later.

The use of formal parameters in a procedure is analogous to the use of the names *defendant* and *plaintiff* in a legal document. The name *defendant* is used in the body of the document to refer to the individual who is accused; the name *plaintiff* is used to refer to the individual doing the accusing. The actual names of the people involved are specified on a separate cover sheet preceding the document.

A formal parameter list describes a template or pattern that is partially filled in. The template described by the formal parameter list for procedure ORDER is shown below. The part that is filled in indicates that formal parameters X and Y are used to represent type REAL variables. The missing entries in the template are the actual variables to be manipulated (*actual parameters*); these entries are filled in when the procedure (call) statement is executed.

Actual Parameters	*Formal Parameters*	*Attributes*
_____	X	REAL variable
_____	Y	REAL variable

The procedure (call) statement below contains an *actual parameter list* enclosed in parentheses.

```
ORDER (NUM1, NUM2)
```

This actual parameter list causes the template to be completed as follows:

Actual Parameters	*Formal Parameters*	*Attributes*
NUM1	X	REAL variable
NUM2	Y	REAL variable

The completed template shows that formal parameters X and Y represent the variables NUM1 and NUM2, respectively. This means that whenever X is referenced in the procedure, the variable NUM1 will actually be manipulated. Thus, the procedure (call) statement

```
ORDER (NUM1, NUM2)
```

can be used to perform step 2.1 of the algorithm: Compare NUM1 and NUM2 and store the smaller number in NUM1 and the larger number in NUM2.

The sequence of the actual parameters is most important. The first actual parameter is paired with the first formal parameter, the second actual parameter is paired with the second formal parameter, etc. The procedure (call) statement

```
ORDER (NUM2, NUM1)
```

would cause the smaller number to be stored in NUM2 and the larger number in NUM1 instead of the other way around. (Complete the partial template above to see why this is so.)

The final program is shown in Fig. 3.9. The main program body contains three procedure statements that call procedure ORDER:

```
ORDER (NUM1, NUM2);    {order the data in NUM1 and NUM2}
ORDER (NUM1, NUM3);    {order the data in NUM1 and NUM3}
ORDER (NUM2, NUM3);    {order the data in NUM2 and NUM3}
```

Since each of these statements contains a different actual parameter list, a different pair of variables will be manipulated each time the procedure is called. We will see how this is done in the next section.

```
program SORT3NUMBERS (INPUT, OUTPUT);

{Reads three numbers and sorts them
 so that they are in increasing order.}

var
    NUM1, NUM2, NUM3 : REAL;                    {a list of three cells}

procedure ORDER (var X, Y : REAL);

{Orders a pair of numbers represented by X and Y so that the
 smaller number is in X and the larger number is in Y.}

var
    TEMP : REAL;                     {copy of number originally in X}

begin {ORDER}
    if X > Y then
       begin {Switch the values of X and Y}
           TEMP := X;                          {store old X in TEMP}
           X := Y;                             {store old Y in X}
           Y := TEMP                           {store old X in Y}
       end {X > Y}
end; {ORDER}

begin {SORT3NUMBERS}
    WRITELN ('Enter 3 numbers to be sorted separated by spaces: ');
    READLN (NUM1, NUM2, NUM3);

    {Sort the numbers}
    ORDER (NUM1, NUM2);               {order the data in NUM1 and NUM2}
    ORDER (NUM1, NUM3);               {order the data in NUM1 and NUM3}
    ORDER (NUM2, NUM3);               {order the data in NUM2 and NUM3}

    {Print the results}
    WRITELN ('The three numbers in order are: ',
             NUM1 :8:2, NUM2 :8:2, NUM3 :8:2)
end. {SORT3NUMBERS}

Enter 3 numbers to be sorted separated by spaces:
8 10 6
The three numbers in order are:
   6.00    8.00   10.00
```

Fig. 3.9 Program to Order Three Numbers

Executing a Procedure with Parameters

Figure 3.10 shows the data areas for the main program and procedure ORDER immediately after the execution of the procedure (call) statement

```
ORDER (NUM1, NUM2);     {order the data in NUM1 and NUM2}
```

This diagram shows the data values read into NUM1, NUM2, and NUM3. It also shows that the local variable TEMP is considered undefined immediately after the procedure is called.

Figure 3.10 also shows the parameter correspondence specified by the actual parameter list above. The double-headed arrows symbolize the connection between formal parameters X and Y and main program variables NUM1 and NUM2, respectively. Whenever Y is referenced in the procedure, the data in variable NUM2 are actually manipulated.

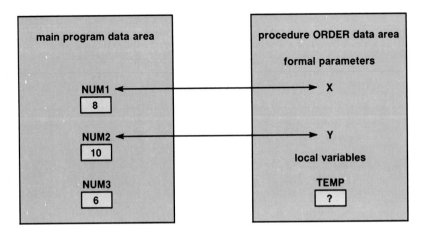

Fig. 3.10 Parameter Correspondence for ORDER (NUM1, NUM2)

The execution of the procedure is traced in Table 3.6. The actual parameter represented by each formal parameter is shown in parentheses at the top of the table. Since the value of NUM1 is less than NUM2, the true alternative is skipped and the variable values are unchanged.

Table 3.6 Trace of Procedure Execution for ORDER (NUM1, NUM2)

Statement in ORDER	X(NUM1)	Y(NUM2)	TEMP	Effect
	8	10	?	
if X > Y then				8 > 10 — false, do nothing

The parameter correspondence specified by the procedure (call) statement

```
ORDER (NUM1, NUM3);
```

is pictured in Fig. 3.11. This time parameter X corresponds to variable NUM1 and parameter Y corresponds to variable NUM3. This means that whenever formal parameter Y is referenced in the procedure, the data in main program variable NUM3 are actually manipulated.

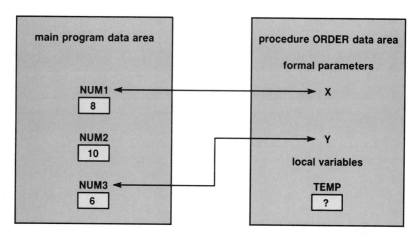

Fig. 3.11 Parameter Correspondence for ORDER (NUM1, NUM3)

The execution of the procedure is traced in Table 3.7. The actual parameter represented by each formal parameter is shown in parentheses at the top of the table. The procedure execution switches the values stored in main program variables NUM1 and NUM3 as desired.

Table 3.7 Trace of Procedure Execution for ORDER (NUM1, NUM3)

Statement in ORDER	X(NUM1)	Y(NUM3)	TEMP	Effect
	8	6	?	
if X > Y then				8 > 6 – true
TEMP := X;			8	Save old NUM1 in TEMP
X := Y;	6			Save old NUM3 in NUM1
Y := TEMP		8		Save old NUM1 in NUM3

Variable and Value Parameters

You have already been using procedure (call) statements with actual parameter lists. READLN and WRITELN are two procedures that are part of the Pascal system. The *input list* for READLN is an actual parameter list; so is the *output list* for WRITELN. Procedure READLN stores new values in its actual parameters whenever it is called; procedure WRITELN displays the values of its actual parameters. Unlike procedures that we declare, the number of parameters used in a call to procedure READLN or WRITELN may vary.

In procedure ORDER, formal parameters X and Y are called *variable parameters* as they correspond to actual parameters that are variables during each execution of the procedure. The reserved word var in the formal parameter list

```
(var X, Y : REAL)
```

indicates that X and Y are variable parameters. The parameters used with procedure READLN are also variable parameters.

As we saw in Table 3.7, it is possible for a procedure execution to change the value of an actual parameter that corresponds to a variable formal parameter. Both NUM1 and NUM3 were changed by the procedure execution traced in this table. Only variables can be used as actual parameters that correspond to variable parameters (e.g., ORDER (5, 3.7) causes a syntax error).

In some situations, a parameter is used only to pass data into a procedure, and we know beforehand that the actual parameter value should not be changed by the procedure (e.g., an actual parameter that is a constant). Pascal provides a second type of parameter, called a *value parameter*, for this purpose. The parameters used with procedure WRITELN are value parameters.

A value parameter may correspond to an actual parameter that is a constant, variable, or expression of the same type as the value parameter. In the procedure (call) statement

```
WRITELN (COUNT, ' is less than ', COUNT + 1)
```

the actual parameter list contains a variable, a string constant, and an expression, in that order.

Pascal allocates a local memory cell in the procedure data area for each formal parameter that is a value parameter. Each local cell is initialized to the value of its corresponding actual parameter when the procedure is called, and there is no further connection between the actual and formal parameter. When a value parameter is referenced within the procedure, the local cell is manipulated. Consequently, even if the local data are modified, the actual parameter value cannot be changed.

The next two examples illustrate the use of value parameters.

Example 3.13 Procedure PRINTLINE in Fig. 3.12 prints a row of asterisks. In the procedure heading

```
procedure PRINTLINE (NUMSTARS : INTEGER);
```

NUMSTARS is declared to be a formal parameter of type INTEGER; NUMSTARS is a value parameter (indicated by the absence of the word var).

Parameter NUMSTARS determines how many asterisks are printed, and its initial value is passed into procedure PRINTLINE when the procedure is called. Since there is no need for the procedure to change its parameter

```
procedure PRINTLINE (NUMSTARS : INTEGER);

{Prints a row of asterisks. The number of asterisks
 printed is determined by NUMSTARS.                  }

const
    STAR = '*';                              {symbol being printed}

var
    COUNTSTAR : INTEGER; {loop control variable for PRINTLINE}

begin
    {Print a row of asterisks}
    for COUNTSTAR := 1 to NUMSTARS do
        WRITE (STAR);
    WRITELN
end;   {PRINTLINE}
```

Fig. 3.12 Procedure PRINTLINE

value, NUMSTARS is declared to be a value parameter. The three procedure (call) statements

```
PRINTLINE (5);
PRINTLINE (3);
PRINTLINE (1)
```

would cause the three lines below to be printed.

```
*****
***
*
```

An integer value (5, 3, or 1) is assigned to NUMSTARS when each procedure (call) statement is executed.

Example 3.14 Procedure TRIANGLE in Fig. 3.13 uses procedure PRINTLINE to draw a triangle. This example shows that a procedure may be declared locally in another procedure and called by that procedure.

```
procedure TRIANGLE (NUMROWS : INTEGER);

{Prints a triangle using procedure PRINTLINE to print lines of
 increasing length—number of lines is determined by NUMROWS. }

var
    ROW : INTEGER;                          {loop control variable for TRIANGLE}

procedure PRINTLINE (NUMSTARS : INTEGER);

{Prints a row of asterisks. The number of asterisks printed is
 determined by NUMSTARS.                                       }

const
    STAR = '*';                                      {symbol being printed}
```

```
var
    COUNTSTAR : INTEGER;              {loop control variable for PRINTLINE}

begin {PRINTLINE}
    {Print a row of asterisks}
    for COUNTSTAR := 1 to NUMSTARS do
        WRITE (STAR);
    WRITELN
end; {PRINTLINE}

begin {TRIANGLE}
    {Print lines of increasing length}
    for ROW := 1 to NUMROWS do
        PRINTLINE (ROW)
end; {TRIANGLE}
```

Fig. 3.13 Procedure TRIANGLE

The for statement in the body of procedure TRIANGLE

```
for ROW := 1 to NUMROWS do
    PRINTLINE (ROW)
```

calls procedure PRINTLINE repeatedly; each time PRINTLINE is called the current value of ROW (1 to NUMROWS) determines how many asterisks will be printed.

The parameter NUMROWS determines the number of lines in the triangle. The procedure (call) statement

```
TRIANGLE (5)
```

assigns a value of 5 to NUMROWS and causes the triangle below to be drawn.

```
*
**
***
****
*****
```

Since procedure PRINTLINE is declared within procedure TRIANGLE, PRINTLINE is considered a local identifier in TRIANGLE, and PRINT-LINE can be called only by TRIANGLE (or by PRINTLINE). *Scope of identifiers* will be discussed in detail in Section 3.6.

When to Use a Variable or Value Parameter

You may be wondering how to tell when to use a variable parameter and when to use a value parameter. Some rules of thumb follow:

- If information is to be passed into a procedure and does not have to be returned, then the formal parameter representing that information can be a value parameter. Such a parameter is called an *input parameter* or a *procedure input* (e.g. NUMSTARS and NUMROWS in Fig. 3.13).

- If information is to be passed out of a procedure, then the formal parameter representing that information must be a variable parameter. Such a parameter is called an *output parameter* or a *procedure output*.

- If information is to be passed into a procedure, perhaps modified, and a new value returned, then the formal parameter representing that information must be a variable parameter. Such a parameter is called an *input/output parameter* (e.g. X and Y in Fig. 3.8).

Remember that it is alright to use a variable, constant, or expression as an actual parameter corresponding to a value parameter; however, only a variable can be used as an actual parameter corresponding to a variable parameter. The reason for this restriction is that an actual parameter corresponding to a variable parameter may be modified when the procedure executes; it is illogical to allow a procedure to change the value of either a constant or expression.

The next example shows a procedure with a value parameter (for input) and a variable parameter (for output).

Example 3.15 Procedure FINDTAX in Fig. 3.14 implements the income tax table (see Table 3.3). The procedure body consists of the if statement first shown in Fig. 3.2. A value is passed into parameter SALARY (a value parameter) when the procedure is called. If SALARY is within the range of the table, a value is assigned to parameter TAX (a variable parameter) during procedure execution. This value is *returned* or passed out of the procedure. The comments {input} and {output} document the use of formal parameters SALARY and TAX, respectively.

```
program DRIVER (INPUT, OUTPUT);

{Tests procedure FINDTAX.}

var
    MYSALARY, MYTAX : REAL;                                {salary and tax}

procedure FINDTAX (SALARY {input} : REAL;
                   var TAX {output} : REAL);

{Computes tax amount (TAX) owed for a salary (SALARY) < $15000.}

begin {FINDTAX}
    if SALARY < 0.0 then
        WRITELN ('Error! Negative salary $', SALARY :10:2)
    else if SALARY < 1500.00 then                          {first range}
        TAX := 0.15 * SALARY
    else if SALARY < 3000.00 then                          {second range}
        TAX := (SALARY - 1500.00) * 0.16 + 225.00
    else if SALARY < 5000.00 then                          {third range}
        TAX := (SALARY - 3000.00) * 0.18 + 465.00
    else if SALARY < 8000.00 then                          {fourth range}
        TAX := (SALARY - 5000.00) * 0.20 + 865.00
```

```
      else if SALARY < 15000.00 then                          {fifth range}
         TAX := (SALARY - 8000.00) * 0.25 + 1425.00
      else
         WRITELN ('Error! Too large salary $', SALARY :10:2)
end; {FINDTAX}

begin {DRIVER}
   WRITE ('Enter a salary less than $15000.00: $');
   READLN (MYSALARY);
   FINDTAX (MYSALARY, MYTAX);
   WRITELN ('The tax on $', MYSALARY :8:2, ' is $', MYTAX :8:2)
end. {DRIVER}

Enter a salary less than $15000.00: $6000.00
The tax on $ 6000.00 is $ 1065.00
```

Fig. 3.14 Driver Program with Procedure FINDTAX

The parameter correspondence specified by the procedure (call) statement

```
FINDTAX (MYSALARY, MYTAX)
```

is shown in Fig. 3.15. The dashed line leading to value parameter SALARY indicates that the connection between the actual and formal parameter is broken after the actual parameter value is stored locally. Assuming a data value of 6000.00 was read into MYSALARY before FINDTAX was called, the value 1065.00 would be assigned to MYTAX during the execution of procedure FINDTAX.

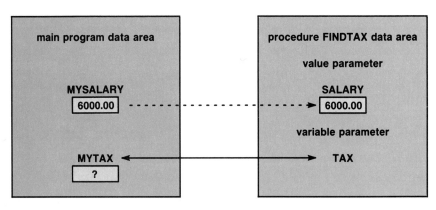

Fig. 3.15 Parameter Correspondence for FINDTAX (MYSALARY, MYTAX)

PROGRAM STYLE

Writing formal parameter lists

The formal parameter list in Fig. 3.14 is written on two lines to improve program readability. The value parameter is written on the first line with the comment {input} inserted to document its use as a procedure input. The variable parameter is written on the second line with the comment {output}.

Generally, we will follow the practice shown here in writing formal parameter lists. Input parameters will be listed first, then the input/output parameters, and any output parameters will be listed last. The order of the actual parameters must correspond to the order of the formal parameters.

PROGRAM STYLE

Writing driver programs to test procedures

The main program body in Fig. 3.14 consists of a statement for data entry, two statements for data display, and a procedure (call) statement. Its sole purpose is to test procedure FINDTAX. Such a program is called a *driver program.*

The use of driver programs to pretest procedures is highly recommended. Generally, the small investment in time and effort required to write a short driver program will pay off by reducing the total time spent debugging a large program system containing several procedures.

The Procedure Data Area

Each time a procedure (call) statement is executed, an area of memory is allocated for storage of that procedure's data. Included in the procedure data area are storage cells for any local variables or constants that may be declared in the procedure. The procedure data area is always erased when the procedure terminates and it is recreated empty (all values undefined) when the procedure is called again.

Memory cells are also allocated in the procedure data area for each formal parameter. These cells are used in different ways for value and variable parameters. For a value parameter, the local cell is used to hold a value; the value of the corresponding actual parameter is placed in this cell when the procedure is called. For a variable parameter, the local cell is used to hold a memory address; this is the address in the calling program data area of the corresponding actual parameter. This information enables the procedure to manipulate data stored in the calling program data area.

Syntax Rules for Procedures and Parameter Lists

In this section we will formally present the syntax rules for procedure declarations and procedure (call) statements with parameters. The displays that follow summarize these rules.

There are certain rules that must be followed when writing parameter lists. The syntax diagram for a formal parameter list follows.

Formal Parameter List

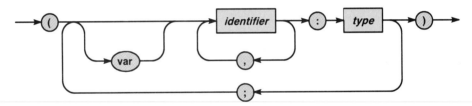

This diagram shows that a *formal parameter list* is always enclosed in parentheses. It consists of one or more lists of identifiers. Each list may be preceded by var. Identifiers are separated by commas, lists of identifiers are separated by semicolons, and each list must end with a colon followed by a data type name (e.g. REAL, CHAR, etc.).

Example 3.16 Two formal parameter lists are shown below. Each list is printed on two or more lines to improve readability.

```
(CH3 : CHAR;
 var X, Y, Z : REAL)

(M, N, O : INTEGER;
 A, B, C : REAL;
 var X, Y, Z : REAL)
```

In both lists above, X, Y, Z are declared to be type REAL variable parameters; CH3 is a type CHAR value parameter in the first list; A, B, C are type REAL value parameters in the second list; M, N, O are type INTEGER value parameters in the second list.

The formal parameter list also determines the form of any actual parameter list that may be used to call the procedure. This form is determined during the translation of the program when the compiler processes the procedure declaration.

Later, when a procedure (call) statement is reached, the compiler checks the actual parameter list for consistency with the formal parameter list. An actual parameter list may be a list of expressions, variables, or constants separated by commas. The actual parameter list must satisfy these rules.

Rules for Parameter List Correspondence

1. There must be the same number of actual parameters as formal parameters.
2. The type of each actual parameter must match the type of its corresponding formal parameter.
3. An actual parameter corresponding to a variable formal parameter must be a variable. An actual parameter corresponding to a value parameter may be a variable, constant, or expression.

Example 3.17 The main program contains the following declarations:

```
var
    X, Y : REAL;
    M : INTEGER;
    NEXT : CHAR;

procedure TEST (A, B : INTEGER;
                var C, D : REAL;
                var E : CHAR);
```

where only the heading for procedure TEST is shown. Any of the procedure statements below would be syntactically correct in the main program.

```
TEST (M + 3, 10, X, Y, NEXT)
TEST (M, MAXINT, Y, X, NEXT)
TEST (35, M * 10, Y, X, NEXT)
```

The correspondence specified by the first parameter list above is shown in Table 3.8.

Table 3.8 Parameter Correspondence for TEST (M + 3, 10, X, Y, NEXT)

Actual Parameter	Formal Parameter	Attributes
M + 3	A	INTEGER, value
10	B	INTEGER, value
X	C	REAL, variable
Y	D	REAL, variable
NEXT	E	CHAR, variable

The last column in Table 3.8 describes each parameter. Table 3.8 shows that an expression (M + 3) or a constant (10) may be associated with a value parameter. All the procedure (call) statements in Table 3.9 contain syntax errors as indicated.

Table 3.9 Invalid Procedure (Call) Statements

Procedure (Call) Statement	Error
TEST (30, 10, M, X, NEXT)	Type of M is not REAL
TEST (M, 19, X, Y)	Not enough actual parameters
TEST (M, 10, 35, Y, 'E')	Constants 35 and 'E' cannot correspond to variable parameters
TEST (M, 3.5, X, Y, NEXT)	Type of 3.5 is not INTEGER
TEST (30, 10, X, X + Y, NEXT)	Expression X + Y cannot correspond to a variable parameter
TEST (30, 10, C, D, E)	C, D, and E are not declared in the main program

The last procedure (call) statement above points out an error that is often made in using procedures. The actual parameter names C, D, E are the same as their corresponding formal parameter names. However, since these names are not declared in the main program, they cannot be used in an actual parameter list in the main program.

When writing relatively long parameter lists such as the ones above, you must be very careful not to transpose two actual parameters. This will result in a syntax error if it causes a violation of a parameter correspondence rule. If no syntax is violated, the procedure execution may generate incorrect results.

Self-check Exercises for Section 3.4

1. Draw the templates specified by the procedure calls

   ```
   ORDER (NUM1, NUM3);
   ORDER (NUM2, NUM3)
   ```

2. Trace the execution of the three procedure statements

   ```
   ORDER (NUM3, NUM2);
   ORDER (NUM3, NUM1);
   ORDER (NUM2, NUM1)
   ```

   for the data sets: 8, 10, 6 and 10, 8, 6. What does this sequence do?

3. Provide a table similar to Table 3.8 for the other correct parameter lists shown in Example 3.17.

4. Correct the syntax errors in the formal parameter lists below.

   ```
   (var A, B : INTEGER, C : REAL)
   (value M : INTEGER; var NEXT : CHAR)
   (var ACCOUNT, REAL; X + Y , REAL)
   ```

5. Assuming the declarations

   ```
   var
       X, Y, Z : REAL;
       M, N : INTEGER;

   procedure MASSAGE (var A, B : REAL;
                           X : INTEGER);
   ```

   what is wrong with each incorrect procedure (call) statement?

a. MASSAGE (X, Y, Z)	g. MASSAGE (A, B, X)
b. MASSAGE (X, Y, 8)	h. MASSAGE (Y, Z, M)
c. MASSAGE (Y, X, N)	i. MASSAGE (Y + Z, Y - Z, M)
d. MASSAGE (M, Y, N)	j. MASSAGE (Z, Y, X)
e. MASSAGE (25.0, 15, X)	k. MASSAGE (X, Y, M, 10)
f. MASSAGE (X, Y, M + N)	l. MASSAGE (Z, Y, MAXINT)

3.5 | Adding Data Flow Information to Structure Charts

Now that we can pass data into and out of procedures, we can make more use of procedures in our programming. Many of the level one subproblems shown in a structure chart will be implemented as separate procedures. Generally, if a subproblem requires more than a few lines of code, it will be written as a procedure.

In this section, we will see how to add *data flow* information to a structure chart and how to practice *top down* design of programs. We will do this by example, reexamining the solution to the General Sum and Average Problem. The problem statement is repeated below, followed by its data description and algorithm.

General Sum and Average Problem

Problem: Write a program to find and print the sum and average of a list of data items.

Discussion: The data requirements and algorithm from Section 2.7 are repeated below.

PROBLEM INPUTS

number of data items to be summed (NUMITEMS : INTEGER)
each data item (ITEM : REAL)

PROBLEM OUTPUTS

sum of data items (SUM : REAL)
average of data items (AVERAGE : REAL)

Algorithm

1. Read the number of items (NUMITEMS).
2. Read each item and add it to the sum (SUM).
3. Find the average (AVERAGE).
4. Print the sum and average.

Step 2 is the only step needing refinement. Rather than refine it now, we will implement it later as procedure FINDSUM.

The structure chart is drawn in Fig. 3.16. The data flow between subproblems is documented in this chart. Downward pointing arrows indicate inputs to a subproblem; upward pointing arrows indicate outputs from a subproblem. The variables involved in the data transfer are listed inside the arrow.

Since the step "Read the number of items" defines the value of the variable NUMITEMS, NUMITEMS is an output of this step. Procedure FINDSUM needs this value in order to know how many data items to read; consequently, NUMITEMS is an input to procedure FINDSUM. The procedure re-

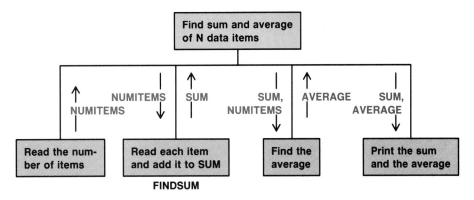

Fig. 3.16 Structure Chart with Data Flow Information

sult SUM is an output of FINDSUM. The variable AVERAGE is an output of the step "Find the average"; SUM and NUMITEMS are inputs to this step. Both SUM and AVERAGE must be provided as inputs to the step that prints them.

Once the data flow information has been added to the structure chart, the main program can be written even if the details of the procedures are not yet known. For example, we know from the data flow information in Fig. 3.16 that the procedure (call) statement

```
FINDSUM (NUMITEMS, SUM)
```

may be used to call FINDSUM. We also know that NUMITEMS should correspond to a value parameter and SUM to a variable parameter.

The program is shown in Fig. 3.17—except for procedure FINDSUM. All the variables that appear in the structure chart are declared in the main program.

```
program SUMITEMS (INPUT, OUTPUT);

{Finds and prints the sum and average of a list of data items.}

var
    NUMITEMS : INTEGER;     {the number of items to be added}
    SUM,                    {the sum being accumulated}
    AVERAGE : REAL;         {the average of the data}

procedure FINDSUM (N {input} : INTEGER;
                   var SUM {output} : REAL);

{Finds the sum of a list of data items. The number of data items
 is passed into N; the result is passed back as SUM.          }
```

```
begin {FINDSUM}
   WRITELN ('Procedure FINDSUM entered.')
end; {FINDSUM}

begin {SUMITEMS}
   {Read the number of items to be summed}
   WRITE ('How many items will be summed? '); READLN (NUMITEMS);

   {Find the sum (SUM) of a list of data items}
   FINDSUM (NUMITEMS, SUM);

   {Find the average (AVERAGE) of the data}
   AVERAGE := SUM / NUMITEMS;

   {Print the sum and average}
   WRITELN ('The sum is ', SUM :8:2);
   WRITELN ('The average is ', AVERAGE :8:2)
end. {SUMITEMS}
```

Fig. 3.17 Main Program with a Stub for Procedure FINDSUM

The declaration for procedure FINDSUM shown in Fig. 3.17 is called a
stub. Including this declaration enables the main program to be compiled,
checked for syntax errors, and even run; however, the program will not
yet generate meaningful results.

Since we already know how to perform the summation operation, it will
be an easy matter to write procedure FINDSUM. The completed procedure,
shown in Fig. 3.18, should replace the stub.

Fig. 3.18 Procedure FINDSUM

```
procedure FINDSUM (N {input} : INTEGER;
                   var SUM {output} : REAL);

{Finds the sum of a list of data items. The number of data items
 is passed into N; the result is passed back as SUM.          }

var
   COUNT : INTEGER;     {count of items added so far}
   ITEM : REAL;         {the next data item to be added}

begin {FINDSUM}
   {Read each data item and add it to SUM}
   SUM := 0.0;
   for COUNT := 1 to N do
      begin
         WRITE ('Next number to be summed? '); READLN (ITEM);
         SUM := SUM + ITEM
      end {for COUNT}
end; {FINDSUM}
```

Since COUNT and ITEM are used only within procedure FINDSUM, they are declared as local variables in FINDSUM. The parameter correspondence specified by the procedure statement

```
FINDSUM (NUMITEMS, SUM);
```

is shown in Fig. 3.19 assuming the value 10 is read into NUMITEMS just before the procedure call.

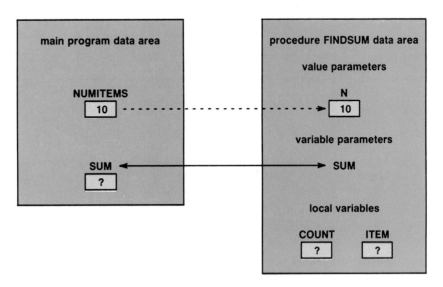

Fig. 3.19 Parameter Correspondence for FINDSUM (NUMITEMS, SUM)

The body of the procedure begins by initializing to zero the main program variable SUM, which corresponds to variable parameter SUM. The for statement causes each data item to be read into the local variable ITEM and added to the main program variable SUM. The procedure exit will occur after 10 items are added.

PROGRAM STYLE

Choosing formal parameter names

The identifiers N and SUM are used as formal parameter names in procedure FINDSUM. In the procedure (call) statement shown, formal parameter SUM happens to correspond to an actual parameter also named SUM. This, of course, is not necessary but it causes no difficulties either.

You should choose meaningful generic names for formal parameters. When a procedure is developed for a particular program system, it is fairly common for a formal parameter to have the same name as its corresponding actual parameter. This may not be true if that procedure is used later with a different program system.

PROGRAM STYLE

Separately testing a program system

In the program shown in Fig. 3.17, a stub is substituted for procedure FINDSUM presumably because FINDSUM is not yet written. When a team of programmers is working on a problem, this is a common practice. Obviously, not all the procedures will be ready at the same time. Still, it would be useful to test and debug those that are available.

Currently, a message is printed when the stub is entered. If the stub was modified to assign some test value (e.g. 100) to its output parameter SUM, then the rest of the program could be tested while procedure FINDSUM was being written. When FINDSUM was completed, it could be tested separately using a driver program.

By testing procedures separately in this fashion, the programming team can be fairly confident that the complete program system will be debugged quickly when it is finally put together. It is also easier to locate and correct errors when dealing with a single, small procedure rather than a complete program system containing several untested procedures.

Self-check Exercises for Section 3.5

1. Add data flow information to the structure chart shown in Fig. 2.13. Implement each subproblem as a procedure with parameters.
2. A procedure has four formal parameters: W, X, Y, and Z (all type REAL). The procedure execution stores the sum of W and X in Y and the product of W and X in Z. Which parameters are inputs and which are outputs? Write the procedure.

3.6 Nested Procedures and Scope of Identifiers

In Fig. 3.17, procedure FINDSUM is nested or contained in program SUMITEMS. It is also possible for one procedure to be nested within another. For example, procedure PRINTLINE is nested within procedure TRIANGLE in Fig. 3.13. Nested procedures occur quite often in Pascal and are a natural consequence of the top down design process.

Each procedure in a nest of procedures has its own declaration part and body; there is also a declaration part and body for the main program. A procedure's parameter list is included in its declaration part.

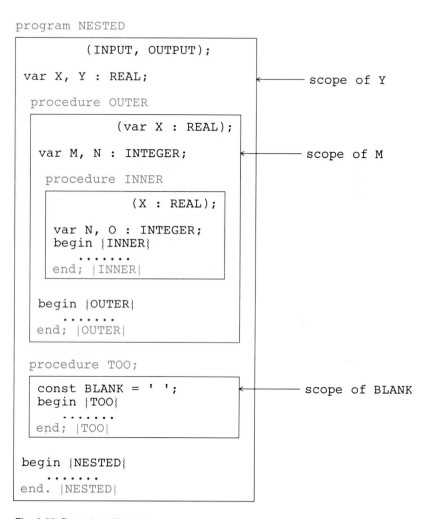

Fig. 3.20 Procedure Nesting

Figure 3.20 displays the organization of procedures in program NESTED. Each box represents a procedure or program *block*. A block consists of the declaration part and body of a program or procedure. The name of the block is indicated just above it.

Figure 3.20 shows procedures OUTER and TOO nested within the main program block. Procedure INNER is shown nested within the block for OUTER.

Scope of Identifiers

The statements in each program or procedure body written so far manipulate only local identifiers. Although we have not done so yet, it is possible in Pascal to reference identifiers that are not declared locally.

The Pascal scope rule below tells us where an identifier may be referenced.

PASCAL SCOPE RULE

An identifier may be referenced only within the block in which it is declared. The declaration of an identifier must precede its first reference.

The *scope of an identifier* is the block in which it is declared. The scope of the constant BLANK (see Fig. 3.20) is the block for procedure TOO; therefore, BLANK may be referenced only in procedure TOO.

Since procedure INNER is nested in procedure OUTER, the scope of an identifier declared in procedure OUTER includes the block for procedure INNER (see Fig. 3.20). Therefore an identifier declared in OUTER (e.g. variable M) may be referenced in the body of either procedure.

Since all procedures are nested within the main program block, an identifier declared in the main program may be referenced anywhere in the program system. For this reason, main program variables are called *global variables*.

Although global variables may be referenced in nested procedures, experience has shown this to be a very dangerous practice. If a procedure references a global variable, then it is possible for the procedure to change the value of that variable in an incorrect way (called a *side effect*). Often, there is no documentation to indicate that the procedure manipulates a global variable; consequently, it may be difficult to find a statement in a nested procedure that is responsible for assigning an incorrect value to a global variable.

The formal parameter list and local declarations for a procedure explicitly document the data that will be manipulated. We will continue to manipulate only identifiers (including parameters) that are declared locally in a procedure.

The only exceptions will be global constants and type identifiers (discussed in later chapters). It is alright to reference a global constant in a procedure because Pascal does not allow the value of a constant to be changed. Hence, there can't be a side effect when a global constant is manipulated.

Multiple Declarations of Identifiers

The same identifier may be declared in more than one place. In Fig. 3.20, for example, X is declared as a global variable in the main program and as a formal parameter in procedures INNER and OUTER. Consequently, when X is referenced in the program system there may be some question in our minds as to which declaration takes precedence. Pascal uses the closest declaration with a scope that includes the point of reference. This will always be the local declaration if one exists.

If the identifier is not declared locally, then a declaration in an outer block containing the point of reference is used. For example, if X is referenced in the body of procedure TOO, what declaration of X would be used? Would it be the declaration of X as a global variable, or its declaration as a formal parameter in one of the other procedures? Since TOO is nested only in the main program block, the declaration of X as a global variable is used.

By this same reasoning, if identifier N is referenced in procedure INNER or procedure OUTER, the corresponding local declaration for identifier N is used. If identifier M is referenced in procedure INNER where it is not declared locally, the declaration for variable M in procedure OUTER is used. A reference to identifier M in either the main program or procedure TOO would cause an "identifier not declared" syntax error. Table 3.10 shows the meaning of each valid reference to an identifier in the blocks of Fig. 3.20. Procedure names are included with other identifiers in this table.

Table 3.10 Valid Identifier References for Fig. 3.20

Block	Meaning of Each Identifier
INNER	X (parameter of INNER) N, O (local variables) M (variable declared in OUTER) INNER (procedure declared in OUTER) Y (variable declared in NESTED) OUTER (procedure declared in NESTED) INPUT, OUTPUT (parameters of NESTED)
OUTER	X (parameter of OUTER) M, N (local variables) INNER (local procedure) Y (variable declared in NESTED) OUTER (procedure declared in NESTED) INPUT, OUTPUT (parameters of NESTED)
TOO	BLANK (local constant) X, Y (global variables) OUTER, TOO (procedures declared in NESTED) INPUT, OUTPUT (parameters of NESTED)
NESTED	X, Y (global variables) INPUT, OUTPUT (parameters of NESTED) OUTER, TOO (procedures declared in NESTED)

Order of Procedures

Since procedure names are identifiers, the Pascal scope rule specifies where a procedure may be referenced or called. Procedure OUTER is declared in the main program so it may be called anywhere. Procedure INNER is declared in procedure OUTER, so it may be called only by procedure OUTER (or INNER itself). A syntax error would result if a call to INNER occurred in the body of procedure TOO or the main program.

Procedure TOO (also declared in the main program) can call procedure OUTER, but OUTER cannot call TOO. This is because an identifier must be declared before it can be referenced and the declaration for procedure TOO comes after the body of procedure OUTER.

As things stand now, only procedure OUTER can call procedure INNER. If it were necessary for procedure TOO also to call procedure INNER, then we would have to make INNER global and declare it in the main program instead of in procedure OUTER. Since Pascal requires that the declaration of an identifier precede its reference, INNER should be the first procedure declared in the main program.

Self-check Exercises for Section 3.6

1. Explain why variable N declared in OUTER cannot be referenced by the main program, procedure INNER, or procedure TOO.
2. What would be the effect of executing the body of INNER shown below? Which identifiers are related and where are they declared?

```
begin {INNER}
    X := 5.5;
    Y := 6.6;
    M := 2;
    N := 3;
    O := 4
end; {INNER}
```

3. If the compound statement above was the body of OUTER, TOO, or NESTED, then some of the assignment statements would be syntactically incorrect. Identify the incorrect statements and indicate the effect of executing all the others in each block.

3.7 Case Studies

In this section we will examine two programming problems that illustrate most of the concepts discussed in this chapter. Each problem contains a nested if statement, a while statement, and makes extensive use of procedures with parameters.

The *top down design* process will be demonstrated in solving these problems. The program solutions will be implemented in a stepwise manner starting at the top of the structure chart, or with the main program.

Balancing a Checkbook

Problem: You have just received a new home computer and would like to write a program to help balance your checkbook. The program will read your initial checkbook balance and each transaction (check or deposit). It will print the new balance after each transaction and a warning message if the balance becomes negative. At the end of the session, the starting and final balances should be printed along with a count of the number of checks and deposits processed.

Discussion: After the starting balance is read, each transaction will be read and processed separately. We can use a simple code ('C' or 'D') to distinguish between checks and deposits. The transaction amount will be a real number. The starting balance must be available at the end so we will save it in variable STARTBAL and use a different variable (CURBAL) to keep track of the current balance.

PROBLEM INPUTS

starting checkbook balance (STARTBAL : REAL)
transaction data
    type of transaction (TRANTYPE : CHAR)
    amount of transaction (AMOUNT : REAL)

PROBLEM OUTPUTS

current balance after each transaction (CURBAL : REAL)
number of checks (NUMCHECK : INTEGER)
number of deposits (NUMDEP : INTEGER)

Algorithm

1. Display the instructions and read the starting balance.
2. For each transaction: read the transaction, update and print the current balance, and increment the count of checks or deposits.
3. Print the starting and final balance and the number of checks and deposits processed.

The structure chart for this algorithm is shown in Fig. 3.21. The level one subproblems will be written as procedures INSTRUCT, PROCESS, and REPORT, respectively. The data flow information shows that STARTBAL is read by INSTRUCT and passed to PROCESS. Procedure PROCESS defines the program results (CURBAL, NUMCHECK, NUMDEP); these results are passed to REPORT and printed.

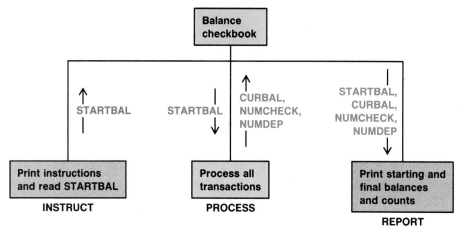

Fig. 3.21 Structure Chart (Level 0 and 1) for Checkbook Problem

The variables shown in the structure chart should be declared in the main program as each variable must be declared at the highest level in which it appears in the structure chart. Variables that are passed between the main program and a level 1 procedure must be declared in the main program.

The data flow information is used to write the parameter lists in the program shown in Fig. 3.22. Since procedures INSTRUCT and REPORT should consist of READ and WRITE statements only, they are written now. Since procedure PROCESS requires further refinement, it is written as a stub.

```
program CHECKBOOK (INPUT, OUTPUT);

{Reads the starting balance for a checking account and processes
 all transactions. Prints the new balance after each transaction is
 processed. Also prints a count of the total number of checks and
 deposits processed.                                              }

var
    STARTBAL,                      {starting balance}
    CURBAL : REAL;                 {current balance}
    NUMCHECK,                      {number of checks}
    NUMDEP : INTEGER;              {number of deposits}

procedure INSTRUCT (var {output} STARTBAL : REAL);

{Displays the instructions to the user and reads starting balance.}

begin {INSTRUCT}
    WRITELN ('Balance your checking account!');
    WRITELN;
    WRITELN ('Enter C (Check), D (Deposit), or Q (Quit)');
    WRITELN ('after prompt C, D, or Q: ');
    WRITELN;
```

```
        WRITELN ('Enter a positive number after prompt AMOUNT $');
        WRITELN;
        WRITE ('Begin by entering your starting balance $');
        READLN (STARTBAL)
end; {INSTRUCT}

procedure PROCESS (STARTBAL {input} : REAL;
                   var CURBAL {output} : REAL;
                   var NUMCHECK, NUMDEP {output} : INTEGER);

{Processes each transaction. Reads each transaction, updates and prints
 the current balance and increments the count of checks or deposits.  }

begin {PROCESS}
    WRITELN ('Procedure PROCESS entered.')
end; {PROCESS}

procedure REPORT (STARTBAL, CURBAL {input} : REAL;
                  NUMCHECK, NUMDEP {input} : INTEGER);

{Prints the starting and final balances and the count of checks and
 deposits.                                                          }

begin {REPORT}
    WRITELN;
    WRITELN ('Starting balance was $', STARTBAL :10:2);
    WRITELN ('Final    balance is  $', CURBAL :10:2);
    WRITELN ('Number of checks written: ', NUMCHECK :3);
    WRITELN ('Number of deposits made : ', NUMDEP :3)
end; {REPORT}

begin {CHECKBOOK}
    {Display user instructions and read STARTBAL}
    INSTRUCT (STARTBAL);

    {Process each transaction}
    PROCESS (STARTBAL, CURBAL, NUMCHECK, NUMDEP);

    {Print starting and final balances and count of checks/deposits}
    REPORT (STARTBAL, CURBAL, NUMCHECK, NUMDEP)
end. {CHECKBOOK}
```

Fig. 3.22 Checkbook Balancing Program with Stub for PROCESS

Procedure PROCESS performs step 2 of the algorithm which requires further refinement.

2. For each transaction: read the transaction, update and print the current balance, and increment the count of checks or deposits.

All program results (NUMCHECK, NUMDEP, and CURBAL) should be initialized in PROCESS before any transactions are processed. The initial value of CURBAL should be the same as STARTBAL. The steps to be carried out by procedure PROCESS are listed below.

Algorithm for PROCESS

1. Set counters to 0 and current balance to starting balance.
2. Read the first transaction.

3. while there are more transactions do

    4. Update balance and increment check or deposit counter.

    5. Read the next transaction.

The structure chart for PROCESS is shown in Fig. 3.23. Procedure READTRANS will perform steps 2 and 5 above, and UPDATE will perform step 4. The new variables, TRANTYPE and AMOUNT, should be declared as local variables in procedure PROCESS; variables passed between a level 1 and level 2 procedure should be declared in the level 1 procedure. The identifiers CURBAL, NUMCHECK, and NUMDEP are declared already as formal parameters of PROCESS.

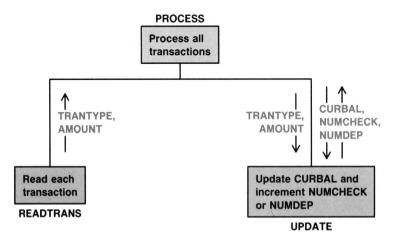

Fig. 3.23 Structure Chart for Procedure PROCESS

Procedure UPDATE will consist of an `if` statement that implements the decision table shown in Table 3.11. Procedure PROCESS is shown in Fig. 3.24; a sample run of program CHECKBOOK is shown in Fig. 3.25.

Table 3.11 Decision table for UPDATE

Condition	Desired Action
TRANTYPE = 'D'	Increment NUMDEP, add AMOUNT to CURBAL
TRANTYPE = 'C'	Increment NUMCHECK, subtract AMOUNT from CURBAL—if CURBAL is negative, print an overdrawn warning

```
procedure PROCESS (STARTBAL {input} : REAL;
                   var CURBAL {output} : REAL;
                   var NUMCHECK, NUMDEP {output} : INTEGER);

{Processes each transaction. Reads each transaction, updates and prints
 the current balance and increments the count of checks or deposits.  }
```

```
const
    SENTINEL = 'Q';          {sentinel value}
var
    TRANTYPE : CHAR;         {transaction type (check or deposit)}
    AMOUNT : REAL;           {transaction amount}
procedure READTRANS (var TRANTYPE {output} : CHAR;
                     var AMOUNT {output} : REAL);

{Reads each transaction—called by PROCESS.}

begin {READTRANS}
    WRITELN;
    WRITE ('C, D, or Q: ');
    READLN (TRANTYPE);
    if TRANTYPE <> SENTINEL then
        begin {Read amount}
            WRITE ('AMOUNT $'); READLN (AMOUNT)
        end {if}
end; {READTRANS}

procedure UPDATE (TRANTYPE {input} : CHAR;
                  AMOUNT {input} : REAL;
                  var CURBAL {input/output} : REAL;
                  var NUMCHECK, NUMDEP {input/output} : INTEGER);

{Updates CURBAL and increments NUMCHECK for a check or NUMDEP for a
 deposit—called by PROCESS.                                          }

begin {UPDATE}
    if TRANTYPE = 'D' then
        begin {deposit}
            CURBAL := CURBAL + AMOUNT;
            NUMDEP := NUMDEP + 1;
            WRITE ('Depositing $', AMOUNT :8:2);
            WRITELN ('   Balance of $', CURBAL :10:2)
        end {deposit}
    else if TRANTYPE = 'C' then
        begin {check}
            CURBAL := CURBAL - AMOUNT;
            NUMCHECK := NUMCHECK + 1;
            WRITE ('Check for $', AMOUNT :8:2);
            WRITELN ('   Balance of $', CURBAL :10:2);
            if CURBAL < 0.0 then
                WRITELN ('Warning! Your account is overdrawn.')
        end {check}
    else {not check or deposit}
        WRITELN ('Invalid transaction type ', TRANTYPE,
                '—transaction ignored')
end; {UPDATE}

begin {PROCESS}
    {Initialize counters to zero and CURBAL to STARTBAL}
    NUMCHECK := 0;  NUMDEP := 0;  CURBAL := STARTBAL;

    {Process each transaction until done}
    READTRANS (TRANTYPE, AMOUNT);                      {read first transaction}
```

```
while TRANTYPE <> SENTINEL do
   begin
      UPDATE (TRANTYPE, AMOUNT, CURBAL, NUMCHECK, NUMDEP);
      READTRANS (TRANTYPE, AMOUNT)                {read next transaction}
   end {while}
end; {PROCESS}
```

Fig. 3.24 Procedure PROCESS for the Checkbook Balancing Program

```
Balance your checking account!

Enter C (Check), D (Deposit), or Q (Quit)
after prompt C, D, or Q:

Enter a positive number after prompt AMOUNT $

Begin by entering your starting balance $1000.00

C, D, or Q: D
AMOUNT $100.00
Depositing $  100.00          Balance of $  1100.00

C, D, or Q: C
AMOUNT $1200.00
Check for $ 1200.00           Balance of $  -100.00
Warning! Your account is overdrawn.

C, D, or Q: X
AMOUNT $500.00
Invalid transaction type X—transaction ignored.

C, D, or Q: Q

Starting balance was $  1000.00
Final     balance is  $  -100.00
Number of checks written: 1
Number of deposits made : 1
```

Fig. 3.25 Sample Run of Checkbook Balancing Program

Procedure PROCESS processes all transactions. PROCESS calls procedure READTRANS to read each transaction and UPDATE to process the transaction just read. Since UPDATE and READTRANS are called by PROCESS only, they are declared inside PROCESS.

Procedure UPDATE contains a nested if statement that differentiates between checks and deposits. When TRANTYPE is 'C', another if statement is executed and is used to detect an overdrawn account (CURBAL < 0.0).

Figure 3.26 shows the structure chart for the entire program system.

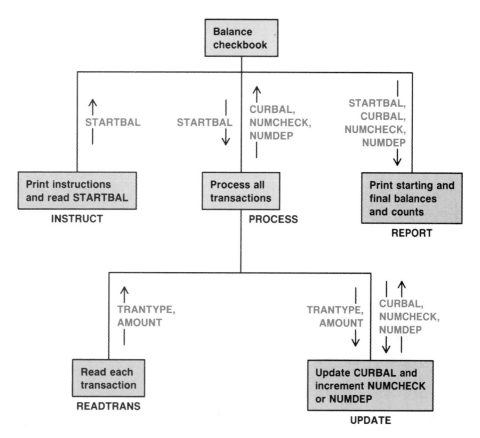

Fig. 3.26 Complete Structure Chart for Checkbook Balancing Program

PROGRAM STYLE

Top down design

The program system for the checkbook problem is a good illustration of the top down design process. It uses procedures to implement each of the subproblems shown in the structure chart. With the exception of procedure PROCESS each procedure is relatively short.

The main program at the bottom of Fig. 3.22 contains three procedure (call) statements. The second procedure (call) statement

```
PROCESS (STARTBAL, CURBAL, NUMCHECK, NUMDEP);
```

is used to process all transactions. Procedure PROCESS calls procedures READTRANS and UPDATE to read each transaction and process each transaction, respectively. Both of these procedures are declared inside procedure PROCESS.

The identifiers SENTINEL, TRANTYPE, and AMOUNT are declared in PROCESS since they are used only by PROCESS and the procedures it calls. NUMCHECK, NUMDEP, and CURBAL are initialized in PROCESS rather than in the main program as this keeps the manipulation of these variables in one place.

The next problem solution further illustrates the top down design process with procedures. It also uses a while statement and if statement.

Grading an Exam

Problem: We wish to write a grading program that will determine the number of exam scores that fall into each of three categories: outstanding, satisfactory, and unsatisfactory. The program will also print the high score on the exam. The program user must specify the minimum satisfactory and outstanding scores, and enter each student's initials and exam score.

Discussion: The program must start by reading in the scale for the exam. The main processing step must then read each student's data, categorize each score, and find the largest score. We will begin by describing the data requirements and the algorithm.

PROBLEM INPUTS

minimum satisfactory score (MINSAT : INTEGER)
minimum outstanding score (MINOUT : INTEGER)
each student's initials (FIRST, LAST : CHAR)
each student's score (SCORE : INTEGER)

PROBLEM OUTPUTS

highest score (HIGH : INTEGER)
number of outstanding scores (NUMOUT : INTEGER)
number of satisfactory scores (NUMSAT : INTEGER)
number of unsatisfactory scores (NUMUNS : INTEGER)

Algorithm

1. Read in the exam scale.
2. Read each student's initials and score, categorize each score, and find the high score.
3. Print the number of scores in each category and the high score.

Step 2 is the main processing step and requires further refinement. Rather than do this now, we will examine the structure chart for the problem shown in Fig. 3.27.

All level 1 subproblems will be implemented as procedures (READ-SCALE, DOSCORES, and REPORT from left to right). The data flow infor-

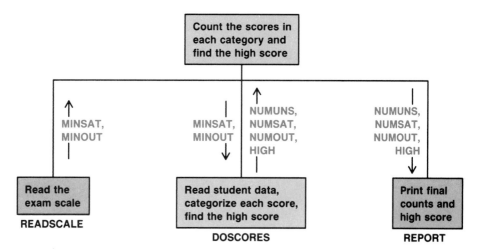

Fig. 3.27 Structure Chart (Level 0 and 1) for Grading Problem

mation shows that the scale boundary values (MINSAT, MINOUT) are defined by procedure READSCALE and passed into procedure DOSCORES. Procedure DOSCORES determines all required output values (NUMUNS, NUMSAT, NUMOUT, and HIGH); these values are then passed into REPORT to be printed.

The variables shown in the structure chart are all declared in the main program (see Fig. 3.28). The data flow information is used to write the parameter lists in the main program. Since procedure DOSCORES requires further refinement before it can be completed, it is written as a stub.

```
program GRADER (INPUT, OUTPUT);

{Reads an exam scale and uses it to find the number of students who
 received outstanding, satisfactory, and unsatisfactory grades on
 an exam. Also, finds the high score on the exam.                   }

var
    MINSAT, MINOUT,             {boundary values for satisfactory category}
    NUMUNS, NUMSAT, NUMOUT,                    {counters for each category}
    HIGH         : INTEGER;                            {high score so far}

procedure READSCALE (var MINSAT, MINOUT {output} : INTEGER);

{Reads the exam scale.}

begin {READSCALE}
    {Enter the exam scale}
    WRITE ('Enter the minimum satisfactory score: ');
    READLN (MINSAT);
    WRITE ('Enter the minimum outstanding score: ');
    READLN (MINOUT)
end; {READSCALE}
```

```
procedure DOSCORES (MINSAT, MINOUT {input} : INTEGER;
              var NUMUNS, NUMSAT, NUMOUT, HIGH {output} : INTEGER);

{Reads each student's initials and score, categorizes each score, and
 finds the high score.                                              }

begin {DOSCORES}
   WRITELN ('Procedure DOSCORES entered.')
end; {DOSCORES}

procedure REPORT (NUMUNS, NUMSAT, NUMOUT, HIGH {input} : INTEGER);

{Prints the final counts and the high score.}

begin {REPORT}
   WRITELN;
   WRITELN ('Number of    outstanding scores: ', NUMOUT :3);
   WRITELN ('Number of    satisfactory scores: ', NUMSAT :3);
   WRITELN ('Number of unsatisfactory scores: ', NUMUNS :3);
   WRITELN;
   WRITELN ('High score on exam: ', HIGH :3)
end; {REPORT}

begin {GRADER}
   {Enter the exam scale}
   READSCALE (MINSAT, MINOUT);

   {Read and categorize all scores and find the high score}
   DOSCORES (MINSAT, MINOUT, NUMUNS, NUMSAT, NUMOUT, HIGH);

   {Print count of scores in each category and the high score}
   REPORT (NUMUNS, NUMSAT, NUMOUT, HIGH)
end. {GRADER}
```

Fig. 3.28 Grading Program with Stub for DOSCORES

Procedure DOSCORES implements step 2 of the initial algorithm:

2. Read each student's initials and score, categorize each score, and find the high score.

The algorithm for DOSCORES follows.

Algorithm for DOSCORES

1. Initialize category counters and high score to 0.
2. Read first student's initials and score.
3. while there are more scores do
   4. Increment the appropriate category counter.
   5. Check whether current score is the highest score so far.
   6. Read next student's initials and score.

Step 4 can be implemented as a multiple-alternative decision as outlined in Table 3.12. This step will be performed by procedure CATEGORIZE.

In order to accomplish step 5 (Check for high score), the program must save the highest score so far in HIGH (initial value 0). If the current score is larger than the highest score so far, then it becomes the new high score. An example of this process is shown in Table 3.13.

Table 3.12 Decision Table for Step 4 of DOSCORES

SCORE	Action
below MINSAT	SCORE is unsatisfactory, increment NUMUNS
MINSAT to MINOUT-1	SCORE is satisfactory, increment NUMSAT
above MINOUT-1	SCORE is outstanding, increment NUMOUT

Table 3.13 Finding the High Score

SCORE	HIGH	Effect of New SCORE
35	0	35 > 0, 35 is the new high score
60	35	60 > 35, 60 is the new high score
47	60	47 < 60, 60 is still the high score
80	60	80 > 60, 80 is the new high score
75	80	75 < 80, 80 is still the high score

Now that the algorithm for DOSCORES is refined, we can draw the system structure chart (see Fig. 3.29) that describes this step and its subproblems. Each subproblem is implemented as a procedure. The structure chart shows that SCORE is an output of procedure READSTU and an input to procedures CATEGORIZE and CHECKHIGH. Since CATEGORIZE must increment a category counter, the counters are input/output parameters for this subproblem. Since HIGH may be modified by CHECKHIGH, it is also an input/output parameter.

Fig. 3.29 Structure Chart for Procedure DOSCORES.

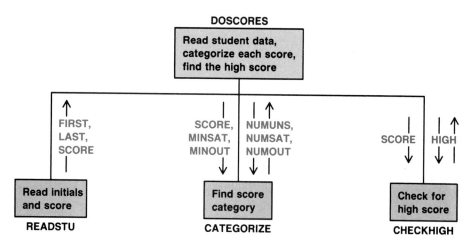

Procedure DOSCORES is shown in Fig. 3.30. FIRST, LAST, and SCORE are declared as local variables in the procedure; SENTINEL is a local constant. Each of the procedures shown in the structure chart for DOSCORES are nested within DOSCORES. A sample run of the complete program is shown in Fig. 3.31.

Procedure DOSCORES begins by initializing all counters and HIGH to zero. It calls READSTU to read each student's initials and score and calls CHECKHIGH to check for the highest score so far.

```
procedure DOSCORES (MINSAT, MINOUT {input} : INTEGER;
                var NUMUNS, NUMSAT, NUMOUT, HIGH {output} : INTEGER);

{Reads each student's initials and score, finds the number of scores in
 each category, and finds the high score.                              }

const
   SENTINEL = '*';                                     {sentinel value}

var
   SCORE : INTEGER;                                    {each exam score}
   FIRST, LAST : CHAR;                             {student's initials}

procedure READSTU (var FIRST, LAST {output} : CHAR;
                var SCORE {output} : INTEGER);

{read a student's initials and score—called by DOSCORES.}

begin {READSTU}
   WRITELN;
   WRITE ('Enter student initials or **: ');
   READLN (FIRST, LAST);                                   {Get initials}
   if FIRST <> SENTINEL then
      begin
         WRITE ('Enter score: ');    READLN (SCORE)          {Get score}
      end {if}
end; {READSTU}

procedure CATEGORIZE (SCORE, MINSAT, MINOUT {input} : INTEGER;
                var NUMUNS, NUMSAT, NUMOUT {input/output} : INTEGER);

{Categorizes SCORE and increments the appropriate counter—called by
 DOSCORES.                                                              }

begin {CATEGORIZE}
   if SCORE < MINSAT then
      begin                                         {unsatisfactory score}
         WRITELN ('Unsatisfactory' :40);
         NUMUNS := NUMUNS + 1
      end {unsatisfactory}
   else if SCORE < MINOUT then
      begin                                           {satisfactory score}
         WRITELN ('Satisfactory' :40);
         NUMSAT := NUMSAT + 1
      end {satisfactory}
   else
```

```
        begin                                              {outstanding score}
            WRITELN ('Outstanding' :40);
            NUMOUT := NUMOUT + 1
        end {outstanding}
end; {CATEGORIZE}

procedure CHECKHIGH (SCORE {input} : INTEGER;
                     var HIGH {input/output} : INTEGER);

{Checks whether SCORE is the highest score so far.}

begin {CHECKHIGH}
    if SCORE > HIGH then
        HIGH := SCORE                                      {Save new high score}
end; {CHECKHIGH}

begin {DOSCORES}
    {Initialize counters and HIGH to zero}
    NUMUNS := 0;  NUMSAT := 0;  NUMOUT := 0;  HIGH := 0;

    {Categorize each score and find HIGH}
    READSTU (FIRST, LAST, SCORE);                          {Read initials and score}
    while FIRST <> SENTINEL do
        begin
            {Categorize SCORE and increment appropriate counter}
            CATEGORIZE (SCORE, MINSAT, MINOUT, NUMUNS, NUMSAT, NUMOUT);
            CHECKHIGH (SCORE, HIGH);                        {Check for high score}
            READSTU (FIRST, LAST, SCORE)                    {Read initials and score}
        end {while}
end; {DOSCORES}
```

Fig. 3.30 Procedure DOSCORES (Replaces the Stub in Fig. 3.28)

Fig. 3.31 Sample Run of Program GRADER

```
Enter the minimum satisfactory score: 75
Enter the minimum outstanding score: 90

Enter student initials or **: EK
Enter score: 100
                                                    outstanding

Enter student initials or **: RK
Enter score: 75
                                                    satisfactory

Enter student initials or **: HH
Enter score: 89
                                                    satisfactory

Enter student initials or **: **

Number of    outstanding scores: 1
Number of    satisfactory scores: 2
Number of unsatisfactory scores: 0

High score on exam: 100
```

Procedure DOSCORES calls procedure CATEGORIZE to find the category of each score. The multiple alternative decision in CATEGORIZE prints the score category and increments a counter. The symbols :40 in each WRITELN statement of CATEGORIZE cause the last character of the category string to be printed in column 40, making it easy to distinguish the program output from the input data.

Self-check Exercises for Section 3.7

1. Modify the checkbook program so that a penalty amount of $15.00 is deducted for each overdrawn check and a count of overdrawn checks is maintained and printed next to each overdrawn check. Reset the count of overdrafts to zero whenever the balance becomes positive.
2. What would be the effect of transposing the parameters MINSAT and MINOUT in the call to procedure DOSCORES or READSCALE in Fig. 3.29? Would the compiler detect this error?
3. What would happen if the person using this program became confused and switched the data values entered for MINSAT and MINOUT? Rewrite procedure READSCALE so that it checks for this error and takes corrective action if it occurs.
4. Draw the procedure nesting diagrams (see Fig. 3.20) for both program systems.

3.8 Debugging a Program System

As the number of modules and statements in a program system grows, the possibility of error also increases. If each module is kept to a manageable size, then the likelihood of error will increase much more slowly. It will also be easier to read and test each module. Finally, the limited use of global variables will minimize the chance of harmful side effects that are always difficult to locate.

Whenever possible, test each procedure separately by writing a short driver program that contains all necessary declarations. The body of the driver program should assign values to the input parameters, call the procedure, and display the procedure results.

Even before all procedures are written, you can test the main program flow by substituting stubs for the missing procedures. If you do this make sure that any procedure outputs needed by the main program are defined in the stub.

A list of suggestions for preventing and debugging errors in a program system follows.

Debugging Tips for Procedures

1. Carefully document each procedure parameter and local identifier using comments. Also describe the procedure operation using comments.
2. During debugging, leave a trace of execution by printing the procedure

name as it is entered. Sometimes a trace showing the currently executing procedure and the procedures that called it is printed by Pascal when a run-time error occurs.

3. During debugging, print the values of all input parameters upon entry to a procedure. Make sure that these values make sense.

4. During debugging, print the values of all output parameters after returning from a procedure. Make sure that all output parameters are declared as variable parameters.

3.9 Common Programming Errors

Remember to bracket each compound statement with begin and end. The compiler will detect a syntax error if either a begin is missing or an end is missing, but not both. If both the begin and end are missing, then your program will be translated, but it will not execute as intended. For example, the while statement below is an infinite (non-terminating) loop since the loop body consists of the assignment statement only.

```
WRITE ('Enter a number: '); READLN (NEXT);
while NEXT <> SENTINEL do
    SUM := SUM + ITEM;
    WRITE ('Enter a number: '); READLN (NEXT)
```

Be very careful when using tests for inequality to control the repetition of a while loop. The loop below is intended to process all transactions for a bank account while the balance is positive.

```
while BALANCE <> 0.0 do
    UPDATE (BALANCE)
```

If the bank balance goes from a positive to a negative amount without being exactly 0.0, the loop will not terminate. The loop below would be safer.

```
while BALANCE > 0.0 do
    UPDATE (BALANCE)
```

Unfortunately, there are many opportunities for error when using procedures with parameter lists. The proper use of parameters is difficult for beginning programmers to master. One obvious pitfall is to be sure that the actual parameter list has the same number of parameters as the formal parameter list. The syntax error "number of parameters does not agree with declaration" will indicate this problem.

Each actual parameter must be the same data type as its corresponding formal parameter. An actual parameter that correponds to a variable formal parameter must be a variable. A violation of either of these rules will result in a syntax error.

A procedure result should be returned to the calling module by assigning a value to a variable parameter. Any value assigned to a value parameter will be stored locally in the procedure and will not be returned. This error cannot be detected by Pascal.

3.10 Chapter Review

Syntax diagrams were introduced in this chapter and we saw how to use them to check the syntax of Pascal statement. A complete set of syntax diagrams for Pascal is provided in Appendix C.

The `if` statement was examined more formally. We saw how to use nested `if` statements to implement decisions with several alternatives.

A conditional looping structure, the `while` statement, was used to implement loops whose repetition is controlled by a condition. The `while` statement is useful when the exact number of repetitions required is not known before the loop begins. Separate Pascal statements are needed for initializing and updating the loop control variable associated with a `while` loop.

One common technique for controlling the repetition of a `while` loop is using a special sentinel value to indicate that all required data have been processed. In this case, the loop control variable is a problem input; it is initialized when the first data value is read (priming read) and updated at the end of the loop when the next data value is read. Loop repetition terminates when the sentinel value is read into the loop control variable.

The use of procedure parameters for passing data to and from procedures was also discussed. The parameter list provides a highly visible communication path between the procedure and the calling program. By using parameters, we can cause different data to be manipulated by a procedure each time we call it. This makes it easier to reuse the procedure in another program system.

There are two types of parameters: value and variable. A value parameter is used only for passing data into a procedure. A variable parameter is used to return results from a procedure. The actual parameter corresponding to a value parameter may be an expression or a constant; the actual parameter corresponding to a variable parameter must be a variable.

We discussed the scope of identifiers. An identifier may be referenced anywhere within the block that declares it. If one block is nested inside another and an identifier is declared in the outer block, then the identifier's meaning in the inner block is determined by its declaration in the outer block. If the identifer is declared in both blocks, then its meaning in the inner block is determined by its declaration in the inner block.

A global variable is one that is declared in the main program; a local variable is one that is declared in a procedure. A local variable is defined only during the execution of the procedure; its value is lost when the procedure is done.

New Pascal Statements

The Pascal statements introduced in Chapter 3 are shown in Table 3.14.

Table 3.14 Summary of New Pascal Statements

Statement	Effect

Multiple alternative decision
``pascal
if SCORE >= 90 then
   begin {A}
      WRITE ('A');
      COUNTA := COUNTA + 1
   end {A}
else if SCORE >= 80 then
   begin {B}
      WRITE ('B');
      COUNTB := COUNTB + 1
   end {B}
else
   begin {C}
      WRITE ('C');
      COUNTC := COUNTC + 1
   end {C}
``
	If SCORE is greater than or equal to 90, then COUNTA is increased by 1; otherwise, if SCORE is greater than or equal to 80, COUNTB is increased; otherwise, COUNTC is increased.

While statement
``pascal
SUM := 0;
while SUM <= MAXSUM do
   begin
      WRITE ('Next integer: ');
      READLN (NEXT);
      SUM := SUM + NEXT
   end {while}
``
	A collection of input data items is read and their sum is accumulated in SUM. This process stops when the accumulated SUM exceeds MAXSUM.

Procedure with parameters
``pascal
procedure A (X : REAL;
            OP : CHAR;
            var XTO3 : REAL);
begin {A}
   if OP = '*' then
      XTO3 := X * X * X
   else if OP = '+' then
      XTO3 := X + X + X
   else
      WRITELN ('Invalid ', OP)
end; {A}
``
	Procedure A has two value parameters (X and OP) and one variable parameter (XTO3). If OP is '*', then the value returned is X * X * X; otherwise, if OP is '+', then the value returned is X + X + X; otherwise, an error message is printed. A result is returned by assigning a new value to the actual parameter (a variable) that corresponds to parameter XTO3.

Procedure (call) statement
``pascal
A (5.5, '+', Y)
``
	Calls procedure A. The value 16.5 is assigned to Y (type REAL).

Review Questions

1. How can syntax diagrams aid a new user in becoming comfortable with an unfamiliar programming language?
2. Given the following syntax diagram, circle the WORDS under the diagram that are valid.

Syntax Diagram for WORDS

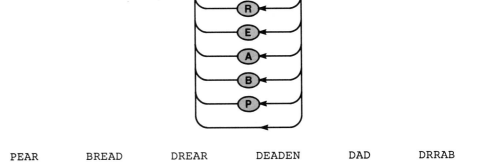

PEAR   BREAD   DREAR   DEADEN   DAD   DRRAB

3. Define a sentinel value.
4. For a sentinel value to be used properly when reading in data, where should the READLN statements appear?
5. Write a program called SUM to sum and print a collection of payroll amounts entered at the standard input device until a sentinel value of −1 is entered. Use a while statement.
6. Hand trace the program below given the following data:

4,2,8,4,   1,4,2,1,   9,3,3,1,   −22,10,8,2

```
program SLOPE (INPUT, OUTPUT);

const
    SENTINEL = 0;

var
    SLOPE, Y2, Y1, X2, X1 : REAL;

begin
    WRITELN ('Enter four real numbers');
    READLN (Y2, Y1, X2, X1);
    SLOPE := (Y2 - Y1) / (X2 - X1);
    while SLOPE <> SENTINEL do
```

```
                    begin
                        WRITELN ('Slope is ', SLOPE :5:3);
                        WRITELN;
                        WRITELN ('Enter four real numbers');
                        READLN (Y2, Y1, X2, X1);
                        SLOPE := (Y2 - Y1) / (X2 - X1)
                    end {while}
            end.
```

7. Explain when it is appropriate to use semicolons within
   a) the variable declaration statement
   b) the constant declaration statement
   c) the program body
   d) an if statement

8. Write the procedure heading statement for a procedure called SCRIPT that accepts three parameters passed to it. The first parameter will be the number of spaces to print at the beginning of a line. The second parameter will be the character to print after the spaces, and the third parameter will be the number of times to print the second parameter on the same line.

9. Write a procedure called LETTERGRADE that has one input parameter called GRADE, and will print out the corresponding letter grade using a straight scale (90 — 100 is an A, 80 — 89 is a B, etc.).

10. Explain the difference between a value parameter and a variable parameter with respect to the parameter's relationship to the variables in the calling program.

11. Explain the allocation of memory cells when a procedure is called.

12. Write the procedure header statement for a procedure named PASS that has two integer parameters. The first parameter should be a value parameter and the second a variable parameter.

13. Explain the use of a stub in refining an algorithm.

14. In the chart below write YES for each procedure on the right that can be referenced (called) by the procedure on the left, and NO for each procedure that is inaccessible.

```
program PROCSCOPE (INPUT, OUTPUT);

procedure A;
   procedure B;
      procedure C;
      .........
      end; {C}
      procedure D;
      .........
      end; {D}
   .........
   end; {B}
.........
end; {A}
.........
end. {PROCSCOPE}
```

calling procedure	callable procedures			
	A	B	C	D
A	X			
B		X		
C			X	
D				X

Programming Projects

1. Write a program that will find the product of a collection of data values. Your program should terminate when a zero value is read.

2. Write a program to read in an integer N and compute $SLOW = i = 1 + 2 + 3 + \ldots + N$ (the sum of all integers from 1 to N). Then, compute $FAST = (N \times (N + 1)) / 2$ and compare FAST and SLOW. Your program should print both FAST and SLOW and indicate whether or not they are equal. (You will need a loop to compute SLOW.) Which computation method is preferable?

3. Write a program to read a list of integer data items and find and print the index of the first occurrence and the last occurrence of the number 12. Your program should print index values of 0 if the number 12 is not found. The index is the sequence number of the data item 12. For example, if the 8th data item is the only 12, then the index value 8 should be printed for the first and last occurrence.

4. Write a program to read in a collection of exam scores ranging in value from 1 to 100. Your program should count and print the number of outstanding scores (90–100), the number of satisfactory scores (60–89), and the number of unsatisfactory scores (1–59). Test your program on the following data:

63	75	72	72	78	67	80	63	75
90	89	43	59	99	82	12	100	

   In addition, print each exam score and its category.

5. Write a program to process weekly employee time cards for all employees of an organization. Each employee will have three data items indicating an identification number, the hourly wage rate, and the number of hours worked during a given week. Each employee is to be paid time-and-a-half for all hours worked over 40. A tax amount of 3.625 percent of gross salary will be deducted. The program output should show the employee's number and net pay.

6. Suppose you own a beer distributorship that sells Piels (ID number 1), Coors (ID number 2), Bud (ID number 3) and Iron City (ID number 4) by the case. Write a program to (a) read in the case inventory for each brand for the start of the week; (b) process all weekly sales and purchase records for each brand; and (c) print out the final inventory. Each transaction will consist of two data items. The first item will be the brand identification number (an integer). The second will be the amount purchased (a positive integer value) or the amount sold (a negative integer value). The weekly inventory for each brand (for the start of the week) will also consist of two items: the identification and initial inventory for that brand. For now, you may assume that you always have sufficient foresight to prevent depletion of your inventory for any brand. (Hint: Your data entry should begin with eight values representing the case inventory. These should be followed by the transaction values.)

7. Write a program to find the largest, smallest, and average value in a collection of N numbers where the value of N will be the first data item read.

8. a) Write a program to process a collection of savings account transactions (deposits or withdrawals). Your program should begin by reading in the previous account balance and then read and process each transaction. Enter a positive value for a deposit and a negative value for a withdrawal. For each transaction, print the message `'WITHDRAWAL'` or `'DEPOSIT'` and the new balance. Print an error message if a withdrawal would result in a negative balance and do not change the balance.

b) Compute and print the number of deposits, the number of withdrawals, the number of invalid withdrawals, and the total dollar amount for each type of transaction.

9. a) Write a program that computes and prints the fractional powers of two (1/2, 1/4, 1/8, etc.). The program should also print the decimal value of each fraction as shown below.

Power	Fraction	Decimal value
1	1/2	0.5
2	1/4	0.25
3	1/8	0.125

Print all values through power equal to ten.

b) Add an extra output column which shows the sum of all decimal values so far. The first three sums are: 0.5, 0.75, 0.875.

10. a) The trustees of a small college are considering voting a pay raise for the twelve faculty. They want to grant a 5.5% pay raise; however, before doing so, they want to know how much this will cost. Write a program that will print the pay raise for each faculty member and the total amount of the raises. Also, print the total faculty payroll before and after the raise. Test your program for the salaries:

$12500	$14029.50	$16000	$13250
$15500	$12800	$20000.50	$18900
$13780	$17300	$14120.25	$14100

b) Redo the program assuming that faculty earning less than $14000 receive a 4% raise, faculty earning more than $16,500 receive a 7% raise, and all others recieve a 5.5% raise. For each faculty member, print the raise percentage as well as the amount.

11. The assessor in your town has estimated the market value of all fourteen properties and would like a program that determines the tax owed on each property and the total tax to be collected. The tax rate is 125 mils per dollar of assessed value. (A mil is 0.1 of a penny.) The assessed value of each property is 28% of its estimated market value. The market values are:

$50000	$48000	$45500	$67000	$37600	$47100	$65000
$53350	$28000	$58000	$52250	$48000	$56500	$43700

12. Patients required to take many kinds of medication often have difficulty in remembering when to take their medicine. Given the following set of medications, write a program that prints an hourly table indicating what medication to take at any given hour. Use a counter variable CLOCK to go through a 24

hour day. Print the table based upon the following prescriptions:

Medication	Frequency
Iron pill	0800, 1200, 1800
Antibiotic	Every 4 hours starting at 0400
Vitamin	0800, 2100
Calcium	1100, 2000

13. A monthly magazine wants a program that will print out renewal notices to its subscribers and cancellation notices when appropriate. Utilize procedures when advisable and write a program that first reads in the current month number (1 through 12) and year. For each subscription processed, read in four data items: the account number, the month and year the subscription started, and the number of years paid for the subscription.

Read in each set of subscription information and print a renewal notice if the current month is either the month prior to expiration or the month of expiration. A cancellation notice should be printed if the current month comes after the expiration month.

Sample input might be:

10, 85	for a current month of October 1985
1364, 4, 83, 3	for account 1364 whose 3 year subscription began in April 1983

14. The square root of a number N can be approximated by repeated calculation using the formula

$$NG = .5(LG + N \ / \ LG)$$

where NG stands for next guess and LG stands for last guess. Write a procedure which implements this process where the first parameter will be a positive real number, the second will be an initial guess of the square root, and the third will be the computed result.

The initial guess will be the starting value of LG. The procedure will compute a value for NG using the formula above. The difference between NG and LG is checked to see whether these two guesses are almost identical. If so, the procedure is exited and NG is the square root; otherwise, the new guess (NG) becomes the last guess (LG) and the process is repeated (i.e. another value is computed for NG, the difference is checked, etc.).

For this program the loop should be repeated until the difference is less than 0.005 (DELTA). Use an initial guess of 1.0 and test the program for the numbers: 4, 120.5, 88, 36.01, 10000.

4

Simple Data Types

4.1 Constant Declarations

4.2 Numeric Data Types—REAL and INTEGER

4.3 Functions in Arithmetic Expressions

4.4 BOOLEAN Variables, Expressions, and Operators

4.5 Character Variables and Functions

4.6 Introduction to Programmer-defined Data Types

4.7 Input/Output Revisited

4.8 Case Study

4.9 Common Programming Errors

4.10 Chapter Review

Thus far in our programming, we have used the four standard data types of Pascal: INTEGER, REAL, CHAR, and BOOLEAN (conditions in if and while statements). In this chapter, we take a closer look at these data types and introduce new operators and operations that can be performed on them. We describe the standard functions of Pascal and demonstrate how they are used to simplify computations.

We also learn how to declare new data types called enumerated types and subrange types. All of the data types in this chapter are *simple* data types, that is, only a single value can be stored in each variable.

Finally we review the input/output operations in Pascal and introduce two new functions, EOLN and EOF, which are often used when reading in data. This chapter also illustrates how to process a data file that was prepared before program execution.

<table>
<tr><td>**4.1**</td><td></td></tr>
</table>

4.1 Constant Declarations

This chapter begins by reexamining constants in Pascal. The syntax diagram for the constant declaration is shown at the top of Fig. 4.1. This diagram shows that each constant definition has the form

$identifier = constant$

where *constant* is described in the syntax diagram at the bottom of Fig. 4.1.

The constant declaration below follows the syntax rules of Fig. 4.1.

```
const
   MAX = 100;
   MIN = -MAX;
   SPEEDOFLIGHT = 2.998E+6;
   NAME = 'Alice';
```

Fig. 4.1 Syntax Diagrams for Constant Declaration

Constant Declaration

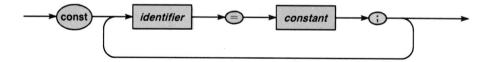

Constant

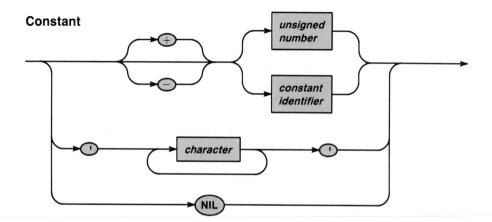

The constant declaration for MIN uses the previously-defined constant MAX. Since MAX has the value 100, MIN has the value −100. The constant SPEEDOFLIGHT is associated with a real value (2998000.0) expressed in scientific notation. The *string value* 'Alice' is associated with the constant NAME; string values are further discussed in Chapter 6. The constant value NIL is discussed in Chapter 10.

4.2 Numeric Data Types—Real and Integer

The data types INTEGER and REAL are used to represent numeric information. We used INTEGER variables as loop counters and to represent data such as exam scores that were whole numbers. In most other instances we used type REAL numeric data.

You may be wondering why it is necessary to have two numeric types? Can the data type REAL be used for all numbers? The answer is yes, but on many computers operations involving integers are faster and less storage space is needed to store integers. Also operations with integers are always precise whereas there may be some loss of accuracy when dealing with real numbers.

These differences result from the way real numbers and integers are represented internally in memory. All data are represented in memory as *binary strings*, strings of 0's and 1's. However, the binary string stored for the integer 13 is not the same as the binary string stored for the real number 13.0. The actual internal representation used is computer dependent; some sample integer and real formats are shown in Fig. 4.2.

integer format	real format	
binary number	mantissa	exponent

Fig. 4.2 Integer and Real Formats

In Fig. 4.2, each integer is represented as a standard binary number. If you are familiar with the binary number system, you know that the integer 13 is represented as the binary number 1101.

Real format is analogous to scientific notation. The storage area occupied by a real number is divided into two sections: the *mantissa* and the *exponent*. The mantissa is a binary fraction between 0.5 and 1.0 (−0.5 and −1.0 for a negative number). The exponent is a power of two. The mantissa and exponent are chosen so that the formula below is correct.

$$real\text{-}number = mantissa \times 2^{exponent}$$

Besides the capability of storing fractions, the range of numbers that may be represented in real format is considerably larger than for integer format. For example, on Control Data Corporation Cyber series computers, real numbers range in value from 10^{-294} (a very small fraction) to 10^{+322}, whereas, the range of positive integers extends from 1 to approximately 10^{15}.

Type of an Arithmetic Result

All the arithmetic operators (+, −, *, /) seen so far can be used with either integer or real operands. Table 4.1 shows the format of the result of an arithmetic operation. If one or both operands are type REAL, then the result always will be type REAL; only when both operands are type INTEGER can the result be type INTEGER. If the operator is /, then the result will be type REAL even when both operands are type INTEGER.

Table 4.1 Data Type of the Result of an Arithmetic Operation

Operands		Operator		
left	right	+, −, *	/	mod, div
REAL	REAL	REAL	REAL	illegal
REAL	INTEGER	REAL	REAL	illegal
INTEGER	REAL	REAL	REAL	illegal
INTEGER	INTEGER	INTEGER	REAL	INTEGER

The operators div and mod require INTEGER operands and compute INTEGER results. They are described in the next section.

Pascal does not allow a type REAL value to be assigned to a type INTEGER variable because the fractional part cannot be represented and will be lost. This means that the assignment statements below will all generate syntax errors if COUNT is a type INTEGER variable. However, either a REAL or INTEGER result may be assigned to a type REAL variable.

```
COUNT := 3.5;       {illegal assignment of a real number to INTEGER}
COUNT := COUNT + 1.0;  {illegal -- 1.0 is REAL so result is REAL}
COUNT := COUNT / 2      {illegal -- result of division is REAL}
```

Arithmetic Operators div and mod

In Table 4.1, there are two new operators, div and mod, that must be used only with type INTEGER operands. The integer division operator, div, computes the integral part of the quotient that results when its first operand is divided by its second operand; the modulo division operator, mod, computes the integer remainder.

For example, the expression 7 div 2 evaluates to 3, which is the integral part of the quotient of 7 divided by 2. The expression 7 mod 2 evaluates to 1, which is the integer remainder of 7 divided by 2 as shown below.

$$\begin{array}{r} 3 \text{ R}1 \\ 2 \overline{)7} \\ \underline{6} \\ 1 \end{array}$$

The operator div may be used to divide two integer values when an integer result is required; any remainder is *truncated* or lost. The sign of the result is positive if both operands have the same sign; otherwise, the sign of the result is negative. The div and mod operators are described in the next display.

OPERATORS DIV AND MOD

$operand_1$ div $operand_2$
$operand_1$ mod $operand_2$

Interpretation: The operator div yields the integral part of the result of $operand_1$ divided by $operand_2$; any remainder is truncated. The operator mod yields the integer remainder of this division. Both operands must be integer constants, variables, or expressions with integer values.

Notes: If $operand_2$ is 0, the result of the div or mod operation is undefined. If $operand_2$ is negative, the result of the mod operation is undefined.

Example 4.1

The integer division operator, div, is illustrated below. The sign of the result is the same as for regular division (operator /). The result is always zero when the magnitude of the first operand is less than the magnitude of the second operand.

```
 3 div 15 = 0        3 div -15 =  0
15 div  3 = 5       15 div  -3 = -5
16 div  3 = 5       16 div  -3 = -5
17 div  3 = 5      -17 div   3 = -5
18 div  3 = 6      -18 div  -3 =  6
```

Example 4.2

The modulo division operator, mod, is illustrated below. Each result is shown in parentheses. The result is always less than the second operand (the divisor). The mod operation is undefined when its second operand is negative or zero. By comparing the second and third columns, we see that M mod N is the negation of -M mod N.

```
3 mod 5 = 3        5 mod 3 = 2        -5 mod 3 = -2
4 mod 5 = 4        5 mod 4 = 1        -5 mod 4 = -1
5 mod 5 = 0       15 mod 5 = 0       -15 mod 5 =  0
6 mod 5 = 1       15 mod 6 = 3       -15 mod 6 = -3
7 mod 5 = 2       15 mod 7 = 1       -15 mod 7 = -1
8 mod 5 = 3       15 mod 8 = 7       -15 mod 8 = -7
```

Example 4.3   Procedure PRINTDIGITS in Fig. 4.3 prints each digit of its parameter DECIMAL in reverse order (e.g. if DECIMAL is 738, the digits printed are 8, 3, 7). This is accomplished by printing each remainder (0 through 9) of DECIMAL divided by 10; the integer quotient of DECIMAL divided by 10 becomes the new value of DECIMAL. DECIMAL must be a positive integer.

The parameter DECIMAL is used as the loop control variable. Within the while loop, the mod operator is used to assign to DIGIT the rightmost digit of DECIMAL, and the div operator is used to assign the rest of the number to DECIMAL. The loop is exited when DECIMAL becomes 0. Since DECIMAL is a value parameter, the actual parameter value is not changed by the procedure execution.

```
procedure PRINTDIGITS (DECIMAL {input} : INTEGER);

{Prints the digits of DECIMAL in reverse order.}

const
    BASE = 10;                                    {number system base}

var
    DIGIT : INTEGER;                              {each digit}

begin {PRINTDIGITS}
    {Find and print successive remainders of DECIMAL divided by 10}
    while DECIMAL <> 0 do
        begin
            DIGIT := DECIMAL mod BASE;            {get next remainder}
            WRITE (DIGIT :1);
            DECIMAL := DECIMAL div BASE           {get next quotient}
        end; {while}
    WRITELN
end; {PRINTDIGITS}
```

Fig. 4.3 Printing Decimal Digits

Table 4.2 shows a trace of the procedure execution for an actual parameter of 43. The digits 3 and 4 are printed.

Expressions with Multiple Operators

To write expressions that compute the desired results, we must know the Pascal rules for evaluating expressions. For example, in the expression A + B * C, is * performed before + or vice versa? Is the expression X / Y * Z evaluated as (X / Y) * Z or X / (Y * Z)?

Some expressions with multiple operators were used in earlier programs. For example,

```
1.8 * CELSIUS + 32
(SALARY - 5000.00) * 0.20 + 1425.00
```

Table 4.2 Trace of Execution of PRINTDIGITS (43)

Statement	DECIMAL	DIGIT	Effect
	43		
while DECIMAL <> 0 do			43 <> 0 is true
DIGIT := DECIMAL mod BASE		3	Remainder is 3
WRITE (DIGIT :1)			Print 3
DECIMAL := DECIMAL div BASE	4		Quotient is 4
while DECIMAL <> 0 do			4 <> 0 is true
DIGIT := DECIMAL mod BASE		4	Remainder is 4
WRITE (DIGIT :1)			Print 4
DECIMAL := DECIMAL div BASE	0		Quotient is 4
while DECIMAL <> 0 do			0 <> 0 is false — exit

In both these cases, the algebraic rule that multiplication is performed before addition is applicable. The use of parentheses in the second expression ensures that subtraction is done first. The rules for expression evaluation in Pascal are based on standard algebraic rules:

a. All parenthesized subexpressions must be evaluated first. Nested parenthesized subexpressions must be evaluated inside out, with the innermost subexpression evaluated first.

b. (*operator precedence*) Operators in the same subexpression are evaluated in the following order:

> *, /, div, mod   first
> +, –   last

c. (*left associative*) Operators in the same subexpression and at the same precedence level (such as + and –) are evaluated left to right.

Example 4.4 The formula for the area of a circle, $a = PI \times r^2$, may be written in Pascal as

```
AREA := PI * RADIUS * RADIUS
```

where PI is the constant 3.14159. The *evaluation tree* for this formula is shown in Fig. 4.4. In this tree, the arrows connect each operand with its operator. The order of operator evaluation is shown by the number to the left of each operator; the rules that apply are shown to the right.

We shall see another way to specify RADIUS * RADIUS in the next section.

Example 4.5 The formula for the average velocity, v, of a particle traveling on a line between points p_1 and p_2 in time t_1 to t_2 is

$$v = \frac{p_2 - p_1}{t_2 - t_1}$$

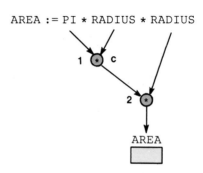

Fig. 4.4 Evaluation Tree for AREA := PI * RADIUS * RADIUS

This formula may be written and evaluated in Pascal as shown in Fig. 4.5.

Inserting parentheses in an expression affects the order of operator evaluation. Parentheses should be used freely to clarify the order of evaluation.

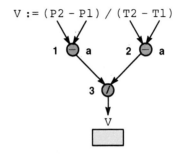

Fig. 4.5 Evaluation Tree for V := (P2 — P1) / (T2 — T1)

Example 4.6   Refer to Fig. 4.6 as you consider the expression

```
Z - (A + B DIV 2) + W * Y
```

containing integer variables only. The parenthesized subexpression (A + B DIV 2) is evaluated first [Rule (a)] beginning with B DIV 2 [[Rule (b)]. Once the value of B DIV 2 is determined, it can be added to A to obtain the value of (A + B DIV 2). Next the multiplication operation is performed [Rule (b)] and the value for W * Y is determined. Then the value of (A + B DIV 2) is subtracted from Z [Rule (c)], and finally this result is added to W * Y.

Writing Mathematical Formulas in Pascal

There are two problem areas in writing a mathematical formula in Pascal; one concerns multiplication and the other concerns division. Multiplication

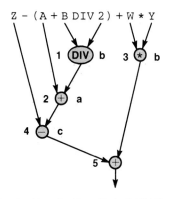

$$Z - (A + B\ DIV\ 2) + W * Y$$

Fig. 4.6 Evaluation Tree for Z − (A + B DIV 2) + W * Y

can often be implied in a mathematical formula by writing the two items to be multiplied next to each other; e.g., a = bc. In Pascal, however, the * operator must always be used to indicate multiplication as in:

```
A := B * C
```

The other difficulty arises in formulas involving division. We normally write the numerator and denominator on separate lines:

$$m = \frac{y - b}{x - a}$$

In Pascal, all assignment statements must be written in a linear form; consequently parentheses are often needed to separate the numerator from the denominator, and to clearly indicate the order of evaluation of the operators in the expression. The formula above would be written as

```
M := (Y - B) / (X - A)
```

Example 4.7 This example illustrates how several mathematical formulas can be written in Pascal.

Mathematical Formula	*Pascal Expression*
a. $b^2 - 4ac$	B * B - 4 * A * C
b. $a + b - c$	A + B - C
c. $\dfrac{a + b}{c + d}$	(A + B) / (C + D)
d. $\dfrac{1}{1 + x^2}$	1 / (1 + X * X)
e. $a \times -(b + c)$	A * (-(B + C))

The points illustrated are summarized as follows:

- Always specify multiplication explicitly by using the operator ∗ where needed (see Example 4.7a).
- Use parentheses when required to control the order of operator evaluation (see Examples 4.7c and d).
- Never write two arithmetic operators in succession; they must be separated by an operand or parentheses (see Example 4.7e).

Self-check Exercises for Section 4.2

1. What happens if BASE is 2 instead of 10 in procedure PRINTDIGITS? What result is generated for PRINTDIGITS(23) and PRINTDIGITS (64) if BASE is 2? Answer these questions if BASE is 8.
2. Evaluate the following expressions with 7 and 22 as operands.

   22 div 7   7 div 22   22 mod 7   7 mod 22

   Repeat this exercise for the pairs of integers:

   15, 16   3, 23   4, 16

3. Given the declarations

   ```
   const
       PI = 3.14159;
       MAXI = 1000;

   var
       X, Y : REAL;
       A, B, I : INTEGER;
   ```

   find the value of each of the valid statements below. Also indicate which are invalid and why. Assume that A is 3, B is 4, and Y is −1.0.

   a. I := A mod B
   b. I := (990 − MAXI) div A
   c. I := A mod Y
   d. X := PI ∗ Y
   e. I := A / B
   f. X := A / B
   g. X := A mod (A / B)
   h. I := B div 0
   i. I := A mod (990 − MAXI)
   j. I := (MAXI − 990) div A
   k. X := A / Y
   l. I := PI ∗ A
   m. X := PI div Y
   n. X := A div B
   o. I := (MAXI − 990) mod A
   p. I := A mod 0
   q. I := A mod (MAXI − 990)

4. What values are assigned by the valid statements in 3 above, assuming A is 5, B is 2, and Y is 2.0?
5. Assume that you have the following variable declarations:

```
var
    COLOR, LIME, STRAW, YELLOW, RED, ORANGE : INTEGER;
    BLACK, WHITE, GREEN, BLUE, PURPLE, CRAYON : REAL;
```

Evaluate each of the statements below given the values: COLOR is 2, BLACK is 2.5, CRAYON is −1.3, STRAW is 1, RED is 3, PURPLE is 0.3E1.
   a. WHITE := COLOR * 2.5 / PURPLE
   b. GREEN := COLOR / PURPLE
   c. ORANGE := COLOR DIV RED
   d. BLUE := (COLOR + STRAW) / (CRAYON + 0.3)
   e. LIME := RED DIV COLOR + RED MOD COLOR
   f. PURPLE := STRAW / RED * COLOR
6. Let A, B, C, and X be the names of four type REAL variables and I, J, and K the names of three type INTEGER variables. Each of the statements below contains a violation of the rules for forming arithmetic expressions. Rewrite each statement so that it is consistent with these rules.
   a. X := 4.0 A * C   d. K := 3(I + J)
   b. A := AC   e. X := 5A / BC
   c. I := 2 * -J   f. I := 5J3

4.3 Functions in Arithmetic Expressions

The function is a feature of Pascal that is helpful in specifying numerical computations. Each function performs a different mathematical operation (square root, cosine, etc.) and computes a single value. Functions are referenced directly in an expression: the value computed by the function is then substituted for the function reference.

Example 4.8   SQRT is the name of a function that computes the square root of a positive value. In the assignment statement

```
Y := 5.7 + SQRT(20.25)
```

the value computed by the function reference SQRT(20.25) is 4.5; this value replaces the function reference in the expression and is added to 5.7. The result of the addition or 10.2 (5.7 + 4.5) is stored in the real variable Y.

Pascal provides a number of standard mathematical functions, such as SQRT, that may be used by the programmer. The names and descriptions of these functions are given in Table 4.3. The function name is always

Table 4.3 Mathematical Functions

Name	Description of Computation	Argument	Result
ABS	The absolute value of the argument	real/integer	same as argument
EXP	The value of e (2.71828) raised to the power of the argument	real/integer	real
LN	The logarithm (to the base e) of the argument	real/integer	real
SQR	The square of the argument	real/integer	same as argument
SQRT	The positive square root of the argument	real/integer (positive)	real
ROUND	The closest integer value to the argument	real	integer
TRUNC	The integral part of the argument	real	integer
ARCTAN	The arc tangent of the argument	real/integer (radians)	real
COS	The cosine of the argument	real/integer (radians)	real
SIN	The sine of the argument	real/integer (radians)	real

followed by its *argument* (an actual parameter) enclosed in parentheses as shown in Example 4.8 (argument is 20.25). Any legal arithmetic expression of the proper type may be used as an argument for these functions.

Example 4.9   The Pascal functions SQR (square) and SQRT may be used to compute the roots of a quadratic equation in X of the form

$$AX^2 + BX + C = 0$$

The two roots are expressed in algebraic form as

$$ROOT_1 = \frac{-B + \sqrt{B^2 - 4AC}}{2A}, \qquad ROOT_2 = \frac{-B - \sqrt{B^2 - 4AC}}{2A}$$

The Pascal implementation is

```
DISC := SQR(B) - 4 * A * C ;
if DISC > 0 then
    begin
        ROOT1 := (-B + SQRT(DISC)) / (2 * A);
        ROOT2 := (-B - SQRT(DISC)) / (2 * A)
    end {if}
```

where the variable DISC represents the *discriminant* $(B^2 - 4AC)$ of the equation.

Except for ABS, SQR, ROUND, and TRUNC, each of the functions listed in Table 4.3 returns (computes) a real value regardless of its parameter type (REAL or INTEGER). The type of the result computed by a reference to ABS or SQR is the same as the type of its parameter.

The functions ROUND and TRUNC require type REAL parameters and always return integer values. These functions determine the integral part of a real-valued expression; consequently the expressions

```
TRUNC(1.5 * GROSS)
ROUND(TOTALSCORE / NUMSTUDENTS)
```

have INTEGER values and may be assigned to INTEGER variables. TRUNC simply truncates, or removes, the fractional part of its parameter; ROUND rounds its parameter to the nearest whole number. For example, TRUNC(17.5) is 17 while ROUND(17.5) is 18; TRUNC(-3.8) is -3 while ROUND(-3.8) is -4.

Example 4.10 The program in Fig. 4.7 illustrates the use of several arithmetic functions. The function references are inserted in the output list of the WRITELN statement. The ABS function is used to find the absolute value of X before the SQRT function is called as the square root of a negative number is undefined.

```
program ARITHFUNC (INPUT, OUTPUT);

{Illustrates the arithmetic functions.}

const
   SENTINEL = 0.0;                              {sentinel value}

var
   X : REAL;                                    {each data value}

begin {ARITHFUNC}
   {Print the table heading.}
   WRITELN ('After each line  enter a real number or 0.0 to stop');
   WRITELN;
   WRITELN ('X', 'TRUNC(X)' :16, 'ROUND(X)' :10, 'ABS(X)' :10,
           'SQR(X)' :10, 'SQRT(ABS(X))' :15);

   {Read and process each value of X.}
   READLN (X);                                  {get first number}
   while X <> SENTINEL do
      begin
         WRITELN (TRUNC(X) :17, ROUND(X) :10, ABS(X) :10:2,
                 SQR(X) :10:2, SQRT(ABS(X)) :10:2);
         READLN (X)                             {get next number}
      end {while}
end. {ARITHFUNC}


After each line enter a real number or 0.0 to stop
```

X	TRUNC(X)	ROUND(X)	ABS(X)	SQR(X)	SQRT(ABS(X))
4.3					
	4	4	4.30	18.49	2.07
-24.78					
	-24	-25	24.78	614.05	4.98
0.0					

Fig. 4.7 Using the Arithmetic Functions

Example 4.11   The program in Fig. 4.8 draws a sine curve. It uses the Pascal function SIN which returns the trigonometric sine of its parameter, an angle expressed in radians. The assignment statement

```
RADIAN := THETA / 180 * PI;
```

computes the number of radians corresponding to the angle THETA (measured in degrees). The value of the loop control variable THETA is increased by eighteen degrees (value of STEP) at the end of each repetition of the loop body.

The assignment statement

```
INDENT := 1 + ROUND(20 * (1 + SIN(RADIAN)));
```

assigns a value between 1 (when SIN(RADIAN) is −1) and 41 (when SIN(RADIAN) is 1) to INDENT. Finally the statement

```
WRITE (STAR :INDENT);      {plot * in column INDENT}
```

plots an asterisk somewhere in columns 1 through 41 as determined by the value of INDENT. Recall that a string (or character) is printed right justified in its field; the value of INDENT determines the size of the output field. The sine value is printed after each asterisk by the statement

```
WRITELN (SIN(RADIAN) :20);      {print sine value}
```

PROGRAM STYLE

Checking boundary values

The discussion for Example 4.11 states that the value of INDENT ranges from 1 to 41 as the sine value goes from −1 to 1. It is always a good idea to check the accuracy of these assumptions; this usually can be done by checking the boundaries of the range as shown below.

```
SIN(RADIAN) is -1, INDENT := 1 + ROUND(20 * (1 + (-1))
                    INDENT := 1 + ROUND(20 * 0)
                    INDENT := 1
```

```
SIN(RADIAN) is +1, INDENT := 1 + ROUND(20 * (1 + 1))
                   INDENT := 1 + ROUND(20 * 2)
                   INDENT := 41
```

Fig. 4.8 Plotting a Sine Curve.

```
program SINECURVE (OUTPUT);

{Plots a sine curve.}

const
   PI = 3.14159;                        {constant Pi}
   STEP = 18;                           {increment in degrees}
   STAR = '*';                          {symbol being plotted}

var
   THETA,                               {angle in degrees}
   RADIAN : REAL;                       {angle in radians}
   INDENT : INTEGER;                    {column of each *}

begin {SINECURVE}
   WRITELN ('Sine curve plot' :28);
   THETA := 0;                          {initial value of THETA}
   while THETA <= 360 do
      begin
         RADIAN := THETA * PI / 180.0;  {compute radians}
         INDENT := 1 + ROUND(20 * (1 + SIN(RADIAN)));
         WRITE (STAR :INDENT);          {plot * in column INDENT}
         WRITELN (SIN(RADIAN) :20);     {print sine value}
         THETA := THETA + STEP          {get next angle}
      end {while}
end. {SINECURVE}
```

```
                    Sine curve plot
                        *                      0
                         *            3.090168E-01
                           *          5.877849E-01
                            *         8.090166E-01
                              *       9.510562E-01
                               *      1.000000E+00
                              *       9.510570E-01
                            *         8.090180E-01
                          *           5.877869E-01
                        *             3.090194E-01
                      *               2.621549E-06
                    *                -3.090146E-01
                  *                  -5.877830E-01
                *                    -8.090152E-01
              *                      -9.510555E-01
             *                       -1.000000E+00
              *                      -9.510579E-01
                *                    -8.090194E-01
                  *                  -5.877893E-01
                    *                -3.090214E-01
                       *             -5.243099E-06
```

There is one additional function that is only used with an integer parameter. It is the function ODD, which determines whether or not an integer variable or expression evaluates to an odd number. The function ODD returns the BOOLEAN value TRUE or FALSE as described in the next display.

FUNCTION ODD

ODD (*argument*)

Interpretation: The function ODD returns the value TRUE if its *argument* evaluates to an odd integer; otherwise, it returns the value FALSE.

Numerical Inaccuracies

One of the problems in processing real numbers is that there is sometimes an error in representing real data. Just as there are certain numbers that cannot be represented exactly in the decimal number system (e.g. the fraction 1/3 is 0.333333 . . .), so there are numbers that cannot be represented exactly in real format. The *representational error* will depend on the number of binary digits (bits) used in the mantissa: the more bits the smaller the error.

The number 0.1 is an example of a real number that has a representational error. The effect of a small error is often magnified through repeated computations. Therefore, the result of adding 0.1 ten times is not exactly 1.0, so the loop below may fail to terminate on some computers.

```
TRIAL := 0.0;
while TRIAL <> 1.0 do
    begin
        . . . . . . . . . . . . . .

        TRIAL := TRIAL + 0.1
    end {while}
```

If the loop repetition test is changed to TRIAL < 1.0, the loop may execute 10 times on one computer and eleven times on another. For this reason, it is best to use integer variables whenever possible in loop repetition tests.

Other problems occur when manipulating very large and very small real numbers. In adding a large number and a small number, the larger number may "cancel out" the smaller number (a *cancellation error*). If X is much larger than Y, then X + Y and X may have the same value (e.g. 1000.0 + 0.0001234 is equal to 1000.0 on some computers).

If two very small numbers are multiplied, the result may be too small to be represented accurately and will become zero. This is called *arithmetic underflow.* Similarly if two very large numbers are multiplied, the result may be too large to be represented. This is called *arithmetic overflow* and is handled in different ways by Pascal compilers. Arithmetic underflow and overflow can occur when processing very large and small integer values as well.

As an illustration of the numerical inaccuracy that may result in performing real computations, examine the sine value for 360 degrees printed in the last line of Fig. 4.8. The actual sine should be zero; the sine value computed is quite small (approximately 10^{-6}) but is not zero. This is because the value of the constant PI is imprecise so the result of any computation involving PI will have a small numerical error.

Self-check Exercises for Section 4.3

1. The numeric constant e is known as Euler's Number. The approximate value of e is 2.71828. Write a procedure that computes

$$e^{a} \times \ln(b)$$

for several different values of a and b where ln is the natural log function. What does this procedure compute?

2. Using the ROUND function, write a Pascal statement to round any real value X to the nearest two decimal places. (Hint: You will have to multiply by 100 before rounding.)

4.4 BOOLEAN Variables, Expressions, and Operators

We introduced the BOOLEAN data type in Chapter 1. We have used BOOLEAN expressions (expressions that evaluate to true or false) to control loop repetition and to select one of the alternatives in an if statement. Some examples of BOOLEAN expressions are:

```
GROSS > TAXBREAK
ITEM <> SENTINEL
TRANTYPE = 'C'
```

The simplest BOOLEAN expression is a BOOLEAN variable or constant. A BOOLEAN variable or constant can be set to either of the BOOLEAN values, TRUE or FALSE. The statement

```
const
    DEBUG = TRUE;
```

specifies that the BOOLEAN constant DEBUG has the value TRUE; the statement

```
var
    SWITCH, FLAG : BOOLEAN;
```

declares `SWITCH` and `FLAG` to be `BOOLEAN` variables; i.e., variables that may be assigned only the values `TRUE` and `FALSE`.

BOOLEAN Operators

A BOOLEAN variable or constant is the simplest form of a BOOLEAN expression (e.g., `SWITCH`). We have used the relational operators (=, <, >, etc.) with numeric data to form conditions or BOOLEAN expressions (e.g. `SALARY < MINSAL`).

There are three BOOLEAN operators: `and`, `or`, `not`. These operators are used with operands that are BOOLEAN expressions.

```
(SALARY < MINSAL) or (NUMDEPEND > 5)
(TEMP > 90) and (HUMIDITY > 90)
ATHLETE and not FAILING
```

The first BOOLEAN expression can be used to determine whether an employee pays income tax. It evaluates to true if either condition in parentheses is true. The second BOOLEAN expression can be used to describe an unbearable summer day: temperature and humidity both above 90. The expression evaluates to true only when both conditions are true. The third BOOLEAN expression manipulates two BOOLEAN variables (`ATHLETE` and `FAILING`). Any individual for whom this expression is true is eligible for intercollegiate sports.

The BOOLEAN operators can be used with BOOLEAN expressions only. They are described in the tables below.

Table 4.4 and Operator

operand1	operand2	operand1 and operand2
true	true	true
true	false	false
false	true	false
false	false	false

Table 4.5 or Operator

operand1	operand2	operand1 or operand2
true	true	true
true	false	true
false	true	true
false	false	false

Table 4.6 not Operator

operand1	not operand1
true	false
false	true

Table 4.4 shows that the and operator yields a true result only when both its operands are true; Table 4.5 shows that the or operator yields a false result only when both its operands are false. The not operator has a single operand; Table 4.6 shows that the not operator yields the *logical complement* or negation of its operand.

The precedence of an operator determines its order of evaluation. Table 4.7 shows the precedence of all operators in Pascal, including the relational operators.

Table 4.7 Operator Precedence

Operator	Precedence
not	highest (evaluated first)
*, /, div, mod, and	
+, -, or	⇓
<, <=, =, <>, >=, >	lowest (evaluated last)

This table shows that the not operator has the highest precedence. Next are the multiplicative operators (including and), the additive operators (including or), and, last, the relational operators. Since the relational operators have the lowest precedence, they should generally be used with parentheses to prevent syntax errors.

Example 4.12   The expression

    X < Y + Z

involving the real variables X, Y, and Z is interpreted as

    X < (Y + Z)

since + has higher precedence than <.

The expression

    X < Y or Z < Y

causes the syntax error "invalid type of operands". It is interpreted as

    X < (Y or Z) < Y

since or has higher precedence than <. This is an error because the type REAL variables Y and Z cannot be operands of the BOOLEAN operator or. The parentheses shown below are required to prevent a syntax error.

```
(X < Y) or (Z < Y)
```

Example 4.13 The following are all legal BOOLEAN expressions if X, Y, and Z are type REAL, and FLAG is type BOOLEAN. The value of each expression is shown in brackets, assuming that X is 3.0, Y is 4.0, Z is 2.0, and FLAG is FALSE.

```
1. (X > Z) and (Y > Z)              [TRUE]
2. (X + Y / Z) <= 3.5               [FALSE]
3. (Z > X) or (Z > Y)               [FALSE]
4. not FLAG                         [TRUE]
5. (X = 1.0) or (X = 3.0)           [TRUE]
6. (0.0 < X) and (X < 3.5)          [TRUE]
7. (X <= Y) and (Y <= Z)            [FALSE]
8. not FLAG or ((Y + Z) >= (X - Z)) [TRUE]
9. not (FLAG or ((Y + Z) >= (X - Z))) [FALSE]
```

Expression 1 gives the Pascal form of the relationship "X and Y are greater than Z." It is often tempting to write this as

```
X and Y > Z
```

However, this is an illegal BOOLEAN expression as the real variable X cannot be an operand of the BOOLEAN operator and. Similarly, expression 5 shows the correct way to express the relationship "X is equal to 1.0 or to 3.0."

Expression 6 is the Pascal form of the relationship 0.0 < X < 3.5, i.e., "X is in the range 0.0 to 3.5." Similarly, expression 7 shows the Pascal form of the relationship X <= Y <= Z; i.e., "Y is in the range X to Z, inclusive."

Finally expression 8 is evaluated in Fig. 4.9; the values given at the beginning of Example 4.13 are shown above the expression.

Example 4.14 We can also write assignment statements that assign a BOOLEAN value to a BOOLEAN variable. The statement

```
SAME := X = Y
```

assigns the value TRUE to the BOOLEAN variable SAME when X and Y are equal; otherwise, the value FALSE is assigned. The assignment above is more efficient than the if statement

```
if X = Y then
    SAME := TRUE
else
    SAME := FALSE
```

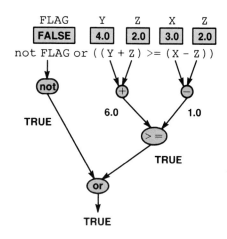

Fig. 4.9 Evaluation Tree for not FLAG or ((Y + Z) >= (X − Z))

which has the same effect.

Example 4.15 Either assignment statement below assigns the value TRUE to EVEN if N is an even number.

```
EVEN := not ODD(N)              EVEN := (N mod 2) = 0
```

The one on the left assigns to EVEN the complement of the value returned by the BOOLEAN function ODD; the one on the right assigns a value of TRUE to EVEN when the remainder of N divided by 2 is 0. (All even numbers are divisible by 2.)

Using BOOLEAN Variables as Program Flags

BOOLEAN variables are often used as *program flags* to signal whether or not a special event occurs in a program. The fact that such an event occurs is important to the future execution of the program. A BOOLEAN variable used as a program flag is initialized to one of its two possible values (TRUE or FALSE) and reset to the other as soon as the event being monitored occurs.

Example 4.16 Procedure READPOS in Fig. 4.10 continues to read integer values until an integer greater than 1 is entered. The BOOLEAN variable POSITIVE is used as a program flag to signal whether or not the event "data entry of an integer greater than 1" has occurred. POSITIVE is initialized to FALSE when the procedure is entered. Inside the while loop, the assignment statement

```
POSITIVE := N > 1
```

resets POSITIVE to TRUE when an integer greater than 1 is entered. The loop is repeated as long as POSITIVE is still FALSE.

```
procedure READPOS (var N {output} : INTEGER);

{Reads an integer greater than 1 into parameter N.}

var
    POSITIVE : BOOLEAN;                   {program flag -- loop control}

begin {READPOS}
    POSITIVE := FALSE;                    {assume N is not an integer > 1}

    {Keep reading until a valid number is read}
    while not POSITIVE do
        begin
            WRITE ('Enter an integer greater than 1: ');
            READLN (N);                   {read next integer into N}
            POSITIVE := N > 1             {set POSITIVE to TRUE if N > 1}
        end {while}
end; {READPOS}
```

Fig. 4.10 Procedure READPOS

Self-check Exercises for Section 4.4

1. Draw the evaluation tree for expression 9 of Example 4.13.
2. Write the following BOOLEAN assignment statements:
   a. Assign a value of TRUE to BETWEEN if the value of N lies between −K and +K, inclusive; otherwise, assign a value of FALSE.
   b. Assign a value of TRUE to UPCASE if CH is an uppercase letter; otherwise, assign a value of FALSE.
3. Assign a value of TRUE to DIVISOR if M is a divisor of N; otherwise, assign a value of FALSE.

4.5 Character Variables and Functions

Pascal provides a character data type that can be used for the storage and manipulation of the individual characters that comprise a person's name, address, etc. Character variables are declared using the data type CHAR in a declaration. A character value consists of a single printable character (letter, digit, punctuation mark, etc.) enclosed in apostrophes. A character value may be assigned to a character variable or associated with a constant identifier as shown below.

```
const
    STAR = '*';

var
    NEXTLETTER : CHAR;

begin
    NEXTLETTER := 'A'
```

The character variable NEXTLETTER is assigned the character value 'A' by the assignment statement above. A single character variable or value may appear on the right-hand side of a character assignment statement. Character values may also be compared, read, and printed.

Example 4.17 The program in Fig. 4.11 reads a sentence ending in a period and counts the number of blanks in the sentence. Each character entered after the prompting message is read into the variable NEXT and tested to see if it is a blank.

The statement

```
READ (NEXT)
```

appears twice in the program and is used to read one character at a time from the data line because NEXT is type CHAR. The while loop is exited when the last character read is a period. Reading character data is discussed in Section 4.7.

Fig. 4.11 Counting Blanks in a Sentence

```
program BLANKCOUNT (INPUT, OUTPUT);

{Counts the number of blanks in a sentence.}

const
    BLANK = ' ';                    {character being counted}
    PERIOD = '.';                   {sentinel character}

var
    NEXT : CHAR;                    {next character in sentence}
    COUNT : INTEGER;               {number of blank characters}

begin {BLANKCOUNT}
    COUNT := 0;                    {initialize COUNT}
    WRITELN ('Enter a sentence ending with a period.');

    {Process each input character up to the period}
    READ (NEXT);                   {get first character}
    while NEXT <> PERIOD do
        begin
            if NEXT = BLANK then
                COUNT := COUNT + 1; {increment blank count}
            READ (NEXT)            {get next character}
        end; {while}

    WRITELN ('The number of blanks is ', COUNT :2)
end. {BLANKCOUNT}

Enter a sentence ending with a period.
There was an old woman who lived in a shoe.
The number of blanks is 9
```

The READ Procedure

The program in Fig. 4.11 uses the standard Pascal READ procedure to read individual characters from a data line. Like the READLN statement, the READ statement causes input data to be stored in the variables specified in its input list. Both statements below

```
READ (NEXT)                    READLN (NEXT)
```

cause one data character to be read into the character variable NEXT; however, there is one important difference. After the READLN statement is executed, the computer automatically skips to the end of the data line (indicated by pressing return); any additional characters entered on that data line before the return key is pressed will not be processed. There is no skip to the end of the line after a READ statement is executed; therefore any additional characters entered on that line will be processed by the next READ or READLN statement.

If READLN (NEXT) is used in Fig. 4.11 instead of READ (NEXT), then the first character in the data line (the letter T) will be read into NEXT before loop entry and the remaining characters in the input sentence will be skipped. When the READLN statement in the loop body is executed, there will be no characters left to process and the computer waits for more data to be entered. We will further detail the differences between these two statements in Section 4.7.

READ STATEMENT

READ (*input-list*)

Interpretation: Data are entered into each variable specified in the *input-list*. There must be one data item for each variable in the *input-list*, and the order of the data must correspond to the order of the variables in the *input-list*. A space should be left between numeric data; character data are entered without intervening spaces. Any data remaining on the current data line will be processed when the next READ or READLN statement is executed.

Using Relational Operators with Characters

In Fig. 4.11, the BOOLEAN expressions

```
NEXT = BLANK
NEXT <> PERIOD
```

are used to determine whether two character variables have the same value or different values. Order comparisons can also be performed on character variables using the relational operators <, <=, >, >=.

To understand the result of an order comparison, we must know something about the way characters are represented internally. Each character has its own unique numeric code; this code is stored as a binary number in a memory cell that has a character value. These binary numbers are compared by the relational operators in the normal way.

Three common character codes are shown in Appendix D. Some of the common features of these codes are that the digits are an increasing sequence of consecutive characters.

```
'0' <'1' <'2' <'3' <'4' <'5' <'6' <'7' <'8' <'9'
```

The uppercase letters are also an increasing sequence of characters.

```
'A' <'B' <'C'< . . . <'X' <'Y' <'Z'
```

However, they are not necessarily consecutive characters. If the lowercase letters are included in the character set, they are also an increasing, but not necessarily consecutive, sequence of characters.

```
'a' <'b' <'c' < . . . <'x' <'y' <'z'
```

In our examples and programs we will assume that the lowercase letters are included.

The Functions ORD, PRED, and SUCC

The data types INTEGER, BOOLEAN, and CHAR are considered *ordinal types*. With ordinal data types, each value (except the first) has a unique predecessor and each value (except the last) has a unique successor (e.g. the predecessor of 5 is 4 and the successor of 5 is 6). The data type REAL is not an ordinal type because a real number such as 3.1415 does not have a unique successor. (Is its successor 3.1416 or 3.14151?)

The order or sequence of an ordinal data type is well defined. For example, −MAXINT is the smallest integer, and the positive integers follow the sequence 0, 1, 2, 3, . . . , MAXINT. The order of the BOOLEAN values is FALSE, TRUE.

The Pascal function ORD determines the *ordinal number* or relative position of an ordinal value in its sequence of values. If the parameter of ORD is an integer, the ordinal number returned is the integer itself. For all other ordinal types, the ordinal number of the first value in the sequence is zero, the ordinal number of the second value is one, etc. Thus ORD(FALSE) is zero and ORD(TRUE) is one. If A and B belong to the same ordinal type and A < B is true, then ORD(A) < ORD(B) must also be true.

The Pascal function PRED returns the predecessor of its parameter, and the Pascal function SUCC returns the successor. These functions, like ORD, can be used only with parameters that are ordinal types.

Example 4.18   Table 4.8 shows the result of using the ORD, SUCC, and PRED functions with an integer or BOOLEAN parameter.

As shown in Table 4.8, there is one value in each ordinal type that does not have a successor (MAXINT, TRUE) and one value that does not have a predecessor (-MAXINT, FALSE).

Although these functions may be used with any of the ordinal types, they are most often used with type CHAR and the user-defined types discussed later in this chapter. The ordinal number of a character is based on the character set code used by Pascal and, therefore, is computer-dependent.

Table 4.8 Result of ORD, SUCC, and PRED

Parameter	ORD	SUCC	PRED
15	15	16	14
0	0	1	-1
-30	-30	-29	-31
-MAXINT	-MAXINT	-MAXINT+1	undefined
MAXINT	MAXINT	undefined	MAXINT-1
FALSE	0	TRUE	undefined
TRUE	1	undefined	FALSE

Example 4.19   Table 4.9 illustrates ORD, SUCC, and PRED for the ASCII code (American Standard Code for Information Interchange) shown in Appendix D.

Table 4.9 Result of ORD, SUCC, and PRED Functions for ASCII Code

Parameter	ORD	SUCC	PRED
'C'	67	'D'	'B'
'7'	55	'8'	'6'
'y'	121	'z'	'x'
' '	32	'!'	unprintable

As shown above, the character '7' has the ordinal number 55 in the ASCII code.

Regardless of which character code is used, the expression

    ORD('7') - ORD('0') = 7

will always be true since the digit characters must be in consecutive sequence. If we assume that the letters are in consecutive sequence as well, then the BOOLEAN expression

```
ORD('C') - ORD('A') = 2
```

will be true.

THE FUNCTION ORD

ORD (*parameter*)

Interpretation: The value returned by ORD is the ordinal number of *parameter*. The *parameter* must be of an ordinal type.

THE FUNCTION PRED

PRED (*parameter*)

Interpretation: PRED returns the value whose ordinal number is one less than the ordinal number of *parameter*. The *parameter* must be of an ordinal type.

Note: If *parameter* evaluates to the first value for its type (-MAXINT for type INTEGER), then the result is undefined.

THE FUNCTION SUCC

SUCC (*parameter*)

Interpretation: SUCC returns the value whose ordinal number is one more than the ordinal number of *parameter*. The *parameter* must be of an ordinal type.

Note: If *parameter* evaluates to the last value for its type (MAXINT for type INTEGER), then the result is undefined.

The Function CHR

The function CHR returns a character as its result. The ordinal number of the character returned is the same as the parameter value (an integer). Therefore, the result of the function reference CHR(67) is the character with ordinal number 67 (the letter 'C' in the ASCII code).

If CH is a type CHAR variable, the *nested function reference*

```
CHR(ORD(CH))
```

has the same value as CH. Therefore, the function CHR is the *inverse* of the ORD function for the characters.

Example 4.20   A *collating sequence* is a sequence of characters arranged by ordinal number. The program in Fig. 4.12 prints part of the Pascal collating sequence. It lists the characters with ordinal numbers 32 through 64, inclusive. The sequence shown is for the ASCII code; the first character printed is a blank (ordinal number 32).

```
program COLLATE (OUTPUT);

{Prints part of the collating sequence.}

const
    MIN = 32;                    {smallest ordinal number}
    MAX = 64;                    {biggest ordinal number}

var
    NEXTORD : INTEGER;           {each ordinal number}

begin {COLLATE}
    {Print characters CHR(32) through CHR(64)}
    for NEXTORD := MIN TO MAX do
        WRITE (CHR(NEXTORD)); {print next character}
    WRITELN
end. {COLLATE}

 !"#$%&'()*+,-./0123456789:;<=>?@
```

Fig. 4.12 Printing Part of a Collating Sequence

Example 4.21   The `if` statement below

```
if (LOWCHAR >= 'a') and (LOWCHAR <= 'z') then
    UPCHAR := CHR(ORD('A') + ORD(LOWCHAR) - ORD('a'))
```

sets UPCHAR to the uppercase form (a capital letter) of the lowercase letter in LOWCHAR. If LOWCHAR is 'c', the BOOLEAN expression will be true, and the assignment statement will be evaluated as:

```
UPCHAR := CHR(ORD('A') + ORD('c') - ORD('a'))
       := CHR(ORD('A') + 2)
       := 'C'
```

The evaluation above assumes that the lowercase and uppercase letters are each consecutive character sets.

Example 4.22 It is sometimes desirable to read a number as a string of individual characters. This enables the program to detect and ignore input errors. For example, if the program user enters a letter instead of a number, this error will be detected and the program will prompt again for a data value. Similarly, if the program user enters $15,400 instead of the number 15400, the extra characters will be ignored.

Procedure READINT in Fig. 4.13 reads in a string of characters ending with the character % and ignores any character that is not a digit. It also computes the value of the number (an integer) formed by the digits only. For example, if the characters $15,43AB0% are entered, the value of NUMDATA will be 15430.

```
procedure READINT (var NUMDATA {output} : INTEGER);

{Reads consecutive characters ending with the symbol %. Computes
the integer value of the digit characters, ignoring non-digits.
Accumulates the integer value in NUMDATA.                        }

const
   BASE = 10;                              {the number system base}
   SENTINEL = '%';                         {the sentinel character}

var
   NEXT : CHAR;                                {each character read}
   DIGIT : INTEGER;            {the value of each numeric character}

begin {READINT}
   {Accumulate the numeric value of the digits in NUMDATA}
   NUMDATA := 0;                            {initial value is zero}
   READ (NEXT);                            {read first character}
   while NEXT <> SENTINEL do
      begin
         if (NEXT >= '0') and (NEXT <= '9') then
            begin {Process digit}
               DIGIT := ORD(NEXT) - ORD('0');    {get digit value}
               NUMDATA := BASE * NUMDATA + DIGIT {add digit value}
            end; {Process digit}
         READ (NEXT)                        {read next character}
      end {while}
end; {READINT}
```

Fig. 4.13 Reading a Number as a String of Characters

In Fig. 4.13, the statements

```
DIGIT := ORD(NEXT) - ORD('0');    {get digit value}
NUMDATA := BASE * NUMDATA + DIGIT {add digit value}
```

assign to DIGIT an integer value between 0 (for character value '0') and 9 (for character value '9'). The number being accumulated in

NUMDATA is multiplied by 10, and the value of DIGIT is added to it. Table 4.10 traces the procedure execution for the input characters 3N5%; the value returned is 35.

Table 4.10 Trace of Execution of Procedure READINT for Data 3N5%

Statement	NEXT	DIGIT	NUMDATA	Effect of Statement
NUMDATA := 0			0	Initialize NUMDATA
READ (NEXT)	'3'			Get character
while NEXT <> SENTINEL do				'3' <> '%' is true
if (NEXT>='0')and(NEXT<='9')				'3' is a digit
DIGIT := ORD(NEXT) - ORD('0')		3		digit value is 3
NUMDATA := BASE*NUMDATA+DIGIT			3	Add 3 to 0
READ (NEXT)	'N'			Get character
while NEXT <> SENTINEL do				'N' <> '%' is true
if (NEXT>='0')and(NEXT<='9')				'N' is not a digit
READ (NEXT)	'5'			Get character
while NEXT <> SENTINEL do				'5' <> '%' is true
if (NEXT>='0')and(NEXT<='9')				'5' is a digit
DIGIT := ORD(NEXT) - ORD('0')		5		digit value is 5
NUMDATA := BASE*NUMDATA+DIGIT			35	Add 5 to 30
READ (NEXT)	'%'			Get character
while NEXT <> SENTINEL do				'%' <> '%' is false

Self-check Exercises for Section 4.5

1. Evaluate the following:
   a. ORD(TRUE)
   b. PRED(TRUE)
   c. SUCC(FALSE)
   d. ORD(TRUE) - ORD(FALSE)
2. Evaluate the following assuming the letters are consecutive characters.
   a. ORD('D') - ORD('A')
   b. ORD('d') - ORD('a')
   c. SUCC(PRED('a'))
   d. CHR(ORD('C'))
   e. CHR(ORD('C')
      - ORD('A') + ORD('a'))
   f. ORD('7') - ORD('6')
   g. ORD('9') - ORD('0')
   h. SUCC(SUCC(SUCC('d')))
   i. CHR(ORD('A') + 5)

4.6 Introduction to Programmer-defined Data Types

One of the features of Pascal that accounts for its widespread use is that it permits the declaration of new data types. Many of these data types will be discussed in later chapters. In this section we will focus on the programmer-defined data types called *enumerated types* and *subrange types*.

Enumerated Types

A payroll program that pays a worker time and a half for all Saturday hours and double time for all Sunday hours may contain a statement such as

```
if DAYNUM = 1 then
    PAYVAL := 2 * RATE * HOURS
else if DAYNUM = 7 then
    PAYVAL := 1.5 * RATE * HOURS
else
    PAYVAL := RATE * HOURS
```

assuming that the days Sunday and Saturday were "coded" as the integers 1 and 7, respectively. In Pascal it is possible to rewrite this statement as

```
if TODAY = SUNDAY then
    PAYVAL := 2 * RATE * HOURS
else if TODAY = SATURDAY then
    PAYVAL := 1.5 * RATE * HOURS
else
    PAYVAL := RATE * HOURS
```

This statement is obviously more readable because it uses values (SATURDAY and SUNDAY) meaningful to the problem rather than an arbitrary code. In order to be able to use this statement, we must first declare an enumerated type as shown next.

Example 4.23   The declaration below are used to declare a data type called DAY and a variable (TODAY) of type DAY.

```
type
    DAY = (SUNDAY, MONDAY, TUESDAY, WEDNESDAY,
            THURSDAY, FRIDAY, SATURDAY);   {days of the week}

var
    TODAY : DAY;                           {current day of the week}
```

The data type DAY is an enumerated type with an ordered list of values SUNDAY, MONDAY, etc. provided in parentheses. Each value is defined as a constant identifier in the block containing the type declaration. The type declaration comes between constant and variable declarations.

The variable TODAY is declared as a variable of type DAY; thus, TODAY may be assigned any of the identifiers in the list for DAY using an assignment statement such as

```
TODAY := TUESDAY
```

No values other than the ones associated with enumerated type DAY may be assigned to TODAY.

Enumerated types are also ordinal types since each value has a clearly defined successor and predecessor. The value of SUCC(MONDAY) is TUESDAY; the value of PRED(MONDAY) is SUNDAY. Both PRED (SUNDAY) and SUCC(SATURDAY) are undefined since SUNDAY is the first value in type DAY and SATURDAY is the last.

The function ORD returns the ordinal number of a value belonging to an ordinal type. The first value in each enumerated type has an ordinal number of 0, the next value has an ordinal number of 1, etc. For type DAY, ORD(SUNDAY) is 0 and ORD(SATURDAY) is 6.

Example 4.24 If variables TODAY and TOMORROW are both declared to be type DAY (see type declaration above), the if statements below assign to TOMORROW the successor value of TODAY.

```
if TODAY = SATURDAY then          if TODAY < SATURDAY then
    TOMORROW := SUNDAY                TOMORROW := SUCC(TODAY)
else                              else
    TOMORROW := SUCC(TODAY)           TOMORROW := SUNDAY
```

When TODAY is SATURDAY, the if statements assign the value SUNDAY to TOMORROW.

The BOOLEAN expression TODAY < SATURDAY is true when ORD(TODAY) is less than ORD(SATURDAY). Since SATURDAY is the last value in the list for DAY, this expression will be true for all values except SATURDAY.

ENUMERATED TYPE DECLARATION

enumerated-type = (*identifier-list*)

Interpretation: A new data type named *enumerated-type* is declared. The values associated with this type are specified in the *identifier-list*. Each value is defined as a constant identifier in the block containing the type declaration.

Note: A particular identifier can appear in only one *identifier-list* in a given block.

As indicated in the above display, an enumerated-type value must be an identifier. Numbers, characters (e.g. 'A'), and strings (e.g. 'Saturday') cannot be used as values for any enumerated type. The scope rules for identifiers apply to enumerated-type values.

The only operators that may be used with enumerated types are the ones shown in this section; these include the assignment and relational operators. Enumerated-type variables and values may be parameters of the standard functions PRED, SUCC, and ORD and programmer-declared procedures and functions. We cannot use READLN and WRITELN with enumerated data types. We will see how to read and write enumerated-type values later in this chapter.

Subrange Types

Subranges are the other kind of simple data type that may be declared by a programmer. A subrange is a subset of values associated with an ordinal type (the *host type*). Subranges are used both to make a program more readable and to enable Pascal to detect when a variable is given a value that is unreasonable in the problem environment.

Example 4.25   Three subranges are declared below.

```
type
    LETTER = 'A'..'Z';
    DAYSINMONTH = 1..31;
    DAY = (SUNDAY, MONDAY, TUESDAY, WEDNESDAY,
           THURSDAY, FRIDAY, SATURDAY);  {days of the week}
    WEEKDAY = MONDAY..FRIDAY;

var
    NEXTCH : LETTER;
    DATE : DAYSINMONTH;
    SCHOOLDAY : WEEKDAY;
```

The first subrange, LETTER, has the host type CHAR. Any character from 'A' to 'Z' inclusive may be stored in a variable of type LETTER. An error message will be printed and the program will stop execution if an attempt is made to store any other character in the variable NEXTCH. (This assumes that the letters are consecutive characters.)

DAYSINMONTH is a subrange with host type INTEGER. A variable of type DAYSINMONTH may be used to keep track of the current date, a value between 1 and 31 inclusive. A "value out of range" error message will be printed and the program will stop execution if a value outside this range is assigned to the variable DATE.

WEEKDAY is a subrange of the enumerated type DAY. Any value listed for DAY except SUNDAY or SATURDAY may be assigned to the variable SCHOOLDAY.

The penalty for an out-of-range value is quite severe as the program stops execution. This happens only if an error is made. If DATE is type INTEGER (instead of DAYSINMONTH), then the program continues to execute regardless of what value is assigned to DATE. In this case, assigning DATE an invalid value, say 100, will cause a later statement to fail. The program user may have a difficult time determining the real cause of this later error: a bad value for DATE.

SUBRANGE TYPE DECLARATION

subrange-type = *minvalue* .. *maxvalue*

Interpretation: A new data type named *subrange-type* is defined. A variable of type *subrange-type* may be assigned a value from *minvalue* through *maxvalue* inclusive. The values *minvalue* and *maxvalue* must belong to the same ordinal type (called the host

---

type), and ORD(*minvalue*) must be less than ORD(*maxvalue*).
Note: minvalue and *maxvalue* may be constant identifiers of the same type.

The scope rules for a subrange type identifier are the same as for other Pascal identifiers. The operations that may be performed on a variable whose type is a subrange are the same as for the host type of the subrange. The host type may be a standard ordinal type (INTEGER, CHAR, or BOOLEAN) or any previously declared enumerated type. The host type is determined by the pair of values used to define the subrange; the ordinal number of the first value must be less than the ordinal number of the second value.

Type and Assignment Compatibility

Two data types are considered *type-compatible* if they are the same type, if one is a subrange of the other, or if they are both subranges of the same host type. The data types CHAR and LETTER (see Example 4.25) are type-compatible.

Operands that are type-compatible may be manipulated by the same operator. For example the expression

```
NEXTCH <> '3'
```

is syntactically correct as long as NEXTCH is type CHAR or LETTER; however, its value must be false if NEXTCH is type LETTER. On the other hand, the expression

```
NEXTCH <> 3
```

is invalid because NEXTCH and the integer 3 are not type-compatible.

The variable DATE declared in Example 4.25 may be manipulated like any type INTEGER variable. It can be used as an actual parameter that corresponds to a formal parameter that is type INTEGER, type DAYSIN-MONTH, or any other subrange with host type INTEGER.

An expression is considered *assignment-compatible* with a variable if their types are compatible. If the variable type is a subrange, then the value of the expression must be within range. If a variable and an expression are assignment-compatible, then the expression may be assigned to the variable without error.

The assignment statement

```
NEXTCH := '3'
```

causes the syntax error "value to be assigned is out of bounds" because the constant value '3' is not assignment-compatible with the variable NEXTCH (type LETTER). If CH is type CHAR, the assignment statement

```
NEXTCH := CH
```

will compile, but it may cause a "value out of range" run time error. This error occurs if the character stored in CH is not an uppercase letter.

There is one exception to the rule that a variable and expression must be type-compatible in order to be assignment-compatible. A type INTEGER expression is assignment-compatible with a type REAL variable. This means that a type INTEGER expression may be assigned to a type REAL variable or may correspond to a value parameter that is type REAL.

Self-check Exercises for Section 4.6

1. Evaluate each of the following:
   a. ORD(MONDAY)   c. SUCC(SUCC(MONDAY))
   b. PRED(SATURDAY)   d. CHR(MONDAY)
2. Identify the illegal subranges below.
   a. SATURDAY..SUNDAY   d. 0..'9'
   b. 'A'..'Z'   e. 15..-15
   c. -15..15   f. 'ACE'..'HAT'

4.7 Input/Output Revisited

In this section we will review some of the rules for input/output in Pascal and will introduce the EOLN and EOF functions. We will begin by explaining how to "read" and "write" enumerated type values.

Reading and Writing Enumerated-Type Values

One disadvantage in using enumerated types is that they cannot be read or written directly. Generally we will assign a value based on the data entry of one or more characters (e.g. enter SA for SATURDAY).

Example 4.26   Given the declarations below

```
type
    COLOR = (RED, GREEN, BLUE, YELLOW);

var
    EYES, HAIR : COLOR;
    VALIDCOLOR : BOOLEAN;
```

Either of the statements

```
READLN (EYES)                            WRITELN (EYES)
```

generates the syntax error message "error in type of standard procedure parameter." This means that EYES cannot be used as a parameter for the standard procedure READLN (or WRITELN) since its type is COLOR.

Although we cannot print an enumerated-type value directly, we can use the if statement below to print a string that represents the value stored in EYES. Make sure you recognize the difference between the string 'BLUE' and the constant identifier BLUE.

```
if EYES = BLUE then
    WRITELN ('BLUE')
else if EYES = RED then
    WRITELN ('RED')
else if EYES = YELLOW then
    WRITELN ('YELLOW')
else if EYES = GREEN then
    WRITELN ('GREEN')
```

The statement

```
WRITELN ('Value of EYES is ', ORD(EYES) :1)
```

may be used as a diagnostic print statement. It does not print the value of EYES, but it displays the ordinal number of that value which is an integer from 0 (for RED) to 3 (for YELLOW).

Example 4.27 The procedure in Fig. 4.14 assigns a value to EYES based on the character read into COLORCHAR. The procedure statement

```
READCOLOR (EYES, VALIDCOLOR)
```

calls this procedure. If BLACK and BROWN are added to the list of values for COLOR, it becomes necessary to read additional characters when the first letter read is B. We will leave this as an exercise.

PROGRAM STYLE

Program flags as procedure results

In Fig. 4.14, the variable parameter VALIDCOLOR is used as a program flag to signal to the calling procedure whether or not a color value was assigned to ITEMCOLOR by the procedure. This information will enable the calling block to take appropriate action based on the value of the BOOLEAN variable corresponding to parameter VALIDCOLOR. This use of the parameter VALIDCOLOR is consistent with our prior usage of BOOLEAN variables as program flags to signal the occurrence of an event.

```
procedure READCOLOR (var ITEMCOLOR {output} : COLOR;
                     var VALIDCOLOR {output} : BOOLEAN);

{Assigns a value to ITEMCOLOR based on an input character.
 Sets VALIDCOLOR to indicate whether or not the assignment
 was made.                                                 }

var
    COLORCHAR : CHAR;                {first letter of color name}

begin {READCOLOR}
    VALIDCOLOR := TRUE;     {Assume valid color will be read}
    WRITE ('Enter first letter of color: ');
    READLN (COLORCHAR);                      {get the letter}

    {Assign the color value}
    if (COLORCHAR = 'R') or (COLORCHAR = 'r') then
        ITEMCOLOR := RED
    else if (COLORCHAR = 'Y') or (COLORCHAR = 'y') then
        ITEMCOLOR := YELLOW
    else if (COLORCHAR = 'G') or (COLORCHAR = 'g') then
        ITEMCOLOR := GREEN
    else if (COLORCHAR = 'B') or (COLORCHAR = 'b') then
        ITEMCOLOR := BLUE
    else
        VALIDCOLOR := FALSE         {valid color was not read}
end; {READCOLOR}
```

Fig. 4.14 Procedure READCOLOR

Reading and Writing BOOLEAN Values

As we indicated earlier, BOOLEAN values may be printed, but they may
not be read directly. We can, however, assign a BOOLEAN value to a
BOOLEAN variable based on an input character as shown next.

```
WRITE ('Enter T (TRUE) or F (FALSE): ');
READLN (BOOLCHAR);
if (BOOLCHAR = 'T') or (BOOLCHAR = 't') then
    SWITCH := TRUE
else if (BOOLCHAR = 'F') or (BOOLCHAR = 'f') then
    SWITCH := FALSE
else
    WRITELN ('Illegal BOOLEAN character ', BOOLCHAR)
```

The EOLN Function

Until now, we have used a sentinel value to indicate the end of a collection of data values. As an example, the statements

```
WRITELN ('Enter characters ending with ', SENTINEL);
READ (NEXTCHAR);
while NEXTCHAR <> SENTINEL do
    READ (NEXTCHAR)
```

may be used to read a string of characters ending with a sentinel character (SENTINEL) into the variable NEXTCHAR. Each character that is read is stored temporarily in NEXTCHAR. The EOLN (end of line) function can be used to detect the end of a data line as shown next.

Example 4.28   The while statement below

```
WRITELN ('Enter characters ending with a return');
while not EOLN do
    READ (NEXTCHAR);
READLN
```

reads one character at a time into NEXTCHAR, stopping at the end of the data line (indicated by pressing Return). The loop repetition test not EOLN is true as long as the last character in the data line has not yet been read into NEXTCHAR. When the end of the line is reached and the next character to be read is the character representing the carriage return, the EOLN function evaluates to true and the while loop is exited.

When the loop is exited, there is still one character remaining to be processed on the current data line; that is the character representing the carriage return. READLN alone (without an input list) is used to skip over the carriage return character so that it will not be processed by the next input operation.

We discussed the difference between READ and READLN in Section 4.5. Assuming A, B, and C are type REAL variables, only the characters in blue below are processed when READ (A, B, C) is executed; the next character (the letter x) will be processed when another READ or READLN is executed.

```
15.34  5.5  8.67xyz   3.333<return>
```

The statements below have the same effect and cause all characters through the <return> to be processed. Only the characters in blue are actually saved in memory.

```
READLN (A, B, C)                   READ (A, B, C);
                                   READLN
```

EOLN FUNCTION (for interactive input/output)

EOLN

Interpretation: The EOLN function returns a value of true if the next character to be read is the carriage return; otherwise, the value returned is false.

Processing a Batch Data File

So far we have stressed interactive programming, assuming that all data are read from file INPUT (the terminal). Pascal was originally designed as a batch-oriented language in which all input was read from keypunched data cards or a separate data file. Files are described in detail in Chapter 9; we will discuss how to read a batch data file in this section.

A *text file* in Pascal consists of a string of characters segmented into lines. The lines may be different lengths, but each line ends with a special character called the *end-of-line mark*. For an interactive program, the data entered at a terminal comprise a text file. Pressing the Return key places the carriage return character in this file which is the same as an end-of-line mark in a batch text file.

A batch text file may be created using the editor in the same way that a program file is created, or it may be keypunched on cards. When using the editor simply type in each line of the text file; pressing the carriage return places an end-of-line mark in the file. If the text file is keypunched on cards, the computer system will insert an end-of-line mark after the last character keypunched on each card.

A sample text file is shown in Fig. 4.15. Each line of this figure represents a line of the file; the shaded symbol at the end of each line denotes the end-of-line mark.

```
Peter Liacouras▩
56000.00   3▩
George Simpleton▩
43000.50   0▩
Caryn Koffman▩
15000.75   5▩
```

Fig. 4.15 A Sample Text File

Example 4.29   The program in Fig. 4.16 reads and echo prints the data in the text file shown in Fig. 4.15. We will assume that this text file is a batch file associated with the name INPUT. In addition to using the EOLN function, this program introduces the EOF (end-of-file) function which is used to determine whether or not the end of a data file is reached.

```
program ECHOFILE (INPUT, OUTPUT);

{Echos all the data on batch file INPUT. Uses procedure
 ECHOLINE to echo each employee name.                              }

var
    SALARY : REAL;                        {a salary amount}
    DEPEND : INTEGER;                     {number of dependents}

procedure ECHOLINE;

{Echos all characters on the current input line.}

var
    NEXTCHAR : CHAR;                          {next input character}

begin {ECHOLINE}
    while not EOLN do                {read to the end of the line}
        begin
            READ (NEXTCHAR);                {read the next character}
            WRITE (NEXTCHAR)               {print the next character}
        end; {while}
    READLN;                        {advance to the next input line}
    WRITELN                         {start a new output line}
end; {ECHOLINE}

begin {ECHOFILE}
    while not EOF do                 {read to the end of the file}
        begin
            ECHOLINE;                      {echo an employee name}
            READLN (SALARY, DEPEND);           {read next line}
            WRITELN ('Salary is ', SALARY :9:2); {echo data read}
            WRITELN ('Number of dependents is ', DEPEND :2);
            WRITELN                            {skip a line}
        end {while}
end. {ECHOFILE}

Peter Liacouras
Salary is 56000.00
Number of dependents is 3

George Simpleton
Salary is 43500.00
Number of dependents is 0

Caryn Koffman
Salary is 15000.75
Number of dependents is 5
```

Fig. 4.16 Program to Echo Print a Data File

In procedure ECHOLINE, the while loop reads all characters on the
current input line. The loop repetition condition not EOLN is true as long
as the next character to be read is not the end-of-line mark.

The EOF function is used in the main program to detect whether or not
the end of file INPUT has been reached. This function returns a value of

true when all characters in the file have been read; otherwise, it returns a value of false. The loop repetition test not EOF evaluates to true as long as there are more characters to be read. This expression will evaluate to false when it is tested after the last value of DEPEND is read and printed.

EOLN FUNCTION (for batch input)

EOLN
or EOLN (*file-name*)

Interpretation: The EOLN function returns a value of true if the next character to be read is the end-of-line mark; otherwise, the value returned is false. The EOLN function may be used with other data files besides file INPUT. If another data file is used, its name must be specified as a parameter in the function reference.

EOF FUNCTION (for batch input)

EOF
or EOF (*file-name*)

Interpretation: The EOF function returns a value of true if all characters were read. If there are any more characters still to be processed, the value returned is false. The EOF function may be used with other data files besides file INPUT. If another data file is used, its name must be specified as a parameter in the function reference.
Note: If a read operation is attempted when the value of EOF is true, a "tried to read past end of input file" error occurs and the program stops.

The Importance of Advancing Past the End-of-Line Mark

When a value is being read into a type CHAR variable, only a single character is read regardless of what that character might be (e.g. letter, digit, blank, end-of-line mark, etc.). If the end-of-line mark is read into a type CHAR variable, it is stored as a blank character on most Pascal systems.

When a value is being read into a numeric variable (type REAL or IN-TEGER), Pascal skips over any leading blanks or end-of-line marks until it encounters a character that is neither a blank nor an end-of-line mark. This character must be a digit; if it is not, then a "non-digit found while reading INPUT" error results and the program stops. If the first character is a digit, then Pascal continues reading characters until it encounters a character that cannot be part of the number (often a blank or end-of-line mark).

It is easy to make an error when reading character data. Many problems are caused by not advancing past the end-of-line mark. As an example, we will replace the last READLN statement in the main program of Fig. 4.16 with

```
READ (SALARY, DEPEND)
```

and trace the execution of the program. The first three lines of the data file are shown below.

```
Peter Liacouras■
56000.00   3■
George Simpleton■
```

The first name (Peter Liacouras) is read and printed by ECHOLINE, and then values of SALARY (56000.00) and DEPEND (3) are read from the second line. Without a READLN, the second end-of-line mark is the next character to be read. When ECHOLINE is called to read the next name, the EOLN function evaluates to true immediately, and no characters are read. After returning from ECHOLINE, the READ statement above attempts to read new values for SALARY and DEPEND. However, the first character following the end-of-line mark is the letter G on the third input line. Since this is not a numeric character, an error results and program execution stops.

A modified version of the data file is shown below. All the data for each employee appears on the same line; the employee's name is at the end of the line.

```
56000.00 3Peter Liacouras■
43000.50 0George Simpleton■
15000.75 5Caryn Koffman■
```

The statements

```
READ (SALARY, DEPEND);
WRITELN ('Salary is ', SALARY :9:2);
WRITELN ('Number of dependents is ', DEPEND :2);
ECHOLINE
```

may be used to read and echo each line of this file. The first READ statement reads both numeric values (a real number and an integer) at the start of each data line; procedure ECHOLINE reads the rest of each line, starting with the first letter of the first name.

Self-check Exercises for Section 4.7

1. What would be the effect of changing READ to READLN in the program fragment above.
2. Rewrite procedure READCOLOR (Fig. 4.14) given the type declaration for COLOR:

```
type
    COLOR = (RED, GREEN, YELLOW, BLUE, BROWN, BLACK)
```

4.8 Case Study

The case study for Chapter 4 involves the manipulation of type INTEGER data. It also illustrates the use of BOOLEAN variables as program flags.

Testing for a Prime Number

Problem: Write a program that tests a positive integer to determine whether or not it is a prime number.

Discussion: A prime number is an integer that has no divisors other than 1 and itself. Examples of prime numbers are the integers 2, 3, 5, 7, 11, etc. Our program will either print a message indicating that its data value is a prime number, or it will print the smallest divisor of the number if it is not prime. The data requirements and the algorithm follow.

PROBLEM INPUTS

the number to be tested for a prime number (N : INTEGER)

PROBLEM OUTPUTS

the smallest divisor if N is not prime (FIRSTDIV : INTEGER)

Algorithm

1. Read in the number to be tested for a prime number.
2. Find the smallest divisor or determine that the number is prime.
3. Print a message that the number is prime or print its smallest divisor.

We will use the BOOLEAN variable PRIME as a program flag to indicate the result of step 2 as described below. The system structure chart is shown in Fig. 4.17.

ADDITIONAL PROGRAM VARIABLES

a program flag that will be set to TRUE if N is prime and will be set to FALSE if N is not prime (PRIME : BOOLEAN)

Step 3 of the algorithm is relatively simple and will be included in the main program. The refinement for step 3 follows.

Step 3 refinement

3.1 if N is prime then
       Print a message that N is prime
   else
       Print the first divisor of N

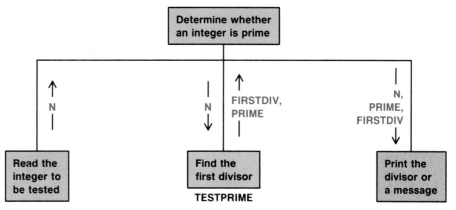

Fig. 4.17 Structure Chart for Prime Number Problem

Step 1 will be implemented by procedure READPOS (see Fig. 4.10) and is included with the main program shown in Fig. 4.18.

Procedure TESTPRIME determines whether or not N has any divisors other than 1 and itself. If N is an even integer, then it is divisible by 2. Therefore, 2 is the only even integer that can be prime, and 2 is the smallest divisor of all other even integers.

If N is an odd integer, then its only possible divisors are the odd integers less than N. In fact, it can be proven that a number is prime if it is not divisible by any odd integer less than or equal to its square root. These considerations form the basis for the algorithm shown next.

Algorithm for TESTPRIME

1. if N = 2 then
   2. N is a prime number
   else if N is even then
   3. 2 is the smallest divisor and N is not prime
   else
   4. Test each odd integer between 3 and the square root of N to see whether it is a divisor of N

The structure chart for procedure TESTPRIME is shown in Fig. 4.19. Step 4 is implemented as procedure TESTODD and is refined next. Procedure TESTPRIME (with nested procedure TESTODD) is shown in Fig. 4.20 and two sample runs are shown in Fig. 4.21.

Algorithm for TESTODD

1. Assume N is a prime number
2. Initialize FIRSTDIV to 3
3. while N is still prime and FIRSTDIV is a possible divisor do
      if FIRSTDIV is a divisor of N then
         N is not a prime number
      else
         Set FIRSTDIV to the next odd number

```
program PRIMENUMBER (INPUT, OUTPUT);

{Prints the smallest divisor (other than 1) of the integer N if a
 divisor exists; otherwise, prints a message that N is prime.      }

var
    N,                              {number being tested as a prime}
    FIRSTDIV : INTEGER;             {first divisor if found}
    PRIME : BOOLEAN;                {flag -- signals whether N is prime
                                     (TRUE) or not prime (FALSE)      }

procedure READPOS (var N {output} : INTEGER);

{Reads an integer greater than 1 into parameter N.}

var
    POSITIVE : BOOLEAN;             {program flag -- loop control}

begin {READPOS}
    POSITIVE := FALSE;              {assume N is not an integer > 1}

    {Keep reading until a valid number is read}
    while not POSITIVE do
        begin
            WRITE ('Enter an integer greater than 1: ');
            READLN (N);             {read next integer into N}
            POSITIVE := N > 1       {set POSITIVE to TRUE if N > 1}
        end {while}
end; {READPOS}

procedure TESTPRIME (N {input} : INTEGER;
                     var FIRSTDIV {output} : INTEGER;
                     var PRIME {output} : BOOLEAN);

{Finds first divisor (FIRSTDIV) of N if it exists. If a divisor
 is found sets PRIME to FALSE; otherwise, sets PRIME to TRUE.      }

begin {TESTPRIME}
    WRITELN ('Procedure TESTPRIME entered')
end; {TESTPRIME}

begin {PRIMENUMBER}
    {Enter an integer to test for a prime number}
    WRITELN ('Enter a number that you think is a prime number.');
    READPOS (N);

    {Find smallest divisor FIRSTDIV or determine that N is a
     prime. Set PRIME to indicate whether or not N is a prime
     number.                                                    }
    TESTPRIME (N, FIRSTDIV, PRIME);

    {Print first divisor or a message that N is prime}
    if PRIME then
        WRITELN (N :5, ' is a prime number')
    else
        WRITELN (FIRSTDIV :5, ' is the smallest divisor of ', N :5)
end. {PRIMENUMBER}
```

Fig. 4.18 Main Program to Test for a Prime Number

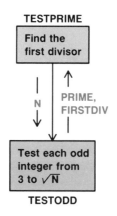

TESTPRIME

Find the
first divisor

N | PRIME,
FIRSTDIV

Test each odd
integer from
3 to $\sqrt{N}$

TESTODD

Fig. 4.19 Structure Chart for TESTPRIME

```
procedure TESTPRIME (N {input} : INTEGER;
                     var FIRSTDIV {output} : INTEGER;
                     var PRIME {output} : BOOLEAN);

{Finds first divisor (FIRSTDIV) of N if it exists. If a divisor
 is found sets PRIME to FALSE; otherwise, sets PRIME to TRUE. }

procedure TESTODD (N {input} : INTEGER;
                   var FIRSTDIV {output} : INTEGER;
                   var PRIME {output} : BOOLEAN);

{Tests each odd integer from 3 to the square root of N as a
 divisor of N. Returns the smallest divisor (FIRSTDIV) if one
 exists. Sets PRIME to FALSE if a divisor is found; otherwise,
 sets PRIME to TRUE.                                              }

begin {TESTODD}
    PRIME := TRUE;                          {assume that N is prime}

    {Test each odd integer from 3 to SQRT(N) as a possible divisor}
    FIRSTDIV := 3;                          {try 3 first}
    while PRIME and (FIRSTDIV <= SQRT(N)) do
        {invariant: FIRSTDIV is in range and N is not divisible by
         any integer less than FIRSTDIV}
        if N mod FIRSTDIV = 0 then
            PRIME := FALSE                  {FIRSTDIV is a divisor}
        else
            FIRSTDIV := FIRSTDIV + 2        {try next odd number}

    {assertion: PRIME is TRUE and FIRSTDIV > SQRT(N) or PRIME is
     FALSE and FIRSTDIV is the smallest divisor of N             }
end; {TESTODD}

begin {TESTPRIME}
    if N = 2 then
        PRIME := TRUE                       {2 is a prime number}
    else if not ODD(N) then
        begin {N is even}
            PRIME := FALSE;
```

```
        FIRSTDIV := 2                        {2 is first divisor}
    end {N is even}
 else {N is odd}
        TESTODD (N, FIRSTDIV, PRIME)         {Test for a divisor}
end; {TESTPRIME}
```

Fig. 4.20 Procedure TESTPRIME with TESTODD

```
Enter a number that you think is a prime number.
Enter an integer greater than 1: 23
   23 is a prime number

Enter a number that you think is a prime number.
Enter an integer greater than 1: 35
    5 is the smallest divisor of     35
```

Fig. 4.21 Two Sample Runs of the Prime Number Program

The program flag PRIME is set within TESTODD or TESTPRIME to indicate whether or not N is a prime number. In TESTODD, PRIME is initialized to TRUE before any candidate divisors are tested. If a divisor is found, PRIME is reset to FALSE and the while loop is exited. If no divisors are found, PRIME will remain TRUE and the loop is exited when FIRSTDIV becomes greater than SQRT(N). The values of PRIME and FIRSTDIV are returned to the main program.

PROGRAM STYLE

Using assertions as comments

In procedure TESTODD, a special kind of comment is used to describe the situation that exists before each repetition of the loop body (the comment beginning with invariant:) and the situation that exists after loop execution is complete (the comment beginning with assertion:). Both of these comments are *assertions* where an assertion is a BOOLEAN statement that must be true.

The BOOLEAN statement.

```
(PRIME and (FIRSTDIV > SQRT(N))
or (not PRIME and FIRSTDIV is the
smallest divisor of N)
```

must be true when the loop is exited. Our comment

```
{assertion: PRIME is TRUE and FIRSTDIV > SQRT(N)
or PRIME is FALSE and FIRSTDIV is the smallest
divisor of N}
```

is a less formal way of phrasing this assertion. The assertion within a loop is called a *loop invariant* and it must be true before each loop repetition begins.

Comments in earlier programs were used to describe the operations performed by a single statement or by a group of statements following the comment. However, an assertion describes a condition that must be true when the point of the assertion is reached.

Many computer scientists encourage the use of assertions as comments because they believe this makes it easier to verify that a program fragment does what it is supposed to do. We will use assertions when they help to make a program easier to understand.

Self-check Exercises for Section 4.8

1. Modify TESTPRIME to print all divisors of N where N may be any positive integer (odd or even). If N is prime, the only divisors printed should be 1 and N.

4.9 Common Programming Errors

A good deal of care is required when working with complicated expressions. It is easy to inadvertently omit parentheses or operators. If an operator or a single parenthesis is omitted, a syntax error will be detected. If a pair of parentheses is omitted then the expression, although syntactically correct, will compute the wrong value.

Sometimes it is beneficial to break a complicated expression into subexpressions that are separately assigned to *temporary variables*, and then to manipulate these temporary variables. For example, it is easier to write correctly the three assignment statements below

```
TEMP1 := SQRT(X + Y);
TEMP2 := 1 + TEMP1;
Z := TEMP1 / TEMP2;
```

than the single assignment statement

```
Z := SQRT(X + Y) / (1 + SQRT(X + Y))
```

that has the same effect. Using three assignment statements is also more efficient because the square root operation is performed only once; it is performed twice in the single assignment statement above.

Be careful to use the correct type of operator with each operand. The arithmetic operators can be used only with type INTEGER or REAL operands. The operator div can be used only with type INTEGER operands.

Only relational operators can be used with type CHAR data. The BOOL-EAN expression

```
3 <> '3'
```

is invalid as it compares an integer to a character value.

The BOOLEAN and and or operators can be used only with BOOLEAN expressions. In the expression

```
FLAG and (X <= Y)
```

the variable FLAG must be type BOOLEAN, and the parentheses shown are required; this statement would be invalid without the parentheses.

Syntax or run-time errors may occur when using the built-in functions. The argument of the functions CHR and ODD must be type INTEGER; the argument of the functions ORD, SUCC, and PRED must be an ordinal type (not type REAL).

If the argument of SQRT or LN is negative, an error will occur. The result of the functions SUCC, PRED, and CHR will be undefined for certain arguments.

In declaring your own enumerated types, make sure that a constant does not appear in more than one type declaration. However, the same constant may appear in more than one subrange declaration. Only the relational operators and the SUCC, PRED, and ORD functions may be used with programmer-defined enumerated types. Their values can neither be read nor written directly.

Subranges can be used to detect erroneous computations or bad data. If a value being assigned is outside the subrange, an "out of range" error occurs. The operations that can be performed on a variable with a subrange type are determined by the host type for that subrange.

When reading individual characters, remember that the carriage return character or end-of-line mark must be accounted for. Make sure to advance past this character using the READLN statement. If you don't skip this character you may cause a later error such as reading a character into a type REAL or INTEGER variable, or causing a loop to execute "forever".

4.10 Chapter Review

This chapter described how to write arithmetic expressions involving several operators and the built-in functions of Pascal. It also discussed the manipulation of other simple data types, including the standard types, BOOLEAN and CHAR, and the programmer-defined types, enumerated types and subranges. Several new operators were introduced, including the operators div and mod for manipulating integer data and the operators and, or, and not for manipulating BOOLEAN data.

The concept of an ordinal number was discussed and the functions PRED, SUCC, and ORD were introduced for the manipulation of ordinal data types. The function CHR, the inverse of ORD, was used to find the character corresponding to a given ordinal number.

In addition, the character-by-character reading of a string of input characters was illustrated. Two functions, EOLN (end of line) and EOF (end of file) were used to facilitate reading a batch data file. The EOLN function evaluates to true when the next character is the end-of-line mark; the EOF function evaluates to true when there are no more characters in the file.

New Pascal Statements

The new Pascal statements introduced in this chapter are described in Table 4.11.

Table 4.11 Summary of New Pascal Statements

Statement	Effect
Arithmetic assignment I := J div K + (L + 5) mod N	Adds the result (an integer) of J div K to the result (an integer) of (L + 5) mod N. J, K, L, and N must be type INTEGER.
Character assignment NEXTCH := 'A'	Assigns the character value 'A' to NEXTCH.
BOOLEAN assignment EVEN := not ODD(N)	If N is an even number, assigns the value TRUE to EVEN; otherwise, assigns the value FALSE to EVEN.
Enumerated type declaration type BCOLOR = (BLUE, BROWN, BLACK)	A data type BCOLOR is declared. The constants BLUE, BROWN, and BLACK are values of this type.
Subrange declaration type DIGIT = '0'..'9'	A subrange of the characters is declared. This subrange (named DIGIT) consists of the character values '0' through '9'.

Table 4.11 Summary of New Pascal Statements (*continued*)

Statement	Effect

Reading a batch file
```while not EOF do```
```   begin```
```   while not EOLN do```
```   begin```
```   READ (CH);```
```   WRITE(CH)```
```   end; {line}```
```   READLN; WRITELN```
```   end {file}```
	Reads every character in a batch input file into CH and echo prints it. READLN is used to skip over every end-of-line mark; WRITELN terminates each output line.

Review Questions

1. What are the advantages of data type INTEGER over data type REAL?
2. Given the following declarations, indicate the data type of the result of each expression below.

```
var
    X, Y : REAL;
    A, B : INTEGER;
```

```
                type
X * Y      _____
A * B      _____
B / Y      _____
B div A    _____
X / Y      _____
A mod B    _____
X mod Y    _____
```

3. Indicate the answer to the operations presented below.

```
11 mod 2    _____        11 div 2     _____
12 mod -3   _____        12 div -3    _____
27 mod 4    _____        -25 div 4    _____
18 mod 6    _____        -18 div -5   _____
```

4. What is the result of the expression (3 + 4 / 2) + 8 - 15 mod 4?
5. Write an assignment statement that rounds a real variable NUM1 to two digits after the decimal point leaving the result in NUM1.
6. Write a procedure called CHANGE that has one real parameter C and four integer parameters Q, D, N, and P. C will be a value parameter and the others will be variable parameters. The procedure will return the number of quarters in Q, the number of dimes in D, the number of

nickels in N, and the number of pennies in P to make change with the minimum number of coins. C (the change amount) is less than $1.00. Hint: Use the mod and div operators.

7. List and explain three computational errors that may occur in type REAL expressions.

8. Write an if statement that will write out TRUE or FALSE according to the following conditions: either FLAG is TRUE or COLOR is RED, or both MONEY is PLENTY and TIME is UP.

9. Write the statement to assign a value of TRUE to the BOOLEAN variable OVERTIME only if a worker's HOURS are greater than 40.

10. Write a BOOLEAN expression using the ORD function that will determine whether the ordinal value for 'a' is greater than the ordinal value for 'Z'. What is the value of this expression in the ASCII character set?

11. Write the Pascal statements necessary to enter an integer between 0 and 9 inclusive and convert it to an equivalent character value (e.g. 0 to '0', 1 to '1') to be stored in a character variable NUM.

12. Write a type declaration for FISCAL as the months from July through June. Declare the subrange WINTER as December through February. Declare the variable CURRENTMONTH as type FISCAL.

13. Enumerated data types can be directly read or written.   T   F

14. Assume that the data looks as follows, and write a Pascal procedure to echo print this file using standard input and output devices. Use the EOLN and EOF functions.

```
ID     AGE    YEARS OF SERVICE
FULL NAME
```

Sample Data

```
1243   23     5
Capone Boiles
```
employee 1

```
4321   35    11
Anthony George
```
employee 2

Programming Projects

1. A company has ten employees, many of whom work overtime (more than 40 hours) each week. They want a payroll program that reads the weekly time records (containing employee name, hourly rate (rate), and hours worked (hours) for each employee) and computes the gross salary and net pay as follows:

$$\text{gross} = \begin{cases} \text{hours} \times \text{rate (if hours } <= 40) \\ 1.5 \text{ rate(hours} - 40) + 40\text{rate (if hours } > 40) \end{cases}$$

$$\text{net} = \begin{cases} \text{gross (if gross } <= \$65) \\ \text{gross} - (15 + 0.45\text{gross}) \text{ (if gross } > \$65) \end{cases}$$

The program should print a five-column table listing each employee's name, hourly rate, hours worked, gross salary, and net pay. The total amount of the payroll should be printed at the end. It can be computed by summing the gross salaries for all employees. Test your program on the following data:

Name	Rate	Hours
IVORY HUNTER	3.50	35
TRACK STAR	4.50	40
SMOKEY BEAR	3.25	80
OSCAR GROUCH	6.80	10
THREE BEARS	1.50	16
POKEY PUPPY	2.65	25
FAT EDDIE	2.00	40
PUMPKIN PIE	2.65	35
SARA LEE	5.00	40
HUMAN ERASER	6.25	52

2. Write a program to read in a collection of integers and determine whether each is a prime number. Test your program with the four integers 7, 17, 35, 96. All numbers should be processed in one run.

3. Let n be a positive integer consisting of up to 10 digits, $d_{10}d_9 \ldots d_1$. Write a program to list in one column each of the digits in the number n. The rightmost digit d_1 should be listed at the top of the column. Hint: If n = 3704, what is the value of digit as computed according to the following formula?

$$\text{digit} = n \bmod 10$$

Test your program for values of n equal to 6, 3704, and 170498.

4. An integer N is divisible by 9 if the sum of its digits is divisible by 9. Use the algorithm developed for project 3) to determine whether or not the following numbers are divisible by 9.

```
N = 154368
N = 621594
N = 123456
```

5. Redo Project 4) by reading each digit of the number to be tested into the type CHAR variable DIGIT. Form the sum of the numeric values of the digits. Hint: The numeric value of DIGIT (type CHAR) is ORD(DIGIT) – ORD('0').

6. Each month a bank customer deposits $50 in a savings account. The account earns 6.5 percent interest, calculated on a quarterly basis (one-fourth of 6.5 percent each quarter). Write a program to compute the total investment, total amount in the account, and the interest accrued, for each of 120 months of a 10-year period. You may assume that the rate is applied to all funds in the account at the end of a quarter regardless of when the deposits were made.

Print all values accurate to two decimal places. The table printed by your program should begin as follows:

MONTH	INVESTMENT	NEW AMOUNT	INTEREST	TOTAL SAVINGS
1	50.00	50.00	0.00	50.00
2	100.00	100.00	0.00	100.00
3	150.00	150.00	2.44	152.44
4	200.00	202.44	0.00	202.44
5	250.00	252.44	0.00	252.44
6	300.00	302.44	4.91	307.35
7	350.00	357.35	0.00	357.35

7. The interest paid on a savings account is compounded daily. This means that if you start with STARTBAL dollars in the bank, then at the end of the first day you will have a balance of

$$STARTBAL \times (1 + rate/365)$$

dollars, where rate is the annual interest rate (0.10 if the annual rate is 10 percent). At the end of the second day, you will have

$$STARTBAL \times (1 + rate/365) \times (1 + rate/365)$$

dollars, and at the end of N days you will have

$$STARTBAL \times (1 + rate/365)^N$$

dollars. Write a program that processes a set of data records, each of which contains values for STARTBAL, rate, and N and computes the final account balance.

8. Compute the monthly payment and the total payment for a bank loan, given:

   1. the amount of the loan
   2. the duration of the loan in months
   3. the interest rate for the loan

   Your program should read in one record at a time (each containing a loan value, months value, and rate value), perform the required computation, and print the values of the loan, months, rate, and the monthly payment, and total payment.
   Test your program with at least the following data (and more if you want).

Loan	Months	Rate
16000	300	12.50
24000	360	13.50
30000	300	15.50
42000	360	14.50
22000	300	15.50
300000	240	15.25

   Notes:

   1. The formula for computing monthly payment is

$$\text{monthly} = \left[\frac{\text{rate}}{1200} \times \left(1 + \frac{\text{rate}}{1200} \right)^{\text{months}} \times \text{loan} \right] \Bigg/ \left[\left(1 + \frac{\text{rate}}{1200} \right)^{\text{months}} - 1 \right]$$

2. The formula for computing the total payment is

$$\text{total} = \text{monthly} \times \text{months}$$

Also, you may find it helpful to introduce additional variables defined below in order to simplify the computation of the monthly payment. You can print the values of ratem and expm to see whether your program's computations are accurate.

$$\text{ratem} = \text{rate}/1200$$
$$\text{expm} = 1 + \text{ratem}$$

Hint: You will need a loop to multiply expm by itself months times.

9. The rate of decay of a radioactive isotope is given in terms of its half-life, "H", the time lapse required for the isotope to decay to one-half of its original mass. The isotope strontium 90 (Sr^{90}) has a half-life of 28 years. Compute and print in table form the amount of this isotope remaining after each year for 50 years, given the initial presence of 50.0 grams. The amount of Sr^{90} remaining can be computed by using the following formula:

$$r = \text{amount} \times C^{(\text{Year}/H)}$$

where "amount" is 50.0 grams as the initial amount, "C" is expressed as $e^{-0.693}$ ($e = 2.71828$), "year" is the number of years elapsed, and "H" is the half-life of the isotope in years.

10. Write a program that will scan a sentence and replace all multiple occurrences of a blank with a single occurrence of a blank.

11. Write a program that will read a sentence and print each word entered on a separate line followed by the number of letters in that word.

12. An employee time card is represented as one long string of characters. Write a program using procedures that processes a collection of these strings.
   a. Compute gross pay using the formula:

$$\text{gross} = \text{regular hours} \times \text{rate} + \text{overtime hours} \times 1.5\text{rate}$$

   b. Compute net pay by subtracting the following deductions:

   federal tax = .14(gross − 13 × dependents)
   social security = 0.052 × gross
   city tax = 4% of gross if employee works in the city
   union dues = 6.75% of gross for union member

The data string for each employee has the form:

Positions	Data
1–10	Employee last name
11–20	Employee first name
21	Contains a C for City Office or S for Suburban Office
22	Contains a U (union) or N (non-union)

23–26	Employee identification number
27	blank
28–29	Number of regular hours (a whole number)
30	blank
31–36	Hourly rate (dollars and cents)
37	blank
38–39	Number of dependents
40	blank
41–42	Number of overtime hours (a whole number)

13. Generate a table indicating the rainfall for the city of Bedrock which can be used to compare the average rainfall for the city with the previous year's rainfall. Assume a maximum monthly rainfall of 15 inches per month when setting up the limits for the table. In addition provide some summary statistics which will indicate: (1) annual rainfall for last year, (2) average annual rainfall, and (3) the difference between the two. The input data will consist of 12 pairs of numbers. The first number in each pair will be the average rainfall for a month and the second number will be what fell the previous year. The first data pair will represent January, second will be February, and so forth. The output should resemble the following:

```
January      !****************
             !%%%%%%%%%%%%%%%%%%%%
             !
February     !***********
             !%%%%%%%%%
             !             .
                           .
                           .
             !----1----2----3----4----5 ...

   * - average rainfall for a given month
   % - previous year's rainfall for a given month
```

The data for the chart above begins with: 3.2 4   (for January)
                                          2.2 1.6 (for February)

14. Read a series of integer numbers and determine the following information about each:

   a. Is it a multiple of 7, 11, or 13?
   b. Is the sum of the digits odd or even?
   c. What is the square root value (if positive)
   d. Is it a prime number?

   You should have at least four procedures and label all output. Some sample input data might be: 104 3773 13 121 77 30751

15. Whatsamata U. offers a service to its faculty in computing grades at the end of each semester. A program will process 3 weighted test scores and will calculate a student's average and letter grade (based on 90–100 is an A, 80–89 is a B, etc.).

Write a program to provide this valuable service. The data will consist of the three test weights followed by three test scores and a student ID number (4 digits) for each student. You should calculate the weighted average for each student and the corresponding grade. This information should be printed along with the initial three test scores. The weighted average for each student is equal to:

$$\text{weight1} \times \text{grade1} + \text{weight2} \times \text{grade2} + \text{weight3} \times \text{grade3}$$

For summary statistics print the "highest average", "lowest average", "average of the averages", and "total number of students processed"
Sample data might be:

```
.35    .25    .40
100    76     88     1014
 96    91     99     2222
 45    15     65     3051
 35    88     86     4067
```

16. As paymaster for the Badwater Brewery, you must determine each worker's gross pay based on the following information:

a. Each person receives a base pay of $800 per month
b. A percentage of pay is added depending upon the following three categories:
   Category 1: Job Classification

Classification	Percent to add
1	5%
2	10%
3	20%

(For example if the employee had a classification of 2 then 10% of $800 or $80 would be added to the base salary.)

Category 2: Years of service
If service is from 0 to 10 add 5% else add 5% plus 1% for every year over 10. For example, 12 years service would earn 7% of $800.
   Category 3: Education

Amount of education	Percent to add
1 - High school	0%
2 - Junior college	5%
3 - University	12%
4 - Graduate school	20%

To calculate someone's wages use the base and calculate the additional amounts for the 3 categories and print out the gross pay. Each set of data will consist of the following information: Employee ID (4 digits), job classification, years of service, and education code. Sample input for an employee might be: 1041 3 12 4.

17. The Fibonacci numbers are defined to be the set of positive integers such that each successive number is equal to the sum of the previous two. The first two numbers in the set are both one. Below is a list of the first seven Fibonacci numbers.

1, 1, 2, 3, 5, 8, 13

Write a program that prints out the first 15 Fibonacci numbers.
Note: How big of an integer (MAXINT) can your system store? This sum can approach that limit quite quickly.

5

More Control Statements

5.1   The case Statement
5.2   Set Values in Decisions
5.3   The General for Statement
5.4   The repeat Statement
5.5   Nested Loops
5.6   User-defined Functions
5.7   Case Studies
5.8   Common Programming Errors
5.9   Chapter Review

In this chapter, more control statements are introduced. We are already familiar with how to use the if statement to implement decisions; the case statement provides us with another way to select among several alternative tasks.

We take another look at the for statement and describe its general form. A new conditional looping statement, the repeat statement is introduced. The use of nested loops is also described.

Until now the procedure was used exclusively to implement separate program modules. We have used the standard Pascal functions to simplify computations. In this chapter, we see how to declare and use our own functions to implement separate modules that return a single result.

5.1 The case Statement

The case statement is used in Pascal to select one of several alternatives. It is especially useful when the selection is based on the value of a single variable or a simple expression. This variable or expression must be an ordinal type.

Example 5.1 The case statement

```
case MOMORDAD of
    'M', 'm' : PRINTMOM;
    'D', 'd' : PRINTDAD
end {case MOMORDAD}
```

has the same behavior as the if statement below when the character stored in MOMORDAD is one of the four letters listed.

```
if (MOMORDAD = 'M') or (MOMORDAD = 'm') then
    PRINTMOM
else if (MOMORDAD = 'D') or (MOMORDAD = 'd') then
    PRINTDAD
```

The procedure (call) statement that is executed depends on the value of the variable MOMORDAD (type CHAR). MOMORDAD is called the *case selector*.

Example 5.2 Procedure PRINTDAY in Fig. 5.1 uses a case statement to print a string indicating the value of a variable whose type is the enumerated type DAY (see Example 4.23).

```
procedure PRINTDAY (DAYVALUE {input} : DAY);

{Prints a string indicating the value of DAYVALUE.}

begin
    case DAYVALUE of
        SUNDAY     : WRITELN ('Sunday');
        MONDAY     : WRITELN ('Monday');
        TUESDAY    : WRITELN ('Tuesday');
        WEDNESDAY  : WRITELN ('Wednesday');
        THURSDAY   : WRITELN ('Thursday');
        FRIDAY     : WRITELN ('Friday');
        SATURDAY   : WRITELN ('Saturday')
    end {case DAYVALUE}
end; {PRINTDAY}
```

Fig. 5.1 Procedure PRINTDAY

Seven different alternatives are shown in Fig. 5.1; the value of DAYVALUE (type DAY) is used to select one of these for execution. The seven possible values of DAYVALUE are listed as *case labels* to the left of each colon; the task for that case label follows the colon. After the WRITELN statement selected is executed, the procedure is exited.

One common error is using a string such as 'SUNDAY' as a case label. Only ordinal values (i.e., characters or integers) or ordinal constants (i.e., identifiers) may appear in case labels.

Example 5.3   The case statement below could be used to compute the numeric value of the hexadecimal digit stored in HEXDIGIT (type CHAR). In the hexadecimal number systems, the valid "digits" are the character values '0' through '9' and 'A' through 'F'. The character values '0' through '9' have the numeric value 0 through 9; the character values 'A' through 'F' have the numeric values 11 (for 'A') through 15 (for 'F').

```
case HEXDIGIT of
   '0','1','2','3','4','5','6','7','8','9' :
                  DECIMAL := ORD(HEXDIGIT) - ORD('0');
   'A','B','C','D','E','F' :
                  DECIMAL := ORD(HEXDIGIT) - ORD('A') + 10
end {case HEXDIGIT}
```

This case statement causes the first assignment statement to be executed when HEXDIGIT is one of the digits '0' through '9'; the second assignment statement is executed when HEXDIGIT is one of the letters 'A' through 'F'. If HEXDIGIT is not one of the characters listed, a "case expression out of range" error occurs, and program execution stops. Note that we cannot abbreviate either case label list as a subrange (e.g. 'A'..'F' or '0'..'9' is an invalid case label).

Example 5.4   The case statement in Fig. 5.2 may be used in a student transcript program that computes grade point average (GPA). For each case shown, the total points (POINTS) earned towards the GPA increases by an amount based on the letter grade (GRADE); the total credits earned towards graduation (GRADCREDITS) increases by 1 if the course is passed. Assuming that the letters are in consecutive order, the expression

```
ORD('A') - ORD(GRADE) + 4
```

evaluates to 4 when GRADE is 'A', 3 when GRADE is 'B', etc.

Fig. 5.2 The case Statement for Student Transcript Program

```
case GRADE of
   'A', 'B', 'C', 'D' :
         begin
            POINTS := POINTS + (ORD('A') - ORD(GRADE) + 4);
            GRADCREDITS := GRADCREDITS + 1
         end;
   'P' : GRADCREDITS := GRADCREDITS + 1;
   'F', 'I', 'W' :
end {case GRADE}
```

In Fig. 5.2, a grade of A through D earns a variable number of points (4 for an A, 3 for a B, etc.) and 1 graduation credit, a grade of P earns 1 graduation credit, and a grade of F, I, or W earns neither graduation credits nor points. The last case must be listed to prevent a "case expression out of range" error even though nothing happens when GRADE assumes one of these values.

The case statement is described in the next display.

CASE STATEMENT

```
case selector of
     label₁ : statement₁;
     label₂ : statement₂;
               .
               .
               .
     labelₙ : statementₙ
end {case}
```

Interpretation: The *selector* (an expression) is evaluated and compared to each of the case labels. Each label is a list of one or more possible values for the *selector*, separated by commas. Only one $statement_i$ will be executed; if the *selector* value is listed in $label_i$, then $statement_i$ is executed. Control is next passed to the first statement following the end {case}. Each $statement_i$ may be a single or compound Pascal statement.

Note 1: If the value of the *selector* is not listed in any case label, an error message is printed and program execution is terminated.

Note 2: A particular *selector* value may appear in, at most, one case label.

Note 3: The type of each *selector* value must correspond to the type of the *selector* expression.

Note 4: Any ordinal data type is permitted as the *selector* type.

As indicated in Note 1 of the case statement display, an error message is printed if the *selector* value does not match a *case label*. Consequently, all possible values of the *selector* must be listed in exactly one *case label*. If no action is to be performed for a particular *case label*, then there should be no statement for that case.

Each $statement_i$ except the last one should be followed by a semicolon; the last *statement* is followed by the word end. Note that there is no corresponding begin for a case statement.

As mentioned earlier, a "case expression out of range" error occurs when the case selector value is not present. On many Pascal systems, the language has been extended to allow the use of an otherwise clause to prevent this error from occurring. The use of this clause is described in Appendix B4.

Comparison of Nested if Statements and the case Statement

Nested if statements are more general than the case statement and always may be used to implement a multiple alternative decision. The case statement, however, is more readable and should be used whenever practical. The case statement cannot be used when the selection criteria involve a type REAL expression.

The case statement should be used when each case label contains a reasonably sized list of values. Nested if statements should be used when the number of possible values for the case selector is large (e.g. more than ten). Nested if statements should also be used when a "case value out of range" error is possible because of a large number of values that require no action to be taken.

Self-check Exercises for Section 5.1

1. Rewrite the case statement in Fig. 5.1 as a nested if statement.
2. If type COLOR is described as the list of identifers (RED, GREEN, BLUE, BROWN, YELLOW), write a case statement that assigns a value to EYES (type COLOR) given that the first two letters of the color name are stored in LETTER1 and LETTER2.

5.2 Set Values in Decisions

This section will introduce the use of set values and the set membership operator in. Sets will be discussed in detail in Chapter 8.

Many of you have studied sets in a mathematics course. In mathematics, a set is represented by a list of *set elements* enclosed in curly braces (square brackets in Pascal). For example, the set of odd integers from 1 through 9 is written as {1, 3, 5, 7, 9} in mathematics and as [1, 3, 5, 7, 9] in Pascal. The order in which elements are listed in a set is immaterial; the Pascal set [9, 5, 7, 1, 3] is equivalent to the set above.

Example 5.5 The case statement in Example 5.3 is rewritten as a nested if statement below.

```
if HEXDIGIT in ['0' .. '9'] then
   DECIMAL := ORD(HEXDIGIT) - ORD('0')
else if HEXDIGIT in ['A', 'B', 'C', 'D', 'E', 'F'] then
   DECIMAL := ORD(HEXDIGIT) - ORD('A') + 10
else
   WRITELN (HEXDIGIT, ' is an invalid Hexadecimal digit.')
```

This statement uses the set ['A', 'B', 'C', 'D', 'E', 'F'] to represent the letters 'A' through 'F'. The set membership operator in is used to test whether or not HEXDIGIT is one of the elements of this set. The BOOLEAN expression

```
HEXDIGIT in ['A', 'B', 'C', 'D', 'E', 'F']
```

evaluates to TRUE if HEXDIGIT is one of the set elements listed; otherwise, the BOOLEAN expression evaluates to FALSE.

This if statement has one advantage over the case statement shown earlier. If the value of HEXDIGIT is not one of the characters listed in the case labels, a "case expression out of range error" occurs and program execution stops. For the if statement, if an invalid character is stored in HEXDIGIT, an error message is printed (by the WRITELN statement) and program execution continues.

The BOOLEAN expression

```
HEXDIGIT in ['0'..'9']
```

uses subrange notation to describe a set whose elements are the digits '0' through '9'. It is possible to use a combination of these techniques as shown below to describe the set of characters that may appear in a real number (the digits, $+$, $-$, E, and the decimal point).

```
['0'..'9', '+', '-', 'E', '.']
```

SET VALUES

[*list-of-elements*]

Interpretation: A set is defined whose set elements are the *list-of-elements* enclosed in brackets. Each set element (an expression) must have the same ordinal type. Commas are used to separate elements in the *list-of-elements*. A group of consecutive elements may be specified using subrange notation (i.e., *minval* .. *maxval* where *minval* and *maxval* are expressions of the same ordinal type and ORD (*minval*) is less than ORD(*maxval*)).

SET MEMBERSHIP OPERATOR IN

element in [*list-of-elements*]

Interpretation: The set membership operator in is used to describe a condition that evaluates to true when *element* is included in the *list-of-elements*; otherwise, the condition evaluates to false. The data type of *element* must be the same ordinal type as the set elements.

Example 5.6   Sets are often used to prevent a "case expression out of range" error. The case statement below is executed in the same way as the nested if shown in the previous example.

```
if HEXDIGIT in ['0'..'9', 'A'..'F'] then
    case HEXDIGIT of
        '0','1','2','3','4','5','6','7','8','9' :
                        DECIMAL := ORD(HEXDIGIT) - ORD('0');
        'A','B','C','D','E','F' :
                        DECIMAL := ORD(HEXDIGIT) - ORD('A') + 10
    end {case HEXDIGIT}
else
    WRITELN (HEXDIGIT, ' is an invalid Hexadecimal digit.')
```

Now the case statement is executed only when HEXDIGIT is valid; an error message is printed when HEXDIGIT is invalid.

Self-check Exercises for Section 5.2

1. Write a set that consists of the special characters that are used for punctuation in Pascal or to denote operators.
2. Write an if statement that prints a message indicating whether or not NEXTCH (type CHAR) is a vowel. Use a set.
3. Write a multiple alternative decision statement that categorizes NEXTCH as a vowel, as any letter, as a digit, or as any special character as defined in exercise 1 above. Your statement should print the category.

5.3 The General for Statement

We have used the for statement to implement counting loops in which the loop control variable (type INTEGER) was always incremented by one. The for statement is more general than the examples we have seen so far and, in fact, the loop control variable may be any ordinal type. It is also possible for the loop control variable to decrease (rather than increase) in value after each loop repetition.

FOR STATEMENT

for *loop-control-variable* := *initial* to *final* do
  loop-body

Interpretation: The *loop-body* is executed once for each value of the *loop-control-variable* (*lcv*) between *initial* and *final* inclusive. *Initial* and *final* may be constants, variables, or expressions; however, *lcv*, *initial*, and *final* must all be the same ordinal type.
Note 1: The value of *lcv* may not be modified in the *loop-body*.
Note 2: The value of *final* is computed once, just before loop entry. Any subsequent changes in the variables that comprise the *final*

---

expression will not change the number of times the loop body is repeated.

Note 3: Upon exit from the `for` loop, the value of *lcv* is considered undefined.

Note 4: If *initial* is greater than *final*, the *loop-body* will not be executed at all.

Note 5: The alternate form

> for *loop-control-variable* := *initial* downto *final* do
>   *loop-body*

may be used to implement a loop that counts down from a larger *initial* value to a smaller *final* value. An example is

```
for I := 5 downto -5 do
   WRITE (I)
```

In the downto form, the *loop-body* will never be executed if *initial* is less than *final*.

Note 6: The variable *lcv* should be declared locally.

Example 5.7   The `for` loop below prints each uppercase letter and its ordinal number. The `for` loop control variable, NEXT, must be type CHAR.

```
for NEXT := 'A' to 'Z' do
   WRITELN (NEXT, ORD(NEXT))
```

Example 5.8   The `for` loop below prints the ordinal number corresponding to each value of the enumerated type DAY (see Example 4.23) from MONDAY to FRIDAY; the integer values from 1 through 5 are printed. The loop control variable TODAY must be declared as type DAY.

```
for TODAY := MONDAY to FRIDAY do
   WRITE (ORD(TODAY) :2)
```

Example 5.9   The `for` loop below may be used to compute and print the Fahrenheit temperature corresponding to each integer Celsius (C) temperature from 5 degrees C downto −10 degrees C (see Example 3.11).

```
for CELSIUS := 5 downto -10 do
   begin
      FAHRENHEIT := 1.8 * CELSIUS + 32;
      WRITELN (CELSIUS :10, FAHRENHEIT :15:1)
   end {for CELSIUS}
```

Self-check Exercises for Section 5.3

1. Write a `for` statement that prints each digit character and its ordinal number on a separate output line.

5.4 The repeat Statement

The repeat statement is used to specify a loop that is repeated until its repetition condition becomes true. Such a loop is called a *repeat-until loop*.

Example 5.10   Both program segments in Fig. 5.3 print the powers of two between one and 1000.

```
POWER := 1;                        POWER := 1;
while POWER < 1000 do              repeat
  begin                               WRITE (POWER :5);
      WRITE (POWER :5);               POWER := POWER * 2
      POWER := POWER * 2          until POWER >= 1000
  end {while}
```

Fig. 5.3 While (left) and repeat (right) Statements

The test used in the repeat-until loop (POWER >= 1000) is the *complement* of the test used in the while loop. The repeat-until loop is repeated until the value of POWER is greater than or equal to 1000. Since loop repetition stops when the condition is true, the test is called a *loop termination test* rather than a loop repetition test. (Note that there is no need for a begin-end bracket around the loop body because the reserved words repeat and until perform this function.)

REPEAT STATEMENT (repeat-until loop)

```
repeat
    loop-body
until termination-condition
```

Interpretation: After each execution of the *loop-body*, the *termination-condition* is evaluated. If the *termination-condition* is true, loop exit occurs and the next program statement is executed. If the *termination-condition* is false, the *loop-body* is repeated.

Example 5.11   A repeat statement is often used to ensure that a data value is in range. For example, some interactive programs print a "menu" of choices from which the program user selects a program operation. The menu for a statistics program might look as follows.

```
1. Compute an average
2. Compute a standard deviation
3. Find the median
4. Find the smallest and largest value
5. Plot the data

Enter your choice (1 through 5):
```

The menu can be displayed using a sequence of WRITELN statements. Procedure GETCHOICE below continues to print the prompt 'Enter your choice...' and to read an integer value until a valid data item is entered. MAXCHOICE (value 5) is a constant.

```
procedure GETCHOICE (var CHOICE {output} : INTEGER);

{Reads a value between 1 and MAXCHOICE (a constant) into CHOICE.}

begin {GETCHOICE}
   repeat
      WRITE ('Enter your choice (1 through ', MAXCHOICE :1, '): ');
      READLN (CHOICE)
   until CHOICE in [1..MAXCHOICE]
end; {GETCHOICE}
```

One important difference between the two conditional loops (while and repeat-until) is that the repeat-until loop is always executed at least once since the *loop-termination-condition* is evaluated after execution of the *loop-body*. This limits the usefulness of the repeat-until loop because many times we would like to have the option of not executing the *loop-body* even once. This is particularly true in loops used for reading a batch data file as illustrated next.

Example 5.12   Procedure GETCHAR in Fig. 5.4 returns the next input character that is not a blank.

```
procedure GETCHAR (var NEXTCHAR {output} : CHAR);

{Returns the next input character that is not a blank. Result
is not defined when the input file contains all blanks or is
empty.                                                         }

const
   BLANK = ' ';                 {character being skipped}

begin {GETCHAR}
   if not EOF then              {find first non-blank}
      repeat
         READ (NEXTCHAR)
      until EOF or (NEXTCHAR <> BLANK)

   {assertion: at end of input file or NEXTCHAR is non-blank.}
end; {GETCHAR}
```

Fig. 5.4 Procedure GETCHAR with a repeat-until Loop.

If the input file is not empty (not EOF is true), when GETCHAR is called, the repeat statement is executed. Characters will be read into NEXTCHAR until NEXTCHAR contains a non-blank character, or the end of the input file is reached. If the input file is empty (not EOF is false) when GETCHAR is called, the repeat statement is skipped.

It is interesting to consider what happens when the if statement is omitted and the body of GETCHAR consists of the repeat statement only.

The procedure works perfectly well as long as the input file is not empty when GETCHAR is called. If the input file is empty, the first READ operation causes a "tried to read past end of input file" error.

Complementing a Condition Involving and, or

Procedure GETCHAR is rewritten in Fig. 5.5 using a while loop. The loop repetition test

    not EOF and (NEXTCHAR = BLANK)

is the complement of the loop termination test

    EOF or (NEXTCHAR <> BLANK)

used in Fig. 5.4.

```
procedure GETCHAR (var NEXTCHAR {output} : CHAR);

{Returns the next input character that is not a blank. Result is
not defined when the input file contains all blanks or is empty.}

const
    BLANK = ' ';                             {character being skipped}

begin {GETCHAR}
    NEXTCHAR := BLANK;                  {make sure a character is read}
    while not EOF and (NEXTCHAR = BLANK) do
        READ (NEXTCHAR)                      {find first non-blank}

    {assertion: at end of input file or NEXTCHAR is non-blank}
end; {GETCHAR}
```

Fig. 5.5 Procedure GETCHAR with a while loop

In Fig. 5.5, the assignment statement

    NEXTCHAR := BLANK;   {make sure a character is read}

is necessary to ensure that at least one character is read if the input file is not empty. Otherwise, if the actual parameter corresponding to NEXTCHAR contains a non-blank character when GETCHAR is called, the READ statement is skipped.

To complement a compound BOOLEAN expression involving the and, or operators, write the complement of each individual BOOLEAN expression and change each and to or and each or to and. Table 5.1 shows the complements of some BOOLEAN expressions.

In Table 5.1, FLAG is a BOOLEAN variable and X, Y, M, and N are type INTEGER. In the complement of the first condition, the operator > is changed to <= and the operator and is changed to or. The last condition is complemented by simply inserting the BOOLEAN operator not in front

Table 5.1 Complements of BOOLEAN Expresions

Condition	Complement
(X > Y) and (X > 0)	(X <= Y) or (X <= 0)
not EOLN or (X <= Y)	EOLN and (X > Y)
(N mod M = 0) and FLAG	(N mod M <> 0) or not FLAG
NEXT in ['A','E','I','O','U']	not (NEXT in ['A','E','I','O','U'])

of the expression. Any BOOLEAN expression can be complemented in this way.

The last complement shows the correct way to write "NEXT is not a vowel" in Pascal. A common error is writing an expression of the form NEXT not in [...], which contains two consecutive operators (not in).

Review of for, while, and repeat Loops

There are three kinds of loops in Pascal: for, while, and repeat. The for loop should be used as a counting loop, i.e. a loop where the number of iterations required can be determined at the beginning of loop execution. The loop control variable of a for loop must belong to an ordinal type.

The while and repeat loops are both conditional loops; i.e. the number of iterations is dependent on whether the value of a condition is true or false. The while loop is repeated as long as its loop repetition condition is true; the repeat loop is repeated until its loop termination condition becomes true.

It is easy to rewrite a while loop as a repeat loop (or vice versa) by simply complementing the condition. However, a repeat loop will always be executed at least once whereas a while or for loop body may be skipped entirely. For this reason a while loop is preferred over a repeat loop unless you are certain that at least one loop iteration must always be performed.

As an illustration of the three loop forms, a simple counting loop is written in Fig. 5.6. (The comment represents the loop body.) The for loop is the best to use in this situation. The repeat loop is nested in an if statement to prevent it from being executed when STARTVALUE is greater than STOPVALUE.

In Fig. 5.6, COUNT, STARTVALUE, and STOPVALUE must all be the same ordinal type. The successor function (SUCC) is used in both the while and repeat loops to update the loop control variable COUNT, although COUNT := COUNT + 1 is preferred if COUNT is type INTEGER. COUNT will be equal to SUCC(STOPVALUE) after the while or repeat loops are executed; COUNT will be equal to STARTVALUE if these loops are skipped. The value of COUNT is considered undefined after execution of the for loop.

```
for COUNT := STARTVALUE to STOPVALUE do
    begin
        { . . . . . . . . .}
    end { for }
```

```
COUNT := STARTVALUE
while COUNT <= STOPVALUE do
    begin
        { . . . . . . . . .}
        COUNT := SUCC(COUNT)
    end { while }
```

```
COUNT := STARTVALUE;
if STARTVALUE <= STOPVALUE then
    repeat
        { . . . . . . . . .}
        COUNT := SUCC(COUNT)
    until COUNT > STOPVALUE
```

Fig. 5.6 Comparison of Three Loop Forms

Self-check Exercises for Section 5.4

1. Write the complements of the conditions below.
   a. (X <= Y) and (X <> 15)
   b. (X <= Y) and (X <> 15) or (Z = 7.5)
   c. (X <> 15) or (Z = 7.5) and (X <= Y)
   d. FLAG or (X <> 15.7)
   e. not FLAG and (NEXTCH in ['A' .. 'H'])
2. The while statement below can be rewritten as a for statement if a new variable is introduced for loop control. Rewrite it as a for statement and a repeat statement.

```
NUM := 10;
while NUM <= 100 do
    begin
        WRITELN (NUM);
        NUM := NUM + 10
    end {while}
```

3. Write a procedure that reads the next character that is not a letter or a digit from an input line. Write two versions: using repeat and using while.

5.5 Nested Loops

In this section, we examine nested loops. We have seen examples of nested loops in our programming so far; however, the nesting was not apparent because the inner loop was contained in a procedure. Nested loops consist of an outer loop with one or more inner loops. Each time the outer loop is repeated, the inner loops are reentered, their loop control parameters are reevaluated, and all required iterations are performed.

Example 5.13   Fig. 5.7 shows a sample run of a program with two nested `for` loops. The outer loop is repeated three times (for I equals 1, 2, 3). Each time the outer loop is repeated, the statement

```
WRITELN ('OUTER' :5, I :7);
```

is executed, the inner loop is entered, and its loop control variable J is reset to 1. The number of times the inner loop is repeated depends on the value of I. Each time the inner loop is repeated, the string 'INNER' and both loop control variables are printed.

```
program NESTLOOP (OUTPUT);

{Illustrates nested for loops.}

type
    SMALLINT = 1..3;

var
    I, J : SMALLINT;                    {loop control variables}
begin {NESTLOOP}
    WRITELN ('I' :12, 'J' :5);             {Print heading}
    for I := 1 to 3 do
        begin {outer loop}
            WRITELN ('OUTER' :5, I :7);
            for J := 1 to I do
                WRITELN ('INNER' :7, I :5, J :5)
        end {outer loop}
end. {NESTLOOP}
```

```
             I     J
OUTER        1
   INNER     1     1
OUTER        2
   INNER     2     1
   INNER     2     2
OUTER        3
   INNER     3     1
   INNER     3     2
   INNER     3     3
```

Fig. 5.7 Nested for Loop Program

In Fig. 5.7, the outer loop control variable I is used as the loop parameter that determines the number of repetitions of the inner loop. This is perfectly valid; however, it is not valid to use the same variable as the loop control variable of both an outer and inner `for` loop in the same nest.

Example 5.14   Program TRIANGLE in Fig. 5.8 prints an isosceles triangle. The program contains an outer loop (loop control variable ROW) and two inner loops. Each time the outer loop is repeated, two inner loops are executed. The first inner loop prints the leading blank spaces; the second inner loop prints one or more asterisks.

```
program TRIANGLE  (OUTPUT);

{Draws an isosceles triangle.}

const
    NUMLINES = 5;                       {number of rows in triangle}
    BLANK = ' '; STAR = '*';            {output characters}

var
    ROW,                    {loop control for outer loop}
    LEADBLANKS,             {loop control for first inner loop}
    COUNTSTARS  : INTEGER;  {loop control for second inner loop}

begin {TRIANGLE}
    for ROW := 1 to NUMLINES do
        begin                                      {draw each row}
            for LEADBLANKS := NUMLINES - ROW downto 1 do
                WRITE (BLANK);             {print leading blanks}
            for COUNTSTARS := 1 to 2 * ROW - 1 do
                WRITE (STAR);                      {print asterisks}
            WRITELN                                {terminate line}
        end {for ROW}
end. {TRIANGLE}
        *
       ***
      *****
     *******
    *********
```

Fig. 5.8 Isosceles Triangle Program

The outer loop is repeated 5 times; the number of repetitions performed by the inner loops is based on the value of ROW. Table 5.2 lists the values of the loop control parameters for each value of ROW. As shown in Table 5.2, 4 blanks and 1 asterisk are printed when ROW is 1, 3 blanks and 3 asterisks are printed when ROW is 2, etc. When ROW is 5, the first inner loop is skipped and 9 (2 * 5 - 1) asterisks are printed.

Table 5.2 Inner Loop Control Parameters

ROW	LEADBLANKS	COUNTSTARS
1	4 downto 1	1 to 1
2	3 downto 1	1 to 3
3	2 downto 1	1 to 5
4	1 downto 1	1 to 7
5	0 downto 1	1 to 9

Example 5.15 The program in Fig. 5.9 prints the addition table for integer values between 0 and 9 (type SMALLINT). For example, the table line beginning with the digit 9 shows the result of adding to 9 each of the digits 0 through 9. The initial for loop prints the table heading, which is the operator + and the list of digits from 0 through 9.

The nested for loops are used to print the table body. The outer for loop (loop control variable ADDEND1) first prints the current value of

Fig. 5.9 Printing an Addition Table

```
program ADDTABLE (OUTPUT);

{Prints an addition table.}

const
    MAXDIGIT = 9;                    {largest digit}

type
    SMALLINT = 0..MAXDIGIT;   {range of digits}

var
    ADDEND1,                         {first addend}
    ADDEND2 : SMALLINT;              {second addend}
    SUM     : INTEGER;               {sum of addends}

begin {ADDTABLE}
    {Print the table heading.}
    WRITE ('+');
    for ADDEND2 := 0 to MAXDIGIT do
        WRITE (ADDEND2 :3);     {print each digit in heading}
    WRITELN;                              {terminate heading}

    {Print the table body.}
    for ADDEND1 := 0 to MAXDIGIT do
        begin                      {print each row of the table}
            WRITE (ADDEND1 :1);           {identify first addend}
            for ADDEND2 := 0 to MAXDIGIT do
                begin
                    SUM := ADDEND1 + ADDEND2;
                    WRITE (SUM :3)           {print sum of addends}
                end; {for ADDEND2}
            WRITELN                          {terminate table row}
        end {for ADDEND1}
end. {ADDTABLE}
```

+	0	1	2	3	4	5	6	7	8	9
0	0	1	2	3	4	5	6	7	8	9
1	1	2	3	4	5	6	7	8	9	10
2	2	3	4	5	6	7	8	9	10	11
3	3	4	5	6	7	8	9	10	11	12
4	4	5	6	7	8	9	10	11	12	13
5	5	6	7	8	9	10	11	12	13	14
6	6	7	8	9	10	11	12	13	14	15
7	7	8	9	10	11	12	13	14	15	16
8	8	9	10	11	12	13	14	15	16	17
9	9	10	11	12	13	14	15	16	17	18

ADDEND1. In the inner for loop, each value of ADDEND2 (0 through 9) is added to ADDEND1 and the individual sums are printed. Each time the outer loop is repeated 10 additions are performed; a total of 100 sums are printed.

Example 5.16 The program in Fig. 5.10 contains a pair of nested while loops that may be used to read and echo print the data on an existing data file. The inner loop reads and echos a line of the file. The outer loop is repeated as long as there are more lines to read.

```
program ECHOTEXT (INPUT, OUTPUT);

{Reads and echos an existing data file.}

var
     NEXTCHAR : CHAR;                   {each character in the file}

begin {ECHOTEXT}
    while not EOF do
        begin                          {echo each line}
            while NOT EOLN do
                begin                  {echo each character}
                    READ (NEXTCHAR);
                    WRITE (NEXTCHAR)
                end; {of line}
            READLN;                    {skip end-of-line mark}
            WRITELN                    {terminate output line}
        end {of file}
end. {ECHOTEXT}
```

Fig. 5.10 Reading and Echoing a File

It is interesting to contemplate the effect of omitting the statement

```
READLN;                                {skip end-of-line mark}
```

Exit from the inner loop occurs when the end-of-line mark at the end of the first line is the next character to be read (not EOLN is false). The outer loop is repeated because there is more data on the file (not EOF is true); however, the inner loop is then skipped because the next character is still the end-of-line mark. An endless loop will result because the outer loop is repeated again, the inner loop skipped again, ad infinitum. If your program reads lines of character data, remember to use the READLN statement to skip over each end-of-line mark.

Self-check Exercises for Section 5.5

1. Write a program that prints the multiplication table. Use separate procedures to print the table heading and table body.
2. Show the output printed by the nested loops below.

```
        for I := 1 to 2 do
            begin
                WRITELN ('OUTER' :5, I :5);
                for J := 1 to 3 do
                    WRITELN ('INNER' :7, I :3, J :3);
                for K := 2 downto 1 do
                    WRITELN ('INNER' :7, I :3, K :3)
            end; {for I}
```

3. Write a nest of loops that causes the output below to be printed.

```
1
1  2
1  2  3
1  2  3  4
1  2  3
1  2
1
```

5.6 User-defined Functions

In the last chapter we introduced some of the functions that are part of Pascal such as ABS, SQRT, ORD. We can also declare our own functions in much the same way that procedures are declared. In fact, a function may be looked upon as a special type of procedure—a procedure that returns exactly one result. Generally, the parameters of a function are value parameters which cannot be modified by the function execution.

Example 5.17   Function POWERS in Fig. 5.11 raises its first parameter, X, to the integer power indicated by its second parameter, N. This is accomplished by multiplying X by itself N times and accumulating the product in PRODUCT.

Fig. 5.11 The Function POWERS

```
function POWERS (X : REAL; N : INTEGER) : REAL;

{Computes the value of X raised to the power N.}

var
    PRODUCT : REAL;                     {the accumulated product}
    COUNT   : INTEGER;                  {loop control variable}

begin {POWERS}
    PRODUCT := 1.0;                     {initialize PRODUCT}
    for COUNT := 1 to ABS(N) do
        PRODUCT := PRODUCT * X ;        {multiply X by itself N times}

    {Define function result}
    if N >= 0 then
        POWERS := PRODUCT               {function result when N >= 0}
    else
        POWERS := 1.0 / PRODUCT         {function result when N < 0}
end; {POWERS}
```

The *function designator* ABS(N) (absolute value of N) ensures that the required number of multiplications are performed even when N is negative.

The function heading

```
function POWERS (X : REAL; N : INTEGER) : REAL;
```

identifies the function name and its parameter list. The formal parameters for a function are generally input parameters so we have not commented them as such. A type identifier after the parameter list indicates the type of the result returned by the function. The result may be any previously-defined simple data type including REAL, INTEGER, BOOLEAN, CHAR, an enumerated type, or a subrange.

Unlike a procedure which returns a result by modifying a variable parameter, a function result is defined by assigning a value to the function name. In Fig. 5.11 if N is positive, the result to be returned is defined by the assignment statement

```
POWERS := PRODUCT
```

If N is negative, the result to be returned is defined by the assignment statement

```
POWERS := 1.0 / PRODUCT
```

You must be careful when using a function name inside its function declaration. A function name should not normally appear in an expression inside the function. For example, the assignment statement

```
POWERS := POWERS * X
```

would be illegal inside function POWERS.

FUNCTION DECLARATION

```
function fname (formal-parameters) : result-type;
local-declaration-section
begin {fname}
    function body
end; {fname}
```

Interpretation: The function *fname* is declared. The list of formal parameters is enclosed in parentheses. The data type of the function result is indicated by the identifier *result-type*.

Any identifiers declared in the *local-declaration-section* are defined only during the execution of the function.

The *function body* describes the data manipulation to be performed by the function. At least one statement that gives a value to *fname* must be executed each time the function is called. The last value giv-

---

en to *fname* is returned as the function result upon completion of the *function body*. This value replaces the function reference in the expression that calls the function.

Note 1: The identifier *result-type* must be the name of a standard data type (BOOLEAN, INTEGER, REAL, or CHAR), a previously-defined enumerated type, a subrange type, or a pointer type (described in Chapter 10).

Note 2: If there are no parameters, the *formal-parameters* and parentheses should be omitted.

PROGRAM STYLE

Checking special cases

What happens in function POWERS if the value of N happens to be zero? If N is zero, the assignment statement

```
PRODUCT := 1.0;
```

is executed and the for loop is skipped. In this case the if statement causes a value of 1.0 to be assigned correctly as the function result.

Often a procedure or function will fail for special cases such as this. It is important to identify special cases and verify that they are handled properly.

Function Designator

A user-defined function is called in the same way as a standard Pascal function—by referencing it in an expression. The assignment statement below computes the actual amount, AMOUNT, in a savings account after N days have passed; DEPOSIT is the initial amount deposited at a daily interest rate of DAILYRATE.

```
AMOUNT := DEPOSIT * POWERS(1 + DAILYRATE, N)
```

This statement is derived from the formula

$$amount = deposit \times (1 + dailyrate)^n$$

The *function designator*

```
POWERS(1 + DAILYRATE, N)
```

calls function POWERS to raise the expression 1 + DAILYRATE to the power N. After execution of the function body, the function result replaces the function designator in the *calling expression*; this result is then multiplied by the value of DEPOSIT and the product is stored in AMOUNT.

FUNCTION DESIGNATOR

fname (*actual-parameters*)

Interpretation: The function *fname* is executed, and its result replaces the function designator. During the function execution, the first actual parameter is associated with the first formal parameter, the second actual parameter with the second formal parameter, etc.
Note: The actual parameters are separated by commas. There should be the same number of actual and formal parameters. Each actual parameter that is an expression is evaluated when *fname* is called; this value is assigned to the corresponding formal parameter. Each actual parameter must be assignment-compatible with its corresponding formal parameter. If there are no formal parameters, the *actual-parameters* and enclosing parentheses should be omitted.

Functions with Nonnumeric Results

A function can return a value belonging to any of the standard types, an enumerated type, a subrange type, or a pointer type (discussed in Chapter 10). In this section we provide examples of functions with different result types.

Example 5.18 Recall that the Pascal READ procedure cannot read data into a variable whose type is an enumerated type. A program can read the first letter or two of an identifier and then use this character data to determine what value should be stored. Function DAYCONVERT in Fig. 5.12 returns a value of enumerated type DAY (see Example 4.23). The parameters CHAR1 and CHAR2 represent the first two letters in the day name.

Fig. 5.12 Function DAYCONVERT

```
function DAYCONVERT (CHAR1, CHAR2 : CHAR) : DAY;

{Returns the day value beginning with the letters
 CHAR1, CHAR2.                                    }

begin {DAYCONVERT}
   case CHAR1 of
      'M', 'm' : DAYCONVERT := MONDAY;
      'W', 'w' : DAYCONVERT := WEDNESDAY;
      'F', 'f' : DAYCONVERT := FRIDAY;
      'S', 's' : case CHAR2 of
                    'A', 'a' : DAYCONVERT := SATURDAY;
                    'U', 'u' : DAYCONVERT := SUNDAY
                 end; {case CHAR2}
      'T', 't' : case CHAR2 of
                    'U', 'u' : DAYCONVERT := TUESDAY;
                    'H', 'h' : DAYCONVERT := THURSDAY
                 end {case CHAR2}
   end {case CHAR1}
end; {DAYCONVERT}
```

The statements below may be used to assign a value to the variable TODAY (type DAY) using function DAYCONVERT.

```
WRITE ('Enter the first two letters of the day name: ');
READLN (CHAR1, CHAR2);
TODAY := DAYCONVERT(CHAR1, CHAR2)
```

Example 5.19   Figure 5.13 shows a function that may be used to determine the number of days in any month of the twentieth century. The data types MONTH, YEARS, and DAYS are defined as follows.

```
type
    MONTH = (JAN, FEB, MAR, APR, MAY, JUN,
             JUL, AUG, SEP, OCT, NOV, DEC);
    YEARS = 1900..1999;
    DAYS  = 1..31;
```

```
function DAYSINMONTH (CURMONTH : MONTH; THISYEAR : YEARS) : DAYS;

{Determines the number of days in a given month and year.}

begin {DAYSINMONTH}
   case CURMONTH of
       APR, JUN, SEP, NOV : DAYSINMONTH := 30;
       JAN, MAR, MAY, JUL, AUG, OCT, DEC : DAYSINMONTH := 31;
       FEB : if THISYEAR mod 4 = 0 then
                 DAYSINMONTH := 29                          {leap year}
             else
                 DAYSINMONTH := 28
   end {case}
end; {DAYSINMONTH}
```

Fig. 5.13 Function DAYSINMONTH

The `if` statement following case label FEB has a condition that is true when THISYEAR is divisible by 4. This condition is true every leap year. An example of a function designator that calls the function DAYSINMONTH is

```
DAYSINMONTH(MAY, 1942)
```

Example 5.20   BOOLEAN functions are often used to make BOOLEAN expressions more readable. The BOOLEAN function UPPERCASE in Fig. 5.14 determines whether its argument is an uppercase letter (returns TRUE) or not (returns FALSE). This function can be used to simplify the writing of if statements that require a test for an uppercase letter. A similar function called LOWERCASE is left as an exercise. (See Exercise 5 at the end of this section.)

Procedure GETLETTER (see Fig. 5.15) returns the next input character that is a letter; the loop is repeated until either an uppercase or lowercase

```
function UPPERCASE (CH : CHAR) : BOOLEAN;

{Returns a result of TRUE if CH is an uppercase letter;
 otherwise, returns a result of FALSE.                    }

begin {UPPERCASE}
   UPPERCASE := CH in ['A'..'Z']
end; {UPPERCASE}
```

Fig. 5.14 Function UPPERCASE

letter is read. It uses functions UPPERCASE and LOWERCASE to test each input character.

```
procedure GETLETTER (var CH {output} : CHAR);

{Returns the next input character that is a letter.
 Result is not defined when there are no letters in
 the input file.                                         }

begin {GETLETTER}
   if not EOF then                      {find first letter}
      repeat
         READ (CH)
      until EOF or UPPERCASE(CH) or LOWERCASE(CH)

   {assertion: at end of input file or CH is a letter.}
end; {GETLETTER}
```

Fig. 5.15 Procedure GETLETTER

Function CHANGECASE (see Fig. 5.16) returns a result that is type CHAR. It changes an uppercase letter to lowercase and vice versa. If its argument CH is an uppercase letter, the assignment statement

```
CHANGECASE := CHR(ORD(CH) - ORD('A') + ORD('a'))
```

is executed. If CH is 'C' and the letters are in consecutive order, then the argument of the function CHR is 2 + ORD('a') and the value 'c' is assigned to CHANGECASE. The analysis is similar when CH is a lowercase letter.

PROGRAM STYLE

When to use a function instead of a procedure

All the function examples shown in this section have the property that they transform one or more input values into a single output. A variety of output types were illustrated: REAL, CHAR, BOOLEAN, DAY.

A procedure should be used when more than one result is to be returned by a program module. Generally a function is used only when

a single result is to be returned. Since a function does not usually return a result by modifying its parameters, the parameters of a function are usually value parameters.

```
function CHANGECASE (CH : CHAR) : CHAR;

{Changes the case of CH when CH is a letter — Uses the
 BOOLEAN functions UPPERCASE and LOWERCASE to test CH.}

begin {CHANGECASE}
    if UPPERCASE(CH) then                {Change to lowercase}
       CHANGECASE := CHR(ORD(CH) - ORD('A') + ORD('a'))
    else if LOWERCASE(CH) then           {Change to uppercase}
       CHANGECASE := CHR(ORD(CH) - ORD('a') + ORD('A'))
    else
       CHANGECASE := CH                  {CH is not a letter}
end; {CHANGECASE}
```

Fig. 5.16 Function CHANGECASE

Self-check Exercises for Section 5.6

1. Write a function that computes the cube of any number.
2. Write a function that computes the tuition owed for a specified number of credit hours taken at a university. Assume that the charge per
   credit is $100 for up to 12 credit hours and that a flat fee of $1000 is
   charged when more than 12 credits are taken.
3. Function POWERS in Fig. 5.11 works perfectly well for an integer exponent; however, the exponent cannot be type REAL. Write a new function that will handle type REAL exponents. Hint: Use the LN and EXP
   functions of Pascal.
4. Write a program that uses function POWERS to compute and print a table showing the powers of two.
5. Write function LOWERCASE.

5.7 Case Studies

In this section we present two problems that illustrate most of the concepts discussed in the last two chapters. The problems involve: analyzing
a passage of text and printing a check.

**Text
Analyzer
Program**

We will begin with a problem that makes use of nested while loops and
the EOLN and EOF functions to process textual data. It also illustrates the
use of sets and program flags.

Problem: Write a program that analyzes a text passage and determines
the number of sentences in the text, the average number of words per sentence, and the average number of letters per word.

Discussion: Every character of the text should be read and echoed. The three special characters **. ! ?** indicate the end of a sentence; the three special characters **, ; :** and the blank and end-of-line mark indicate the end of a word. The data requirements follow.

PROBLEM INPUTS

the text passage (a batch file)

PROBLEM OUTPUTS

count of sentences (SENTCOUNT : INTEGER)
average number of words per sentence (AVEWORD : INTEGER)
average number of letters per word (AVELETTER : INTEGER)

It is necessary to maintain a count of words and letters in order to compute the averages requested. Descriptions of these variables and the algorithm follow.

ADDITIONAL PROGRAM VARIABLES

count of words (WORDCOUNT : INTEGER)
count of letters (LETTERCOUNT : INTEGER)

Algorithm

1. Read the text and count the number of letters, words, and sentences.
2. Compute the average number of words per sentence and letters per word.
3. Print the count of sentences and the two averages.

The system structure chart is shown in Fig. 5.17. Step 1 is implemented as procedure COUNTCHARS; steps 2 and 3 are included in the main program body shown in Fig. 5.18.

Fig. 5.17 Structure Chart for Text Analyzer Program

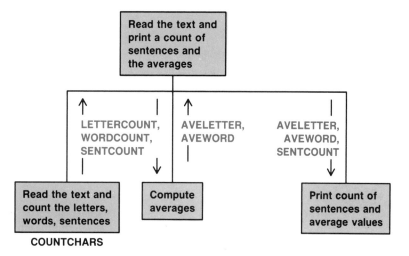

```
program TEXTANALYZE (INPUT, OUTPUT);

{Analyzes a body of text printing the number of sentences, the
 average number of words per sentence, and the average number
 of letters per word.                                          }

var
    SENTCOUNT,              {count of sentences}
    WORDCOUNT,              {count of words}
    LETTERCOUNT,            {count of letters}
    AVEWORD,                {average number of words/sentence}
    AVELETTER : INTEGER;    {average number of letters/words}

procedure COUNTCHARS (var SENTCOUNT {output},
                          WORDCOUNT {output},
                          LETTERCOUNT {output} : INTEGER);

{Reads the text and counts the number of sentences, words, and
 letters in the input text.                                    }

begin {COUNTCHARS}
    WRITELN ('Procedure COUNTCHARS entered.');
    SENTCOUNT := 10;  WORDCOUNT := 100;  LETTERCOUNT := 1000
end; {COUNTCHARS}

begin {TEXTANALYZE}
    {Read the text and count the letters, words, and sentences.}
    COUNTCHARS (SENTCOUNT, WORDCOUNT, LETTERCOUNT);

    {Find the averages.}
    AVEWORD := ROUND(WORDCOUNT / SENTCOUNT);
    AVELETTER := ROUND(LETTERCOUNT / WORDCOUNT);

    {Print the sentence count and the averages.}
    WRITELN;
    WRITELN ('There are ', SENTCOUNT :2, ' sentences with an');
    WRITELN ('average of ', AVEWORD :2, ' words / sentence');
    WRITELN ('and ', AVELETTER :2, ' letters / word.')
end. {TEXTANALYZE}
```

Fig. 5.18 Main Program for Text Analysis with a Stub for COUNTCHARS

In most text processing situations, it is easier to process the text on a line-by-line basis. The algorithm for procedure COUNTCHARS follows.

Algorithm for Procedure COUNTCHARS

1. Initialize all counters to zero
2. while there are more lines to process do
    3. Process each line of the text

Procedure COUNTCHARS calls procedure SCANLINE to perform step 3 above. SCANLINE uses procedure CHECKTERM to categorize each character as a terminator, letter, or other character. The structure chart for COUNTCHARS is shown in Fig. 5.19.

Procedure SCANLINE reads and echoes each character of the text. It uses procedure CHECKTERM to check for the occurrence of one or more of

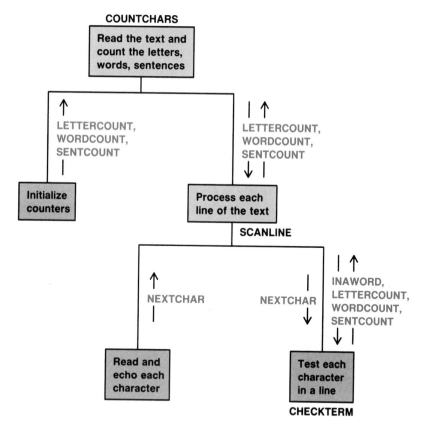

Fig. 5.19 Structure Chart for COUNTCHARS

the special terminator characters mentioned earlier. Both the sentence count and word count should be incremented by one whenever a sentence terminator is read. The count of words should be incremented by one whenever a word terminator is read or the end-of-line mark is reached.

The count of letters is incremented for each character that is a letter. All other characters are only echo printed.

If a sequence of consecutive terminator characters occurs, only the first in the sequence affects the counter values; e.g. if a period is followed by two blanks then the count of words and sentences are increased by one when the period is read but not the blanks. A program flag (INAWORD) is used to indicate whether the last character processed is part of a word (INAWORD is TRUE) or a terminator (INAWORD is FALSE).

The local variables declared in procedure SCANLINE and the algorithm for SCANLINE follow.

LOCAL VARIABLES FOR SCANLINE

each letter read from the text (NEXTCHAR : CHAR)
program flag that indicates whether or not the last character processed
was part of a word or a terminator (INAWORD : BOOLEAN)

Algorithm for Procedure SCANLINE

1. Set INAWORD to FALSE.
2. while the end of the input line is not reached do
   3. Read and echo the next character (NEXTCHAR).
   4. Categorize the next character as a terminator, letter, or other character. Update INAWORD and the counters.
5. if the end-of-line mark follows a word then
   6. Increment the count of words.
7. Skip over the end-of-line mark and terminate the output line.

Step 4 above is performed by procedure CHECKTERM. The algorithm for CHECKTERM follows. Procedures COUNTCHARS, SCANLINE, and CHECK-TERM are shown in Fig. 5.20 and a sample run is shown in Fig. 5.21.

Algorithm for CHECKTERM

1. if NEXTCHAR is an initial sentence terminator then
   2. Increment count of words and sentences and set INAWORD to FALSE.
   else if NEXTCHAR is an initial word terminator then
   3. Increment the count of words and set INAWORD to FALSE.
   else if NEXTCHAR is a letter then
   4. Increment the count of letters and set INAWORD to TRUE.

```
procedure COUNTCHARS (var SENTCOUNT {output},
                          WORDCOUNT {output},
                          LETTERCOUNT {output} : INTEGER);

{Reads the text and counts the number of sentences, words,
 and letters in the input text. Uses procedure SCANLINE.  }

procedure SCANLINE (var SENTCOUNT {input/output},
                        WORDCOUNT {input/output},
                        LETTERCOUNT {input/output} : INTEGER);

{Adds the count of sentences, words, and letters on the
 current input line to the counts being accumulated. Uses
 CHECKTERM.                                                }

var
    NEXTCHAR : CHAR;     {each input character}
    INAWORD : BOOLEAN;    {flag indicating whether last character
                 was in a word (TRUE) or was a terminator (FALSE)}

procedure CHECKTERM (NEXTCHAR {input} : CHAR;
                        var SENTCOUNT {input/output},
                            WORDCOUNT {input/output},
                            LETTERCOUNT {input/output} : INTEGER;
                        var INAWORD {input/output} : BOOLEAN);

{Checks whether current character is a terminator or letter or
 other character. Increments counters and updates INAWORD.    }

begin {CHECKTERM}
    if (NEXTCHAR in ['.', '!', '?']) and INAWORD then
```

```
            begin                                      {initial sentence terminator}
                SENTCOUNT := SENTCOUNT + 1;
                WORDCOUNT := WORDCOUNT + 1;
                INAWORD := FALSE                           {no longer in a word}
            end
        else if (NEXTCHAR in [',', ';', ':', ' ']) and INAWORD then
            begin                                        {initial word terminator}
                WORDCOUNT := WORDCOUNT + 1;
                INAWORD := FALSE                           {no longer in a word}
            end
        else if NEXTCHAR in ['A'..'Z', 'a'..'z'] then
            begin                                                      {letter}
                LETTERCOUNT := LETTERCOUNT + 1;
                INAWORD := TRUE                              {now in a word}
            end
end; {CHECKTERM}

begin {SCANLINE}
    INAWORD := FALSE;          {Assume not in a word at start of line}
    while not EOLN do
        begin
            READ (NEXTCHAR);                      {read next character}
            WRITE (NEXTCHAR);                     {echo next character}

            {Check whether NEXTCHAR is a terminator or letter.}
            CHECKTERM (NEXTCHAR, SENTCOUNT, WORDCOUNT,
                       LETTERCOUNT, INAWORD)
        end; {while not EOLN}

    {assertion: at end-of-line mark}
    if INAWORD then
        WORDCOUNT := WORDCOUNT + 1;              {process word terminator}
    READLN;                                       {skip end-of-line mark}
    WRITELN                                        {terminate output line}
end; {SCANLINE}

begin {COUNTCHARS}
    {Initialize counters to zero}
    SENTCOUNT := 0;  WORDCOUNT := 0;  LETTERCOUNT := 0;

    {Process each character in the text}
    while not EOF do
        SCANLINE (SENTCOUNT, WORDCOUNT, LETTERCOUNT)
end; {COUNTCHARS}
```

Fig. 5.20 Procedure COUNTCHARS with Nested Procedures SCANLINE and CHECKTERM

```
I never saw a purple cow.
I never hope to see one.
But, I can tell you anyhow:
I'd rather see than be one!

There are 3 sentences with an
average of 8 words / sentence
and 3 letters / word.
```

Fig. 5.21 Sample Run of Text Analysis Program

The next problem illustrates the use of the case statement. It also uses two subrange types.

Problem: As part of a check writing program, it would be desirable to have a procedure that writes a check amount in words. Some examples of the desired procedure output are shown below.

Amount	Output
43.55	forty three dollars and fifty five cents
62.05	sixty two dollars and five cents
15.20	fifteen dollars and twenty cents
0.95	zero dollars and ninety five cents
35.00	thirty five dollars and zero cents

Discussion: The procedure must separate the check amount into two integers, DOLLARS and CENTS. Once this is done, DOLLARS can be printed followed by the string ' dollars and ', the value of CENTS, and the string ' cents'. For the sake of simplicity, we will restrict the check writing procedure to amounts less than $100. A description of the procedure data requirements and algorithm follow.

PROBLEM INPUTS

check amount as a real number (CHECK : REAL)

PROBLEM OUTPUTS

description of check amount in words

LOCAL VARIABLES FOR PRINTCHECK

dollar amount (DOLLARS : 0..99)
number of cents (CENTS : 0..99)

Algorithm for PRINTCHECK

1. if check amount is invalid then
   2. Print an error message
   else
   3. Separate check amount into DOLLARS and CENTS
   4. Print DOLLARS in words
   5. Print ' dollars and '
   6. Print CENTS in words
   7. Print ' cents'

The structure chart for procedure PRINTCHECK is shown in Fig. 5.22. Procedure PETTYCASH is called twice: first to print the value of DOLLARS in words and then to print the value of CENTS in words. Procedure PRINTCHECK is shown in Fig. 5.23 with a stub for procedure PETTYCASH.

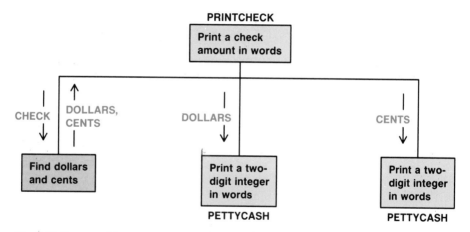

Fig. 5.22 Structure Chart for Procedure PRINTCHECK

Fig. 5.23 Procedure PRINTCHECK with a Stub for PETTYCASH

```pascal
procedure PRINTCHECK (CHECK {input} : REAL);

{Prints a check amount in words. Uses procedure PETTYCASH
to first print the dollars amount and then the cents
amount.                                                      }

type
    SMALLINT = 0..99;              {range of check amount}

var
    DOLLARS,                       {the dollar amount}
    CENTS  : SMALLINT;             {the cents amount}

procedure PETTYCASH (AMOUNT : SMALLINT);

{Prints an integer AMOUNT less than 100 in words.}

begin {PETTYCASH}
    WRITELN ('Procedure PETTYCASH entered.')
end; {PETTYCASH}

begin {PRINTCHECK}
    if (CHECK < 0) or (CHECK > 99.99) then
        WRITELN ('Check amount ', CHECK, ' is invalid.')
    else
        begin {valid amount}
            DOLLARS := TRUNC(CHECK);   {get amount in dollars}
            CENTS := ROUND(100 * (CHECK - DOLLARS));
                                       {get amount in cents}
            PETTYCASH (DOLLARS);       {print dollar amount}
            WRITE (' dollars and ');
            PETTYCASH (CENTS);         {print cents amount}
            WRITELN (' cents')
        end {valid amount}
end; {PRINTCHECK}
```

In Fig. 5.23 the assignment statements

```
DOLLARS := TRUNC(CHECK);     {get amount in dollars}
CENTS := ROUND(100 * (CHECK - DOLLARS));
                             {get amount in cents}
```

are used to determine the value of DOLLARS and CENTS (e.g. if CHECK is 95.63 then DOLLARS is 95 and CENTS is 63). The ROUND function ensures that an integer value is assigned to CENTS.

Procedure PETTYCASH prints an integer value less than 100 in words. Its parameter value is separated into a 10's digit (stored in TENS) and a units digit (stored in UNITS). Once this separation is performed the two digits are printed in words. The data requirements and algorithm for PETTYCASH follow.

PROCEDURE INPUTS

a number less than 100 (AMOUNT : 0..99)

PROCEDURE OUTPUTS

a two digit integer printed in words

LOCAL VARIABLES FOR PETTYCASH

the tens digit (TENS : 0..9)
the units digit (UNITS : 0..9)

Algorithm for PETTYCASH

1. If AMOUNT = 0 then
    2. Print 'zero'
   else
    3. Separate AMOUNT into TENS and UNITS
    4. Print TENS and UNITS in words

The structure chart is shown in Fig. 5.24. Step 4 above is performed by procedure PRINT2DIGITS which calls procedure PRINTADIGIT to print the word corresponding to a single digit value.

Procedure PRINT2DIGITS must be able to print amounts that are less than 10 (TENS is 0), in the teens (TENS is 1), and above (TENS >= 2). The algorithm below should handle all cases. Procedure PETTYCASH and nested procedures PRINT2DIGITS and PRINTADIGIT are shown in Fig. 5.25.

Algorithm for PRINT2DIGITS

1. case TENS of
    0 : print UNITS value
    1 : select and print a string based on the UNITS value
    2 : print 'twenty' followed by the UNITS value
    3 : print 'thirty' followed by the UNITS value
    4 : print 'forty' followed by the UNITS value

5 : print 'fifty' followed by the UNITS value
6, 7, 8, 9 : print the TENS value
            print 'ty '
            print the UNITS value

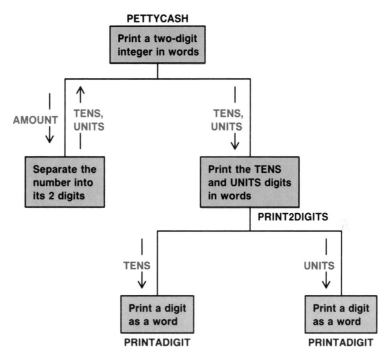

Fig. 5.24 Structure Chart for PETTYCASH

```
procedure PETTYCASH (AMOUNT {input} : SMALLINT);

{Prints an AMOUNT less than 100 in words. Uses
 PRINT2DIGITS.                                       }

type
   DIGIT = 0..9;

var
   TENS,                    {tens digit}
   UNITS : DIGIT;           {units digit}

procedure PRINT2DIGITS (TENS, UNITS {input} : DIGIT);

{Prints the 2 digits of a number in words. Uses
 PRINTADIGIT.                                        }

procedure PRINTADIGIT (INDIGIT {input} : DIGIT);

{Prints a single digit number (INDIGIT) as a word.}
```

```
   begin {PRINTADIGIT}
      case INDIGIT of
         0 : {Print nothing};
         1 : WRITE ('one');
         2 : WRITE ('two');
         3 : WRITE ('three');
         4 : WRITE ('four');
         5 : WRITE ('five');
         6 : WRITE ('six');
         7 : WRITE ('seven');
         8 : WRITE ('eight');
         9 : WRITE ('nine')
      end {case}
end; {PRINTADIGIT}

   begin {PRINT2DIGITS}
      case TENS of
         0 : PRINTADIGIT (UNITS);    {Print units digit only}
         1 : case UNITS of           {Print the special case teens}
               0 : WRITE ('ten');
               1 : WRITE ('eleven');
               2 : WRITE ('twelve');
               3 : WRITE ('thirteen');
               5 : WRITE ('fifteen');
               4, 6, 7, 8, 9 : begin {Print ...teen}
                                  PRINTADIGIT (UNITS);
                                  if UNITS <> 8 then
                                     WRITE ('t');
                                  WRITE ('een')
                               end {print ...teen}
            end; {case UNITS}
         2 : begin                              {print twenty ...}
               WRITE ('twenty ');
               PRINTADIGIT (UNITS)
            end; {2}
         3 : begin                              {print thirty ... }
               WRITE ('thirty ');
               PRINTADIGIT (UNITS)
            end; {3}
         4 : begin                              {print forty ... }
               WRITE ('forty ');
               PRINTADIGIT (UNITS)
            end; {4}
         5 : begin                              {print fifty ... }
               WRITE ('fifty ');
               PRINTADIGIT (UNITS)
            end; {5}
         6, 7, 8, 9 : begin                     {print ...ty ... }
                         PRINTADIGIT (TENS);
                         if TENS <> 8 then
                            WRITE ('t');
                         WRITE ('y');
                         PRINTADIGIT (UNITS)
                      end {6, 7, 8, 9}
      end {case TENS}
   end; {PRINT2DIGITS}
```

```
begin {PETTYCASH}
   if AMOUNT = 0 then
      WRITE ('zero')
   else
      begin {nonzero amount}
         TENS  := AMOUNT div 10;                    {Get tens digit}
         UNITS := AMOUNT mod 10;                     {Get units digit}
         PRINT2DIGITS (TENS, UNITS){Print the 2 digits in words}
      end {nonzero amount}
end; {PETTYCASH}
```

Fig. 5.25 Procedure PETTYCASH with Nested Procedures PRINT2DIGITS and PRINTADIGIT

In the above procedures, the subrange SMALLINT is declared in
PRINTCHECK and is used as the data type of the formal parameter for
PETTYCASH. Similarly the subrange DIGIT is declared in PETTYCASH
and is used as the data type of the formal parameters for PRINT2DIGITS.
The data type INTEGER is the host type for both of these subranges; they
are used to limit the range of parameter values that may be passed to
each procedure.

A common error in a programmer-defined data type is to specify the
type declaration in the procedure header statement. The procedure header
statement

```
procedure PRINT2DIGITS (TENS, UNITS {input} : 0..9);
```

causes a syntax error because a parameter type must be an identifier, not
a subrange.

Self-check Exercises for Section 5.7

1. Verify that the assignment statements in PETTYCASH that assign values to TENS and UNITS are correct.

5.8 Common Programming Errors

When using a case statement, make sure the case selector and labels
are of the same ordinal type. Remember that only lists of ordinal values
may be used as case labels and that no value may appear in more than
one case label. If the selector evaluates to a value not listed in any of the
case labels, an error occurs and your program stops. Be sure to insert the
end {case}; there is no matching begin.

The main problem in using a repeat statement is the possibility of too
many loop repetitions. A repeat-until loop can execute forever if its
conditional test remains false. This is indicated by a program exceeding
its time limit or running out of input data. Remember that a repeat-
until loop is always executed at least once because the loop termination
test follows the loop body.

Be sure to trace each nest of loops carefully, checking all loop parameter values. A loop control variable for a `for` statement cannot be changed inside the loop body. It is also illegal to use the same loop control variable for two nested `for` statements.

When using functions, make sure that the function result is defined for all valid parameter values. Do not use the function name in an expression inside the function body.

5.9 Chapter Review

The `case` statement was introduced in this chapter as a convenient means of implementing decisions with several alternatives. We saw how to use the `case` statement to implement decisions that are based on the value of a variable or simple expression (the `case` selector). The `case` selector must have an ordinal data type.

The `repeat` statement was used to implement conditional loops. The `repeat` statement can be used to implement a loop that will always execute at least one time.

Nested loops were analyzed. Every inner loop of a nest is reentered and executed to completion each time an outer loop is repeated.

Functions were used to implement modules that return a single result. The parameters of a function are generally value parameters. Usually a function result is defined by assigning a value to the function name inside the function body. A function is called by using it in an expression in the calling program; the function name and actual parameters (function arguments) are inserted directly in the expression.

New Pascal Statements

The new Pascal statements introduced in this chapter are shown in Table 5.3.

Table 5.3 Summary of New Pascal Statements

Statement	Effect

Case statement
```case NEXTCH of```
``` 'A', 'a' : WRITELN ('Excellent');```
``` 'B', 'b' : WRITELN ('Good');```
``` 'C', 'c' : WRITELN ('O.K.');```
``` 'D', 'd', 'F', 'f' :```
```   begin```
```   WRITELN ('Poor');```
```   PROBATION (IDNUM)```
```   end```
```end {case}```
	One of four messages is printed based on the value of NEXTCH (type CHAR). If NEXTCH is 'D', 'd' or 'F', 'f', procedure PROBATION is also called with IDNUM as an actual parameter.

Table 5.3 Summary of New Pascal Statements (*continued*)

Statement	Effect

Set values and operator in
`if CURMONTH in [DEC, JAN, FEB] then`
`    WRITELN ('Winter storm watch')`
	The message `'Winter storm watch'` is printed if the value of CURMONTH is one of the three constants listed. CURMONTH and the constants must belong to the same enumerated data type.

General for statement
`for CURMONTH := JAN to DEC do`
`  begin`
`    READ (MONTHSALES);`
`    YEARSALES := YEARSALES +`
`                MONTHSALES`
`  end {for}`
	The loop body is repeated for each value of CURMONTH from JAN through DEC, inclusive. For each month, the value of MONTHSALES is read and added to YEARSALES.

Repeat statement
`repeat`
`  READLN (NEXTNUM);`
`  WRITELN (SQR(NEXTNUM))`
`until NEXTNUM < 0`
	Reads each number and prints its square. Loop is exited after the first negative number is processed.

Declaring a function
`function SIGN (X : REAL) : CHAR;`
 	
`{Finds the sign ('+' or '-') of X.}`
 	
`begin`
`  if X >= 0 then`
`      SIGN := '+'`
`  else`
`      SIGN := '-'`
`end; {SIGN}`
	Returns a character value that indicates the sign (`'+'` or `'-'`) of its type REAL argument.

Review Questions

1. When should a nested `if` statement be used instead of a `case` statement?

2. Write a `case` statement to select an operation based on INVENTORY. Increment TOTALPAPER by PAPERORDER if INVENTORY is `'B'` or `'C'`; increment TOTALRIBBON by RIBBONORDER if INVENTORY is `'L'`, `'T'`, or `'D'`; increment TOTALLABEL by LABELORDER if INVENTORY is `'A'` or `'X'`. Do not take any action if INVENTORY is `'M'`.

3. a) Write the `for` statement that displays the character values of the ordinal numbers 21 through 126, inclusive. Use ORDNUM as the loop control variable.

b) What is the value of ORDNUM, above, after completion of the loop?

4. Write a `repeat` statement that will only accept a valid response to a menu. A valid response would be any of the following: `'A'`, `'a'` or `'B'`, `'b'`.

5. Write the complement of each BOOLEAN expression below.

```
FLAG and (I < 20)
(ORD(NEXTCH) = 0) or EOLN

not (VOWEL and CONSONANT)
(ROUND(N) = N) OR (N < SQR(M))
```

6. a) Write an `if` statement that tests to see if TODAY is a working day. Print either the message `'Workday'` or `'Weekend'`. Assume that TODAY is type DAY, an enumerated type which has the days of the week as its values.
   b) Write an equivalent `case` statement.

7. Write a `for` statement that runs from `'Z'` down to `'A'` and prints out only the consonants. Test each character against the set of vowels.

8. Write a nested loop that prints the first six letters of the alphabet on a line, the first five letters on the next line, the first four letters on the next line, etc., down to and including the first two letters on the last line. Use either upper- or lowercase letters.

9. Write a function called FINDGROSS that computes a worker's weekly gross pay given HOURS (an INTEGER) and RATE (a REAL) as input parameters. Pay time and a half for any hours worked over 40 along with subtracting 30% for taxes. For 30 or more hours but less than 40, subtract 20% for taxes. For 20 or more hours but less than 30, subtract 10% for taxes. Do not deduct any taxes for under 20 hours. Be sure to check for a valid number of hours (0 <= HOURS <= 168).

Programming Projects

1. Write a program that reads in a positive real number and finds and prints the number of digits to the left and right of the decimal point. Hint: Separate both parts and repeatedly divide or multiply by 10. Test the program with the following data:

   4703.62   0.01   0.47   5764   10.12   40000

2. Write a program that finds the largest value, the smallest value, and the sum of the input data. After all data are processed, call two functions to find the average value and the range of values in the data collection. Print these results.

3. Write a program that will provide change for a dollar for any item purchased that costs less than one dollar. Print out each unit of change (quarters, dimes, nickels, or pennies) provided. Always dispense the biggest denomination coin possible. For example, if there are 37 cents left in change, dispense a quarter which leaves 12 cents in change, then dispense a dime, then two pennies.

4. The function $SIN(X)$ increases in value starting at $X = 0$ radians. Write a program to determine the value of X for which $SIN(X)$ begins to decrease. Calculate the value of $SIN(X)$ beginning at $X = 0$ for intervals of .01 radians, and watch for a decrease. Print a two-column table of X and $SIN(X)$ as long as the increase continues. At the point of decrease, simply print X and stop.

5. The Norecall Auto Company keeps sales records for each employee. Each time an automobile is sold the following data are entered into the record:

Salesperson Name	Make of Car	Date of Sale	Amount of Sale
For example:			
LITTLE NELL	CADILLAC	6/24	$8532.67

Each month the company must collect the sales records for each employee, add up the number of sales and the sales amount, and compute the employee commission as follows

For sales up to $30,000,	5% commission.
For sales between $30,000–$50,000,	5% of first $30,000, 8% of the rest.
For sales over $50,000,	5% of first $30,000, 8% of next $20,000, 15% of the rest.

Write a program to perform these computations. For each employee, your program should print employee name, total sales count, total dollar amount of sales, and total commission. At the end, print grand totals of sales count, dollar amount, and commissions. Use a function to compute the commission.

Insert tests in your program to ensure that the sales date and amount are meaningful. The month being processed should be entered at the start of execution.

6. Write a program to read in a collection of positive integers and print all divisors of each, except for 1 and the number itself. If the number has no divisors, print a message indicating that it is prime. Use a procedure to determine all of the divisors of each integer read. This procedure should set a flag, PRIME, to indicate whether or not an integer is prime. The main program should test the flag to decide whether or not to print the prime message.

7. Redo Project 6 of Chapter 3 using the enumerated type

```
type
   BRAND = (PIELS, COORS, BUD, IRONCITY);
```

Enter a single character to indicate which kind of beer is being sold and write a function that converts to one of the values above. Your program should also use a case statement with these values as labels.

8. Shown below is the layout of a string that the registrar uses as input for a program to print the end-of-the-semester final grade report for each student.

Positions	Data Description
1–6	Student number
7–19	Last name
20–27	First name
28	Middle initial
29	Academic year:
	1 = Fr, 2 = So, 3 = Jr, 4 = Sr
30–32	First course—Department ID (3 letters)
33–35	First course—Number (3 digits)
36	First course—Grade A, B, C, D, or F
37	First course—Number of credits: 0–7
40–42	
43–45	
46	Second course: data as described above
47	
50–52	
53–55	
56	Third course data
57	
60–62	
63–65	
66	Fourth course data
67	
70–72	
73–75	
76	Fifth course data
77	

Write a program to print the following grade report sheet for each student.

```
Line 1                      MAD RIVER COLLEGE
Line 2                      YELLOW GULCH, OHIO
Line 3
Line 4              GRADE REPORT, SPRING SEMESTER
Line 5
Line 6      (student number)   (year)   (student name)
            _____   ____     _____
Line 7
Line 8                      GRADE SUMMARY
Line 9                COURSE
Line 10         DEPT     NMBR     CREDITS     GRADE
Line 11      1. ____     ____        __          __
Line 12      2. ____     ____        __          __
Line 13      3. ____     ____        __          __
Line 14      4. ____     ____        __          __
Line 15      5. ____     ____        __          __
Line 16
Line 17   SEMESTER GRADE POINT AVERAGE = _____
```

Your program should work for students taking anywhere from 1 to 5 courses.

9. Write a program to read in a string of up to 10 characters representing a number in the form of a Roman numeral. Print the Roman numeral form and then convert to Arabic form (an integer). The character values for Roman numerals are

M	1000
D	500
C	100
L	50
X	10
V	5
I	1

Test your program on the following data: LXXXVII (87), CCXIX (219), MCCCLIV (1354), MMDCLXXIII (2673), MCDLXXVI (?)

10. An equation of the form

(1) $mx + b = 0$

(where m and b are real numbers) is called a linear equation in one unknown, x. If we are given the values of both m and b, then the value of x that satisfies this equation may be computed as

(2) $x = -b/m$

Write a program to read in N different sets of values for m and b and compute x. Test your program for the following five sets of values:

m	b
−12.00	3.0
0.0	18.5
100.0	40.0
0.0	0.0
−16.8	0.0

Hint: There are three distinct possibilities concerning the values of x that satisfy the equation $mx + b = 0$.
(1) As long as $m <> 0$, the value of x that satisfies the original equation 1 is given by equation 2.
(2) If both b and m are 0, then any real number satisfies the equation.
(3) If $m = 0$ and $b = <> 0$ then no real number x satisfies this equation.

11. Each year the legislature of a state rates the productivity of the faculty of each of the state-supported colleges and universities. The rating is based on reports submitted by each faculty member indicating the average number of hours worked per week during the school year. Each faculty member is ranked, and the university also receives an overall rank.

The faculty productivity rank is computed as follows:

(1) Faculty members averaging over 55 hours per week are considered highly productive.
(2) Faculty members averaging between 35 and 55 hours a week, inclusive, are considered satisfactory.
(3) Faculty members averaging fewer than 35 hours a week are considered overpaid.

The productivity rating of each school is determined by first computing the faculty average for the school and then comparing the faculty average to the category ranges above.

Write a program to rank the following faculty;

Name	Hours
HERM	63
FLO	37
JAKE	20
MO	55
SOL	72
TONY	40
AL	12

Your program should print a three-column table giving the name, hours and productivity rank of each faculty member. It should also compute and print the school's overall productivity ranking.

12. Write a savings account transaction program that will process the following set of data

ADAM	1054.37	group 1
W	25.00	
D	243.35	
W	254.55	
Z		
EVE	2008.24	group 2
W	15.55	
Z		
MARY	128.24	group 3
W	62.48	
D	13.42	
W	84.60	
Z		
SAM	7.77	group 4
Z		
JOE	15.27	group 5
W	16.12	
D	10.00	
Z		
BETH	12900.00	group 6
D	9270.00	
Z		

The first record in each group (header) gives the name for an account and the starting balance in the account. All subsequent records show the amount of each withdrawal (W) or deposit (D) that was made for that account followed by a sentinel value (Z). Print out the final balance for each of the accounts processed. If a balance becomes negative, print an appropriate message and take whatever corrective steps you deem proper. If there are no transactions for an account, print a message so indicating.

13. Write a program to print a table of the following form.

Home loan mortgage interest payment table

Rate (Percent)	Duration (Years)	Monthly Payment	Total Payment
10.00	20	_____	_____
10.00	25	_____	_____
10.00	30	_____	_____
10.25	20	_____	_____

Your program should print a table showing the monthly and total payments on a loan of $1,000 for interest rates from 10% to 14% with increments of 0.25%. The loan duration should be 20, 25, and 30 years. Your program should contain nested loops, some of which may be inside separate procedures, depending upon your solution. Be careful to remove all redundant computations from inside your loops.

14. The equation of the form

(1) $ax^2 + bx + c = 0$ (a, b, c real numbers, with a $<>$ 0)

is called a quadratic equation in x. The real roots of this equation are those values of x for which

$$ax^2 + bx + c$$

evaluates to zero. Thus, if a = 1, b = 2, and c = −15, then the real roots of

$$x^2 + 2x - 15$$

are +3 and −5, since

$$(3)^2 + 2(3) - 15 = 9 + 6 - 15 = 0$$

and

$$(-5)^2 + 2(-5) - 15 = 25 - 10 - 15 = 0$$

Quadratic equations of the form (1) have either 2 real and different roots, 2 real and equal roots, or no real roots. The determination as to which of these three conditions holds for a given equation can be made by evaluating the discriminant d of the equation, where

$$d = b^2 - 4ac$$

There are three distinct possibilities:

1. If d > 0, then the equation has two real and unequal roots.
2. If d = 0, the equation has two real and equal roots.
3. If d < 0, the equation has no real roots.

Write a program to compute and print the real roots of quadratic equations having the following value of a, b, and c.

a	b	c
1.0	2.0	−15.0
1.0	−1.25	−9.375
1.0	0.0	1.0
1.0	−80.0	−900.0
1.0	−6.0	9.0

If the equation has no real roots for a set of a, b and c, print an appropriate message and read the next set. Hint: If the equation has two real and equal roots, then the root values are given by the expression

$$\text{Root 1} = \text{Root 2} = -b/2a$$

If the equation has two real and unequal roots, their values may be computed as

$$\text{Root 1} = \frac{-b + \sqrt{d}}{2a}$$

$$\text{Root 2} = \frac{-b - \sqrt{d}}{2a}$$

15. At Bob's Bank, Bob senior would like to keep some information on his employees readily available. Bob junior suggested he keep the data on the computer so that it would be available anytime someone ran a program. As the sole computer programmer you are to write a program which will read in the employee data and print a report. The data entered for each employee and the output corresponding to each data item are described next.

Data	Corresponding output
Initials	same as entered
Class	This will be a character A, B, C which you will convert to print one of the classifications A—MANAGEMENT B—SUPERVISOR C—CLERICAL
Age	This will be the employee's actual age, but you will print out the group that the employee falls in according to the ranges given below: < 25 : Group 1 25 – 40 : Group 2 41 – 65 : Group 3 > 65 : Group 4
License number	This is a 4 digit number, but you will print out 'EVEN' or 'ODD'. (This is for possible gas rationing).
Code	This is to be calculated by adding up the digits of the employee license number. (For example 14, is the code number for license number 5432.)

The report line shown below is generated for the data: SCS, B, 37, 4436

NAME	POSITION	AGE GROUP	LICENSE	CODE NUMBER
SCS	SUPERVISOR	25 – 40	EVEN	17

Use the following data in your program.

```
TGP C 18 4737
JWW A 25 9630
TMS C 41 7000
MLH B 67 2468
```

16. One of the simplest and most often used means of encoding data is the principle of shifting the alphabet some number of letters in one direction or another. For the sake of simplicity assume all the letters of some message are capitalized and all punctuation and blanks are not encoded.

Write a program that will read in a series of words and convert each to some other word and then print it. The first letter that you read will indicate what the shift will be. For example if the first letter was a J then all A's would be converted to J's, B's to K's, C's to L's, etc. The amount to shift in the alphabet can be determined by calculating the difference of the ordinal value of A and the ordinal value of this first letter.

When a shift exceeds Z the program should start over at A. Hint: Add the excess over the ordinal value of Z to the ordinal value of A minus 1.

Sample input might be:

F NIGHTS OF FUTURE'S PAST

where F would be used to substitute for A, G for B, etc.
Test this program with the example above.
(What would need to be done to the program to decode the message back again?)

17. A problem encountered in writing compilers or determining efficient means of storing data on disks is converting a name into a unique or a reasonably unique numeric value. This procedure is called hashing. Several algorithms are used to accomplish this task.

One of the simpler methods is to use the numeric representation of each letter in some type of equation. In this problem you are to convert a word into a reproducible integer value between 0 and 500. To get this value, add each ordinal value of a letter times that letter's position within the word. This should generate a rather large number which may not be within the required range. To calculate a number within the range, determine the modulus of this large number and 500. For example the number for ACE would be: 1 * 65 + 2 * 67 + 3 * 69 or 406.

Test your program with several words and print out the calculated value for each word.

18. Often in doing a statistical analysis a calculation that is required is the standard deviation (sd). It is derived by summing a series of numbers and doing a few additional calculations which are depicted in the following equation. *Note:* The symbol $\sum_{i=1}^{n}$ represents a summation of values from 1 to n which can easily be implemented as a `for` loop. The first summation under the square root sign is the sum $x_1^2 + x_2^2 + ... + x_n^2$ where x_i is the ith data item and n is the count of the number of items read.

$$sd = \sqrt{\frac{\sum_{i=1}^{n} X_i^2 - \frac{1}{n}\left(\sum_{i=1}^{n} X_i\right)^2}{n-1}}$$

For this problem, read in a series of real numbers and determine

(1) the standard deviation
(2) the largest and smallest values
(3) the range of the numbers
(4) the average value

Use functions in cases where only one value is being returned.

19. Write a procedure that reads in a string of characters representing a real number. The procedure will skip any leading blanks and then read all characters through the first character that cannot be part of the number. If an illegal real value is read, a program flag will be set to indicate this; otherwise the value of the number entered will be returned as a procedure result. (Unlike the standard Pascal READ procedure, the first character following the number is also read.) *Hint:* This procedure must recognize all valid forms of real data including integers, real numbers, and scientific notation. The numeric value returned is type REAL. Examples of the desired procedure outputs are shown next

Input Characters	Real Value	Valid Flag
−1.345	−1.345	TRUE
1.354E02	135.4	TRUE
15E−3	0.015	TRUE
999	999.0	TRUE
17.	17.0	TRUE
.012	undefined	FALSE
1.35Ew	undefined	FALSE
x	undefined	FALSE

6

Arrays

6.1 Declaring and Referencing Arrays

6.2 Arrays with Integer Subscripts

6.3 Case Study

6.4 Manipulating Entire Arrays

6.5 Reading Part of an Array

6.6 General Arrays

6.7 Character Strings

6.8 Multidimensional Arrays

6.9 Case Study

6.10 Common Programming Errors

6.11 Chapter Review

In the programs written so far, each variable was associated with a single memory cell. These variables are called simple variables, and their data types are simple types. In this chapter, we will begin the study of data structures. A *data structure* is a grouping of related data items in memory. The items in a data structure can be processed individually although some operations may be performed on the structure as a whole. Generally, the form of a data structure is declared in a type declaration statement.

The *array* is a data structure used for storing a collection of data items that are all the same type (e.g. all the exam scores for a class). By using an array, we can associate a single variable name (e.g. SCORES) with an entire collection of data. This enables us to save the entire collection of data in adjacent cells of main memory (one item per memory cell) and to easily reference individual items. To process an individual item, we need to specify the array name and indicate which array element is being manipulated (e.g. SCORES[3] references the third item in the array SCORES).

Since each score is saved in a separate cell in main memory, we can process the individual items more than once and in any order we wish. In previous programs we reused the same cell to store each exam score. Consequently, we could no longer access the third score after the fourth score was read.

We will see that the use of arrays also makes it easier for us to process textual data. Text will be stored in special arrays called strings. Some simple string manipulation operations will be discussed.

6.1 Declaring and Referencing Arrays

Usually, we first describe the structure of an array in an *array type declaration*. Then we may allocate storage for one or more arrays of that type. The array type REALARRAY is declared below followed by the declaration of array X of type REALARRAY.

```
type
    REALARRAY = array [1..8] of REAL;

var
    X : REALARRAY;
```

Pascal allocates eight memory cells for the name X; these memory cells will be adjacent to each other in memory. Each element of array X may contain a single real value so a total of eight real values may be stored and referenced using the array name X.

In order to process the data stored in an array, we must be able to reference each individual element. The *array subscript* is used to differentiate between elements of the same array; the subscript is written in brackets after the array name. For example, if X is the array with eight elements declared above, then we may refer to the elements of the array X as shown in Fig. 6.1. The *subscripted variable* X[1] (read as X sub 1) references the first element of the array X (value is 16.0), X[2] references

Fig. 6.1 The Eight Elements of the Array X.

	array X						
X[1]	X[2]	X[3]	X[4]	X[5]	X[6]	X[7]	X[8]
16.0	12.0	6.0	8.0	2.5	12.0	14.0	−54.5

First element   Second element   Third element   Eighth element the second element (value is 12.0), and X[8] references the eighth element (value is −54.5).

Example 6.1   Let X be the array shown in Fig. 6.1. Some statements that manipulate this array are shown in Table 6.1.

Table 6.1 Statements that Manipulate Array X

Statement	Explanation
WRITELN (X[1])	Displays the value of X[1] or 16.0.
X[4] := 25.0	Stores the value 25.0 in X[4].
SUM := X[1] + X[2]	Stores the sum of X[1] and X[2] or 28.0 in the variable SUM.
SUM := SUM + X[3]	Adds X[3] to SUM. The new SUM is 34.0.
X[4] := X[4] + 1.0	Adds 1.0 to X[4]. The new X[4] is 26.0.
X[3] := X[1] + X[2]	Stores the sum of X[1] and X[2] in X[3]. The new X[3] is 28.0.

The contents of array X, after execution of these statements, is shown below. Only X[3] and X[4] are changed

array X

X[1]	X[2]	X[3]	X[4]	X[5]	X[6]	X[7]	X[8]
16.0	12.0	28.0	26.0	2.5	12.0	14.0	−54.5

First element   Second element   Third element   Eighth element

Example 6.2   Two array types (BOOLARRAY and SCOREARRAY) and two arrays (AN-SWERS and SCORES) are declared below.

```
type
    BOOLARRAY = array [1..10] of BOOLEAN;
    SCOREARRAY = array [1..50] of 0..100;

var
    ANSWERS : BOOLARRAY;
    SCORES : SCOREARRAY;
```

The array ANSWERS has 10 elements and each element can store a BOOLEAN value. This array may be used to store the 10 answers for a true-false quiz (e.g. ANSWERS[1] is TRUE, ANSWERS[2] is FALSE).

The array SCORES has 50 elements and each element can store an integer value from 0 to 100. This array may be used to store exam scores for up to 50 students (e.g. SCORES[1] is 90, SCORES[2] is 65).

It is important to realize that no storage space is allocated when the array-type is declared. The array-type describes the structure of an array only; storage space is allocated when a variable of this type is declared.

Self-check Exercise for Section 6.1

1. Execute the statements in Table 6.1 for array X shown after the table.

6.2 Arrays with Integer Subscripts

As indicated in section 6.1, the subscript-type may be any ordinal type (except type `INTEGER`) or a subrange. The subscript (sometimes called an *index*) used to reference an array element must be an expression that is assignment-compatible with the subscript-type. Very often, the subscript-type is a subrange whose host type is `INTEGER`. In this case, the subscript must be an integer expression whose value is in the range specified by the subscript-type. For the array `SCORES` declared in Example 6.2, the allowable subscript values are the integers from 1 through 50.

Example 6.3   Table 6.2 shows some sample statements using the array X shown in Fig. 6.1. I is assumed to be a type `INTEGER` variable with value 6. Be sure you understand each statement.

There are two illegal attempts to display element X[12], which is not in the array. These attempts will result in an "index expression out of bounds" run-time error.

The last `WRITE` statement uses `TRUNC(X[5])` (or `TRUNC(2.5)`) as a subscript expression. Since this evaluates to 2, the value of X[2] (and not

Table 6.2 Sample Statements for Array X in Fig. 6.1 (I is 6)

Statement	Effect
WRITE (5, X[5])	Displays 5 and 2.5 (value of X[5]).
WRITE (I, X[I])	Displays 6 and 12.0 (value of X[6]).
WRITE (X[I] + 1)	Displays 13.0 (value of 12.0 + 1).
WRITE (X[I] + I)	Displays 18.0 (value of 12.0 + 6).
WRITE (X[I+1])	Displays 14.0 (value of X[7]).
WRITE (X[I+I])	Illegal attempt to display X[12].
WRITE (X[2*I])	Illegal attempt to display X[12].
WRITE (X[2*I-4])	Displays −54.5 (value of X[8]).
WRITE (X[TRUNC(X[5])])	Displays 12.0 (value of X[2]).
X[I-1] := X[I]	Assigns 12.0 (value of X[6]) to X[5].
X[I] := X[I+1]	Assigns 14.0 (value of X[7]) to X[6].
X[I] - 1 := X[I]	Illegal assignment statement

X[5]) is printed. If the value of TRUNC(X[5]) is outside the range 1 through 8, this would be an illegal subscript expression.

ARRAY REFERENCE

name [*subscript*]

Interpretation: The *subscript* must be an expression that is assignment-compatible with the *subscript-type* specified in the declaration for array *name*. If the expression is the wrong data type, then the syntax error "index type is not compatible with declaration" will be detected. If the expression value is not in range, then the run-time error "index expression out of bounds" will occur.

Often we wish to process the elements of an array in sequence, starting with the first element. For example we might enter data into the array or print its contents. This can be accomplished using a for loop whose loop control variable (e.g. I) is also used as the array subscript (e.g. X[I]). Increasing the value of the loop control variable by 1 causes the next array element to be processed.

Example 6.4   The array CUBE declared below will be used to store the cubes of the first 10 integers (e.g. CUBE[1] is 1, CUBE[10] is 1000).

```
type
    INTARRAY = array [1..10] of INTEGER;

var
    CUBE : INTARRAY;                    {array of cubes}
    I : INTEGER;                        {loop control variable}
```

The for statement

```
for I := 1 to 10 do
    CUBE[I] := I * I * I
```

initializes this array as shown below

array CUBE

[1]	[2]	[3]	[4]	[5]	[6]	[7]	[8]	[9]	[10]
1	8	27	64	125	216	343	512	729	1000

Example 6.5   The program in Fig. 6.2 uses three for loops to process the array X. The loop control variable I (1 <= I <= 8) is also used as the array subscript in each loop. The first for loop

```
for I := 1 to MAXITEMS do
    READ (X[I]);
```

is used to read one data value into each array element (the first item is stored in X[1], the second item in X[2], etc.) The READ statement is repeated for each value of I from 1 to 8; each repetition causes a new data value to be read and stored in X[I]. The subscript I determines which array element receives the next data value. The data line shown in the sample run causes the array to be initialized as in Fig. 6.1.

The second for loop is used to accumulate (in SUM) the sum of all values stored in the array; this loop will be traced later. The last for loop

```
for I := 1 to MAXITEMS do
    WRITELN (I :4, X[I] :8:1, X[I]-AVERAGE :14:1)
```

is used to display a table showing a subscript (I), the array element with that subscript (X[I]), and the difference between that element and the average value (X[I]-AVERAGE).

```
program SHOWDIFF (INPUT, OUTPUT);

{Computes the average value of an array of data and
 prints the difference between each value and the average.}

const
    MAXITEMS = 8;                       {number of data items}

type
    REALARRAY = array [1..MAXITEMS] of REAL;
```

```
var
   X : REALARRAY;                              {array of data}
   AVERAGE,                                    {average value of data}
   SUM        : REAL;                          {sum of the data}
   I : INTEGER;                                {loop control variable}

begin {SHOWDIFF}
   {Enter the data.}
   WRITE ('Enter ', MAXITEMS :2, ' numbers: ');
   for I := 1 to MAXITEMS do
      READ (X[I]);
   READLN;

   {Compute the average value.}
   SUM := 0.0;                                 {initialize SUM}
   for I := 1 to MAXITEMS do
      SUM := SUM + X[I];                     {add each element to SUM}
   AVERAGE := SUM / MAXITEMS;                   {get average value}
   WRITELN ('The average value is ', AVERAGE :8:1);

   {Display the difference between each item and the average.}
   WRITELN ('Table of differences between X[I] and the average');
   WRITELN ('I' :4, 'X[I]' :8, 'Difference' :14);
   for I := 1 to MAXITEMS do
      WRITELN (I :4, X[I] :8:1, X[I]-AVERAGE :14:1)
end.   {SHOWDIFF}

Enter 8 numbers: 16   12   6   8   2.5   12   14   -54.5
The average value is        2.0
Table of differences between X[I] and the average
   I    X[I]      Difference
   1    16.0          14.0
   2    12.0          10.0
   3     6.0           4.0
   4     8.0           6.0
   5     2.5           0.5
   6    12.0          10.0
   7    14.0          12.0
   8   -54.5         -56.5
```

Fig. 6.2 Printing a Table of Differences

The program fragment

```
SUM := 0.0;                                 {initialize SUM}
for I := 1 to MAXITEMS do
   SUM := SUM + X[I];                     {add each element to SUM}
```

accumulates the sum of all eight elements of array X in the variable SUM. Each time the for loop is repeated, the next element of array X is added to SUM. The execution of this program fragment is traced in Table 6.3 for the first three repetitions of the loop.

In Fig. 6.2, the subscripted variable X[I] is an actual parameter for the standard Pascal READ or WRITELN procedure. It is always necessary to read data into an array one element at a time as shown in this example.

Table 6.3 Partial Trace of for Loop

Statement Part	I	X[I]	SUM	Effect
SUM := 0.0;			0.0	Initializes SUM
for I := 1 to MAXITEMS do	1	16.0		Initializes I to 1
SUM := SUM + X[I]			16.0	Add X[1] to SUM
increment and test I	2	12.0		2 <= 8 is true
SUM := SUM + X[I]			28.0	Add X[2] to SUM
increment and test I	3	6.0		3 <= 8 is true
SUM := SUM + X[I]			34.0	Add X[3] to SUM

In most instances it is also necessary to display one array element at time; however, this requirement may be waived when dealing with packed arrays (see Section 6.7).

6.3 Case Study

We have written programs that accumulate the sum of all input data items in a single variable. Often, we have different categories of data items and we might want to accumulate a separate total for each category rather than one grand total for all the items. The problem that follows uses an array to accomplish this.

Home Budget Problem

Problem: We would like to write a program that keeps track of our monthly expenses in each of 10 categories. The program should read each expense amount, add it to the appropriate category total, and print the total expenditures by category. The input data consists of the category number and amount of each purchase made during the past month.

Discussion: There are 10 separate totals to be accumulated; each total can be associated with a different element of a 10-element array. The program must read each expenditure, determine its correct category, and then add that expenditure to the appropriate array element. When finished with all expenditures, the program can print a table showing each category and its accumulated total. As in all programs that accumulate a sum, each total must be initialized to zero. The problem inputs and outputs and algorithm follow.

PROBLEM INPUTS

each expenditure and its category

the array of ten expenditure totals (BUDGET)

Algorithm

1. Initialize all category totals to zero.
2. Read each expenditure and add it to the appropriate total.
3. Print the accumulated total for each category.

The structure chart in Fig. 6.3 shows the relationship between the three steps. The array BUDGET is manipulated by all three procedures. Procedures INITIALIZE and POST store information in this array; this information is displayed by procedure REPORT. The main program and procedures INITIALIZE and REPORT are shown in Fig. 6.4.

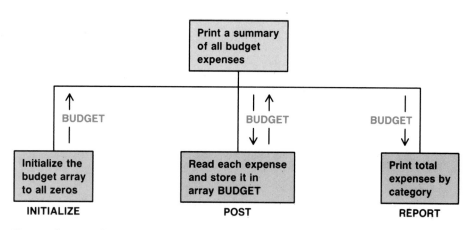

Fig. 6.3 Structure Chart for Home Budget Problem

```
program HOMEBUDGET (INPUT, OUTPUT);

{Prints a summary of all expenses by budget category.}

const
    NUMCATEGORY = 10;                          {number of categories}

type
    INDEX = 1..NUMCATEGORY;                    {subscript type}
    BUDGETARRAY = array [INDEX] of REAL;       {array type}

var
    BUDGET : BUDGETARRAY;                      {array of ten totals}

procedure INITIALIZE (var BUDGET {output} : BUDGETARRAY);

{Initializes array BUDGET to all zeros.}

var
    NEXTCAT : INDEX;                           {loop control variable—
                                                array subscript}
```

```
begin {INITIALIZE}
    for NEXTCAT := 1 to NUMCATEGORY do
        BUDGET[NEXTCAT] := 0.0
end; {INITIALIZE}

procedure POST (var BUDGET {input/output} : BUDGETARRAY);

{Reads each expenditure amount and adds it to the appropriate
 element of array BUDGET.                                      }

begin {POST}
    WRITELN ('Procedure POST entered')
end; {POST}

procedure REPORT (BUDGET {input} : BUDGETARRAY);

{Prints the expenditures in each budget category.}

var
    NEXTCAT : INDEX;                              {loop control variable—
                                                  array subscript}

begin {REPORT}
    WRITELN ('Category' :10, 'Expenses' :15);              {print heading}

    {Print each category number and the expenditure}
    for NEXTCAT := 1 to NUMCATEGORY do
        WRITELN (NEXTCAT :10, BUDGET[NEXTCAT] :15:2)            {print row}
end; {REPORT}

begin {HOMEBUDGET}
    {Initialize array BUDGET to all zeros.}
    INITIALIZE (BUDGET);

    {Read and process each expenditure.}
    POST (BUDGET);

    {Print the expenditures in each category.}
    REPORT (BUDGET)
end. {HOMEBUDGET}
```

Fig. 6.4 Home Budget Main Program

The main program (shown in Fig. 6.4) contains declarations for a constant NUMCATEGORY and two types (INDEX and BUDGETARRAY) as well as the array BUDGET. The array BUDGET (type BUDGETARRAY) appears in each parameter list shown in Fig. 6.4 and is passed between each procedure and the main program. When passing an entire array, no subscript is used. Later we will say more about the use of arrays as parameters.

The constant NUMCATEGORY determines the number of repetitions of the for loop in each procedure. The loop control variable NEXTCAT (type INDEX) is declared as a local variable in each procedure.

In procedure INITIALIZE, the assignment statement in the loop

```
    for NEXTCAT := 1 to NUMCATEGORY do
        BUDGET[NEXTCAT] := 0.0
```

is repeated once for each value of NEXTCAT from 1 to 10 and is used to set each element of BUDGET to zero. In procedure REPORT, the statement

```
    for NEXTCAT := 1 to NUMCATEGORY do
        WRITELN (NEXTCAT :10, BUDGET[NEXTCAT] :15:2)
```

is used to print each category number (from 1 to 10) and its expense total.

Procedure POST must read each expenditure and add it to the appropriate array element. The total of all expenditures in category 1 is accumulated in BUDGET[1], all expenditures in category 2 are accumulated in BUDGET[2], etc. Procedure POST is shown in Fig. 6.5; it uses procedure READEXPENSE to read in the category (CATEGORY) and amount (EXPENSE) for each expenditure.

```
procedure POST (var BUDGET {input/output} : BUDGETARRAY);

{Reads each expenditure amount and adds it to the appropriate
 element of array BUDGET.                                       }

const
    SENTINEL = 0;                                    {sentinel category}

type
    CATRANGE = 0..NUMCATEGORY;

var
    CATEGORY : CATRANGE;                            {expenditure category}
    EXPENSE : REAL;                                 {expenditure amount}

procedure READEXPENSE (var CATEGORY {output} : CATRANGE;
                       var EXPENSE {output} : REAL);

{Reads the category and amount of each expenditure.}

var
    TEMPCAT : INTEGER;

begin {READEXPENSE}
    {Read the category.}
    repeat
        WRITE ('Enter a budget category (1 to ', NUMCATEGORY :2,
               ') or 0 to stop: ');
        READLN (TEMPCAT);
    until TEMPCAT in [0..NUMCATEGORY];
    CATEGORY := TEMPCAT;                            {return valid category}

    {Read the amount.}
    if CATEGORY <> SENTINEL then
```

```
      begin
          WRITE ('Enter the expenditure amount $');
          READLN (EXPENSE)
      end
end; {READEXPENSE}

begin {POST}
    {Read each expenditure and add it to an element of BUDGET.}
    READEXPENSE (CATEGORY, EXPENSE);              {read first expense data}
    while CATEGORY <> SENTINEL do
        begin
            BUDGET[CATEGORY] := BUDGET[CATEGORY] + EXPENSE;
            READEXPENSE (CATEGORY, EXPENSE)         {read next expense data}
        end {while}
end; {POST}
```

Fig. 6.5 Procedure POST for Home Budget Problem.

An advantage to using arrays in Fig. 6.5 is that there is no need to process each expense category as a separate case using an if or case statement. In procedure POST, the assignment statement

```
BUDGET[CATEGORY] := BUDGET[CATEGORY] + EXPENSE;
```

adds the expense amount to the element of array BUDGET that is selected by the subscript CATEGORY.

A sample run of the Home Budget Program is shown in Fig. 6.6. As illustrated, it is not necessary for the data to be in order by category.

Fig. 6.6 Sample Run of Home Budget Program

```
Enter a budget category (1 to 10) or 0 to stop: 4
Enter the expenditure amount $10.00
Enter a budget category (1 to 10) or 0 to stop: 10
Enter the expenditure amount $15.00
Enter a budget category (1 to 10) or 0 to stop: 4
Enter the expenditure amount $35.00
Enter a budget category (1 to 10) or 0 to stop: 0
        Category          Expenses
            1               0.00
            2               0.00
            3               0.00
            4              45.00
            5               0.00
            6               0.00
            7               0.00
            8               0.00
            9               0.00
           10              15.00
```

Sequential versus Random Access to Arrays

The Home Budget Program illustrates two common ways of selecting array elements for processing. Often, we need to manipulate all elements of an array in a uniform manner (e.g. initialize them all to zero). In situations like this, it makes sense to process the array elements in sequence (*sequential access*), starting with the first and ending with the last. In procedures INITIALIZE and REPORT, this is accomplished by using a for loop whose loop control variable is also the array subscript.

In procedure POST the order in which the array elements are accessed is completely dependent on the order of the data. The value read into CATEGORY determines which element is incremented. This is called *random access* since the order is not predictable beforehand.

Self-check Exercises for Section 6.3

1. Write a procedure that copies each value stored in one array to the corresponding element of another array. (i.e. If the arrays are INAR-

RAY and OUTARRAY, then copy INARRAY[1] to OUTARRAY[1], next copy INARRAY[2] to OUTARRAY[2], etc.)

2. Write a procedure that reverses the values stored in an array. If array X has N elements, then Y[1] will become X[N], Y[2] will become X[N-1], etc. X and N should be procedure inputs; Y should be a procedure output.

6.4 Manipulating Entire Arrays

Most Pascal operators can manipulate only one array element at a time. Consequently an array name in an expression will generally be followed by its subscript.

One exception is the *array copy* operation. It is possible to copy the contents of one array to another array provided the arrays are the same array type. Given the declarations

```
const
    MAXSIZE = 100;

type
    INDEX = 1..MAXSIZE;
    TESTARRAY = array [INDEX] of REAL;

var
    X, Y, Z : TESTARRAY;
```

the assignment statement

```
    X := Y                              {array copy statement}
```

copies each value in array Y to the corresponding element of array X (i.e. Y[1] is copied to X[1], Y[2] to X[2], etc.).

Arrays as Parameters

If several elements of an array are being manipulated by a procedure, it is generally better to pass the entire array of data instead of individual array elements. In Fig. 6.4, the procedure (call) statements

```
    INITIALIZE (BUDGET);
    POST (BUDGET);
    REPORT (BUDGET)
```

pass the entire array BUDGET to each procedure. BUDGET is declared as a variable parameter in procedures INITIALIZE and POST and as a value parameter in procedure REPORT.

In all three procedures, the formal parameter is declared as type

BUDGETARRAY. This is necessary since the formal and actual parameter must be the same array type. The procedure heading

```
procedure INITIALIZE (var BUDGET : array [INDEX] of REAL);
```

is invalid because an identifier must be used to specify the parameter type.

When an array is used as a variable parameter, Pascal passes the address of the first actual array element into the procedure data area. Since the array elements are stored in adjacent memory cells, the entire array of data can be accessed directly by the procedure.

When an array is used as a value parameter, a local copy of the array is made when the procedure is called. The local array is initialized so that it contains the same values as the corresponding actual array. The procedure manipulates the local array, and the changes made to the local array are not reflected in the actual array.

The next two examples illustrate the use of arrays as parameters, assuming the declarations below.

```
const
    MAXSIZE = 5;

type
    INDEX = 1..MAXSIZE;
    TESTARRAY = array [INDEX] of REAL;

var
    X, Y, Z : TESTARRAY;
```

Example 6.6 Although it is possible to use a single assignment statement to copy one array to another, the assignment statement

```
Z := X + Y          {illegal addition of arrays}
```

is invalid because the operator + cannot have an array as an operand. Procedure ADDARRAY in Fig. 6.7 may be used to add two arrays of type TESTARRAY.

```
procedure ADDARRAY (A, B {input} : TESTARRAY;
                    var C {output} : TESTARRAY);

{Stores the sum of A[I] and B[I] in C[I]. Array
 elements with subscripts 1..MAXSIZE are summed,
 element by element.                            }

var
    I : INDEX;                  {loop control variable and
                                 array subscript}
```

```
begin {ADDARRAY}
   {Add corresponding elements of each array}
   for I := 1 to MAXSIZE do
      C[I] := A[I] + B[I]
end; {ADDARRAY}
```

Fig. 6.7 Procedure ADDARRAY

The parameter correspondence established by the procedure (call) statement

ADDARRAY (X, Y, Z)

is shown in Fig. 6.8. Arrays A and B in the procedure data area are local copies of arrays X and Y in the calling program. As indicated by the solid arrow, array parameter C is connected to array Z in the main program. The procedure results are stored directly in array Z. After execution of the procedure, $Z[1]$ will contain the sum of $X[1]$ and $Y[1]$ or 3.5, $Z[2]$ will contain 6.7, etc; arrays X and Y will be unchanged.

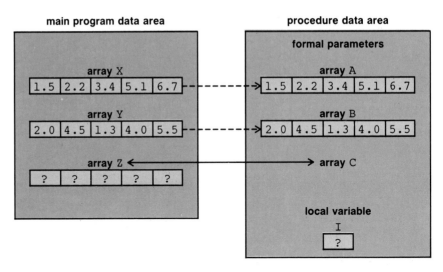

Fig. 6.8 Parameter Correspondence for ADDARRAY (X, Y, Z)

Example 6.7   Function SAMEARRAY in Fig. 6.9 is used to determine whether two arrays of type TESTARRAY are identical. Two arrays are considered identical if the first element of one is the same as the first element of the other, the second element of one is the same as the second element of the other, etc.

We can determine that the arrays are not identical by finding a single pair of unequal elements. Consequently, the repeat-until loop may be executed anywhere from one time (first elements unequal) to MAXSIZE times. The loop is exited when a pair of unequal elements is found (A[I] <> B[I]) or when all elements have been tested (I = MAXSIZE). The subscript I is initialized to 0; however, it becomes 1 before the first test of the until condition.

```
function SAMEARRAY (A, B : TESTARRAY) : BOOLEAN;

{Returns a value of TRUE if the arrays A, B are identical; otherwise,
 returns a value of FALSE.                                          }

var
    I : 0..MAXSIZE;                    {array subscript}

begin {SAMEARRAY}
    I := 0;              {I is incremented before first array reference}

    {Test corresponding elements of arrays A and B.}
    repeat
        {invariant: I < MAXSIZE and elements
         with subscripts 1..I are equal}
        I := I + 1                     {advance to next elements}
    until (A[I] <> B[I]) or (I = MAXSIZE);

    {assert: an unequal pair was found or arrays are identical}
    SAMEARRAY := A[I] = B[I]
end; {SAMEARRAY}
```

Fig. 6.9 Function SAMEARRAY

The BOOLEAN assignment statement

```
        SAMEARRAY := A[I] = B[I]
```

defines the function result. If the repeat-until loop is exited because the elements with subscript I are unequal, then SAMEARRAY will be FALSE; otherwise, SAMEARRAY will be TRUE.

As an example of how function SAMEARRAY may be used, the if statement

```
        if SAMEARRAY(X, Y) then
            Z := X
        else
            ADDARRAY (X, Y, Z)
```

either copies array X to array Z (X and Y are identical) or stores the sum of arrays X and Y in array Z (X and Y are not identical).

PROGRAM STYLE

Efficiency of variable parameters versus protection of value parameters

Parameters A and B in Fig. 6.9 are declared as value parameters because they are used only to store data passed into procedure ADDARRAY; and their values should not be changed by ADDARRAY.

Pascal must create a local copy of these two arrays each time procedure ADDARRAY is called. This uses valuable computer time and memory space. If the arrays being copied are very large, the program may terminate with an error because all of its memory space has been used. To conserve time and memory space, experienced programmers sometimes declare arrays that are used only for input as variable parameters instead of value parameters. However, this means that the array is no longer protected from accidental modification by the procedure. Any changes (either by accident or design) are made directly to an actual array that corresponds to a variable parameter. If an array corresponds to a value parameter, the changes are made to a local copy, and the actual array is unaffected.

Individual Array Elements as Parameters

It is also correct to use a single array element as an actual parameter. For example, the expression

```
ROUND(BUDGET[5])
```

rounds the value stored in the fifth element of array BUDGET where the subscripted variable BUDGET[5] is the actual parameter passed to function ROUND.

Example 6.8 Procedure EXCHANGE in Fig. 6.10 exchanges the values of its two type REAL parameters.

Fig. 6.10 Procedure EXCHANGE

```
procedure EXCHANGE (var P, Q {input/output} : REAL);

{Exchanges the values of P and Q.}

var
   TEMP : REAL;          {temporary variable for the exchange}

begin  {EXCHANGE}
   TEMP := P;   P := Q;   Q := TEMP
end; {EXCHANGE}
```

The procedure (call) statement

```
EXCHANGE (X[1], X[2])
```

uses this procedure to exchange the contents of the first two elements (type REAL) of array X. The actual parameter X[1] corresponds to formal parameter P; the actual parameter X[2] corresponds to formal parameter Q. Figure 6.11 shows this correspondence for the array X shown earlier in Fig. 6.8.

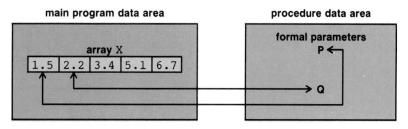

Fig. 6.11 Parameter Correspondence for EXCHANGE (X[1], X[2])

It is illegal to use a subscripted variable as a formal parameter. For example, the procedure header

```
procedure EXCHANGE (var X[I], X[J] {input/output} : REAL);
```

will cause a syntax error.

Type Compatibility Revisited

Three arrays (X, Y, and Z) are declared below. Each array can be used to store 100 real numbers. The declaration for array Z shows that it is not necessary to declare the array type before declaring the array itself; however, this is not recommended.

```
const
    MAXSIZE = 100;

type
    INDEX = 1..MAXSIZE;
    TESTARRAY = array [INDEX] of REAL;

var
    X, Y : TESTARRAY;
    Z : array [INDEX] of REAL;
```

X and Y are both declared to be the same array type; consequently, the array copy statement

```
X := Y       {copy array Y to array X}
```

can be executed without error. However, the array copy statement

```
X := Z        {invalid array copy}
```

may cause a syntax error as array Z is not considered the same type as array X (type TESTARRAY) even though both arrays have 100 type REAL elements.

If the variable declaration is rewritten as

```
var
    X, Y, Z : TESTARRAY;
```

the array copy

```
X := Z        {copy array Z to array X}
```

is valid. We recommend that you follow this convention of using array type identifiers particulary when there is a possibility that the array may be used as a procedure parameter.

Self-check Exercises for Section 6.4

1. Write a procedure that assigns a value of TRUE to element I of the output array only if element I of one input array has the same value as element I of the other input array.

6.5 Reading Part of an Array

Usually we don't know exactly how many elements will be in an array. For example, if we are processing exam scores, there may be 150 students in one class, 200 in the next, etc. In this situation, we should declare an array that can accommodate the largest anticipated class. Only part of this array will actually be processed for a smaller class.

Example 6.9   The array SCORES declared below can accommodate a class of up to 250 students. Each array element may contain an integer value between 0 and 100.

```
const
    MAXSIZE = 250;

type
    CLASSINDEX = 1..MAXSIZE;
    SCOREARRAY = array [CLASSINDEX] of 0..100;
    CLASSRANGE = 0..MAXSIZE;

var
    SCORES : SCOREARRAY;
    CLASSIZE : CLASSRANGE;
```

Procedure READSCORES in Fig. 6.12 reads up to 250 exam scores. It prints a warning message when the array is filled. The actual number of scores read is returned as the value of CLASSIZE.

```
procedure READSCORES (var SCORES {output} : SCOREARRAY;
                      var CLASSIZE {output} : CLASSRANGE);

{Reads an array of exam scores (SCORES) for a class of up to
 MAXSIZE students and returns the number (CLASSIZE) of array
 elements actually read.                                      }

const
    SENTINEL = -1;                                    {sentinel value}

var
    TEMPSCORE : -1..100;              {temporary storage for a score}

begin  {READSCORES}
    CLASSIZE := 0;                              {initial class size}

    {Read each array element until done.}
    repeat
        WRITE ('Enter next score or -1 to stop: ');
        READLN (TEMPSCORE);
        if TEMPSCORE <> SENTINEL then
            begin  {save}
                CLASSIZE := CLASSIZE + 1;         {increment CLASSIZE}
                SCORES[CLASSIZE] := TEMPSCORE            {save the score}
            end  {save}
    until (TEMPSCORE = SENTINEL) or (CLASSIZE = MAXSIZE);

    {Assert: Sentinel read or array is filled.}
    if CLASSIZE = MAXSIZE then
        WRITELN ('Array is filled.')
end;  {READSCORES}
```

Fig. 6.12 Reading Part of an Array

In any subsequent processing of array SCORES, the variable CLASSIZE should be used to limit the number of array elements processed. Only the subarray with subscripts 1..CLASSIZE is defined. All array elements with subscripts larger than CLASSIZE are still undefined and should not be manipulated.

6.6 General Arrays

The subscript type of each array examined so far was a subrange of the integers. This, of course, is not required in Pascal as the subscript type may be any enumerated type (except INTEGER) or a subrange. Several different array types are described in Table 6.4.

Table 6.4 Some Array Types and Applications

Array	Application
NAME : array [1..10] of CHAR;	NAME[1] := 'A'; storing a person's name (up to 10 letters)
FAHREN : array [-10..10] of REAL;	FAHREN[-10] := 14.0; storing Fahrenheit temperatures corresponding to −10 through 10 degrees Celsius
LETCOUNT : array ['A'..'Z'] of INTEGER;	LETCOUNT['A'] := 0; storing the number of times each letter occurs
LETFOUND : array ['A'..'Z'] of BOOLEAN;	LETFOUND['X'] := FALSE; storing a set of flags indicating which letters occurred (flag is TRUE)
ANSWERS : array [BOOLEAN] of INTEGER;	ANSWERS[TRUE] := 15; storing the number of TRUE answers and FALSE answers for a quiz

The array NAME has 10 elements and may be used to store the letters of a person's name. The array FAHREN has 21 elements and may be used to store the Fahrenheit temperature corresponding to each Celsius temperature in the range −10 through +10 degrees Celsius. For example, FAHREN [0] would be the Fahrenheit temperature, 32.0, corresponding to 0 degrees Celsius.

The arrays LETCOUNT and LETFOUND have the subscript type 'A'..'Z'. Hence, there is an array element for each uppercase letter. LETCOUNT['A'] can be used to count the number of occurrences of the letter A in a line; LETFOUND['A'] can be used to indicate whether or not the letter A occurs. If the letter A occurs, LETFOUND['A'] will be TRUE; otherwise, LETFOUND['A'] will be FALSE.

Example 6.10 The program in Fig. 6.13 uses the arrays LETCOUNT and LETFOUND described above to count and print the number of occurrences of each letter in a line of text. The first for loop initializes the two arrays. The while loop reads each character into NEXTCHAR and updates the corresponding array elements if the character is a letter. The last for loop prints the number of times each letter occurs; only counts greater than zero are printed.

```
program CONCORDANCE (INPUT, OUTPUT);

{Finds and prints the number of occurrences of each letter.}

type
    LETTER = 'A'..'Z';
```

```
var
    LETCOUNT : array [LETTER] of INTEGER;              {array of counts}
    LETFOUND : array [LETTER] of BOOLEAN;              {array of flags}
    NEXTCHAR : CHAR;                                   {the next character}

begin {CONCORDANCE}
    {Initialize LETCOUNT and LETFOUND.}
    for NEXTCHAR := 'A' to 'Z' do
        begin
            LETCOUNT[NEXTCHAR] := 0;                   {initialize counts}
            LETFOUND[NEXTCHAR] := FALSE                {initialize flags}
        end; {for}

    {Count the letters in a line.}
    WRITELN ('Type in a line of text using uppercase letters.');
    while not EOLN do
        begin
            READ (NEXTCHAR);                           {get next character}
            if NEXTCHAR in ['A'..'Z'] then
                begin {letter}
                    LETCOUNT[NEXTCHAR] := LETCOUNT[NEXTCHAR] + 1;
                    LETFOUND[NEXTCHAR] := TRUE         {set letter flag}
                end {letter}
        end; {while}
    READLN;  WRITELN;

    {Print counts of letters that are in the line.}
    WRITELN ('Letter', 'Occurrences' :16);
    for NEXTCHAR := 'A' to 'Z' do
        if LETFOUND[NEXTCHAR] then
            WRITELN (NEXTCHAR :6, LETCOUNT[NEXTCHAR] :16)
end. {CONCORDANCE}

Type in a line of text using uppercase letters.
THIS IS IT!

Letter      Occurrences
     H                1
     I                3
     S                2
     T                2
```

Fig. 6.13 Counting Letters in a Line.

Example 6.11   The array MONTHSALES declared below can be used to keep track of the amount of sales in each month. The subscript type is MONTH; the subscript values are the constants JAN to DEC.

```
type
    MONTH = (JAN,FEB,MAR,APR,MAY,JUN,JUL,AUG,SEP,OCT,NOV,DEC);
    SALESARRAY = array [MONTH] of REAL;

var
    CURMONTH : MONTH;
    MONTHSALES : SALESARRAY;
    CURSALES : REAL;
```

The statement

```
for CURMONTH := JAN to DEC do
   MONTHSALES[CURMONTH] := 0.0
```

initializes this array to all zeros. The statement

```
MONTHSALES[CURMONTH] := MONTHSALES[CURMONTH] + CURSALES
```

adds the value of CURSALES to the element of MONTHSALES selected by the subscript CURMONTH.

Example 6.12 The program in Fig. 6.14 generates cryptograms. A cryptogram is a coded message formed by substituting a code character for each letter of an original message. The substitution is performed uniformly throughout the original message, i.e., all A's might be replaced by S, all B's by P, etc. All punctuation (including blanks between words) remains unchanged.

The program uses array CODE (subscript type 'A'..'Z') to hold the code symbol corresponding to each uppercase letter (e.g. CODE['A'] is the code symbol for the letter A). The code symbols are read in by the for statement in procedure READCODE, starting with the code symbol for the letter A.

Procedure ENCRYPT reads each message character into NEXTCHAR. If NEXTCHAR is an uppercase letter, its code symbol is printed next to it; otherwise, NEXTCHAR is printed again. The original message is in the first output column in blue type; the cryptogram appears in the second column.

```
program CRYPTOGRAM (INPUT, OUTPUT);

type
   LETTER = 'A'..'Z';
   CODEARRAY = array [LETTER] of CHAR;

var
   CODE : CODEARRAY;                        {array of code symbols}

procedure READCODE (var CODE {output} : CODEARRAY);

{Reads in the code symbol for each letter.}

var
   NEXTLETTER : LETTER;                     {each letter}

begin {READCODE}
   WRITELN ('Enter a code symbol under each letter.');
   WRITELN ('ABCDEFGHIJKLMNOPQRSTUVWXYZ');

   {Read each code symbol into array CODE.}
   for NEXTLETTER := 'A' to 'Z' do
      READ (CODE[NEXTLETTER]);

   READLN;                                  {terminate input line}
   WRITELN                                  {skip a line}
end; {READCODE}
```

```
procedure ENCRYPT (CODE {input} : CODEARRAY);

{Reads each character and prints it or its code symbol.}

const
    SENTINEL = '@';                          {sentinel character}

var
    NEXTCHAR : CHAR;                         {each message character}

begin {ENCRYPT}
    WRITELN ('Enter each message character. Use uppercase letters.');
    WRITELN ('Enter the symbol "@" after your message.');
    repeat
        READ (NEXTCHAR);
        if NEXTCHAR in ['A'..'Z'] then
            WRITELN (CODE[NEXTCHAR] :5)       {print code symbol}
        else
            WRITELN (NEXTCHAR :5)             {print nonletter}
    until NEXTCHAR = SENTINEL
end; {ENCRYPT}

begin {CRYPTOGRAM}
    {Read in the code symbol for each letter.}
    READCODE (CODE);

    {Read each character and print it or its code symbol.}
    ENCRYPT (CODE)
end. {CRYPTOGRAM}

Enter a code symbol under each letter.
ABCDEFGHIJKLMNOPQRSTUVWXYZ
BCDEFGHIJKLMNOPQRSTUVWXYZA

Enter each message character. Use uppercase letters.
Enter the symbol "@" after your message.
A        B

T        U
I        J
N        O
Y        Z

O        P
N        O
E        F
!        !
@        @
```

Fig. 6.14 Cryptogram Generator

The program in Fig. 6.14 must be modified slightly for computers that use the EBCDIC character set. This character set contains some special characters between the letters I and J and between the letters R and S. One possibility is to replace the for statement in procedure READCODE with the one shown next.

```
for NEXTCHAR := 'A' to 'Z' do
    if NEXTCHAR in ['A'..'I', 'J'..'R', 'S'..'Z'] then
        READ (CODE [NEXTLETTER]);
```

The if statement causes the READ statement to be skipped when
NEXTCHAR is a special character.

Self-check Exercises for Section 6.6

1. Describe the following array types:
a) array [1..20] of CHAR
b) array ['0'..'9'] of BOOLEAN
c) array [-5..5] of REAL
d) array [BOOLEAN] of CHAR

6.7 Character Strings

Until now, our use of character data has been quite limited. Variables of
type CHAR were used to hold single character values. In this section, we
shall discuss the manipulation of character arrays.

The variable declaration

```
var
    NAME : array [1..10] of CHAR;
    I : INTEGER;
```

declares a character array NAME with 10 elements; a single character can
be stored in each array element.

The program fragment below first reads a sequence of characters, one at
a time, into the array NAME and then prints out the array NAME.

```
for I := 1 to 10 do
    READ (NAME[I]);
for I := 1 to 10 do
    WRITE (NAME[I])
```

If the characters A.C. Jones are entered, then the array NAME would
be defined as shown next. NAME[5] contains the blank character (shown
as ▢).

Array NAME

[1]	[2]	[3]	[4]	[5]	[6]	[7]	[8]	[9]	[10]
A	.	C	.	▢	J	o	n	e	s

As with any other array, a loop must be used to read and print each individual array element. In the next section, we will introduce a special

type of array that will enable us to print character arrays without using a loop.

Storing Character Strings in Packed Arrays

A *packed array* can be used to store a sequence or *string* of characters. When an array is packed some compilers can store more than one character in each memory cell. Thus less storage space is needed for storing a character string in a packed array. Another important benefit is that Pascal makes it easier for the programmer to manipulate character strings stored in packed arrays. For example, the arrays NAME1 and NAME2 declared below may each be used to store a character string of *length* STRINGSIZE (10 characters).

```
const
    STRINGSIZE = 10;

type
    STRING = packed array [1..STRINGSIZE] of CHAR;

var
    NAME1, NAME2 : STRING;
```

The statement

```
NAME1 := 'A.C. Jones';       {assign a string to NAME1}
```

stores the string value 'A.C. Jones' in the packed array NAME1 ('A' in NAME1[1], '.' in NAME1[2], etc.). If NAME1 is not a packed array, this statement causes a syntax error.

The string value being assigned must be the same type as the packed array receiving the string; this means that the number of characters in the string value must match exactly the size (STRINGSIZE) of the array. The string assignments

```
NAME1 := 'Jones';          {invalid-string too short}
NAME1 := 'A.C. Johnson'    {invalid-string too long}
```

cause a "type conflict of operands" syntax error.

The assignment statement

```
NAME2 := NAME1;            {Copy NAME1 to NAME2}
```

copies the string stored in NAME1 to NAME2. The statement

```
NAME2[1] := 'K'            {change A.C. to K.C.}
```

changes only the first character stored in array NAME2 to 'K'. The statements

```
WRITELN (NAME1);
WRITELN (NAME2)
```

display the lines

```
A.C. JONES
K.C. JONES
```

As shown above, a packed array of characters can be used as a parameter in a WRITELN statement. When this is done, the characters are printed as a single string. Note that these WRITELN statements are only valid for packed arrays. Unfortunately, there is no shortcut for reading a string into a packed array. A loop must be used to read individual characters as it is for a regular array.

Example 6.13 Procedure READSTRING in Fig. 6.15 uses a while loop to read in a data string of up to STRINGSIZE (a global constant) characters. The data string will be stored in the first actual parameter (type STRING); the string length (actual number of characters read) will be stored in the second actual parameter.

Fig. 6.15 Procedure READSTRING

```
procedure READSTRING (var INSTRING {output} : STRING;
                      var LENGTH   {output} : INTEGER);

{Reads a data string into INSTRING. The end of the string is
 indicated by an end-of-line mark. The string length (number of
 characters read) is assigned to LENGTH. A string that is shorter
 than STRINGSIZE is padded with blanks.                           }
const
   BLANK = ' ';                              {character used for padding}

var
   I : 0..STRINGSIZE;                            {loop control variable}

begin {READSTRING}
   {Read each character and store it in the next array element.}
   LENGTH := 0;                                 {no characters read}

   while not EOLN and (LENGTH < STRINGSIZE) do
   begin
      {invariant: not at end of line and array is not filled}
      LENGTH := LENGTH + 1;                        {increment subscript}
      READ (INSTRING[LENGTH])                    {store next character}
   end; {while}

   {assert: at end of line or array is filled}
   READLN;                                       {advance to the next line}

   {If LENGTH < STRINGSIZE, pad rest of string with blanks}
   for I := LENGTH+1 to STRINGSIZE do
      INSTRING[I] := BLANK
end; {READSTRING}
```

Procedure READSTRING assumes that the string being read is at the end of the line. You indicate the end of the line by pressing the carriage return. The while condition calls the standard function EOLN (see Section 4.7) to test whether the end of the line is reached. The while loop is exited when the EOLN function returns TRUE (at end of line) or the array is filled (LENGTH is STRINGSIZE). After loop exit occurs, the READLN statement processes the carriage return thereby advancing to the next line.

A data string may have fewer characters than the declared length, STRINGSIZE, of the array receiving it. If the data string length (LENGTH) is less than STRINGSIZE, then a blank character should be stored in all array elements that did not receive data. This is called *padding a string with blanks* and, in Fig. 6.15, is performed by the for statement. The for loop body is skipped if LENGTH is equal to STRINGSIZE (array is filled with data). If the data string is longer than STRINGSIZE, only the first STRINGSIZE characters will be read and stored; the rest will be skipped.

Due to the different ways in which interactive input occurs in Pascal, procedure READSTRING may have to be modified for your system. Your instructor will tell you if any changes are necessary.

Some Pascal compilers provide a special STRING data type which may be used for storing character strings. This data type is discussed in Appendixes B.3 and B.4.

Now that we have a way to store character strings in memory, we can improve our capability to manipulate textual data. One of the things we might like to do is write a program that prints form letters.

Example 6.14   The three lines below may be used to begin a series of letters inquiring about a summer job.

Dear _____,

I would be interested in applying for the position of _____ at _____ this summer. I am currently a junior at Temple University.

If the rest of the letter is relatively long, then it's wise to write a program to generate these letters. The procedure that fills in the three blanks in the preamble above is shown in Fig. 6.16.

```
procedure PREAMBLE;

{Prints the preamble of a job inquiry letter.}

var
    BOSS, JOBTITLE, COMPANY : STRING;          {three data strings}
    BOSSLEN, JOBLEN, COMPLEN : INTEGER;        {their lengths}

begin {PREAMBLE}
    {Get data needed to fill in the blanks.}
    WRITE ('Name of prospective employer: ');
    READSTRING (BOSS, BOSSLEN);
    WRITE ('Job desired: ');
    READSTRING (JOBTITLE, JOBLEN);
    WRITE ('Company name: ');
    READSTRING (COMPANY, COMPLEN);
```

```
{Display the preamble}
PAGE;
WRITELN ('Dear ', BOSS :BOSSLEN, ',');  WRITELN;
WRITE ('I would be interested in applying for the ');
WRITELN ('position of ', JOBTITLE :JOBLEN);
WRITE ('at ', COMPANY :COMPLEN, ' this summer.  ');
WRITELN ('I am currently a junior at Temple University.')
end;   {PREAMBLE}
```

Fig. 6.16 Procedure PREAMBLE

Procedure PREAMBLE calls procedure READSTRING to read a string into the variables BOSS, JOBTITLE, and COMPANY (type STRING). The WRITE and WRITELN statements at the bottom of PREAMBLE determine where these data strings are displayed in the program output. The number of characters used to display each string is determined by its length (e.g. BOSS :BOSSLEN); consequently, only the characters read in are displayed, not the blank padding.

Procedure PREAMBLE displays its output on the system output device. In Chapter 8, we will learn how to write data to a separate output file.

Comparing Character Strings

Function SAMEARRAY in Fig. 6.9 determines whether or not two arrays of real numbers are identical. It is much easier to determine this for packed character arrays. Assuming the declarations

```
type
    STRING = packed array [1..3] of CHAR;

var
    ALPHASTR, BETASTR : STRING;      {strings being compared}
    SAME, DIFFER : BOOLEAN;          {BOOLEAN flags}
```

the statement

```
    SAME := ALPHASTR = BETASTR        {are strings identical?}
```

assigns the value TRUE to SAME when ALPHASTR and BETASTR contain the same string. The assignment statement

```
    DIFFER := ALPHASTR <> BETASTR     {are strings different?}
```

assigns the value TRUE to DIFFER when ALPAHSTR and BETASTR contain different strings. Finally, the assignment statement

```
    SAME := ALPHASTR = 'Rob'
```

assigns the value TRUE to SAME when ALPHASTR contains the string 'Rob'.

It is also possible to compare packed arrays and strings of the same type for *lexicographic* or alphabetical order using the relational operators <, <=, >, >=. The result of such a comparison is based on the collating sequence (order of characters) for your computer. For example, the condition

    ALPHASTR < BETASTR

is true if the string stored in ALPHASTR is considered less than the string stored in BETASTR. This is determined by comparing corresponding characters in both strings, starting with the first pair. If the characters are the same, then the next pair is checked. If the characters in position i are the first different pair, then ALPHASTR is less than BETASTR if ALPHASTR [i] is less than BETASTR[i].

Example 6.15 The conditions shown in Table 6.5 are true for all character codes shown in Appendix D. The reason each condition is true is explained in the last column.

Table 6.5 Some True String Comparisons

ALPHASTR	Operator	BETASTR	Reason condition is true
'AAA'	<	'ZZZ'	'A' < 'Z'
'AZZ'	<	'ZZZ'	'A' < 'Z'
'ZAZ'	<	'ZZA'	'A' < 'Z'
'AZZ'	<	'BAA'	'A' < 'B'
'B11'	>	'A99'	'B' > 'A'
'B11'	<	'B12'	'1' < '2'
'ACE'	<	'AID'	'C' < 'I'
'123'	>	'103'	'2' > '0'
'123'	>=	'123'	all characters equal
'30 '	>=	'123'	'3' > '1'

The last line of Table 6.5 shows the curious result that '30 ' >= '123' is true. This is because the condition result is based solely on the relationship between the first pair of different characters, '3' and '1'. To avoid these kinds of results, it is best to replace any blanks in numeric strings with zeros. The condition

    '300' >= '123'

is true while the condition

    '030' >= '123'

is false as expected.

In summary, the following operations can be performed on the packed array ALPHASTR (type is packed array [1..3] of CHAR).

- A packed array can be assigned a string value. e.g.
  ```
  ALPHASTR := 'ABC'
  ```
- A packed array can be written without using a loop. e.g.
  ```
  WRITE ('Alpha is ', ALPHASTR :3)
  ```
- A packed array can be compared to another packed array or a string.
  e.g.   `ALPHASTR <> 'ZZZ'`

Arrays of Strings

So far, each array element has been used to store a simple data value. Array elements can also be data structures. One application that comes to mind is an array whose elements are character strings.

Example 6.16   The array MONTHNAME declared below can be used to store 12 character strings. Each element of MONTHNAME is a packed array of length 9 (type STRING).

```
type
    MONTH = (JAN,FEB,MAR,APR,MAY,JUN,JUL,AUG,SEP,OCT,NOV,DEC);
    STRING = packed array [1..9] of CHAR;
    NAMEARRAY = array [MONTH] of STRING;

var
    MONTHNAME : NAMEARRAY;                    {array of month names}
    CURMONTH : MONTH;
```

If the name of each month is stored in this array as shown in Fig. 6.17 (e.g. MONTHNAME[SEP] is 'September'), the statement

```
WRITE (MONTHNAME[CURMONTH])
```

prints the string corresponding to the value of CURMONTH (e.g. If CURMONTH is FEB, the string 'February ' is printed.) In this way, we can print the value of a variable whose type is an enumerated type. This array can be initialized by a series of assignment statements of the form

```
MONTHNAME[JAN] := 'January  ';   MONTHNAME[FEB] := 'February ';
```

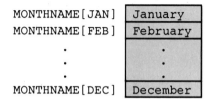

Fig. 6.17 Array MONTHNAME

The array MONTHNAME is an array of arrays. Such a data structure is called a *two-dimensional array* and is the subject of the next section.

1. Write a function that finds the actual length of a string that is padded with blanks. The blank padding should not be included in the actual length.
2. Write a procedure that stores the reverse of an input string parameter in its output parameter. (e.g. if the input string is 'happy   ', the output string should be 'yppah   '.) The actual length of the string being reversed (excluding blank padding) should also be an input parameter.
3. Write a program that uses the procedure in Exercise 2 above to determine whether or not a string is a palindrome. A palindrome is a string that reads the same way from left to right as it does from right to left. (e.g. 'LEVEL' is a palindrome.)

6.8 Multidimensional Arrays

In this section, we will see how to store tables of data and how to represent multidimensional objects using arrays. A two-dimensional object we are all familiar with is a tic-tac-toe board. The declarations

```
type
    BOARDROW = array [1..3] of CHAR;
    BOARDARRAY = array [1..3] of BOARDROW;

var
    TICTACTOE : BOARDARRAY;
```

allocate storage for the array TICTACTOE shown in Fig. 6.18. This array has nine storage cells arranged in three rows and three columns. A character value may be stored in each cell.

In the declarations above, BOARDROW is declared as an array type with three elements of type CHAR; BOARDARRAY is declared as an array type with three elements of type BOARDROW. Consequently, the variable TIC-TACTOE (type BOARDARRAY) is an array of arrays, or a two-dimensional array.

Fig. 6.18 A Tic-Tac-Toe Board Stored as Array TICTACTOE

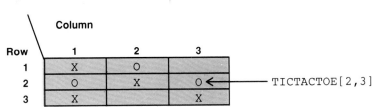

Usually, it is clearer to use one type declaration for an array type that is multidimensional. The declarations

```
type
    BOARDARRAY = array [1..3, 1..3] of CHAR;

var
    TICTACTOE : BOARDARRAY;
```

are equivalent to the ones above in that they allocate storage for a two-dimensional array (TICTACTOE) with three rows and three columns. This array has nine elements, each of which must be referenced by specifying a row subscript (1, 2, or 3) and a column subscript (1, 2, or 3). Each array element contains a character value. The array element TICTACTOE[2,3] pointed to in Fig. 6.18 is in row 2, column 3 of the array; it contains the character 'O'. The diagonal line consisting of array elements TICTACTOE[1,1], TICTACTOE[2,2], and TICTACTOE[3,3] represents a win for player X because each cell contains the character 'X'.

ARRAY TYPE (Multidimensional)

array [*subscript*$_1$] of array [*subscript*$_2$]...
    of array [*subscript*$_n$] of *element-type*

or   array [*subscript*$_1$, *subscript*$_2$, ..., *subscript*$_n$] of *element-type*

Interpretation: *Subscript*$_i$ represents the subscript-type of dimension i of a multidimensional array. The subscript-type may be BOOLEAN, CHAR, an enumerated type, or a subrange. The *element-type* may be any standard data type or a previously-defined data type.

Although we will focus our discussion on arrays with two and three dimensions, there is no limit on the number of dimensions allowed in Pascal.

Example 6.17   The array TABLE declared below

```
var
    TABLE : array [1..7, 1..5, 1..6] of REAL;
```

consists of three dimensions: The first subscript may take values from 1 to 7; the second, from 1 to 5; and the third, from 1 to 6. A total of $7 \times 5 \times 6$, or 210 real numbers may be stored in the array TABLE. All three subscripts must be specified in each reference to array TABLE (e.g. TABLE[2,3,4]).

Manipulation of Two-dimensional Arrays

A row and column subscript must be specified in order to reference an element of a two-dimensional array. The type of each subscript must be compatible with the corresponding subscript type specified in the array declaration.

If I is type INTEGER, the statement

```
for I := 1 to 3
    WRITE (TICTACTOE[1,I])
```

displays the first row of array TICTACTOE (TICTACTOE[1,1], TICTACTOE[1,2], and TICTACTOE[1,3]) on the current output line. The statement

```
for I := 1 to 3 do
    WRITELN (TICTACTOE[I,2])
```

displays the second column of TICTACTOE (TICTACTOE[1,2], TICTACTOE[2,2], and TICTACTOE[3,2]) in a vertical line.

Nested loops may be used to access all elements in a multidimensional array in a predetermined order. In the next examples, the outer loop determines the row being accessed, starting with row 1; the inner loop cycles through the elements of that row. This is called *row-major order*.

Example 6.18   Procedure PRINTBOARD in Fig. 6.19 displays the current status of a tic-tac-toe board. A sample output of this procedure is also shown in Fig. 6.19.

Fig. 6.19 Procedure PRINTBOARD with Sample Output

```
procedure PRINTBOARD (TICTACTOE {input} : BOARDARRAY);

{Displays the status of a tic-tac-toe board (array TICTACTOE).}

var
    ROW, COLUMN : 1..3;

begin {PRINTBOARD}
    WRITELN ('-------');
    for ROW := 1 TO 3 do
        begin {row}
            {Print all columns of current row}
            for COLUMN := 1 TO 3 do
                WRITE ('!', TICTACTOE[ROW,COLUMN]);
            WRITELN ('!');
            WRITELN ('-------')
        end {row}
end; {PRINTBOARD}


-------
!X!O! !
-------
!O!X!O!
-------
!X! !X!
-------
```

Example 6.19   Function BOARDFILLED in Fig. 6.20 returns a value of TRUE if a tic-tac-toe board is all filled up; it returns a value of FALSE if there is at least one empty cell (contains a blank). In a tic-tac-toe program, function BOARDFILLED could be called before each move to determine whether there were any possible moves left. The if statement below prints an appropriate message when there are no moves.

```
if BOARDFILLED(TICTACTOE) then
    WRITELN ('Game is a draw!')
```

```
function BOARDFILLED (TICTACTOE : BOARDARRAY) : BOOLEAN;

{Returns TRUE if the array TICTACTOE is filled;
 otherwise, returns FALSE.                          }

const
    EMPTY = ' ';

var
    ROW, COLUMN : 1..3;

begin {BOARDFILLED}
    BOARDFILLED := TRUE;                   {assume the board is filled}

    {Reset BOARDFILLED to FALSE if an empty cell is found}
    for ROW := 1 TO 3 do
        for COLUMN := 1 TO 3 do
            if TICTACTOE[ROW,COLUMN] = EMPTY then
                BOARDFILLED := FALSE
end; {BOARDFILLED}
```

Fig. 6.20 Function BOARDFILLED

Example 6.20   Procedure ENTERMOVE in Fig. 6.21 is used to enter a move into the array TICTACTOE. The character value stored ('X' or 'O') is determined by the value of PLAYER. Procedure ENTERMOVE reads the move coordinates (MOVEROW, MOVECOLUMN). Function VALIDMOVE is used to test whether the coordinates are valid (i.e. they are in-range and the selected cell is currently empty).

```
procedure ENTERMOVE (PLAYER {input} : CHAR;
                     var TICTACTOE {input/output} : BOARDARRAY);

{Stores an X or O (identity of PLAYER) in the array TICTACTOE.}

var
    MOVEROW, MOVECOLUMN : INTEGER;      {coordinates of selected move}

function VALIDMOVE (MOVEROW, MOVECOLUMN : INTEGER) : BOOLEAN;

{Tests whether the move coordinates (MOVEROW, MOVECOLUMN) are O.K..
 References array TICTACTOE declared as a parameter of ENTERMOVE. }
```

```
const
   EMPTY = ' ';

begin {VALIDMOVE}
   if (MOVEROW in [1..3]) and MOVECOLUMN in [1..3]) then
      VALIDMOVE := TICTACTOE[MOVEROW, MOVECOLUMN] = EMPTY
   else
      VALIDMOVE := FALSE
end; {VALIDMOVE}

begin {ENTERMOVE}
   repeat
      WRITE ('Enter your move coordinates');
      WRITELN ('Enter the row first and then the column: ');
      READLN (MOVEROW, MOVECOLUMN)
   until VALIDMOVE(MOVEROW, MOVECOLUMN);

   {Assert: A valid move is entered}
   TICTACTOE[MOVEROW, MOVECOLUMN] := PLAYER          {Place X or O in cell}
end; {ENTERMOVE}
```

Fig. 6.21 Procedure ENTERMOVE with Function VALIDMOVE

If either move coordinate is out-of-range, the statement

```
VALIDMOVE := FALSE
```

is executed and function VALIDMOVE returns a value of FALSE. When both coordinates are in-range, the statement

```
VALIDMOVE := TICTACTOE[MOVEROW, MOVECOLUMN] = EMPTY
```

is executed, and the function result depends on whether the cell selected is empty.

PROGRAM STYLE

Referencing a nonlocal array

Function VALIDMOVE references the array TICTACTOE which is declared as a parameter in procedure ENTERMOVE. This is the first instance of a function referencing an identifier that is not declared locally. The reason for this is to save the time and memory space required to make a local copy of array TICTACTOE each time VALIDMOVE is called. Since VALIDMOVE is a local function used only by ENTERMOVE, it is reasonable to allow this reference to an identifier declared in ENTERMOVE. Another alternative would be to declare TICTACTOE as a variable parameter in VALIDMOVE.

Multidimensional Arrays with Noninteger Subscripts

The subscript type for each dimension of the multidimensional array TICTACTOE is a subrange of type INTEGER. It is not necessary for the subscript types to have the same host type. The arrays in the next example have a different subscript type for each dimension.

Example 6.21 A university offers 50 courses at each of five campuses. We can conveniently store the enrollments of these courses in the array ENROLL declared below.

```
const
    MAXCOURSE = 50;                {maximum number of courses}

type
    CAMPUS = (MAIN, AMBLER, CENTER, DELAWARE, MONTCO);

var
    ENROLL : array [1..MAXCOURSE, CAMPUS] of INTEGER;
```

This array consists of 250 elements (see Fig. 6.22). ENROLL[1, CENTER] represents the number of students in course 1 at CENTER campus.

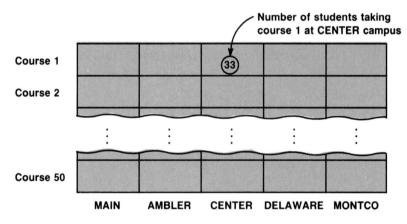

Fig. 6.22 Two-dimensional Array ENROLL

If we wish to have this enrollment information broken down further according to student rank, we would need a three-dimensional array with 1000 elements. This array is declared below and shown in Fig. 6.23.

```
const
    MAXCOURSE = 50;                        {maximum number of courses}

type
    CAMPUS = (MAIN, AMBLER, CENTER, DELAWARE, MONTCO);
    RANK = (FRESHMAN, SOPHOMORE, JUNIOR, SENIOR);
```

```
var
    CLASSENROLL : array [1..MAXCOURSE, CAMPUS, RANK] of INTEGER;
    CURCAMPUS : CAMPUS;                            {current campus}
    CLASSRANK : RANK;                                {current rank}
    TOTAL : INTEGER;                               {student totals}
```

The subscripted variable CLASSENROLL[1, CENTER, SENIOR] represents the number of seniors taking course 1 at CENTER campus.

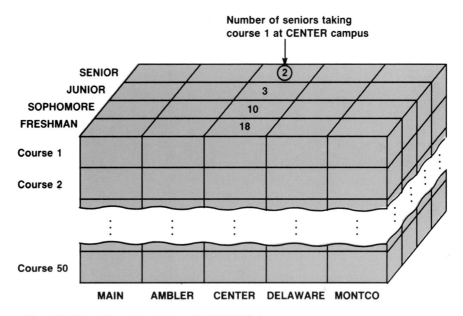

Fig. 6.23 Three-Dimensional Array CLASSENROLL

Example 6.22   The program segment

```
TOTAL := 0;
for CLASSRANK := FRESHMAN to SENIOR do
    TOTAL := TOTAL + CLASSENROLL[1, CENTER, CLASSRANK]
```

computes the total number of students of all ranks in course 1 at CENTER campus.

The program segment

```
TOTAL := 0;
for CURCAMPUS := MAIN to MONTCO do
    for CLASSRANK := FRESHMAN to SENIOR do
        TOTAL := TOTAL + CLASSENROLL[1, CURCAMPUS, CLASSRANK]
```

computes the total number of students in course 1 (regardless of rank or campus).

Self-check Exercises for Section 6.8

1. Explain why the `if` statement below cannot replace the `if` statement in function VALIDMOVE (see Fig. 6.21).

```
if (MOVEROW in [1..3]) and (MOVECOLUMN in [1..3])
      and (TICTACTOE[MOVEROW, MOVECOLUMN] = EMPTY) then
   VALIDMOVE := TRUE
else
   VALIDMOVE := FALSE
```

2. Redefine MAXCOURSE as 5 and write and test program segments that perform the following operations:
   a) Enter the enrollment data for CLASSENROLL.
   b) Find the number of juniors in all classes at all campuses. Students will be counted once for each course in which they are enrolled.
   c) Find the number of sophomores on all campuses who are enrolled in course 2.
   d) Compute and print the number of students at MAIN campus enrolled in each course and the total number of students at MAIN campus in all courses. Students will be counted once for each course in which they are enrolled.
   e) Compute and print the number of upper-class students in all courses at each campus, as well as the total number of upper-class students enrolled. (Upper-class students are juniors and seniors.) Again, students will be counted once for each course in which they are enrolled.

6.9 Case Study

At this point you have learned a lot about Pascal and programming. Knowledge of arrays will enable you to write fairly sophisticated programs. In this section, we will develop a general program that could be used by a company to analyze sales figures.

Sales Analysis Problem

Problem: The High Risk Software Company has employed us to develop a general sales analysis program that can be marketed to many different companies. This program will be *menu-driven*, which means that each user will be given a choice of options to perform. The menu format follows.

```
GENERAL SALES ANALYSIS—choose an option

1. Enter sales data
```

```
2. Display sales table
3. Tabulate sales data by year
4. Tabulate sales data by month
5. Graph sales data by year
6. Graph sales data by month
7. Exit the program
```

We need to write a program that can perform these operations.

Discussion: An examination of the menu shows that the central data structure will be an array of sales data organized by year and month. Since this is a general program, we should make the array large enough to accommodate many companies that are likely to use this product. A good choice would be the array type SALESARRAY below.

```
type
    YEARRANGE = 1900..1999;
    MONTH = (JAN,FEB,MAR,APR,MAY,JUN,JUL,AUG,SEP,OCT,NOV,DEC);
    SALESARRAY = array [YEARRANGE, MONTH] of REAL
```

By storing the names of the months in an array of strings (e.g. MONTH-NAME[1] is 'January ', MONTHNAME[2] is 'February '), we can simplify printing a month name. We also need two BOOLEAN flags (MONTHDONE and YEARDONE) to keep track of whether or not the monthly sums and annual sums have been computed.

The problem data requirements and algorithm follow.

PROBLEM INPUTS

the sales data
each selected option

PROBLEM OUTPUTS

The sales array with sums by year or month and graphic displays

---

LOCAL VARIABLES

an array of month names
(MONTHNAME : array [MONTH] of STRING)
a program flag indicating if month sums are computed
(MONTHDONE : BOOLEAN)
a program flag indicating if year sums are computed
(YEARDONE : BOOLEAN)

Algorithm

1. Initialize the month name array and flags.
2. Read in each option selected and perform it.

The structure chart is shown in Fig. 6.24. The array SALES is declared in procedure DOCHOICE and passed to the level two procedures that are used to carry out each menu option. The main program is shown in Fig. 6.25.

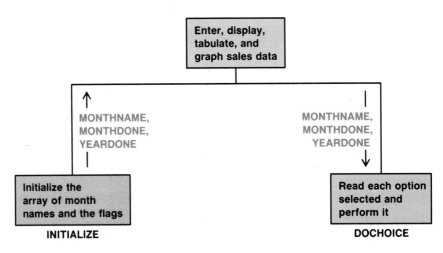

Fig. 6.24 Structure Chart for Sales Analysis Problem

```
program ANALYZE (INPUT, OUTPUT);

{Analyzes an array of sales data. A menu is used to determine
 which operations are performed. The choices include: reading the
 sales data, displaying the data, tabulating sums by year or month,
 and graphing the tabulated sums.                                  }

const
    EXITCHOICE = 7;

type
    SMALLINT = 1..EXITCHOICE;
    MONTH = (JAN,FEB,MAR,APR,MAY,JUN,JUL,AUG,SEP,OCT,NOV,DEC);
    STRING = packed array [1..9] of CHAR;
    NAMEARRAY = array [MONTH] of STRING;

var
    MONTHNAME : NAMEARRAY;              {array of month names}
    YEARDONE : BOOLEAN;                {program flag for year sums}
    MONTHDONE : BOOLEAN;               {program flag for month sums}

procedure INITIALIZE (var MONTHNAME {output} : NAMEARRAY;
                      var MONTHDONE, YEARDONE {output} : BOOLEAN);
```

```
{Initializes the array of month names and the program flags.}
begin {INITIALIZE}
    MONTHNAME[JAN] := 'JANUARY  ';  MONTHNAME[FEB] := 'FEBRUARY ';
    MONTHNAME[MAR] := 'MARCH    ';  MONTHNAME[APR] := 'APRIL    ';
    MONTHNAME[MAY] := 'MAY      ';  MONTHNAME[JUN] := 'JUNE     ';
    MONTHNAME[JUL] := 'JULY     ';  MONTHNAME[AUG] := 'AUGUST   ';
    MONTHNAME[SEP] := 'SEPTEMBER';  MONTHNAME[OCT] := 'OCTOBER  ';
    MONTHNAME[NOV] := 'NOVEMBER ';  MONTHNAME[DEC] := 'DECEMBER ';
    MONTHDONE := FALSE;
    YEARDONE  := FALSE
end;  {INITIALIZE}

procedure DOCHOICE  (var MONTHNAME {input} : NAMEARRAY;
                     MONTHDONE, YEARDONE {input} : BOOLEAN);

{Reads in each option selected and perform it.}

begin {DOCHOICE}
    WRITELN ('Procedure DOCHOICE entered.')
end; {DOCHOICE}

begin {ANALYZE}
    {Initialize MONTHNAME array and flags.}
    INITIALIZE (MONTHNAME, MONTHDONE, YEARDONE);

    {Process all user choices.}
    DOCHOICE (MONTHNAME, MONTHDONE, YEARDONE)
end. {ANALYZE}
```

Fig. 6.25 Main Program for Sales Analysis Problem

The array SALES will be local to procedure DOCHOICE. There will also be local arrays used to store the sales totals by year (SUMBYYEAR) and the sales totals by month (SUMBYMONTH). Procedure DOCHOICE must read the option selected and call a level 2 procedure to process the array SALES. The local variables and algorithm for DOCHOICE are described next.

LOCAL VARIABLES FOR DOCHOICE

the array of sales data (SALES : SALESARRAY)
an array of sums by year
    (SUMBYYEAR : array [YEARRANGE] of REAL)
an array of sums by month
    (SUMBYMONTH : array [MONTH] of REAL)
the first sales year processed (FIRSTYEAR : YEARRANGE)
the last sales year processed (LASTYEAR : YEARRANGE)
each option selected (CHOICE : SMALLINT)

Algorithm for DOCHOICE

1. repeat
    2. Read and validate the user's choice.
    3. Process the option selected.
   until the user is done

Step 3 above will be implemented as a `case` statement that selects a procedure based on the value of CHOICE. The structure chart for DOCHOICE (see Fig. 6.26) shows the level-two procedures that may be called in step 3 except for TABMONTH (similar to TABYEAR) and GRAPHMONTH (similar to GRAPHYEAR). The level-two procedures are relatively straightforward to implement. We will show them nested in DOCHOICE in Fig. 6.27 and discuss them afterwards.

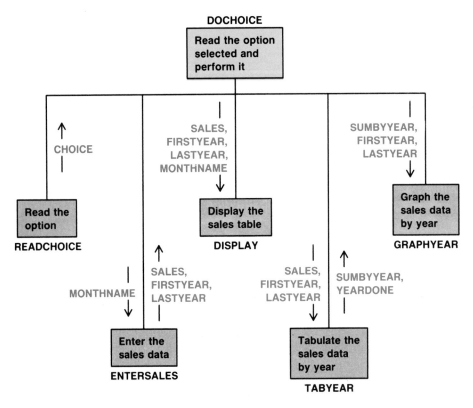

Fig. 6.26 Structure Chart for DOCHOICE

```
procedure DOCHOICE (var MONTHNAME {input} : NAMEARRAY;
                    MONTHDONE, YEARDONE {input} : BOOLEAN);

{Reads in each option selected and perform it.}
```

```
type
    YEARRANGE = 1900..1999;
    SALESARRAY = array [YEARRANGE, MONTH] of REAL;
    YEARARRAY = array [YEARRANGE] of REAL;
    MONTHARRAY = array [MONTH] of REAL;

var
    SALES : SALESARRAY;                  {table of sales data}
    SUMBYYEAR : YEARARRAY;               {sales totals for each year}
    SUMBYMONTH : MONTHARRAY;             {sales totals for each month}
    FIRSTYEAR, LASTYEAR : YEARRANGE;     {period covered}
    CHOICE : SMALLINT;                   {each option selected}

procedure READCHOICE (var CHOICE {output} : SMALLINT);

{Reads and validates the user's choice.}

var
    TEMPCHOICE : INTEGER;                {a possible choice}

procedure PRINTMENU;

{Prints the menu.}

begin {PRINTMENU}
    WRITELN ('Procedure PRINTMENU entered.')
end;  {PRINTMENU}

begin  {READCHOICE}
    PRINTMENU;                           {display the menu}
    repeat
        WRITE ('Select an option (1 through 7): ');
        READLN (TEMPCHOICE)
    until TEMPCHOICE in [1..EXITCHOICE];
    CHOICE := TEMPCHOICE                 {return valid choice}
end; {READCHOICE}

procedure ENTERSALES (var MONTHNAME {input} : NAMEARRAY;
                      var SALES {output} : SALESARRAY;
                      var FIRSTYEAR, LASTYEAR {output} : YEARRANGE);

{Reads the sales data into the array SALES. The first and last
 years stored are read into FIRSTYEAR and LASTYEAR. Uses array
 MONTHNAME to prompt for monthly sales.                         }

var
    CURMONTH : MONTH;                                    {current month}
    CURYEAR : YEARRANGE;                                 {current year}

begin {ENTERSALES}
    {Enter first and last years of sales data.}
    WRITE ('Enter first year of sales data: ');  READLN (FIRSTYEAR);
    WRITE ('Enter last year of sales data: ');   READLN (LASTYEAR);
    WRITELN;

    {Enter table data.}
    for CURYEAR := FIRSTYEAR to LASTYEAR do
```

```
        begin
            WRITELN ('For year ', CURYEAR :4);
            WRITELN ('Enter sales amount for each month or 0');
            for CURMONTH := JAN to DEC do
                begin
                    WRITE (MONTHNAME[CURMONTH], ' sales $');
                    READLN (SALES[CURYEAR, CURMONTH])          {get amount}
                end; {for CURMONTH}
            WRITELN
        end {for CURYEAR}
end; {ENTERSALES}

procedure DISPLAY (var SALES {input} : SALESARRAY;
                   FIRSTYEAR, LASTYEAR {input} : YEARRANGE;
                   MONTHNAME {input} : NAMEARRAY);

{Displays the sales data as a table. Due to line length limits,
 the first 6 months and last 6 months of each year are shown in
 separate tables. Uses SHOWHALF to display each table.            }

procedure SHOWHALF (var SALES {input} : SALESARRAY;
                    FIRSTYEAR, LASTYEAR {input} : YEARRANGE;
                    FIRSTMONTH, LASTMONTH {input} : MONTH);

{Displays the sales amounts by year for each of the months from
 FIRSTMONTH to LASTMONTH.                                         }

var
    CURMONTH : MONTH;                   {loop control variable}
    CURYEAR : YEARRANGE;                {loop control variable}

begin {SHOWHALF}
    {Print table heading for 6 months of each year.}
    WRITE ('YEAR');
    for CURMONTH := FIRSTMONTH to LASTMONTH do
        WRITE (MONTHNAME[CURMONTH] :12);                {print month names}
    WRITELN;                                            {end the heading}

    {Print sales figures for 6 months of each year.}
    for CURYEAR := FIRSTYEAR to LASTYEAR do
        begin
            WRITE (CURYEAR :4);
            for CURMONTH := FIRSTMONTH to LASTMONTH do
                WRITE (SALES[CURYEAR, CURMONTH] :12:2);
            WRITELN
        end {for CURYEAR}
end; {SHOWHALF}

begin {DISPLAY}
    {Display first 6 months of array SALES.}
    SHOWHALF (SALES, FIRSTYEAR, LASTYEAR, JAN, JUN);
    WRITELN;

    {Display last 6 months of array SALES.}
    SHOWHALF (SALES, FIRSTYEAR, LASTYEAR, JUL, DEC)

end; {DISPLAY}
```

```
procedure TABYEAR (var SALES {input} : SALESARRAY;
                   FIRSTYEAR, LASTYEAR {input} : YEARRANGE;
                   var SUMBYYEAR {output} : YEARARRAY;
                   var YEARDONE {output} : BOOLEAN);

{Tabulates sales totals by year. Sums are printed and stored in
 array SUMBYYEAR. YEARDONE is set to TRUE.                     }

var
    CURMONTH : MONTH;                     {loop control variable}
    CURYEAR : YEARRANGE;                  {loop control variable}
    SUM : REAL;                           {sum for each year}

begin {TABYEAR}
    {Print heading.}
    WRITELN ('Total sales by year');
    WRITELN ('YEAR', 'TOTAL' :13);

    {Find and print each annual total.}
    for CURYEAR := FIRSTYEAR to LASTYEAR do
        begin
            {Accumulate sum for 12 months}
            SUM := 0.0;
            for CURMONTH := JAN to DEC do
                SUM := SUM + SALES[CURYEAR, CURMONTH];
            WRITELN (CURYEAR :4, SUM :13:2);       {print sales total}
            SUMBYYEAR[CURYEAR] := SUM              {store sales total}
        end; {for CURYEAR}

    YEARDONE := TRUE                              {set program flag}
end;  {TABYEAR}

procedure TABMONTH (var SALES {input} : SALESARRAY;
                    var MONTHNAME {input} : NAMEARRAY;
                    FIRSTYEAR, LASTYEAR {input} : YEARRANGE;
                    var SUMBYMONTH {output} : MONTHARRAY;
                    var MONTHDONE {output} : BOOLEAN);

{Tabulates sales totals by month. Sums are printed and stored in
 array SUMBYMONTH. MONTHDONE is set to TRUE.                     }

begin {TABMONTH}
    WRITELN ('Procedure TABMONTH entered.')
end; {TABMONTH}

procedure GRAPHYEAR (var SUMBYYEAR {input} : YEARARRAY;
                     FIRSTYEAR, LASTYEAR {input} : YEARRANGE);

{Plots the annual sales totals (stored in SUMBYYEAR) as a bar
 graph. One line is plotted for each year from LASTYEAR to
 FIRSTYEAR. The graph is scaled so that the longest line is
 approximately 50 characters. Uses function FINDMAX to find
 the largest value in the array SUMBYYEAR.                   }

const
    STAR = '*';              {symbol plotted}
    MAXPOINTS = 50;          {longest line length}
```

```
var
    MAXDOLLARS,                      {the largest value plotted}
    PLOTVAL : REAL;                  {the amount plotted so far}
    DOLLARINC : INTEGER;             {the amount represented by each point}
    CURYEAR : YEARRANGE;             {loop control variable}

function FINDMAX (var SUMBYYEAR : YEARARRAY;
                  FIRSTYEAR, LASTYEAR : YEARRANGE) : REAL;

{Finds the largest element in array SUMBYYEAR. Examines elements
 with subscripts FIRSTYEAR through LASTYEAR.                      }

var
    MAXSOFAR : REAL;                 {largest value found so far}
    CURYEAR : YEARRANGE;             {loop control variable}

begin {FINDMAX}
    {Initialize MAXSOFAR to first array element.}
    MAXSOFAR := SUMBYYEAR[FIRSTYEAR];

    {Compare each element to MAXSOFAR. If current element is larger
     than MAXSOFAR, redefine MAXSOFAR as current element.          }
    for CURYEAR := FIRSTYEAR + 1 to LASTYEAR do
        if SUMBYYEAR[CURYEAR] > MAXSOFAR then
            MAXSOFAR := SUMBYYEAR[CURYEAR];              {redefine MAXSOFAR}

    FINDMAX := MAXSOFAR                                  {define result}
end; {FINDMAX}

begin {GRAPHYEAR}
    {Define the scale for the horizontal axis.}
    MAXDOLLARS := FINDMAX (SUMBYYEAR, FIRSTYEAR, LASTYEAR);
    DOLLARINC := ROUND(MAXDOLLARS / MAXPOINTS);
    WRITELN ('Each point on the horizontal scale represents $',
             DOLLARINC :9);

    {Plot the bar graph.}
    WRITELN ('YEAR                        AMOUNT');        {print heading}
    {Print a bar for each element of SUMBYYEAR, start with last one}
    for CURYEAR := LASTYEAR downto FIRSTYEAR do
        begin
            WRITE (CURYEAR :4);                               {print the year}

            {Plot points until value plotted exceeds element value.}
            PLOTVAL := DOLLARINC;                    {initialize sum plotted}
            while PLOTVAL <= SUMBYYEAR[CURYEAR] do
                begin
                    WRITE (STAR);                             {plot a new point}
                    PLOTVAL := PLOTVAL + DOLLARINC       {add to sum plotted}
                end; {while}
            WRITELN (SUMBYYEAR[CURYEAR] :12:2)          {print value of bar}
        end {for CURYEAR}
end; {GRAPHYEAR}

procedure GRAPHMONTH (var SUMBYMONTH {input} : MONTHARRAY;
                      var MONTHNAME {input} : NAMEARRAY);

{Plots the sales totals for each month as a bar graph.}
```

```
begin {GRAPHMONTH}
    WRITELN ('Procedure GRAPHMONTH entered.')
end; {GRAPHMONTH}

begin {DOCHOICE}
    repeat
        {Read and validate the user's choice.}
        READCHOICE (CHOICE);

        {Process the option selected.}
        case CHOICE of
            1 : ENTERSALES (MONTHNAME, SALES, FIRSTYEAR, LASTYEAR);
            2 : DISPLAY (SALES, FIRSTYEAR, LASTYEAR, MONTHNAME);
            3 : TABYEAR (SALES,FIRSTYEAR,LASTYEAR,SUMBYYEAR,YEARDONE);
            4 : TABMONTH (SALES, MONTHNAME, FIRSTYEAR, LASTYEAR,
                            SUMBYMONTH, MONTHDONE);
            5 : if YEARDONE then
                    GRAPHYEAR (SUMBYYEAR, FIRSTYEAR, LASTYEAR)
                else
                    WRITELN ('Tabulate sums before graphing.');
            6 : if MONTHDONE then
                    GRAPHMONTH (SUMBYMONTH, MONTHNAME)
                else
                    WRITELN ('Tabulate sums before graphing.');
            7 : WRITELN ('Sales analysis completed.')
        end {case}
    until CHOICE = EXITCHOICE
end; {DOCHOICE}
```

Fig. 6.27 Procedure DOCHOICE with Nested Procedures

During each repetition of the loop in DOCHOICE, procedure READ-
CHOICE is called to print the menu (performed by PRINTMENU) and read
the user's next choice (CHOICE). The case statement in DOCHOICE selects a level 2 procedure based on the value of CHOICE. Since the array
SUMBYYEAR (or SUMBYMONTH) cannot be graphed before it is tabulated,
an error message is printed if option 5 is selected before option 3 (or option 6 is selected before option 4).

Procedure DISPLAY calls procedure SHOWHALF twice. The first time
the data in array SALES for the first six months of each year are printed;
the second time the data for the last six months are printed. This is because many output devices can only display 80 characters per line.

Procedure GRAPHYEAR calls function FINDMAX to find the largest value
in the array SUMBYYEAR. FINDMAX examines each element in the array,
saving the largest element found so far in MAXSOFAR. The largest value is
returned (saved in MAXDOLLARS) and divided by MAXPOINTS (50) to get
the value represented by each point plotted. For each year being
displayed, the while loop in GRAPHYEAR continues to plot points until
the value plotted exceeds the sales total for that year. Hence, the largest
value will be plotted as a bar of length 50; all other bars will be smaller.

Procedures TABMONTH and GRAPHMONTH are similar to TABYEAR and
GRAPHYEAR; they are left as exercises. A sample run of the sales analysis
program is shown in Fig. 6.28. Only part of the data entry process and the

first half of the sales table display are shown. Only the first menu display
is shown.

```
GENERAL SALES ANALYSIS—choose an option

1. Enter sales data
2. Display sales table
3. Tabulate sales data by year
4. Tabulate sales data by month
5. Graph sales data by year
6. Graph sales data by month
7. Exit the program

Select an option (1 through 7): 1

Enter first year of sales data: 1984
Enter last year of sales data: 1985

For year 1984
Enter sales amount for each month or 0
JANUARY    sales    $1012
FEBRUARY   sales    $13
            .
            .
            .

Select an option (1 through 7): 2

YEAR    JANUARY   FEBRUARY   MARCH     APRIL     MAY       JUNE
1984    1012.00      13.00    144.00    155.00   1000.00      0.00
1985    2125.00       0.00      0.00    120.00   4230.00    815.00

Select an option (1 through 7): 3

Total sales by year
YEAR          TOTAL
1984         5220.00
1985        10425.00

Select an option (1 through 7): 5

Each point on the horizontal scale represents $      209
YEAR                            AMOUNT
1985*****************************************************  $    10425.00
1984**********************  $     5220.00

Select an option (1 through 7): 7

Sales analysis completed.
```

Fig. 6.28 Sample Run of the Sales Analysis Program

Self-check Exercises for Section 6.9

1. Write procedures PRINTMENU, TABMONTH, and GRAPHMONTH.

6.10 Common Programming Errors

The most common error made when using arrays is a subscript range error. This occurs when the subscript value is outside the subrange specified for that array type. Subscript range errors are not syntax errors; they will not be detected until program execution begins. They are usually caused by an incorrect subscript expression, a loop parameter error, or a nonterminating loop. Before considerable time is spent in debugging, all questionable subscript calculations should be carefully checked for out-of-range errors. This is easily done by inserting diagnostic output statements in your program in order to print subscript values that may be out-of-range.

If an out-of-range subscript occurs inside a loop, you should make sure that the loop is terminating properly. If the loop control variable is not being updated as expected, then the loop may be repeated more often than required. This can happen, for example, if the update step follows the loop end statement or if the loop begin and end are erroneously omitted.

You should also double-check the subscript values at the loop boundaries. If these values are in-range, it is likely that all other subscript references in the loop will also be in-range.

As with all Pascal data types, make sure that there are no type inconsistencies. The subscript type and element type used in all array references must correspond to the types specified in the array declaration. Similarly, the types of two arrays used in an array copy statement or as corresponding parameters must be the same. Remember to use only identifiers without subscripts as array parameters and to specify the types of all array parameters using identifiers.

When using multidimensional arrays, the subscript for each dimension must be consistent with its declared type. If nested for loops are used to process the array elements, make sure that loop control variables used as subscripts are in the correct order.

6.11 Chapter Review

In this chapter we introduced the array which is a data structure used to simplify the storage and manipulation of a collection of like data items. We discussed how to declare an array type and how to reference an individual array element by placing a subscript in brackets following the array name.

The for statement enables us to easily reference the elements of an array in sequence. We used for statements to initialize arrays, read and print arrays, and to control the manipulation of individual array elements.

Packed arrays were used for storage of character strings. We saw that operations such as array comparison, array assignment, and array printing are performed more easily on a packed array since the entire array can be processed as a unit rather than element by element.

Arrays of arrays, or multidimensional arrays, were used to represent tables of information and game boards. Nests of loops are needed to manipulate the elements of a multidimensional array in a systematic way. The correspondence between the loop control variables and the array subscripts determines the sequence in which the array elements are processed.

New Pascal Statements

The new Pascal statements introduced in this chapter are described in Table 6.6.

Review Questions

1. Identify the error in the Pascal fragment below.

```
type
    ANARRAY = array [1..8] of INTEGER;

var
    X : ANARRAY;
    I : INTEGER;

begin
    for I := 1 to 9 DO
        X[I] := I
end.
```

When will the error be detected?

2. Declare an array of reals called WEEK that can be referenced by using any day of the week as a subscript, where SUNDAY is the first subscript.

3. Identify the error in the Pascal fragment below.

```
type
    ANARRAY = array [CHAR] of REAL;

var
    X : ANARRAY;
    I : INTEGER;

begin
    I := 1;
    X[I] := 8.384
end.
```

4. The statement {a} in the following Pascal program segment is a valid Pascal statement—TRUE or FALSE?

```
type
    REALARRAY = array [1..8] of REAL;
```

Table 6.6 Summary of New Pascal Statements

Statement	Effect

Array declaration
`type`
    `INTARRAY = array [1..10] of INTEGER;`
`var`
    `CUBE, COUNT : INTARRAY;`
	The data type `INTARRAY` describes an array with 10 type `INTEGER` elements. CUBE and COUNT are arrays with this structure.

Packed array declaration
`type`
    `STRING = packed array [1..10] of CHAR;`
`var`
    `NAME : STRING;`
	The data type `STRING` describes a packed array of 10 characters. NAME is an array with this structure.

Multidimensional array declaration
`type`
    `DAY = (SUN,MON,TUE,WED,THU,FRI,SAT);`
    `MATRIX = array [1..52, DAY] of REAL;`
`var`
    `SALES : MATRIX;`
	`MATRIX` describes a two-dimensional array with 52 rows and seven columns (days of the week). SALES is an array of this type and can store 364 real numbers.

Array references
`for I := 1 to 10 do`
    `CUBE[I] := I * I * I`
	Saves I^3 in the Ith element of array CUBE ($1 \leq I \leq 10$).

`if CUBE[5] > 100 then`	Compares `CUBE[5]` to 100.
`WRITE (CUBE[1], CUBE[2])`	Displays the first two cubes.
`WRITE (SALES[3, MON])`	Displays the element of SALES for week 3 and day Monday.

`for WEEK := 1 to 52 do`
    `for TODAY := SUN to SAT do`
        `SALES[WEEK, TODAY] := 0.0`
	Initializes each element of SALES to zero.

`READ (SALES[1, SUN])`	Reads the value for week 1 and day Sunday into SALES.
Array copy `COUNT := CUBE`	Copies contents of array CUBE to array COUNT.
Operations on packed arrays `NAME := 'R. Koffman'`	Saves `'R. Koffman'` in NAME.
`WRITELN (NAME)`	Displays `'R. Koffman'`.
`if NAME = 'Daffy Duck' then`	Compares NAME to `'Daffy Duck'`.

```
var
    X : REALARRAY;
    I : INTEGER;

begin
    I := 1;
    X(I) := 8.384  {a}
end.
```

5. What are the two common ways of selecting array elements for processing?
6. Write a Pascal fragment to print out the index of the smallest and the largest numbers in an array X of 20 integers. Array X has a range of values of 0 to 100. Assume array X already has values assigned to each element.
7. The parameters for a procedure are two arrays (type REALARRAY) and an integer representing the length of the arrays. The procedure copies the first array in the parameter list to the other array in reverse order using a loop structure. Write the procedure.
8. List two advantages to using packed character arrays.
9. Define row-major order.
10. Declare an array that can be used to store each title of the TOP40 hits for each week of the year, given that the TITLELENGTH will be 20 characters.
11. Declare an array YEARLYHOURS for storing the hours five employees work each day of the week, each week of the year.

Programming Projects

1. Write a program to read N data items into two arrays X and Y of size 20. Store the product of corresponding elements of X and Y in a third array Z, also of size 20. Print a three-column table displaying the arrays X, Y, and Z. Then compute and print the square root of the sum of the items in Z. Make up your own data, with N less than 20.

2. Let A be an array containing 20 integers. Write a program that first reads up to 20 data items into A, and then finds and prints the subscript of the largest item in A and that item.

3. Each year the Department of Traffic Accidents receives accident count reports from a number of cities and towns across the country. To summarize these reports, the Department provides a frequency-distribution printout that gives the number of cities reporting accident counts in the following ranges: 0–99, 100–199, 200–299, 300–399, 400–499, 500 and above. The Department needs a computer program to read the number of accidents for each reporting city or town and to add one to the count for the appropriate accident range. After all the data have been processed, the resulting frequency counts are to be printed.

4. Assume for the moment that your computer has the very limited capability of

being able to read and print only single-decimal digits at a time and to add together two integers consisting of one decimal digit each. Write a program to read in two integers of up to 10 digits each, add these numbers together, and print the result. Test your program on the following numbers.

$$X = 1487625$$
$$Y = 12783$$

$$X = 60705202$$
$$Y = 30760832$$

$$X = 1234567890$$
$$Y = 9876543210$$

Hints: Store the numbers X and Y in two character arrays X, Y, of size 10, one decimal digit per element. If the number is less than 10 digits in length, enter enough leading zeros (to the left of the number) to make the number 10 digits long.

array X

[1]	[2]	[3]	[4]	[5]	[6]	[7]	[8]	[9]	[10]
0	0	0	1	4	8	7	6	2	5

array Y

[1]	[2]	[3]	[4]	[5]	[6]	[7]	[8]	[9]	[10]
0	0	0	0	0	1	2	7	8	3

You will need a loop to add together the digits in corresponding array elements, starting with the element with subscript 10. Don't forget to handle the carry if there is one! Use a BOOLEAN variable CARRY to indicate whether or not the sum of the last pair of digits is greater than nine.

5. Write a program for the following problem. You are given a collection of scores for the last exam in your computer course. You are to compute the average of these scores, and then assign grades to each student according to the following rule.

If a student's score is within 10 points (above or below) of the average, give the student a grade of SATISFACTORY. If the score is more than 10 points higher than the average, give the student a grade of OUTSTANDING. If the score is more than 10 points below the average, give the student a grade of UNSATISFACTORY. Test your program on the following data:

RICHARD LUGAR	55
FRANK RIZZO	71
DONALD SCHAEFFER	84
KEVIN WHITE	93
JAMES RIEHLE	74
ABE BEAME	70
TOM BRADLEY	84
WALTER WASHINGTON	68

```
        RICHARD DALEY              64
        RICHARD HATCHER           82
```

Hint: The output from your program should consist of a labelled three-column list containing the name, exam score, and grade of each student.

6. Write a program to read N data items into each of two arrays X and Y of size 20. Compare each of the elements of X to the corresponding element of Y. In the corresponding element of a third array Z, store:

$$+1 \quad \text{if X is larger than Y}$$
$$0 \quad \text{if X is equal to Y}$$
$$-1 \quad \text{if X is less than Y}$$

Then print a three-column table displaying the contents of the arrays X, Y, and Z, followed by a count of the number of elements of X that exceed Y, and a count of the number of elements of X that are less than Y. Make up your own test data with N less than 20.

7. It can be shown that a number is prime if there is no smaller prime number that divides it. Consequently, in order to determine whether N is prime, it is sufficient to check only the prime numbers less than N as possible divisors (see Section 4.8). Use this information to write a program that stores the first 100 prime numbers in an array. Then have your program print the array.

8. The results of a true-false exam given to a Computer Science class have been coded for input to a program. The information available for each student consists of a student identification number and the students' answers to 10 true-false questions. The available data are as follows:

Student identification	Answer string
0080	FTTFTFTTFT
0340	FTFTFTTTFF
0341	FTTFTTTTTT
0401	TTFFTFFTTT
0462	TTFTTTFFTF
0463	TTTTTTTTTT
0464	FTFFTFFTFT
0512	TFTFTFTFTF
0618	TTTFFTTFTF
0619	FFFFFFFFFF
0687	TFTTFTTFTF
0700	FTFFTTFFFT
0712	FTFTFTFTFT
0837	TFTFTTFTFT

Write a program that first reads in the answer string representing the 10 correct answers (use FTFFTFFTFT as data). Next, for each student, read the student's data and compute and store the number of correct answers for each student in one array, and store the student ID number in the corresponding element of another array. Determine the best score, BEST. Then print a three-column table displaying the ID number, score, and grade for each student. The grade should be determined as follows: If the score is equal to BEST or BEST−1, give an A; if it is BEST−2 or BEST−3, give a C. Otherwise, give an F.

9. The results of a survey of the households in your township have been made available. Each record contains data for one household, including a four-digit integer identification number, the annual income for the household, and the number of members of the household. Write a program to read the survey results into three arrays and perform the following analyses:

a) Count the number of households included in the survey and print a three-column table displaying the data read in. (You may assume that no more than 25 households were surveyed.)

b) Calculate the average household income, and list the identification number and income of each household that exceeds the average.

c) Determine the percentage of households having incomes below the poverty level. The poverty level income may be computed using the formula

$$P = \$6500.00 + \$750.00 \times (m - 2)$$

where m is the number of members of each household. This formula shows that the poverty level depends on the number of family members, m, and the poverty level increases as m gets larger.

Test your program on the following data.

Identification number	Annual income	Household members
1041	12,180	4
1062	13,240	3
1327	19,800	2
1483	22,458	8
1900	17,000	2
2112	18,125	7
2345	15,623	2
3210	3,200	6
3600	6,500	5
3601	11,970	2
4725	8,900	3
6217	10,000	2
9280	6,200	1

10. Write a program which, given the taxable income for a single taxpayer, will compute the income tax for that person. Use Schedule X shown in Fig. 6.29 on the page. Assume that "line 34," referenced in this schedule, contains the taxable income. Example: If the individual's taxable income is $8192, your program should use the tax amount and percent shown in column 3 of line 5 (see arrow). The tax in this case is $692 + 0.19(8192 − 6500) = $1013.48. For each individual processed, print taxable earnings and the total tax. Hint: Set up three arrays, one for the base tax (column 3), one for the tax percent (column 3), and the third for the excess base (column 4). Your program must then compute the correct index to these arrays, given the taxable income.

11. Write a program that removes all of the blanks from a character string and

Tax Rate Schedule

Schedule X

Single Taxpayers

Use this schedule if you checked **Filing Status Box 1** on Form 1040 —

If the amount on Form 1040, line 34 is:		Enter on line 2 of the worksheet on this page:	
Over—	But not Over—		of the amount over—
$0	$2,300	—0—	
2,300	3,400	. . . . .14%	$2,300
3,400	4,400	$154 + 16%	3,400
4,400	6,500	314 + 18%	4,400
6,500	8,500	692 + 19%	6,500
8,500	10,800	1,072 + 21%	8,500
10,800	12,900	1,555 + 24%	10,800
12,900	15,000	2,059 + 26%	12,900
15,000	18,200	2,605 + 30%	15,000
18,200	23,500	3,565 + 34%	18,200
23,500	28,800	5,367 + 39%	23,500
28,800	34,100	7,434 + 44%	28,800
34,100	41,500	9,766 + 49%	34,100
41,500	55,300	13,392 + 55%	41,500
55,300	81,800	20,982 + 63%	55,300
81,800	108,300	37,677 + 68%	81,800
108,300	. . . . .	55,697 + 70%	108,300

Fig. 6.29 Schedule X (from IRS Form 1040)

compacts all nonblank characters in the string so that all the blanks are at the end. You should only have to scan the input string once from left to right.

12. Assume a set of sentences is to be processed. Each sentence consists of a sequence of words, separated by one or more blank spaces. Write a program that will read these sentences and count the number of words with one letter, two letters, etc., up to ten letters.

13. Write a program to read in a collection of character strings of arbitrary length. For each string read, your program should do the following:
    a) Print the length of the string.
    b) Count the number of occurrences of four letter words.
    c) Replace each four letter word with a string of four asterisks and print the new string.

14. Write an interactive program that plays the game of HANGMAN. Read the word to be guessed into successive elements of the packed array WORD. The player must guess the letters belonging to WORD. The program should termi-

nate when either all letters have been guessed correctly (player wins) or a specified number of incorrect guesses have been made (computer wins). Hint: Use a packed array SOLUTION to keep track of the solution so far. Initialize SOLUTION to a string of symbols '*'. Each time a letter in WORD is guessed, replace the corresponding '*' in SOLUTION with that letter.

15. Write a program that reads in a tic-tac-toe board and determines the best move for player X. Use the following strategy: Consider all squares that are empty and evaluate potential moves into them. If the move fills the third square in a row, column, or diagonal that already has two X's, add 50 to the score; if it fills the third square in a row, column or diagonal with two O's, add 25 to the score; for each row, column, or diagonal containing this move that will have two X's and one blank, add 10 to the score; add eight for each row, column or diagonal through this move that will have one O, and X, and one blank; add four for each row, column or diagonal that will have one X and the rest blanks. Select the move that scores the highest.

The possible moves for the board below are numbered. Their scores are shown to the right of the board. Move five is selected.

1	O	X
2	X	3
O	4	5

1—10 + 8 = 18
2—10 + 8 = 18
3—10 + 10 = 20
4—8
5—10 + 10 + 8 = 28

16. Write a program that reads the five cards representing a poker hand into a two-dimensional array (first dimension is suit, second dimension is rank). Evaluate the poker hand using procedures to determine whether the hand is a flush (all one suit), a straight (five consecutive cards), a straight flush (five consecutive cards of one suit), four-of-a-kind, a full house (three-of-a-kind, two of another), three-of-a-kind, two pair, or one pair.

17. Write a set of procedures to manipulate a pair of matrices. You should provide procedures for addition, subtraction, and multiplication. Each procedure should validate its input parameters (i.e., check all matrix dimensions) before performing the required data manipulation.

18. The results from the mayor's race have been reported by each precinct as follows:

Precinct	Candidate A	Candidate B	Candidate C	Candidate D
1	192	48	206	37
2	147	90	312	21
3	186	12	121	38
4	114	21	408	39
5	267	13	382	29

Write a program to do the following:

a) Print out the table with appropriate headings for the rows and columns.
b) Compute and print the total number of votes received by each candidate and the percent of the total votes cast.

c) If any one candidate receives over 50% of the votes, the program should print a message declaring that candidate the winner.

d) If no candidate receives 50% of the votes, the program should print a message declaring a run-off between the two candidates with the highest number of votes; the two candidates should be identified by their letter names.

e) Run the program once with above data and once with candidate C receiving only 108 votes in precinct 4.

19. The game of Life, invented by John H. Conway, is supposed to model the genetic laws for birth, survival, and death. (See *Scientific American*, October, 1970, p. 120.) We will play it on a board consisting of 25 squares in the horizontal and vertical directions. Each square can be empty or contain an X indicating the presence of an organism. Each square (except the border squares) has eight neighbors. The small square shown in the segment of the board drawn below connects the neighbors of the organism in row three, column three.

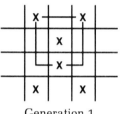

Generation 1

The next generation of organisms is determined according to the following criteria:

1. Birth: An organism will be born in each empty location that has exactly three neighbors.

2. Death: An organism with four or more organisms as neighbors will die from overcrowding. An organism with fewer than two neighbors will die from loneliness.

3. Survival: An organism with two or three neighbors will survive to the next generation. Generations 2 and 3 for the sample follow:

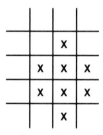

Generation 2

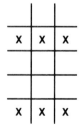

Generation 3

Read in an initial configuration of organisms. Print the original game array, calculate the next generation of organisms in a new array, copy the new array into the original game array and repeat the cycle for as many generations as you wish. *Hint:* Assume that the borders of the game array are infertile regions where organisms can neither survive nor be born; you will not have to process the border squares.

20. The results of a multiple-choice exam are recorded in a computer. It is often useful to provide a simple item analysis of a set of questions to determine their effectiveness. Read the 10 answers for each exam and process the following information: (a) determine if each answer is correct, accumulate the number of correct answers, and (b) increment a respective counter for the appropriate answer whether right or wrong.

Assume all of the answers are of the range of A-E. The output should consist of each question number, the correct answer, number of correct responses, number of incorrect responses, and a count of the number of A's, B's, C's, D's, and E's.

Use the following sample data:

(1)	(2)	(3)	(4)	(5)	(6)	(7)	(8)	(9)	(10)
A	B	C	E	A	B	C	D	B	B
E	C	C	E	D	A	B	A	D	E
C	A	B	B	C	D	E	D	B	B
E	A	D	A	D	A	D	A	D	A
C	C	B	B	A	A	D	D	B	E
E	D	C	B	A	A	B	C	D	E
E	A	C	C	D	A	C	A	B	A
B	B	A	C	B	A	B	B	B	D

And use as the key: E C C B E A D A B C

21. An amusing program consists of a sentence generator that will read a series of four numbers and print out a sentence. Provide three arrays containing eight words each (maximum of 10 characters to each word) called NOUN, VERB, and ADJECTIVE. Fill each of these arrays with some appropriate words and then read four numbers (each in a range from 1-8). Write out a short sentence in which each number is the appropriate subscript from arrays in the following order:

NOUN, VERB, ADJECTIVE, NOUN

An example would be to read 4, 5, 2, 6. This will print the strings NOUN[4], VERB[5], ADJECTIVE[2], and NOUN[6]. If their contents are:

```
NOUN[4] is 'JOHN      '
VERB[5] is 'LIKES     '
ADJECTIVE[2] is 'CRAZY     '
NOUN[6] is 'BREAD     '
```

The sentence

JOHN LIKES CRAZY BREAD.

would be printed. A trailing blank should not be printed; however, one blank between each word is needed and a period should be supplied at the end.

22. The INDEX function is useful in character string manipulation. This function locates the first appearance of the second string within the first string and returns the subscript of this location. Parameters to this function are:

```
(STRING1, STRING2 : STRING; LEN1, LEN2 : INTEGER)
```

where STRING is an array type sufficiently large enough to hold each string. The length parameters (LEN1, LEN2) are used to indicate how many characters of each string should be used in the processing.

If no match is found the function returns a zero. Some examples are included below:

Given:

```
var
    A, B:   STRING;
    X : INTEGER;

begin
    A := 'ABCDEFGHIJK';
    B := 'DEF        ';
    X := INDEX(A, B, 11, 3);
    .
    .
```

X would have a value of 4.

For the same A if B contained:

```
B := ' ABD         ';
X := INDEX(A, B, 11, 4);
```

X would be asigned 0 since ' ABD' is not contained (in order) in string A. Test your function with several sets of data.

23. Write the appropriate procedures to process a standard address and extract the following information. First read an address of the form:

LINE1: <Title> <First name> <Middle name> <Last name>
LINE2: <Street address>
LINE3: <City>, <State> <Zipcode>

For example: Dr. John E. Smith
           111 Chestnut Street
           Kalamazoo, MI 49001

Determine and print the (a) Title, (b) Last name, (c) State, and (d) Zipcodes for each label.

7

Records

7.1 Declaring a Record
7.2 Manipulating Individual Fields of a Record
7.3 Manipulating an Entire Record
7.4 Arrays of Records
7.5 Case Study
7.6 Searching an Array
7.7 Sorting an Array
7.8 General Data Structures
7.9 Record Variants
7.10 Manipulating Strings Stored in Records
7.11 Common Programming Errors
7.12 Chapter Review

In the previous chapter we introduced the array, a data structure fundamental to programming and included in almost every high-level programming language. In this chapter we will introduce an additional data structure, the record, that is available in Pascal, but not in all other high-level languages. The use of records makes it easier to organize and represent information in Pascal. This is a major reason for the popularity of the Pascal language.

A record, like an array, is a collection of related data items. However, unlike an array, the individual components of a record can contain data of different types. We can use a record to store a variety of kinds of information about a person, such as the person's name, marital status, age, date of birth, etc. Instead of using a subscript, we refer to the information in a record by using a field name.

7.1 Declaring a Record

Normally a record is declared in two stages, as is an array. We first declare the structure or form of a record in a record type declaration. Next, we declare one or more record variables of this record type. The record type declaration specifies the name and type of each record component or *field*.

Example 7.1 We wish to store the descriptive information shown below in a computerized payroll program.

```
NAME: Danielson
SEX : FEMALE
SOCIAL SECURITY NUMBER: 035-20-1111
NUMBER OF DEPENDENTS : 2
HOURLY SALARY RATE : 3.98
TAXABLE SALARY (for 40 hour week): 130.40
```

We will declare a record type EMPLOYEE with six distinct fields and a record variable, CLERK, for storage of the data above.

```
const
    STRINGSIZE = 11;

type
    STRING = packed array [1..STRINGSIZE] of CHAR;
    EMPLOYEE = record
        NAME : STRING;
        SEX : (FEMALE, MALE);
        SOCSECNUM : STRING ;
        NUMDEPEND : INTEGER;
        RATE,
        TAXSAL : REAL
    end; |EMPLOYEE|

var
    CLERK : EMPLOYEE;
```

The record variable CLERK is structured as defined in the declaration for record type EMPLOYEE. Thus the memory allocated for CLERK consists of storage space for two character strings (maximum length 11), a scalar value (FEMALE or MALE), an integer value, and two real values.

The record variable CLERK (see Fig. 7.1) assumes the values shown earlier are stored in memory.

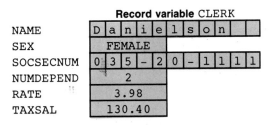

Fig. 7.1 Record Variable CLERK

As illustrated in the type declaration for EMPLOYEE, it is possible to specify record fields corresponding to any standard or user-defined type. In addition, the type declaration of a field can be included within the record declaration, e.g. (FEMALE, MALE). The record type declaration is described in the next display.

RECORD TYPE DECLARATION

$rec\text{-}type$ = record
    $id\text{-}list_1$: $type_1$;
    $id\text{-}list_2$: $type_2$;
             .
             .
             .
    $id\text{-}list_n$: $type_n$
end;

Interpretation: The identifier $rec\text{-}type$ is the name of the record structure being described. Each $id\text{-}list_i$ is a list of one or more field names separated by commas; the data type of each field in $id\text{-}list_i$ is specified by $type_i$.

Note: $type_i$ may be any standard or user-defined data type including a structured type such as an array or another record. If $type_i$ is a user-defined data type, it can either be defined before the record or as part of the record description.

Self-check Exercises for Section 7.1

1. A catalogue listing for a textbook consists of the author's name, title, publisher, and year of publication. Define a record type CATALOGUE for storage of this information.

2. Each part in an inventory is represented by its part number, a descriptive name, the quantity on hand, and price. Define a record type PART.

7.2 Manipulating Individual Fields of a Record

In most instances, each field of a record must be individually manipulated. We can reference a record field by using a field selector consisting of the record variable name followed by the field name. A period is used to separate the field name and the record name.

Example 7.2

Fig. 7.1 gives an example of the record variable CLERK. The data shown earlier can be stored in CLERK through the sequence of assignment statements

```
CLERK.NAME := 'Danielson    ';
CLERK.SEX := FEMALE;
CLERK.SOCSECNUM := '035-20-1111';
CLERK.NUMDEPEND := 2;
CLERK.RATE := 3.98
```

Once data are stored in a record, they can be manipulated in the same way as other data in memory. For example, the statements

```
WRITE ('The clerk is ');
case CLERK.SEX of
   FEMALE : WRITE ('Ms. ');
   MALE   : WRITE ('Mr. ')
end; {case}
WRITELN (CLERK.NAME)
```

print the character string stored in the NAME field of CLERK following an appropriate message. For the data above, the output would be

```
The clerk is Ms. Danielson
```

The field selector CLERK.NAME[1] references the first character ('D') stored in the NAME field (a string) of the record variable CLERK.

The assignment statement

```
CLERK.TAXSAL := 40.0 * CLERK.RATE - 14.40 * CLERK.NUMDEPEND
```

computes the clerk's taxable salary by deducting $14.40 for each dependent from the gross salary (40.0 * hourly rate). The computed result is saved in the record field named CLERK.TAXSAL.

The with Statement

It becomes tedious to write the complete field selector each time we reference a field of a record. The with statement can be used to shorten the field selector.

```
with CLERK do
    begin
        WRITE ('The clerk is ');
        case SEX of
            FEMALE : WRITE ('Ms. ');
            MALE   : WRITE ('Mr. ')
        end; {case}
        WRITELN (NAME);

        TAXSAL := 40.0 * RATE - 14.40 * NUMDEPEND;
        WRITELN ('The clerk''s taxable salary is $', TAXSAL :7:2)
    end {with}
```

As shown, it is not necessary to specify both the record variable and field names inside a with statement. The record variable CLERK is identified in the with statement header; consequently, only the field name is needed inside the with statement, not the complete field selector (e.g., RATE instead of CLERK.RATE). The with statement is particularly useful when several fields of the same record variable are being manipulated, as in this example.

WITH STATEMENT

with *record-var* do
    statement

Interpretation: The *statement* may be a single or compound statement. *Record-var* is the name of a record variable. Within the statement body, any field of *record-var* may be referenced by specifying its field name only.

Example 7.3   The program in Fig. 7.2 computes the distance from an arbitrary point on the X-Y plane to the origin (intersection of X axis and Y axis). The values of the X and Y coordinates are entered as data and stored in the fields XCOORD and YCOORD of the record variable POINT1. The formula used to compute the distance from the origin to an arbitrary point (X, Y) is

$$\text{distance} = \sqrt{X^2 + Y^2}$$

Since the record variable POINT1 is specified in the with statement header, only the field names XCOORD and YCOORD are needed to reference the coordinates of the data point. Each coordinate is read separately since it is illegal to use a record variable by itself in a READ(READLN) or WRITE(WRITELN) statement (i.e., only individual fields of a record variable may be read or displayed at a terminal, not the entire record).

```
program DISTORIGIN (INPUT, OUTPUT);

{Finds the distance from a point to the origin.}

type
   POINT = record
      XCOORD, YCOORD : REAL
   end; {POINT}

var
   POINT1 : POINT;         {the data point}
   DISTANCE : REAL;        {its distance from the origin}

begin
   with POINT1 do
      begin
         WRITE ('X: '); READLN (XCOORD);
         WRITE ('Y: '); READLN (YCOORD);
         DISTANCE := SQRT(SQR(XCOORD) + SQR(YCOORD));
         WRITELN ('Distance to origin is ', DISTANCE :5:2)
      end {with}
end. {DISTORIGIN}

X: 3.00
Y: 4.00
Distance to origin is 5.00
```

Fig. 7.2 Distance from Point to Origin.

PROGRAM STYLE

A word of caution about the with *statement*

Although the with statement shortens program statements that manipulate record components, it can also reduce the clarity of these statements. For example, in Fig. 7.2 it is not obvious that the statement

```
DISTANCE := SQRT(SQR(XCOORD) + SQR(YCOORD));
```

is passing two record fields (POINT1.XCOORD and POINT1.YCOORD) to the function SQR and not two variables.

The possibility of confusion and error increases when two record variables (e.g. POINT1 and POINT2) are being manipulated. In this case if the field name XCOORD is referenced by itself, it is not clear whether we mean POINT1.XCOORD or POINT2.XCOORD. Pascal uses the record variable specified in the header of the closest containing with.

1. Write the Pascal statements required to print the values stored in CLERK in the form shown in Fig. 7.1.

7.3 Manipulating an Entire Record

Since arithmetic and logical operations must be performed on individual memory cells, record variables cannot be used as the operands of arithmetic and relational operators. These operators must be used with individual fields of a record as shown in the previous section. This is also true now for the standard procedures READ(READLN) and WRITE(WRITELN). In the next chapter we will learn how to read and write entire record variables to certain types of files.

Copying One Record to Another

All the fields of one record variable can be copied to another record variable of the same type using a record copy (assignment) statement. If CLERK and JANITOR are both record variables of type EMPLOYEE, the statement

```
CLERK := JANITOR          {copy JANITOR to CLERK}
```

copies each field of JANITOR into the corresponding field of CLERK.

Records as Parameters

A record variable can be passed as a parameter to a function or procedure. As always, the actual parameter must be the same type as its corresponding formal parameter. The use of records as parameters can shorten parameter lists considerably because only one parameter (the record variable) has to be passed instead of several.

Example 7.4   In a grading program, the vital statistics about an exam might consist of the highest and lowest scores, the average score, and the standard deviation. In previous problems these data would be stored in separate variables; however, it makes sense to group them together as a record.

```
type
    EXAMSTATS = record
        LOW, HIGH : 0..100;
        AVERAGE, STANDARDDEV : REAL
    end; {EXAMSTATS}

var
    EXAM : EXAMSTATS;
```

A procedure that computes one of these results (e.g. AVERAGE) could be passed a single record field (e.g. EXAM.AVERAGE). A procedure that manipulates more than one of these fields could be passed the entire record. An example would be procedure REPORT shown in Fig. 7.3.

```
procedure REPORT (EXAM {input} : EXAMSTATS);

{Prints the exam statistics.}

begin {REPORT}
   with EXAM do
      begin
         WRITELN ('High score: ', HIGH :3);
         WRITELN ('Low score: ', LOW :3);
         WRITELN ('Average: ', AVERAGE :5:1);
         WRITELN ('Standard deviation: ', STANDARDDEV :5:1)
      end {with}
end; {REPORT}
```

Fig. 7.3 Procedure REPORT

Example 7.5 In computer simulations we need to keep track of the time of day during the progress of a simulated event or experiment. Normally the time of day is updated after a certain time period has elapsed. The record type TIME is declared below assuming a 24-hour clock.

```
type
   TIME = record
      HOUR : 0..23;
      MINUTE, SECOND : 0..59
   end; {TIME}
```

Procedure CHANGETIME in Fig. 7.4 updates the time of day, TIMEOFDAY (type TIME), after a time interval, ELAPSEDTIME, expressed in seconds. Each statement that uses the mod operator updates a particular field of the record represented by TIMEOFDAY. The mod operator ensures that each updated value is within the required range; the div operator converts multiples of 60 seconds to minutes and multiples of 60 minutes to hours.

Reading a Record

Normally we use a procedure to read data into a record. Procedure READEMPL in Fig. 7.5 be used to read data into the first five fields of a record variable of type EMPLOYEE. Since we can pass a record variable to READEMPL, only one parameter is needed, not five. The procedure (call) statement

```
READEMPL (CLERK)
```

causes the data read to be stored in record variable CLERK.

```
procedure CHANGETIME (ELAPSEDTIME {input} : INTEGER;
                      var TIMEOFDAY {input/output} : TIME);

{Updates the time of day, TIMEOFDAY, assuming a 24-hour clock and
 an elapsed time of ELAPSEDTIME in seconds.                        }

var
    NEWHOUR, NEWMIN, NEWSEC : INTEGER;                  {temporary variables}

begin {CHANGETIME}
    with TIMEOFDAY do
        begin
            NEWSEC := SECOND + ELAPSEDTIME;            {total seconds}
            SECOND := NEWSEC mod 60;                   {seconds mod 60}
            NEWMIN := MINUTE + (NEWSEC div 60);         {total minutes}
            MINUTE := NEWMIN mod 60;                   {minutes mod 60}
            NEWHOUR := HOUR + (NEWMIN div 60);           {total hours}
            HOUR := NEWHOUR mod 24                      {hours mod 24}
        end {with}
end; {CHANGETIME}
```

Fig. 7.4 Procedure CHANGETIME

Fig. 7.5 Procedure READEMPL

```
procedure READEMPL (var ONEEMPL {output} : EMPLOYEE);

{Reads one employee record into ONEEMPL. Uses procedure
 READSTRING to read in a string of up to 11 characters.}

var
    LENGTH : INTEGER;      {actual length of data string}
    SEXCHAR : CHAR;        {letter indicating sex}

{Insert procedure READSTRING here.}

begin {READEMPL}
    with ONEEMPL do
        begin
            WRITE ('Name: ');  READSTRING (NAME, LENGTH);
            WRITE ('Sex (F or M): ');   READ (SEXCHAR);
            case SEXCHAR of
                'F', 'f' : SEX := FEMALE;
                'M', 'm' : SEX := MALE
            end; {case}
            WRITE ('Social Security number: ');
            READSTRING (SOCSECNUM, LENGTH);
            WRITE ('Number of dependents: ');  READLN (NUMDEPEND);
            WRITE ('Hourly rate: ');  READLN (RATE)
        end {with}
end; {READEMPL}
```

The two procedure (call) statements

```
READSTRING (NAME, LENGTH);
READSTRING (SOCSECNUM, LENGTH);
```

use procedure READSTRING (see Fig. 6.15) to enter a data string. READSTRING returns a character string and an integer value. The first actual parameter in each procedure (call) statement specifies which record field (ONEEMPL.NAME or ONEEMPL.SOCSECNUM) receives the data string.

The second parameter of READSTRING represents the length of the string read. The string length is stored in local variable LENGTH but is not saved in the employee's record.

7.4 Arrays of Records

In Chapter 6, we manipulated arrays with one or more dimensions. We found the array to be a useful data structure for storing a large collection of data items of the same type. We were able to represent game boards and tables of sales figures using arrays.

Often a data collection contains items of different types. For example, the data representing the performance of a class of students on an exam might consist of the student names, exam scores, and grades assigned.

One approach to organizing these data is to allocate separate arrays for the names, scores, and grades as shown in Fig. 7.6. These arrays are called *parallel arrays* because all the data items with the same subscript (for example I) pertain to a particular student (the Ith student). Related data items have the same color in the arrays shown in Fig. 7.6. The data for the first student are stored in NAMES[1], SCORES[1], and GRADES[1].

Fig. 7.6 Three Parallel Arrays

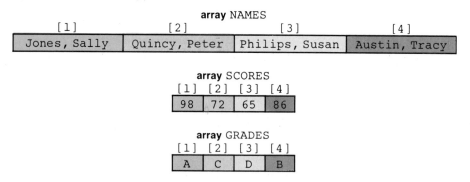

A more natural organization of the class performance data is to group all the information pertaining to a particular student in a record. Then a single array of records can be used to represent the class. This array of records is illustrated in Fig. 7.7 below.

array CLASS

	NAME	SCORE	GRADE
CLASS [1]	Jones, Sally	98	A
CLASS [2]	Quincy, Peter	72	C
CLASS [3]	Philips, Susan	65	D
CLASS [4]	Austin, Tracy	86	B

Fig. 7.7 Array of Records

The data for the first student are stored in the record CLASS[1]; her individual data items are CLASS[1].NAME, CLASS[1].SCORE, and CLASS[1].GRADE. This particular data organization is used next.

7.5 Case Study

The next problem illustrates the use of an array of records.

Student Grading Problem Revisited

Problem: In Section 3.7 we wrote a program to assign grades to each student taking an exam. Since we could not save strings, only the student's initials were read as data. The grade category (outstanding, satisfactory, unsatisfactory) was determined by comparing the student's exam score to the data values MINOUT and MINSAT. We would like to improve this program to read and display the student's last name, to display the low score, high score, average score, and standard deviation, and to assign letter grades more equitably based on the class average and standard deviation.

Discussion: The input data for the new grading program consists of a name (a string) and exam score (an integer) for each student; the output consists of the exam statistics and the grade (a character) assigned to each student. The record variable EXAM can be used to provide storage for the grade statistics (see Example 7.4).

Since we will have to find the class average before assigning a grade, it will be necessary to process the exam scores more than one time. Consequently we should save all the student data (name, score, and grade) in an array.

If the items being stored were all the same data type, a two-dimensional array or table could be used. Since the individual items are not all the same type, we can organize the data for a single student as a record; the data for the entire class can then be stored in an array of records (CLASS). Each student record should contain storage space for the student's name, score, and the grade to be assigned.

PROBLEM INPUTS

The name and score of each student taking the exam (CLASS)

PROBLEM OUTPUTS

The exam statistics including the low score, high score, average score, and standard deviation (EXAM : EXAMSTATS)
The grade assigned to each student (stored in CLASS)

PROGRAM VARIABLES

The number of students taking the exam (NUMSTU : INTEGER)

Algorithm
1. Read the student data.
2. Compute the exam statistics.
3. Assign letter grades to each student.
4. Print the exam statistics.
5. Print the data and grade for each student.

The structure chart for this problem is shown in Fig. 7.8; The main program is shown in Fig. 7.9

Fig. 7.8 Structure Chart for Improved Grading Problem

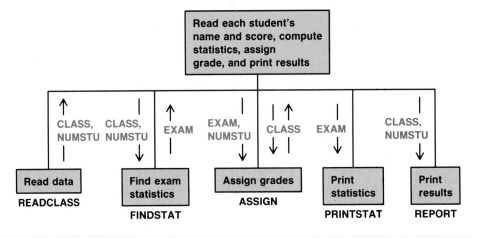

```
program NEWGRADER (INPUT, OUTPUT);

{Reads student names and scores and computes exam statistics such
 as low score, high score, average, standard deviation. Assigns
 letter grades based on the average score. Prints these results.}

const
    STRINGSIZE = 20;              {Maximum length of each name string}
    CLASSIZE = 200;              {maximum number of students}

type
    STRING = packed array [1..STRINGSIZE] of CHAR;
    STUDENT = record
        NAME : STRING;
        SCORE : 0..100;
        GRADE : 'A'..'E'
    end; {STUDENT}
    CLASSRANGE = 1..CLASSIZE;
    STUDENTARRAY = array [CLASSRANGE] of STUDENT;

    EXAMSTATS = record
        LOW, HIGH : 0..100;
        AVERAGE, STANDARDDEV : REAL
    end; {EXAMSTAT}

var
    CLASS : STUDENTARRAY;         {array of student records}
    EXAM : EXAMSTATS;             {statistics for exam}
    NUMSTU : 0..CLASSIZE;         {number of students}

{Insert procedures READCLASS, FINDSTAT, ASSIGN, PRINTSTAT, REPORT.}

begin {NEWGRADER}
    {Read the student data.}
    READCLASS (CLASS, NUMSTU);

    {Compute the exam statistics.}
    FINDSTAT (CLASS, NUMSTU, EXAM);

    {Assign letter grades to each student.}
    ASSIGN (NUMSTU, EXAM, CLASS);

    {Print the exam statistics.}
    PRINTSTAT (EXAM);

    {Print the data and grade for each student.}
    REPORT (CLASS, NUMSTU)
end. {NEWGRADER}
```

Fig. 7.9 Main Program for Improved Grading Problem

Rather than show stubs for the five level one procedures, we have simply indicated by a comment where these procedures belong in the main program. We will discuss some of the level two procedures next and leave the rest as exercises.

Procedure READCLASS in Fig. 7.10 is used to enter the data (student name and exam score) for the class. It also returns a count of students (NUMSTU) taking the exam.

Fig. 7.10 Procedure READCLASS

```
procedure READCLASS (var CLASS {output} : STUDENTARRAY;
                     var NUMSTU {output} : INTEGER);

{Reads all student records and stores them in consecutive elements
 of the array CLASS. Returns the count of students in NUMSTU.      }

const
    SENTINEL = '                    ';    {string of 20 blanks}

var
    NEXTSTUDENT : STUDENT;                 {current student record}

procedure READSTUDENT (var NEXTSTUDENT {output} : STUDENT);

{Reads a single student record. Reads a blank string for the NAME
 field if there are no more student records.                    }

var
    LENGTH : 0..STRINGSIZE;                {actual length of name string}

{Insert procedure READSTRING here.}

begin {READSTUDENT}
    with NEXTSTUDENT do
        begin
            WRITE ('NAME: ');  READSTRING (NAME, LENGTH);
            if NAME <> SENTINEL then
                begin
                    WRITE ('SCORE: ');  READLN (SCORE)
                end {if}
        end {with}
end; {READSTUDENT}

begin {READCLASS}
    WRITELN ('Enter the data requested for each student.');
    WRITELN ('Press return (after prompt NAME: ) when done.');

    NUMSTU := 0;                                {initial count of students}
    repeat
        READSTUDENT (NEXTSTUDENT);                      {read next student}
        if NEXTSTUDENT.NAME <> SENTINEL then
            begin
                NUMSTU := NUMSTU + 1;                       {increase count}
                CLASS[NUMSTU] := NEXTSTUDENT          {save the data in CLASS}
            end {if}
    until (NEXTSTUDENT.NAME = SENTINEL) or (NUMSTU = CLASSIZE);

    {assert: no more students or array is filled}
    if NUMSTU = CLASSIZE then
        WRITELN ('Array is filled with student data.')
end; {READCLASS}
```

Procedure READCLASS is similar to procedure READSCORES in Fig. 6.12. It uses procedure READSTUDENT to read each student's data (name and exam score only) into the local record variable NEXTSTUDENT. Entering a blank name (by pressing <Return>) indicates that there are no more records. If a nonblank name is read into NEXTSTUDENT.NAME, procedure READCLASS increments the array subscript NUMSTU by 1, and the assignment statement

```
CLASS[NUMSTU] := NEXTSTUDENT      {save the data in CLASS}
```

copies the record in NEXTSTUDENT into the array of records.

The student data can be manipulated in the usual way after being stored in array CLASS. Procedure FINDSTAT will call a different level two function to find each of the four individual exam statistics. Procedure FINDSTAT is shown in Fig. 7.11 along with one of these functions (FINDAVE).

Fig. 7.11 Procedure FINDSTAT with Function FINDAVE

```
procedure FINDSTAT (var CLASS {input} : STUDENTARRAY;
                        NUMSTU {input} : INTEGER;
                        var EXAM {output} : EXAMSTATS);

{Finds the exam statistics: low score, high score, average, and
 standard deviation.                                             }

function FINDAVE (var CLASS : STUDENTARRAY;
                     NUMSTU : INTEGER) : REAL;

{Finds the average score assuming NUMSTU students took the exam.}

var
    SCORESUM : INTEGER          {sum of scores}
    CURSTU : CLASSRANGE;        {loop control variable}

begin {FINDAVE}
    {Accumulate sum of scores in SCORESUM.}
    SCORESUM := 0;                                       {initialize sum}
    for CURSTU := 1 to NUMSTU do
        SCORESUM := SCORESUM + CLASS[CURSTU].SCORE;      {add next score}

    {Define result.}
    if NUMSTU <> 0 then
        FINDAVE := SCORESUM / NUMSTU                     {compute average}
    else
        FINDAVE := 0.0                                   {average undefined}
end; {FINDAVE}

{Insert functions FINDHIGH, FINDLOW, FINDSTDEV here.}
```

(continued)

```
begin {FINDSTAT}
    with EXAM do
        begin
            {Find the average score.}
            AVERAGE := FINDAVE(CLASS, NUMSTU);

            {Find the low score.}
            LOW := FINDLOW(CLASS, NUMSTU);

            {Find the high score.}
            HIGH := FINDHIGH(CLASS, NUMSTU);

            {Find the standard deviation.}
            STANDARDDEV := FINDSTDEV(CLASS, NUMSTU, AVERAGE)
        end {with}
end; {FINDSTAT}
```

In procedure FINDSTAT, the assignment statement

```
AVERAGE := FINDAVE(CLASS, NUMSTU);
```

calls function FINDAVE, assigning the function result to EXAM.AVERAGE. Function FINDAVE uses a for statement to accumulate the sum of all exam scores in the local variable SCORESUM. Each score is referenced by the field selector CLASS[CURSTU].SCORE, where CURSTU is the loop control variable. Next, the average is defined by dividing the sum by the number of students.

Procedure ASSIGN assigns a letter grade to each student. The grade can be determined by comparing the student's score to the class average and standard deviation. The decision table below specifies the grade to be assigned for each possible score.

Table 7.1 Decision Table for Assigning Letter Grades

Score Range	Grade
>= AVERAGE + 2 * STANDARDDEV	A
>= AVERAGE + STANDARDDEV	B
>= AVERAGE - STANDARDDEV	C
>= AVERAGE - 2 * STANDARDDEV	D
< AVERAGE - 2 * STANDARDDEV	E

Procedure ASSIGN is shown in Fig. 7.12. The nested if statement implements the decision table above. The for loop causes this if statement to be executed once for each student.

```
procedure ASSIGN (NUMSTU {input} : INTEGER;
                  EXAM {input} : EXAMSTATS;
                  var CLASS {input/output} : STUDENTARRAY);

{Assigns a letter grade to each student based on the
 student's score and the average score and standard deviation.}

var
    CURSTU : CLASSRANGE;                              {loop control variable}

begin {ASSIGN}
    with EXAM do
        for CURSTU := 1 to NUMSTU do
            if CLASS[CURSTU].SCORE >= AVERAGE + 2 * STANDARDDEV then
                CLASS[CURSTU].GRADE := 'A'
            else if CLASS[CURSTU].SCORE >= AVERAGE + STANDARDDEV then
                CLASS[CURSTU].GRADE := 'B'
            else if CLASS[CURSTU].SCORE >= AVERAGE - STANDARDDEV then
                CLASS[CURSTU].GRADE := 'C'
            else if CLASS[CURSTU].SCORE >= AVERAGE - 2 * STANDARDDEV then
                CLASS[CURSTU].GRADE := 'D'
            else
                CLASS[CURSTU].GRADE := 'E'
end; {ASSIGN}
```

Fig. 7.12 Procedure ASSIGN

Procedure REPORT (see Fig. 7.13) displays the information stored in array CLASS. The with statement selects the record variable, CLASS [CURSTU], to be printed. Since the with statement is nested inside the for statement and CURSTU is the loop control variable, a different student's record is printed on each output line. It would be an error to attempt to nest the for statement inside the with statement.

Fig. 7.13 Procedure REPORT

```
procedure REPORT (var CLASS {input} : STUDENTARRAY;
                  NUMSTU {input} : INTEGER);

{Prints a report of student results.}

var
    CURSTU : CLASSRANGE;                              {loop control variable}

begin
    WRITELN ('Table of ', NUMSTU :3, ' students follows:');
    WRITELN ('Name' :20, 'Score' :10, 'Grade' :10); {Print heading}

    {Print each student's data.}
    for CURSTU := 1 to NUMSTU do
        with CLASS[CURSTU] do
            WRITELN (NAME :20, SCORE :10, GRADE :10)          {Print student}
end; {REPORT}
```

The array CLASS is declared as a variable parameter in FINDSTAT, FINDAVE, and REPORT even though it is used for input only. This saves the extra time and memory required to make a local copy of this rather large array.

Self-check Exercises for Section 7.5

1. Why must FINDSTAT be a procedure and not a function?
2. Write functions FINDLOW, FINDHIGH, and FINDSTDEV. Function FINDSTDEV should implement the formula

$$\text{standard deviation} = \sqrt{\frac{\sum_{i=1}^{N} \text{score}_{i}^{2}}{N} - \text{average}^2}$$

where $\sum_{i=1}^{N} \text{score}_i^2$ is the sum of the square of each score and N is the number of scores.

7.6 Searching an Array

A common problem in dealing with arrays is *searching* an array to determine whether or not a particular data item is in the array. If the array elements are records, then we must compare a particular field of each record, called the *record key*, to the data item that we are seeking. Once we have located the item in question, we can display or update the associated record.

Example 7.6 Function SEARCH in Fig. 7.14 searches the array CLASS for a *target name*, represented by STUNAME. If the target name is located, SEARCH returns the index of the student record with that name. Otherwise, it returns a value of 0. For the array CLASS shown in Fig. 7.7, the value returned would be 3 for the target name 'Philips, Susan   '; the value returned would be 0 for the target name 'Philips, Sue   '.

Each time the while loop is repeated, the student name selected by CURSTU is compared to the target name. If they are equal, the BOOLEAN flag FOUND is set to TRUE and the loop will be exited when the while condition is retested; otherwise, CURSTU is increased by 1 so that the next student name can be checked.

The while loop is exited after all names are checked (if not before). The if statement following the loop defines the search result as the subscript of the target name (FOUND is TRUE) or 0 (FOUND is FALSE).

```
function SEARCH (var CLASS : STUDENTARRAY;
                     STUNAME : STRING;
                     NUMSTU : INTEGER) : INTEGER;

{Searches for STUNAME in the NAME field of array CLASS. If found,
 returns the subscript of STUNAME; otherwise, returns 0.          }

var
    CURSTU : INTEGER;               {array subscript}
    FOUND : BOOLEAN;                {flag indicating success or failure}

begin {SEARCH}
    FOUND := FALSE;                              {initially target not found}

    {Compare the NAME field of each record to STUNAME until done.}
    CURSTU := 1;                                 {start with first record}
    while not FOUND and (CURSTU <= NUMSTU) do
        {invariant: STUNAME not found and CURSTU is in range.}
        if CLASS[CURSTU].NAME = STUNAME then
            FOUND := TRUE                              {target is found}
        else
            CURSTU := CURSTU + 1;                 {check next record}

    {assert: STUNAME found or CURSTU is out of range.}
    {Define the function result.}
    if FOUND then
        SEARCH := CURSTU                         {return target subscript}
    else
        SEARCH := 0                                  {return 0}
end; {SEARCH}
```

Fig. 7.14 Function SEARCH

Example 7.7   In the grading program, we wish to be able to change the exam score and/or grade of a particular student. We can use function SEARCH to locate the student whose name matches the target name. Then we can modify the rest of the data stored for that student. This is accomplished by procedure CHANGERECORD shown in Fig. 7.15.

First, procedure READSTUDENT is called to store the new student data in record TARGET. Next, function SEARCH is called to locate the target name. If the target name is found, the statement

```
CLASS[INDEX] := TARGET              {Update the record}
```

copies the new student data into the element of array CLASS selected by INDEX. If the target name is not found (INDEX is 0), then an appropriate message is printed.

```
procedure CHANGERECORD (var CLASS |input/output| : STUDENTARRAY;
                            NUMSTU |input| : INTEGER);

|Changes the record stored in CLASS for a particular student.
 Calls procedure READSTUDENT and function SEARCH.            |

var
    TARGET : STUDENT;              |data for record being updated|
    INDEX : 0 .. CLASSIZE;         |subscript of target record or 0|

|Insert procedure READSTUDENT and function SEARCH|

begin |CHANGERECORD|
    |Enter the new student data.|
    WRITELN ('Enter the name of the student whose record'|;
    WRITELN ('is being changed and the new data for that student.')
    READSTUDENT (TARGET);

    |Search for the target name in the array CLASS.|
    INDEX := SEARCH (CLASS, TARGET.NAME, NUMSTU);

    |If the target name is found, update the record.|
    if INDEX <> 0 then
        CLASS[INDEX] := TARGET                     |update the record|
    else
        WRITELN ('Student ', TARGET.NAME, ' is not in the class. ')
end; |CHANGERECORD|
```

Fig. 7.15 Procedure CHANGERECORD

Self-check Exercise for Section 7.6

1. Write a procedure to count the number of students with a passing grade on the exam (D or higher).

7.7 Sorting an Array

In Section 3.4 we discussed a simple sort operation involving three numbers. We performed the sort by examining pairs of numbers and exchanging them if they were out of order. There are many times when we need to sort the elements in an entire array. For example, we might prefer to have a grade report printed out in alphabetical order, or in order by score.

In this section, a fairly simple (but not very efficient) algorithm called the *bubble sort* will be discussed. The bubble sort compares adjacent array elements and exchanges their values if they are out of order. In this way the smaller values "bubble" up to the top of the array (toward the first element) while the larger values sink to the bottom of the array; hence the name bubble sort. The data requirements and algorithm for a bubble sort procedure follow.

the array being sorted
the number of array elements

the sorted array

Algorithm for Bubblesort Procedure

1. repeat
   2.   Examine every pair of adjacent array elements and exchange any values that are out of order.
   until the array is sorted

As an example we will trace through one execution of step 2 above, that is one *pass* through an array being sorted. By scanning the diagrams in Fig. 7.16a from left to right we see the effect of each comparison. The pair of array elements being compared is shown in a darker color in each diagram. The first pair of values (M[1] is 60, M[2] is 42) is out of order so the values are exchanged. The next pair of values (M[2] is now 60, M[3] is 75) is compared in the second array shown in Fig. 7.16a; this pair is in order and so is the next pair (M[3] is 75, M[4] is 83). The last pair (M[4] is 83, M[5] is 27) is out of order so the values are exchanged as shown in the last diagram.

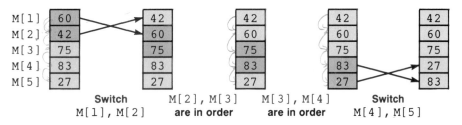

Fig. 7.16a One Pass of Bubble Sort of Array M

The last array shown in Fig. 7.16a is closer to being sorted than the original. The only value that is out of order is the number 27 in M[4]. Unfortunately, it will be necessary to complete three more passes through the entire array before this value bubbles up to the top of the array (we warned you the sort was inefficient!). In each of these passes, only one pair of values will be out of order so only one exchange will be made. The exchanges made and the contents of array M after the completion of each pass are shown in Fig. 7.16b.

We can tell by looking at the contents of the array at the end of pass 4 that the array is now sorted; however, the computer can only recognize this by making one additional pass with no exchanges. If no exchanges are made, then all pairs must be in order. This is the reason for the extra pass shown in Fig. 7.16b and for the BOOLEAN flag NOEXCHANGES described next.

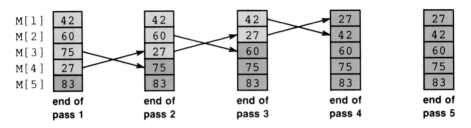

Fig. 7.16b Array M after Completion of Each Pass

flag to indicate whether or not any exchanges were made in a pass (NOEXCHANGES : BOOLEAN)
loop control variable and subscript (FIRST : INTEGER)
number of the current pass starting with 1 (PASS : INTEGER)

Refinement of step 2 of Bubble Sort

2.1   Initialize NOEXCHANGES to TRUE
2.2   for each pair of adjacent array elements do
    2.3   if the values in a pair are out of order then
        2.4   Exchange the values
        2.5   Set NOEXCHANGES to FALSE

Step 2.2 will be implemented as a for statement. The for loop control variable, FIRST, will also be the subscript of the first element in each pair; consequently, FIRST+1 will be the subscript of the second element in each pair. During each pass, the initial value of FIRST is 1. The final value of FIRST must be less than the number of array elements so that FIRST+1 will be in range.

For an array of N elements, the final value of FIRST can be N−PASS, where PASS is the number of the current pass, starting with 1 for the first pass. The reason is that at the end of pass 1 the last array element must be in its correct place; at the end of pass 2 the last 2 array elements must be in their correct places; at the end of pass 3 the last 3 array elements must be in their correct places, etc. There is no need to examine array elements already in place. The section of the array already sorted at the end of each pass is shown in a darker color in Fig. 7.16b.

Procedure BUBBLESORT in Fig. 7.17 performs a bubble sort on the array CLASS. Because the array is being sorted on the NAME field, CLASS[FIRST].NAME is compared to CLASS[FIRST+1].NAME. If the student names are out of order, the statement

```
SWITCH (CLASS[FIRST], CLASS[FIRST+1]);   {Switch data}
```

calls procedure SWITCH to exchange the records of the two array elements listed as actual parameters. Note that the entire records are switched, not just the names. If only the names are switched, the scores and grades will be associated with the wrong students. When BUBBLE-SORT is completed, the array of records will be in alphabetical order by student name.

```
procedure BUBBLESORT (var CLASS {input/output} : STUDENTARRAY;
                      NUMSTU {input} : INTEGER);

{Sorts the data in array CLASS by student name.}

var
    NOEXCHANGES : BOOLEAN;              {any exchanges in current pass?}
    FIRST,                             {first element of a pair}
    PASS : INTEGER;                    {number of current pass}

procedure SWITCH (var STU1, STU2 {input/output} : STUDENT);

{Switches records STU1 and STU2.}

var
    TEMPSTU : STUDENT;                 {temporary student record}

begin {SWITCH}
    TEMPSTU := STU1;  STU1 := STU2;  STU2 := TEMPSTU
end; {SWITCH}

begin {BUBBLESORT}
    PASS := 1;                                       {start with pass 1}
    repeat
        NOEXCHANGES := TRUE;                          {no exchanges yet}

        {Compare student names in each pair of adjacent elements}
        for FIRST := 1 to NUMSTU-PASS do
            if CLASS[FIRST].NAME > CLASS[FIRST+1].NAME then
                begin {exchange}
                    SWITCH (CLASS[FIRST], CLASS[FIRST+1]);     {switch data}
                    NOEXCHANGES := FALSE                        {reset flag}
                end; {exchange}

        PASS := PASS + 1                          {increment pass number}
    until NOEXCHANGES                    {until no exchanges in last pass}

    {assert: array is sorted}
end; {BUBBLESORT}
```

Fig. 7.17 Bubblesort Procedure

Self-check Exercises for Section 7.7

1. What changes would be needed to sort the array CLASS by exam score instead of student name? How could you have the scores arranged in descending order (largest score first)?

7.8 General Data Structures

In solving any programming problem, data structures must be selected that enable us to efficiently represent in the computer a variety of information. The selection of data structures is a very important part of the problem solving process. The data structures used can have a profound effect on the efficiency and simplicity of the algorithm and program.

The data structuring facilities in Pascal are quite powerful and general. In the last sample, we used a data type consisting of an array of records. It is also possible to declare a record type with fields that are arrays or other records.

Fig. 7.18 Record Type NEWEMPLOYEE and Record Variable PROGRAMMER

```
const
   STRINGSIZE = 11;
   DIGITSIZE = 5;

type
   STRING = packed array [1..STRINGSIZE] of CHAR;
   DIGITSTRING = packed array [1..DIGITSIZE] of '0'..'9';
   MONTH = (JAN,FEB,MAR,APR,MAY,JUN,JUL,AUG,SEP,OCT ,NOV,DEC);

   EMPLOYEE = record
      NAME : STRING;
      SEX : (FEMALE, MALE);
      SOCSECNUM : STRING ;
      NUMDEPEND : INTEGER;
      RATE : REAL;
      TAXSAL : REAL
   end; {EMPLOYEE}

   ADDRESS = record
      STREET, CITY, STATE : STRING;
      ZIPCODE : DIGITSTRING
   end; {ADDRESS}

   DATE = record
      MONTHVAL : MONTH;
      DAY : 1..31;
      YEAR : 1900..1999
   end; {DATE}

   NEWEMPLOYEE = record
      PAYDATA : EMPLOYEE;
      HOME : ADDRESS;
      STARTDATE, BIRTHDATE : DATE
   end; {NEWEMPLOYEE}

var
   PROGRAMMER : NEWEMPLOYEE;
   DAYOFYEAR : DATE;
```

We began our study of records by introducing a record type EMPLOYEE. In this section we will modify this record by adding new fields for storage of the employee's address, starting date, and date of birth. The record type NEWEMPLOYEE as well as two additional record types, DATE and ADDRESS, are declared in Fig. 7.18.

The hierarchical structure of PROGRAMMER, a record variable of type NEWEMPLOYEE, is shown in Fig. 7.19. This is not a structure diagram, but is used to provide a graphic display of the record form.

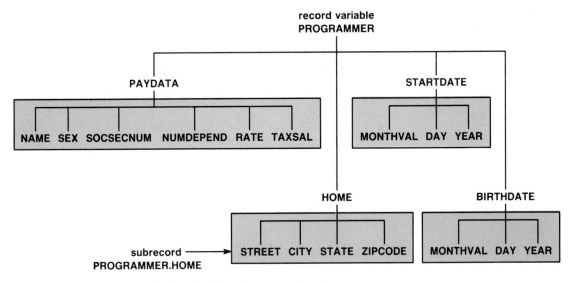

Fig. 7.19 Record Variable PROGRAMMER (Type NEWEMPLOYEE)

This diagram shows that PROGRAMMER is a record with fields PAYDATA, HOME, STARTDATE, BIRTHDATE. Each of these fields is itself a record (called a *subrecord*) of PROGRAMMER. Each subrecord is shaded in Fig. 7.19. As shown, there are 4 data fields (STREET, CITY, etc.) in the subrecord PROGRAMMER.HOME.

In order to reference a field in this diagram, we must trace a complete path to it starting from the top of the diagram. For example, the field selector

PROGRAMMER.STARTDATE

references the entire subrecord STARTDATE (type DATE) of the variable PROGRAMMER. The field selector

PROGRAMMER.STARTDATE.YEAR

references the YEAR field (type INTEGER) of the subrecord PROGRAMMER.STARTDATE. The field selector

```
PROGRAMMER.YEAR
```

is incomplete (which YEAR field?) and will cause a syntax error.

The record copy statement

```
PROGRAMMER.STARTDATE := DAYOFYEAR
```

is legal if DAYOFYEAR is a record variable of type DATE. This statement copies each field of DAYOFYEAR into the corresponding field of the subrecord PROGRAMMER.STARTDATE. Three values are copied.

In many situations, the with statement can be used to shorten the field selector. The statement

```
with PROGRAMMER.STARTDATE do
    WRITELN ('Year started: ', YEAR,
            'Day started: ', DAY)
```

prints two fields of the subrecord PROGRAMMER.STARTDATE. The computation for taxable salary could be written as

```
with PROGRAMMER.PAYDATA do
    TAXSAL := 40.0 * RATE - 14.40 * NUMDEPEND
```

You can use a list of field names in a with statement. The statement

```
with PROGRAMMER, PAYDATA, HOME, STARTDATE do
    WRITELN (NAME, ' lives in ', CITY,
            ' and started in ', YEAR :4)
```

displays one field of each subrecord PROGRAMMER.PAYDATA, PROGRAM-MER.HOME, and PROGRAMMER.STARTDATE. This is equivalent to

```
with PROGRAMMER do
    WRITELN (PAYDATA.NAME, ' lives in ', HOME.CITY,
            ' and started in ', STARTDATE.YEAR :4)
```

You can also nest with statements. The nested with statement below is equivalent to those just discussed.

```
with PROGRAMMER do
    with PAYDATA do
        with HOME do
            with STARTDATE do
                WRITELN (NAME, ' lives in ', CITY,
                        ' and started in ', YEAR :4)
```

The record variable name (PROGRAMMER) must precede the subrecord names as shown above. The order of the field names PAYDATA, HOME, and STARTDATE is not important.

Procedure READNEWEMP in Fig. 7.20 can be used to read in a record of type NEWEMPLOYEE. It calls procedures READEMPL (see Fig. 7.5), READDATE, and READDRESS.

```
procedure READNEWEMP (var NEWEMP {output} : NEWEMPLOYEE);

{Reads a record into record variable NEWEMP. Uses
 procedures READEMPL, READDATE, and READADDRESS.  }

begin {READNEWEMP}
   with NEWEMP do
      begin
         WRITELN ('Enter employee payroll data.');
         READEMPL (PAYDATA);
         WRITELN ('Enter Address.');
         READADDRESS (HOME);
         WRITELN ('Enter starting date.');
         READDATE (STARTDATE);
         WRITELN ('Enter birthday.');
         READDATE (BIRTHDATE)
      end {with}
end; {READNEWEMP}
```

Fig. 7.20 Procedure READNEWEMP

Finally, we can extend our declarations to include an array (PERSONNEL) with record type NEWEMPLOYEE.

```
const
   STRINGSIZE = 11;  DIGITSIZE = 5;
   MAXEMP = 300;

type
   .}
   .}      insert declarations from Fig. 7.18
   .}
   EMPRANGE = 1..MAXEMP;
   EMPARRAY = array [EMPRANGE] of NEWEMPLOYEE;

var
   PERSONNEL : EMPARRAY;
   NUMEMP, CUREMP : EMPRANGE;
```

The for statement below can be used to fill this array with data for the number of employees specified by NUMEMP.

```
for CUREMP := 1 to NUMEMP do
   READNEWEMP (PERSONNEL[CUREMP])
```

Each record read will be stored in the array element selected by CUREMP.

Self-check Exercises for Section 7.8

1. Write procedures READDATE and READADDRESS.

7.9 Record Variants*

All record variables of type NEWEMPLOYEE have the same form and structure. However, it is possible to define record types that have some fields that are the same for all variables of that type (fixed part) and some fields that may be different (variant part).

For example, we might wish to include additional information about an employee based on the employee's marital status. For all married employees, we might want to know the spouse's name and number of children. For all divorced employees, we might want to know the date of the divorce. For all single employees, we might want to know whether or not the employee lives alone.

This new employee type, EXECUTIVE, is declared in Fig. 7.21. It uses several data types declared earlier in Fig. 7.18 for type NEWEMPLOYEE.

The fixed part of a record always precedes the variant part. The fixed part of record type EXECUTIVE has the form of record type NEWEMPLOYEE. The variant part begins with the phrase

```
case MS : MARITALSTAT of
```

defining a special field MS, of type MARITALSTAT, that is called the *tag field*. The value of the tag field (MARRIED, DIVORCED, or SINGLE) indicates the form of the remainder of the record. If the value of the tag field is MARRIED, there are two additional fields, SPOUSENAME and NUMKIDS; otherwise, there is only one additional field, DIVORCEDATE (type DATE) or LIVESALONE (type BOOLEAN).

Some samples of record variable BOSS are shown below. Only the tag field and variant part are shown since the fixed parts all have the same form.

BOSS.MS	MARRIED
BOSS.SPOUSENAME	J A N E
BOSS.NUMKIDS	2

BOSS.MS	DIVORCED
BOSS.DIVORCEDATE.MONTHVAL	MAY
BOSS.DIVORCEDATE.DAY	20
BOSS.DIVORCEDATE.YEAR	1975

BOSS.MS	SINGLE
BOSS.LIVESALONE	TRUE

---

*This section is optional and may be omitted.

```
const
    STRINGSIZE = 11;
    DIGITSIZE = 5;

type
    STRING = packed array [1..STRINGSIZE] of CHAR;
    DIGITSTRING = packed array [1..DIGITSIZE] of '0'..'9';
    MONTH = (JAN,FEB,MAR,APR,MAY,JUN,JUL,AUG,SEP,OCT,NOV,DEC);

    EMPLOYEE = record
        NAME : STRING;
        SEX : (FEMALE, MALE);
        SOCSECNUM : STRING ;
        NUMDEPEND : INTEGER;
        RATE : REAL;
        TAXSAL : REAL
    end; {EMPLOYEE}

    ADDRESS = record
        STREET, CITY, STATE : STRING;
        ZIPCODE : DIGITSTRING
    end; {ADDRESS}

    DATE = record
        MONTHVAL : MONTH;
        DAY : 1..31;
        YEAR : 1900..1999
    end; {DATE}

    NEWEMPLOYEE = record
        PAYROLLDATA : EMPLOYEE;
        HOME : ADDRESS;
        STARTDATE, BIRTHDATE : DATE
    end; {NEWEMPLOYEE}

    MARITALSTAT = (MARRIED, DIVORCED, SINGLE);
    EXECUTIVE = record
        {fixed part}
        PAYDATA : EMPLOYEE;
        HOME : ADDRESS;
        STARTDATE, BIRTHDATE : DATE;

        {variant part}
        case MS : MARITALSTAT of
            MARRIED : (SPOUSENAME : STRING;
                        NUMKIDS : INTEGER);
            DIVORCED : (DIVORCEDATE : DATE);
            SINGLE : (LIVESALONE : BOOLEAN)
    end; {EXECUTIVE}

var
    BOSS : EXECUTIVE;
```

Fig. 7.21 Record Type EXECUTIVE and Record Variable BOSS

For each variable of type EXECUTIVE, the compiler will allocate sufficient storage space to accommodate the largest of the record variants. However, only one of the variants is defined at any given time; this particular variant is determined by the tag field value.

For example, if the value of BOSS.MS (the tag field) is MARRIED, then only the variant fields BOSS.SPOUSENAME and BOSS.NUMKIDS may be correctly referenced; all other variant fields are undefined. The statement

```
with BOSS do
    begin
        WRITELN ('Spouse is ', SPOUSENAME);
        WRITELN ('They have ', NUMKIDS, ' children.')
    end; {with}
```

can only be executed without error when BOSS.MS is MARRIED.

The programmer must ensure that the variant fields that are referenced are consistent with the tag field value. For this reason, a case statement is often used in processing the variant part of a record. By using the tag field as the case selector, we can ensure that only the currently defined variant is manipulated. The case statement below will execute correctly for any valid tag field value. The value of BOSS.MS determines what information will be displayed.

```
with BOSS do
    case MS of
        MARRIED   : begin
                        WRITELN ('Spouse is ', SPOUSENAME);
                        WRITELN ('They have ', NUMKIDS :2, ' children.')
                    end; {MARRIED}
        DIVORCED  : with DIVORCEDATE do
                        WRITELN ('Date of divorce: ',
                            ORD(MONTHVAL)+1 :2, '/', DAY :2, '/', YEAR :4);
        SINGLE    : if LIVESALONE then
                        WRITELN ('Lives alone')
                    else
                        WRITELN ('Does not live alone')
    end {case}
```

The syntax for a record with fixed and variant parts is described in the next display.

RECORD TYPE WITH VARIANT PART

$rec\text{-}type$ = record

$\quad id\text{-}list_1$: $type_1$;

$\quad id\text{-}list_2$: $type_2$;

$\qquad\qquad \cdot$

$\qquad\qquad \cdot$ } fixed part

$\qquad\qquad \cdot$

$\quad id\text{-}list_n$: $type_n$;

```
    case tag : tag-type of
        label₁ : (field-list₁) ;
        label₂ : (field-list₂) ;
                .                        ⎫
                .                        ⎬  variant part
                .                        ⎭
        labelₖ : (field-listₖ)
    end;
```

Interpretation: The *field-list* for the fixed part is declared first. The variant part starts with the reserved word case. The identifier *tag* is the name of the tag field of the record; the tag field name is separated by a colon from its type (*tag-type*), which must be a previously-defined enumerated type or subrange.

The case labels (*label₁, label₂ ,...., labelₖ*) are lists of values of the tag field as defined by *tag-type*. *Field-list$_i$* describes the record fields associated with *label$_i$*. Each element of *field-list$_i$* specifies a field name and its type; the elements in *field-list$_i$* are separated by semicolons. *Field-list$_i$* is enclosed in parentheses.

Note 1: All field names must be unique. The same field name may not appear in the fixed and variant parts or in two field lists of the variant part.

Note 2: An empty field list (no variant part for the case label) is indicated by an empty pair of parentheses, ( ).

Note 3: It is possible for *field-list$_i$* to also have a variant part. If so, it must follow the fixed part of *field-list$_i$*.

Note 4: There is only one end for the record type declaration; there is no separate end for the case.

When initially storing data into a record with a variant part, the tag field value should be read first. Once the value of the tag field is defined, data can be read into the variant fields associated with that value.

Example 7.8   The record type FIGURE can be used to represent a geometric object. It has three variants, one for each type of object. There is no fixed part in the declaration of FIGURE.

```
type
    FIGKIND = (RECTANGLE, SQUARE, CIRCLE);
    FIGURE = record
        case FIGSHAPE : FIGKIND of
            RECTANGLE : (WIDTH, HEIGHT : REAL);
            SQUARE : (SIDE : REAL);
            CIRCLE : (RADIUS : REAL)
    end; {FIGURE}
```

The program in Fig. 7.22 enters data describing a geometric figure and computes its perimeter and area. The first letter entered (R, S, or C) indicates the type of figure to be processed. This letter is converted by function FIGCONVERT (not shown) to a scalar value of type FIGKIND (RECTANGLE, SQUARE, CIRCLE, ILLEGAL) where the scalar value ILLEGAL has been added to signal an illegal input character.

```pascal
program GEOMETRY (INPUT, OUTPUT);

{Computes the area and perimeter of a geometric figure.}

const
   PI = 3.14159;

type
   FIGKIND = (RECTANGLE, SQUARE, CIRCLE, ILLEGAL);
   FIGURE = record
      case FIGSHAPE : FIGKIND of
         RECTANGLE : (WIDTH, HEIGHT : REAL);
         SQUARE : (SIDE : REAL);
         CIRCLE : (RADIUS : REAL);
         ILLEGAL : ()
   end; {FIGURE}

var
   OBJECT : FIGURE;          {object being processed}
   FIGCHAR : CHAR;           {indicates shape of object}
   PERIMETER,                {perimeter of object}
   AREA        : REAL;       {area of object}

function FIGCONVERT (FIGCHAR : CHAR) : FIGKIND;

{Converts FIGCHAR (a letter) to a scalar value of type FIGKIND.}

begin {FIGCONVERT}
   WRITELN ('Function FIGCONVERT entered.')
end; {FIGCONVERT}

begin {GEOMETRY}
   WRITELN ('Enter object shape.');
   WRITE ('Enter R (rectangle), S (square), or C (circle): ');
   READLN (FIGCHAR);

   {Process the object denoted by FIGCHAR}
   with OBJECT do
      begin
         FIGSHAPE := FIGCONVERT(FIGCHAR);          {define the tag field}

         {Select the proper variant and compute area and perimeter}
         case FIGSHAPE of
            RECTANGLE : begin
                        WRITE ('Enter width and height: ');
                        READLN (WIDTH, HEIGHT);
                        AREA := WIDTH * HEIGHT;
                        PERIMETER := 2 * (WIDTH + HEIGHT);
                        WRITELN ('Area is ', AREA :7:2,
                                 ' Perimeter is ', PERIMETER :7:2)
                    end; {RECTANGLE}
```

```
            SQUARE      : begin
                             WRITE ('Enter length of side: ');
                             READLN (SIDE);
                             AREA := SQR(SIDE);
                             PERIMETER := 4 * SIDE;
                             WRITELN ('Area is ', AREA :7:2,
                                     ' Perimeter is ', PERIMETER :7:2)
                          end; {SQUARE}
            CIRCLE      : begin
                             WRITE ('Enter circle radius: ');
                             READLN (RADIUS);
                             AREA := PI * SQR(RADIUS);
                             PERIMETER := 2 * PI * RADIUS;
                             WRITELN ('Area is ', AREA :7:2,
                                      ' Perimeter is ', PERIMETER :7:2)
                          end; {CIRCLE}
            ILLEGAL     : WRITELN ('Figure ', FIGCHAR, ' is invalid')
        end {case}
    end {with}
end. {GEOMETRY}


Enter object shape.
Enter R (rectangle), S (square), or C (circle) : R
Enter width and height: 5 6.5
Area is  32.50    Perimeter is  23.00
```

Fig. 7.22 Program to Compute Areas and Perimeters.

Self-check Exercises for Section 7.9

1. Add the variant

```
TRIANGLE : (SIDE1, SIDE2, ANGLE : REAL);
```

to FIGURE and modify the program in Fig. 7.22 to process triangles.

2. Write the function FIGCONVERT.

7.10 Manipulating Strings Stored in Records

In this Chapter and in Chapter 6, we have been storing character strings in packed arrays of characters. The maximum size of each string that could be stored was specified by the global constant STRINGSIZE; however, in many cases the actual string stored was shorter than the maximum. The record type LINE declared below has a separate field, LENGTH, for saving the actual string length. The character string itself is stored in the field INFO.

```
type
    LINE = record
        INFO : packed array [1..STRINGSIZE] of CHAR;
        LENGTH : 0..STRINGSIZE
    end; {LINE}
```

```
var
    S1, S2, S3 : LINE;
```

Most programming languages provide special string manipulation procedures and functions. In fact, several extended versions of Pascal include such features. However, standard Pascal does not. In this section, we will discuss how to perform some common operations on strings in standard Pascal. (See Appendixes B.3 and B.4.)

Example 7.9   Procedure READLINE in Fig. 7.23 is based on procedure READSTRING in Fig. 6.15. Only one parameter is passed because the character string read and its length are both saved in the record variable corresponding to INSTRING (type LINE).

```
procedure READLINE (var INSTRING {output} : LINE);

{Reads a string of characters into INSTRING.INFO. The string
 length is saved in INSTRING.LENGTH.                          }

const
    BLANK = ' ';                              {character used for padding}

var
    I : 1..STRINGSIZE;                        {loop control variable}

begin {READLINE}
    with INSTRING do
        begin
            {Read each character and store it in field INFO.}
            LENGTH := 0;                             {no characters read}
            while not EOLN and (LENGTH < STRINGSIZE) do
                begin
                    {invariant: not at end of line and INFO not filled}
                    LENGTH := LENGTH + 1;                {increase LENGTH}
                    READ (INFO[LENGTH])            {store next character}
                end; {while}

            {assert: at end of line or INFO is filled}
            READLN;                            {advance to the next line}

            {Pad rest of INFO with blanks.}
            for I := LENGTH+1 to STRINGSIZE do
                INFO[I] := BLANK
        end {with}
end; {READLINE}
```

Fig. 7.23 Procedure READLINE

If the characters I am a string.<Return> are entered at the keyboard when the procedure (call) statement

```
READLINE (S1)
```

is executed, S1 will be defined as shown below. Those parts of S1 that contain data are in a darker color. STRINGSIZE is 20.

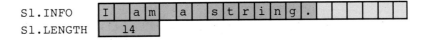

| S1.INFO | I | a m | a | s t r i n g . |
| S1.LENGTH | 14 |

The rest of the material in this section is rather detailed. You may wish to skip it on a first reading.

Example 7.10 Procedure COPY in Fig. 7.24 copies a portion of its source string (SOURCE) to its destination string (DESTIN). The *substring* copied, starting at position INDEX in the source string, will begin at position 1 in DESTIN. The parameter SIZE represents the length of the substring being copied.

A result of the procedure (call) statement

```
COPY (S1, 3, 2, S2)
```

follows, assuming S1 is defined as shown earlier. Only the characters in cells 3 and 4 of S1.INFO are copied to S2.INFO; S1 is unchanged.

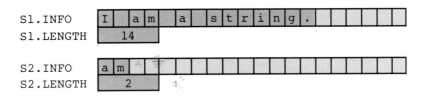

| S1.INFO | I | a m | a | s t r i n g . |
| S1.LENGTH | 14 |

| S2.INFO | a m |
| S2.LENGTH | 2 |

Fig. 7.24 String Copy Procedure

```
procedure COPY (SOURCE {input} : LINE;
                INDEX, SIZE {input} : INTEGER;
                var DESTIN {output} : LINE);

{Copies a substring of SOURCE to DESTIN. The substring copied
 starts at position INDEX of SOURCE. The length of the substring
 copied is specified by SIZE.                                      }

var
    I : 1..STRINGSIZE;                          {loop control variable}

begin {COPY}
    if (INDEX < 1) or (SIZE < 1) or
       (INDEX + SIZE - 1 > SOURCE.LENGTH) then
          WRITELN ('Illegal integer parameter. Copy aborted.')
    else
        begin {copy operation}
           for I := 1 to SIZE do
              DESTIN.INFO[I] := SOURCE.INFO[INDEX+I-1];
           DESTIN.LENGTH := SIZE
        end {copy operation}
end; {COPY}
```

The `if` condition in Fig. 7.24 validates the parameters INDEX and SIZE. Both parameters must be positive and the last character to be copied (at position INDEX+SIZE-1 in SOURCE.INFO) must be defined.

The `for` statement copies SIZE characters from the source string to the destination string. When the loop control variable I is 1, the character at position INDEX of the source string is copied; when I is SIZE, the character at position INDEX+SIZE-1 is copied. The assignment statement

```
DESTIN.LENGTH := SIZE
```

defines the actual length, SIZE, of the destination string.

Example 7.11   Procedure CONCAT in Fig. 7.25 *concatenates* or joins its two source strings together. The destination string, DESTIN, will contain the string in SOURCE1 followed by the string in SOURCE2. A result of the procedure (`call`) statement

```
CONCAT (S1, S2, S3)
```

follows assuming S1 and S2 are defined as shown below.

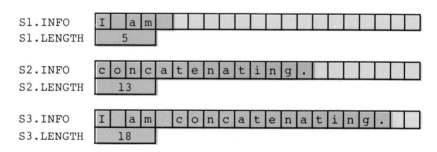

Procedure CONCAT begins by checking that the concatenated string will fit in DESTIN. If so, the assignment statement

```
DESTIN.INFO := SOURCE1.INFO;            {copy SOURCE1 first}
```

copies the string in SOURCE1.INFO to DESTIN.INFO. This defines the characters in positions 1 through SOURCE1.LENGTH of DESTIN.INFO. The `for` statement copies each character in SOURCE2.INFO to DESTIN.INFO. The first character in SOURCE2.INFO is stored at position SOURCE1.LENGTH+1, or just after the string SOURCE1.INFO. Finally, the length of the string in DESTIN is defined as the sum of the lengths of the two strings that were concatenated.

Example 7.12   The final string operation we will discuss is a string search. It is often necessary to locate the starting position of a particular target string in a source string. This is done by "sliding" the target string over the source string until each character in the target string matches the source string

```
procedure CONCAT (SOURCE1, SOURCE2 {input} : LINE;
                  var DESTIN {output} : LINE);

{Concatenates the strings in SOURCE1 and SOURCE2; the resulting
 string in stored in DESTIN.                                    }

var
   I : 1..STRINGSIZE;                           {loop control variable}

begin {CONCAT}
   if (SOURCE1.LENGTH + SOURCE2.LENGTH > STRINGSIZE) then
      WRITELN ('Strings too long. Concatenation aborted.')
   else
      begin {join strings}
         DESTIN.INFO := SOURCE1.INFO;           {copy SOURCE1 first}

         {Copy SOURCE2 after SOURCE1.}
         for I := 1 to SOURCE2.LENGTH do
            DESTIN.INFO[SOURCE1.LENGTH + I] := SOURCE2.INFO[I];
         DESTIN.LENGTH := SOURCE1.LENGTH + SOURCE2.LENGTH
      end {join strings}
end; {CONCAT}
```

Fig. 7.25 Concatenation Procedure

character under it. For the example shown below, there is a match when the target string, S1.INFO, is over positions 3 and 4 of the source string, S2.INFO, so the function designator POS(S1,S2) returns a value of 3. If there is no match, then the function result will be 0 (e.g. POS(S2,S1) returns 0). Function POS in Fig. 7.26 implements the string search operation.

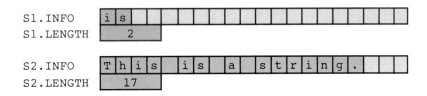

Function POS begins by validating the parameters TARGET.LENGTH and SOURCE.LENGTH. If either the source or target string length is not positive or if the target string is longer than the source string the BOOLEAN flag MATCHED is set to FALSE.

If the parameters are valid, then each substring in SOURCE.INFO of length TARGET.LENGTH is compared to TARGET.INFO using function MATCH. Function MATCH is similar to function SAMEARRAY (see Fig. 6.9), which determines whether or not two arrays are identical. MATCH returns a value of TRUE if the substring of SOURCE.INFO starting at position START is the same as the string TARGET.INFO; otherwise, MATCH returns a value of FALSE. Function POS continues sliding START to the right until either a match occurs or START is so large that there are less than TARGET.LENGTH characters in the substring of SOURCE.INFO starting at START.

```
function POS (TARGET, SOURCE : LINE) : INTEGER;

{Returns the starting position of the first occurrence
 of the string TARGET in string SOURCE. Returns 0 if TARGET is not a
 substring of SOURCE.                                                    }

var
   START : 0..STRINGSIZE;                    {the starting position in SOURCE}
   MATCHED : BOOLEAN;                        {indicator of success or failure}

function MATCH (TARGET, SOURCE : LINE;
                START : INTEGER) : BOOLEAN;

{Returns TRUE if TARGET.INFO matches the substring in SOURCE.INFO
 starting at position START; otherwise, returns FALSE.                   }

var
   NEXT : 0..STRINGSIZE;                           {subscript for TARGET.INFO}

begin {MATCH}
   NEXT := 0;                             {NEXT will be increased by 1}

   {Compare corresponding characters in TARGET and SOURCE
    starting with TARGET.INFO[1] and SOURCE.INFO[START].}
   repeat
      {invariant: all pairs tested match
       and NEXT < TARGET.LENGTH}
      NEXT := NEXT + 1                                     {advance to next pair}
   until (TARGET.INFO[NEXT] <> SOURCE.INFO[START+NEXT-1]) or
         (NEXT = TARGET.LENGTH);

   {assert: an unequal pair is found or strings match}
   MATCH := TARGET.INFO[NEXT] = SOURCE.INFO[START+NEXT-1]
end; {MATCH}

begin {POS}
   if (TARGET.LENGTH < 1) or (SOURCE.LENGTH < 1) or
      (TARGET.LENGTH > SOURCE.LENGTH) then
         MATCHED := FALSE                                  {invalid parameter}
   else
      begin {slide and match}
         START := 0;                        {START will be increased by 1}
         repeat
            {invariant : TARGET is not matched
             and START is in range.}
            START := START + 1;                            {slide to right}
            MATCHED := MATCH(TARGET, SOURCE, START)
         until MATCHED or (START > SOURCE.LENGTH - TARGET.LENGTH);

         {assert: TARGET is matched or START is too large}
      end; {slide and match}
   {Define function result.}
   if MATCHED then
      POS := START                              {target string begins at START}
   else
      POS := 0                                  {target string is not found}
end; {POS}
```

Fig. 7.26 String Search Function POS

Self-check Exercises for Section 7.10

1. Write a procedure DELETE that can be used to delete a substring of a string. The procedure parameters are the source string, the starting position of the substring to be deleted, and the length of the substring.
2. Write a procedure to insert a new string into a source string. The parameters are the two strings and the position in the source string where the new string is to be inserted. Verify that the expanded string will fit before doing the insertion.
3. Exercises 1 and 2 can both be solved by using procedures COPY and CONCAT. Provide alternate solutions that utilize these procedures to extract and concatenate substrings. Hint: To delete, copy the substring following the one to be deleted to a local variable, shorten the original string by changing its length, and then concatenate the modified original string and the local string. To insert, copy the substring following the point of insertion to a local string, shorten the original string by changing its length, and then concatenate the modified original string, the new string, and the local string.

7.11 Common Programming Errors

The most common error when using records is to incorrectly specify the record field to be manipulated. The full field selector (record variable and field name) must be used unless the record reference is nested inside a with statement, or the entire record is to be manipulated. So far we have discussed the latter option only for record copy statements and for records passed as parameters. When reading or writing records at the terminal, each field must be processed separately.

If a record variable name is listed in a with statement header, then only the field name is required to reference fields of that record inside the with statement. The full field selector must still be used to reference fields of any other record variable.

When an array of records is manipulated, the array subscript must be included in the field selector. If a with statement is being used, then the array name and subscript must be listed in the with statement header. If the subscript is updated in a loop, then the with statement must be nested inside the loop; otherwise, the array element (record) being manipulated will not change as the subscript value changes.

If a record has both a fixed and a variant part, be sure to define the fixed part first. Remember that the value of the tag field determines the form of the variant part that is currently defined. Consequently, the variant part should be manipulated in a case statement with the tag field as the case selector in order to ensure that the proper form is being manipulated. This is the programmer's responsibility because the compiler does not check to make sure that the variant part is being manipulated correctly.

7.12 Chapter Review

In this chapter we studied the record data type. Records were shown to be useful for organizing a collection of related data items of different types. We were able to create some very general data structures to model our "real world" data organization through hierarchical combinations of arrays and records.

In processing records, we learned how to reference each individual component through the use of a field selector consisting of the record variable name and field name separated by a period. The with statement was introduced as a means of shortening the field selector. If a record variable name is specified in a with statement header, then the field name may be used alone inside the with statement.

We also studied arrays of records as well as records that contained array fields. In both cases, we found that the subscript should be included as part of the field selector.

Each individual component of a record must be manipulated separately in a READ(READLN) or WRITE(WRITELN) statement or an arithmetic expression. However, it is permissable to assign one record variable to another record variable of the same type (record copy statement), to pass a record as a parameter to a procedure or function, or to compare two records. In the next chapter, we will learn how to read and write complete records to external files of records.

We also learned how to search an array to see if a desired value or key was present. An array search involves examining each element in sequence until either the key is found or all elements are examined without success. If the latter situation occurs, then the desired key is not present in the array.

Another important application discussed in this chapter is sorting an array. We introduced one technique, the bubble sort, to order the elements of an array of records based on the values of a particular field.

Finally, we discussed storing strings in records and wrote some procedures and a function to manipulate such strings.

New Pascal Statements

The new Pascal statements introduced in this chapter are described in Table 7.2.

Review Questions for Chapter 7

1. Declare a record called SUBSCRIBER which contains the fields NAME, STREETADDRESS, MONTHLYBILL (how much the subscriber owes), and which paper the subscriber receives (MORNING, EVENING, or BOTH).
2. Write a Pascal program to enter and then print out the data in record COMPETITION declared following Table 7.2.

Table 7.2 Summary of New Pascal Statements

Statement	Effect
Record declaration	

```
type
   PART = record
      ID : packed array [1..6] of CHAR;
      QUANTITY : INTEGER;
      PRICE : REAL
   end; {PART}
var NUTS, BOLTS : PART;
```
A record type PART is declared with fields that can store a character string, integer, and real number. NUTS and BOLTS are record variables of type PART.

Record variant declaration
```
type
   CHILDKIND = (GIRL, BOY);
   CHILD = record
      NAME : packed array [1..20] of CHAR;
      AGE : INTEGER;
      case KIND : CHILDKIND of
         GIRL : (SUGAR, SPICE : REAL);
         BOY :
            (SNAKES, SNAILS, TAILS : INTEGER)
   end; {CHILD}
var KID : CHILD;
```
A record type with a variant part is declared. Each record variable can store a string and an integer. Besides the fixed part, one variant can store 2 real numbers and the other can store 3 integers. The record variable KID is type CHILD. The tag field, KIND, is type CHILDKIND.

Record reference
```
NUTSVALUE := NUTS.QUANTITY * NUTS.PRICE;
```
Multiplies 2 fields of NUTS.

```
WRITELN ('Part ID is ', BOLTS.ID);
```
Prints 1 field of BOLTS.

Record copy
```
BOLTS := NUTS
```
Copies record NUTS to BOLTS.

with statement
```
with BOLTS do
   WRITE ('Part ', ID, ' costs $', PRICE)
```
Prints 2 fields of BOLTS.

Referencing a record variant
```
with KID do
   case KIND of
      GIRL :
         begin
            WRITE ('Enter pounds of sugar:');
            READLN (SUGAR)
         end; {GIRL}
      BOY :
         begin
            WRITE ('Enter count of snakes:');
            READLN (SNAKES)
         end {BOY}
   end {case}
```
Uses a case statement to read data into the variant part of record variable KID. If tag field KIND is GIRL, reads a value into the field SUGAR. If tag field KIND is BOY, reads a value into the field SNAKES.

```
type
   STRING = packed array [1..15] of CHAR;
   OLYMPICEVENT = record
      EVENT : STRING;
      ENTRANT : STRING;
      COUNTRY : STRING;
      PLACE : INTEGER
end; {OLYMPICEVENT}

var
     COMPETITION : OLYMPICEVENT;
```

3. Explain the use of the with statement.
4. Identify and correct the errors in the following Pascal program segment.

```
program REPORT (INPUT, OUTPUT);

type
   STRING = packed array [1..15] of CHAR;
   SUMMERHELP = record
      NAME : STRING;
      STARTDATE : packed array of [1..9];
      HOURSWORKED : REAL
   end; {SUMMERHELP}

var
   OPERATOR : SUMMERHELP;

begin
   with SUMMERHELP do
      begin
         NAME := 'Stoney Vic';
         STARTDATE := '01-JUN-84';
         HOURSWORKED := 293
      end;
   WRITELN (OPERATOR)
end.
```

5. Write the declarations for the array CPUARRAY that will hold 20 records of type CPU. The record CPU has the following fields: IDNUMBER (11 characters in length), MAKE (five characters), LOCATION (15 characters), and PORTS (integer).

6. Write the function TOTALGROSS that will return the total gross pay paid given the data stored in array EMPLOYEES.

```
const
   TOTALEMPLOYEES = 20;

type
   EMPLOYEE = record
      ID: INTEGER;
      RATE,
      HOURS : REAL
   end; {EMPLOYEE}
```

```
      EMPARRAY = array [1..TOTALEMPLOYEES] of EMPLOYEE;
   var
      EMPLOYEES : EMPARRAY;
```

7. Declare the proper data structure to store the following student data: GPA, MAJOR, and ADDRESS, which consists of STREETADDRESS, CITY, STATE, ZIPCODE; and CLASSCHEDULE, which consists of up to six class records each of which has DESCRIPTION, TIME, and DAYS fields. Use whatever data types are most appropriate for each field.

8. Write the variant declaration for SUPPLIES. SUPPLIES consist of either PAPER, RIBBON, or LABELS. If paper is chosen then the information needed is the number of sheets per box and the size of the paper. If RIBBON is chosen then the size, color, and kind (CARBON or CLOTH) are needed. If LABELS is chosen then the size and number per box is needed. For each item, the cost, number on hand, and the reorder point must also be included. Use whatever variable types are appropriate for each field.

9. Write the variant declaration for VEHICLE. If the vehicle is a TRUCK then bedsize and cabsize are needed. If the vehicle is a wagon then third seat or not is needed (BOOLEAN). If a sedan then the information needed is 2-door or 4-door, manual or automatic transmission. For all vehicles store air conditioning, power steering, power brakes (all BOOLEAN), and miles per gallon. Use whatever data types are appropriate for each field.

10. Write a procedure that replaces a substring of a source string with a new string. The procedure should be passed the source string, the string to be replaced, and the new string. Call function POS, and procedures COPY and CONCAT to do the replacement (see Section 7.10).

Programming Projects

1. An examination has been administered to a class of students, and the scores for each student have been provided as data along with the student's name. Write a program to do the following:

   a) Determine and print the class average for the exam.
   b) Find the median grade.
   c) Scale each student's grade so that the class average will become 75. For example, if the actual class average is 63, add 12 to each student's grade.
   d) Assign a letter grade to each student based on the scaled grade:
      90–100 (A), 80–89 (B), 70–79 (C), 60–69 (D), 0–59 (E).
   e) Print out each student's name in alphabetical order followed by the scaled grade and the letter grade.
   f) Count the number of grades in each letter grade category.

2. An array may be used to contain descriptions of people including name, height, weight, sex, color of hair, color of eyes, religion. Write a program that reads and stores data into this array, sorts the array in alphabetical order by name, and prints its contents.

3. Write a program that searches an array of records of type EMPLOYEE (see Section 7.1) to find and print the data stored for all employees who match a target description. Modify the record type by adding a third category (UN-KNOWN) for the sex field. The array of employee data should be read in first and then the target data. A blank target name or Social Security number indicates that this field should be ignored during the matching process. Enter a range of values for each numeric target field. A lower bound of −1 should indicate that this particular numeric field should be ignored.

4. A number expressed in scientific notation is represented by its mantissa (a fraction) and its exponent. Write a procedure that reads two character strings representing numbers in Pascal scientific notation and stores each number in a record with two fields. Write a procedure that prints the contents of each record as a real value. Also write a procedure that computes the sum, product, difference, and quotient of the two numbers. Hint: The string—0.1234E20 represents a number in scientific notation. The fraction—0.1234 is the mantissa and the number 20 is the exponent.

5. Write a program that generates the Morse code equivalent of a sentence. First, read the Morse code for each letter and punctuation character and save it in an array of records of type LINE (see Section 7.10). Next, read and convert the sentence. Your program should print the Morse code for each word on a separate line.

6. Write a set of procedures to delete a substring from a source string, to insert a new string in a source string at a specified position, to indicate where a specified target string occurs in the source string, and to replace the first occurrence of a specified substring in a source string with another. Test these procedures by writing a text editor and performing several editing operations. The editor should be driven by the menu below.

    Enter the first letter of an edit operation described below:
    D — Delete a substring
    E — Enter a source string to be edited
    I — Insert a substring
    L — Locate a substring
    P — Print the source string
    R — Replace one substring with another
    S — Show the menu
    Q — Quit

7. Write a more complete text editor (see the previous project) that will edit a page of text. Store each line of the page in a separate element of an array of strings. Maintain a pointer (index) to the line currently being edited. In addition to the edit commands, include commands that move the index to the top of the page, the bottom of the page, or up or down a specified number of lines. Your program should also be able to delete an entire line, insert a new line preceding the current line, or replace the current line with another. The first two of these new operations will require moving a portion of the array of strings up or down by one element.

8. At a grocery store, certain categories of food have been established and this information is to be comuterized. Write a procedure to read and store information into a variant record with appropriately-designed types.

The first letter read will either be a M, F, or V (indicating a kind of meat, fruit, or vegetable). The second set of information (until a blank is encountered) will be the name of the item (maximum of 20 letters). The third item read will be cost/unit. The fourth item read will be the unit (either O for ounces or P for pounds).

The last field (5th) read will be one character indicating information depending upon the M, F, or V read earlier. For meat the valid input values are:

R for red meat, P for poultry and F for fish
For fruit the valid input values are:

T for tropical and N for nontropical
For vegetables the valid input values are:

B for beans, P for potatoe, O for other
The procedure should check to see if all input read is valid before assigning a value to the record parameter. Also write procedures to print the data stored for all the meats and another to print the data stored for all the potatoes.

(Points to ponder: How could you generalize the selection process so a procedure is not needed for every combination of searches?)

9. The selection sort is similar to the bubble sort presented in Section 7.6, in that repeated passes are made through the data until it is sorted. The fundamental difference between the two is that in the bubble sort adjacent elements are compared and switched while in the selection sort one element is compared against the others.

In the selection sort the first pass through the array finds the largest value in the collection and stores the location (subscript) of this element. At the completion of the pass the item at this subscript location is switched with the one in the last position in the array. This puts the largest value in the last position, where it belongs, much like the bubble sort. The process is then repeated (the second pass) but the last position is not included in the search for the largest value. After the second pass, the second largest value in the array is now known and can be inserted in the second position from the end of the array. This continues until each item is in its correct location.

Write a program to implement this method on an array of names. Write out the before and after contents of the array to verify success.

10. By adding additional comparisons to the `if` statement in the bubble sort, it can be used to sort any field of the records in an array of records. Assume each record contains a NAME (20 characters), ADDRESS (20 characters), CITY (20 characters), STATE (2 characters), ZIPCODE (5 characters). Provide a sort that will sort the records in either NAME, STATE, or ZIPCODE order. The sort should be written as a procedure which has a parameter of type (NAME, STATE, ZIPCODE) to indicate the field to sort. Call the procedure for all three cases and write the array of records after each call to verify the procedure.

11. Write a program that will read 400 characters into a 20 by 20 array. Afterwards read in a character string of a maximum of 10 characters which will be used to search the "table" of characters. Indicate how many times the second string occurs in the 20 by 20 array. This should include horizontal, vertical, and right diagonal occurrences. (Right diagonal means only going down and to the right for the search.)

12. The inventory for a certain warehouse is to be kept on a computer. In addition, shipments into and from the warehouse (transactions) are to be processed. Each item will contain an ID number (3 digits), name (maximum of 10 characters), initial quantity on hand, and cost per item. Write a procedure that will read and store the initial quantities of items into an appropriate array of records until an ID number of 0 is read. At this point write the initial contents of the warehouse.

Now process the transactions, which will consist of the ID number for the item and the quantity of items shipped or received (if negative, the quantity was shipped; otherwise, the items were received). Process these transactions until done.

Each transaction processed should generate a message indicating the item name, quantity shipped or received, and new quantity on hand. The program should check to make sure that more items are not shipped than are on hand and that the ID number requested for a transaction matches one in the warehouse.

After all transactions are processed, print a list of all items in the warehouse. Show how many of each remain and the approximate total value of each item in the inventory.

Sample input might be:

376	BOLTS	350	0.05
142	NUTS	425	0.03
261	HAMMERS	100	10.45
0			
142	-27		
142	104		
261	-75		

Sets and Files

8.1 Set Data Type and Set Operators

8.2 RESET, REWRITE, and the File Position Pointer

8.3 TEXT Files

8.4 Case Studies

8.5 User-defined File Types

8.6 Case Study—File Merge

8.7 Case Study—Data Base Inquiry

8.8 File Buffer Variable

8.9 Common Programming Errors

8.10 Chapter Review

In this chapter, we will complete the study of the set data type. Sets were first introduced in Chapter 5, and we have used sets and the set member-ship operator in to simplify conditions. We will learn how to perform the operations of set union, set intersection, and set difference in Pascal and how to test for subsets, supersets, and set equality.

Sets, like arrays and records, are internal data structures; i.e. they are stored in main memory. We will also study the file, the only data structure that is stored in external memory (e.g. disk or tape storage).

In our programming so far, data items were either read from the key-board or from a batch file associated with the system file INPUT. Each data item could be read only once. Furthermore, all output generated was printed on the screen and could not be processed at a later time.

In this chapter, we will learn how to save output generated by a program as a permanent file on disk. This file can be sent to a printer or used as input data for another program at a later time. We will also learn how to read data from more than one input file and merge these data together into a single output file.

Like an array, a file is a collection of elements that are all the same type. Since files are located in secondary memory rather than in the main computer memory, files can be much larger than arrays.

The elements of an array can be accessed in arbitrary (random) order. Files in standard Pascal can only be accessed in sequential order. This means that file component 1, component 2, . . . , component n−1 must all be accessed before file component n can be accessed.

8.1 Set Data Type and Set Operators

The use of set values in conditional statements was introduced in Chapter 5. Until now, we have only used the set membership operator in with set values. In this section, we will examine the other set operators and learn how to declare and manipulate set variables.

Example 8.1 The statements below define a set type DIGIT and two set variables named ODD and EVEN. Each set variable of type DIGIT can contain between zero and nine elements chosen from the integers in the subrange 1..9. The set variables ODD and EVEN represent the set of odd digits and even digits in the range 1 through 9.

```
type
    DIGIT = set of 1..9;

var
    ODD, EVEN : DIGIT;

begin
    ODD := [1,3,5,7,9];
    EVEN := [2,4,6,8]
```

The set type declaration is described below.

SET TYPE DECLARATION

set-type = set of *base-type*

Interpretation: The identifier *set-type* is defined over the values specified in *base-type*. A variable declared to be of type *set-type* is a set whose elements are chosen from the values in *base-type*. The *base-type* must be an ordinal type.

Notes: Most implementations impose a limit on the number of values in the *base-type* of a set. In many implementations this limit is the same as the number of values in the data type CHAR (64, 128, or 256). This allows the programmer to use CHAR as a *base-type*. Given this limitation, the data type INTEGER may not be used as a *base-type*; however, a subrange of type INTEGER is allowed.

Set Assignment, Empty Set and Universal Set

An existing set can be modified using the set operators, which will be discussed in the next section. Before a set can be manipulated, its initial elements must be defined using a set assignment statement.

Example 8.2   The statements below specify two sets defined over the base type MONTH.

```
type
    MONTH = (JAN,FEB,MAR,APR,MAY,JUN,JUL,AUG,SEP,OCT,NOV,DEC);
    MONTHSET = SET OF MONTH;

var
    WINTER, SUMMER : MONTHSET;

begin
    WINTER := [DEC,JAN,FEB];
    SUMMER := [JUN..AUG];
```

Each assignment statement consists of a set variable on the left and a set value on the right. A set value is indicated by a pair of brackets and a list of values from the base type of the set being defined. As shown in the assignment statement for SUMMER, a list of consecutive values may be denoted as a subrange (see Section 5.2).

It is also possible to have a set variable on the right of the assignment statement, provided that both set variables have compatible base types. The value of the set variable on the right would be assigned to the set variable on the left.

Often we wish to denote that a set is empty, that is, it has no elements. The *empty set* is indicated by a pair of brackets [].

```
    SUMMER := []              {a very long winter!}
```

A set variable must always be initialized before it can be used with any of the set operators. Very often, a set variable is initialized to the empty set or the *universal set*, the set consisting of all values of the base type. The universal set for a set of type MONTHSET would be denoted as [JAN..DEC].

The general form of the set assignment statement is shown in the display below. As indicated, it is possible to write set expressions involving set manipulation operators. These operators are described in the next section.

SET ASSIGNMENT

set-var := *set-expression*

Interpretation: The variable, *set-var*, is defined as the set whose elements are determined by the value of *set-expression*. The *set-expression* may be a set value, or another set variable. Alternatively, a *set-expression* may specify the manipulation of two or more sets using the set operators. The base type of *set-var* and *set-expression* must be type compatible, and all the elements in *set-expression* must be included in the base type of *set-var*.

Set Union, Intersection, and Difference

The set operators union, intersection, and difference require two sets of the same type as operands.

- The *union* of two sets (set operator +) is defined as the set of elements that are contained in either set or both sets.

```
[1,3,4] + [1,2,4] is [1,2,3,4]
[1,3] + [2,4] is [1,2,3,4]
['A','C','F'] + ['B','C','D','F'] is ['A','B','C','D','F']
['A','C','F'] + ['A','C','D','F'] is ['A','C','D','F']
```

- The *intersection* of two sets (set operator *) is defined as the set of all elements that are common to both sets:

```
[1,3,4] * [1,2,4] is [1,4]
[1,3] * [2,4] is []
['A','C','F'] * ['B','C','D','F'] is ['C','F']
['A','C','F'] * ['A','C','D','F'] is ['A','C','F']
```

- The *difference* of set A and set B (set operator −) is defined as the set of elements that are in set A but not in set B:

```
[1,3,4] - [1,2,4] is [3]
[1,3] - [2,4] is [1,3]
['A','C','F'] - ['B','C','D','F'] is ['A']
['A','C','F'] - ['A','C','D','F'] is []
```

The operators +, *, and − are treated as set operators when their operands are sets. These operators can be used to combine two sets to form a third set. If more than one set operator is used in an expression, the normal precedence rules for the operators +, *, and − will be followed (see Table 4.7 in Section 4.4). When in doubt, it is best to use parentheses to specify the intended order of evaluation.

Often we wish to insert a new element in an existing set. This is accomplished by forming the union of the existing set and the *unit set* containing only the new element. The set [2] below is a unit set.

[1,3,4,5] + [2] is [1,2,3,4,5]

A common error is omitting the brackets around a unit set. The expression

[1,3,4,5] + 2

is invalid because one operand is a set and the other is an integer constant.

SET OPERATORS

Intersection: $set_1 * set_2$
Union: $set_1 + set_2$
Difference: $set_1 - set_2$

Interpretation: set_1 and set_2 are either set variables or set values (a list of elements enclosed in square brackets). The normal definitions for set intersection, union, and difference apply. The set operators return sets as values. Set_1 and set_2 must have compatible base types.

Example 8.3   Procedure BUILDSETS in Fig. 8.1 returns a set of odd numbers (ODD) and a set of even numbers (EVEN) in the range 1 to MAXNUM assuming the declarations

```
const
    MAXNUM = 60;

type
    INTSET = set of 1..MAXNUM;

var
    ODD, EVEN : INTSET;
```

Procedure BUILDSETS uses the set operators + (union) and – (difference).

```
procedure BUILDSETS (var ODD, EVEN {output} : INTSET);

{Builds a set of odd integers (ODD) and a set of even
 integers (EVEN) in the range 1 to MAXNUM.              }

var
    I : INTEGER;                              {loop control variable}

begin {BUILDSETS}
```

```
   ODD := [ ];                        {initialize ODD to the empty set}

{Build a set of odd integers.}
   I := 1;                            {initialize I to first odd integer}
   while I <= MAXNUM do
      begin
           ODD := ODD + [I];          {union next odd integer with ODD}
           I := I + 2                 {get next odd integer}
      end; {while}

      EVEN := [1..MAXNUM] - ODD       {assign integers not in ODD to EVEN}
end; {BUILDSETS}
```

Fig. 8.1 Procedure BUILDSETS

Set Relational Operators

Sets may also be compared through the use of the relational operators =, <= , etc. Both operands of a set relational operator must have the same base type. The operators = and <> are used to test whether or not two sets contain the same elements.

```
[1,3] = [1,3] is TRUE     |  [1,3] <> [1,3] is FALSE
[1,3] = [2,4] is FALSE    |  [1,3] <> [2,4] is TRUE
[1,3] = [3,1] is TRUE     |  [1,3] <> [3,1] is FALSE
  [] = [1]   is FALSE     |    [] <> [1]   is TRUE
```

As the next to last example above illustrates, the order in which the elements of a set are listed is not important ([1,3] and [3,1] denote the same set). However, we will usually list the elements of a set in ordinal sequence.

Other relational operators are used to determine subset and superset relationships.

- Set A is a *subset* of set B (A <= B) if every element of set A is also an element of set B.

```
[1,3]       <= [1,2,3,4] is TRUE
[1,3]       <= [1,3]     is TRUE
[1,2,3,4] <= [1,3]       is FALSE
[1,3]       <= []        is FALSE
[]          <= [1,3]     is TRUE
```

As the last example above illustrates, the empty set, [ ], is a subset of every set.

- Set A is a *superset* of set B (A >= B) if every element of B is also an element of A.

```
[1,3]       >= [1,2,3,4] is FALSE
[1,3]       >= [1,3]     is TRUE
[1,2,3,4]   >= [1,3]     is TRUE
[1,3]       >= []        is TRUE
[]          >= [1,3]     is FALSE
```

The set relational operators are summarized in the next display.

SET RELATIONAL OPERATORS

Equality	: $set_1 = set_2$
Inequality	: $set_1 <> set_2$
Subset	: $set_1 <= set_2$
Superset	: $set_1 >= set_2$

Interpretation: Set_1 and set_2 are either set variables or set values. The value of a set relation (TRUE or FALSE) corresponds to the standard set-theoretic definitions of set equality, subset, superset, etc. Note: The base type of set_1 and set_2 must be compatible.

Reading and Writing Sets

Like most other data structures, a set cannot be a parameter of the standard READ or WRITE procedures. Data items to be stored in a set must be read individually and inserted in an initially empty set using the set union operator.

Example 8.4   Procedure READSET in Fig. 8.2 reads a sequence of uppercase letters terminated by a * and inserts them in the set represented by parameter LETTERS (set type LETTERSET). Given the declarations below

```
type
    LETTERSET = set of 'A'..'Z';
```

```
var
    MYLETTERS : LETTERSET;
```

The procedure (call) statement READSET (MYLETTERS) could be used to
enter data in the set MYLETTERS.

```
procedure READSET (var LETTERS {output} : LETTERSET);

{Reads a set of uppercase letters terminated by *
 and stores them in LETTERS.                                        }

const
    SENTINEL = '*';                                    {sentinel character}

var
    NEXTCHAR : CHAR;                                   {next input character}

begin {READSET}
    LETTERS := [];                                     {initialize LETTERS}
    WRITELN ('Enter a set of uppercase letters followed by "*".');
    READ (NEXTCHAR);                                   {read first data item}
    while NEXTCHAR <> SENTINEL do
        begin
            if NEXTCHAR in ['A'..'Z'] then
                LETTERS := LETTERS + [NEXTCHAR];        {insert next letter}
            READ (NEXTCHAR)                             {read next data item}
        end {while}
end; {READSET}
```

Fig. 8.2 Procedure READSET

When printing a set every value in the base type must be tested to see
whether or not it is a set element. Only values that are set elements
should be printed.

Example 8.5   Procedure PRINTSET in Fig. 8.3 prints the uppercase letters that are in the
set represented by its parameter LETTERS.

Fig. 8.3 Procedure PRINTSET

```
procedure PRINTSET (LETTERS {input} : LETTERSET);

{Prints the uppercase letters in set LETTERS.}

var
    NEXTLETTER : 'A'..'Z';                             {loop control variable}

begin {PRINTSET}
    for NEXTLETTER := 'A' to 'Z' do
        if NEXTLETTER in LETTERS then
            WRITE (NEXTLETTER)                          {print a set member}
end; {PRINTSET}
```

A complete case study using sets and set operators appears in Section 8.4.

Self-check Exercises for Section 8.1

1. A is the set [1,3,5,7], B is the set [2,4,6], and C is the set [1,2,3]. Evaluate the following:

   a. A + (B - C)
   b. A + (B * C)
   c. A + B + C
   d. (C - A) <= B

   e. C + (A - C)
   f. C - (A - B)
   g. (C - A) - B
   h. (B + C) = (A + C)

2. Modify PRINTSET to print a set of type DIGIT.

8.2 Reset, Rewrite, and the File Position Pointer

Files may be used to store large quantities of data on a secondary storage device such as a disk. All components of a file are the same type, and the file components are always accessed in sequential order, starting with the first. Associated with each file is a *file position pointer*, which indicates the current position in the file; i.e. the next component to be processed.

At any given time a file may be used either for input or for output, but not both simultaneously. If a file is being used for input, then its components may be read as data. If a file is being used for output, then new components may be written to the file.

If INFILE is the name of a file, the statement

    RESET (INFILE)

calls the standard procedure RESET to prepare file INFILE for input. The file position pointer is moved to the beginning of file INFILE so that the first file component will be read by the next READ operation. The file position pointer is automatically advanced after each READ operation.

If OUTFILE is the name of a file, the statement

    REWRITE (OUTFILE)

calls the standard procedure REWRITE to prepare file OUTFILE for output. If OUTFILE is a new file, it is initialized to an empty file. If OUTFILE is an existing file in disk storage, its file position pointer is returned to the beginning. In this way OUTFILE becomes an empty file and the data previously associated with the file are lost.

Each subsequent WRITE operation appends a new component to the end of file OUTFILE. The file position pointer is at the end of file OUTFILE, following the last file component.

Example 8.6   Assume that INFILE and OUTFILE are both files whose individual components are characters and NEXTCHAR is a type CHAR variable. The statements

```
RESET (INFILE);
REWRITE (OUTFILE);
READ (INFILE, NEXTCHAR);
WRITE (OUTFILE, NEXTCHAR)
```

read the first character from file INFILE and write it to file OUTFILE. The status of both files (after the RESET and REWRITE statements are executed) is shown below. File OUTFILE is an empty file.

After RESET and REWRITE

The READ statement stores 'A' in NEXTCHAR; the WRITE statement copies it to OUTFILE. The file position pointer for file INFILE is advanced to the next file component ('C'). The file position pointer for file OUTFILE remains at the end of the file. The status of both files after the READ and WRITE is shown next.

After READ and WRITE

The first parameter in the READ and WRITE statements indicates the name of the file to be processed. If this parameter is omitted it is assumed to be INPUT (for READ) or OUTPUT (for WRITE). A read operation can only be performed on a file that is being used as an input file (after RESET). A write operation can only be performed on a file that is being used as an output file (after REWRITE).

RESET PROCEDURE

RESET (*infile*)

Interpretation: File *infile* is prepared for input and the file position pointer for *infile* is moved to the first file component. The RESET operation is automatically performed on system file INPUT, so RESET (INPUT) is not required and may cause an error on some Pascal systems.

REWRITE PROCEDURE

REWRITE (*outfile*)

Interpretation: File *outfile* is prepared for output and *outfile* is initialized to an empty file. Any data previously associated with file *outfile* are lost. The REWRITE operation is automatically performed on system file OUTPUT, so REWRITE (OUTPUT) is not required and may cause an error on some Pascal systems.

8.3 Text Files

The file type TEXT is predefined in Pascal. The individual components of a file of type TEXT are the Pascal characters (type CHAR) and a special character called the end-of-line mark (see Section 4.7). The end-of-line mark is used to group sequences of characters into lines. You have been using two files of type TEXT, INPUT, and OUTPUT. In this section we will see how to declare and use other files of type TEXT.

Files of type TEXT can be created using the system editor in the same way that you create a Pascal program. The individual characters are entered at the keyboard; the end-of-line mark is entered in the file by pressing <Return>. Once the file is completely entered it can be saved as a permanent file on disk and retrieved as needed.

Example 8.7   The program in Fig. 8.4 makes a copy of a file of type TEXT. Each character of the input file INFILE is written to the output file OUTFILE.

The program statement

```
program COPY (INFILE, OUTFILE);
```

identifies INFILE and OUTFILE as file parameters for program COPY. These names will be used in program COPY to reference the files being processed and are declared as type TEXT in the variable declaration statement. It is possible to associate these names with other external file names; however, the details of accomplishing this are system dependent.

The EOF and EOLN functions are used to test for the end of a file and the end of a line, respectively (see Section 4.7). The function parameter indicates which input file is being tested. If there is no parameter, then the system file INPUT is assumed. If the file position pointer for INFILE has advanced past the last character in INFILE, the function designator EOF(INFILE) evaluates to TRUE. If the file position pointer for file INFILE is at an end-of-line mark, the function designator EOLN (INFILE) evaluates to TRUE.

The outer while loop is repeated once for every line in file INFILE.

```
program COPY (INFILE, OUTFILE);

{Makes a copy, OUTFILE, of file INFILE.}

var
    INFILE, OUTFILE : TEXT;                      {two files of type TEXT}
    NEXTCHAR : CHAR;                             {each character of INFILE}

begin {COPY}
    {Prepare INFILE for input and OUTFILE for output.}
    RESET (INFILE);
    REWRITE (OUTFILE);

    {Copy each character of INFILE to OUTFILE, one line at a time.}
    while not EOF(INFILE) do
        begin
            while not EOLN(INFILE) do
                begin
                    READ (INFILE, NEXTCHAR);         {get next character}
                    WRITE (OUTFILE, NEXTCHAR)        {write it to OUTFILE}
                end; {line}
            WRITELN (OUTFILE);                       {insert end-of-line mark}
            READLN (INFILE)                          {skip end-of-line mark}
        end {file}
end. {COPY}
```

Fig. 8.4 Program COPY

Inside the inner while loop, the statements

```
    READ (INFILE, NEXTCHAR);                      {get next character}
    WRITE (OUTFILE, NEXTCHAR)                      {write it to OUTFILE}
```

copy each character on the current line of file INFILE to file OUTFILE. The inner while loop is exited when the file position pointer for file INFILE is at an end-of-line mark (EOLN(INFILE) is TRUE). This situation is depicted below.

End-of-line mark reached

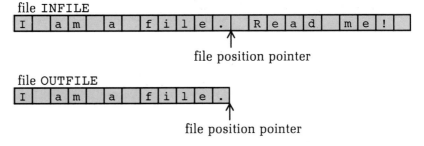

All characters in the first line of INFILE are copied to OUTFILE, and the file position pointer for INFILE is at the end-of-line mark (denoted by ▯). Since EOLN(INFILE) is TRUE, the inner while loop is exited, and the statements

```
WRITELN (OUTFILE);              {insert end-of-line mark}
READLN (INFILE)                 {skip end-of-line mark}
```

are executed. The WRITELN statement inserts an end-of-line mark in file OUTFILE; the READLN statement advances the file position pointer for INFILE to the next line as shown below.

After first execution of WRITELN and READLN

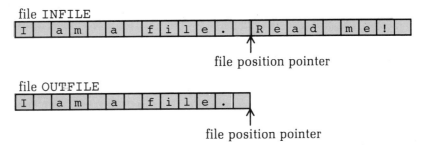

It is interesting to contemplate the effect of omitting either of these statements. If WRITELN (OUTFILE) is deleted, then the end-of-line mark will not be written in file OUTFILE whenever the end of a line is reached in file INFILE. Consequently, OUTFILE will contain all the characters in file INFILE, but on one line.

If READLN (INFILE) is omitted, the end-of-line mark will not be skipped. Consequently, EOLN(INFILE) will remain true, the inner loop will be exited immediately, and another end-of-line mark will be written to file OUTFILE. This will continue "forever" or until the program is terminated by the program user or its time-limit is exceeded.

The situation after the second execution of WRITELN and READLN is depicted below. At this point, the file position pointer for INFILE has advanced past the last character in the file. The value of EOF(INFILE) is true so the while condition is false and the outer loop is exited.

After second execution of WRITELN and READLN

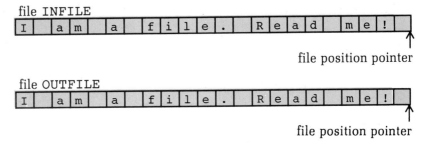

The standard input/output procedures work the same way for other TEXT files as they do for the system files INPUT and OUTPUT. Consequently, it is not necessary to read and write only single characters. The READ and READLN statements can be used to read a sequence of numeric characters in a TEXT file into an integer or real variable. Similarly the WRITE and WRITELN statements can be used to write an integer, real, or string value as a sequence of numeric characters in a TEXT file. Whenever READLN is used, the file position pointer is always advanced to the beginning of the next line after the required data are read; whenever WRITELN is used an end-of-line mark is always inserted in the file after the output characters are written.

READ, READLN PROCEDURES (for text files)

        READ   (*infile*, *input-list*)
    or   READLN (*infile*, *input-list*)

Interpretation: A sequence of characters is read from file *infile* into the variables specified in *input-list*. The type of each variable in *input-list* must be CHAR, INTEGER, a subrange of CHAR or INTEGER, or REAL. If the data type of a variable is CHAR, only a single character is read into that variable; if the data type of a variable is INTEGER or REAL, a sequence of numeric characters is read, converted to a binary value, and stored in that variable. If READ is used, the file position pointer for *infile* is advanced past the last character read. If READLN is used, the file position pointer for *infile* is advanced to the start of the next line.
Notes: If *infile* is omitted, it is assumed to be the system file INPUT. File *infile* must first be prepared for input via RESET (*infile*) except when *infile* is INPUT. An error will result if EOF(*infile*) is true before the read operation.

WRITE, WRITELN PROCEDURES (for text files)

        WRITE   (*outfile*, *output-list*)
    or   WRITELN (*outfile*, *output-list*)

Interpretation: The characters specified by *output-list* are written to the end of file *outfile*. The type of each expression in *output-list* must be one of the standard data types (BOOLEAN, CHAR, INTEGER, REAL), a subrange of a standard data type, or a character string. If an expression is type CHAR, a single character is written to file *outfile*; otherwise, a sequence of characters may be written. If WRITELN is used, an end-of-line mark is written as the last character in *outfile*. The file position pointer for *outfile* is at the end of the file.
Notes: If *outfile* is omitted, it is assumed to be the system file OUTPUT. File *outfile* must first be prepared for output via REWRITE (*outfile*) except when *outfile* is OUTPUT.

EOF FUNCTION (for text files)

EOF (*filename*)

Interpretation: The function result is TRUE if the file position pointer has passed the last component of file *filename*; otherwise, the function result is FALSE.
Note: If *filename* is omitted, it is assumed to be the system file IN-PUT.

EOLN FUNCTION (for text files)

EOLN (*filename*)

Interpretation: The function result is TRUE if the file position pointer is at an end-of-line mark; otherwise, the function result is FALSE.
Notes: If *filename* is omitted, it is assumed to be the system file IN-PUT. It is an error to call the EOLN function if EOF(*filename*) is TRUE.

Self-check Exercises for Section 8.3

1. Making a copy of a file is analogous to echo printing a batch data file. Consequently, there is a great deal of similarity between program COPY and a program that displays each character of a batch input file (represented by INPUT) at the terminal (represented by OUTPUT). Modify COPY to perform this task.

8.4 Case Studies

In Section 6.7 we considered writing a series of letters inquiring about the availability of summer jobs. Now that we know about files, we can automate the process.

Form Letter Problem Revisited

Problem: Write a program that can be used to send individualized letters to prospective employers. Assume that the letter body is already saved as a file called LETTER, and that each employer name and address is saved in a file called EMPLOYER. We wish to create a file of letters that can eventually be sent to a printer and printed.

Discussion: The data for each employer will occupy four consecutive lines of file EMPLOYER: the first line is the individual being contacted, the second line is the company name, and the next two lines are the address. Each letter will begin with today's date (read from the keyboard), the

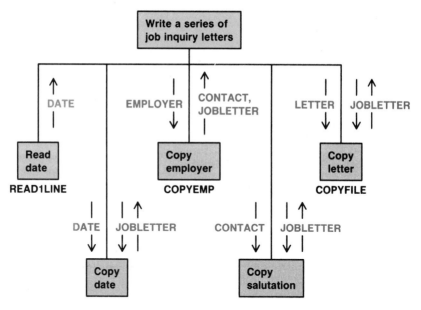

Fig. 8.5 Structure Chart for Job Inquiry Letter Program

company data, a salutation (Dear ____), and the letter body (including the closing).

A sample letter is shown below. The date is read from the keyboard, the next four lines are from file EMPLOYER, and the letter body is from file LETTER.

```
                                           March 25, 1986

    Mr. Kermit Frog
    Muppet Madness
    15 Times Square
    New York, New York 10020

    Dear Mr. Kermit Frog,

         I am a student at Temple University and would like
    to apply for a summer job with your company ...
```

The problem inputs, outputs, and algorithm follow.

PROBLEM INPUTS

today's date (a string read from the terminal)
four lines of data per employer (file EMPLOYER)
each line of the letter body and closing (file LETTER)

PROBLEM OUTPUTS

a file of letters ready to be printed (file JOBLETTER)

1. Enter today's date
2. while there are more employers do
    3. Write today's date to file JOBLETTER.
    4. Copy the employer data (the addressee) to JOBLETTER.
    5. Write the salutation.
    6. Copy file LETTER to file JOBLETTER.

Steps 3 through 6 write the different parts of each letter. Step 3 is performed by a WRITELN statement that prints the date string read in step 1; step 5 is performed by a WRITELN statement that prints the first line of the employer data (CONTACT) read in step 4. The structure chart is shown in Fig. 8.5; the program is shown in Fig. 8.6.

```
program JOBS (LETTER, EMPLOYER, JOBLETTER, INPUT, OUTPUT);

{Writes a series of job inquiry letters to file JOBLETTER. Each
 letter consists of a date, the employer's data (from file
 EMPLOYER) and the letter itself (from file LETTER).            }

const
    STRINGSIZE = 65;                        {maximum length of each line}
    PAD = ' ';                              {character for padding date line}

type
    STRING = packed array [1..STRINGSIZE] of CHAR;
    LINE = record
        INFO : STRING;                          {the data on a line}
        LENGTH : 0..STRINGSIZE                  {length of the line}
    end;   {LINE}

var
    LETTER,                                 {file containing letter body}
    EMPLOYER,                               {file of prospective employers}
    JOBLETTER : TEXT;                       {file of complete letters}
    DATE,                                   {today's date}
    CONTACT : LINE;                         {the employer's contact person}

procedure READ1LINE (var INFILE {input file} : TEXT;
                     var NEXTLINE {output} : LINE);

{Reads the next line of data from file INFILE. Returns data
 and length in fields INFO and LENGTH of record NEXTLINE.  }

const
    PAD = ' ';                                             {pad character}

var
    I : 1..STRINGSIZE;                                     {loop control variable}

begin {READ1LINE}
    with NEXTLINE do
        begin
            {Read and store each character in the next array element.}
            LENGTH := 0;                       {initial string length}
            while not EOLN(INFILE) and (LENGTH < STRINGSIZE) do
```
(continued)

```
            begin
                LENGTH := LENGTH + 1;                    {increment LENGTH}
                READ (INFILE, INFO[LENGTH])             {save next character}
            end;  {while}

        {assert: at end of line or array is filled}
        READLN (INFILE);                              {skip end-of-line mark}

        {Pad rest of INFO with blanks.}
        for I := LENGTH+1 to STRINGSIZE do
            INFO[I] := PAD
      end  {with}
end;  {READ1LINE}

procedure COPYEMP (var INFILE {input file},
                       OUTFILE {output file} : TEXT;
                   var CONTACT {output} : LINE);

{Copies the next NUMLINES lines of file INFILE to file OUTFILE.
 Stores the first line read and its length in record CONTACT.  }

const
    NUMLINES = 4;                               {number of employer data lines}

var
    NEXTLINE : LINE;                            {the next line of file INFILE}
    COUNTLINE : INTEGER;                             {loop control variable}

begin {COPYEMP}
    {Read the first line into CONTACT and copy it to OUTFILE.}
    READ1LINE (INFILE, CONTACT);
    WRITELN (OUTFILE, CONTACT.INFO :CONTACT.LENGTH);

    {Copy the rest of the lines to OUTFILE.}
    for COUNTLINE := 2 to NUMLINES do
        begin
            READ1LINE (INFILE, NEXTLINE);
            WRITELN (OUTFILE, NEXTLINE.INFO :NEXTLINE.LENGTH)
        end {for}
end;  {COPYEMP}

procedure COPYFILE (var INFILE {input file} : TEXT;
                    var OUTFILE {output file} : TEXT);

{Appends file INFILE to the end of file OUTFILE.}

var
    NEXTLINE : LINE;                            {the next line of file INFILE}

begin {COPYFILE}
    RESET (INFILE);                        {reset the file position pointer}
    {Copy each line of file INFILE to OUTFILE.}
    while not EOF(INFILE) do
        begin
            READ1LINE (INFILE, NEXTLINE);
            WRITELN (OUTFILE, NEXTLINE.INFO :NEXTLINE.LENGTH)
        end {while}
end;  {COPYFILE}
```

```
begin {JOBS}
    {Prepare file EMPLOYER for input and file JOBLETTER for output.}
    RESET (EMPLOYER);  REWRITE (JOBLETTER);

    {Enter today's date.}
    WRITE ('Enter the date as you would like it printed: ');
    READ1LINE (INPUT, DATE);

    {Write a letter for each employer.}
    while not EOF(EMPLOYER) do
        begin
            PAGE (JOBLETTER);                              {start a new page}
            {Copy the date to file JOBLETTER}
            WRITE (JOBLETTER, PAD :STRINGSIZE - DATE.LENGTH);
            WRITELN (JOBLETTER, DATE.INFO :DATE.LENGTH);

            {Copy the employer data (the addressee) to file JOBLETTER}
            WRITELN (JOBLETTER);
            COPYEMP (EMPLOYER, JOBLETTER, CONTACT);
            {Write the salutation}
            WRITELN (JOBLETTER);
            WRITELN (JOBLETTER, 'Dear ',
                    CONTACT.INFO :CONTACT.LENGTH, ';');

            {Copy the letter body and closing to file JOBLETTER}
            WRITELN (JOBLETTER);
            COPYFILE (LETTER, JOBLETTER)
        end {while}
end. {JOBS}
```

Fig. 8.6 Program to Write a File of Job Letters

The program begins by reading the date string from the keyboard using procedure READ1LINE. The date string is saved as a record (type LINE) with an INFO field (the data) and a LENGTH field. Procedure READ1LINE is used in program JOBS to read one line from a designated input file (INPUT, EMPLOYER, or JOBLETTER) that is represented by parameter INFILE. READ1LINE is a general version of procedure READLINE (see Fig. 7.23) which can only read data from file INPUT. In READ1LINE, the file being read is passed as parameter INFILE to the standard procedures READ, READLN, and EOLN.

Within the main program while loop, the PAGE procedure causes each letter of inquiry to start on a new page of program output when file JOBLETTER is printed. The statements

```
WRITE (JOBLETTER, PAD :STRINGSIZE - DATE.LENGTH);
WRITELN (JOBLETTER, DATE.INFO :DATE.LENGTH);
```

cause string (DATE.INFO) to be printed right-justified (preceded by blanks) at the top of each letter in file JOBLETTER. The statement

```
WRITELN (JOBLETTER);
```

is used to skip a line in the output file JOBLETTER.

Procedure COPYEMP copies the next four lines of file EMPLOYER (the addressee) to file JOBLETTER. COPYEMP begins by calling READ1LINE to read the first line of the input file into the main program record variable CONTACT. This line and the next three lines of file EMPLOYER (the employer address) are written to file JOBLETTER. After returning to the main program, the string stored in CONTACT is written to JOBLETTER a second time as part of the salutation.

Procedure COPYFILE appends all lines of file LETTER to the end of file JOBLETTER. COPYFILE does the same job as program COPY (see Fig. 8.4); however, COPYFILE reads and writes one line at a time rather than individual characters. Procedure COPYFILE begins by resetting the file-position pointer for LETTER (its first actual parameter) back to the beginning. Procedure READ1LINE reads each line from LETTER into NEXTLINE; the WRITELN statement writes the line just read to file JOBLETTER.

PROGRAM STYLE

Files as variable parameters

Several file parameters are declared in the procedures shown in Fig. 8.6. Each of these is declared as a variable parameter regardless of whether it represents a file used for input or for output. This is required in Pascal because it is not possible to make a local copy of a complete file in main memory.

Wheel of Fortune Problem

In the game show "The Wheel of Fortune" three contestants attempt to guess a phrase. The contestants select consonants that they think are in the phrase. If a consonant that is chosen occurs in the phrase it is inserted in its proper place. Contestants may also "buy" vowels; if the vowel occurs in the phrase it is also inserted.

Problem: The game show producers would like a computer program they can use to help select phrases. Since the consonants are key, it will help the producers if they can see what the phrase looks like without vowels. The program will read a phrase entered at the keyboard and then display that phrase with a minus sign inserted in place of every vowel. A list of vowels and consonants occurring in the phrase will be printed underneath it. The input phrase

```
THIS IS A SAMPLE
PHRASE WITH
VOWELS REMOVED
```

would generate the output

```
TH-S -S - S-MPL-
PHR-S- W-TH
V-W-LS R-M-V-D
```

```
The consonants are: DHLMPRSTVW
The vowels are: AEIO
```

Discussion: We will read each line of the phrase, substitute a minus sign for each vowel, and write each converted line to a file (SCRATCH). Each individual letter in a line will be added to a set of consonants or vowels. After the phrase is completed, file SCRATCH will be echo printed. The problem inputs and outputs and algorithm follow.

PROBLEM INPUTS

phrase to be processed (uppercase letters)

PROBLEM OUTPUTS

phrase with vowels removed (SCRATCH : TEXT)
set of consonants in the phrase (CONSONANTS : set of 'A'..'Z')
set of vowels in the phrase (VOWELS : set of 'A'..'Z')

Algorithm

1. Classify each character as a consonant or vowel, substitute the minus sign for each vowel, and write the phrase to a scratch file.
2. Echo print the scratch file.
3. Print the set of consonants.
4. Print the set of vowels.

The structure chart in Fig. 8.7 uses separate procedures to accomplish steps 1 through 4. The main program is shown in Fig. 8.8.

Fig. 8.7 Structure Chart for Wheel of Fortune Problem

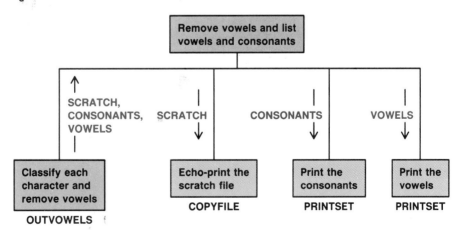

```
program WHEEL (INPUT, OUTPUT);

{Displays a phrase with vowels removed. Also
 lists the consonants and vowels in the phrase.}

const
    STRINGSIZE = 65;                                  {maximum length of each line}

type
    STRING = packed array [1..STRINGSIZE] of CHAR;
    LINE = record
        INFO : STRING;                               {the data on a line}
        LENGTH : 0..STRINGSIZE                   {actual length of the line}
    end; {LINE}
    LETTERSET = set of 'A'..'Z';                           {set of letters}

var
    CONSONANTS,                                        {set of consonants}
    VOWELS : LETTERSET;                                    {set of vowels}
    SCRATCH : TEXT;                                      {a scratch file}

{Insert procedure READ1LINE here.}
{Insert procedures OUTVOWELS, COPYFILE, and PRINTSET here.}

begin
    {Classify each character as a consonant or vowel, substitute
     - for each vowel, and write the scratch file.                    }
    OUTVOWELS (SCRATCH, CONSONANTS, VOWELS);

    {Echo print the scratch file.}
    COPYFILE (SCRATCH, OUTPUT);

    {Print the set of consonants.}
    WRITE ('The consonants are: ');
    PRINTSET (CONSONANTS);
    WRITELN;

    {Print the set of vowels.}
    WRITE ('The vowels are: ');
    PRINTSET (VOWELS)
end.   {WHEEL}
```

Fig. 8.8 Main Program for Wheel of Fortune Problem

This program uses three procedures that are already written. Procedure READ1LINE and COPYFILE (see Fig. 8.6) are used to echo print the file SCRATCH. Procedure PRINTSET (see Fig. 8.3) prints the sets VOWELS and CONSONANTS. However, first procedure OUTVOWELS must write the file SCRATCH and define the sets VOWELS and CONSONANTS. The local variables and algorithm for OUTVOWELS follow.

LOCAL VARIABLES FOR OUTVOWELS

each line of the phrase (NEXTLINE : LINE)

Algorithm for OUTVOWELS

1. Prepare SCRATCH for output.
2. Initialize CONSONANTS and VOWELS to empty sets.
3. Print the user instructions.
4. Read the first line of the phrase.
5. while there are more lines in the phrase do
   6. Replace each vowel in the current line with − and add the vowel to VOWELS. Add each consonant to CONSONANTS.
   7. Write the modified line to file SCRATCH.
   8. Read the next line of the phrase.

Procedure READ1LINE is used to enter each line of the phrase and its length into the record NEXTLINE. Procedure CLASSIFY performs step 5. The structure chart for OUTVOWELS is shown in Fig. 8.9; procedure OUTVOWELS is shown in Fig. 8.10.

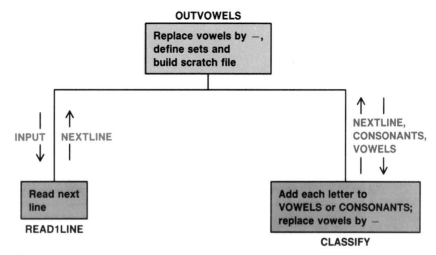

Fig. 8.9 Structure Chart for Procedure OUTVOWELS

```
procedure OUTVOWELS (var SCRATCH      {output} : TEXT;
                     var CONSONANTS {output},
                         VOWELS      {output} : LETTERSET);

{Classifies each character as a consonant or vowel, substitutes
 − for each vowel, and writes the scratch file.            }

var
    NEXTLINE : LINE;                                {the next data line}

procedure CLASSIFY (var NEXTLINE     {input/output} : LINE;
                    var CONSONANTS {input/output},
                        VOWELS      {input/output} : LETTERSET);

{Adds each letter in NEXTLINE to the set CONSONANTS or VOWELS.
 Replaces each vowel in NEXTLINE with −.                   }

const
    MINUS = '−';                                    {minus sign}
```

```
var
    ALLVOWELS,                                          {set of all vowels}
    ALLCONSONANTS : LETTERSET;                       {set of all consonants}
    NEXTCHAR : CHAR;                               {each character in the line}
    I : 1..STRINGSIZE;                              {loop control variable}

begin {CLASSIFY}
    {Initialize ALLVOWELS and ALLCONSONANTS}
    ALLVOWELS := ['A','E','I','O','U'];
    ALLCONSONANTS := ['A'..'Z'] - ALLVOWELS;                 {rest of alphabet}

    {Replace each vowel with -; update vowel and consonant sets.}
    for I := 1 to NEXTLINE.LENGTH do
        begin
            NEXTCHAR := NEXTLINE.INFO[I];                  {save next character}
            if NEXTCHAR in ALLVOWELS then
                begin {vowel}
                    VOWELS := VOWELS + [NEXTCHAR];            {insert vowel}
                    NEXTLINE.INFO[I] := MINUS                 {replace vowel}
                end {vowel}
            else if NEXTCHAR in ALLCONSONANTS then
                CONSONANTS := CONSONANTS + [NEXTCHAR]        {add consonant}
        end {for}
end; {CLASSIFY}

begin {OUTVOWELS}
    REWRITE (SCRATCH);                          {prepare SCRATCH for output}
    CONSONANTS := [];  VOWELS := [];                    {initialize sets}

    {Print user instructions.}
    WRITELN ('Enter each line of the text phrase.');
    WRITELN ('Press return twice when done.');

    {Read each line, convert it, and write it to SCRATCH.}
    READ1LINE (INPUT, NEXTLINE);                          {get the first line}
    while NEXTLINE.LENGTH <> 0 do
        begin
            {Replace vowels with - and update CONSONANTS and VOWELS.}
            CLASSIFY (NEXTLINE, CONSONANTS, VOWELS);

            {Write converted line to scratch file.}
            WRITELN (SCRATCH, NEXTLINE.INFO :NEXTLINE.LENGTH);
            READ1LINE (INPUT, NEXTLINE)                  {get the next line}
        end {while}
end; {OUTVOWELS}
```

Fig. 8.10 Procedure OUTVOWELS

The length of the input line, NEXTLINE.LENGTH, is used to control rep-etition of the while loop in procedure OUTVOWELS. A length of zero indi-cates that the <Return> key was pressed twice. The line length also determines the number of characters that are written to file SCRATCH by the statement

```
WRITELN (SCRATCH, NEXTLINE.INFO :NEXTLINE.LENGTH);
```

The sets ALLVOWELS and ALLCONSONANTS are defined in CLASSIFY as the set of all vowels and consonants, respectively. The assignment statement

```
ALLCONSONANTS := ['A'..'Z'] - ALLVOWELS;    {rest of alphabet}
```

defines ALLCONSONANTS properly when the letters are consecutive characters. If this is not the case on your system, you may wish to represent the set ['A'..'Z'] differently. (For example, in the EBCDIC code use ['A'..'I','J'..'R','S'..'Z']).

In CLASSIFY, the assignment statements

```
VOWELS := VOWELS + [NEXTCHAR];           {insert vowel}
NEXTLINE.INFO[I] := MINUS                 {replace vowel}
```

insert a letter (NEXTCHAR) that is a vowel in the set VOWELS and replace that letter with a minus sign in the string NEXTLINE.INFO. A letter that is a consonant is inserted in the set CONSONANTS by the statement

```
CONSONANTS := CONSONANTS + [NEXTCHAR]     {add consonant}
```

PROGRAM STYLE

Use of scratch files

File SCRATCH is created by procedure OUTVOWELS and echo printed by procedure COPYFILE. Since it is completely processed during the execution of program WHEEL, there is no need to retain it in secondary storage after WHEEL is finished. For this reason, the identifier SCRATCH was not listed as a file parameter in the program statement. Files that are defined only during the execution of a program are called *scratch files*. The space used by a scratch file on a disk may be reallocated after the program is done.

It would have been just as easy to use an array of records to store each line of the phrase being processed instead of a scratch file. A scratch file was used for two reasons. First, to demonstrate its use and, secondly, because the number of lines in the input phrase is unknown. Because of limitations on available memory, it might be impossible to store a very long phrase in an array of records; however, this would be no problem using a scratch file.

Self-check Exercises for Section 8.4

1. Discuss the changes that would be needed in the Wheel of Fortune program to save the phrase in an array of records instead of using a scratch file.

8.5 User-defined File Types

We can declare file types with components that are any standard or user-defined data type, except for another file type. Files with components other than type CHAR are called *binary files* as the binary values stored in memory are copied directly to the disk. In a TEXT file, the file components are characters from the Pascal character set; consequently, only binary character codes can be copied to the disk. Pascal converts a numeric value in memory to a sequence of character codes before writing it to a TEXT file; this conversion is not performed when a numeric value is written from memory to a binary file.

Example 8.8   Program ECHOFILE in Fig. 8.11 creates and echo prints a file of integer values from 1 to 1000. The file type declaration

```
type
   NUMBERFILE = file of INTEGER;
```

identifies NUMBERFILE as a file type whose components are integer values. The binary file that is processed is named NUMBERS and is shown below.

file NUMBERS

| 1 | 2 | 3 | 4 | 5 | 6 | . . . | 999 | 1000 |

ECHOFILE begins by preparing file NUMBERS for output (the REWRITE statement). The for loop with loop control variable I is used to create a file of integer values. The statement

```
WRITE (NUMBERS, I);        {write each integer to NUMBERS}
```

copies each value of I (1 to 1000) to file NUMBERS.

Next, file NUMBERS is prepared for input (the RESET statement). The while loop echo prints each value stored in NUMBERS until the end of file NUMBERS is reached (EOF(NUMBERS) is TRUE). Within the loop, the statement

```
READ (NUMBERS, NEXTINT); {read next integer into NEXTINT}
```

reads the next file component (an integer value) into variable NEXTINT. The statement

```
WRITELN (NEXTINT)                            {display it}
```

displays this value on the screen (system file OUTPUT).

The above example shows how the standard procedures READ and WRITE can be used with binary files. The file name must be the first pa-

```
program ECHOFILE (NUMBERS, OUTPUT);

{Creates a file of integer values and echo prints it.}

const
    NUMINT = 1000;                          {number of integers in the file}

type
    NUMBERFILE = file of INTEGER;

var
    NUMBERS : NUMBERFILE;                              {file of integers}
    I,                                          {loop control variable}
    NEXTINT : 1..NUMINT;                {each integer read from file NUMBERS}

begin {ECHOFILE}
    {Create a file of integers.}
    REWRITE (NUMBERS);                   {initialize NUMBERS to an empty file}
    for I := 1 to NUMINT do
        WRITE (NUMBERS, I);                 {write each integer to NUMBERS}

    {Echo print file NUMBERS.}
    RESET (NUMBERS);                           {prepare NUMBERS for input}
    while not EOF(NUMBERS) do
        begin
            READ (NUMBERS, NEXTINT);       {read next integer into NEXTINT}
            WRITELN (NEXTINT)                              {display it}
        end {while}
end. {ECHOFILE}
```

Fig. 8.11 Program ECHOFILE

rameter. For the READ procedure, a single variable of the same type as the file components must follow the file name. For the WRITE procedure, a single expression of the same type as the file components must follow the file name.

The EOF function may be used to test for the end of a binary file in the same way that it tests for the end of a TEXT file. The file name must be passed as a parameter to the function.

Unlike TEXT files, binary files cannot be segmented into lines. Consequently, the standard procedures READLN, WRITELN, and EOLN cannot be used with binary files.

FILE DECLARATION

file-type = file of *component-type*

Interpretation: A new type *file-type* is declared whose components must be type *component-type*. Any standard or previously-declared data type may be the *component-type* except for another file type or a structured type with a file type as one of its fields.

READ PROCEDURE (for binary files)

READ (*infile*, *variable*)

Interpretation: The READ procedure reads the current component of file *infile* into *variable* and then advances the file position pointer to the next file component. The type of *variable* must correspond to the component type for *infile*. The value of EOF(*infile*) must be FALSE before the read operation occurs.

WRITE PROCEDURE (for binary files)

WRITE (*outfile*, *expression*)

Interpretation: The WRITE procedure appends the value of *expression* to file *outfile*. The type of *expression* must correspond to the component type for *outfile*.

Creating a File of Records

The components of a binary file may be any simple or structured type except for another file type. Often the components of a binary file are records. In this section we will see how to create a binary file of records.

Unlike a TEXT file, a binary file cannot be created by using the system editor. Instead, a binary file must be created by executing a program. Normally, the data to be stored in the file are read from the keyboard (or another TEXT file) into a record variable; then the contents of the record variable is written to the binary file.

Example 8.9   The program in Fig. 8.12 creates a binary file, INVENTORY, that represents the inventory of a bookstore. Each file component is a record of type BOOK since INVENTORY is declared as type BOOKFILE (file of BOOK). The information saved in each component consists of a four-digit stock number, the author and title (strings), the price, and the quantity on hand. The program also computes and prints the total value of the inventory.

Procedure READBOOK is called to enter the data for each book from the terminal into record variable ONEBOOK. READBOOK calls procedure READSTRING (see Fig. 6.15) to read the author and title strings.

Once ONEBOOK is defined, the main program statement

```
WRITE (INVENTORY, ONEBOOK); {copy the book to INVENTORY}
```

copies the internal, binary form of the entire record ONEBOOK to file INVENTORY. Contrast this with the statement

```
           with ONEBOOK do
               WRITELN (STOCKNUM :4, AUTHOR, TITLE, PRICE`:10:2, QUANTITY :5)
```

that would be needed to display each individual record field as a sequence of characters on the terminal (the TEXT file OUTPUT). The binary file created by the program run shown in Fig. 8.12 is sketched below.

file INVENTORY

1234	7654
Robert Ludlum	Blaise Pascal
The Parsifal Mosaic	Pascal Made Easy
17.95	50.00
10	1

```
program BOOKINVENTORY (INVENTORY, INPUT, OUTPUT);

{Creates an inventory file, INVENTORY, from data entered at the
 terminal. Also computes and prints the total inventory value. }

const
   STRINGSIZE = 20;                            {size of each string}
   SENTINEL = 9999;                            {sentinel stock number}

type
   STOCKRANGE = 1111..9999;                    {range of stock numbers}
   STRING = packed array [1..STRINGSIZE] of CHAR;
   BOOK = record
      STOCKNUM : STOCKRANGE;
      AUTHOR,
      TITLE  : STRING;
      PRICE : REAL;
      QUANTITY : INTEGER
   end; {BOOK}
   BOOKFILE = file of BOOK;

var
   INVENTORY : BOOKFILE;                       {the new inventory file}
   ONEBOOK : BOOK;                                      {each book}
   INVVALUE : REAL;                            {value of inventory}

procedure READBOOK (var ONEBOOK {output} : BOOK);

{Reads a book from the keyboard into ONEBOOK.
 Uses procedure READSTRING.                        }

var
   LENGTH : INTEGER;                           {length of a data string}

{Insert procedure READSTRING here.}

begin {READBOOK}
   with ONEBOOK do
      begin
         WRITE ('Stock number: ');  READLN (STOCKNUM);
```

```
            if STOCKNUM <> SENTINEL then
                begin
                    WRITE ('Author: ');      READSTRING (AUTHOR, LENGTH);
                    WRITE ('Title: ');       READSTRING (TITLE, LENGTH);
                    WRITE ('Price: $');      READLN (PRICE);
                    WRITE ('Quantity: ');    READLN (QUANTITY)
                end {if}
        end {with}
end; {READBOOK}

begin {BOOKINVENTORY}
    REWRITE (INVENTORY);                     {prepare INVENTORY for output}
    INVVALUE := 0.0;                            {initialize inventory value}

    {Read and copy each book until done.}
    WRITELN ('Enter the data requested for each book.');
    WRITELN ('Enter a stock number of 9999 when done.');
    READBOOK (ONEBOOK);                              {read first book}
    while ONEBOOK.STOCKNUM <> SENTINEL do
        begin
            WRITE (INVENTORY, ONEBOOK);          {copy the book to INVENTORY}
            {Update inventory value}
            INVVALUE := INVVALUE + ONEBOOK.PRICE * ONEBOOK.QUANTITY;
            READBOOK (ONEBOOK)                          {read next book}
        end; {while}

    {Print inventory value.}
    WRITELN;
    WRITELN ('Inventory value is $', INVVALUE :9:2)
end. {BOOKINVENTORY}


Enter the data requested for each book.
Enter a stock number of 9999 when done.
Stock Number: 1234
Author: Robert Ludlum
Title: The Parsifal Mosaic
Price: $17.95
Quantity: 10
Stock Number: 7654
Author: Blaise Pascal
Title: Pascal Made Easy
Price: $50.00
Quantity: 1
Stock Number: 9999

Inventory value is $   229.50
```

Fig. 8.12 Creating a Bookstore Inventory File

Self-check Exercises for Section 8.5

1. Write a program that echo prints file INVENTORY at the terminal.
2. Modify procedure BOOKINVENTORY so that a special sentinel record is added at the end. This record should have a stock number field of 9999; the remaining field values are immaterial.

8.6 Case Study—File Merge

Like most data structures, a file often needs to be modified or updated after it has been created. We may want to modify one or more fields of an existing record, delete a record, insert a new record, or simply display the current field values for a record.

Unlike a TEXT file, a binary file cannot be modified by an editor. Instead, we must create a new file whose records are based on the original file. In order to do this, we must read each existing record, perhaps modify it, and then write it to the new file.

The next problem discusses how to merge two files with similar components into one larger file.

File Merge Problem

Problem: Whenever our bookstore receives a new shipment of books a file (UPDATE) is prepared that describes the new shipment. In order to keep our inventory file (INVENTORY) up-to-date, we need a program to combine or merge the information on these two files, assuming the records on both files are the same type (BOOK).

Discussion: Merging two files is a common data processing operation. To perform this and most other tasks involving sequential files efficiently, we will assume that the records on both files are in order by stock number. We will also reserve the largest stock number (9999) as a special sentinel record always found at the end of each file (see Exercise 2 above).

Our task is to create a third file (NEWINVEN) that contains all data appearing on the two existing files. If a stock number appears on only one of the files, then its corresponding record will be copied directly to NEWINVEN. If a stock number appears on both files, then the data from file UPDATE will be copied to NEWINVEN, since that is most recent; however, the QUANTITY field of the record written to NEWINVEN must be the sum of both QUANTITY fields, i.e., the quantity shipped plus the quantity on hand. The records on the new file should also be in order by stock number.

Table 8.1 illustrates the desired result of merging two small sample files. For simplicity, only the STOCK and QUANTITY fields of all three files are shown. The only stock numbers appearing on all three files are 4234 and the sentinel stock number (9999).

The data requirements and algorithm for a MERGE procedure are described next. Since we are writing a procedure, the type declarations should appear in the main program; they will be similar to those in Fig. 8.12.

PROBLEM INPUTS

the current inventory file (INVENTORY : BOOKFILE)
the file of new books received (UPDATE : BOOKFILE)

Table 8.1 Sample File Merge Operation

File INVENTORY		File UPDATE		File NEWINVEN	
STOCK	QUANTITY	STOCK	QUANTITY	STOCK	QUANTITY
1111	30	4234	55	1111	30
4234	15	6345	10	4234	70
8955	90	7789	22	6345	10
9999	?	9999	?	7789	22
				8955	90
				9999	?

PROBLEM OUTPUTS

the new inventory file (NEWINVEN : BOOKFILE)

LOCAL VARIABLES

the current record from INVENTORY (INVENBOOK : BOOK)
the current record from UPDATE (UPDATEBOOK : BOOK)

Algorithm

1. Prepare files INVENTORY and UPDATE for input and file NEWINVEN for output.
2. Read the first record from INVENTORY into INVENBOOK and from UPDATE into UPDATEBOOK.
3. Copy all records that appear on only one input file to NEWINVEN. If a record appears on both input files, sum both QUANTITY values before copying record UPDATEBOOK to NEWINVEN.

In step 3 above, the records currently stored in INVENBOOK and UPDATEBOOK are compared. Since the records on file NEWINVEN must be in order by stock number, the record with the smaller stock number is written to NEWINVEN. Another record is then read from the file containing the record just written and the comparison process is repeated. If the stock numbers of UPDATEBOOK and INVENBOOK are the same (a record appears on both files), the new value of UPDATEBOOK.QUANTITY is computed, the modified record is written to NEWINVEN, and the next records are read from both input files. (See refinement at top of next page.)

What happens when the end of one input file is reached? The stock number for the current record of that file will be 9999 (the maximum) so each record read from the other input file will be copied directly to file NEWINVEN. When the end of both input files is reached, the while loop is exited and the sentinel record is written to file NEWINVEN (step 3.5).

Procedure COPYSMALLER implements the if statement shown in the refinement of step 3. The three files are global identifiers referenced by

Step 3 refinement **3.1** while there are more records to copy do
if INVENBOOK.STOCKNUM < UPDATEBOOK.STOCKNUM then
   3.2 Write INVENBOOK to NEWINVEN and read the next record of INVENTORY into INVENBOOK.
else if INVENBOOK.STOCKNUM > UPDATEBOOK.STOCKNUM then
   3.3 Write UPDATEBOOK to NEWINVEN and read the next record of UPDATE into UPDATEBOOK.
else
   3.4 Modify the QUANTITY field of UPDATEBOOK, write UPDATEBOOK to NEWINVEN, and read the next record from INVEN and UPDATE.
3.5 Write the sentinel record to NEWINVEN.

COPYSMALLER. The structure chart for the MERGE procedure is shown in Fig. 8.13; procedure MERGE is shown in Fig. 8.14.

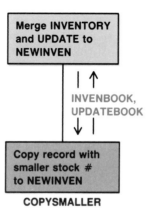

Fig. 8.13 Structure Chart for Procedure MERGE

```
procedure MERGE (var INVENTORY, UPDATE {input} : BOOKFILE;
                 var NEWINVEN {output} : BOOKFILE);

{Merges the data on files INVENTORY and UPDATE to file NEWINVEN.
 All records are in order by stock number (field STOCKNUM). If the
 same stock number appears on both input files, the new QUANTITY
 field value is the sum of the old QUANTITY field values.            }

var
    INVENBOOK,                          {current record of file INVENTORY}
    UPDATEBOOK : BOOK;                     {current record of file UPDATE}

procedure COPYSMALLER (var INVENBOOK,
                       UPDATEBOOK {input/output} : BOOK);

{Compares the stock numbers of the current records, writes the
 record with the smaller stock number to NEWINVEN, and reads the
```

next record from the file whose record was written. If both records have the same stock number, sums the quantity fields before writing the record, and reads new records from each file.}

```
begin {COPYSMALLER}
   if INVENBOOK.STOCKNUM < UPDATEBOOK.STOCKNUM then
      begin {<}
         WRITE (NEWINVEN, INVENBOOK);                    {copy INVENBOOK}
         READ (INVENTORY, INVENBOOK)                     {read INVENTORY}
      end {<}
   else if INVENBOOK.STOCKNUM > UPDATEBOOK.STOCKNUM then
      begin {>}
         WRITE (NEWINVEN, UPDATEBOOK);                   {copy UPDATEBOOK}
         READ (UPDATE, UPDATEBOOK)                       {read UPDATE}
      end {>}
   else
      begin {=}
         UPDATEBOOK.QUANTITY := UPDATEBOOK.QUANTITY +
                                INVENBOOK.QUANTITY;
         WRITE (NEWINVEN, UPDATEBOOK);                   {copy UPDATEBOOK}
         READ (INVENTORY, INVENBOOK);  READ(UPDATE, UPDATEBOOK)
      end {=}                                            {read both}
end; {COPYSMALLER}

begin {MERGE}
   {Prepare INVENTORY and UPDATE for input, NEWINVEN for output.}
   RESET (INVENTORY);  RESET (UPDATE);  REWRITE (NEWINVEN);

   {Read the first record from INVENTORY and UPDATE.}
   READ (INVENTORY, INVENBOOK);  READ(UPDATE, UPDATEBOOK);

   {Copy all records from file INVENTORY and UPDATE to NEWINVEN.}
   while not EOF(UPDATE) or not EOF(INVENTORY) do
      COPYSMALLER (INVENBOOK, UPDATEBOOK);

   {Write the sentinel record to NEWINVEN.}
   WRITE (NEWINVEN, INVENBOOK);
   WRITELN ('File merge completed')
end; {MERGE}
```

Fig. 8.14 Procedure MERGE

The only output displayed as a result of executing procedure MERGE is the message 'File merge completed'. After the procedure's execution you may wish to echo print file NEWINVEN. Once you are certain file NEWINVEN is correct, you can rename it file INVENTORY, using an operating system command. It can then be used as the input inventory file and merged with another UPDATE file at a later time.

The merge procedure can be adapted to perform other update operations. For example, a file representing the daily sales of all books (file SALES) can be merged with file INVENTORY to generate an updated inventory file at the end of each day. If the quantity sold is represented as a negative number in file SALES, then the sum of the quantity fields will indicate the quantity remaining in stock. It is even possible to delete records whose quantity fields become negative or zero by simply not copying such records to NEWINVEN.

PROGRAM STYLE

Analysis of the merge procedure

A number of questions can be asked about the merge procedure shown in Fig. 8.14. For example, what happens if an input file is empty or only contains the sentinel record? Since procedure MERGE always reads at least one record, an execution error will occur if either input file is empty. If a file contains only the sentinel record, then only the sentinel record will be read from that file and all the records in the other file will be copied directly to file NEWINVEN. If both input files contain only the sentinel record, then the while loop will be exited immediately and the sentinel record only will be copied to file NEWINVEN after loop exit.

There is also a question as to whether or not the if statement is executed when both records (INVENBOOK and UPDATEBOOK) contain the sentinel stock number 9999. If it is, then the sentinel record will be copied to NEWINVEN, and an execution error will occur when Pascal attempts to read the next pair of records. Fortunately, this does not happen because immediately after the second sentinel stock number is read the while condition is tested. Since the end of both input files is reached, the while condition is false and the loop is exited immediately.

Finally, we must question the efficiency of the merge procedure when the end of one file is reached much sooner than the other. This will result in the stock number 9999 being repeatedly compared to the stock numbers on the file that is not yet finished. It is more efficient to exit the while loop when the end of one file is reached and then copy all remaining records on the other file directly to file NEWINVEN. This modification is left as an exercise.

Self-check Exercises for Section 8.6

1. Modify procedure MERGE as described in the program style display above.

8.7 Case Study—Data Base Inquiry

Computerized matching of data against a file of records is becoming very common. For example, many real estate companies maintain a large file of property listings. This file can be processed to locate the most desirable properties for a client. Similarly, computerized dating services maintain a file of clients from which compatible matches can be made.

These large files of data are called *data bases*. In this section we will write a program that searches a data base to find all records that match a proposed set of requirements.

Data Base Inquiry Problem

Problem: One reason for storing the bookstore inventory as a computer file is to facilitate answering questions regarding this data base. Some questions of interest might be:

- What books by Robert Ludlum are in stock?
- What books in the price range $5.95 to $8.00 are in stock?
- What is the stock number of the book *Pascal Made Easy* and how many copies are in stock?
- What books priced over $25 are in stock in quantities greater than 10?

These questions and others can be answered providing we know the correct way to ask them.

Discussion: A data base inquiry program has two phases: setting the search parameters and searching for records that satisfy the parameters. In our program we will assume that all of the record fields can be involved in the search. The program user must enter low and high bounds for each field. The sample dialogue below sets the search parameters to answer the question:

What are the books by Tennyson that cost less than $11 and for which 2 or more copies are in stock?

We are assuming that there are never more than 5000 copies of a book in stock and that the price of a book does not exceed $1000.

```
Enter the low bound for stock number or 1111: 1111
Enter the high bound for stock number or 9999: 9999
Enter the low bound for author name or AAA: Tennyson
Enter the high bound for author name or ZZZ: Tennyson
Enter the low bound for title or AAA: AAA
Enter the high bound for title or ZZZ: ZZZ
Enter the low bound for price or $0: $0
Enter the high bound for price or $1000: $10.99
Enter the low bound for quantity or 0: 2
Enter the high bound for quantity or 5000: 5000
```

The data description and algorithm for the data base inquiry problem follow.

PROBLEM INPUTS

the search parameter bounds
the inventory file (INVENTORY : BOOKFILE)

all books that satisfy the search parameters

Algorithm
1. Prepare file NEWINVENTORY for input.
2. Enter the search parameters.
3. Display all books that match the parameters.

To simplify parameter passing between the procedures that implement steps 1 and 2, we will store the search parameters in a record variable (PARAMS). The structure chart for the data base inquiry problem is shown in Fig. 8.15; the main program with procedure ENTERPARAMS is shown in Fig. 8.16.

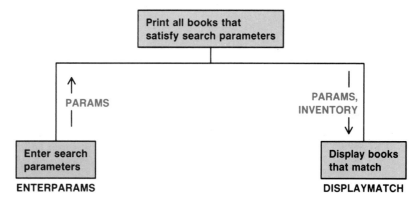

Fig. 8.15 Structure chart for data base inquiry problem

```
program INQUIRE (INVENTORY, INPUT, OUTPUT);

{Prints all books that satisfy the search parameters specified
 by the program user.                                           }

const
    STRINGSIZE = 20;                        {size of each string}
    MAXQUANTITY = 5000;                      {maximum quantity}
    MAXPRICE = 1000.00;                      {maximum book price}
    MINSTOCK = 1111;                        {minimum stock number}
    MAXSTOCK = 9999;                        {maximum stock number}

type
    STRING = packed array [1..STRINGSIZE] of CHAR;
    STOCKRANGE = MINSTOCK..MAXSTOCK;
    BOOK = record
        STOCKNUM : STOCKRANGE;                     {four-digit stock number}
        AUTHOR,
        TITLE : STRING;
        PRICE : REAL;
        QUANTITY : INTEGER
    end; {BOOK}

    BOOKFILE = file of BOOK;
```

```
SEARCHPARAMS = record                          {search parameter bounds}
    LOWSTOCK, HIGHSTOCK : STOCKRANGE;
    LOWAUTHOR, HIGHAUTHOR,
    LOWTITLE, HIGHTITLE : STRING;
    LOWPRICE, HIGHPRICE : REAL;
    LOWQUANT, HIGHQUANT : INTEGER
  end; {SEARCHPARAMS}

var
   INVENTORY : BOOKFILE;                        {the inventory file}
   PARAMS : SEARCHPARAMS;                        {the search parameters}

procedure ENTERPARAMS (var PARAMS {output} : SEARCHPARAMS);

{Enters the search parameters and validates them. The low bound
for a parameter must be <= the high bound and both bounds must be
in range.                                                           }

begin {ENTERPARAMS}
   WRITELN ('Procedure ENTERPARAMS entered.')
end; {ENTERPARAMS}

procedure DISPLAYMATCH (var INVENTORY {input} : BOOKFILE;
                        PARAMS {input} : SEARCHPARAMS);

{Displays all records of INVENTORY that satisfy search parameters.}

begin {DISPLAYMATCH}
   WRITELN ('Procedure DISPLAYMATCH entered.')
end; {DISPLAYMATCH}

begin {INQUIRE}
   {Prepare INVENTORY for input.}
   RESET (INVENTORY);

   {Enter the search parameters.}
   ENTERPARAMS (PARAMS);

   {Display all books that match the search parameters.}
   DISPLAYMATCH (INVENTORY, PARAMS)
end. {INQUIRE}
```

Fig. 8.16 Main Program for Data Base Inquiry Problem

Procedure ENTERPARAMS is left as an exercise. As an example of how this might be implemented, procedure BOUNDSTOCK in Fig. 8.17 enters and validates the stock number boundary values. The procedure (call) statement

```
BOUNDSTOCK (PARAMS.LOWSTOCK, PARAMS.HIGHSTOCK)
```

can be used in ENTERPARAMS to set the stock number boundary values. Procedures similar to BOUNDSTOCK can be used to set the other search parameters.

```
procedure BOUNDSTOCK (var LOWSTOCK,
                          HIGHSTOCK {output} : STOCKRANGE);

{Enters and validates the search boundaries for stock number.}

var
    LOWVALUE, HIGHVALUE : INTEGER;                    {unvalidated boundary values}

begin {BOUNDSTOCK}
    repeat
        WRITE ('Enter the low bound for stock number or ',
                MINSTOCK :4, ': ');   READLN (LOWVALUE);
        WRITE ('Enter the high bound for stock number or ',
                MAXSTOCK :4, ': ');   READLN (HIGHVALUE)
    until (LOWVALUE <= HIGHVALUE) and (LOWVALUE >= MINSTOCK) and
            (HIGHVALUE <= MAXSTOCK);

    {assert: search boundaries are valid}
    LOWSTOCK := LOWVALUE;   HIGHSTOCK := HIGHVALUE
end; {BOUNDSTOCK}
```

Fig. 8.17 Procedure BOUNDSTOCK

Procedure DISPLAYMATCH must examine each file record with stock number less than or equal to the upper bound. If a record satisfies the search parameters it is displayed. DISPLAYMATCH will also print a message if no matches are found. The local variables and algorithm for procedure DISPLAYMATCH follow.

LOCAL VARIABLES FOR DISPLAYMATCH

the current book (NEXTBOOK : BOOK)
a program flag indicating whether or not there are any matches
(NOMATCHES : BOOLEAN)

Algorithm for
DISPLAYMATCH
1. Initialize NOMATCHES to TRUE.
2. Read the first book record.
3. while the current stock number is in range do
    4. If the search parameters match then
        5. Display the book and set NOMATCHES to FALSE.
    6. Read the next book record.
7. if there were no matches then
    8. Print a "no books available" message

The structure chart for DISPLAYMATCH is shown in Fig. 8.18. The BOOLEAN function MATCH is used to implement step 4; procedure SHOW is used to implement step 5. The program is shown in Fig. 8.19.

Function MATCH uses a local BOOLEAN variable, MATCHED, to indicate whether or not each search parameter is satisfied. There are five assignment statements, one per parameter, that assign a value to MATCHED. If a search parameter is not satisfied, its corresponding assignment statement

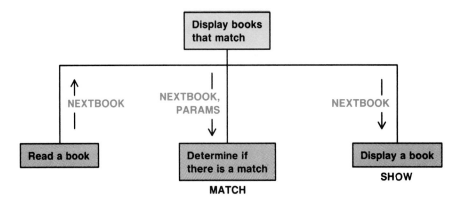

Fig. 8.18 Structure Chart for DISPLAYMATCH

```
procedure DISPLAYMATCH (var INVENTORY {input} : BOOKFILE;
                        PARAMS {input} : SEARCHPARAMS);

{Displays all books that match the search parameters.}

var
    NEXTBOOK : BOOK;                              {the current record}
    NOMATCHES : BOOLEAN;            {indicates if there were any matches}

function MATCH (NEXTBOOK : BOOK;
                PARAMS : SEARCHPARAMS) : BOOLEAN;

{Returns TRUE if the current record (NEXTBOOK) satisfies search
 parameters (PARAMS); otherwise returns FALSE.                     }

var
    MATCHED : BOOLEAN;                              {local BOOLEAN flag}

begin {MATCH}
    with PARAMS do
        begin
            {NEXTBOOK matches if it satisfies all search parameters.}
            MATCHED := (NEXTBOOK.STOCKNUM >= LOWSTOCK);
            MATCHED := MATCHED and (NEXTBOOK.AUTHOR >= LOWAUTHOR) and
                    (NEXTBOOK.AUTHOR <= HIGHAUTHOR);
            MATCHED := MATCHED and (NEXTBOOK.TITLE >= LOWTITLE) and
                    (NEXTBOOK.TITLE <= HIGHTITLE);
            MATCHED := MATCHED and (NEXTBOOK.PRICE >= LOWPRICE) and
                    (NEXTBOOK.PRICE <= HIGHPRICE);
            MATCHED := MATCHED and (NEXTBOOK.QUANTITY >= LOWQUANT)
                    and (NEXTBOOK.QUANTITY <= HIGHQUANT)
        end; {with}

    {Define function result.}
    MATCH := MATCHED
end; {MATCH}

procedure SHOW (var NEXTBOOK {input} : BOOK);

{Displays each field of NEXTBOOK at the terminal. Leaves a line
 space after each book.                                            }
```

```
begin {SHOW}
   WRITELN ('Procedure SHOW entered.')
end; {SHOW}

begin {DISPLAYMATCH}
   NOMATCHES := TRUE;                       {assume no matches to start}
   READ (INVENTORY, NEXTBOOK);                {read the first record}

   {Display each book that satisfies the search parameters.}
   WRITELN ('Books that satisfy the search parameters follow.');
   while (NEXTBOOK.STOCKNUM <= PARAMS.HIGHSTOCK)
      and not EOF(INVENTORY) do
      begin
         if MATCH(NEXTBOOK, PARAMS) then
            begin {match}
               NOMATCHES := FALSE;                {signal a match}
               SHOW (NEXTBOOK)                 {print matched record}
            end; {match}
         READ (INVENTORY, NEXTBOOK)             {read the next record}
      end; {while}

   {assert: all records in range are searched or end of file reached}
   if NOMATCHES then
      WRITELN ('Sorry, no books are available.')
end; {DISPLAYMATCH}
```

Fig. 8.19 Procedure DISPLAYMATCH

sets MATCHED to FALSE. Since MATCHED is "anded" with the result of each parameter test, once MATCHED is set to FALSE it remains FALSE. Consequently, in order for the function result to be TRUE, NEXTBOOK must satisfy all search parameters.

Self-check Exercises for Section 8.7

1. Write the search parameters needed to answer the questions listed at the beginning of this section.
2. Write procedures ENTERPARAMS and SHOW described in the data base inquiry problem.
3. Explain why NEXTBOOK.STOCKNUM is not compared to PARAMS.HIGHSTOCK in function MATCH.

8.8 File Buffer Variable

Unlike other Pascal data structures, a file is located in secondary storage rather than main memory. For this reason, it is less convenient to access data stored in a file. The file component must first be transferred into main memory by a READ operation before the data in that component can be manipulated.

To simplify file access, Pascal allocates a *buffer variable* in main memory for each file declared in a program. The buffer variable acts as a "window" through which file data can be accessed. The buffer variable for a file being read contains a copy of the file component currently selected by the file position pointer. Data in the buffer variable can be manipulated just like any other data in main memory. Data in the buffer variable can also be appended to the end of a file that is being written.

The file buffer variable is denoted by writing the file name followed by a caret (^) or an arrow (↑), depending on the Pascal system. Therefore, INVENTORY^ or INVENTORY↑ represents the file buffer variable for file INVENTORY. The field selector INVENTORY^.AUTHOR may look strange, but it correctly references the AUTHOR field of the file buffer variable. The with statement

```
with INVENTORY^ do
   begin
      WRITELN ('Stock number of book sold is ', STOCKNUM :4);
      QUANTITY := QUANTITY - 1;
      SALESTOTAL := SALESTOTAL + PRICE
   end
```

manipulates the STOCKNUM, PRICE, and QUANTITY fields of the record currently in the file buffer variable.

GET and RESET

The RESET operator moves the file position pointer to the beginning of a file. It also initializes the file buffer variable for that file. The effect of the statement

```
RESET (INVENTORY)
```

is shown below.

file position pointer

As indicated, the file buffer variable contains the data stored in the first file component after RESET. The statement

```
GET (INVENTORY)
```

advances the file position pointer to the next file component and updates the file buffer variable as shown next.

```
INVENTORY^              file INVENTORY
┌──────────────┐    ┌──────────────┬──────────────┬──────────────┐
│ 1234         │    │ 1111         │ 1234         │ 1345         │
│ Baker        │    │ Ashenhurst   │ Baker        │ Carnegie     │
│    •         │    │    •         │    •         │    •         │
│    •         │    │    •         │    •         │    •         │
│    •         │    │    •         │    •         │    •         │
└──────────────┘    └──────────────┴──────────────┴──────────────┘
                                          ↑
                              file position pointer
```

When the file position pointer is at the last file component, the next GET operation causes the buffer variable to become undefined and EOF(INVENTORY) becomes true.

RESET PROCEDURE (effect on file buffer variable)

   RESET (*infile*)

Interpretation: The file position pointer for file *infile* is moved to the beginning of file *infile*. The first file component is stored in the file buffer variable *infile^*.
Note: The RESET operation is automatically performed on system file INPUT, so RESET (INPUT) is not needed and may cause an error on some Pascal systems.

GET OPERATOR

   GET (*infile*)

Interpretation: The file position pointer for file *infile* is advanced and the next file component is stored in the file buffer variable *infile^*.
Note: The effect of the GET operation is undefined if EOF(*infile*) is true before or after the GET is executed. The first GET must be preceded by a RESET operation (except for system file INPUT).

PUT and REWRITE

We write a file in Pascal by appending data to the end of the file. Data stored in a file buffer variable can be appended using the PUT operator. Whenever the statement

   PUT (*outfile*)

is executed, the current contents of the file buffer variable *outfile^* is appended to the end of file *outfile*. The data to be transferred must be stored in the file buffer variable *outfile^* before the PUT is executed. The statement

REWRITE (*outfile*)

must be executed before the first PUT operation.

Example 8.10   Procedure BUILDSMALL in Fig. 8.20 creates an abbreviated inventory file, SMALLINV, which consists of the stock number and quantity only of every record in file INVENTORY. File types BOOKFILE and SMALLBOOKFILE must be declared in the calling program.

```
procedure BUILDSMALL (var INVENTORY {input} : BOOKFILE;
                      var SMALLINV {output} : SMALLBOOKFILE);

{Creates a new inventory file (SMALLINV) containing only stock
 numbers and quantities of the records in INVENTORY.          }

begin {BUILDSMALL}
   {Initialize buffer variable for INVENTORY and prepare SMALLINV.}
   RESET (INVENTORY);  REWRITE (SMALLINV);

   {Copy stock number and quantity from INVENTORY to SMALLINV.}
   while not EOF(INVENTORY) do
      begin
         SMALLINV^.STOCKNUM := INVENTORY^.STOCKNUM;
         SMALLINV^.QUANTITY := INVENTORY^.QUANTITY;
         PUT (SMALLINV);                    {append data to SMALLINV}
         GET (INVENTORY)                         {access next record}
      end {while}
end; {BUILDSMALL}
```

Fig. 8.20 Procedure BUILDSMALL

Each assignment statement

```
SMALLINV^.STOCKNUM := INVENTORY^.STOCKNUM;
SMALLINV^.QUANTITY := INVENTORY^.QUANTITY;
```

copies one field from the file buffer variable for INVENTORY to the file buffer variable for SMALLINV. The statement

```
PUT (SMALLINV);                    {append data to SMALLINV}
```

appends the data just copied to file SMALLINV. The statement

```
GET (INVENTORY)                         {access next record}
```

updates the file buffer variable for INVENTORY so the next record can be transferred.

Note that it is no longer necessary to allocate local variables in BUILDSMALL for storage of a single record of each file. The buffer variables INVENTORY^ and SMALLINV^ are used for this purpose.

GET and PUT versus READ and WRITE

GET and READ may both be used to access data stored in a file. The READ procedure enters the current file component into a local variable of the same type. The statement

```
READ ( INVENTORY, NEXTBOOK )
```

stores the next component of file INVENTORY in the variable NEXTBOOK and advances the file position pointer for INVENTORY.

A local variable is not needed when using GET because the data in the file buffer variable may be accessed directly. However, data can still be stored in a local variable, if desired. The statements

```
NEXTBOOK := INVENTORY^;
GET ( INVENTORY )
```

have the same effect as the READ above; the current file component (stored in INVENTORY^) is copied into NEXTBOOK and the file position pointer is advanced.

The statement

```
WRITE ( NEWINVEN, NEXTBOOK )
```

writes the data stored in variable NEXTBOOK to file NEWINVEN. This can also be accomplished using the statements

```
NEWINVEN^ := NEXTBOOK;
PUT (NEWINVEN)
```

The assignment statement defines the file buffer variable NEWINVEN^; the PUT operation appends this data to the end of file NEWINVEN.

Self-check Exercises for Section 8.8

1. Rewrite procedure BUILDSMALL to copy every other record of file INVENTORY to file SMALLINV.
2. Indicate how you would modify procedures MERGE and COPY-SMALLER (see Fig. 8.14) to use GET and PUT instead of READ and WRITE. Also, manipulate the file buffer variables directly instead of local variables UPDATEBOOK and INVENBOOK.

8.9 Common Programming Errors

Remember that a set variable, like any variable, must be initialized before it can be manipulated. It is tempting to assume that a set is empty and begin processing it without initializing it to the empty set, [ ], through an explicit assignment.

The operands of the set manipulation operators must all be sets. Remember to use a unit set (a set of one element) when inserting or deleting a set element. The set union operation in the expression below is incorrect.

```
['A', 'E', 'O', 'U'] + 'I'          {incorrect set union}
```

It should be rewritten as

```
['A', 'E', 'O', 'U'] + ['I']        {valid set union}
```

It is not possible to use a set as an operand of the standard READ or WRITE procedure. The elements of a set must be read in individually and inserted in an initially empty set using the set union operator. To print a set, each value in the base type of a set must be tested for set membership. Only those values that are in the set should be printed.

File processing in any programming language tends to be difficult to master and Pascal is no exception. Remember to include the name of each permanent file that you wish to process in the program statement. This is the name that will be used in the program and it may differ from the actual external name of the associated disk file. All file types (except TEXT) must be declared as well as all file names (except INPUT and OUTPUT).

Do not forget to prepare a file for input or output using the RESET or REWRITE procedure (except for system files INPUT and OUTPUT). If you

REWRITE an existing file, the data on that file may be lost. Make sure that you do not inadvertently place the RESET or REWRITE statement in a loop. If you do, a read operation in the loop will repeatedly read the first file component; a write operation in the loop will repeatedly write the first file component.

The READ (READLN) procedure can be used only after a file has been prepared for input. Similarly, the WRITE (WRITELN) procedure can be used only after a file has been prepared for output. Be sure to specify the file name as the first procedure parameter; otherwise, the system file IN-PUT or OUTPUT will be assumed. An "attempt to read beyond end of file" error occurs if a read operation is performed when the file position pointer for a file has passed the last file component.

There are a number of operations that can be performed with TEXT files that cannot be performed with binary files, since binary files are not segmented into lines. The EOLN function and READLN and WRITELN procedures cannot be used with binary files. Also, you cannot create or modify a binary file using an editor.

Binary files do have an advantage in that an entire record can be transferred between a binary file and a variable in main memory. The variable involved in the data transfer must be the same type as the components of the binary file.

When processing TEXT files, sequences of characters are transferred between main memory and disk storage. The data type of a variable used in an input list must be CHAR or INTEGER (or a subrange thereof) or REAL. The data type of an expression used in an output list must be CHAR or INTEGER (or a subrange thereof), BOOLEAN, REAL, or a character string.

The file buffer variable can be used to directly access the current file component. A common error is writing the operators that manipulate the file buffer variable as GET(*infile^*) or PUT(*outfile^*). The carat should be deleted and the operators written as GET(*infile*) or PUT(*outfile*).

8.10 Chapter Review

Set and file data types can be used for storing a collection of elements of the same type. A set is stored in main memory, whereas a file is stored in secondary memory. The base type of a set specifies which values may belong to the set. Each value in the base type of a set is either a member of the set or it is not. Unlike an array or file, a value can only be saved once in a set and there is no way to determine the time sequence in which the values were stored in the set (e.g. [1,5,2,4] is the same set as [1,2,4,5]).

Whereas the elements of a set must be simple values, the components of a file may be any simple or structured type except for another file type. The file type TEXT is predefined and its components are the Pascal characters and a special character designated the end-of-line mark. The EOLN function can be used to test for an end-of-line mark, and the WRITELN statement places one in a TEXT file. If an end-of-line mark is read into a type CHAR variable, it is stored as a blank character.

We also learned how to declare and manipulate binary files whose components were not individual characters. We created a file of records and merged two files of records into a third file. We also searched a data base to retrieve file records that matched a specified set of search parameters.

New Pascal Statements

The new Pascal statements introduced in this chapter are summarized in Table 8.2.

Table 8.2 Summary of New Pascal Statements

Statement	Effect

Set type declaration
`type`
    `DIGITSET = set of 0..9;`
`var`
    `DIGITS, PRIMES : DIGITSET;`
	Declares a set type `DIGITSET` whose base type is the set of digits from 0 through 9. `DIGITS` and `PRIME` are set variable of type `DIGITSET`.

Set assignment
`DIGITS := [];`
`PRIMES := [2,3,5] + [7];`
`DIGITS := DIGITS + [1..3];`
`DIGITS := [0..9] - [1,3,5,7,9];`
`DIGITS := [1,3,5,7,9] * PRIMES`
	`DIGITS` is the empty set.
	`PRIMES` is the set [2,3,5,7].
	`DIGITS` is the set [1,2,3].
	`DIGITS` is the set [0,2,4,6,8].
	`DIGITS` is the set [3,5,7].

Set relations
`PRIMES <= DIGITS`
`PRIMES = []`
`PRIMES <> []`
`[1,2,3] = [3,2,1]`
	True if `PRIMES` is a subset of `DIGITS`.
	True for the empty set [ ].
	True if `PRIMES` contains any element.
	True because order does not matter.

File type declaration
`type`
    `DIGITFILE = file of INTEGER;`
`var`
    `MOREDIGITS : DIGITFILE;`
    `MORECHARS : TEXT;`
    `I : INTEGER;`
    `NEXTCH : CHAR;`
	Declares a file type `DIGITFILE` whose components are integers. `MOREDIGITS` is a file of type `DIGITFILE`. `MORECHARS` is a file of type `TEXT`.

RESET and REWRITE procedures
`RESET (MOREDIGITS);`
`REWRITE (MORECHARS);`
	`MOREDIGITS` is prepared for input and `MORECHARS` is prepared for output.

Table 8.2 Summary of New Pascal Statements (*continued*)

Statement	Effect

READ and WRITE procedures
`READ (MOREDIGITS, I);`
`WRITELN (MORECHARS, 'number: ', I)`
	The next integer is read from file MOREDIGITS into variable I (type INTEGER). A sequence of characters representing a string and the value of I are written to MORECHARS.

EOF function
`while not EOF(MOREDIGITS) do`
   `begin`
      `READ (MOREDIGITS, I);`
      `WRITELN (MORECHARS, I)`
   `end {while}`
	Every integer value on file MOREDIGITS is written as a sequence of characters on a separate line of file MORECHARS.

EOLN function
`RESET (MORECHARS);`
`while not EOLN do`
   `begin`
      `READ (MORECHARS, NEXTCH);`
      `WRITE (NEXTCH)`
   `end {while}`
	File MORECHARS is prepared for input. Each character on the current line is read into NEXTCH and displayed on the terminal screen.

GET operator
`RESET (MOREDIGITS);`
`I := MOREDIGITS^;`
`GET (MOREDIGITS);`
`WRITE (MOREDIGITS^)`
	The first integer in file MOREDIGITS is placed in the file buffer variable and assigned to variable I. The second integer is displayed.

PUT operator
`MORECHARS^ := 'A';`
`PUT (MORECHARS)`
	The letter A is appended to file MORECHARS.

Review Questions

1. Given the declarations below, indicate how FISCAL year from JULY to JUNE would be declared as a set of type MONTHSET.

```
type
    MONTHS = (JAN,FEB,MAR,APR,MAY,JUN,JUL,AUG,SEP,OCT,NOV,DEC);
    MONTHSET = SET OF MONTHS;
```

2. Write the Pascal statements to find and print the intersection, union, and difference of the two sets defined in the last two lines below.

```
type
    LETTERSET = set of 'A'..'Z';
```

```
var
    VOWEL,
    LETTER : LETTERSET;

procedure PRINTSET (ASET : LETTERSET);

{Prints the elements of set ASET.}

var
    NEXTCH : 'A'..'Z';

begin {PRINTSET}
    for NEXTCH := 'A' to 'Z' do
        if NEXTCH in ASET then
            WRITE(NEXTCH);
        WRITELN
end; {PRINTSET}

begin
    VOWEL := ['Y','U','O','I'];
    LETTER := ['A'..'P'];
```

3. List three advantages to using files for input and output as opposed to the standard input and output devices used thus far in the text.
4. Where are files stored?
5. Modify the COPY program given in the text to accept data from the system file INPUT and write the data out to both the file OUTFILE and the system file OUTPUT.
6. There is an EMPSTAT file (type TEXT) that contains records for up to 15 employees. The data for each employee consists of the employee's name (maximum length of 20), social security number (length of 11 characters), gross pay for the week (real), taxes deducted (real), and the net pay (real) for the week. Each data item is on a separate line of file EMPSTAT. Write a program called PAYREPORT that will create a TEXT file REPORTFILE with the heading line:

       NAME SOC.SEC.NUM. GROSS TAXES NET

   followed by two blank lines and then the pertinent information under each column heading. REPORTFILE should contain up to 18 lines of information after PAYREPORT is executed.
7. Define a scratch file.
8. Describe the characteristics of a binary file.
9. Write the type and variable declaration for a file that will consist of multiple records of type STUDENTSTATS. The statistics kept on each student are the GPA, MAJOR, ADDRESS—consisting of NAME, STREETADDRESS, CITY, STATE, ZIPCODE, and CLASSCHEDULE—consisting of up to six records of CLASS each containing DESCRIPTION, TIME, and DAYS fields. Use variable types that are appropriate for each field.
10. Explain the use and manipulation of a file buffer variable.

11. What Pascal statement would be used to advance the file position pointer in a file being used for input?

12. Write a Pascal procedure LASTNAME that will accept a file of names of the form Lastname, firstname (example: Drend, Jane) and PUT only the length of the last name and the last name in the file LAST-ONLY. Assume the declarations below are in the main program.

Hint: Write a function that returns the position of the comma.

```
program GETLAST (NAMES {input}, LASTONLY {output});

const
    MAXNAME = 30;

type
    STRING = packed array [1..MAXNAME] of CHAR;
    NAMERECS = record
        NAME : STRING
    end;

    LASTNAMES = record
        LENGTH : INTEGER;
        LAST : STRING
    end;

    NAMEFILE = file of NAMERECS;
    LASTNAMEFILE = file of LASTNAMES;

var
    NAMES : NAMEFILE;
    LASTONLY : LASTNAMEFILE;
```

Programming Projects

1. Write a procedure that reads in a hand of cards and stores it in an array of sets, one set for each suit. Each card is represented using a pair of characters. The first character represents the rank of the card: the digits 2 through 9 stand for themselves, and the letters T, J, Q, K, A stand for ten, jack, queen, king, ace, respectively. The second character denotes the suit: C, D, H, or S. Check for invalid cards and duplicate cards.

2. Extend the program in 1), assuming that the cards read represent a bridge hand. Count the point value of the hand assuming the following point count method:

rank	points
2 .. 10	0
jack	1
queen	2
king	3
ace	4

Also, add one point for each suit that has only one card but not a jack, queen, king, or ace; add two points for each suit that is void (no cards for that suit).

3. Assume that you have a file of records each containing a person's last name, first name, birth date, and sex. Create a new file of records containing only first names and sex. Also print out the complete name of every person whose last name begins with the letter A, C, F, or P through Z, and was born in a month beginning with the letter J.

4. Create separate files of saleswomen and salesmen. For each employee on these files, there is an employee number (four digits), a name, and a salary. Each file should be in order by employee number. Merge these two files into a third file that also has a gender field containing one of the values in the type (FEMALE, MALE). After the file merge operation, find the average salary for all employees. Then search the new file and print a list of all female employees over the average and a separate list of all male employees over the average. Hint: You will have to search the new file once for each list.

5. Write a procedure that will merge the contents of three sorted files by ID number and write the merged data to an output file. The parameters to the procedure will be the three input files and the one output file. Data will be of the form

```
DATA = record
    ID : INTEGER;
    NAME : STRING;
    LENGTH : INTEGER;
    SALARY : REAL
end;
```

Assume a sentinel ID number of 9999 is at the end of each file. Test your procedure with some sample data.

6. Cooking recipes can be stored on a computer and with the use of files, can be quickly referenced.
   a) Write a procedure that will create a TEXT file of recipes from information entered at the terminal. The format of the data to be stored is:

   1. Recipe type (e.g. DESSERT, MEAT, etc.)
   2. Subtype (e.g. for DESSERT: CAKE, PIE or BROWNIES)
   3. Name (e.g. GERMAN CHOCOLATE, for a cake)
   4. Number of lines in the recipe to follow
   5. Actual recipe

   Items 1, 2, 3, and 4 should be on separate lines.
   b) Write a procedure that will accept as parameters a file and a record of search parameters that will cause all recipes of a type, all recipes of a subtype, or a specific recipe to be written.

7. A local weather station keeps daily statistics on its weather. This weather data is stored in files by months (one file per month). The data is also in chronological order; therefore, no date is stored within the file. The information stored consists of the high and low temperature, rainfall, and snowfall reading.

a) Write a procedure that will write the day of the month with the highest temperature, the day with the lowest temperature, the day with the most rainfall, and the day with the most snowfall.

b) Write a procedure that will write the total rainfall and snowfall for a month.

All procedures will have as parameters the file to search, and the number of days in that month. Test your procedures with a few months worth of data. A main program can request the month to search.

8. The college football teams need a service to keep track of all the records and vital statistics for various teams. Write a program that will maintain this information on a file. Every week an update file is "posted" against this master file. The update file updates all team statistics and records. All of the information in both files will be stored in order by ID number. Each master record will contain the ID number, team name, number of games won, lost and tied, total yards gained by the team's offense, total yards gained by the other teams against this one, total points scored by this team, and total points scored by the other teams against this one.

For this program, use the master file TEAMS and update TEAMS from file WEEKLY. The updated information should be written to a file called NEWTEAMS. In addition, each record of the weekly file should be echo printed. When files are finished being processed, write a message indicating the number of weekly scores processed, the team that scored the most points, and the team with the most offensive yardage for this week.

9. Write a program that takes a master file of college football information and prints out teams that match a specified set of search parameters. The bounds on the search parameters can be presented in the format described in the section on Data Base Inquiry (see Section 8.7). Some information to be printed can be: all teams with a won/lost percentage in a certain range, all teams within a certain range of points scored or scored upon, or yardage gained and given up, or number of games won, tied or lost. (Note: the won/lost percentage is calculated by dividing number of games won by total games played where ties count as half a game won.)

10. Write a program to scan a line of characters containing an equation and calculates the result. Assume all numeric values are integer. Tests should be made to determine if the equation is valid.

Valid operations are +, −, /, *, ^ where +, −, /, * perform their normal functions and ^ indicates the left value is raised to the power of the right operand (must be positive).

Numbers may be negative and all operations are done in left to right order (no operator precedence). For example:

```
2 + 3 ^ 2 + 36 * -1
```

would be

```
5 ^ 2 + 36 * -1 = 25 + 36 * -1 = 61 * -1 = -61
```

Use sets to verify the operations and ignore all blanks. Output should consist of the echo printing of the equation followed by an equal sign (=) and then the answer. If an equation is invalid display the message `'** IN-VALID **'`.

11. Write a program that updates a file of type BOOKFILE (see Section 8.6). Your program should be able to modify an existing record, insert a new record, or delete an existing record. Assume that the update requests are in order by stock number and that they are of the form shown below.

```
type
   CHANGEKIND = (DELETE, INSERT, MODIFY);
   UPDATEREQ = record
      case CHANGE : CHANGEKIND of
         DELETE : (STOCKNUMBER : STOCKRANGE);
         INSERT : (NEWBOOK : BOOK);
         MODIFY : (MODBOOK : BOOK)
      end
```

Each update request should be read from a binary file. Only the stock number appears in an update request for a deletion. The new book record is supplied for a request to insert a record or modify an existing record. Your program should also print an error message for invalid requests such as an attempt to delete a record that does not exist, an attempt to insert a new record with the same stock number as an existing record, or an attempt to modify a record that does not exist.

9

Recursion, Searching, and Sorting

9.1 The Nature of Recursion
9.2 Recursive Procedures
9.3 Recursive Functions
9.4 Binary Search of an Array
9.5 Searching by Hashing
9.6 Additional Sorting Algorithms
9.7 Case Study—The Quicksort Algorithm
9.8 Common Programming Errors
9.9 Chapter Review

A recursive procedure or function is one that calls itself. This ability to call itself enables a recursive procedure to be repeated with different parameter values. Recursion may be used as an alternative to iteration (looping). Generally, a recursive solution is less efficient in terms of computer time than an iterative one; however, in many instances the use of recursion enables us to specify a natural, simple solution to a problem that would otherwise be very difficult to solve. For this reason, recursion is an important and powerful tool in problem solving and programming.

We will also discuss additional techniques for searching and sorting arrays. We will study two new techniques for searching an array and several algorithms for sorting an array. The efficiency of various sorting algorithms will be compared.

9.1 The Nature of Recursion

Problems that lend themselves to a *recursive* solution have the following characteristics:

- There are one or more simple cases of the problem (called *stopping cases*) that have a simple solution.
- The other cases can be solved by substituting one or more reduced cases of the problem that are closer to a stopping case.
- Eventually the problem can be reduced to stopping cases only, all of which are relatively easy to solve.

The Towers of Hanoi problem is an example of a problem that has these characteristics. In the version of the problem shown in Fig. 9.1 there are five discs (numbered 1 through 5) and three towers or pegs (lettered A, B, C). The goal is to move the five disks from peg A to peg C, according to the following rules:

1. Only one disc may be moved at a time and this disc must be the top disc on a peg.
2. A larger disc can never be placed on top of a smaller disc.

The stopping cases of the problem involve moving one disc only (e.g. move disc 2 from peg A to peg C). It is simpler to solve the problem for four discs than five. Therefore, we want to redefine the original problem (which was to move five discs) in terms of moving four discs, even if this means we have additional steps. If we use peg B as an intermediary, we get the recursive solution:

Algorithm

1. Move 4 discs from peg A to peg B.
2. Move disc 5 from peg A to peg C.
3. Move 4 discs from peg B to peg C.

Fig. 9.1 Towers of Hanoi

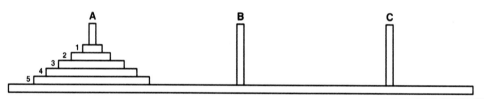

To verify the validity of substituting these three steps for the original problem, we show the status of the three towers after completing steps 1 and 2 in Fig. 9.2. It should be clear that performing step 3 above will lead to the desired result.

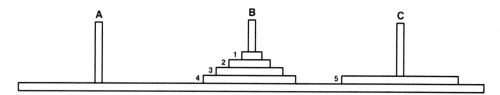

Fig. 9.2 Towers of Hanoi after Steps 1 and 2

Unfortunately, we still don't know how to perform step 1 or 3. (Step 2 is easy because it's a stopping case.) Both these steps involve four discs instead of five so they are simpler than the original problem. Using peg C as an intermediary, we can generate the recursive solution to step 1 shown below.

Step 1 refinement 1.1 Move 3 discs from peg A to peg C.
 1.2 Move disc 4 from peg A to peg B.
 1.3 Move 3 discs from peg C to peg B.

By repeating the process for three discs and then for two discs we will finally reach only cases of moving one disc, which we know how to solve. Later, we will write a Pascal procedure that does this.

Tracing a Recursive Procedure

Recursive procedures are used to implement *recursive* algorithms. We cannot use conventional techniques for tracing the execution of a recursive procedure. We will illustrate how to do this by studying a recursive procedure next.

Example 9.1 Procedure PALINDROME in Fig. 9.3 is a recursive procedure that reads in a string of length N and prints it out backwards. If the procedure (call) statement

```
PALINDROME (5)
```

is executed, the five characters entered will be printed in reverse order. If the characters abcde are entered when this procedure is called, the line

```
abcde edcba
```

will appear on the screen. The letters in blue are entered as data and the letters in black are printed. If the procedure (call) statement

PALINDROME (3)

is executed instead, only three characters will be read and the line

abccba

will appear on the screen if abc are the data.

```
procedure PALINDROME (N : INTEGER);

{Echo prints a string of length N in
 reverse of the order in which it is entered.}

var
    NEXT : CHAR;                              {next data character}

begin {PALINDROME}
   if N = 1 then
      begin {stopping case}
         READ (NEXT);
         WRITE (NEXT)
      end {stopping case}
   else
      begin {recursion}
         READ (NEXT);
         PALINDROME (N-1);
         WRITE (NEXT)
      end {recursion}
end; {PALINDROME}
```

Fig. 9.3 Procedure PALINDROME

Like most recursive procedures, the body of procedure PALINDROME consists of an if statement that evaluates a *terminating condition*, N = 1. When the terminating condition is true, the problem has reached a stopping case. If so, the READ and WRITE statements are executed immediately, causing a single character to be read and echo printed. The procedure end statement is then reached and control is returned back from the procedure.

If the terminating condition is false (N is greater than 1), the recursive step (following else) is executed. The READ statement enters the next data character. The procedure (call) statement

PALINDROME (N-1);

calls the procedure recursively with the parameter value decreased by 1.

The character just read is printed later. This is because the WRITE statement comes after the recursive procedure call; consequently, the WRITE statement cannot be performed until after the procedure execution is completed and control is returned back to the WRITE statement. For example, the character that is read when N is 3 is not echo printed until after the procedure execution for N equal to 2 is completed. Hence, this character is printed after the characters that are read when N is 2 and N is 1.

To fully illustrate this it is necessary to trace the execution of the procedure (call) statement

PALINDROME (3)

This trace is shown in Fig. 9.4, assuming the letters abc are entered as data.

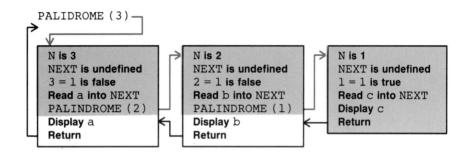

Fig. 9.4 Trace of PALINDROME (3)

The trace shows three separate *activation frames* for procedure PALINDROME. Each activation frame begins with a list of the initial values of N and NEXT for that frame. The value of N is passed into the procedure when it is called since N is a value parameter; the value of NEXT is initially undefined since NEXT is a local variable.

The statements in blue are executed first, starting with the frame on the left. Each recursive call to PALINDROME transfers control to a new activation frame as indicated by the blue arrows. A procedure return occurs when the procedure end statement is reached. In Fig. 9.4 this is indicated by the word Return and by a black arrow that points to the statement in the calling frame to which the procedure returns. Tracing the blue arrows and then the black arrows gives us the sequence of events listed next. All the statements for a particular activation frame are indented to the same column.

Call PALINDROME with N equal to 3.
   Read the first character (a) into NEXT.
   Call PALINDROME with N equal to 2.
      Read the second character (b) into NEXT.
      Call PALINDROME with N equal to 1.
         Read the third character (c) into NEXT.
         Display the third character (c).
         Return from third call.
      Display the second character (b).
      Return from second call.
   Display the first character (a).
   Return from original call.

As shown above, there are three calls to procedure PALINDROME, each with a different parameter value. The procedure returns always occur in the reverse order of the procedure calls; i.e. we return from the last call first, then we return from the next to last call, etc. After we return from a particular execution of the procedure, we display the character that was read into NEXT just prior to that procedure call.

Parameter and Local Variable Stacks

You may be wondering how Pascal keeps track of the values of N and NEXT at a given point. Pascal uses a special data structure called a *stack*, which is analogous to a stack of dishes or trays. In a cafeteria, clean dishes are always placed on top of a stack of dishes. When we need a dish, we always remove the one most recently placed on the stack. This causes the next to last dish placed on the stack to move to the top of the stack.

Whenever a new procedure call occurs, the parameter value associated with that call is placed on the top of the parameter stack. Also, a new cell whose value is initially undefined is placed on top of the stack that is maintained for the local variable NEXT. Whenever N or NEXT is referenced, the value at the top of the corresponding stack is always used. When a procedure return occurs, the value currently at the top of each stack is removed and the next lower value moves to the top.

As an example we will look at the two stacks immediately after the first call to PALINDROME. There is one cell on each stack as shown below.

After first call to PALINDROME

The letter a is read into NEXT just before the second call to PALIN-DROME.

However, the top of the stack for NEXT becomes undefined immediately after the second call occurs as shown below. The darker color cells represent the top of each stack.

After second call to PALINDROME

```
 N      NEXT
┌─┐    ┌───┐
│2│    │ ? │
├─┤    ├───┤
│3│    │ a │
└─┘    └───┘
```

The letter b is read into NEXT just before the third call to PALINDROME.

```
 N      NEXT
┌─┐    ┌───┐
│2│    │ b │
├─┤    ├───┤
│3│    │ a │
└─┘    └───┘
```

However, NEXT becomes undefined again right after the third call.

After third call to PALINDROME

```
 N      NEXT
┌─┐    ┌───┐
│1│    │ ? │
├─┤    ├───┤
│2│    │ b │
├─┤    ├───┤
│3│    │ a │
└─┘    └───┘
```

During this execution of the procedure, the letter c is read into NEXT, and c is echo printed immediately since N is 1 (the stopping case).

```
 N      NEXT
┌─┐    ┌───┐
│1│    │ c │
├─┤    ├───┤
│2│    │ b │
├─┤    ├───┤
│3│    │ a │
└─┘    └───┘
```

The procedure return causes the values at the top of the stack to be removed as shown below.

After first return

```
 N      NEXT
┌─┐    ┌───┐
│2│    │ b │
├─┤    ├───┤
│3│    │ a │
└─┘    └───┘
```

Since control is returned to a WRITE statement, the value of NEXT (b) at the top of the stack is then displayed. Another return occurs, causing the values currently at the top of the stack to be removed.

After second return

Again control is returned to a WRITE statement and the value of NEXT (a) at the top of the stack is displayed. The third return removes the last pair of values from the stack.

We will see how to declare and manipulate stacks in the next chapter. Since Pascal does this automatically, we can write recursive procedures without worrying about the stacks.

Self-check Exercises for Section 9.1

1. Why must N be a value parameter in Fig. 9.3?
2. Assume the characters *+-/ are entered for the procedure (call) statement

   ```
   PALINDROME (4)
   ```

   What output line would appear on the screen? Show the contents of the stacks immediately after each procedure call and return.

9.2 Recursive Procedures

In this section, we will examine two familiar problems and implement recursive procedures to solve them. Both of these problems involve printing the contents of an array and can easily be solved using iteration. We will also solve the Towers of Hanoi problem, which is not easily solved using iteration.

Printing an Array Backwards

Problem: Provide a recursive solution to the problem of printing the elements of an array in reverse order.

Discussion: If the array X has elements with subscripts 1 .. N, then the element values should be printed in the sequence X[N], X[N-1], X[N-2], . . . , X[2], X[1]. The stopping case is printing an array with 1 element (N is 1); the solution is to print that element. For larger arrays, the recursive step is to print the last array element (X[N]) and then print the subarray with subscripts 1 .. N-1 backwards. The data description and algorithm are shown next.

PROBLEM INPUTS

an array of integer values (X : INTARRAY)
the number of elements in the array (N : INTEGER)

PROBLEM OUTPUTS

the array values in reverse order (X[N], X[N-1], . . . , X[2], X[1])

Algorithm

1. if N is 1 then
   2. Print X[1]
   else
   3. Print X[N]
   4. Print the subarray with subscripts 1 .. N-1

Procedure PRINTBACK in Fig. 9.5 implements this algorithm.

```
procedure PRINTBACK (var X {input} : INTARRAY;
                         N {input} : INTEGER);

{Print an array of integers (X) with subscripts 1..N.}

begin {PRINTBACK}
   if N = 1 then
      WRITELN (X[1])                        {stopping case}
   else
      begin {recursive step}
         WRITELN (X[N]);
         PRINTBACK (X, N-1)
      end {recursive step}
end; {PRINTBACK}
```

Fig. 9.5 Procedure PRINTBACK

Given the declarations

```
type
   INTARRAY = array [1..20] of INTEGER;

var
   TEST : INTARRAY;
```

and the procedure (call) statement

```
PRINTBACK (TEST, 3)
```

three WRITELN statements will be executed in the order indicated below and the elements of TEST will be printed backwards as desired.

```
WRITELN (TEST[3]);
WRITELN (TEST[2]);
WRITELN (TEST[1])
```

Figure 9.6 verifies this by tracing the execution of the procedure (call) statement above. Tracing the blue and then the black arrows leads to the sequence of events listed below.

Call PRINTBACK with parameters TEST and 3.
Print TEST[3].
Call PRINTBACK with parameters TEST and 2.
Print TEST[2].
Call PRINTBACK with parameters TEST and 1.
Print TEST[1].
Return from third call.
Return from second call.
Return from original call.

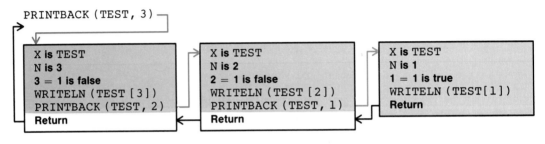

Fig. 9.6 Trace of PRINTBACK (TEST, 3)

As shown above, there are three calls to procedure PRINTBACK, each with different parameters. The procedure returns always occur in the reverse order of the procedure calls; i.e. we return from the last call first, then we return from the next to last call, etc. This time there are no statements left to execute after the returns because the recursive call

PRINTBACK (X, N-1)

occurs at the end of the recursive step.

Printing an Array in Normal Order

Problem: Provide a recursive procedure that prints the elements of an array in usual order.

Discussion: We can use the approach just followed to print the elements of an array in normal order. Again, the stopping case is an array with just one element. The data description and algorithm follow.

PROBLEM INPUTS

an array of integer values (X : INTARRAY)
the number of elements in the array (N : INTEGER)

---

the array values in normal order (X[1], X[2], ..., X[N-1], X[N])

Algorithm

1. if N is 1 then
   2. Print X[1]
   else
      3. Print the subarray with subscripts 1 .. N-1
      4. Print X[N]

The only difference between this algorithm and the one shown earlier is that steps 3 and 4 are transposed. Procedure PRINTNORMAL is shown in Fig. 9.7.

```
procedure PRINTNORMAL (var X {input} : INTARRAY;
                            N {input} : INTEGER);

{Print an array of integers (X) with subscripts 1..N.}

begin {PRINTNORMAL}
   if N = 1 then
      WRITELN (X[1])                            {stopping case}
   else
      begin {recursive step}
         PRINTNORMAL (X, N-1);
         WRITELN (X[N])
      end {recursive step}
end; {PRINTNORMAL}
```

Fig. 9.7 Procedure PRINTNORMAL

The trace of PRINTNORMAL (TEST, 3) is shown in Fig. 9.8. The black return arrows to each activation frame point to the WRITELN statement; therefore, the WRITELN statement is executed after the return. Following the blue and then the black arrows results in the sequence of events listed below. This time there are no statements that precede the recursive calls.

Call PRINTNORMAL with parameters TEST and 3.
    Call PRINTNORMAL with parameters TEST and 2.
        Call PRINTNORMAL with parameters TEST and 1.
            Print TEST[1].
            Return from third call.
        Print TEST[2].
        Return from second call.
    Print TEST[3].
    Return from original call.

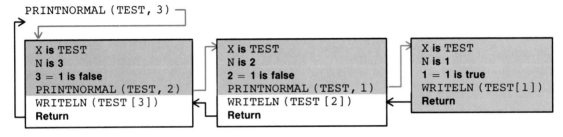

Fig. 9.8 Trace of PRINTNORMAL (TEST, 3)

PROGRAM STYLE

Effect of variable array parameters in recursive procedures

X is declared as a variable parameter in both procedures PRINT-BACK and PRINTNORMAL even though it is used for input only. If X were a value parameter instead, then each recursive call would generate a local copy of the actual array corresponding to X in each activation frame. This can result in a tremendous waste of time and memory space. For example, if X corresponds to an array with 10 elements and we want to print the entire array (N is 10), then there will be 10 activation frames so storage space will be needed for 100 integer values. If N is 100, then storage space is needed for 100 × 100 or 10,000 integer values.

The next case study is considerably more complicated than the preceding ones. It leads to a recursive procedure that solves the Towers of Hanoi problem introduced in Section 9.1.

Towers of Hanoi Problem

Problem: Solve the Towers of Hanoi problem for N discs where N is a parameter.

Discussion: The solution to the Towers of Hanoi problem consists of a printed list of individual disk moves. A general recursive procedure is needed that can be used to move any number of discs from one peg to another using the third peg as an auxiliary. The data description and algorithm for this procedure follow.

PROBLEM INPUTS

the number of discs to be moved (N : INTEGER)
the *from* peg (FROMPEG : 'A'..'C')
the *to* peg (TOPEG : 'A'..'C')
the *auxiliary* peg (AUXPEG : 'A'..'C')

---

a list of individual disc moves

Algorithm

1. if N is 1 then
     2. Move disc 1 from the *from* peg to the *to* peg
   else
       3. Move N-1 discs from the *from* peg to the *auxiliary* peg using the *to* peg.
       4. Move disc N from the *from* peg to *to* peg.
       5. Move N-1 discs from the *auxiliary* peg to the *to* peg using the *from* peg.

The recursive step (following else) will generate the three subproblems listed earlier when N is 5, the *from* peg is 'A', the *to* peg is 'C', and the *auxiliary* peg is 'B'. The implementation of this algorithm is shown as procedure TOWER in Fig. 9.9. Procedure TOWER has four parameters. The stopping case (move disc 1) is handled by the first WRITELN statement. Each recursive step consists of a WRITELN statement sandwiched between two calls to procedure TOWER. The first recursive call moves N-1 discs to the *auxiliary* peg. The WRITELN statement moves disc N to the *to* peg. The second recursive call moves the N-1 discs from the *auxiliary* peg to the *to* peg.

```
procedure TOWER (FROMPEG,
                 TOPEG,
                 AUXPEG    {input} : CHAR;
                 N         {input} : INTEGER);

{Moves N discs from FROMPEG to TOPEG using AUXPEG as an auxiliary.}

begin {TOWER}
   if N = 1 then
      WRITELN ('Move disc 1 from peg ', FROMPEG,
               ' to peg ', TOPEG)

   else
      begin {recursive step}
         TOWER (FROMPEG, AUXPEG, TOPEG, N-1);
         WRITELN ('Move disc ', N :1, ' from peg ', FROMPEG,
                  ' to peg ', TOPEG);
         TOWER (AUXPEG, TOPEG, FROMPEG, N-1)
      end {recursive step}
end;   {TOWER}
```

Fig. 9.9 Recursive Procedure TOWER

The procedure (call) statement

```
TOWER ('A', 'C', 'B', 5)
```

generates the solution to the original problem. The procedure (call) statement

TOWER ('A', 'C', 'B', 3)

solves the simpler three disc problem. Its execution is traced in Fig. 9.10. The output generated is shown below. Verify for yourself that this solves the three disc problem.

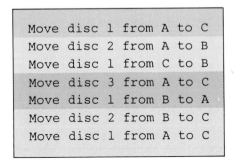

```
Move disc 1 from A to C
Move disc 2 from A to B
Move disc 1 from C to B
Move disc 3 from A to C
Move disc 1 from B to A
Move disc 2 from B to C
Move disc 1 from A to C
```

Fig. 9.10 Trace of TOWER ('A', 'C', 'B', 3)

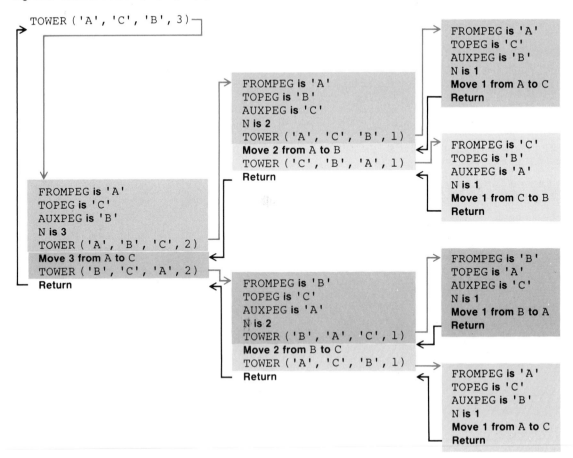

Comparison of Iteration and Recursive Procedures

It is interesting to consider that procedure TOWER in Fig. 9.9 will solve the Tower of Hanoi problem for any number of discs. The three disc problem results in a total of seven calls to procedure TOWER and is solved by seven moves. The five disc problem would result in a total of 31 calls to procedure TOWER and is solved in 31 moves.

Since each procedure call requires the allocation and initialization of a local data area in memory, the computer time and memory requirements increase exponentially with the problem size (2^3 is 8, 2^5 is 32). This is different than for an iterative solution where the computer time required is generally proportional to the number of cases being processed, so the time requirements increase linearly rather than exponentially. The memory required for an iterative solution does not necessarily increase when there are more cases to process.

This means that recursion is generally inefficient in its use of computer resources. In cases where an iterative solution can easily be implemented, the iterative solution is preferred. For example, it would be quite easy to write iterative solutions to the problems "Print the values in an array backwards" and "Print the values in an array in normal order." In fact, we have solved the latter problem many times.

We have provided the recursive solutions to these simple problems to demonstrate recursion, but we would not use them in practice. On the other hand, the Towers of Hanoi problem would be very difficult to program iteratively. Yet the recursive procedure TOWERS is a very natural solution to the problem and results in a compact program that is easy to read.

Self-check Exercises for Section 9.2

1. Write a main program that reads in a data value for N (the number of discs) and calls procedure TOWER.
2. Show the solution that would be generated for the four disc problem.
3. Provide an iterative procedure that is equivalent to PRINTBACK in Fig. 9.5.

9.3 Recursive Functions

The process demonstrated in the previous section can also be followed to write recursive functions. This process involves identifying the stopping cases of a problem. For the other cases, there must be a means of reducing the problem to one that is closer to a stopping case.

A difference between recursive functions and procedures is that the recursive function calls appear in an expression. Also, a result or value is passed back from each activation frame to an earlier frame. These results must be combined in some way to produce the final result.

Summing the Values in an Array	**Problem:** We want to write a recursive function that finds the sum of the values in an array X with subscripts 1 . . N.

Discussion: The stopping case occurs when N is 1—the sum is X[1]. If N is not 1, then we must add the sum of the values in the subarray with subscripts 1 . . N−1 to X[N].

PROBLEM INPUTS

an array of integer values (X : INTARRAY)
the number of elements in the array (N : INTEGER)

PROBLEM OUTPUTS

the sum of the array values

Algorithm

1. if N is 1 then
    2. The sum is X[1]
  else
    3. Add X[N] to the sum of values in the subarray with subscripts 1 . . N−1

Function FINDSUM in Fig. 9.11 implements this algorithm. The result of calling FINDSUM for a small array (N is 3) is also shown.

A trace of the function call FINDSUM(X, 3) is shown in Fig. 9.12. As before, each recursive function call is in blue, and a blue arrow points to the activation frame for a recursive call. The black arrows indicate the return point (the operator +) after each function execution. The value returned is indicated alongside the arrow. The value returned for the original call, FINDSUM(X, 3), is 8.

Functions that return BOOLEAN values (TRUE or FALSE) can also be written recursively. These functions do not perform a computation; however, the function result is still determined by evaluating a BOOLEAN expression containing a recursive call. We will write recursive functions that search an array and compare two arrays.

Example 9.2

The BOOLEAN function MEMBER in Fig. 9.13 returns the value TRUE if the argument TARGET is in the array X with subscripts 1..N; otherwise, it returns the value FALSE. If N is 1 (the stopping case), the result is determined by comparing X[1] and TARGET. If N is not 1 (the recursive step), then the result is true if either X[N] is TARGET or TARGET occurs in the subarray with subscripts 1 . . N−1. The recursive step is implemented as the assignment statement

```
MEMBER := (X[N] = TARGET) or MEMBER(X, TARGET, N-1)
```

in Fig. 9.13

```
program TESTFINDSUM (INPUT, OUTPUT);

{Tests function FINDSUM.}

type
    INTARRAY = array [1..20] of INTEGER;

var
    N : INTEGER;
    X : INTARRAY;

function FINDSUM (var X : INTARRAY;
                      N : INTEGER) : INTEGER;

{Finds the sum of the values in elements 1..N of array X.}

begin {FINDSUM}
    if N = 1 then
        FINDSUM := X[1]
    else
        FINDSUM := X[N] + FINDSUM(X, N-1)
end; {FINDSUM}

begin {TESTFINDSUM}
    N := 3;
    X[1] := 5;  X[2] := 10;  X[3] := -7;
    WRITELN ('The array sum is ', FINDSUM(X, 3) :3)
end. {TESTFINDSUM}

The array sum is 8
```

Fig. 9.11 Using Recursive Function FINDSUM

Fig. 9.12 Trace of FINDSUM(X, 3)

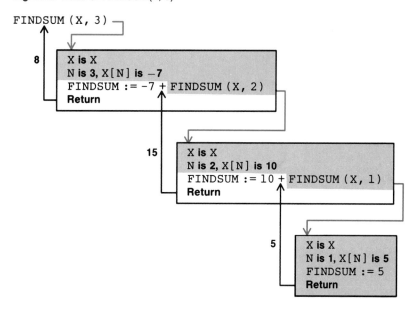

```
function MEMBER (var X : INTARRAY;
                     TARGET,
                     N       : INTEGER) : BOOLEAN;

{Returns a value of TRUE if TARGET is located in array X with
 subscripts 1..N. Otherwise, it returns FALSE.                     }

begin {MEMBER}
    if N = 1 then
        MEMBER := X[1] = TARGET
    else
        MEMBER := (X[N] = TARGET) or MEMBER(X, TARGET, N-1)
end; {MEMBER}
```

Fig. 9.13 Recursive Function MEMBER

The function designator MEMBER(X, 10, 3) is traced in Fig. 9.14 for
the array X defined in Fig. 9.11 (i.e. X[1] is 5, X[2] is 10, X[3] is −7).
The value returned is TRUE since the expression X[N] = TARGET is
TRUE when N is 2.

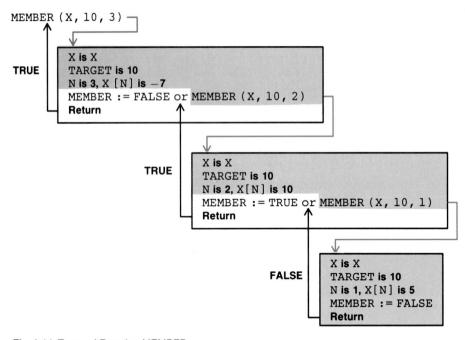

Fig. 9.14 Trace of Function MEMBER

Example 9.3   The BOOLEAN function EQUAL returns the value TRUE if two arrays,
X and Y, of N elements are the same (i.e. X[1] = Y[1], X[2] =
Y[2], . . . , X[N] = Y[N]). This function (see Fig. 9.15) is similar to function MEMBER. For the stopping case, single element arrays, the function result depends on whether or not X[1] = Y[1]. For larger arrays, the
result is TRUE if X[N] = Y[N] and the subarrays with subscripts 1 . .
N−1 are equal.

```
function EQUAL (var X, Y : INTARRAY;
                    N : INTEGER) : BOOLEAN;

{Returns a value of TRUE if arrays X and Y with
 subscripts 1..N are equal. Otherwise, returns FALSE.}

begin {EQUAL}
   if N = 1 then
      EQUAL := X[1] = Y[1]
   else
      EQUAL := (X[N] = Y[N]) and EQUAL(X, Y, N-1)
end; {EQUAL}
```

Fig. 9.15 Recursive Function EQUAL

Comparison of Iterative and Recursive Functions

It is interesting to consider the iterative version of MEMBER shown in Fig.
9.16. A for loop is needed to examine each array element. Without recursion it is not possible to use the function name in an expression, so a local variable, FOUND, is needed to represent the result so far. Before returning from the function, the final value of FOUND is assigned as the function result.

```
function MEMBER (var X : INTARRAY;
                     TARGET,
                     N        : INTEGER) : BOOLEAN;

{Returns a value of TRUE if TARGET is located in array X
 with subscripts 1..N. Otherwise, returns FALSE.      }

var
    FOUND : BOOLEAN;                    {local flag}
    I : INTEGER;                        {loop control variable}

begin {MEMBER}
    FOUND := FALSE;                              {assume TARGET not found}

    {Search array X for TARGET.}
    for I := 1 to N do
       FOUND := (X[I] = TARGET) or FOUND;

    MEMBER := FOUND                              {define result}
end; {MEMBER}
```

Fig. 9.16 Iterative Function MEMBER

This is somewhat different than the iterative array search shown earlier
(see Fig. 7.14). We could make it more efficient by using a while loop and exiting from the loop when FOUND becomes TRUE; however, the version shown in Fig. 9.16 would still execute faster than the recursive version.

It can be argued that the recursive version is esthetically more pleasing. It is certainly more compact (a single `if` statement) and requires no local variables. Once you are used to thinking recursively you will find it somewhat easier to read and understand than the iterative form.

Some programmers like to use recursion as a conceptual tool. Once the recursive form of a function or procedure is written it can always be translated into an iterative version if run-time efficiency is a major concern. This translation is necessary when programming in older languages that do not support recursion.

Recursive Definitions of Mathematical Functions

Many mathematical functions are defined recursively. An example is the fractorial of a number n (n!).

- 0! is 1
- n! is n $\times$ (n−1)! for n > 0

Thus 4! is 4 $\times$ 3 $\times$ 2 $\times$ 1 or 24. It is easy to implement this definition as a recursive function in Pascal.

Example 9.4 Function FACTOR in Fig. 9.17 computes the factorial of its argument N. The recursive step

```
FACTOR := N * FACTOR(N-1)
```

implements the second line of the factorial definition above. This means that the result of the current call (argument N) is determined by multiplying the result of the next call (argument N−1) by N.

```
function FACTOR (N : INTEGER) : INTEGER;

{Recursively computes the factorial of N.}

begin {FACTOR}
   if N = 0 then
      FACTOR := 1
   else
      FACTOR := N * FACTOR(N-1)
end; {FACTOR}
```

Fig. 9.17 Function FACTOR

A trace of

```
FACT := FACTOR(3)
```

is shown in Fig. 9.18. The value returned from the original call, FACTOR(3), is 6, and this value is assigned to FACT.

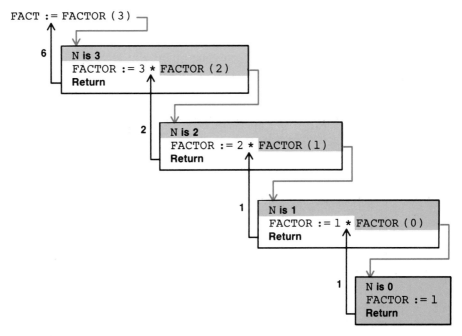

Fig. 9.18 Trace of FACT := FACTOR(3)

Example 9.5   The Fibonacci numbers are a number sequence that have varied uses. They were originally intended to model the growth of a rabbit colony. Although we will not go into details of the model here, the Fibonacci sequence 1,1,2,3,5,8,13,21,34, . . . certainly seems to increase rapidly enough. The fifteenth number in the sequence is 610. (That's a lot of rabbits!)

The Fibonacci sequence is defined below.

- Fib_1 is 1
- Fib_2 is 1
- Fib_n is $Fib_{n-2} + Fib_{n-1}$ for n > 2

Verify for yourself that the sequence of numbers shown in the paragraph above is correct. A recursive function that computes the Nth Fibonacci number is shown in Fig. 9.19.

Fig. 9.19 Recursive Function FIBONACCI

```
function FIBONACCI (N : INTEGER) : INTEGER;

{Computes the Nth Fibonacci number.}

begin {FIBONACCI}
   if (N = 1) or (N = 2) then
      FIBONACCI := 1
   else
      FIBONACCI := FIBONACCI(N-2) + FIBONACCI(N-1)
end; {FIBONACCI}
```

Although easy to write, the FIBONACCI function is not efficient because each recursive step generates two calls to function FIBONACCI. This is similar to procedure TOWER shown earlier, in that time and memory requirements grow exponentially as N increases.

Example 9.6   Euclid's algorithm for finding the greatest common divisor of two integers, GCD(M,N), is defined recursively below. The *greatest common divisor* of two integers is the largest integer that divides them both.

- GCD(M, N) is N if N <= M and N divides M
- GCD(M, N) is GCD(N, M) if M < N
- GCD(M, N) is GCD(N, M mod N) otherwise

This algorithm states that the GCD is N if N is the smaller number and N divides M. If M is the smaller number, the GCD determination should be performed with the arguments transposed. If N does not divide M, then the answer is obtained by finding the GCD of N and the remainder of M divided by N. The declaration and use of the Pascal function GCD is shown in Fig. 9.20.

Fig. 9.20 Euclid's Algorithm for the Greatest Common Divisor

```
program FINDGCD (INPUT, OUTPUT);

{Prints the greatest common divisor of two integers.}

var
    M, N : INTEGER;                                    {two input items}

function GCD (M, N : INTEGER) : INTEGER;

{Finds the greatest common divisor of M and N.}

begin {GCD}
    if (N <= M) and (M mod N = 0) then
        GCD := N
    else if M < N then
        GCD := GCD(N, M)
    else
        GCD := GCD(N, M mod N)
end; {GCD}

begin {FINDGCD}
    WRITE ('Enter two positive integers separated by a space: ');
    READLN (M, N);
    WRITELN ('Their greatest common divisor is ', GCD (M, N) :6)
end. {FINDGCD}
```

```
Enter two positive integers separated by a space: 24 84
Their greatest common divisor is      12
```

The next problem is a good illustration of the power of recursion. Its solution is relatively easy to write recursively but would be much more difficult without using recursion.

Counting Cells in a Blob

Problem: We have a two-dimensional grid of cells, each of which may be empty or filled. The filled cells that are connected (adjacent in a vertical, horizontal, or diagonal direction) form a blob. There may be several blobs on the grid. We would like a function that accepts as input the coordinates of a particular cell and returns the size of the blob containing the cell.

There are three blobs in the sample grid below (indicated by the shading). If the function parameters represent the X and Y coordinates of a cell, the result of BLOBCOUNT(3, 4) is 5; the result of BLOBCOUNT(1, 2) is 2; the result of BLOBCOUNT(5, 5) is 0; the result of BLOB-COUNT(5, 1) is 4.

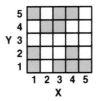

Discussion: Function BLOBCOUNT must test the cell specified by its arguments to see whether it is filled. There are two stopping cases: the cell (X, Y) is not on the grid or the cell (X, Y) is empty; in either case, the vaue returned by BLOBCOUNT is 0. If the cell is on the grid and filled, then the value returned is 1 plus the size of the blobs containing each of its eight neighbors. To avoid counting a cell more than once, we will mark it as empty once it has been counted. The data description and algorithm follow.

PROBLEM INPUTS

the grid (a global array)
the X and Y coordinates of the point being tested (X, Y : INTEGER)

PROBLEM OUTPUTS

the number of the cells in the blob containing point X, Y

Algorithm

1. if cell (X, Y) is not in the array then
    2. BLOBCOUNT is 0
  else if cell (X, Y) is empty then

3. BLOBCOUNT := 0

else

    4. Mark cell (X, Y) as empty

    5. Add 1 to the size of the blobs containing the 8 neighbors of cell (X, Y)

The recursive function BLOBCOUNT is shown in Fig. 9.21, assuming the declarations below. The global array GRID is type BLOBARRAY with element values EMPTY or FILLED. The constants MAXX and MAXY represent the largest X and Y coordinate, respectively.

```
const
    MAXX = 100;
    MAXY = 100;

type
    BLOBARRAY = array [1..MAXX, 1..MAXY] of (FILLED, EMPTY);

var
    GRID : BLOBARRAY;
```

```
function BLOBCOUNT (X, Y : INTEGER) : INTEGER;

{Counts the number of filled cells in the blob containing
point (X, Y). Resets each cell in array GRID that is part of
this blob from FILLED to EMPTY.                              }

begin {BLOBCOUNT}
   if (X < 1) or (X > MAXX) or (Y < 1) or (Y > MAXY) then
      BLOBCOUNT := 0                              {cell not in grid}
   else if GRID[X, Y] = EMPTY then
      BLOBCOUNT := 0                              {cell is empty}
   else {cell is filled}
      begin {recursive step}
         GRID[X, Y] := EMPTY;
         BLOBCOUNT := 1 + BLOBCOUNT(X-1, Y+1) + BLOBCOUNT(X, Y+1) +
                     BLOBCOUNT(X+1, Y+1) + BLOBCOUNT(X+1, Y) +
                     BLOBCOUNT(X+1, Y-1) + BLOBCOUNT(X, Y-1) +
                     BLOBCOUNT(X-1, Y-1) + BLOBCOUNT(X-1, Y)
      end {recursive step}
end; {BLOBCOUNT}
```

Fig. 9.21 The Function BLOBCOUNT

In the recursive step, function BLOBCOUNT is called eight times with the neighbors of the current cell passed as arguments. For example, if the current cell is (1, 2), its eight neighbors would be: (0,3), (1,3), (2,3), (2,2), (2,1), (1,1), (0,1), (0,2). The cells are passed in a clockwise manner with the neighbor above and to the left passed first. If a cell is off the grid (e.g. (0,3), (0,2), (0,1)) or empty, a value of zero will be returned immediately. The function result is defined as the sum of all values returned plus 1 (for the current cell).

The sequence of operations performed in function BLOBCOUNT is very important. The `if` statement tests whether the cell (X, Y) is on the grid before testing whether (X, Y) is empty. If the order is reversed, the error "out of bounds subscript" occurs whenever (X, Y) is off the grid.

Also, the recursive step resets GRID[X, Y] to EMPTY before checking the neighbors of point (X, Y). If this were not done first, then cell (X, Y) would be counted more than once since it is a neighbor of all its neighbors. A more serious problem is that the recursion would not terminate. When each neighbor of the current cell is tested, BLOBCOUNT is called again with the coordinates of the current cell as arguments. If the current cell is EMPTY, an immediate return occurs. If the current cell is still FILLED, then the recursive step would be executed erroneously. Eventually, the program will run out of time or memory space; the latter is often indicated by a "stack overflow" message.

A side effect of the function execution is that all cells that are part of the blob being processed are reset to EMPTY. It would be necessary to save a copy of array GRID before the first call to BLOBCOUNT if its original status was important. This could also be achieved by making GRID a value parameter in procedure BLOBCOUNT; however, this wastes memory because each time BLOBCOUNT is called a new copy of array GRID is made.

Self-check Exercises for Section 9.3

1. Write the recursive function FINDMIN that finds the smallest value in an integer array X with subscripts 1..N.
2. Trace the execution of function BLOBCOUNT for the coordinate pair (1,2) in the sample grid.

9.4 Binary Search of an Array

We discussed searching an array in Section 7.6 and wrote a function that returned the index of a target value in an array or the value 0 if the target was not present. In order to do this it was necessary to compare array element values to the target value, starting with the first array element value. The comparison process was terminated when the target value was found or the end of the array was reached.

Often we want to search an array that is already sorted in ascending (increasing) order. We can take advantage of the fact that the array is sorted and terminate our search when an array element value greater than or equal to the target value is reached. Since the array is sorted, there is no need to look any further in the array as all other values will be too large.

Computer scientists are very concerned about the efficiency of an algorithm as it relates to the number of elements being processed. If there are N elements in the array, then on the average N/2 of the elements will need to be examined to either locate the target or to determine that it is not in the array using our improved search algorithm. In the original algorithm, all N elements need to be examined when the target is not in the array.

The array search described above is called a *linear search* because its execution time increases linearly with the number of array elements. This can be a problem when searching large arrays (N > 100). Consequently, when searching large sorted arrays we often use the *binary search algorithm* described below.

Binary Search   **Problem:**   The binary search algorithm may be used to search an ordered array. It takes advantage of the fact that the array is ordered to eliminate half of the array elements with each probe into the array. Consequently, if the array has 1000 elements, it will either locate the target value or eliminate 500 elements with its first probe, 250 elements with its second probe, 125 elements with its third probe, etc. It turns out that only ten probes will be needed to completely search an array with 1000 elements. (Why?) The binary search algorithm can be used to find a name in a large metropolitan telephone book using thirty probes or less.

Discussion: Since the array is ordered, all we have to do is compare the target value with the middle element of the subarray we are searching. If their values are the same, then we are done. If the middle value is larger than the target, then we should search the lower half of the array next; otherwise, we should search the upper half of the array next.

The subarray to be searched has subscripts FIRST..LAST. The variable MIDDLE is the subscript to the middle element in this range. The portion of the array with subscripts MIDDLE..LAST is eliminated by the first probe shown in the diagram below.

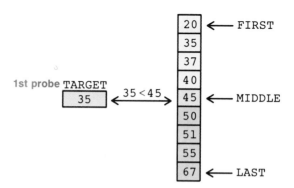

LAST should be reset to MIDDLE−1 to define the new subarray left to be searched, and MIDDLE should be redefined as shown below. The target value, 35, would be found on this probe.

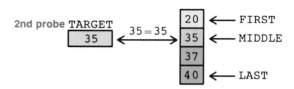

The binary search algorithm can be stated clearly using recursion. The stopping cases are:

- The array bounds are improper (FIRST > LAST)
- The middle value is the target value

In the first case above, the function result is zero; in the second case, the function result is MIDDLE. The recursive step is to search the appropriate subarray. The data requirements and algorithm for a recursive binary search function follow.

PROBLEM INPUTS

array to be searched (TABLE : INTARRAY)
target being searched for (TARGET : INTEGER)
the first subscript in the subarray (FIRST : INTEGER)
the last subscript in the subarray (LAST : INTEGER)

PROBLEM OUTPUTS

the location of the TARGET value or 0 if not found

Algorithm

1. Compute the subscript of the middle element
2. if the array bounds are improper then
    3. Return a result of 0
   else if the middle value is the target then
    4. Return the subscript of the middle element
   else if the middle value is larger than the target
    5. Search the subarray with subscripts FIRST..MIDDLE-1
   else
    6. Search the subarray with subscripts MIDDLE+1..LAST

For each of the recursive steps (steps 5 and 6), the bounds of the new subarray must be listed as actual parameters in the recursive call. The actual parameters define the search limits for the next probe into the array.

In the initial call to the recursive procedure, FIRST and LAST should be defined as the first and last elements of the entire array, respectively. For example, the procedure (call) statement

```
BINARYSEARCH (X, 35, 1, 9)
```

could be used to search the elements of array X with subscripts 1 . . 9 for the target value 35 (assuming X is type INTARRAY). Function BINARYSEARCH is shown in Fig. 9.22.

```
function BINSEARCH (var TABLE : INTARRAY;
                        TARGET : INTEGER;
                        FIRST, LAST : INTEGER) : INTEGER;

{Performs a recursive binary search of an ordered array of integer
 values with subscripts FIRST..LAST. Returns the subscript of
 TARGET if found in array TABLE; otherwise, returns a value of 0. }

var
    MIDDLE : INTEGER;                       {the subscript of the middle element}

begin {BINSEARCH}
    MIDDLE := (FIRST + LAST) div 2;                         {define MIDDLE}

    {Determine if TARGET is found or missing or redefine subarray.}
    if FIRST > LAST then
        BINSEARCH := 0                      {stopping case: TARGET missing}
    else if TABLE[MIDDLE] = TARGET then
        BINSEARCH := MIDDLE                  {stopping case: TARGET found}
    else if TABLE[MIDDLE] > TARGET then          {search lower subarray}
        BINSEARCH := BINSEARCH(TABLE, TARGET, FIRST, MIDDLE-1)
    else                                          {search upper subarray}
        BINSEARCH := BINSEARCH(TABLE, TARGET, MIDDLE+1, LAST)
end;  {BINSEARCH}
```

Fig. 9.22 Recursive Binary Search Function

Fig. 9.23 Iterative Binary Search Function

```
function BINSEARCH (var TABLE : INTARRAY;
                        TARGET : INTEGER;
                        FIRST, LAST : INTEGER) : INTEGER;

{Performs an iterative binary search of an array of integer values
 with subscripts FIRST..LAST. Returns the subscript of TARGET
 if found in array TABLE; otherwise, returns a value of 0.          }

var
    MIDDLE : INTEGER;                   {the subscript of the middle element}

begin {BINSEARCH}
    {Compare TARGET to middle element and reduce subarray to search}
    repeat
        MIDDLE := (FIRST + LAST) div 2;                    {define MIDDLE}
        if TABLE[MIDDLE] > TARGET then
            LAST := MIDDLE - 1                      {search lower subarray}
        else
            FIRST := MIDDLE + 1                     {search upper subarray}
    until (FIRST > LAST) or (TABLE[MIDDLE] = TARGET);

    {Assert: improper array bounds or TARGET is found.}
    if TABLE[MIDDLE] = TARGET then
        BINSEARCH := MIDDLE                                 {TARGET is found}
    else
        BINSEARCH := 0                                     {TARGET not found}
end;  {BINSEARCH}
```

The assignment statement

```
MIDDLE := (FIRST + LAST) div 2;           {define MIDDLE}
```

computes the subscript of the middle element by finding the average of FIRST and LAST. This value has no meaning when FIRST is greater than LAST, but it does no harm to compute it.

An iterative version of the binary search function is shown in Fig. 9.23.

Self-check Exercises for Section 9.4

1. Trace the search of the array TABLE shown in this section for a TARGET of 40. Specify the values of FIRST, MIDDLE, and LAST during each recursive call.
2. Assume each character string terminates in a dollar sign ($) and that the null string (length 0) starts with a $. Write a recursive function that finds the length of its character string argument. *Hint:* Call this function with a parameter, NEXT, that equals 1. Increase NEXT with each recursive call.

9.5 Searching by Hashing

So far we have discussed the advantages of using the binary search technique to retrieve information stored in a large array. Binary search can be used only when the contents of the array are ordered.

An additional technique used for storing data in an array so it can be retrieved in an efficient manner is called *hashing*. This technique consists of implementing a *hash function*, which accepts as its input a designated field of a record, the *record key*, and returns as its output an integer, the *hash index*. The hash index selects the particular array element that will be used to store the new data. To retrieve the item at a later time, it is only necessary to recompute the hash index and access the item in that array location. This process is illustrated in the diagram below. The hash index is 3.

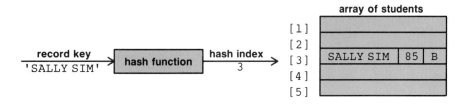

As an example, let's assume we have up to 100 student records to maintain and each record (type STUDENT) has a string field (NAME) of 20 characters or less, an exam score, and a grade. The student data can be stored in an array with subscripts 1 . . 100. The record key must be unique for each record; hence, we can use the student's name as the record key. One possible hash function would simply add up the ordinal values of each nonblank character in the student's name and then use the mod function to convert this sum to an integer in the range 1 to 100. Figure 9.24 shows such a function, assuming that STRINGSIZE (20), BLANK (' '), and CLASSIZE (100) are all declared as global constants and STRING is a packed array of STRINGSIZE characters.

```
function HASH (KEY : STRING) : INTEGER;

{Computes an integer value between 1 and CLASSIZE
 based on the nonblank characters in KEY.          }
const
   BLANK = ' ';

var
   I : 1..STRINGSIZE;                              {loop control variable}
   HASHINDEX : INTEGER;                            {accumulated hash value}

begin {HASH}
   HASHINDEX := 0;                                 {initialize sum}
   {Add ordinal values for all non-blank characters in string KEY.}
   for I := 1 to STRINGSIZE do
      if KEY[I] <> BLANK then
         HASHINDEX := HASHINDEX + ORD(KEY[I]);      {increment sum}

   HASH := HASHINDEX mod CLASSIZE + 1              {define result}
end; {HASH}
```

Fig. 9.24 Function HASH

Inserting a student record then becomes a matter of passing its key to function HASH and storing the record in the array element selected by HASH. After all records are stored in the array, we can retrieve a particular student's record by passing the student's name to function HASH and accessing the array element selected by HASH. The net result is that it will usually take only one probe into the array to get the record we are seeking. Sometimes it will take more than one probe, as explained next.

Effect of Collisions

The hashing technique described above works well as long as HASH never returns the same hash index for two different keys. However, the names 'SILLY SAM' and 'SALLY SIM' would both yield the same hash index since they contain the same letters. It would be easy to improve the hash function so this situation is avoided (see Exercise 2); however, regardless of what hash function is used there is always a possibility that two different keys will hash to the same index. This is called a *collision*.

One way to handle collisions is to insert a new record in the element selected by function HASH only if that slot is currently empty. If that slot is filled, then advance to the next empty slot in the array and place the record in that location. The record keys could all be initialized to blank strings to indicate that they are initially empty.

To retrieve a record, we first examine the element selected by the hash index. If the record we are seeking is there, then we are finished. If the element selected by the hash index is filled with other data, then we keep searching until we find the record we are seeking or we reach an empty cell. If we reach an empty cell, the record we are seeking is not present in the array.

Procedure INSERT (see Fig. 9.25) is used to insert a student record (NEXTSTU) in an array CLASS. Function FINDSTU (see Fig. 9.26) returns the subscript of the record specified by KEY if it is in the array; otherwise, it returns a value of 0. Both these modules assume that BLANKSTRING is a global constant (all blanks).

Both modules use the assignment statement

```
INDEX := INDEX mod CLASSIZE + 1;        {get next element}
```

to increment the value of INDEX. If the current value of INDEX is CLASSIZE, the new value will be 1; otherwise, the new value will be one more than the current value.

Procedure INSERT assumes that the same name cannot appear twice in the array. If the new student name matches one in the array, then the new data replace the old data and a message is printed.

Both procedures use the local variable PROBE to count the number of probes into the array. If the array is completely filled it would be possible to search forever for an empty slot. The while condition (PROBE <= CLASSIZE) prevents this from happening.

Fig. 9.25 Procedure INSERT

```
procedure INSERT (var CLASS {input/output} : STUDENTARRAY;
                  NEXTSTU {input} : STUDENT);

{Inserts a new student record (NEXTSTU) in the array of student
 records CLASS using hashing. Function HASH computes the hash
 index based on the student's name.                           }

var
    INDEX : 1..CLASSIZE;                          {index to array}
    PROBE : INTEGER;                     {number of probes into array}

begin {INSERT}
    INDEX := HASH(NEXTSTU.NAME);                  {compute hash index}
```

```
{Place NEXTSTU in first empty slot or
 update data if student is in the array.}
PROBE := 1;
while (CLASS[INDEX].NAME <> BLANKSTRING) and
      (CLASS[INDEX].NAME <> NEXTSTU.NAME) and
      (PROBE <= CLASSIZE) do
    begin
        INDEX := INDEX mod CLASSIZE + 1;
        PROBE := PROBE + 1                          {get next element}
    end; {while}

{assert: first empty slot reached or student found
        or the array is filled.                    }
if CLASS[INDEX].NAME = BLANKSTRING then
    CLASS[INDEX] := NEXTSTU                      {insert new student data}
else if CLASS[INDEX].NAME = NEXTSTU.NAME then
    begin {in array}
        CLASS[INDEX] := NEXTSTU;                     {update student data}
        WRITELN (NEXTSTU.NAME, ' in array -- record updated.')
    end {in array}
else
    WRITELN ('Array is filled -- insertion is not possible.')
end;  {INSERT}
```

Fig. 9.26 Function FINDSTU

```
function FINDSTU (var CLASS : STUDENTARRAY;
                 KEY : STRING) : INTEGER;

{Returns the index of the student whose name field matches KEY.
 Returns 0 if the student is not in the array CLASS.
 Calls function HASH to determine the search start point.        }

var
    INDEX : 1..CLASSIZE;                                {index to array}
    PROBE : INTEGER;

begin {FINDSTU}
    INDEX := HASH(KEY);                         {starting point for search}

    {Search for student whose name is KEY.}
    PROBE := 1;
    while (CLASS[INDEX].NAME <> KEY) and
          (CLASS[INDEX].NAME <> BLANKSTRING) and
          (PROBE <= CLASSIZE) do
        begin
            INDEX := INDEX mod CLASSIZE + 1;                {get next element}
            PROBE := PROBE + 1
        end; {while}

    {assert: current NAME field matches KEY or empty slot reached
            or all array elements searched without success.     }
    if CLASS[INDEX].NAME = KEY then
        FINDSTU := INDEX                                 {student at INDEX}
    else
        FINDSTU := 0                                 {student not found}
end; {FINDSTU}
```

1. Assume that the ordinal number for the letter A is 1, B is 2, etc. and CLASSIZE is 10 (array CLASS has 10 elements). Compute the hash values for the following names and indicate where each name would be stored in the array: 'SAL', 'BIL', 'JILL', 'LIB', 'HAL', 'ROB'

2. Rewrite HASH so that the ordinal value for each letter is multiplied by its position in the string (e.g. for 'SAL', multiply ORD('S') by 1, ORD('A') by 2, etc). Why is this a better hash function? Answer Exercise 1 for this new function.

3. An improved way of handling collisons is called quadratic hashing where 1 is added to the hash index after probe 1, 4 (2^2) is added after probe 2, 9 (3^2) is added after probe 3, etc. Modify INSERT and FINDSTU to use this technique.

9.6 Additional Sorting Algorithms

The binary search algorithm may be used to search a sorted array. We discussed one of the simplest and least efficient sorting algorithms, the Bubble Sort, in Section 7.7. In this section, we will discuss other algorithms for sorting an array.

The first algorithm discussed is quite natural and involves finding the largest element in the array and making it the last element, finding the next largest element in the array and making it the next to last element, etc. This is called the *selection sort*.

Example 9.7

The selection sort process lends itself to a recursive solution as described below, for an array with subscripts 1..N.

Algorithm

1. If the subarray being sorted has one element then
      the subarray is already sorted
   else
      2. Find the largest value in the subarray and switch it with the value in the last element of the subarray.
      3. Sort the subarray with subscripts 1..N-1.

As indicated above, there is nothing to do if the array has only one element (stopping case) since such an array is sorted by definition. For a larger array, it is necessary to switch the largest value with the last value and then sort the subarray with subscripts 1..N-1. A trace of the effect of this algorithm for an array of four elements is shown in Fig. 9.27; the subarray being sorted at each point is in the lighter color. The procedure is shown in Fig. 9.28.

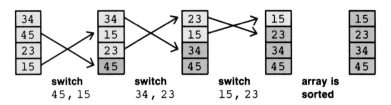

Fig. 9.27 Trace of Selection Sort

Fig. 9.28 Procedure SELECTSORT

```
procedure SELECTSORT (var TABLE {input/output} : INTARRAY;
                          N {input} : INTEGER);

{Performs a selection sort on array TABLE with subscripts 1..N.}

var
    MAXPOSITION : INTEGER;              {position of largest element}

function FINDMAXPOS (var TABLE : INTARRAY;
                         N : INTEGER) : INTEGER;

{Returns the subscript of the largest value in TABLE.
 Examines the element values with subscripts 1..N.    }

var
    I,                                {loop control variable}
    MAXPOS : INTEGER;                 {position of largest so far}

begin {FINDMAXPOS}
    MAXPOS := 1;                      {assume first element is largest}
    for I := 2 to N do
        if TABLE[I] > TABLE[MAXPOS] then
            MAXPOS := I;              {value at I is larger}
    FINDMAXPOS := MAXPOS              {define result}
end; {FINDMAXPOS}

procedure EXCHANGE (var X, Y {input/output} : INTEGER);

{Switches the values in X and Y.}

var
    TEMP : INTEGER;                   {temporary cell for exchange}

begin {EXCHANGE}
    TEMP := X;    X := Y;     Y := TEMP
end; {EXCHANGE}

begin {SELECTSORT}
    if N > 1 then
        begin {recursion step}
            MAXPOSITION := FINDMAXPOS(TABLE, N);
            EXCHANGE (TABLE[MAXPOSITION], TABLE[N]);
            SELECTSORT (TABLE, N-1)
        end {recursion step}
end; {SELECTSORT}
```

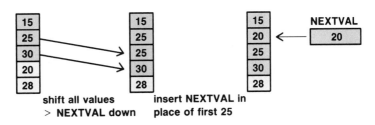

Fig. 9.29 Inserting the Fourth Array Element Value

Example 9.8 The next sorting algorithm we will discuss is used by card players to sort their cards. They keep the cards dealt so far in sorted order. As each new card is dealt they insert it in its proper place. The algorithm is called the *insertion sort*.

Algorithm
1. for each element value after the first do
   2. Make room for the next value by shifting all larger values down one position.
   3. Insert the next value in place of the last value moved.

This process is illustrated in Fig. 9.29 for the array shown on the left of the diagram. The subarray with subscripts 1 .. 3 is sorted and we wish to insert the next value, 20, into its proper place (in element 2). Since 30 and 25 are greater than 20, both these values starting with 30, are shifted down one place. After the shift occurs (middle diagram), there will temporarily be two copies of the value 25 in the array. The first of these is erased when 20, saved in NEXTVAL, is moved into its correct position (rightmost diagram). The shift and insert operations should then be repeated to insert the new next value (28) where it belongs.

The structure chart for procedure INSERTSORT is shown in Fig. 9.30. Procedure SHIFTBIGGER is called to perform the shift operation and de-

Fig. 9.30 Structure Chart for Procedure INSERTSORT

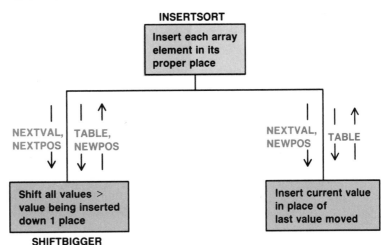

termine the correct position for the array element currently being inserted (NEXTVAL). Procedure INSERTSORT is shown in Fig. 9.31.

```
procedure INSERTSORT (var TABLE {input/output} : INTARRAY;
                          N {input} : INTEGER);

{Performs an insertion sort on array TABLE with subscripts 1..N.}

var
    NEXTPOS,          {subscript of the next element to be inserted}
    NEWPOS,           { subscript of this element after insertion}
    NEXTVAL : INTEGER;  {temporary storage for next element value}

procedure SHIFTBIGGER (var TABLE {input/output} : INTARRAY;
                           NEXTPOS, NEXTVAL {input} : INTEGER;
                           var NEWPOS {output} : INTEGER);

{Shifts each array element value in the sorted subarray
 1..NEXTPOS-1 that is greater than NEXTVAL down 1 element.
 NEWPOS is set to indicate the position of last value moved.}

begin {SHIFTBIGGER}
    WRITELN ('Procedure SHIFTBIGGER entered.')
end; {SHIFTBIGGER}

begin {INSERTSORT}
    for NEXTPOS := 2 to N do
        begin
            {invariant: subarray 1..NEXTPOS-1 is sorted}
            NEXTVAL := TABLE[NEXTPOS];                {save next element}

            {Shift all values > NEXTVAL down one element.}
            SHIFTBIGGER (TABLE, NEXTPOS, NEXTVAL, NEWPOS);

            {Insert NEXTVAL in location NEWPOS.}
            TABLE[NEWPOS] := NEXTVAL
        end {for}
end; {INSERTSORT}
```

Fig. 9.31 Procedure INSERTSORT

Procedure SHIFTBIGGER must move all array element values larger than NEXTVAL, starting with the array element at position NEXTPOS-1. The shift operation terminates when all array elements are moved (NEXTVAL is the smallest value so far) or a value less than or equal to NEXTVAL is reached. NEXTVAL should then be inserted in the position formerly occupied by the last value that was moved. The algorithm for SHIFTBIGGER follows; the procedure is shown in Fig. 9.32.

Algorithm

1. Start with the element in position NEXTPOS-1.
2. while first element not reached and element value > NEXTVAL do
    3. Move element value down one position.
    4. Check next smaller element value.
5. Define NEWPOS as the position of the last value moved.

```
procedure SHIFTBIGGER (var TABLE {input/output} : INTARRAY;
                       NEXTPOS, NEXTVAL {input} : INTEGER;
                       var NEWPOS {output} : INTEGER);

{Shifts each array element value in the sorted subarray
 1..NEXTPOS-1 that is greater than NEXTVAL down 1 element.
 NEWPOS is set to indicate the correct position of NEXTVAL.}

begin {SHIFTBIGGER}
   {Shift all values > NEXTVAL. Start with element at NEXTPOS-1.}
   while (NEXTPOS > 2) and (TABLE[NEXTPOS-1] > NEXTVAL) do
      begin
         TABLE[NEXTPOS] := TABLE[NEXTPOS-1];      {shift value down}
         NEXTPOS := NEXTPOS - 1                   {try next element}
      end; {while}

   {assert: NEXTPOS is 2 or NEXTVAL belongs at position NEXTPOS}
   {Shift TABLE[1] if necessary and define NEWPOS.}
   if TABLE[1] > NEXTVAL then
      begin
         TABLE[2] := TABLE[1];                    {move TABLE[1] down}
         NEWPOS := 1                        {NEXTVAL is the smallest so far}
      end
   else
      NEWPOS := NEXTPOS                            {define NEWPOS}
end; {SHIFTBIGGER}
```

Fig. 9.32 Procedure SHIFTBIGGER

The while statement in Fig. 9.32 compares and shifts all values greater than NEXTVAL in the subarray with subscripts 2..NEXTPOS-1. The if statement in Fig. 9.32 is used to compare only the first array element value to NEXTVAL and possibly shift it. This seemingly extra statement is needed because an "out of bounds subscript" error occurs if the while condition is evaluated for NEXTPOS = 1 (NEXTPOS-1 = 0). The if statement also defines the value of NEWPOS.

So far, we have studied three sorting algorithms: bubble sort, selection sort, and insertion sort. In each of these algorithms the time required to sort an array increases with the square of the number of array elements, or, the time required to sort an array of N elements is proportional to N^2. Consequently, these algorithms are not particularly efficient for large arrays (i.e. N >= 100). A much faster sorting procedure will be discussed in the next section.

Self-check Exercises for Section 9.6

1. Rewrite the selection sort without using recursion.
2. Assume the values 10, 5, 7, −3, 4, 9, 7, −3, −5 are stored in consecutive array elements. Trace the execution of SELECTSORT and INSERTSORT on this array. Show the array just before each recursive call to SELECTSORT and just before each repetition of the for statement in INSERTSORT.

The time required to sort an array using a simple sorting algorithm increases with the square of the number of array elements. This means that the time required to sort an array with N elements is proportional to N^2.

Quicksort

Problem: A faster algorithm is needed for sorting an array. We would like to see an improvement similar to that provided by binary search over simple search.

Discussion: The quicksort algorithm works in the following way. Given an array with subscripts FIRST..LAST to sort, it rearranges this array so that all element values smaller than a selected *pivot value* are first, followed by the pivot value, followed by all element values larger than the pivot value. After this rearrangement (called a *partition*), the pivot value is in its proper place. All element values smaller than the pivot value are closer to where they belong as they precede the pivot value. All element values larger than the pivot value are closer to where they belong as they follow the pivot value.

An example of this process is shown below. We will assume that the first array element is arbitrarily selected as the pivot. A possible result of the partitioning process is shown beneath the original array.

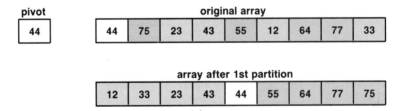

After the partitioning process, the fifth array element contains the pivot value, 44. All values less than 44 are in the left subarray (blue area); all values greater than 44 are in the right subarray (grey area) as desired. The next step is to apply quicksort recursively to both subarrays. The data requirements and algorithm for quicksort follow. We will describe how to do the partitioning later.

PROBLEM INPUTS

the array being sorted (TABLE : INTARRAY)
the first subscript (FIRST : INTEGER)
the last subscript (LAST : INTEGER)

the sorted array (TABLE : INTARRAY)

the subscript of the pivot value after partitioning
(PIVINDEX : INTEGER)

Algorithm

1. if FIRST < LAST then
   2. Partition the elements in the subarray FIRST..LAST so that the pivot value is in place (subscript is PIVINDEX)
   3. Apply quicksort to the subarray FIRST..PIVINDEX-1
   4. Apply quicksort to the subarray PIVINDEX+1..LAST

The recursive algorithm above shows that nothing is done for the simple case FIRST >= LAST. If FIRST > LAST is true, then the array bounds are improper; if FIRST = LAST is true, then a one-element array exists which is sorted by definition. The implementation of procedure QUICK-SORT is shown in Fig. 9.33. The procedure (call) statement

QUICKSORT (TABLE, 1, N)

could be used to sort an array TABLE (type INTARRAY) with subscripts 1..N.

The two recursive calls to QUICKSORT in Fig. 9.33 will cause the QUICKSORT procedure to be applied to the subarrays that are separated by the value at PIVINDEX. If any subarray contains just one element (or zero elements), an immediate return will occur.

Procedure PARTITION selects the pivot and performs the partitioning operation. When the arrays are randomly ordered to begin with, any element may be used as the pivot value. For simplicity, we will choose the element with subscript FIRST. We will then search for the first value at the left end of the subarray being sorted that is greater than the pivot value. When we find it, we search for the first value at the right end of the subarray that is less than or equal to the pivot value. These two values are exchanged and we repeat the search and exchange operations. This is illustrated below with UP pointing to the first value greater than the pivot and DOWN pointing to the first value less than or equal to the pivot value.

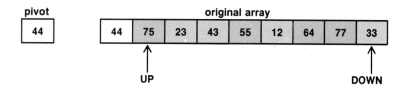

```
procedure QUICKSORT (var TABLE {input/output} : INTARRAY;
                     FIRST, LAST {input} : INTEGER);

{Recursive procedure to sort the subarray of TABLE with
 subscripts FIRST..LAST. Uses procedure PARTITION to split the
 array into two subarrays such that the pivot value is in its
 proper place (subscript PIVINDEX) preceded by all smaller values
 and followed by all larger values.                              }

var
    PIVINDEX : INTEGER;            {subscript of pivot value-
                                    returned by PARTITION}

procedure PARTITION (var TABLE {input/output} : INTARRAY;
                     FIRST, LAST {input} : INTEGER;
                     var PIVINDEX {output} : INTEGER);

{Partitions the subarray of TABLE with subscripts FIRST..LAST into
 two subarrays. All values less than or equal to TABLE[PIVINDEX]
 are in the left subarray; all values greater than TABLE[PIVINDEX]
 are in the right subarray.                                      }

begin {PARTITION}
    WRITELN ('Procedure PARTITION entered.')
end;  {PARTITION}

begin {QUICKSORT}
    if FIRST < LAST then
        begin
            {Split into two subarrays separated by value at PIVINDEX}
            PARTITION (TABLE, FIRST, LAST, PIVINDEX);
            QUICKSORT (TABLE, FIRST, PIVINDEX-1);
            QUICKSORT (TABLE, PIVINDEX+1, LAST)
        end
end;  {QUICKSORT}
```

Fig. 9.33 Procedure QUICKSORT

Seventy-five is the first value at the left end of the array that is larger than 44; thirty-three is the first value at the right end that is less than or equal to 44 so these two values are exchanged. The *pointers* UP and DOWN are then advanced from their current positions to the positions below.

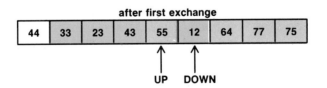

Fifty-five is the next value at the left end that is larger than 44; twelve is the next value at the right end that is less than or equal to 44, so these two values are exchanged, and UP and DOWN are advanced again.

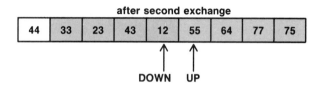

After second exchange

| 44 | 33 | 23 | 43 | 12 | 55 | 64 | 77 | 75 |

DOWN   UP

After the second exchange above, the first five array element values are all less than or equal to the pivot; the last four element values are all larger than the pivot. Fifty-five is selected by UP once again as the next element larger than the pivot; twelve is selected by DOWN as the next element less than or equal to the pivot. Since UP has now "passed" DOWN, these values are not exchanged. Instead, the pivot value (subscript is FIRST) and the value at position DOWN are exchanged. This puts the pivot value in its proper position (new subscript is DOWN) as shown below.

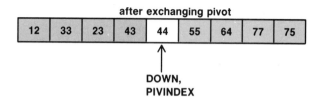

after exchanging pivot

| 12 | 33 | 23 | 43 | 44 | 55 | 64 | 77 | 75 |

DOWN,
PIVINDEX

The partitioning process is now complete, and the value of DOWN is returned as the pivot index (PIVINDEX). QUICKSORT will be called recursively to sort the left subarray and the right subarray. The algorithm for PARTITION follows.

This algorithm is implemented in Fig. 9.34.

Algorithm for PARTITION

1. Define the pivot value as the contents of TABLE[FIRST].
2. Initialize UP to FIRST and DOWN to LAST.
3. repeat
    4. Assign the subscript of the first element greater than the pivot value to UP.
    5. Assign the subscript of the first element less than or equal to the pivot value to DOWN.
    6. if UP < DOWN then
        7. Exchange their values.
    until UP meets or passes DOWN
8. Exchange TABLE[FIRST] and TABLE[DOWN].
9. Define PIVINDEX as DOWN.

```
procedure PARTITION  (var TABLE {input/output} : INTARRAY;
                      FIRST, LAST {input} : INTEGER;
                      var PIVINDEX {output} : INTEGER);

{Partitions the subarray of TABLE with subscripts FIRST..LAST into
two subarrays. All values less than or equal to TABLE[PIVINDEX]
are in the left subarray; all values greater than TABLE[PIVINDEX]
are in the right subarray.                                         }

var
    PIVOT,                      {the pivot value}
    UP,                         {pointer to values > PIVOT}
    DOWN : INTEGER;             {pointer to values <= PIVOT}

procedure EXCHANGE (var X, Y {input/output} : INTEGER);

{Switches the values in X and Y.}

var
    TEMP : INTEGER              {temporary cell for exchange}

begin {EXCHANGE}
    TEMP := X;  X := Y;  Y := TEMP
end; {EXCHANGE}

begin {PARTITION}
    PIVOT := TABLE[FIRST];          {define leftmost element as the pivot}

    {Find and exchange values that are out of place.}
    UP := FIRST;                {set UP to point to leftmost element}
    DOWN := LAST;               {set DOWN to point to rightmost element}
    repeat
        {Move UP to the next value larger than PIVOT.}
        while (TABLE[UP] <= PIVOT) and (UP < LAST) do
            UP := UP + 1;
        {assert: TABLE[UP] > PIVOT or UP is equal to LAST}

        {Move DOWN to the next value less than or equal to PIVOT.}
        while TABLE[DOWN] > PIVOT do
            DOWN := DOWN - 1;
        {assert: TABLE[DOWN] <= PIVOT}

        {Exchange out of order values.}
        if UP < DOWN then
            EXCHANGE (TABLE[UP], TABLE[DOWN])
    until UP >= DOWN;                       {until UP meets or passes DOWN}

    {Assert: values <= PIVOT have subscripts <= DOWN and
             values > PIVOT have subscripts > DOWN}
    {Put pivot value where it belongs and define PIVINDEX.}
    EXCHANGE (TABLE[FIRST], TABLE[DOWN]);
    PIVINDEX := DOWN
end; {PARTITION}
```

Fig. 9.34 Procedure PARTITION

The two while loops in Fig. 9.34 are used to advance pointers UP and DOWN to the right and left, respectively. Since TABLE[FIRST] is equal to PIVOT, the second loop will stop if DOWN reaches the left end of the array (DOWN is FIRST). The extra condition (UP < LAST) is added to the first while loop to ensure that it also stops if UP reaches the right end of the array.

The quicksort procedure works better for some arrays than for others. It works best when the partitioning process splits each subarray into two subarrays of almost the same size. The worst behavior results when one of the subarrays has 0 elements and the other has all the rest except for the pivot value. Ironically, this worst case behavior results when QUICKSORT is applied to an array that is already sorted. The pivot value remains in position FIRST, and the rest of the elements will be in one subarray.

The relationship between the number of array elements, N, and the time required to perform QUICKSORT is on the order of $N \times \log_2 N$ as compared to $N \times N$ for bubble sort. Table 9.1 lists the values of these formulas for different N. By moving down a column of the table, we see the relative effect of increasing N; obviously $N \times \log_2 N$ increases much more slowly than does $N \times N$.

Table 9.1 Comparison of Effect of N on Simple Sorts and QUICKSORT

N	$N \times N$ (simple sorts)	$N \times \log_2 N$ (QUICKSORT)
32	1024	160
64	4096	384
128	16384	896
256	65536	2048
512	262144	4608

Self-check Exercises for Section 9.7

1. Complete the trace of QUICKSORT for the subarrays remaining after the first partition.
2. If an array contains some values that are the same, in which subarray (left or right) will all values equal to the pivot value be placed?

9.8 Common Programming Errors

The most common problem with a recursive procedure is that it does not terminate properly. For example, if the terminating condition is not correct or is incomplete, the procedure may call itself indefinitely or until all available memory is used up. Normally, a "stack overflow" run-time error is an indicator that a recursive procedure is not terminating. Be sure to identify all stopping cases and provide a terminating condition for each one. Also be sure that each recursive step leads to a situation that is closer to a stopping case and that repeated recursive calls will eventually lead to stopping cases only.

The use of large arrays as value parameters can quickly consume all available memory. Unless absolutely essential for data protection, arrays should be passed as variable parameters. An expression such as N-1 must be passed as a value parameter.

Debugging Recursive Procedures

Sometimes it is difficult to observe the result of a recursive procedure execution. If each recursive call generates many output lines and there are many recursive calls, the output will scroll down the screen more quickly than it can be read. On most systems it is possible to stop the screen temporarily by pressing a control character sequence (e.g. Control S). If this cannot be done, it is still possible to cause your output to stop temporarily by printing a prompting message followed by a READLN. Your program will resume execution when you press the carriage return character.

One problem with sort and search procedures is the possibility of going beyond the bounds of a subarray. Make sure that your Pascal system checks for subscript range errors. On some systems this important check must be activated by the programmer; otherwise, subscript range violations are not detected. If this is the case on your system, make sure that you activate this feature when debugging any program that manipulates arrays, particularly a search or sort.

When debugging a search or sort procedure it is best to use relatively small arrays (e.g. 10 elements). Make sure that you print the new contents of the array after each pass through a sort procedure.

9.9 Chapter Review

This chapter provided many examples of recursive procedures and functions. Hopefully, studying them has given you some appreciation of the power of recursion as a problem solving and programming tool and has provided you with valuable insight regarding its use. It may take some time to feel comfortable thinking in this new way about programming, but it is certainly worth the effort.

We discussed a minor improvement to an array search and also studied the binary search technique, which provides significant improvement for larger arrays. The relationship between the number of array elements, N, and the time required to perform a binary search is on the order of $\log_2 N$. This means that the time required to perform a binary search increases very slowly. For example, it should only take about twice as long to perform a binary search on an array with 256 elements ($\log_2 256$ is 8) as it would take to perform a binary search on an array with 16 elements ($\log_2 16$ is 4).

Searching an array using hashing was also discussed. In the absence of collisions, this technique enables a target to be found with a single probe regardless of the array size.

We also discussed three new sorting algorithms. The selection sort and insertion sort are considered N × N sorts just like the bubble sort. This means that the time required to sort an array using one of these techniques is proportional to the square of the number of elements. For larger arrays, it is best to use the recursive QUICKSORT algorithm described in Section 9.7. The relationship between this algorithm and the number of array elements, N, is expressed by the formula N × $\log_2$N.

Review Questions

1. Explain the nature of a recursive problem.
2. Discuss the efficiency of recursive procedures.
3. Differentiate between stopping cases and a terminating condition.
4. Write a Pascal program with a procedure that has a character string parameter (maximum length of six). The procedure should print the accumulating sum of ordinal values corresponding to each character in the string until a blank is encountered or all six characters have been summed.
5. Write a Pascal program with a function that will return the sum of ordinal values corresponding to the characters in a character string parameter (maximum length of six). The function should add up the ordinal values until a blank is encountered or all six characters have been summed.
6. Convert the Pascal program below from an iterative process to a recursive function that calculates an approximate value for e, the base of the natural logarithms, by summing the series

```
1 + 1/1!  + 1/2!  + ...  1/N!
```

until additional terms do not affect the approximation.

```
program ELOG (OUTPUT);

var
    ENL, DELTA, FACT : REAL;
    N : INTEGER;

begin {ELOG}
    ENL := 1.0;
    N := 1;
    FACT := 1.0;
    DELTA := 1.0;
    repeat
       ENL := ENL + DELTA;
       N := N + 1;
       FACT := FACT * N;
       DELTA := 1 / FACT;
    until ENL = (ENL + DELTA);
    WRITE ('The value of e is ', ENL :18:15)
end. {ELOG}
```

7. Write a function that will recursively search a string of maximum length of 30 characters and return the position of the first comma in the string. If the string does not contain a comma, then return 30.

8. Discuss the major differences between hashing and binary search.

Programming Projects

1. Write a procedure that reads each row of an array as a string and converts it to a row of GRID (see Fig. 9.21). The first character of row one corresponds to GRID[1,1], the second character to GRID[1,2], etc. Set the element value to EMPTY if the character is blank; otherwise, set it to FILLED. The number of rows in the array should be read first. Use this procedure in a program that reads in cell coordinates and prints the number of cells in the blob containing each coordinate pair.

2. The expression for computing C(n,r), the number of combinations of n items taken r at a time is

$$c(n,r) = \frac{n!}{r!\,(n-r)!}$$

Write and test a function for computing c(n,r) given that n! is the factorial of n.

3. A palindrome consists of a word that reads the same forward or backward, such as level, deed, and mom. Write a recursive function that returns the BOOLEAN value TRUE if a word, passed as a parameter, is a palindrome.

4. Write a recursive function that returns the value of the following recursive definition:

```
F(X,Y) = X - Y              if X or Y < 0
F(X,Y) = F(X-1,Y) + F(X,Y-1)    otherwise
```

5. Write a recursive routine that lists all the pairs of positive integers that are the sum of a given number. For example:

```
7 = 6+1, 5+2, and 4+3
```

Do not repeat any pairs (ie. not both 6+1 and 1+6).

6. Write a routine that lists all the pairs of subsets for a given set of letters. For example

```
['A', 'C', 'E', 'G'] ⟶ ['A', 'C'], ['A', 'E'],
                        ['A', 'G'],
                        ['C', 'E'], ['C', 'G'],
                        ['E', 'G']
```

7. Write two recursive routines that add the numerical equivalents of two character strings and save the result in a third string. The first recursive routine will accept five parameters: two strings of digits, right-justified with leading blanks, the length of each string, and a RESULT string. The routine will add each corresponding set of digits, from the right, and calculate the sum. At this point, each digit calculated by this ADDER procedure will be inserted into a character string for the RESULT. At the completion of this routine, the answer will be in reverse order in the string RESULT.

   The second recursive routine will take the string RESULT and reverse the digits and right-justify the answer with leading blanks.

   An example would be:

   ```
   After Routine #1:
      STRING1 = '   368'
      STRING2 = '  4162'
      RESULT  = '0354  '   if all are size 6
   ```

   After Routine #2:

   ```
   ORIGINAL RESULT = '0354  '
   PROCESSED RESULT = '  4530'
   ```

8. Write a routine that converts a character string consisting of numbers, letters, spaces, and punctuation symbols into a compressed and symbolic representation of the original string. Each consecutive string of digits, letters, blanks, or punctuation symbols will be converted to one specially defined character. Use the following conversion scheme:

   • Letters convert to an 'L'
   • Digits convert to a '#'
   • Blanks convert to a blank
   • Anything else converts to a '?'

   For example the following string would be converted as indicated:

   ```
   INITIAL STRING = 'HELLO,  MY.,NUMBER  IS 2716..'
   ```

   would convert to: 'L? L?L L #?'

9. Write a routine that accepts an 8 by 8 array of characters that represent a MAZE. Each position can contain either an 'X' or a blank. Starting at position [1,1], list any path through the maze to get to location [8,8]. Only horizontal and vertical moves are allowed (no diagonal moves). If no path exists, write a message indicating this. Moves can only be made to locations that contain a blank. Encountering an 'X' means the path is blocked and another must be chosen. Use recursion.

10. One method of solving a continuous numerical function for a root implements a technique similar to the binary search. Given a numerical function defined as F(X), and two values of X that are known to bracket one of the roots, we can approximate this root through a method of repeated division of this bracket.

For a set of values of X to bracket a root, the value of the function for one X must be negative and the other must be positive, as illustrated in the diagram below, which plots F(X) for values of X between X1 and X2.

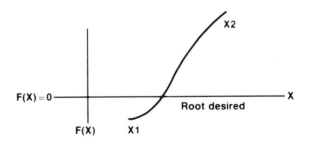

The algorithm requires that the midpoint between the left X and the right X be evaluated in the function; if it equals zero the root is found; otherwise, the left X(X1) or right X (X2) is set to this midpoint. To determine whether to replace either X1 or X2, the sign of the midpoint is compared against the signs of the values of F(X1) and F(X2). The midpoint replaces the X (X1 or X2) whose function value has the same sign as its function value.

This routine can be written recursively. The terminating conditions are true when either the midpoint evaluated in the function is zero or the absolute value of the left minus the right X is less than some small predetermined value (e.g. 0.0005). If the second condition occurs then the root is said to be approximately equal to the midpoint of the last set of left and right X's.

11. We can use the file merge technique demonstrated in Section 8.6 to sort two arrays. The *mergesort* begins by taking adjacent pairs of array values and ordering the values in each pair. It then forms groups of four elements by merging adjacent pairs (first pair with second pair, third pair with fourth pair, etc.) into another array. It then takes adjacent groups of four elements from this new array and merges them back into the original array as groups of eight, etc. The process terminates when a single group is formed that has the same number of elements as the array. MERGESORT is illustrated in Fig. 9.35 for an array with eight elements. Write a MERGESORT procedure.

Fig. 9.35 Illustration of MERGESORT

original array	pairs ordered	merged pairs	merged quads
5	5	3	1
8	8	5	3
7	3	7	5
3	7	8	5
9	9	1	7
12	12	5	8
5	1	9	9
1	5	12	12

12. Many compilers use the recursive descent technique for compiling. This technique consists of writing a recursive procedure for each syntactic element of the language. To determine whether or not an input line is a particular kind of statement it is parsed by the procedure for that statement. If the procedure is able to successfully process every element in the input line, then the line is accepted as satisfying the syntax of that statement.

Write a parser that determines whether or not its input string is a Pascal expression. Assume that all characters of the string are squeezed together (no blanks) and that all unsigned constants are single digits and all variables are individual uppercase letters. The operators mod, div, and, or, not are represented by single lowercase letters (m for mod, d for div, etc.). Also, ignore sets and functions as possible syntactic elements. The symbol $ will appear at the end of each string to be parsed. The string 'X+(Y*2m4)$' represents the expression X + (Y * 2 mod 4) which is syntactically valid. The string 'X+(Y*2m4$' should not be accepted as valid (missing parenthesis).

To write your parser, provide a procedure corresponding to each relevant syntax diagram in Appendix C. Each procedure should return TRUE if its syntax is satisfied and should also return the length of the string that it accepted; otherwise, it should return FALSE. We will start you off with the procedure for *expression* in Fig. 9.36. An *expression* is either a *simple expression* (accepted by procedure SIMPEXPR) or two *simple expressions* separated by a relational operator. (For simplicity, the relational operators are <, >, = only.)

```
procedure EXPRESSION (INSTRING {input} : STRING;
                      START {input} : INTEGER;
                      var EXPRLENGTH {output} : INTEGER;
                      var ISEXPR {output} : BOOLEAN);

{Attempts to recognize an expression in INSTRING starting at
 position START. If an expression exists, ISEXPR is set to TRUE
 and EXPRLENGTH indicates the length of the expression. Otherwise,
 ISEXPR is set to FALSE. Calls SIMPEXPR.                         }

var
    POSITION,                      {current position in INSTRING}
    SIMPEXPRLENGTH : INTEGER;      {length of last simple expression}
    ISSIMPEXPR : BOOLEAN;          {is a simple expression found?}

begin {EXPRESSION}
    POSITION := START;                         {initial position}
    ISEXPR := FALSE;                           {assume not an expression}

    {An expression must start with a simple expression.}
    SIMPEXPR (INSTRING, POSITION, SIMPEXPRLENGTH, ISSIMPEXPR);
    if ISSIMPEXPR then
       begin {first simple expression}
          EXPRLENGTH := SIMPEXPRLENGTH;              {define length}
          POSITION := POSITION + SIMPEXPRLENGTH;     {advance in string}
```

```
     {Check whether next character is a relational operator.}
     if not (INSTRING[POSITION] in [' <','>','=']) then
        ISEXPR := TRUE                    {is an expression without rel op}
     else                                 {next character is rel op}
        begin {rel op}
          {A simple expression must follow relational operator.}
          POSITION := POSITION + 1;
          SIMPEXPR (INSTRING,POSITION, SIMEXPRLENGTH,ISSIMPEXPR);
          if ISSIMPEXPR then
             begin {second simple expression}
                ISEXPR := TRUE;           {is an expression with rel op}
                {Its length is sum of simple lengths + 1 (rel op)}
                EXPRLENGTH := EXPRLENGTH + SIMPEXPRLENGTH + 1
             end {second simple expression}
        end {rel op}
     end {first simple expression}
end;   {EXPRESSION}
```

Fig. 9.36 Procedure EXPRESSION

You will need procedures for *simple expressions, factors, terms, variables,* and *unsigned constants.* Your main program should read the input string and call the procedure EXPRESSION. If the value returned is TRUE and the next character is '$', the string is a valid expression

Pointer Variables and Dynamic Data Structures

10.1   The NEW Statement and Pointer Variables
10.2   Understanding Dynamic Allocation
10.3   Introduction to Linked Lists
10.4   Manipulating Linked Lists Using Pointer Variables
10.5   Case Study—Maintaining a Linked List
10.6   Stacks and Queues
10.7   Multiple-linked Lists and Trees
10.8   Case Study—Maintaining a Binary Search Tree
10.9   Common Programming Errors
10.10 Chapter Review

In this chapter, we shall see how Pascal can be used to create *dynamic data structures*. Dynamic data structures are data structures that "grow" as a program executes. A dynamic data structure is a collection of elements (called *nodes*) that are normally records. Unlike an array that always contains storage space for a fixed number of elements, a dynamic data structure expands and contracts during program execution based on the data storage requirements of the program.

Dynamic data structures are used for storage of real world data that are constantly changing. An example would be an airline passenger list. If this list were maintained in alphabetical order in an array, it would be necessary to move all passenger records that alphabetically followed a new passenger in order to make room for that passenger's data in the array. This would require using a loop to copy the data record for each passenger being moved to the next array element. If a dynamic data structure is used instead, the new passenger data can simply be inserted between two existing passenger records with a minimum of effort.

Dynamic data structures are extremely flexible. As described above, it is relatively easy to add new information by creating a new node and inserting it between two existing nodes. We shall see that it is also relatively easy to modify dynamic data structures by removing or deleting an existing node. This is more convenient than modifying an array of records, where each record is in a fixed position relative to the others as determined by its subscript.

This chapter discusses four dynamic data structures: lists, stacks, queues, and trees. We will learn how to insert and delete elements from each of these data structures. We will also learn how to search a list and a tree. Before beginning our study of these data structures, we will introduce dynamic storage allocation in Pascal.

10.1 The NEW Statement and Pointer Variables

Since we don't know beforehand the order or number of *nodes* (elements) in a dynamic data structure, we cannot allocate storage for a dynamic data structure in the conventional way (using a variable declaration statement). Instead, we must allocate storage for each individual node as needed and, somehow, join this node to the rest of the structure. The *NEW statement* is used to allocate storage for a new node.

We must also have some way of referencing each new node that is allocated in order to store data in it. Pascal provides a special type of variable, called a *pointer variable* (or *pointer*), for this purpose.

Example 10.1 The declarations

```
Type
  STRING = packed array [1..3] of CHAR;
  NODE = record
    WORD : STRING;
    PLACE : INTEGER
  end; {NODE}
  NODEPOINTER = ^NODE;

var
  P, Q, R : NODEPOINTER;
```

declare a record type NODE and a pointer type, NODEPOINTER, to records of type NODE. The variables P, Q, and R are defined as pointer variables of type NODEPOINTER.

The statements

```
NEW (P);
NEW (Q);
```

allocate storage for two records that are "pointed to" (referenced) by pointers P and Q. Since P and Q are type NODEPOINTER, these new records must be type NODE as illustrated below. The value of a pointer variable is really the address in memory of a particular node. We will represent a pointer value by drawing an arrow to the node referenced by the pointer. Both fields of these new nodes are initially undefined.

```
P^.WORD := 'ACE';
Q^.WORD := 'BOY';
```

define the WORD field of P^ (the node referenced by pointer P) and Q^ (the node referenced by pointer Q) as shown next.

The diagram shows that P points to a record of type NODE whose first field contains the string 'ACE' and Q points to a record of type NODE whose first field contains the string 'BOY'. The second field of both records is still undefined.

The statements

```
P^.PLACE := 25;
Q^.PLACE := 37;
```

define the PLACE fields as shown next.

In the example above, we used pointers P and Q to reference two different nodes. The pointer that references each node was determined when the node was created. We shall demonstrate next that it is possible to change the node referenced by a particular pointer, or to have the same node referenced by more than one pointer.

Example 10.2 The pointer assignment statement

```
R := P;
```

copies the value of pointer P into pointer R. This means that pointers P and R contain the same memory address and now point to the same node as shown below.

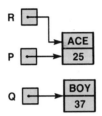

The pointer assignment statements

```
P := Q;
Q := R;
```

would have the effect of exchanging the nodes pointed to by P and Q as shown below.

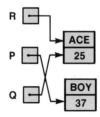

The statement

```
WRITE (P^.WORD, Q^.WORD, R^.WORD)
```

displays the WORD field (a character string) of the records pointed to by P, Q and R. The output printed would be

```
BOYACEACE
```

Pointers P, Q and R are similar to subscripts in that they select particular nodes or elements of a data structure. Unlike subscripts, their range of values is not declared and their values (memory cell addresses) may not be printed.

It is important to understand the difference between using P and P^ in a program. P is a pointer variable (type NODEPOINTER) and is used to store the address of a data structure of type NODE. P can be assigned a new value through a pointer assignment or execution of a NEW statement. P^ is the name of the record pointed to by P and can be manipulated like any other record in Pascal. The field selectors P^.WORD and P^.PLACE can be used to reference data (a string and integer) stored in this record.

Throughout the chapter, we will represent the value of a pointer variable by drawing an arrow to a box that denotes a record. The actual point of contact of the arrowhead with the box is not important. The arrow in the diagram below represents the value of P; the value of P^.WORD is 'BOY' and P^.PLACE is 37.

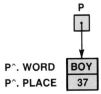

In this section, we discussed how to declare pointer variables and manipulate pointer values. We also saw how to create nodes and reference nodes using pointer variables. These operations are described in the displays that follow.

POINTER TYPE

pointer-id = ^*node-id*

Interpretation: The identifier *pointer-id* is defined as a pointer type to elements of type *node-id* where *node-id* is a data type name.

NEW STATEMENT

NEW (*pointer*)

Interpretation: The procedure NEW allocates storage for a data structure that is pointed to by the pointer variable *pointer*. The type of data structure allocated is determined by the type of *pointer*.

REFERENCING A FIELD USING A POINTER

pointer^.*field-name*

Interpretation: The field specified by *field-name* of the node currently pointed to by pointer variable *pointer* is referenced.

POINTER ASSIGNMENT

$pointer_1 := pointer_2$

Interpretation: The address contained in variable *pointer₂* is assigned to variable *pointer₁*. The result is that pointer variable *pointer₁* now points to (references) the same node as *pointer₂*. *Pointer₁* and *pointer₂* must be the same pointer type.

Self-check Exercises for Section 10.1

1. For the last diagram in this section, explain the effect of each legal assignment statement below.
   a) R^.WORD := 'CAT'
   b) P^ := R^
   c) P.WORD := 'HAT'
   d) P := 54
   e) P^.PLACE := 0
   f) P := R
   g) P^.WORD := -10
   h) Q^.PLACE := R^.PLACE

2. The sequence of assignment statements

   ```
   R := P;
   P := Q;
   Q := R
   ```

   was used to exchange the values of pointer variables P and Q so that P points to the element containing 'BOY' and Q points to the element containing 'ACE'. What would the sequence

   ```
   R^.WORD := P^.WORD;
   P^.WORD := Q^.WORD;
   Q^.WORD := R^.WORD
   ```

   do? What is the difference between these two sequences?

10.2 Understanding Dynamic Allocation

As mentioned above, a new record is created whenever the NEW statement (a standard procedure) is executed. You may be wondering where in memory the new record is stored. Pascal maintains a *storage pool* of available memory cells; memory cells from this pool are allocated whenever a NEW statement is executed.

The statement

```
NEW (P)
```

in Example 10.1 has pointer variable P as its parameter. Since P is declared as a pointer to records of type NODE, the execution of this statement causes the allocation of memory space for the storage of three characters and an integer variable. These cells are originally undefined (they retain whatever data was last stored in them) and the address of the first cell allocated is stored in P. The cells allocated are no longer considered part of the storage pool of available cells. The only way to reference these cells is through pointer variable P (e.g. P^.WORD or P^.PLACE).

Fig. 10.1 shows the pointer variable P and the storage pool before and after the execution of NEW (P). The before diagram shows pointer variable P as undefined before the execution of NEW (P). The after diagram shows P pointing to the first of two memory cells that were allocated for the new record (assuming that three characters and an integer can be stored in two cells). The cells considered part of the storage pool have the darker color in Fig. 10.1

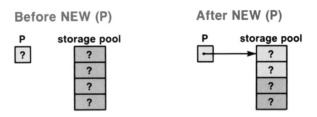

Fig. 10.1 Storage Pool before and after NEW (P)

As an example, if the memory cells with addresses 1000 through 1003 were originally in the storage pool, then after the execution of NEW (P) only the memory cells with addresses 1002 and 1003 would be considered part of the storage pool. The address 1000 would be stored in pointer variable P and that cell and cell 1001 can only be referenced through P.

10.3 Introduction to Linked Lists

A *linked list* or simply *list* is a sequence of nodes in which each node is linked or connected to the node following it. A list with three nodes is shown below.

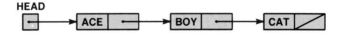

Each node in the list above has two fields: the first field contains data and the second field is a pointer (represented by an arrow) to the next list element. There is a pointer (HEAD) to the first list element or *list head*. The symbol / is always found in the pointer field of the last list element.

Lists are important data structures because they can easily be modified. For example, a new node containing the string 'BYE' can be inserted between the strings 'BOY' and 'CAT' by changing only one pointer value (the one from 'BOY') and defining the pointer from the new node. This is true regardless of how many elements there may be in the list. The list is shown below after the insertion; the pointer values that are new are shown in blue.

Similarly, it is easy to delete a list element. Only one pointer value has to be changed—the pointer that currently points to the element being deleted. The linked list is redrawn below, after deleting the string 'BOY' by changing the pointer from the node 'ACE' (new value shown in blue; old value in grey). The node containing string 'BOY' is effectively disconnected from the list since there is no longer a pointer to it. The new list consists of the strings 'ACE', 'BYE', 'CAT'.

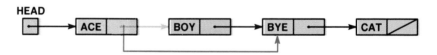

Implementing Linked Lists in Arrays

Two methods are commonly used to implement linked lists. In older programming languages, linked lists are implemented using arrays. Nodes are stored in parallel arrays or arrays of records. The node value is stored in one field, and the subscript of the next list element is stored in the pointer field. A pointer value of 0 indicates the end of the list. The original three-element list is shown at the left of Fig. 10.2. Since HEAD is 1, the first array element represents the first node in the list. The third array element is the last list node.

Fig. 10.2 Representing Lists in Arrays

HEAD				HEAD				HEAD		
1	ACE	2		1	ACE	2		1	ACE	4
	BOY	3			BOY	4			BOY	4
	CAT	0			CAT	0			CAT	0
	?	?			BYE	3			BYE	3

| original list | list after inserting 'BYE' | list after deleting 'BOY' |

The array element pointed to by each subscript is indicated by an arrow. The original list ('ACE', 'BOY', 'CAT') can be traced by following the arrows. The list is shown in the middle diagram after inserting 'BYE' ('ACE', 'BOY', 'BYE', 'CAT'); the list is shown in the diagram on the right after deleting 'BOY' ('ACE', 'BYE', 'CAT'). Note that the node containing 'BOY' is still in the array (second element), but it is no longer considered part of the list.

One of the disadvantages of storing lists in arrays is that we must declare an array that is big enough to hold the largest possible list regardless of how many nodes are actually used. In Pascal, we can use pointer variables and dynamic allocation to ensure that we only allocate enough memory to store the actual list. We will see how to do this next.

10.4 Manipulating Linked Lists Using Pointer Variables

In order to implement a linked list using pointer variables, we must declare a record with at least one field that is a pointer. The record type LISTNODE declared below describes a node in our sample list.

```
type
    STRING = packed array [1..3] of CHAR;
    LISTPOINTER = ^LISTNODE;
    LISTNODE = record
        WORD : STRING;
        LINK : LISTPOINTER
    end; {LISTNODE}
```

A pointer type, LISTPOINTER, that points to elements (records) of type LISTNODE is declared. Each element of type LISTNODE contains a field named LINK that is also type LISTPOINTER. The above declaration is circular in that the record type LISTNODE appears in the declaration of LISTPOINTER; similarly, the pointer type LISTPOINTER appears in the declaration of LISTNODE. Pascal requires the pointer type to be declared first.

Creating a List

Let us see how we might create the list described at the start of Section 10.3. First of all, we must have some way of referencing the list. This is usually done by establishing a pointer to the list head. We will declare HEAD, Q and R as variables of type LISTPOINTER and use HEAD as the pointer to the list head.

```
var
    HEAD, Q, R : LISTPOINTER;
```

In the discussion below, each statement that defines a pointer has a number comment. This comment identifies the pointer in a diagram.
The statements

```
{1} NEW(HEAD);
     HEAD^.WORD := 'ACE';
```

define the WORD field of a new list element referenced by pointer HEAD.

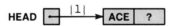

The LINK field of this element must point to the next element of our list. The statements

```
{2} NEW(Q);
{3} HEAD^.LINK := Q;
```

have the effect shown below.

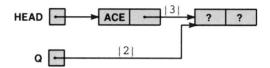

As indicated, a new element is created that is pointed to by Q. The value of Q is then copied into the link field of our first node {3} thereby connecting the two elements.
The sequence of statements

```
     Q^.WORD := 'BOY';
{4} NEW(R);
{5} Q^.LINK := R;
     R^.WORD := 'CAT';
```

completes the linked list. The first statement copies 'BOY' into the WORD field of the second element. The next statement {4} creates a third element pointed to by R. This element is then joined to the second {5}, and the value of its WORD field is defined as 'CAT'. The new data structure is shown below.

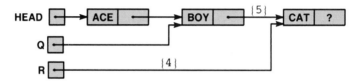

The only thing left to do is to indicate that the element pointed to by R is, in fact, the last element of the list and points to no other. This is accomplished by the statement

```
R^.LINK := NIL
```

The reserved word NIL is a predefined constant in Pascal that is used to designate the end of a list.

The extra pointers, Q and R, in the list above may be ignored. The final list is shown below.

Obviously, we do not want to go through this process each time we create a new linked list. Hence, we will write a procedure to do this for us later.

Traversing a list

In many list processing operations, each node in the list must be processed in sequence; this is called *traversing* a list. In order to traverse a list, we must start at the list head and follow the list pointers. This is illustrated in the next two examples.

Example 10.3 Procedure PRINTLIST in Fig. 10.3 displays the WORD fields of each node in a list starting with the node pointed to by HEAD. Consequently, PRINTLIST may be used to print the words stored in our sample list.

```
procedure PRINTLIST (HEAD {input} : LISTPOINTER);

{Prints out the list pointed to by HEAD.}

begin
    {Traverse the list until the end is reached.}
    while HEAD <> NIL do
        begin
            WRITELN (HEAD^.WORD);       {print the node value}
            HEAD := HEAD^.LINK          {advance to next node}
        end {while}
end; {PRINTLIST}
```

Fig. 10.3 Procedure PRINTLIST

For our original sample list, the output of PRINTLIST would be

```
ACE
BOY
CAT
```

The statement

```
HEAD := HEAD^.LINK       {advance to next node}
```

advances the pointer HEAD to the next list element, which is pointed to by the LINK field of the current list element. The while loop is exited when

HEAD becomes NIL. Since HEAD is a value parameter, a local copy of the pointer to the first list element is established when the procedure is entered. This local pointer is updated; however, the corresponding pointer in the calling program remains unchanged.

Example 10.4   List processing operations can be formulated very naturally using recursion. As an example, we will consider the problem of searching a list to find a string TARGET. The result will be a pointer to the list element containing TARGET or NIL if TARGET is not found. One stopping state would be an empty list; in this case the TARGET cannot be present. The other stopping state would be finding TARGET at the head of the list. The recursion step is to search the rest of the list (excluding the current list head) for TARGET. This algorithm is summarized below; function SEARCH is shown in Fig. 10.4.

Algorithm for
List Search

1. if the list is empty then
     2. TARGET is not present.
   else if TARGET is in the list head then
     3. The result is a pointer to the list head.
   else
     4. Search for TARGET in the rest of the list.

```
function SEARCH (HEAD : LISTPOINTER;
                 TARGET : STRING) : LISTPOINTER;

{Searches a list for a specified TARGET string. Returns
 a pointer to TARGET if found. Returns NIL if TARGET is
 not in the list.                                       }

begin {SEARCH}
   if HEAD = NIL then
      SEARCH := NIL                         {empty list—TARGET not found}
   else if HEAD^.WORD = TARGET then
      SEARCH := HEAD                            {TARGET is in HEAD}
   else
      SEARCH := SEARCH(HEAD^.LINK, TARGET)    {search rest of list}
end;   {SEARCH}
```

Fig. 10.4 Function SEARCH

As indicated by the function header, a pointer value may be returned as a function result. In the recursive step

```
SEARCH := SEARCH(HEAD^.LINK, TARGET)  {search rest of list}
```

the function SEARCH is called again to search the rest of the list that is pointed to by HEAD^.LINK. Eventually, a stopping state will be reached and a value will be assigned to the function identifier. The value returned from a lower level call is not modified; it is simply passed up as the function result.

A trace of

```
P := SEARCH(HEAD, 'BOY')
```

is shown in Fig. 10.5 for our sample list 'ACE', 'BOY', 'CAT'. Since the TARGET string 'BOY' is in the second list element, there is one recursive call to SEARCH after the original function call. The result, as desired, is a pointer to the node containing the string 'BOY'. The address of this node is saved in pointer variable P.

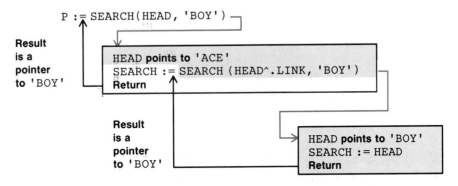

Fig. 10.5 Trace of P := SEARCH(HEAD, 'BOY')

PROGRAM STYLE

Testing for an empty list

The order of evaluation of the terminating conditions in Fig. 10.4 is very important. The value of HEAD^.WORD is not defined if the list is empty (HEAD is NIL); consequently, the terminating condition HEAD = NIL must be evaluated before HEAD^.WORD = TARGET. In all list processing operations, you must make sure that your program does not attempt to reference a field pointed to by NIL. This illegal reference to undefined data is a very common error.

Self-check Exercises for Section 10.4

1. Write procedure PRINTLIST as a recursive procedure.
2. Write an iterative version of function SEARCH.
3. Write a recursive function that finds the length of a list.

10.5 Case Study—Maintaining a Linked List

We stated earlier that lists are very flexible data structures and can easily be modified. In this section we will show how to keep a list up to date and in alphabetical order while performing list insertions and deletions.

Problem: We wish to maintain a data base that contains up-to-date information about the passengers on a particular airline flight. The passenger data at the start of each day is available on a disk file. In order to be able to process new data rapidly, we would like to transfer the passenger data into main memory, process the changes that occur during the day by modifying the passenger data in main memory, and save the updated passenger data in a new disk file. Both the original passenger file and the new passenger file should be in alphabetical order by passenger name.

Discussion: Since the list of passengers on an airline flight is changed frequently, a linked list is a good choice for an internal data structure. We will create a linked list by reading the passenger data from an external file. This linked list will be updated during the day as new data are entered. At the end of the day, each record stored in the linked list will be copied to another external file.

We will need to provide procedures that create the original linked list, copy this list to an external file, and perform whatever updates may be required. For now, we will assume that the update operations consist of deleting passengers from the list and inserting new passenger records. We also want to be able to display the record of a particular passenger or print the entire passenger list.

The data for each passenger will be stored in a record of type PASSENGER as described below.

```
type
    STRING = packed array [1..STRINGSIZE] of CHAR;
    PASSENGER = record
        NAME : STRING;
        CLASS : (ECONOMY, FIRSTCLASS);
        NUMSEATS : 1..MAXSEATS
    end; {PASSENGER}
```

Each list element will contain a passenger record as described above (field PASSINFO) and a pointer (field LINK) to the next passenger record in the list.

```
{rest of type declarations}
PASSPOINTER = ^PASSNODE;
PASSNODE = record
    PASSINFO : PASSENGER;
    LINK : PASSPOINTER
end; {PASSNODE}
```

An entire record of type PASSENGER can be stored in a record of type PASSNODE. Assuming NEXT is type PASSPOINTER and ONEPASS is type PASSENGER, the statements

```
NEW (NEXT);
NEXT^.PASSINFO := ONEPASS
```

copy the record variable ONEPASS into the PASSINFO field of the new node pointed to by NEXT.

To simplify the list processing operations, we will assume that the passenger file always begins with a record whose NAME field is 'AA...A' and always ends with a record whose NAME field is 'ZZ...Z'. The reason for these dummy elements will be discussed later. An empty passenger list will contain only these two elements, as shown below.

An empty passenger list

The problem inputs and outputs and algorithm follow.

PROBLEM INPUTS

the file of passenger records in alphabetical order by NAME field beginning with 'AA...A' and ending with 'ZZ...Z'.
(PASSFILE : FLIGHTFILE)

PROBLEM OUTPUTS

the updated file of passengers (NEWPASSFILE : FLIGHTFILE)

Algorithm

1. Create a linked list corresponding to the original passenger file (PASSFILE).
2. Process each update request.
3. Copy the passenger records in the updated list to a new passenger file (NEWPASSFILE).

Procedure CREATELIST performs step 1 and is described next. Procedure COPYLIST performs step 3 and is based on procedure PRINTLIST shown earlier (see Fig. 10.3). To perform step 2, we must first print a menu of update choices and then call a procedure to read each choice and perform it. We will call procedures PRINTMENU and MODLIST, respectively, to perform these tasks. The structure chart is shown in Fig. 10.6; the main program and COPYLIST are shown in Fig. 10.7.

Procedure CREATELIST must allocate a new node for storage of each passenger record and then read the passenger data into that node. It should return a pointer, HEAD, to the first passenger record (NAME field 'AA...A'). The procedure inputs, outputs, and algorithm follow.

PROCEDURE INPUTS

the file of passenger data in alphabetical order by NAME field beginning with 'AA...A' and ending with 'ZZ...Z'.
(PASSFILE : FLIGHTFILE)

(*continued on p. 491*)

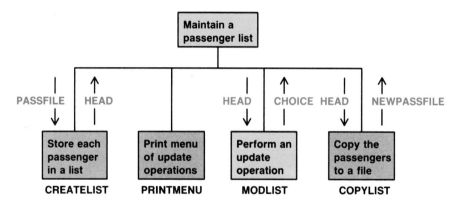

Fig. 10.6 Structure Chart for Passenger List Problem

```
program MAINTAIN (PASSFILE, NEWPASSFILE, INPUT, OUTPUT);

{Stores the data in file PASSFILE in a linked list and updates
 the linked list by performing insertions and deletions.  When
 done, copies the records in the linked list to file NEWPASSFILE.}

const
   DONE = 5;                              {finished list update}
   MAXSEATS = 350;                        {number of seats in airplane}
   STRINGSIZE = 10;                       {maximum length of a string}

type
   STRING = packed array [1..STRINGSIZE] of CHAR;
   PASSENGER = record                     {each passenger record}
      NAME : STRING;
      CLASS : (ECONOMY, FIRSTCLASS);
      NUMSEATS : 1..MAXSEATS
   end; {PASSENGER}
   FLIGHTFILE = file of PASSENGER;        {file of passenger records}

   PASSPOINTER = ^PASSNODE;
   PASSNODE = record                      {each list element}
      PASSINFO : PASSENGER;
      LINK : PASSPOINTER
   end; {PASSNODE}

var
   HEAD : PASSPOINTER;                     {pointer to head of list}
   PASSFILE, NEWPASSFILE : FLIGHTFILE;     {old and new files}
   CHOICE : INTEGER;                       {option selected}

procedure COPYLIST (HEAD {input} : PASSPOINTER;
                    var NEWPASSFILE {output} : FLIGHTFILE);

{Copies each node of the list pointed to by HEAD to NEWPASSFILE.}

begin {COPYLIST}
   REWRITE (NEWPASSFILE);                  {prepare NEWPASSFILE for output}
```

```
      while HEAD <> NIL do
         begin
            WRITE (NEWPASSFILE, HEAD^.PASSINFO);       {copy current node}
            HEAD := HEAD^.LINK                    {advance to next node}
         end {while}
end;   {COPYLIST}
```

{Insert procedures CREATELIST, PRINTMENU, MODLIST here.}

```
begin
   {Read the passenger data from PASSFILE into the linked list.}
   CREATELIST (PASSFILE, HEAD);

   {Process each update request.}
   repeat
      PRINTMENU;                                  {display the option}
      MODLIST (HEAD, CHOICE)          {read and perform user's choice}
   until CHOICE = DONE;

   {Copy each passenger record from the linked list to NEWPASSFILE.}
   COPYLIST (HEAD, NEWPASSFILE)
end. {MAINTAIN}
```

Fig. 10.7 Main Program and COPYLIST

PROCEDURE OUTPUTS

a pointer to the list head (HEAD : PASSPOINTER)

LOCAL VARIABLES

a pointer to the last list node (LAST : PASSPOINTER)

Algorithm for CREATELIST

1. Prepare PASSFILE for input.
2. Allocate a node for storage of the first list element, point HEAD to this node, and read the first record into it.
3. Initialize the pointer to the last list node (LAST) to HEAD.
4. while there are more passenger records do
   5. Attach a new node to the end of the list and read the next passenger's data into it.
   6. Reset LAST to point to the new node.

In step 2, the pointer HEAD is set to point to the first node that is allocated and the first passenger record is read into this node. The local pointer variable LAST always points to the current end of the list. In step 5, a new node is allocated and attached to the current end of the list; the next passenger's data are read into the new node. Procedure CREATENODE is called to perform steps 2 and 5; procedure CREATELIST is shown in Fig. 10.8.

```
procedure CREATELIST (var PASSFILE {input} : FLIGHTFILE;
                      var HEAD {output} : PASSPOINTER);

{Reads each passenger record from PASSFILE into a linked list.
 The pointer HEAD is set to point to the first list node.     }

var
   LAST : PASSPOINTER;                          {pointer to last list node}

procedure CREATENODE (var PASSFILE {input} : FLIGHTFILE;
                      var NEXT {output} : PASSPOINTER);

{Allocates a new node that is pointed to by NEXT for storage of
 the next passenger's data.  Reads the data from PASSFILE.       }

begin {CREATENODE}
{1} NEW (NEXT);                                 {point NEXT to a new node}
    READ (PASSFILE, NEXT^.PASSINFO);            {save the data in new node}
{2} NEXT^.LINK := NIL                      {set LINK field of new node to NIL}
end; {CREATENODE}

begin {CREATELIST}
    RESET (PASSFILE);                           {prepare PASSFILE for input}
    CREATENODE (PASSFILE, HEAD);            {point HEAD to the first record}

    {Read each record and add it to the end of the list.}
    LAST := HEAD;                       {initialize last node to list head}
    while not EOF(PASSFILE) do
        begin
            CREATENODE (PASSFILE, LAST^.LINK);          {attach a new node
                                                         to the last node}
        {3}LAST := LAST^.LINK                {make the new node the last node}
        end {while}
end; {CREATELIST}
```

Fig. 10.8 Procedures CREATELIST and CREATENODE

In CREATENODE, the statement

```
    {1}NEW (NEXT);                              {point NEXT to a new node}
```

allocates a new node and points the parameter represented by NEXT to this node. The first statement below

```
    READ (PASSFILE, NEXT^.PASSINFO);     {save the data in new node}
    {2}NEXT^.LINK := NIL                 {set LINK field of new node to NIL}
```

reads the next record from file PASSFILE into the record NEXT^. PASSINFO, thereby defining the PASSINFO field of the new node. Statement {2} initializes the LINK field of each new node to NIL.

In CREATELIST, the procedure (call) statement

```
    CREATENODE (PASSFILE, HEAD);  {point HEAD to the first record}
```

creates the list head and reads the first passenger record (name 'AA...A') into it. Within the while loop, the first statement below

```
CREATENODE (PASSFILE, LAST^.LINK);      {attach a new node
                                          to the last node}
{3}LAST := LAST^.LINK      {make the new node the last node}
```

calls CREATENODE to attach a new node to the current last node; the next passenger's data are read into the new node. Then statement {3} advances LAST to point to the new list node. The last node attached before CREATELIST is exited will have a NAME field of 'ZZ...Z' and a link field of NIL.

The process of adding a new node to the end of the list is illustrated below. The current last node contains passenger 'ALPHARD' and passenger 'ATKINSON' is being added. The blue lines show the new pointer values; the grey lines show the original values of pointers that are changed. The comments identify the statement in Fig. 10.8 that caused the change.

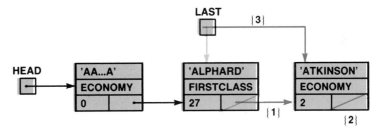

Procedure PRINTMENU simply prints out the menu of update choices (1—insert, 2—delete, 3—print passenger, 4—print passenger list, 5—quit) and is not shown. Procedure MODLIST reads the user's choice and attempts to process it. The data requirements and algorithm for MODLIST are shown below.

PROCEDURE INPUTS

a pointer to the head of the passenger list (HEAD : PASSPOINTER)

PROCEDURE OUTPUTS

the update operation selected (CHOICE : INTEGER)

LOCAL VARIABLES

the passenger data to be inserted (NEWPASS : PASSENGER)
the name of a passenger to be processed (TARGET : STRING)
the length of the passenger's name (LENGTH : INTEGER)
a pointer to a particular node in the list (TARGPOINT : PASSPOINTER)

a BOOLEAN flag indicating whether or not a passenger was deleted
(DELETED : BOOLEAN)

Algorithm for MODLIST

1. Read the user's update choice into CHOICE.
2. case CHOICE of
   - **1:** Read the new passenger data into NEWPASS.
     Insert NEWPASS in the list.
   - **2:** Read the name of the passenger to be deleted into TARGET.
     Delete the designated passenger from the list.
   - **3:** Read the name of the passenger to be displayed into TARGET.
     Find the passenger and display the passenger's data.
   - **4:** Traverse the passenger list and print each passenger's data.
   - **5:** Do nothing

The structure chart for MODLIST is shown in Fig. 10.9. The procedure is shown in Fig. 10.10.

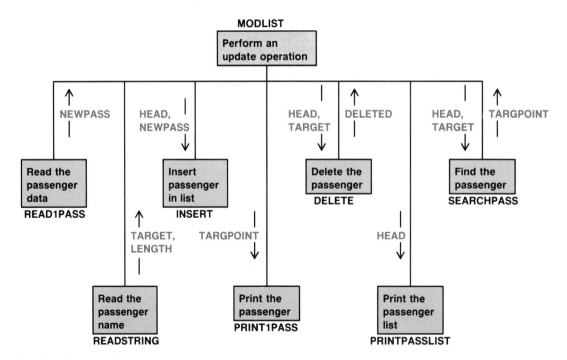

Fig. 10.9 Structure Chart for MODLIST

```
procedure MODLIST (HEAD {input} : PASSPOINTER;
                   var CHOICE {output} : INTEGER);

{Reads each update choice (CHOICE) and performs it.}

var
    TARGPOINT : PASSPOINTER;        {pointer to a target node}
    NEWPASS : PASSENGER;            {a passenger record}
```

```
        TARGET : STRING;                    {a passenger name}
        LENGTH : INTEGER;                   {length of a name}
        DELETED : BOOLEAN;                  {BOOLEAN flag}

{Insert READSTRING, READ1PASS, PRINT1PASS here.}
{Insert SEARCHPASS, PRINTPASSLIST, INSERT, DELETE here.}

begin {MODLIST}
    WRITE ('Select an option 1 through 5: ');   READLN (CHOICE);
    if CHOICE in [1..5] then
        case CHOICE of
            1:  begin
                    WRITELN ('Enter the data for the new passenger.');
                    READ1PASS (NEWPASS);                    {read new passenger}
                    INSERT (HEAD^.LINK, NEWPASS, HEAD)      {insert in list}
                end; {1}
            2:  begin
                    WRITE ('Enter name of passenger to delete: ');
                    READSTRING (TARGET, LENGTH);
                    DELETE (HEAD^.LINK, TARGET, HEAD, DELETED);
                    if not DELETED then
                        WRITELN (TARGET :LENGTH, ' not found.')
                end; {2}
            3:  begin
                    WRITE ('Enter name of passenger to display: ');
                    READSTRING (TARGET, LENGTH);
                    TARGPOINT := SEARCHPASS(HEAD, TARGET);
                    if TARGPOINT = NIL then
                        WRITELN (TARGET, ' not found.')
                    else
                        PRINT1PASS (TARGPOINT^.PASSINFO)        {show the data}
                end; {3}
            4:  begin
                    WRITELN ('CURRENT PASSENGER LIST');
                    WRITELN ('Name' :10, 'Seats' :10, 'Class' :10);
                    PRINTPASSLIST (HEAD)
                end; {4}
            5:  WRITELN ('Passenger list update complete for today.')
        end {case}
end; {MODLIST}
```

Fig. 10.10 Procedure MODLIST

Procedure MODLIST consists of a long case statement. Each case label implements a different option. Working backwards, option 5 simply
prints a message and returns. Option 4 calls procedure PRINTPASSLIST
(similar to procedure PRINTLIST in Fig. 10.3) to echo print each passenger's data. Option 3 reads a passenger's name into TARGET and then calls
function SEARCHPASS (similar to function SEARCH in Fig. 10.4) to set
TARGPOINT to point to the record containing this passenger's data. Procedure PRINT1PASS is then called to display the passenger information. All
of these procedures are similar to earlier procedures and are left as exercises.

We will discuss cases 1 and 2 next. In case 1, insert a new passenger, procedure READ1PASS is first called to read the passenger's data from the keyboard. We have written many similar procedures already. Procedure INSERT is then called to insert this passenger's data where it belongs in the list.

In case 2, delete a passenger, procedure READSTRING is called to read the name of the passenger to be deleted. Procedure DELETE is called to delete the corresponding passenger record from the list. If the passenger to be deleted is not in the list, an error message is printed after returning from DELETE. We will write procedures DELETE and INSERT in the next sections.

Deleting a List Node

We stated earlier that deleting a list node is simply a matter of changing a single pointer value. The LINK field of the predecessor of the node being deleted must be reset to point to the successor of the node being deleted. A recursive algorithm for deleting a node follows.

Algorithm for DELETE

1. If the list is empty then
    2. TARGET cannot be deleted.
  else if TARGET is in the list head then
    3. Delete the list head.
  else
    4. Delete TARGET from the rest of the list.

Fig. 10.11 Procedure DELETE

```
procedure DELETE (NEXT {input} : PASSPOINTER;
                  TARGET {input} : STRING;
                  PRED {input} : PASSPOINTER;
                  var DELETED {output} : BOOLEAN);

{Deletes the passenger with name TARGET from the list pointed to
by NEXT. The predecessor of the list head is pointed to by PRED.
DELETED is a flag that is set to indicate whether or not the
deletion is performed (DELETED is TRUE if performed).        }

begin {DELETE}
   if NEXT = NIL then
      DELETED := FALSE                       {empty list—TARGET not found}
   else if NEXT^.PASSINFO.NAME = TARGET then
      begin
       {1}PRED^.LINK := NEXT^.LINK;  {reset LINK field of predecessor}
          DELETED := TRUE;                {set flag to indicate deletion}
          DISPOSE (NEXT)                    {return node to storage pool}
      end
   else
      DELETE (NEXT^.LINK, TARGET, NEXT, DELETED)    {try rest of list}
end; {DELETE}
```

Procedure DELETE is shown in Fig. 10.11. The parameter NEXT represents a pointer to the head of the list being searched; the parameter PRED represents a pointer to the predecessor of the list head. The BOOLEAN parameter DELETED is used to signal that the TARGET was found and removed from the list (DELETED set TRUE) or that the TARGET was not found (DELETED set FALSE).

The assignment statement

```
{1}PRED^.LINK := NEXT^.LINK;  {reset LINK field of predecessor}
```

performs the list deletion by changing the LINK field of the predecessor of node NEXT to point to the successor of node NEXT. The statement

```
DISPOSE (NEXT)
```

returns the memory cells allocated to the node pointed to by NEXT to the storage pool.

If the TARGET string is not found, the recursive step

```
DELETE (NEXT^.LINK, TARGET, NEXT, DELETED) {try rest of list}
```

is used to search the rest of the list for TARGET. The current head (pointed to by NEXT) becomes the predecessor; the current second element (pointed to by NEXT^.LINK) becomes the new list head. The search is terminated when the end of the list is reached.

For the original procedure (call) statement

```
DELETE (HEAD^.LINK, NEWPASS, HEAD, DELETED);
```

the first actual list element is pointed to by NEXT and the dummy node with NAME field 'AA..A' is pointed to by PRED as shown below.

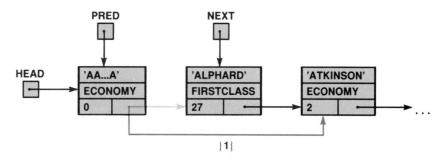

If the string in TARGET is 'ALPHARD', the value of PRED^.LINK would be changed as shown by the blue arrow labeled {1}; otherwise, the recursive step would cause PRED and NEXT to advance down the list. The original value of PRED^.LINK is shown by the grey arrow. Note that the value of PRED^.LINK can be changed even though PRED is a value parameter.

Without the dummy element at the head of the list there would be no predecessor to the first actual element. Consequently, the algorithm as shown could not be used because the deletion of the first actual element would have to be treated as a special case.

DISPOSE STATEMENT

DISPOSE (*pointer*)

Interpretation: The memory space allocated to the node pointed to by *pointer* is returned to the storage pool and may be reallocated later. Note: It is an error to perform the DISPOSE operation when the value of *pointer* is NIL or undefined.

Inserting a Node in a List

We stated earlier that it was relatively easy to insert a new node in a list. We must locate the first node that alphabetically follows the new node (the successor of the new node). The LINK field of the new node must be set to point to its successor; the LINK field of the new node's predecessor should be changed to point to the new node.

The insertion algorithm is written below using recursion to search the list for the correct position of the new passenger. Step 2 assumes that there cannot be two passenger's with the same NAME field. If the new passenger's name matches a name already in the list, then that record is updated with the new data. Step 3 inserts a new node between two existing nodes. Step 4 is the recursive step and is executed until one of the two stopping conditions becomes true. The second stopping condition must eventually be true (i.e. 'ZZ...Z' follows all actual passenger names).

Algorithm for INSERT

1. if the name at the list head matches the new passenger's then
   2. Replace the passenger's data with the new data.
   else if the name at the list head follows the new name then
   3. Insert the new passenger just before the list head.
   else
   4. Insert the new passenger in the rest of the list.

Procedure INSERT is shown in Fig. 10.12. The parameter NEXT represents a pointer to the head of the list being searched; the parameter PRED represents a pointer to the predecessor of the list head.

```
procedure INSERT (NEXT {input} : PASSPOINTER;
                  NEWPASS {input} : PASSENGER;
                  PRED {input} : PASSPOINTER);

{Inserts a new passenger (NEWPASS) in the list pointed to by NEXT.
 The predecessor of the list head is pointed to by PRED.          }
```

```
var
   TEMP : PASSPOINTER;                                    {a temporary pointer}

begin {INSERT}
   if NEXT^.PASSINFO.NAME = NEWPASS.NAME then
      NEXT^.PASSINFO := NEWPASS
   else if NEXT^.PASSINFO.NAME > NEWPASS.NAME then
      begin {insert}
      {1}NEW (TEMP);                                      {allocate a new node}
         TEMP^.PASSINFO := NEWPASS;                       {store new passenger data}
      {2}TEMP^.LINK := NEXT;                              {join new node to successor}
      {3}PRED^.LINK := TEMP                               {join new node to predecessor}
      end {insert}
   else
      INSERT (NEXT^.LINK, NEWPASS, NEXT)                  {insert in rest of list}
end; {INSERT}
```

Fig. 10.12 Procedure INSERT

In Fig. 10.12, the statements

```
{1}NEW (TEMP);                            {allocate a new node}
   TEMP^.PASSINFO := NEWPASS;   {store new passenger data}
```

allocate a new node that is pointed to by the local pointer variable `TEMP`. Next, the new passenger data (stored in record `NEWPASS`) is copied into the `PASSINFO` field of this new node. The assignment statements

```
{2}TEMP^.LINK := NEXT;        {join new node to successor}
{3}PRED^.LINK := TEMP         {join new node to predecessor}
```

insert the new node in the list. If the original list is in alphabetical order, then so must the new list because all insertions maintain the alphabetical ordering.

For the original procedure (call) statement

```
INSERT (HEAD^.LINK, NEWPASS, HEAD)           {insert in list}
```

the first actual list element is pointed to by `NEXT` and the dummy node with `NAME` field `'AA..A'` is pointed to by `PRED`. Fig. 10.13 illustrates the insertion of a new first passenger, `'ARNOLD'`. The new pointer values are shown as blue arrows; the original values of pointers that are changed appear as grey arrows. Again, the inclusion of the dummy first element allows us to use this algorithm to insert a node at the head of the actual passenger list.

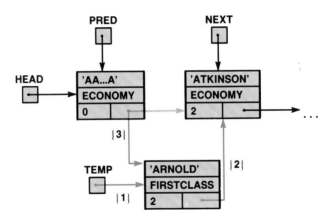

Fig. 10.13 Inserting Passenger 'ARNOLD'

1. Write procedures READ1PASS, PRINTPASSLIST, and PRINT1PASS called in Fig. 10.10. PRINTPASSLIST should use procedure PRINT1PASS.

10.6 Stacks and Queues

In this section we will discuss two kinds of linked lists that find wide application in the design of compilers and operating systems, stacks and queues. We introduced stacks in Section 9.1 and described their role in implementing recursion. A stack may be thought of as a linked list in which each new node is inserted at the head of the list and each deletion removes the current head of the list. Inserting a node is a *push* operation and deleting a node is *popping the stack*.

We might also want to determine whether a stack is *empty* (i.e. has no elements) or examine the element currently on top of the stack. The latter operation is easy since the top of the stack is always pointed to by the list head pointer.

A stack created by inserting the character values '2', '+', 'C', '*' in that order is shown below.

The character '*' is at the top of the stack. If each character is stored in a field named DATA, then the top of the stack is referenced as TOP^. DATA. The element at the top of the stack is the last element placed on the stack and is the first one that will be removed. For this reason a stack is sometimes called a *LIFO (Last In First Out) list.* The character value

'2' is at the bottom of the stack and will be the last one removed; its pointer value is NIL.

Example 10.5   Procedure PUSH in Fig. 10.14 is used to push a new value (type CHAR) onto a stack. We are assuming the following declarations.

```
type
    STACKPOINTER = ^STACKNODE;
    STACKNODE = record
        DATA : CHAR;
        LINK : STACKPOINTER
    end; {STACKNODE}

procedure PUSH (NEXTCHAR {input} : CHAR;
                var TOP {output} : STACKPOINTER);

{Pushes the data stored in NEXTCHAR onto the top of the
 stack pointed to by TOP.                                 }

var
    TEMP : STACKPOINTER;                        {local pointer}

begin {PUSH}
  {1}NEW (TEMP);                      {point TEMP to a new node}
     TEMP^.DATA := NEXTCHAR;          {save the next character}
  {2}TEMP^.LINK := TOP;                 {connect it to old top}
  {3}TOP := TEMP                     {redefine top of the stack}
end; {PUSH}
```

Fig. 10.14 Procedure PUSH

The stack of characters is redrawn below after execution of the procedure (call) statement

```
PUSH ('X', TOP)
```

The character value 'X' is the new top of the stack. The value of TOP before the push operation is shown by the grey arrow.

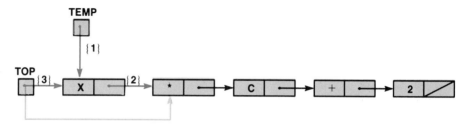

Example 10.6   Procedure POP in Fig. 10.15 returns the top of the stack pointed to by TOP. The pointer TOP is reset to point to the current second element that becomes the new top of the stack. The BOOLEAN function EMPTYSTACK is called by POP to determine whether the stack is currently empty

(EMPTYSTACK returns TRUE). An error message is printed if procedure
POP is called when the stack is empty.

```
function EMPTYSTACK (TOP : STACKPOINTER) : BOOLEAN;

{Returns TRUE if the stack pointed to by TOP is empty.}

begin {EMPTYSTACK}
   EMPTYSTACK := TOP = NIL
end; {EMPTYSTACK}

procedure POP (var ITEM {output} : CHAR;
               var TOP {input/output} : STACKPOINTER);

{Pops the top of the stack pointed to by TOP. ITEM is assigned the
current top item. TOP is reset to point to the current second item. An
error message is printed if the stack is empty. Calls function
EMPTYSTACK.                                                           }

begin {POP}
   if EMPTYSTACK(TOP) then
      WRITELN ('Stack underflow error.')           {stack is empty}
   else
      begin
         ITEM := TOP^.DATA;                            {get ITEM}
         TOP := TOP^.LINK                             {reset TOP}
      end
end; {POP}
```

Fig. 10.15 Procedure POP

Example 10.7   The program in Fig. 10.16 reads a sequence of characters ending with ' # '
and echo prints the string in reverse order. The line

PALINDROME#EMORDNILAP

appears on the screen when the characters in blue are entered.

Fig. 10.16 Using a Stack to Print Characters Backwards

```
program USESTACK (INPUT, OUTPUT);

{Uses a stack of characters to print out a data string backwards.}

const
   SENTINEL = '#';             {sentinel character}

type
   STACKPOINTER = ^STACKNODE;
   STACKNODE = record
      DATA : CHAR;
      LINK : STACKPOINTER
   end; {STACKNODE}
```

```
var
    TOP : STACKPOINTER;          {pointer to stack top}
    NEXTCHAR : CHAR;             {next character}

{Insert function EMPTYSTACK here.}
{Insert procedures PUSH and POP here.}

begin {USESTACK}
    TOP := NIL;                               {initially stack is empty}

    {Push each input character onto the stack.}
    READ (NEXTCHAR);
    while NEXTCHAR <> SENTINEL do
        begin
            PUSH (NEXTCHAR, TOP);             {push next character}
            READ (NEXTCHAR)
        end; {while}

    {Pop each character and display it.}
    while not EMPTYSTACK(TOP) do
        begin
            WRITE (NEXTCHAR);                 {print last item popped}
            POP (NEXTCHAR, TOP)               {pop the stack}
        end; {while}
    WRITELN
end. {USESTACK}
```

Queues

A queue is a linked list used to model things such as a line of customers waiting at a checkout counter or a stream of jobs waiting to be printed by a line printer in a computer center. In a queue, all insertions are done at one end (the rear of the queue) and all deletions are made from the other end (the front of the queue).

A queue of three passengers on a waiting list for an airline flight is shown below. The name of the passenger who has been waiting the longest is 'BROWN' (pointed to by FRONT); the name of the most recent arrival is 'CARSON' (pointed to by REAR). The passenger pointed to by FRONT will be the first one removed. Since this is also the passenger who has been waiting the longest, a queue is sometimes called a *FIFO (First In First Out) list.* The last passenger who will be removed is the one pointed to by REAR. The pointer field of this passenger's node contains NIL.

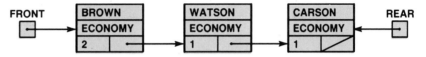

Note that the passengers above are listed in order of arrival into the queue rather than in alphabetical order. If an opening occurs on the flight, then passenger 'BROWN' will be removed from the queue and inserted into the flight list, and FRONT will be reset to point to passenger 'WATSON'. If another passenger is added to the waiting list, the new passenger will be linked to passenger `'CARSON'`, and REAR will be reset to point to the new passenger.

Example 10.8 Procedure ENQUEUE in Fig. 10.17 is used to add a new passenger (NEWPASS) to a waiting list of passengers assuming the declarations shown in Section 10.5. The pointer REAR is reset to point to the new passenger's data.

The BOOLEAN function EMPTYQUEUE is used to test whether the queue was empty just prior to the insertion (EMPTYQUEUE returns TRUE). If so, FRONT is also reset to point to the new passenger since there is only one passenger in the queue.

```
function EMPTYQUEUE (FRONT : PASSPOINTER) : BOOLEAN;

{Returns TRUE if the queue pointed to by FRONT is empty.}

begin {EMPTYQUEUE}
   EMPTYQUEUE := FRONT = NIL
end; {EMPTYQUEUE}

procedure ENQUEUE (NEWPASS {input} : PASSENGER;
                   var FRONT,
                       REAR {input/output} : PASSPOINTER);

{Inserts the passenger data stored in NEWPASS in the queue. REAR is
reset to point to the new passenger. If the queue is empty, FRONT is
assigned the same value as REAR. Calls EMPTYQUEUE.            }

var
    TEMP : PASSPOINTER;            {temporary pointer}

begin
  {1}NEW (TEMP);                              {allocate a new node}
     TEMP^.PASSINFO := NEWPASS;          {store new passenger data}
  {2}REAR^.LINK := TEMP;        {attach new node to old end of list}
  {3}TEMP^.LINK := NIL;            {new node is the new end of list}
  {4}REAR := TEMP                         {reset REAR to new node}
     if EMPTYQUEUE(FRONT) then
         FRONT := REAR                       {single element queue}
end; {ENQUEUE}
```

Fig. 10.17 Procedure ENQUEUE

The queue is shown in Fig. 10.18 after passenger `'MCMANN'` has been added to the waiting list. The original values of pointers that are changed appear as grey arrows.

Example 10.9 Procedure DEQUEUE in Fig. 10.19 is used to remove from the queue the passenger who has been waiting the longest (pointed to by FRONT). FRONT is reset to point to the passenger who has been waiting the second longest amount of time. If there is only one passenger in the queue when DEQUEUE is called, the queue becomes empty and FRONT and REAR are

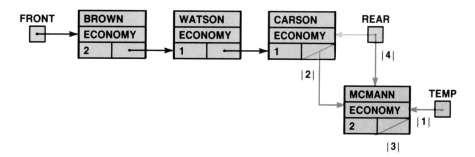

Fig. 10.18 Adding a Passenger to a Queue

reset to NIL. An error message is printed if the queue is empty when DEQUEUE is called.

```
procedure DEQUEUE (var NEXTPASS {input/output} : PASSENGER;
                   var FRONT,
                       REAR {input/output} : PASSPOINTER);
```

{Assigns to NEXTPASS the passenger record pointed to be FRONT. Resets FRONT to point to the next passenger at the front of the list. If the queue is initially empty, an error message is printed. If the queue becomes empty, sets both FRONT and REAR to NIL. Calls EMPTYQUEUE.   }

```
begin {DEQUEUE}
   if EMPTYQUEUE(FRONT) then
      WRITELN ('Queue underflow error.')          {queue is already empty}
   else
      begin {remove}
         NEXTPASS := FRONT^.PASSINFO;             {remove passenger at front}
      {1}FRONT := FRONT^LINK;                      {advance next passenger to front}
         if EMPTYQUEUE(FRONT) then
            REAR := NIL                                   {queue becomes empty}
      end {remove}
end;   {DEQUEUE}
```

Fig. 10.19 Procedure DEQUEUE

    The queue is shown below after deletion of the passenger at the front of the queue. Passenger `'WATSON'` is now at the front of the queue. The new value of FRONT is shown by the blue arrow; the original value is shown by the grey arrow.

    A main program should initialize pointers FRONT and REAR to NIL before any insertions or deletions are performed on the queue. The first call to procedure ENQUEUE will insert a new node in the queue, resetting both FRONT and REAR to point to this node.

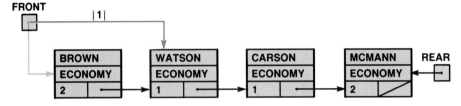

Fig. 10.20 Deleting a Passenger from a Queue

Self-check Exercises for Section 10.6

1. Draw the stack for Fig. 10.16 after the last push operation is performed. Use the data string HELLO#. Answer this question assuming the string is stored in a queue instead of a stack.
2. Modify POP and DEQUEUE so that the node removed is returned to the storage pool. Use DISPOSE.
3. Discuss how to implement a stack using an array.
4. Discuss how to implement a queue using an array.

10.7 Multiple-linked Lists and Trees

All the examples seen so far have involved list elements or nodes with a single pointer field. It is possible to have lists of elements with more than one link. For example, each element in the list shown below has a forward pointer that points to the next list element and a backward pointer that points to the previous list element. This allows us to traverse the list in either the left or right direction.

This structure is called a *doubly linked list*. The declarations below declare a list element of this general form.

```
type
   LINK = ^MULTINODE;
   MULTINODE = record
               •
               •      data fields
               •
      LEFT, RIGHT : LINK;
   end; {MULTINODE}
```

Introduction to Trees

A special kind of multiple-linked list that has wide applicability in computer science is a data structure called a *binary tree*. A sample tree is drawn in Fig. 10.21.

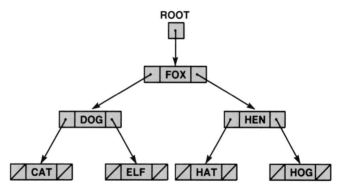

Fig. 10.21 A Sample Tree

Trees in computer science actually grow from the top down rather than from the ground up. The topmost element is called the *root of the tree*. The pointer, ROOT, points to the root of the tree drawn in Fig. 10.21. Each tree node shown has a single data field and two pointer fields called the *left branch* and *right branch*, respectively. Any node with both pointer fields equal to NIL is called a *leaf*.

The node containing the string 'HEN' is the *parent* of the nodes containing the strings 'HAT' and 'HOG'. Similarly, the nodes 'HAT' and 'HOG' are *siblings* since they are both children of the same parent node. The root of the tree is an *ancestor* of all other nodes in the tree and they, in turn, are all *descendants* of the root node.

Each node in a tree may be thought of as the root node of its own *subtree*. Since each node has two branches, it spawns two subtrees, a *left subtree* and a *right subtree*. Its *left child* is the root node of the left subtree, and its *right child* is the root node of the right subtree.

The declarations below describe the form of a tree node.

```
type
  STRING = packed array [1..3] of CHAR;
  BRANCH = ^TREE;
  TREE = RECORD
    WORD : STRING;
    LEFT, RIGHT : BRANCH
  end; {TREE}
```

Trees may be used for representing expressions in memory. For example, the expression

```
(X + Y)  *  (A - B)
```

could be represented as the tree drawn in Fig. 10.22.

The root node contains the operator (*) that is evaluated last. Each subtree that is itself an expression has an operator in its root node. The left subtree of the root node represents the expression (X + Y); the right subtree represents the expression (A - B).

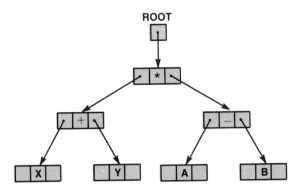

Fig. 10.22 Tree Form of Expression (X+Y) * (A−B)

Trees are also used to organize related data items as a hierarchical data structure in order to facilitate efficient search and retrieval for a desired item. For example, the *binary search tree* shown in Fig. 10.21 is arranged so that the left descendent of each node alphabetically precedes its parent and the right descendant alphabetically follows its parent. Hence, in searching for a particular key at any level of this tree, the left branch should be followed if the key value is "less than" the current node value, and the right branch should be followed if the key value is "greater than" the current node value. (What if the key value equals the current node value?) This effectively reduces the search space by a factor of two each time since all the descendants (children and grandchildren) in the branch not chosen are ignored.

Traversing a Tree

In order to process the data stored in a tree, we need to be able to traverse the tree, or visit each and every node in a systematic way. The first approach that will be illustrated is called an *inorder traversal*. The algorithm for an inorder traversal is described below.

Algorithm

1. Traverse the left subtree.
2. Visit the root node and print its data.
3. Traverse the right subtree.

Recall that the left subtree of any node is the part of the tree whose root is the left child of that node. The inorder traversal for the tree shown in Fig. 10.23 would visit the nodes in sequence

'CAT' 'DOG' 'ELF' 'FOX' 'HAT' 'HEN' 'HOG'

In Fig. 10.23, a numbered circle is drawn around each subtree. The subtrees are numbered in the order that they are traversed. Subtree 1 is the left subtree of the root node. Its left subtree (number 2) has no left subtree (or right subtree); hence, the string 'CAT' would be printed first. The root node for subtree 1 would then be visited and 'DOG' would be printed. Its right subtree consists of the leaf node containing the string 'ELF' (number 3). After 'ELF' is printed, the root node for the complete

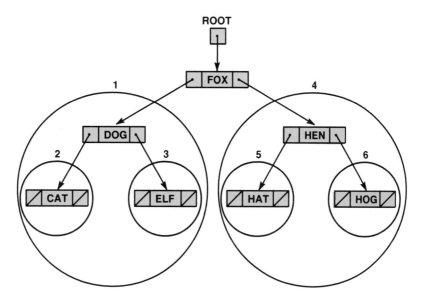

Fig. 10.23 Subtrees of a Tree.

tree is visited ('FOX' is printed) and the right subtree of the root node (number 4) is traversed in a like manner.

Procedure INORDER in Fig. 10.24 is a recursive procedure that performs an inorder traversal of a tree and displays each node's data. The parameter ROOT represents the pointer to the root node of the tree being traversed. If the tree is empty (ROOT = NIL) an immediate return occurs. Procedure INORDER is much simpler than any nonrecursive procedure that might be written to traverse a tree.

```
procedure INORDER (ROOT {input} : BRANCH);

{Performs an inorder traversal of the tree
 pointed to by ROOT. Prints each node visited.}

begin {INORDER}
    if ROOT <> NIL then
        begin {recursive step}
            INORDER (ROOT^.LEFT);                    {traverse left subtree}
            WRITELN (ROOT^.WORD);                      {print root value}
            INORDER (ROOT^.RIGHT)                    {traverse right subtree}
        end {recursive step}
end; {INORDER}
```

Fig. 10.24 Procedure INORDER

As we saw earlier an inorder traversal of the tree shown in Fig. 10.23 would visit the nodes in alphabetical sequence. If we performed an inorder traversal of the expression tree in Fig. 10.22, the nodes would be visited in the sequence

```
X + Y * A - B
```

Except for the absence of parentheses, this is the form in which we would normally write the expression. The expression above is called an *infix* expression because each operator is between its operands.

Switching the sequence of the three statements in the `if` statement shown in Fig. 10.24 will produce rather different results. The sequence

```
WRITELN (ROOT^.WORD);         {print root value}
INORDER (ROOT^.LEFT);         {traverse left subtree}
INORDER (ROOT^.RIGHT)         {traverse right subtree}
```

displays the root node before traversing its subtrees; consequently, the root value will be displayed before the values in its subtrees. This is called a *preorder* traversal. The nodes in Fig. 10.23 would be visited in the sequence

```
'FOX'  'DOG'  'CAT'  'ELF'  'HEN'  'HAT'  'HOG'
```

The nodes in the expression tree in Fig. 10.22 would be visited in the sequence

```
* + X Y - A B
```

The expression above is called a *prefix* expression because each operator precedes its operands. The operands of + are X and Y; the operands of − are A and B; the operands of * are the two triples + X Y and − A B.

Finally, the sequence

```
INORDER (ROOT^.LEFT);         {traverse left subtree}
INORDER (ROOT^.RIGHT);        {traverse right subtree}
WRITELN (ROOT^.WORD)          {print root value}
```

displays the root node after traversing each of its subtrees; consequently, each root value will be printed after all values in its subtrees. This is called a *postorder* traversal. The nodes in Fig. 10.23 would be visited in the sequence

```
'CAT'  'ELF'  'DOG'  'HAT'  'HOG'  'HEN'  'FOX'
```

The nodes in the expression tree in Fig. 10.22 would be visited in the sequence

```
X Y + A B - *
```

The expression above is called a *postfix* expression because each operator follows its operands. The operands of + are X and Y; the operands of − are A and B; the operands of * are the two triples X Y + and A B −.

Note that the left subtree is always traversed before the right subtree for all three methods discussed above.

Self-check Exercises for Section 10.7

1. Draw the binary tree representation of the expression below.

   ```
   X * Y / (A + B) * C
   X * Y / A + B * C
   ```

2. What would be printed by the inorder, preorder, and postorder traversals of the tree below?

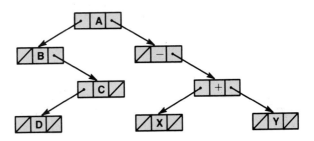

10.8 Case Study—Maintaining a Binary Search Tree

We mentioned earlier that the tree in Fig. 10.23 is a binary search tree. A binary search tree has the property that for any node, all values less than that node's value are in its left subtree and all values greater than that node's value are in its right subtree.

Trying to locate an item in a binary search tree is analogous to performing a binary search on an array that has already been sorted. To find a particular item or *key*, we compare the key to the value of the root node. If the key is less than the root node, then we can eliminate the right subtree and search only the left subtree, thereby reducing by half the number of nodes to be searched. For this reason, the time required to search a binary tree of N nodes is proportional to $\log_2 N$. The algorithm for searching a binary tree is shown below.

Algorithm for binary tree search

1. if the tree is empty then
   2. The key is not in the tree.
   else if the key matches the root node data then
   3. The key is found in the root node.
   else if the key is less than the root node data then
   4. Search the left subtree.
   else
   5. Search the right subtree.

Steps 2 and 3 are stopping steps. We will leave the writing of this procedure as an exercise and describe how to build and maintain a binary search tree next.

Maintaining a Binary Search Tree

Problem: We want to write a concordance program that counts the number of times each word appears in a large TEXT file. After the file is completely read, an alphabetized list of the words and their occurrence counts should be printed.

Discussion: For simplicity, we will assume that each word is on a separate line of the TEXT file. We can use an array of records or a binary search tree to store the words in memory. One advantage of using a binary search tree is that it is already ordered and does not need to be sorted. Each new word that is read will be entered in its proper place in the tree with an initial occurrence count of 1. If the word is already in the tree, its occurrence count should be increased by 1. Once the tree is completed, performing an inorder traversal will enable the nodes to be printed in alphabetical order. The problem inputs, outputs, and algorithm follow.

PROBLEM INPUTS

the file of words, one word per line (WORDS : TEXT)

PROBLEM OUTPUTS

an alphabetized list of words and occurrence counts

Algorithm

1. Store each word in its appropriate place in a binary search tree together with its occurrence count.
2. Perform an inorder traversal of the tree and print each word and its occurrence count.

We can modify procedure INORDER to perform step 2. Step 1 will be performed by procedure BUILDTREE. Each node of the tree must have storage space for a character string, an integer value, and two pointers. The main program variable ROOT will point to the root of the tree. The structure chart is shown in Fig. 10.25; the main program is shown in Fig. 10.26.

We will leave the modification of procedure INORDER as an exercise and discuss procedure BUILDTREE next. Procedure BUILDTREE should store the first word in the node pointed to by ROOT. Each subsequent word should be read and inserted in the tree if it is not already there. The data requirements and algorithm for BUILDTREE follow.

PROCEDURE INPUTS

the file of words (WORDS : TEXT)

a pointer to the root of the tree being formed (ROOT : BRANCH)

the next word in file WORDS (NEXTWORD : LINE)
a pointer to each ancestor of the word being inserted
(ANCESTOR : BRANCH)

Algorithm for BUILDTREE

1. Prepare file WORDS for input.
2. Store the first word in the root of the tree.
3. while there are more words do
   4. Read the next word into NEXTWORD.
   5. Insert NEXTWORD in the tree or increment its occurrence count if NEXTWORD is already in the tree.

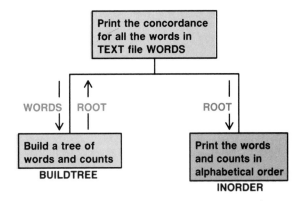

Fig. 10.25 Structure Chart for Concordance Program

```
program CONCORD (WORDS, INPUT, OUTPUT);

{Prints the words in file WORDS and their number of occurrences
 in alphabetical order.                                         }

const
    STRINGSIZE = 10;              {maximum length of a word}

type
    STRING = packed array [1..STRINGSIZE] of CHAR;
    BRANCH = ^TREENODE;
    TREENODE = record
       WORD : STRING;
       COUNT : INTEGER;
       LEFT, RIGHT : BRANCH
    end; {TREENODE}

var
    ROOT : BRANCH;               {pointer to tree root}
    WORDS : TEXT;                {file of words in text}
```

```
{Insert procedures BUILDTREE and INORDER here.}

begin {CONCORD}
   {Build the binary search tree.}
   BUILDTREE (WORDS, ROOT);

   {Print the words and their counts in alphabetical order.}
   WRITELN ('Word' :10, 'Occurrences' :15);
   INORDER (ROOT)
end. {CONCORD}
```

Fig. 10.26 Concordance Program

Procedure READ1LINE (see Fig. 8.6) can be used to read each line of file WORDS. Step 2 will be performed by procedure ATTACHNODE. Step 5 will be performed by procedure PUTINTREE. The structure chart for procedure BUILDTREE is shown in Fig. 10.27; the procedure is written in Fig. 10.28.

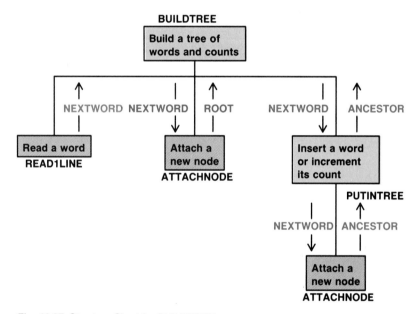

Fig. 10.27 Structure Chart for BUILDTREE

```
procedure BUILDTREE (var WORDS {input} : TEXT;
                     var ROOT {output} : BRANCH);

{Builds a tree of words and occurrence counts based on the words in
 file WORDS. Returns ROOT as a pointer to this tree.                 }

type
   LINE = record
      INFO : STRING;
      LENGTH : 0..STRINGSIZE
   end; {LINE}
```

```
var
    NEXTWORD : LINE;            {each word in WORDS}
    ANCESTOR : BRANCH;         {local pointer}

procedure ATTACHNODE (NEXTWORD {input} : LINE;
                      var ANCESTOR {output} : BRANCH);

{Attaches a new tree node to the pointer ANCESTOR. The WORD field is
defined as the string in NEXTWORD. The COUNT field is 1. Both pointer
fields are initialized to NIL.                                       }

begin {ATTACHNODE}
    NEW (ANCESTOR);                      {attach new tree node to its parent}
    with ANCESTOR^ do
        begin
            WORD := NEXTWORD.INFO;                    {store the word}
            COUNT := 1;                               {initialize COUNT}
            LEFT := NIL;  RIGHT := NIL                {initialize pointers}
        end
end; {ATTACHNODE}

{Insert procedures READ1LINE, PUTINTREE here.}

begin {BUILDTREE}
    RESET (WORDS);                       {prepare WORDS for input}
    READ1LINE (WORDS, NEXTWORD);         {get first word}
    ATTACHNODE (NEXTWORD, ROOT);         {place it in root}

    {Insert rest of words in the tree.}
    while not EOF(WORDS) do
        begin
            READ1LINE (WORDS, NEXTWORD);
            ANCESTOR := ROOT;            {root is first ancestor}
            PUTINTREE (NEXTWORD, ANCESTOR)    {insert next word}
        end {while}
end; {BUILDTREE}
```

Fig. 10.28 Procedure BUILDTREE

After reading the first word into NEXTWORD, procedure BUILDTREE calls ATTACHNODE to attach this word to the pointer ROOT. The remaining words are inserted in the tree by procedure PUTINTREE. After each word is read by READ1LINE, the local pointer variable ANCESTOR is reset to ROOT and is then passed to PUTINTREE. This local variable is needed to prevent PUTINTREE from redefining the tree root whenever it inserts a new node in the tree. The algorithm for PUTINTREE follows.

Algorithm for PUTINTREE

1. if the subtree being searched is empty then
  2. Attach the next word to the parent of this subtree.
   else if the next word is in the subtree root then
  3. Increment the occurrence count by 1.
   else if the next word is alphabetically < the subtree root word then
  4. Insert the next word in the left subtree.
   else
  5. Insert the next word in the right subtree.

Steps 2 and 3 are stopping steps. We will trace this algorithm for the list of words 'the', 'week', 'of', 'the', 'start'. The word 'the' is placed in the root node as shown below.

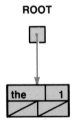

The next string 'week' is alphabetically greater than 'the' so the right pointer from the root node is followed. This subtree is empty so 'week' is attached as the right subtree of the root node. The pointers represented by ANCESTOR during the search are in color.

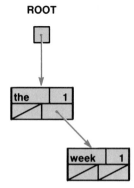

The next string 'of' is alphabetically less than 'the' so the left pointer from the root node is followed. This subtree is empty so 'of' is attached as the left subtree of the root node.

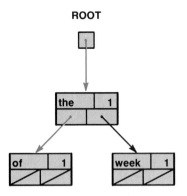

The next word is 'the'. It is found in the root so its count is increased to 2.

The next word is 'start'. It is alphabetically less than 'the' so the left pointer from the root node is followed. The word 'start' is alphabetically greater than 'of' so the right pointer from 'of' is followed. This subtree is empty so 'start' is attached as the right subtree of the node containing 'of'. Procedure PUTINTREE is shown in Fig. 10.29.

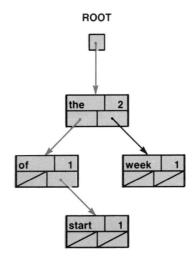

```
procedure PUTINTREE (NEXTWORD {input} : LINE;
                     var ANCESTOR {input/output} : BRANCH);

{Inserts the string in NEXTWORD in the tree if it is not already in the
 tree pointed to by ANCESTOR. Otherwise, increments its count. Uses
 procedure ATTACHNODE to attach a new node.                          }

begin {PUTINTREE}
   if ANCESTOR = NIL then
      ATTACHNODE (NEXTWORD, ANCESTOR)          {attach word to its parent}
   else if NEXTWORD.INFO = ANCESTOR^.WORD then
      ANCESTOR^.COUNT := ANCESTOR^.COUNT + 1          {increase count by 1}
   else if NEXTWORD.INFO < ANCESTOR^.WORD then
      PUTINTREE (NEXTWORD, ANCESTOR^.LEFT)          {follow left pointer}
   else
      PUTINTREE (NEXTWORD, ANCESTOR^.RIGHT)          {follow right pointer}
end; {PUTINTREE}
```

Fig. 10.29 Procedure PUTINTREE

If the value of ANCESTOR becomes NIL, procedure PUTINTREE calls procedure ATTACHNODE (see Fig. 10.28) to attach a new node to the tree. ATTACHNODE changes the value of the pointer represented by ANCESTOR so that it points to a newly allocated node.

Self-check Exercises for Section 10.8

1. Modify procedure INORDER as needed to print the words and their counts.
2. Continue to grow the tree in this section by processing the words: 'of', 'the', 'first', 'semester', 'is', 'next', 'week'.

Draw the tree.

3. Write the algorithm for searching a binary tree as a function. Return a pointer to the node containing the key or NIL. Hint: See Fig. 10.4.

10.9 Common Programming Errors

It is often very difficult to debug a program involving pointer variables since the value of a pointer variable represents a memory cell address and cannot normally be printed. Hence, if a pointer value is invalid or incorrect, there may be no way of finding out what this erroneous value happens to be.

Make sure that the symbol ^ follows each pointer variable used to designate a particular node or record. The ^ must always be written when you wish to manipulate a field of a node. If the pointer variable appears without the ^, the compiler will maniplate the pointer value itself (an address) rather than the node pointed to by the pointer variable.

Another potential source of error involves attempting to reference a field of a node pointed to by a pointer whose value is NIL. This, of course, is illegal since the NIL pointer is a special value used to indicate the end of a list.

An additional error may arise if your program gets stuck in a loop during the creation of a dynamic data structure. In this case, the number of cells allocated may exceed the memory space available in your Pascal system. This condition will result in a "stack overflow" error message.

When traversing a list, make sure that the pointer to the list head is advanced down the list. The while statement below

```
while HEAD <> NIL do
   WRITE (HEAD^.WORD);
   HEAD := HEAD^.LINK
```

will execute forever because the pointer assignment statement is not included in the loop body so HEAD will not be advanced down the list.

Debugging Tips

Because the value of a pointer variable cannot be printed, it is difficult to debug programs that manipulate pointers. You will have to trace the execution of such a program by printing an information field that identifies the list element referenced by the pointer instead of printing the pointer value itself.

When writing driver programs it is often helpful to create a sample linked structure using the technique shown at the beginning of Section 10.4. The information and pointer fields of the structure can be defined using assignment statements.

10.10 Chapter Review

In this chapter, we introduced several dynamic data structures. We discussed the use of pointers to reference and connect elements of a dynamic data structure. The procedure NEW was used to allocate additional elements or nodes of a dynamic data structure.

Many different aspects of manipulating linked lists were covered. We showed how to build or create a linked list, how to traverse a linked list, and how to insert and delete linked list elements.

We also described how to implement stacks and queues. Procedures were written to add and remove elements from these data structures.

The tree was shown to be a special list form with two links. We showed how to create a binary search tree and how to perform three kinds of tree traversal: inorder, preorder, and postorder. If you continue your study of computer science, all of these subjects will be covered in much more detail in a future course on data structures.

New Pascal Statements

The new Pascal statements introduced in this chapter are described in Table 10.1.

Table 10.1 Summary of New Pascal Statements

Statement	Effect

Pointer type declaration
`type`
`    POINT = ^NODE;`
`    NODE = record`
`        INFO : INTEGER;`
`        LINK : POINT`
`    end;`
`var`
`    HEAD : POINT;`
	The identifier `POINT` is declared as a pointer to a record of type NODE where NODE is a record type containing a field (`LINK`) of type `POINT`. HEAD is a pointer variable of type `POINT`.

NEW statement `    NEW (HEAD)`	A new record is allocated of type NODE. This record is pointed to by HEAD and may be referenced as record variable HEAD^.
DISPOSE statement `    DISPOSE (HEAD)`	The memory space occupied by the record HEAD^ is returned to the storage pool.
Pointer assignment `    HEAD := HEAD^.LINK`	The pointer HEAD is advanced to the next node in the dynamic data structure pointed to by HEAD.

Review Questions

1. Differentiate between dynamic and nondynamic data structures.
2. What kind of value is contained in a pointer variable?
3. Give the necessary statements to create a pointer variable Q that points to a record type NUMBERS consisting of three integer fields called A, B, and C. Also indicate at what point actual space is allocated for Q and one occurrence of NUMBERS.
4. Define a simple linked list. Indicate how the pointers are utilized to establish a link between nodes. Also indicate any other variables that would be needed to reference the linked list.
5. Write a procedure that will link a node into an existing list. Parameters will be the HEAD of the linked list and a pointer to the node to be inserted. Assume a dummy record exists at the beginning and end of the linked list and there are no duplicate records.

   Given the following record definition, insert the new element preserving ID order:

   ```
   type
       PTR = ^NODE;
       NODE = record
           ID : INTEGER;
           NAME : STRING;
           GPA : REAL;
           LINK : PTR
       end;
   ```

6. Write an algorithm to remove a node (identified by TARGETID) from an ordered list that does not contain a dummy record at the beginning.
7. Write the necessary procedures to duplicate all elements with a GPA of 3.5 or above in one linked list in another linked list. The original list is ordered by ID number; the new list should be ordered by GPA. Do not remove nodes from the existing list. Assume the list nodes are type NODE as described below.

   Parameters will be the head of the existing list (HEAD) and the head of the new linked list (GPAHEAD).

   ```
   type
       PTR = ^NODE;
       NODE = record
           ID : INTEGER;
           NAME : STRING;
           GPA : REAL;
           LINK : PTR
       end;
   ```

8. Declare a node for a two-way or doubly linked list, and indicate how a traversal would be made in reverse order (from the last list element to the list head). Include any variables or fields that are necessary.
9. Discuss the differences between a simple linked list and a binary tree. Consider such things as numbers of pointer fields per node, search technique, and insertion algorithm.

10. Write a procedure to delete all males over 25 from an existing linear linked list, given the following global statements (assume no dummy records).

```
type
    PTR = ^NODE;
    NODE = record
        NAME : STRING;
        AGE : INTEGER;
        SEX : (MALE,FEMALE);
        LINK : PTR
    end;
```

The procedure parameter is the head of the list.

11. How can you determine whether a node is a leaf?

12. Traverse the tree below in inorder, preorder, and postorder.

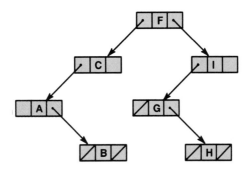

Provide one sequence that would create this ordered binary tree. Are there any letters that must occur before other letters?

13. Discuss how you might delete a node from a binary tree. Consider nodes with 0 or 1 child first.

Programming Projects

1. Write a main program that first builds an airline passenger list in alphabetical order from passenger data provided on an input file. The program should next process commands read from system file INPUT to modify this list. The first letter of each command indicates what is to be done with any passenger data on that input line (I—Insert, D—Delete, R—Replace flight data, P—Print all passengers, Q—Quit). After the Q command is entered, the program system should display the final passenger list.

2. Redo the problem in Section 10.5 using a tree to store the passenger data. When deleting a passenger, simply blank out the information fields and leave the passenger node in the tree. Use an extra data field to indicate whether a node is still in the tree or deleted.

3. Write a program to moniter the flow of an item into and out of a warehouse. The warehouse will have numerous deliveries and shipments for this item (a

widget) during the time period covered. A shipment out is billed at a profit of 50% over the cost of a widget. Unfortunately, each shipment received may have a different cost associated with it. The accountants for the firm have instituted a first-in, first-out system for filling orders. This means that the newest widgets are the first ones sent out to fill an order. This method of inventory can be represented using a stack. The PUSH procedure will add a shipment received. The POP procedure will be used for a shipment out. Each data record will consist of:

S or O — for shipment received or an order to be sent
\# — a quantity received or shipped out
Cost — the cost per widget (for a shipment received only)
Vendor — character string naming company sent to or received from.

Write the necessary procedures to store the shipments received and process orders. The output for an order will consist of the total cost for all the widgets in the order as well as the quantity. *Hint:* Each widget price is 50% higher than its cost. The widgets used to fill an order may come from multiple shipments with different costs.

4. Redo Project 3, assuming the widgets are shipped using a first-in, first-out strategy. Use a queue to store the widget orders.

5. At Bob's Bank a program is needed to store the checks processed during a month for a customer. Since the checks will be processed daily, but not in numerical order, it is best to store them in a simple linked list by check number.
   Write a program that will input a check number, date of transaction, amount of check, and the name of the person receiving the check. Insert the checks into a list and after all checks have been entered, display all of the checks with all associated information, and a final total for all the checks written during the month.

6. In preparing mailing lists, it is often useful to be able to reference the information by using either the person's name or zipcode. This can be done if each list node has a pointer to the next node by name and a pointer to the next node by zipcode. The nodes representing each person's data should be linked together in both name and zipcode order; there should only be one copy of the data for each person.
   First the information can be inserted in a list by name order using a pointer field called NEXTNAME. Then the pointer field NEXTZIPCODE can be defined so that the new list node is also in zipcode order. There should be a list head that points to the first person in name order and a second list head that points to the first person in zipcode order.
   Write a program that reads a record containing first name (character 10), last name (character 15), street address (character 50), city (character 20), state (character 2), and zipcode (character 6) and inserts each record into the lists. After all of the information has been entered, provide a list of the information in name order and a second list in zipcode order.

7. The set capability is limited in the number of elements that can be stored in a set (often only 255). A more universal system can be implemented using list representation to store sets.

Write the necessary routines needed to insert and delete integer values from a set. Also write the routines necessary to implement the set difference, intersection, and union operations. To verify the results, list the contents of the sets before and after each operation.

8. Many card games require that each of four players receive 13 cards of a 52 card deck (for example: bridge). The computer can be utilized to shuffle a deck of cards and then deal them.

To accomplish this first place all 52 cards into a linked list. Afterwards, "deal" the cards to 4 players by generating a random number between 1 and the size of the list remaining. Traverse the linked list and delete the selected card from the list. Each player's hand will consist of a record that has pointers to a list of hearts, diamonds, clubs, and spades in ascending order. (i.e. You will need 4 pointer fields). After all cards are dealt, list the contents (by suit) of each hand.

9. In this chapter we wrote recursive procedures to perform preorder, inorder, and postorder tree traversals. A tree traversal can be written without using recursion. In this case it is necessary to push the address of a tree node that is reached during the traversal onto a stack. The node will be popped off later when it is time to traverse the tree rooted at this node. For example, the algorithm for a nonrecursive preorder traversal follows.

1. Push NIL onto the stack.
2. Assign the root node as the current node.
3. while the current node is not NIL do
    4. Print the current node.
    5. if the current node has a right subtree then
        Push the right subtree root onto the stack.
    6. If the current node has a left subtree then
        Make it the current node
      else
        Pop the stack and make the node removed the
        current node.

In this algorithm each right subtree pointer that is not NIL is pushed onto the stack; the stack is popped when the current left subtree pointer is NIL.

Implement and test a nonrecursive procedure for preorder traversal. Write a nonrecursive algorithm for inorder traversal and implement and test it as well.

10. If an arithmetic expression is written in prefix or postfix notation, then there is no need to use parentheses to specify the order of operator evaluation. For this reason, some compilers translate infix expressions to postfix notation first and then evaluate the postfix string.

Write a procedure that simulates the operation of a calculator. The input will consist of an expression in postfix notation. The operands will all be single digit numbers. Your program should print the expression value. For example, if the input string is '54+3/', the result printed should be ((5 + 4) / 3) or 3.

To accomplish this, examine each character in the string in left to right order. If the character is a digit, push its numeric value onto a stack. If the character is an operator, pop the top two operands, apply the operator to them, and push the result onto the stack. When the string is completely scanned there should only be one number on the stack and that should be the expression value. Besides the operators +, −, *, and /, use the operator ^ to indicate exponentiation.

11. There are many applications in which a two-dimensional matrix with large dimensions must be stored in memory. If a majority of the elements in the matrix are zero, the matrix is called a sparse matrix. A sparse matrix may be more efficiently represented using a one-dimensional array of pointers where each element of this array, ROW, points to a linked list. ROW[I] would point to a list whose nodes indicate the value and column number for each nonzero element in row I. For example, if row 3 is (25 0 0 0 −14 0 0), then the third element of this array would point to the list shown below.

ROW[3]

This list indicates that there are two nonzero elements in the third row of the sparse matrix at columns 1 and 5. Write procedures to read a sparse matrix and store it as shown, to add together two sparse matrices and to print a sparse matrix.

12. A polynomial may be represented as a linked list where each node contains the coefficient and exponent of a term of the polynomial. The polynomial $4x^3 + 3x^2 − 5$ would be represented as the linked list.

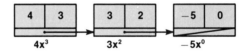

$4x^3$ $3x^2$ $−5x^0$

Write a program system that reads two polynomials, stores them as linked lists, adds them together, and prints the result as a polynomial. The result should be a third linked list. Hint: Traverse both polynomials. If a particular exponent value is present in either of the two polynomials being summed, then it should be present in the answer. If it is present in both polynomials, then its coefficient is the sum of the corresponding coefficient in both polynomials. (If this sum is zero, the term should be deleted.)

13. Assume that the registration data for a class of students is stored as the array of records shown below.

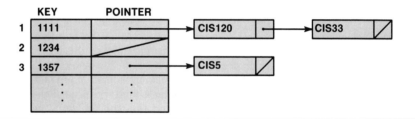

KEY   POINTER

The first field in each record contains the student ID number (four digits) and the second field contains a pointer to all classes for which the student is registered. Write a program system that builds this array from a file of randomly arranged data and prints it out. Assume each data line starts with an I (insert) or D (delete), followed by the student ID and course identification string.

14. Write a program system that represents the Morse code as a binary tree. The symbol · should cause a branch to the left and the symbol − a branch to the right. The information field of each node should be the letter represented by the corresponding code. The first three levels of the tree are shown below.

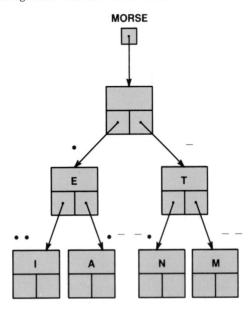

The Morse code should be read from an input file where each file component consists of a letter, and the corresponding code string. After building the tree, read a coded message and translate it into English.

15. Use two stacks (OPERATOR and OPERAND) and procedures PUSH and POP to help in "compiling" a simple arithmetic expression without parentheses. For example, the expression

$$A + B * C - D$$

should be compiled as the table:

OPERATION	OPERAND1	OPERAND2	RESULT
*	B	C	Z
+	A	Z	Y
−	Y	D	X

The above table shows the order of the three operations (*, +, −) and their operands. The result column gives the name of an identifier selected to hold the result.

Your procedure should read each character (NEXTCHAR) and process it as follows: If it is a blank, then ignore it; otherwise, if it is an operand (A—F), then push it onto the OPERAND stack; otherwise, if it is not an operator (+, −, *, /), then print an error message. If the character is an operator, then it should be pushed onto the OPERATOR stack if its precedence is greater than the operator currently at the top of the stack (e.g., when * is read in the example above, it is pushed onto the stack because + is on the top) or if the operator stack is empty. Otherwise, a line of the output table should be written by popping the OPERATOR stack and removing the first two elements of the OPERAND stack (two pops). A new symbol is used to hold the result (Z—G), and this symbol is pushed onto the operand stack. The process of generating output table lines continues until the precedence of NEXTCHAR is greater than the precedence of the operator at the top of the stack or the operator stack is empty. At this point, NEXTCHAR should be pushed onto the operator stack. When the end of the input line is reached, any remaining operators and operands should be popped as described above.

Appendixes

Appendix A
Reserved Words, Standard Identifiers, Operators, Functions, and Procedures

Reserved words

and	end	nil	set
array	file	not	then
begin	for	of	to
case	function	or	type
const	goto	packed	until
div	if	procedure	var
do	in	program	while
downto	label	record	with
else	mod	repeat	

Standard identifiers

Constants:
  FALSE, TRUE, MAXINT

Types:
  INTEGER, BOOLEAN, REAL, CHAR, TEXT

Program parameters:
  INPUT, OUTPUT

Functions:
  ABS, ARCTAN, CHR, COS, EOF, EOLN, EXP, LN, ODD, ORD,
  PRED, ROUND, SIN, SQR, SQRT, SUCC, TRUNC

Procedures:
  GET, NEW, PACK, PAGE, PUT, READ, READLN, RESET,
  REWRITE, UNPACK, WRITE, WRITELN

Table A.1 Table of Operators

Operator	Operation	Type of Operand(s)	Result type
:=	assignment	any type except file types	—
arithmetic:			
+ (unary)	identity	integer or real	same as
– (unary)	sign inversion		operand
+	addition	integer or real	integer or real
–	subtraction		
*	multiplication		
div	integer division	integer	integer
/	real division	integer or real	real
mod	modulus	integer	integer
relational:			
=	equality	scalar, string, set,	
<>	inequality	or pointer	
<	less than	scalar or string	BOOLEAN
>	greater than		
<=	less than or equal	scalar or string	
	-or-		
	subset	set	
>=	greater than or equal	scalar or string	
	-or-		
	superset	set	
in	set membership	first operand is any scalar, the second is its set type	
logical:			
not	negation		
or	disjunction	BOOLEAN	BOOLEAN
and	conjunction		
set:			
+	union		
–	set difference	any set type T	T
*	intersection		

Table A.2 Standard Functions

Name	Description of Computation	Argument	Result
ABS	The absolute value of the argument	real/integer	same as argument
EXP	The value of e (2.71828) raised to the power of the argument	real/integer	real
LN	The logarithm (to the base e) of the argument	real/integer	real
SQR	The square of the argument	real/integer	same as argument
SQRT	The positive square root of the argument	real/integer (positive)	real
ROUND	The closest integer value to the argument	real	integer
TRUNC	The integral part of the argument	real	integer
ARCTAN	The arc tangent of the argument	real/integer (radians)	real
COS	The cosine of the argument	real/integer (radians)	real
SIN	The sine of the argument	real/integer (radians)	real
CHR	Returns the character whose ordinal number is its argument	integer	CHAR
ODD	Returns TRUE if its argument is an odd number; otherwise returns FALSE	integer	BOOLEAN
ORD	Returns the ordinal number of its argument	ordinal	integer
PRED	Returns the predecessor of its argument	ordinal	ordinal
SUCC	Returns the successor of its argument	ordinal	ordinal

Table A.3 Table of Standard Procedures

Procedure Call	Description
DISPOSE (P)	Returns the record pointed to by pointer variable P to free storage.
GET (F)	Advances the file position pointer for file F to its next component and assigns the value of the component to F^.
NEW (P)	Creates a record of the type pointed to by pointer P and saves its address in P.
PACK (U, I, P)	Copies the elements in unpacked array U, starting with U[I], to packed array P, starting with the first element.
PAGE (F)	Advances the printer to a new page before printing the next line of file F.
PUT (F)	Appends the current contents of F^ to file F.
READ (F, *variables*)	Reads data from file F to satisfy the list of *variables*. Only one component of file F can be read unless F is a text file. If F is not specified, file INPUT is read.
READLN (F, *variables*)	Reads data from text file F to satisfy the list of *variables*. Skips any characters at the end of the last line read.
RESET (F)	Resets the file position pointer for file F to the beginning. File F may then be read.
REWRITE (F)	Resets the file position pointer for file F to the beginning; any prior contents are lost. File F may then be written.
UNPACK (P, U, I)	Copies the elements in packed array P, starting with the first element, to unpacked array U, starting with U[I].
WRITE (F, *outputs*)	Writes the data in the order specified by *outputs* to file F. Only one output item can be written unless F is a text file. If F is not specified, the data are written to file OUTPUT.
WRITELN (F, *outputs*)	Writes the data in the order specified by *outputs* to text file F. Writes an end-of-line mark after the data.

Appendix B
Additions and Extensions to Pascal

B.1 Additional Features of ANSI/IEEE Pascal

This appendix describes additional features of the ANSI/IEEE Pascal standard not covered in the text.

Forward Declarations

Given the procedure declarations below, procedure B can call A, but procedure A cannot call B. This is because the declaration for procedure B is not processed until after procedure A is translated.

```
procedure A (var X : REAL);
. . . . . . . . .
end; {A}

procedure B (var Y : REAL);
. . . . . . . . .
end; {B}
```

If a *forward declaration* for procedure B is inserted before procedure A, then A can also call B.

```
procedure B (var Y : REAL); FORWARD;

procedure A (var X : REAL);
. . . . . . . . .
end; {A}

procedure B;
. . . . . . . . .
end; {B}
```

As shown above, the forward declaration for procedure B consisting of only the procedure heading comes first, followed by the declaration of procedure A, and finally the declaration for procedure B. The parameter list for procedure B appears only in the forward declaration. Now procedure A can call B, and procedure B can call A; so A and B are called *mutually recursive*.

Functions and Procedures as Parameters

A procedure or function may be passed as a parameter to another procedure or function. As an example, we may wish to compute the sum below for the integers 1 through N where f represents a function that is applied to each integer.

$$f(1) + f(2) + f(3) + ... + f(N)$$

If f is the function SQR (square), then we wish to compute the sum
a) $1 + 2^2 + 3^2 + ... + N^2$

If f is the function SQRT (square root), then we wish to compute the sum
b) $\sqrt{1} + \sqrt{2} + \sqrt{3} + ... + \sqrt{N}$

In function SUMINT below, the function F is declared as a *function parameter*. The function designator

```
SUMINT (SQR, 10)
```

computes sum a) above for N = 10; the function designator

```
SUMINT (SQRT, 10)
```

computes sum b) above for N = 10.

```
function SUMINT (function F(X : INTEGER) : REAL;
                 N : INTEGER) : REAL;

{Computes F(1) + F(2) + . . . + F(N).}

var
    SUM : REAL;                      {the partial sum}
    I : INTEGER;                     {loop control variable}

begin {SUMINT}
    SUM := 0.0;                      {initialize SUM}

    for I := 1 to N do
        SUM := SUM + F(I);

    SUMINT := SUM                    {define result}
end;   {SUMINT}
```

The parameter of function F is represented by X in the heading for function SUMINT; any identifier may be used. F can also represent a user-defined function with one type INTEGER parameter.

GOTO Statements and Labels

The GOTO statement is used to transfer control from one program statement to another. The label (a positive integer) is used to indicate the statement to which control is transferred. Labels must be declared in label declaration statements at the beginning of a block. In function SAMEARRAY below, the GOTO statement is used to exit a for loop before the specified number of repetitions (N) are performed.

```
function SAMEARRAY (A, B : REALARRAY;
                    N : INTEGER) : BOOLEAN;
{Returns TRUE if arrays A[1..N] and B[1..N] are the same array.}

label 100;

var
    I : INTEGER;                    {loop control variable}

begin {SAMEARRAY}
    SAMEARRAY := FALSE;            {assume arrays are not the same}

    {Compare elements 1..N until an unequal pair is found.}
    for I := 1 to N do
       if A[I] <> B[I] then
          GOTO 100;

    {assert: arrays A and B are equal.}
    SAMEARRAY := TRUE;

100: {return from function}
    end; {SAMEARRAY}
```

The function result is initialized to FALSE and corresponding array elements are compared in the for loop. If an unequal pair of elements is found, the loop is exited via an immediate transfer of control to label 100. If all pairs are equal, the loop is exited after the Nth pair is tested and the function result is set to TRUE. This function can easily be implemented without using the GOTO (see Fig. 6.9 and 9.15); computer scientists generally avoid using the GOTO except when absolutely necessary.

PACK and UNPACK

The standard procedures PACK and UNPACK are used to transfer data between packed and unpacked arrays. Given the declarations

```
var
    PA : packed array [1..N] of CHAR;
    UA : array [1..M] of CHAR;
    I : INTEGER;
```

the procedure (call) statement

```
PACK (UA, I, PA)
```

copies elements from unpacked array UA (starting with UA[I]) to packed array PA (starting with PA[1]). The procedure (call) statement

```
UNPACK (PA, UA, I)
```

copies elements from packed array PA (starting with PA[1]) to unpacked array UA (starting with UA[I]). Arrays PA and UA do not have to be the same size.

B.2 ISO Pascal

This appendix describes a feature of the Pascal standard approved by the International Organization for Standardization (ISO Pascal) that is not included in the ANSI/IEEE standard.

Conformant Array Parameters

One of the principal frustrations in using ANSI/IEEE standard Pascal is the fact that a function or procedure that manipulates an array of one type cannot also manipulate an array of a similar type. For example, a procedure that manipulates array NAME declared below cannot manipulate array FLOWER because the arrays have different types.

```
type
    STRING1 = packed array [1..20] of CHAR;
    STRING2 = packed array [1..8] of CHAR;

var
    NAME : STRING1;
    FLOWER : STRING2;
```

Even though the only difference between these two arrays is their size (number of elements), separate procedures would have to be written to read data into them.

In ISO Pascal, the *conformant array schema*

```
packed array [U..V : INTEGER] of CHAR
```

describes a packed array of characters whose subscript type is a subrange of type INTEGER. The use of this schema in the procedure header below enables procedure READSTRING to read data into a packed array of characters (represented by INSTRING) of any size (represented by STRINGSIZE).

```
procedure READSTRING (SIZE {input} : INTEGER;
    var INSTRING {output} : packed array [U..V : INTEGER] of CHAR);
```

In ISO Pascal, the procedure (call) statement

```
READSTRING (20, NAME)
```

could be used to read up to twenty characters into array NAME; the procedure (call) statement

```
READSTRING (8, FLOWER)
```

could be used to read up to eight characters into array FLOWER.

Any identifiers can be used in the declaration of the index-type specification [U..V : INTEGER] for INSTRING. The data type listed (INTEGER) must be an ordinal type.

Conformant array schemas can be used with packed and unpacked arrays of any element type, not just CHAR. Conformant array schemas can also be used with multidimensional arrays. The two-dimensional conformant array schema below is valid if MONTH is declared as an enumerated type.

```
array [U..V : INTEGER; J..K : MONTH] of REAL;
```

The corresponding actual parameter must be a two dimensional array of type REAL values. The first subscript type must be a subrange of the integers; the second subscript type must be a subrange of type MONTH.

B.3 UCSD Pascal*

UCSD Pascal is a complete operating system that includes facilities for editing and saving files as well as a Pascal compiler. This section covers some of the differences between UCSD Pascal and standard Pascal with emphasis on string and file processing.

Identifiers in UCSD Pascal

There are a number of additional reserved words and standard identifiers in UCSD Pascal. The reserved words are listed below followed by the standard identifiers discussed in this section.

Additional reserved words

external	implementation	interface	process	segment
separate	unit	uses		

Selected standard identifiers

CLOSE	CONCAT	COPY	CRUNCH	DELETE	INSERT
INTERACTIVE	LENGTH	LOCK	NORMAL	POS	PURGE
STRING					

UCSD Pascal uses only the first eight characters of an identifier to determine uniqueness. The underscore character (_) can appear in an identifier but it is not considered one of the eight characters (i.e. TOP_SCORE and TOPSCORE are the same identifier).

String Manipulation in UCSD Pascal

One of the most important extensions of UCSD Pascal is the inclusion of the data type STRING. In UCSD Pascal, the declarations

---

*UCSD Pascal is a trademark of the regents of the University of California.

```
var
    PUPILNAME, TEACHERNAME : STRING;
```

allocate space for storage of two character strings of up to eighty characters each. The procedure READLN can be used to read data into a variable of type STRING.

```
WRITE ('Enter the name of the teacher: ');
READLN (TEACHERNAME);
```

After the prompt above is displayed, all characters (up to 80) entered before pressing the <Return> key are stored in TEACHERNAME.

UCSD Pascal keeps track of the actual length of the string stored in TEACHERNAME. The string length can change dynamically as the string is manipulated. The assignment statement

```
TEACHERNAME := 'Mr. Chips'
```

replaces the string stored in TEACHERNAME with a new string. The function LENGTH can be used to determine the current string length. The statement

```
WRITELN ('The number of characters in ', TEACHERNAME, ' is ',
    LENGTH(TEACHERNAME) :2)
```

displays the line

```
The number of characters in Mr. Chips is 9
```

It is possible to set the maximum string size at any length up to 255 characters. The declarations below provide storage space for one string of up to ten characters and one string of up to 255 characters.

```
var
    WORD : STRING[10];
    PARAGRAPH : STRING[255];
```

Strings of different sizes can be manipulated together. The first assignment statement below stores the string shown on the right in PARAGRAPH. The second assignment statement stores the ten character substring 'This is a ' in WORD. This substring replaces the string originally saved in PARAGRAPH when the third assignment statement is executed.

```
PARAGRAPH := 'This is a very, very long string';
WORD := PARAGRAPH;
PARAGRAPH := WORD
```

Because the STRING data type is part of UCSD Pascal, it is not necessary to declare your own data type STRING or to write procedures such as READSTRING (see Fig. 6.15) and READLINE (see Fig. 7.23) to enter string data. Consequently, the programs in Chapters 6 through 10 that manipulate strings can all be rewritten to take advantage of this. The type declaration

```
type
    STRING = packed array [1..STRINGSIZE] of CHAR;
```

should be deleted since STRING is a predefined data type. The procedure READLN can be used to enter each data string instead of READSTRING or READLINE.

In Section 7.10, we wrote a number of procedures that manipulate character strings. These operations are all performed by standard functions in UCSD Pascal as described in Table B.1. All arguments ending with *-string* are type STRING; all other arguments are type INTEGER.

Table B.1 Table of String Manipulation Functions

Function	Description
CONCAT (*string-list*)	Returns a string formed by concatenating the strings in *string-list*. The *string-list* consists of any number of strings separated by commas.
CONCAT ('X', ' + ', 'y')	Result is 'X + y'.
COPY (*source-string*, *index, size*)	Returns a string of *size* characters taken from *source-string* starting at position *index*. The *source-string* is unchanged.
COPY ('HI HO', 4, 2)	Result is 'HO'.
POS (*target-string*, *source-string*)	Returns the starting position (an integer) of the first occurrence of *target-string* in *source-string*. Returns 0 if *target-string* is not found.
POS ('Find me', 'me')	Result is 6.

There are two string-manipulation procedures in UCSD Pascal. They are described in Table B.2 and illustrated. The examples assume that STR1 is 'Mr. & Mrs. Jones' and STR2 is 'The day'.

To illustrate the use of these functions and procedures, we will write two versions of procedure REPLACE. Procedure REPLACE replaces all occurrences of a *target-string* in a *source-string* with a *pattern-string*. For example, the procedure (call) statement

```
REPLACE ('Pascal', 'UCSD Pascal', TEXTSTRING)
```

would replace all occurrences of 'Pascal' in TEXTSTRING by 'UCSD Pascal'.

The first implementation (see Fig. B.1) uses the standard functions; the second implementation (see Fig. B.2) uses the standard procedures. In both

Table B.2 Table of String Manipulation Procedures

Procedure	Description
DELETE (*source-string*, *index*, *size*)	Removes the next *size* characters from *source-string* starting with the character at position *index*.
DELETE (STR1, 5, 7)	The new value of STR1 is 'Mr. Jones'.
INSERT (*pattern-string*, *source-string*, *index*)	Inserts the *pattern-string* at position *index* of *source-string*.
INSERT (STR2, 'next', 5)	The new value of STR2 is 'The next day'.

implementations, the while loop is repeated as long as the string TARGET is still present in the string SOURCE. The loop body replaces each occurrence of TARGET with PATTERN and finds the next occurrence of TARGET in SOURCE.

```
procedure REPLACE (TARGET, PATTERN {input} : STRING;
                   var SOURCE {input/output} : STRING);

{Replaces each occurrence of TARGET in SOURCE by PATTERN.}

var
   INDEX : INTEGER;      {the position of TARGET if found}
   HEAD,                 {the substring of SOURCE preceding TARGET}
   TAIL : STRING;        {the substring of SOURCE following TARGET}

begin {REPLACE}
   {Find each occurrence of TARGET and replace it with PATTERN.}
   INDEX := POS(TARGET, SOURCE);                {find first occurrence}
   while INDEX <> 0 do
      begin
         {Get the head of the string SOURCE.}
         HEAD := COPY(SOURCE, 1, INDEX-1);
         {Get the tail of the string SOURCE.}
         TAIL := COPY(SOURCE, INDEX+LENGTH(TARGET),
                   LENGTH(SOURCE)-INDEX-LENGTH(TARGET)+1);
         {Concatenate HEAD, PATTERN, and TAIL.}
         SOURCE := CONCAT(HEAD, PATTERN, TAIL);
         INDEX := POS(TARGET, SOURCE)           {find next occurrence}
      end {while}
end; {REPLACE}
```

Fig. B.1 Procedure REPLACE Using Standard Functions

Fig. B.2 Procedure REPLACE Using Standard Procedures

```
procedure REPLACE (TARGET, PATTERN {input} : STRING;
                   var SOURCE {input/output} : STRING);

{Replaces each occurrence of TARGET in SOURCE by PATTERN.}
```

```
var
    INDEX : INTEGER;        {the position of TARGET if found}
    HEAD,                   {the substring of SOURCE preceding TARGET}
    TAIL : STRING;          {the substring of SOURCE following TARGET}

begin {REPLACE}
    {Find each occurrence of TARGET and replace it with PATTERN.}
    INDEX := POS(TARGET, SOURCE);               {find first occurrence}
    while INDEX <> 0 do
        begin
            DELETE (SOURCE, INDEX, LENGTH(TARGET));     {delete TARGET}
            INSERT (PATTERN, SOURCE, INDEX);            {insert PATTERN}
            INDEX := POS(TARGET, SOURCE)            {find next occurrence}
        end {while}
end; {REPLACE}
```

Compiler Directives in UCSD Pascal

A special form of comment called a *pseudo comment* may be used to set *option switches* in the UCSD Pascal compiler. Each pseudo comment begins with the symbol $. One particulary useful option switch directs the compiler to insert a disk file into the source program being compiled. The comment

```
{$I PROCESS}
```

causes the file PROCESS to be inserted where the comment occurs in the program. This enables the programmer to save procedures and functions in separate files and pull these files together at a later time.

Sequential File Manipulation in UCSD Pascal

There are a few differences in the way sequential files are processed in UCSD Pascal. There are two predefined file types in UCSD Pascal: TEXT and INTERACTIVE. The system files INPUT and OUTPUT are predeclared as type INTERACTIVE. If CH is type CHAR, the operation READ (CH) is implemented as

```
GET (INPUT);
CH := INPUT^
```

This is the reverse of the order for a TEXT file (see Section 8.8) and facilitates interactive data entry in UCSD Pascal.

The RESET and REWRITE statements have a slightly different form in UCSD Pascal. The first statement on Ap-14 associates the internal file name INFILE with the directory name 'MYDATA' and prepares this file for input. The second statement Ap-14 associates the internal file name OUTFILE with the directory name 'NEWDATA' and prepares this file for output.

```
RESET (INFILE, 'MYDATA');          {prepare INFILE for input}
REWRITE (OUTFILE, 'NEWDATA');    {prepare OUTFILE for output}
```

The internal file names must be referenced in the program. The if statement

```
if not EOF(INFILE) then
   begin
      READ (INFILE, NEXT_RECORD);
      WRITE (OUTFILE, NEXT_RECORD)
   end;
```

copies a record from file INFILE to file OUTFILE using NEXT_RECORD as an intermediary.

After file processing is finished, the statements

```
CLOSE (INFILE, NORMAL);
CLOSE (OUTFILE, LOCK)
```

should be used to update the disk directory. Failure to do so may result in a newly created file being lost.

The second parameter of the CLOSE statement specifies the disposition of the file being closed as explained in Table B.3. The LOCK parameter should be used to save a newly created file. If the program does not close an opened file, the system performs a CLOSE(*file*, NORMAL) operation on that file.

Table B.3 Table of CLOSE Options

CLOSE *Statement*	*Effect*
CLOSE (*file*, NORMAL) CLOSE (*file*)	The *file* is closed and has the same contents that it had before it was opened.
CLOSE (*file*, LOCK)	The *file* is closed and its contents as changed by the program is saved.
CLOSE (*file*, PURGE)	The *file* is closed and is removed from the disk directory.
CLOSE (*file*, CRUNCH)	The *file* is closed and all records following the last one accessed are deleted.

The directory name may be read into a string variable during program execution. If INNAME is type STRING, then the statements below associate the directory file specified by the program user with file INFILE.

```
WRITE ('Enter directory name of file to be copied: ');
READLN (INNAME);                  {read the directory name}
RESET (INFILE, INNAME)            {prepare INFILE for input}
```

TURBO Pascal*

TURBO Pascal is another version of Pascal that is available on personal computers. Like UCSD Pascal, TURBO Pascal provides facilities for editing and saving files. The text editor in TURBO Pascal uses many of the commands found in the popular WordStar[†] word processing program.

Identifiers in TURBO Pascal

There are a number of additional reserved words and standard identifiers in TURBO Pascal. The reserved words are listed below followed by the standard identifiers discussed in this section.

Additional reserved words
```
absolute    external    inline    shl    shr    string    xor
```

Selected standard identifiers
```
CLOSE    CONCAT    COPY    DELETE    INSERT    LENGTH    POS
```

An identifier may consist of up to 127 characters. The underscore character (_) can appear in an identifier.

The case Statement in TURBO Pascal

The case statement in TURBO Pascal has been extended to include an else clause. This clause is executed when the case selector value does not match any of the case labels. If the value of OPERATOR (type CHAR) is not one of the four characters listed, the WRITELN statement following else is executed in TURBO Pascal.

```
case OPERATOR of
    '+' : RESULT := OPERAND1 + OPERAND2;
    '-' : RESULT := OPERAND1 - OPERAND2;
    '/' : RESULT := OPERAND1 / OPERAND2;
    '*' : RESULT := OPERAND1 * OPERAND2
else
    WRITELN ('Invalid symbol ', OPERATOR)
end {case}
```

The word otherwise is sometimes used instead of else in other extended versions of Pascal. The rest of the case statement would be unchanged.

---

* TURBO Pascal is a trademark of Borland International, Inc.

[†] WordStar is a trademark of MicroPro International, Inc.

String Manipulation in TURBO Pascal

The string data type and string processing features of UCSD Pascal are also provided in TURBO Pascal. You should read the section entitled String Manipulation in UCSD Pascal at the beginning of Appendix B.3.

There are two significant differences between the STRING data type in UCSD Pascal and TURBO Pascal. First, STRING is a reserved word in TURBO Pascal and cannot be redefined; STRING is a standard identifier in UCSD Pascal. Second, the maximum length of a string variable must always be specified in TURBO Pascal; there is no default value. The declarations

```
var
    WORD : STRING[10];
    LINE : STRING[80];
    PARAGRAPH : STRING[255];
```

allocate space for storage of three strings; the maximum length of each string is specified.

The programs that manipulate character strings in Chapters 6 through 10 must be modified to run in TURBO Pascal. The declaration

```
type
    STRING = packed array [1.. STRINGSIZE] of CHAR;
```

is invalid because STRING is a reserved word in TURBO Pascal. Replace this declaration with

```
type
    A_STRING = STRING[STRINGSIZE];
```

and substitute A_STRING for each occurrence of the type identifier STRING. The READLN procedure can be used to read up to STRINGSIZE characters into a variable of type A_STRING.

The string manipulation procedures and functions described for UCSD Pascal are also implemented in TURBO Pascal. Procedure REPLACE shown in Fig. B.1 and B.2 will run in TURBO Pascal provided the type identifier A_STRING is declared and used in place of STRING as described above. Also, the statement

```
SOURCE := HEAD + PATTERN + TAIL;
```

can be used in Fig. B.1 to concatenate the three strings listed on the right because the operator + means concatenation when used with string operands in TURBO Pascal.

Compiler Directives in TURBO Pascal

There are a number of compiler options which are set to default values of + or − in TURBO Pascal. In order to change the default value, the programmer must specify the new value for a *compiler directive*. This new value is provided in the form of a *pseudo comment*.

TURBO Pascal does not normally check for subscript range errors. The pseudo comment {$R+} changes the value of the R compiler directive from – to + and enables subscript checking and should be used while debugging programs. This comment should appear before the first reference to an array element.

The pseudo comment {$I PROCESS.PAS} instructs the compiler to include the file PROCESS.PAS in the source program at the point where the comment occurs. The I compiler directive is necessary for compiling large programs. It enables the programmer to save procedures and functions as separate files and then pull these files together at a later time.

Sequential File Manipulation in TURBO Pascal

The system file INPUT may correspond to either of two *logical devices* in TURBO Pascal. In normal operation, the system file INPUT corresponds to the console device. This is fine for entering numeric data and allows the user to edit the data string before pressing the < Return > key. The disadvantage is that the EOLN functions and EOF functions will not work properly and character data are not read as expected.

The pseudo comment {$B–} resets the value of the B compiler directive from + to –. The effect is to assign the system file INPUT to the terminal device instead of the console device. This enables data entry to proceed as described in the text. This comment must precede the program statement.

When processing disk files, two additional statements must be used in TURBO Pascal. The ASSIGN statements below associate the internal file name INFILE with the directory name 'MYDATA.TXT' and the internal file name OUTFILE with the directory name 'NEWDATA.TXT'.

```
ASSIGN (INFILE, 'MYDATA.TXT');
ASSIGN (OUTFILE, 'NEWDATA.TXT');
```

The ASSIGN statement for a file must precede any statement that manipulates the file.

The internal file names may be manipulated as before. The statements below

```
RESET (INFILE);
REWRITE (OUTFILE);
if not EOF(INFILE) then
    begin
        READ (INFILE, NEXT_RECORD);
        WRITE (OUTFILE, NEXT_RECORD)
    end;
```

prepare INFILE and OUTFILE for input and output, respectively, and copy the first record of INFILE to OUTFILE using NEXT_RECORD as an intermediary.

After file processing is finished, the statements

```
CLOSE (INFILE);
CLOSE (OUTFILE)
```

should be used to update the disk directory. Failure to do so may result in a newly created file being lost.

The directory name may be read into a string variable during program execution. If INNAME is type STRING[11], then the statements below associate the directory file specified by the program user with file INFILE.

```
WRITE ('Enter directory name of file to be copied: ');
READLN (INNAME);              {read the directory name}
ASSIGN (INFILE, INNAME);
RESET (INFILE)                   {prepare INFILE for input}
```

Appendix C
Pascal Syntax Diagrams

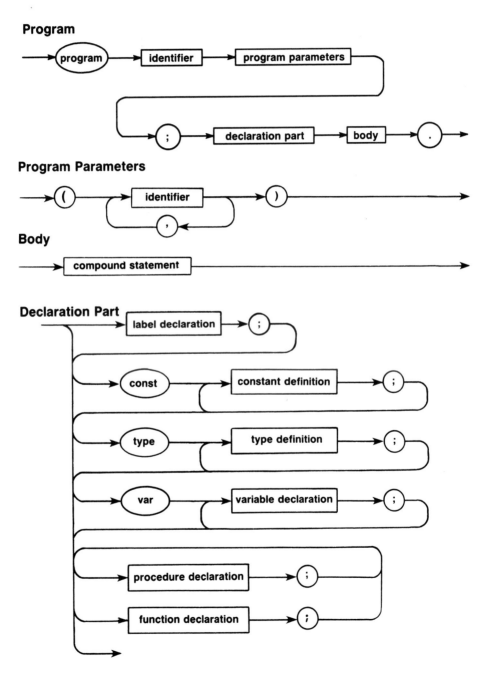

Program

Program Parameters

Body

Declaration Part

Label Declaration

Constant Definition

Type Definition

Variable Declaration

Statement Label

Constant

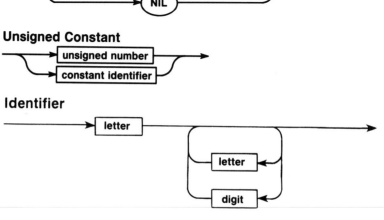

Unsigned Constant

Identifier

Function Declaration

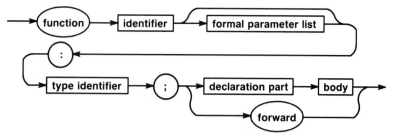

Procedure Declaration

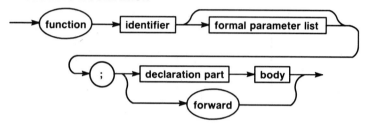

Formal Parameter List

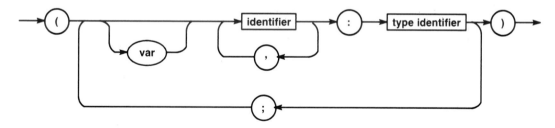

Type

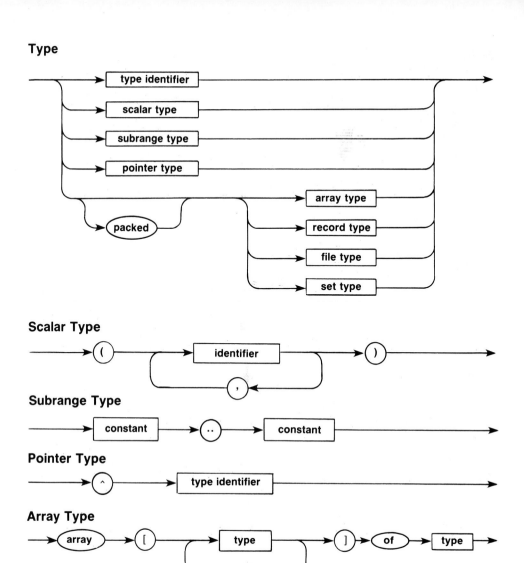

Scalar Type

Subrange Type

Pointer Type

Array Type

Record Type

Field List

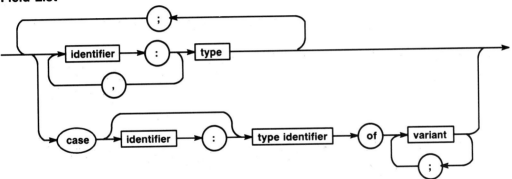

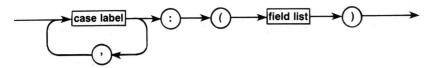

Variant

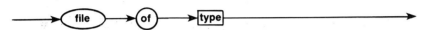

File Type

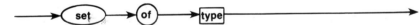

Set Type

Compound Statement

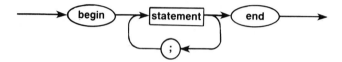

Statement

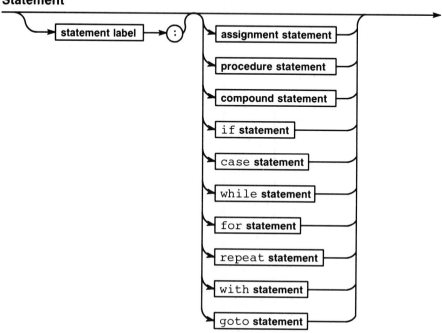

Assignment Statement

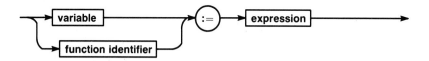

Procedure (Call) Statement

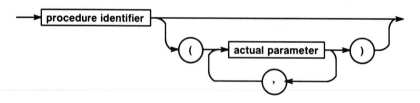

if Statement

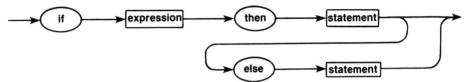

while Statement

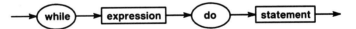

for Statement

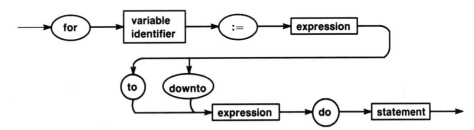

case Statement

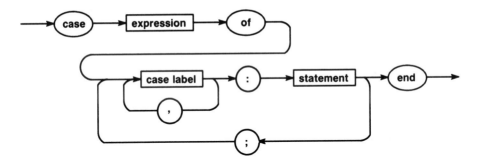

case Label

repeat Statement

with Statement

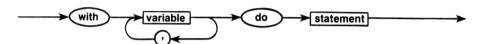

goto Statement

Actual Parameter

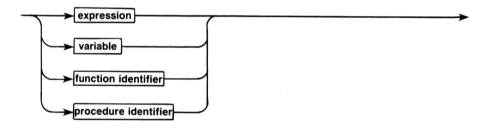

Expression

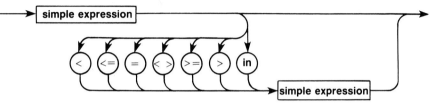

Simple Expression

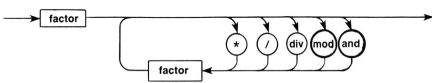

Term

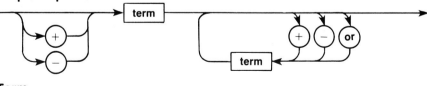

Factor

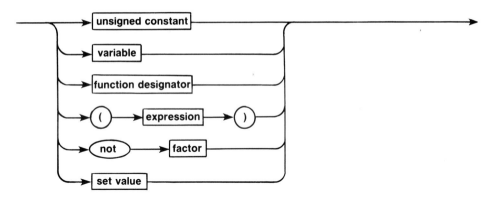

Function Designator

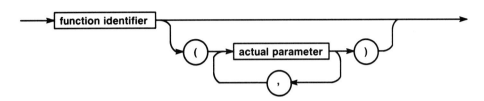

Set Value

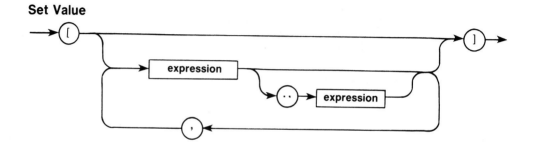

Variable

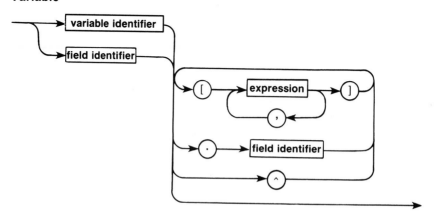

Unsigned Number

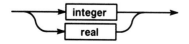

Integer

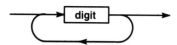

Real

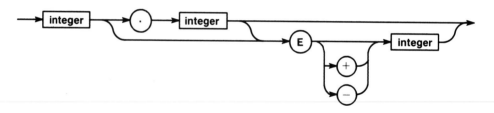

Appendix D
Character Sets

The following charts show the ordering of the character sets: ASCII (American Standard Code for Information Interchange), EBCDIC (Extended Binary Coded Decimal Interchange Code), and CDC* Scientific. Only printable characters are shown. The ordinal number for each character is shown in decimal. The blank character is denoted by a "□".

Left Digit(s) / Right Digit	ASCII									
	0	1	2	3	4	5	6	7	8	9
3			□	!	"	#	$	%	&	'
4	(	)	*	+	,	−	.	/	0	1
5	2	3	4	5	6	7	8	9	:	;
6	<	=	>	?	@	A	B	C	D	E
7	F	G	H	I	J	K	L	M	N	O
8	P	Q	R	S	T	U	V	W	X	Y
9	Z	[	\	]	^	—	`	a	b	c
10	d	e	f	g	h	i	j	k	l	m
11	n	o	p	q	r	s	t	u	v	w
12	x	y	z	{			}				

Codes 00-31 and 127 are nonprintable control characters.

---

* CDC is a trademark of Control Data Corporation.

Left Digit(s) \ Right Digit	0	1	2	3	4	5	6	7	8	9
								EBCDIC			
6					□					
7					¢	.	<	(	+	|
8	&									
9	!	$	*	)	;	¬	-	/		
10							^	,	%	—
11	>	?								
12			:	#	@	'	=	"		a
13	b	c	d	e	f	g	h	i		
14						j	k	l	m	n
15	o	p	q	r						
16			s	t	u	v	w	x	y	z
17								\	{	}
18	[	]								
19				A	B	C	D	E	F	G
20	H	I								J
21	K	L	M	N	O	P	Q	R		
22							S	T	U	V
23	W	X	Y	Z						
24	0	1	2	3	4	5	6	7	8	9

Codes 00-63 and 250-255 are nonprintable control characters.

Left Digit(s) \ Right Digit	0	1	2	3	4	5	6	7	8	9
								CDC			
0	:	A	B	C	D	E	F	G	H	I
1	J	K	L	M	N	O	P	Q	R	S
2	T	U	V	W	X	Y	Z	0	1	2
3	3	4	5	6	7	8	9	+	−	*
4	/	(	)	$	=	□	,	.	≡	[
5	]	%	≠	↦	∨	∧	↑	↓	<	>
6	≤	≥	¬	;						

Appendix E
Error Number Summary

```
 1: error in simple type
 2: identifier expected
 3: 'program' expected
 4: ')' expected
 5: ':' expected
 6: illegal symbol
 7: error in parameter list
 8: 'of' expected
 9: '(' expected
10: error in type
11: '[' expected
12: ']' expected
13: 'end' expected
14: ';' expected
15: integer expected
16: '=' expected
17: 'begin' expected
18: error in declaration part
19: error in field-list
20: ',' expected
21: '*' expected

50: error in constant
51: ':=' expected
52: 'then' expected
53: 'until' expected
54: 'do' expected
55: 'to'/'downto' expected
56: 'if' expected
57: 'file' expected
58: error in factor
59: error in variable
60: identifier not declared

101: identifier declared twice
102: low bound exceeds highbound
103: identifier is not of appropriate class
104: identifier not declared
105: sign not allowed
106: number expected
107: incompatible subrange types
108: file not allowed here
109: type must not be real
110: tagfield type must be scalar or subrange
111: incompatible with tagfield type
112: index type must not be real
113: index type must be scalar or subrange
114: base type must not be real
115: base type must be scalar or subrange
```

```
116: error in type of standard procedure parameter
117: unsatisfied forward reference
118: forward reference type identifier in variable
     declaration
119: forward declared; repetition of parameter list
     not allowed
120: function result type must be scalar, subrange or
     pointer
121: file value parameter not allowed
122: forward declared function; repetition of result
     type not allowed
123: missing result type in function declaration
124: F-format for real only
125: error in type of standard function parameter
126: number of parameters does not agree with
     declaration
127: illegal parameter substitution
128: result type of parameter function does not agree
     with declaration
129: type conflict of operands
130: expression is not of set type
131: tests on equality allowed only
132: strict inclusion not allowed
133: file comparison not allowed
134: illegal type of operand(s)
135: type of operand must be Boolean
136: set element type must be scalar or subrange
137: set element types not compatible
138: type of variable is not array
139: index type is not compatible with declaration
140: type of variable is not record
141: type of variable must be file or pointer
142: illegal parameter substitution
143: illegal type of loop control variable
144: illegal type of expression
145: type conflict
146: assignment of files not allowed
147: label type incompatible with selecting
     expression
148: subrange bounds must be scalar
149: index type must not be integer
150: assignment to standard function is not allowed
151: assignment to formal function is not allowed
152: no such field in this record
153: type error in read
154: actual parameter must be a variable
155: control variable must neither be formal nor non
     local
156: multidefined case label
157: too many cases in case statement
158: missing corresponding variant declaration
159: real or string tagfields not allowed
160: previous declaration was not forward
161: again forward declared
162: parameter size must be constant
163: missing variant in declaration
164: substitution of standard proc/func not allowed
```

```
165: multidefined label
166: multideclared label
167: undeclared label
168: undefined label
169: error in base set
170: value parameter expected
171: standard file was redeclared
172: undeclared external file
173: Fortran procedure or function expected
174: Pascal procedure or function expected
175: missing file "input" in program heading
176: missing file "output" in program heading

201: error in real constant: digit expected
202: string constant must not exceed source line
203: integer constant exceeds range
204: 8 or 9 in octal number

250: too many nested scopes of identifiers
251: too many nested procedures and/or functions
252: too many forward references of procedure entries
253: procedure too long
254: too many long constants in this procedure
255: too many errors on this source line
256: too many external references
257: too many externals
258: too many local files
259: expression too complicated

300: division by zero
301: no case provided for this value
302: index expression out of bounds
303: value to be assigned is out of bounds
304: element expression out of range

398: implementation restriction
399: feature not implemented
```

Answers to Selected Exercises

Chapter 1

Section 1.2

1. -27.2, 75.62. Memory cells : 998, 2.

Section 1.4

2. Add A, B, and C and store result in X.
Divide Y by Z and store result in X.
Subtract B from C and then add A and store result in D.

Section 1.5

1. The programmer creates the source file. The compiler produces the object file from a syntactically correct source file. The loader processes the object file

Section 1.6

1. Pascal reserved words: `END, PROGRAM, BEGIN, CONST`
standard identifiers: `READLN`
identifiers: `BILL, RATE, OPERATE, START, XYZ123,`
`THISISALONGONE`
invalid identifiers: `SUE'S, 123XYZ, Y=Z`

2.
```
program SMALL (INPUT, OUTPUT);

var
    X,Y,Z : REAL;   {X,Y,Z are declared variables with real contents}

begin
    Y := 15.0;      {the value 15.0 is assigned to variable Y     }
    Z := -Y + 3.5;  {the negative of contents in Y is added to 3.5
                     and assigned to variable Z                   }
    X := Y + Z;     {the contents of Y is added to contents of Z
                     and assigned to variable X                   }
    WRITELN (X,Y,Z){the contents of variables X, Y, Z are printed}
end.
```

```
3.500000     1.500000E1    -1.150000E1
```
3. `WRITELN ('The value of X is ', X, ' pounds.')`

2.

```
program COUNTCOINS (INPUT, OUTPUT);

var
    QUARTERS, DIMES, NICKELS, PENNIES, COINS, CENTS : INTEGER;

begin
    WRITE ('How many quarters do you have?'); READLN (QUARTERS);
    WRITE ('How many dimes do you have?'); READLN (DIMES);
    WRITE ('How many nickels do you have?'); READLN (NICKELS);
    WRITE ('How many pennies do you have?'); READLN (PENNIES);
    COINS := QUARTERS + DIMES + NICKELS + PENNIES;
    CENTS := 25 * QUARTERS + 10 * DIMES + 5 * NICKELS + PENNIES;
    WRITELN ('You have ', COINS :2, ' coins.');
    WRITELN ('Their value is ', CENTS :3, ' cents.')
end.
```

3. –15.5640
    –15.564
    –15.56
    –15.6
    –16
    –16

Section 1.10

1. Integer, string, character, invalid character, real, invalid real, integer, invalid real, character, invalid character, character, string

Chapter 2

Section 2.1

2. Problem inputs
    the list price of an item (LISTPRICE : REAL)
    the rate of discount as a percentage (RATE : REAL)

Problem outputs
    the discounted price of the item (DISPRICE : REAL)

Algorithm for computation of discounted price of an item
1. Read the values of LISTPRICE and RATE.
2. Determine actual discount.
    2.1 Multiply RATE by 0.01 and store in DISCRATE.
3. Computed discounted price of item.
    3.1 Multiply LISTPRICE by DISCRATE, save result in DISCOUNT.
    3.2 Subtract DISCOUNT from LISTPRICE, save result in DISPRICE.
4. Print value of DISPRICE.

Section 2.2

2. program HIHO;
    {Print the words "HI HO" in block letters.}
    {Insert procedures PRINTH, PRINTI, PRINTO here.}

```
begin {HIHO}
    {Print the word "HI".}
    PRINTH;
    PRINTI;

    {Print three blank lines}
    WRITELN;
    WRITELN;
    WRITELN;

    {Print the word "HO".}
    PRINTH;
    PRINTO
end. {HIHO}
```

Structure Chart

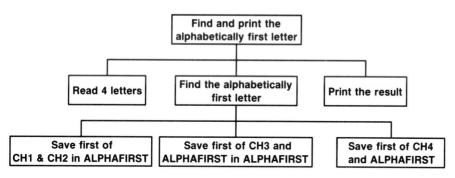

Section 2.3

2. *Structure chart*

```
program FIRSTLETTER (INPUT, OUTPUT);
{Finds and prints the alphabetically first letter.}

var
    CH1, CH2, CH3, CH4 : CHAR;    {four letters read in}
    ALPHAFIRST : CHAR;            {alphabetically first letter}

begin   {FIRSTLETTER}
    {Read four letters}
    WRITE ('Enter any four letters: ');
    READLN (CH1, CH2, CH3, CH4);
```

```
      {Store the alphabetically first of CH1 and CH2 in ALPHAFIRST}
      if CH1 < CH2 then
         ALPHAFIRST := CH1
      else
         ALPHAFIRST := CH2;

      {Store the alphabetically first of CH3 and ALPHAFIRST}
      if CH3 < ALPHAFIRST then
         ALPHAFIRST := CH3;

      {Store the alphabetically first of CH4 and ALPHAFIRST}
      IF CH4 < ALPHAFIRST then
         ALPHAFIRST := CH4;

      {Print the result}
      WRITELN (ALPHAFIRST, ' is the first letter alphabetically.')
   end.   {FIRSTLETTER}
```

3. a)
```
   if ITEM <> 0 then
      PRODUCT := PRODUCT * ITEM;
   WRITELN (PRODUCT)
```
b)
```
   if (X - Y) > 0 then
      Z := X - Y
   else
      Z := Y - X;
```
c)
```
   if X = 0 then
      ZEROCOUNT := ZEROCOUNT + 1
   else if X < 0 then
      MINUSSUM := MINUSSUM + X
   else
      PLUSSUM := PLUSSUM = X;
```

Section 2.4

1. Rearrange letters T, H, and E between CH1, CH2, and CH3 so that all the possibilities of the two if statements can be examined. When all three letters are the same then ALPHAFIRST will be assigned the value of that letter through variable CH2 in the else statement. When all letters are the same neither of the conditions is true.

2. Trace of program from figure 2.10 where HOURS is 30.0 and RATE is 5.00.

Program statement	HOURS	RATE	GROSS	NET	Effect
WRITE ('Hours worked?');					print prompt
READLN (HOURS);	30.0				data read into HOURS
WRITE ('Hourly rate?');					print prompt
READLN (RATE);		5.00			data read into RATE
GROSS := HOURS * RATE;			150.00		product saved in GROSS
if GROSS > TAXBRACKET then					Is GROSS larger than TAXBRACKET? Yes, expression is true.
NET := GROSS - TAX				125.00	difference saved in NET

```
WRITELN ('Gross salary is $'...);                    gross salary printed
WRITELN ('Net salary is $'...);                      net salary printed
```

Section 2.5

2. *Algorithm combining steps 2 and 2A*
1. Enter hours worked and hourly rate
2. Compute gross salary including double pay for overtime
3. Compute net salary
4. Print gross salary and net salary

step 2 refinement
```
2.1 if HOURS > MAXHOURS then
       GROSS := (MAXHOURS * RATE) + ((HOURS - MAXHOURS) * RATE * 2)
    else
       GROSS := HOURS * RATE
```
3. *Revision of Figure 2.14*
```
    if CLAIMS = 0 then
       DIVIDEND := (PREMIUM * FIXEDRATE) + (PREMIUM * BONUSRATE)
    else
       DIVIDEND := PREMIUM * FIXEDRATE
```

Section 2.6

1.
```
program SUMINTEGERS (INPUT, OUTPUT);
{Finds and compares summation of integers by two methods.}

var
   N,                  {the last integer to be added to the sum}
   SUM1,               {the sum being accumulated with a loop}
   SUM2,               {the sum being accumulated without a loop}
   NEXTINT : INTEGER;  {the next integer to be added to sum}

begin    {SUMINTEGERS}
   {Read in an integer}
   WRITE ('Enter a number to be summed: ');
   READLN (N);

   {Compute the summation using a loop}
   SUM1 := 0;                                     {initialize SUM1}
   For NEXTINT := 1 to N do
      SUM1 := SUM1 + NEXTINT;

   {Compute summation using formula}
   SUM2 := (N * (N + 1)) DIV 2;                   {DIV means division—
                                                   yields integer result}

   {Print out results}
   WRITELN ('The sum computed using a loop is ', SUM1 :5);
   WRITELN ('The sum computed by a formula is ', SUM2 :5);
```

```
{Print out comparison message}
if SUM1 = SUM2 then
    WRITELN ('The sums computed differently are the same.')
else
    WRITELN ('The sums computed differently are not the same.')
end.     {SUMINTEGERS}
```

Section 2.7

1.
```
program FINDPRODUCT (OUTPUT, INPUT);
{Computes and prints the product of a list of nonzero data items}

var
    NUMITEMS,           {the number of data items to be summed}
    COUNT : INTEGER;    {count of the items multiplied so far}
    ITEM,               {the next data item to be multiplied}
    PRODUCT : REAL;     {the product of the computation}

begin    {FINDPRODUCT}
    {Enter the number of data items to be multiplied}
    WRITE ('Enter the number of data items: ');
    READLN (NUMITEMS);

    {Find the product of items entered}
    PRODUCT := 1;     {Initialize PRODUCT to one}
    for COUNT := 1 to NUMITEMS do
        begin
            WRITE ('Please enter data item: ');
            READLN (ITEM);

            {Process valid data ignoring value of 0}
            if ITEM <> 0 then
                PRODUCT := PRODUCT * ITEM
        end;     {for COUNT}

    {Print the final product of data items}
    WRITELN ('The product of all nonzero data items is ', PRODUCT :8:2)
end.     {FINDPRODUCT}
```

Chapter 3

Section 3.1

1. for statement, identifier, expression, simple expression, term, factor,
variable, statement, assignment statement. I is a variable identifier and
also a term. SUM is a variable and also a term. N is an expression.

Section 3.2

2.
```
if X > Y then
    begin
        LARGER := X;
        SMALLER := Y;
        WRITELN ('X LARGER')
    end   {if}
else
    begin
```

```
          LARGER := Y;
          SMALLER := X;
          WRITELN ('Y LARGER')
      end;  {else}
5. {correct grade assignment}
   if SCORE < 60 then
      WRITE ('F')
   else if SCORE < 70 then
      WRITE ('D')
   else if SCORE < 80 then
      WRITE ('C')
   else if SCORE < 90 then
      WRITE ('B')
   else
      WRITE ('A')
6. {assign correct grade}
   if GPA >= 3.5 then
      WRITELN ('Highest honors for the semester')
   else if GPA >= 3.0 then
      WRITELN ('Deans list for the semester')
   else if GPA <= 0.99 then
      WRITELN ('Failed semester—registration suspended')
   else if GPA <= 1.99 then
      WRITELN ('On probation for next semester');
```

Section 3.3

1. 2, 4, 8, 16, 32, 64, 128, 256, 512, 1024

2.

```
program POWERS (INPUT, OUTPUT);
{Prints all powers of N with a value less than 1000}

const
   MAXPOWER = 1000;        {the largest possible power}
var
   NEXTPOWER,              {the value of the next power of N}
   COUNT,                  {the present power of N}
   N : INTEGER;            {an integer}

begin  {POWERS}
   WRITELN ('This program prints all powers of an integer with a');
   WRITE   ('value less than 1000. Enter an integer: ');
   READLN (N);
   NEXTPOWER := 1;         {Initialize NEXTPOWER to the zero power}
   COUNT := 0;             {Initialize COUNT to zero power}

   {Print table heading}
   WRITELN ('POWER    VALUE');
   {Print each power of N less than MAXPOWER and its value}
   while NEXTPOWER < MAXPOWER do
      begin
         WRITELN (COUNT :3, MAXPOWER :8);
         NEXTPOWER := NEXTPOWER * N;
         COUNT := COUNT + 1
      end     {while}
end.    {POWERS}
```

```
4. CELSIUS := MINCEL;
   for LCV := 1 to 8 do
      begin
         FAHREN := 1.8 * CELSIUS + 32;
         WRITELN (CELSIUS :10, FAHREN :15:1);
         CELSIUS := CELSIUS + CELSTEP
      end     {for}
```

Section 3.4

1.

actual parameters	formal parameters	attributes
NUM1	X	REAL variable
NUM3	Y	REAL variable

actual parameters	formal parameters	attributes
NUM2	X	REAL variable
NUM3	Y	REAL variable

4. (var A, B : INTEGER; var C : REAL);
   (M : INTEGER; var NEXT : CHAR);
   (var ACCOUNT : REAL; X, Y : REAL);

5. a) type REAL of Z does not correspond to type INTEGER of formal pa-
      rameter X
   b) procedure call is correct
   c) procedure call is correct
   d) type INTEGER of M does not correspond to type REAL of formal pa-
      rameter A
   e) 25.0 and 15.0 cannot correspond to variable parameters
   f) procedure call is correct
   g) parameter names A, B have not been declared in main program
   h) procedure call is correct
   i) expressions (Y + Z) or (Y - Z) may not correspond to a vari-
      able parameter
   j) type REAL of actual parameter X does not correspond with type
      INTEGER of formal parameter X
   k) 4 actual parameters are one too many for 3 formal parameters
   l) procedure call is correct

Section 3.5

2. procedure STORE (W {input}, X {input} : REAL;
                    var Y {output}, Z {output} : REAL);
   {Sums and multiplies two numbers entered}

   begin
      Y := W + X;
      Z := W * X
   end;   {STORE}

Section 3.6

1. The scope of variable N is procedure OUTER only. Since INNER is nested in OUTER, it is permissible for INNER to reference N. However, there is a local declaration for N in INNER which takes precedence.

2.
```
begin  {INNER}
    X := 5.5;   {local value parameter X is set to 5.5}
    Y := 6.6;   {global variable Y is set to 6.6}
    M := 2;     {variable M declared in OUTER is set to 2}
    N := 3;     {local variable N is set to 3}
    O := 4      {local variable O is set to 4}
end.   {INNER}
```

Section 3.7

2. Such a transposition would result in only categories of Outstanding or Unsatisfactory being given. Anyone with less than the minimum score for Outstanding would be classified as Unsatisfactory. Since both variables are type INTEGER, the compiler would not detect the error.

Chapter 4

Section 4.2

1. If base 2 is used in PRINTDIGITS instead of base 10 a binary number is printed in reverse (11101 — reverse of 23 in Base 2). PRINTDIGITS (64) in base 2 prints 0000001 which is the reverse of 64 in base 2. If the base is 8, data printed is 72 and 001 respectively.

2. 3, 0, 1 , 7
  0, 1, 15, 1
  0 7, 3, 2
  0, 4, 4, 0

3. a) 3 b) −3 c) undefined because of negative mod operand d) −3.14159 e) invalid, assigning REAL value to INTEGER variable I f) 0.75 g) invalid, REAL operand (A/B) for mod operator h) invalid, result of division by 0 is undefined i) invalid, undefined because of negative mod operand (990−1000) j) 3 k) −3.0 l) invalid, assigning REAL value to INTEGER variable I m) invalid, REAL operand for div operator n) 0 o) 1 p) invalid, result of division by 0 is undefined q) 3

4. a) 1 b) −2 d) 6.28138 f) 2.5 i) −5 j) 2 k) 2.5 n) 2.0 o) 0 q) 5

5. a) WHITE := 1.6666... b) GREEN := 0.6666... c) ORANGE := 0 d) BLUE := −3.0 e) LIME := 2 f) PURPLE := 0.6666...

6. a) X := 4.0 * A * C
  b) A := A * C
  c) I := 2 * (−J)
  d) K := 3 * (I + J)
  e) X := (5 * A) / (B * C)
  f) I := 5 * J * 3

Section 4.3

1. procedure EULER (BASE, APOWER : INTEGER;
   var EXPON : REAL);
   {Computes the value of a number raised to a power}
   begin   {EULER}
      EXPON := EXP(APOWER * LN(BASE))
   end;   {EULER}
2. ROUNDX := ROUND (100 * X) / 100.0

Section 4.4

2. a) BETWEEN := N <= ABS(K)
   b) UPCASE := CH in ['A'..'Z']
3. DIVISOR := N mod M = 0

Section 4.5

1. a) 1 b) FALSE c) TRUE d) 1
2. a) 3 b) 3 c) a d) C e) c f) 1 g) 9 h) g i) F

Section 4.6

1. a) 1 b) FRIDAY c) WEDNESDAY d) CHR(MONDAY) is undefined
2. a) illegal unless declared in a type declaration where SATURDAY precedes SUNDAY b) legal subrange c) legal subrange d) illegal. Quotes
   must be added to 0 or removed from '9'. e) illegal subrange. The first
   value must be less than the last value. f) illegal. String values may not
   be used as identifiers in a subrange

Section 4.7

1. The salary and number of dependents would be read and the rest of
   the line would be discarded. Then procedure ECHOLINE will echo print
   the entire next line.

Chapter 5

Section 5.1

1. if (DAYVALUE = SUNDAY) then
      WRITELN ('Sunday')
   else if (DAYVALUE = MONDAY) then
      WRITELN ('Monday')
   else if (DAYVALUE = TUESDAY) then
      WRITELN ('Tuesday')
   else if (DAYVALUE = WEDNESDAY) then
      WRITELN ('Wednesday')
   else if (DAYVALUE = THURSDAY) then
      WRITELN ('Thursday')
   else if (DAYVALUE = FRIDAY) then
      WRITELN ('Friday')
   else if (DAYVALUE = SATURDAY) then
      WRITELN ('Saturday')
2. case LETTER1 of

```
    'R','r' : EYES := RED;
    'G','g' : EYES := GREEN;
    'B','b' : case LETTER2 of
                'L','l' : EYES := BLUE
                'R','r' : EYES := BROWN
            end;   {case LETTER2}
    'Y','y' : EYES := YELLOW
end    {case LETTER1}
```

Section 5.2

1. OPERCHARSET := ['+','-','/','*','=','<','>'];

2.
```
if NEXTCH in ['A','E','I','O','U','a','e','i','o','u'] then
    WRITELN ('The next character ', NEXTCH,' is a vowel.')
else
    WRITELN ('The next character ', NEXTCH, ' is not a vowel.')
```

Section 5.3

1. {Print each digit and its ordinal number}
```
    for CH := '0' to '9' do
        WRITELN (CH, ' ', ORD(CH))
```

Section 5.4

1. a) (X > Y) or (X = 15)
   b) ((X > Y) or (X = 15)) and (Z <> 7.5)
   c) (X = 15) and ((Z <> 7.5) or (X > Y))
   d) not FLAG and (X = 15.7)
   e) FLAG or not (NEXTCH in ['A'..'H'])

2.
```
NUM := 10;                      NUM := 10;
for LCV := 1 to 10 do           repeat
    WRITELN (NUM * LCV)             WRITELN (NUM);
                                    NUM := NUM + 10
                                until NUM > 100
```

Section 5.5

2.
```
OUTER     1
    INNER     1   1
    INNER     1   2
    INNER     1   3
    INNER     1   2
    INNER     1   1
OUTER     2
    INNER     2   1
    INNER     2   2
    INNER     2   3
    INNER     2   2
    INNER     2   1
```
3. for I := 1 to 4 do

```
      begin
          for J := 1 to I do
              WRITE (J :2);
          WRITELN
      end;    {for I}
   for I := 3 downto 1 do
      begin
          for J := 1 to I do
              WRITE (J :2);
          WRITELN
      end    {for I}
```

Section 5.6

1. function CUBE (NUM : REAL) : REAL;
{Computes the cube of any number.}

```
begin
    CUBE := NUM * NUM * NUM
end;    {CUBE}
```

2.

function TUITION (CREDHOURS : INTEGER) : INTEGER;
{Computes the tuition for a certain number of credit hours taken
 at the university.   }

```
const
    MINCHARGE = 100;    {minimum charge per class hour taken}
    MAXCHARGE = 1000;   {maximum charge for 12 hours or more}

begin
    if CREDHOURS > 0 then
        if CREDHOURS <= 11 then
            TUITION := CREDHOURS * MINCHARGE
        else
            TUITION := MAXCHARGE
    else
        TUITION := 0
end;    {TUITION}
```

3. function EXPONENT (NUMBER, POWER : REAL) : REAL;
{Computes the value of a number to a given power}

```
begin
    EXPONENT := EXP(POWER * LN(NUMBER))
end;    {EXPONENT}
```

5.

function LOWERCASE (CH : CHAR) : BOOLEAN;
{Returns a result of TRUE if CH is a lowercase letter and FALSE if not}

```
begin  {LOWERCASE}
    LOWERCASE := CH in ['a'..'z']
end;  {LOWERCASE}
```

Chapter 6

Section 6.1

1. Array X is unchanged. The new value of SUM is 56.0

Section 6.3

1.
```
procedure COPY (INARRAY {input} : ANARRAY;
                SIZE {input} : INTEGER;
                var OUTARRAY {output} : ANARRAY);
  {Copies each value in array INARRAY to array OUTARRAY.}

  var
      I : INTEGER;

  begin {COPY}
      for I := 1 to SIZE do
          OUTARRAY[I] := INARRAY[I]
  end; {COPY}
```
2.
```
procedure REVERSE (X {input} : ANARRAY;
                   N {input} : INTEGER;
                   var Y {output} : ANARRAY);
  {Reverses the values stored in an array.}

  var
      I : INTEGER;

  begin {REVERSE}
      {Copy X[N] to Y[1], X[N-1] to Y[2], etc.}
      for I := 1 to N do
          Y[I] := X[N+1-I]
  end; {REVERSE}
```

Section 6.4

1.
```
type
    INDEX = 1..MAXSIZE;
    ANARRAY = array [INDEX] of REAL;
    BOOLARRAY = array [INDEX] of BOOLEAN;

procedure COMPARE (X, Y {input} : ANARRAY;
                   N {input} : INTEGER;
                   var Z {output} : BOOLARRAY);
  {Assigns TRUE to Z[I] if X[I] = Y[I]; assigns false if X[I] <> Y[I]}

  var
      I : INTEGER;

  begin {COMPARE}
      for I := 1 to N do
          Z[I] := X[I] = Y[I]
  end; {COMPARE}
```

Section 6.7

1.
```
function LENGTH (INSTRING : STRING) : INTEGER;
{Finds the actual length of INSTRING excluding blank padding.}

const
   BLANK = ' ';

var
   I : INTEGER;                            {character being tested}

begin {LENGTH}
   {Find first non-blank.}
   I := STRINGSIZE;                        {start at right end of string}
   while (INSTRING[I] = BLANK) and (I > 1) do
      I := I - 1;                          {test character to the left}

   {assert: at left end of string or at a non-blank character}
   if INSTRING[I] = BLANK then
      LENGTH := 0                          {at left end of a string of all blanks}
   else
      LENGTH := I
end; {LENGTH}
```

2. See exercise 2 in Section 6.3.

3. Use the program body below where READSTRING is shown in Fig. 6.15 and REVERSE is the solution to exercise 2. INSTRING and OUTSTRING should both be type STRING.

```
   begin
      READSTRING (INSTRING, STRINGLENGTH);
      REVERSE (INSTRING, STRINGLENGTH, OUTSTRING);
      WRITE (INSTRING :STRINGLENGTH, ' is ');
      if INSTRING <> OUTSTRING then
         WRITE ('not ');
      WRITELN ('a palindrome.')
   end.
```

Section 6.8

1. If MOVEROW or MOVECOLUMN is greater than 3 (or less than 1), a subscript range error will occur.

2. Declare CAMPUSNAME and CLASSNAME as arrays of strings and initialize them so that CAMPUSNAME[DELAWARE] is 'DELAWARE' and CLASSNAME[JUNIOR] is 'JUNIOR'.

a)
```
{Enter the enrollment data.}
for CURCAMPUS := MAIN to MONTCO do
   for I := 1 to MAXCOURSE do
      for CLASSRANK := FRESHMAN to SENIOR do
         begin
            WRITE ('Enter No. of ', CLASSNAME[CLASSRANK],
                   ' in class #', I :2, ' at ',
                   CAMPUSNAME[CURCAMPUS], ' campus: ');
```

```
                READLN (CLASSENROLL[I,CURCAMPUS,CLASSRANK])
            end {for CLASSRANK}
```

b)
```
CLASSUM := 0;
for CURCAMPUS := MAIN to MONTCO do
   for I := 1 to MAXCOURSE do
       CLASSUM := CLASSUM + CLASSENROLL[I,CURCAMPUS,JUNIOR]
```

c)
```
CLASSUM := 0;
for CURCAMPUS := MAIN to MONTCO do
   CLASSUM := CLASSUM + CLASSENROLL[2,CURCAMPUS,SOPHOMORE]
```

d)
```
STUDENTOTAL := 0;
WRITELN ('ENROLLMENT AT MAIN CAMPUS');
WRITELN ('-------------------------');
WRITELN (' COURSE#       STUDENTS');
for I := 1 to MAXCOURSE do
   begin
       CLASSUM := 0;
       for CLASSRANK := FRESHMAN to SENIOR do
           CLASSUM := CLASSUM + CLASSENROLL[I,MAIN,CLASSRANK];
       WRITELN (I :5, CLASSUM :14);
       STUDENTOTAL := STUDENTOTAL + CLASSUM
   end;   {for I}
WRITELN ('Total students enrolled at Main campus : ',
         STUDENTOTAL :4)
```

e)
```
UPPERCLASSTOTAL := 0;
WRITELN ('ENROLLMENT OF UPPERCLASS STUDENTS BY CAMPUS')
WRITELN ('-------------------------------------------');
WRITELN ('      CAMPUS              ENROLLMENT');
for CURCAMPUS := MAIN to MONTCO do
   begin
       CLASSUM := 0;
       for CLASSRANK := JUNIOR to SENIOR do
           for I := 1 to MAXCOURSE do
               CLASSUM := CLASSUM +
                          CLASSENROLL[I,CURCAMPUS,CLASSRANK];
       WRITELN (CAMPUSNAME[CURCAMPUS] :16, CLASSUM :15);
       UPPERCLASSTOTAL := UPPERCLASSTOTAL + CLASSUM
   end;   {for CURCAMPUS}
WRITELN ('Total enrolled upperclass students is ',
         UPPERCLASSTOTAL :5)
```

Section 6.9

1. PRINTMENU is implemented as a sequence of WRITELN statements. TABMONTH must compute and save the sales amounts for January of all years covered in SUMBYMONTH[JAN], etc. It will be similar to

TABYEAR except that the order of the loop control variables should be reversed. GRAPHMONTH will plot the values in the array SUMBYMONTH for each month from January to December and is similar to GRAPHYEAR. Both TABMONTH and GRAPHMONTH are passed the array MONTHNAME so that the name of each month can be displayed.

Chapter 7

Section 7.1

```
1. CATALOGUE = record
       TITLE : STRING;
       AUTHOR : STRING;
       PUBLISHER : STRING;
       PUBDATE : INTEGER
   end;   {CATALOGUE}
2. PART = record
       NAME : STRING;
       SERIALNUM = STRING;
       INVENTORY : INTEGER;
       PRICE : REAL
   end;   {PART}
```

Section 7.5

2.
```
function FINDLOW (var CLASS {input} : STUDENTARRAY;
                  NUMSTU {input} : INTEGER) : INTEGER;
{Returns the lowest score of NUMSTU students              }

var
    CURSTU : CLASSRANGE;        {loop control variable}
    LOW : INTEGER;             {contains lowest score}

begin  {FINDLOW}
    LOW := 100;
    for CURSTU := 1 to NUMSTU do
        if CLASS[CURSTU].SCORE < LOW then
            LOW := CLASS[CURSTU].SCORE;
    FINDLOW := LOW
end;    {FINDLOW}

function FINDSTAND (CLASS {input} : STUDENTARRAY;
                    NUMSTU {input} : INTEGER;
                    AVERAGE {input} : REAL) : REAL;
{Determines standard deviation for scores of NUMSTU students   }

var
    SUMSQSCORE : INTEGER;       {sum of the squares of NUMSTU scores}
    CURSTU : CLASSRANGE;        {loop control variable}

begin  {FINDSTAND}
    SUMSQSCORE := 0;
    for CURSTU := 1 to NUMSTU do
        SUMSQSCORE := SUMSQSCORE+SQR(CLASS[CURSTU].SCORE);
    if NUMSTU > 0 then
        FINDSTAND := SQRT(SUMSQSCORE  / NUMSTU-SQR(AVERAGE))
end;    {FINDSTAND}
```

Section 7.7

1. Change the condition in the if statement to

```
if CLASS[FIRST].SCORE > CLASS[FIRST+1].SCORE then
```

For descending ordr, change the operator > to <

Section 7.9

2.
```
function FIGCONVERT (FIGCHAR : CHAR) : FIGKIND;
{Converts FIGCHAR (a letter) to a value of type FIGKIND.}

 begin  {FIGCONVERT}
    if FIGCHAR in ['R','S','C','T'] then
       case FIGCHAR of
          'R' : FIGCONVERT := RECTANGLE;
          'S' : FIGCONVERT := SQUARE;
          'C' : FIGCONVERT := CIRCLE;
          'T' : FIGCONVERT := TRIANGLE
       end  {case}
    else
       FIGCONVERT := ILLEGAL
 end;  {FIGCONVERT}
```

Section 7.10

1.
```
procedure DELETE (var SOURCE1 {input/output} : LINE;
                  STARTINDEX, SIZE {input} : INTEGER);
{Deletes a substring of SOURCE1 of length SIZE at STARTINDEX.}


var
    I : 1..STRINGSIZE;                    {loop control variable}

begin  {DELETE}
   if (STARTINDEX < 1) or (SIZE < 1) or
      (STARTINDEX+SIZE-1 > SOURCE1.LENGTH) then
      WRITELN ('Illegal integer parameter—deletion aborted.')
   else
      begin  {deletion}
         for I := STARTINDEX to STARTINDEX+SIZE-1 do
            SOURCE.INFO[I] := SOURCE.INFO[I+SIZE];
         SOURCE.LENGTH := SOURCE.LENGTH - SIZE    {adjust LENGTH}
      end  {deletion}
end;  {DELETE}
```
3.
```
procedure DELETE (var SOURCE1 {input/output} : LINE;
                  STARTINDEX, SIZE {input} : INTEGER );
{Deletes a substring of SOURCE1 of length SIZE at STARTINDEX.}

var
    TAIL : LENGTH;                {substring at end of SOURCE1,
                                   following the one to be deleted}
    TAILINDEX,                    {starting point of TAIL in SOURCE1}
    TAILLENGTH : 0..STRINGSIZE;   {length of TAIL}
```

```
begin  {DELETE}
    if (STARTINDEX < 1) or (SIZE < 1) or
        (STARTINDEX+SIZE-1 > SOURCE1.LENGTH) then
        WRITELN ('Illegal integer parameter—deletion aborted.')
    else
        begin  {deletion}
            TAILINDEX := STARTINDEX + SIZE;
            TAILLENGTH := SOURCE1.LENGTH - TAILINDEX + 1;
            COPY (SOURCE1, TAILINDEX, TAILLENGTH, TAIL); {define TAIL}
            SOURCE1.LENGTH := STARTINDEX - 1;        {"shorten" SOURCE1}
            CONCAT (SOURCE1, TAIL, SOURCE1)
        end  {deletion}
end;  {DELETE}
```

Chapter 8

Section 8.1

a) [1,3,4,5,6,7] b) [1,2,3,5,7] c) [1,2,3,4,5,6,7] d) TRUE e) [1,2,3,5,7] f) [2]
g) [ ] h) FALSE

2.
```
procedure PRINTSET (DIGITS {input} : DIGITSET);
{Prints the digits in set DIGITS}

var
    NEXTDIGIT : '0'..'9';
begin   {PRINTDIGIT}
    for NEXTDIGIT := '0' to '9' do
        if NEXTDIGIT in DIGITS then
            WRITE (NEXTDIGIT)
end;   {PRINTSET}
```

Section 8.5

1.
```
program ECHOFILE (INVENTORY,INPUT,OUTPUT);

{Echoes file INVENTORY at the terminal}

type
    STOCKRANGE = 1111.9999;
    BOOK = RECORD
        STOCKNUM : STOCKRANGE;
        AUTHOR,
        TITLE: STRING;
        PRICE : REAL;
        QUANTITY : INTEGER
    end; {Record}
    BOOKFILE = FILE OF BOOK;

var
    INVENTORY : BOOKFILE;
    ONEBOOK : BOOK;

begin
    RESET (INVENTORY);
    READ (INVENTORY,ONEBOOK);
    if not EOF(INVENTORY) then
```

```
        begin
            WRITELN ('INVENTORY LISTING OF BOOKS ON HAND');
            WRITELN ('-----------------------------------');
            WRITELN
        end;  {if}
    while not EOF (INVENTORY) do
        begin
            with ONEBOOK do
                begin
                    WRITELN ('StockNumber: ',STOCKNUM);
                    WRITELN ('Title: ', TITLE);
                    WRITELN ('Author: ', AUTHOR);
                    WRITELN ('Price: ',PRICE:10:2,' Quantity: ',QUANTITY:5)
                end;
            READ (INVENTORY, ONEBOOK)
        end
end.    {ECHOFILE}
```

Section 8.6

1.

```
begin  {MERGE}
    {Prepare INVENTORY and UPDATE for input, NEWINVEN for output.}
    RESET (INVENTORY); RESET (UPDATE); REWRITE (NEWINVEN);

    {Read the first record from INVENTORY and UPDATE.}
    READ (INVENTORY, INVENBOOK); READ (UPDATE, UPDATEBOOK);

    {While not EOF for both files copy INVENTORY and UPDATE to NEWINVEN}
    while not EOF (UPDATE) and not EOF (INVENTORY) do
        COPYSMALLER (INVENBOOK, UPDATEBOOK);

    {Copy remainder of whichever file remains to NEWINVEN}
    while not EOF (UPDATE) do
        begin
            WRITE (NEWINVEN, UPDATEBOOK);
            READ (UPDATE, UPDATEBOOK)
        end;
    while not EOF (INVENTORY) do
        begin
            WRITE (NEWINVEN, INVENBOOK);
            READ (INVENTORY, INVENBOOK)
        end;

    {Write the sentinel record to NEWINVEN.}
    WRITE (NEWINVEN, INVENBOOK);
    WRITELN ('File merged completed.')
end;    {MERGE}
```

Section 8.7

2. a)

```
procedure ENTERPARAMS (var PARAMS {output} : SEARCHPARAMS);

{Enters the search parameters and validates them. The low bound for a
 parameter must be <= the high bound and both bounds must be in range.}

{Insert procedures BOUNDSTOCK, BOUNDAUTHOR, BOUNDTITLE, BOUNDPRICE,
 BOUNDQUANTITY                                                      }
```

```
begin {ENTERPARAMS}
    with PARAMS do
        begin
            BOUNDSTOCK (LOWSTOCK, HIGHSTOCK);
            BOUNDAUTHOR (LOWAUTHOR, HIGHAUTHOR);
            BOUNDTITLE (LOWTITLE, HIGHTITLE);
            BOUNDPRICE (LOWPRICE, HIGHPRICE);
            BOUNDQUANTITY (LOWQUANT, HIGHQUANT)
        end    {with}
end;    {ENTERPARAMS}
```

2. b)
```
procedure SHOW (NEXTBOOK {input} : BOOK);

{Displays each field of NEXTBOOK at the terminal. Leaves a line space
 after each book.                                                     }

begin    {SHOW}
    with NEXTBOOK do
        WRITELN (STOCKNUM :4,' ',TITLE,' ',AUTHOR,PRICE:10:2,QUANTITY:5);
    WRITELN
end;    {SHOW}
```
3. NEXTBOOK.STOCKNUM is compared to PARAMS.HIGHSTOCK in the
condition of the while loop within which function MATCH is called.

Section 8.8

1. At bottom of while not EOF (INVENTORY) loop do GET (INVENTORY)
twice

Chapter 9

Section 9.1

1. The actual parameter in the procedure call PALINDROME (N-1) is an
expression and must correspond to a variable parameter.

Section 9.2

1.
```
program TESTHANOI (INPUT, OUTPUT);
{Tests the Towers of Hanoi procedure.}

var
    NUMDISCS : INTEGER;                      {number of discs to be moved}

{Insert procedure TOWER here.}

begin {TESTHANOI}
    WRITE ('How many discs do you wish moved?');    READLN (NUMDISCS);
    TOWER ('A', 'C', 'B', NUMDISCS)
end. {TESTHANOI}
```

Section 9.3

1.
```
function FINDMIN (var X : INARRAY; N : INTEGER) : INTEGER;
{Finds the smallest value in X[1]..X[N].}
```

```
var
    MINOFREST : INTEGER;                        {minimum of rest of array}

begin {FINDMIN}
    if N = 1 then
        FINDMIN := X[1]
    else
        begin  {recursive step}
            MINOFREST := FINDMIN(X, N-1);
            if MINOFREST < X[N] then
                FINDMIN := MINOFREST
            else
                FINDMIN := X[N]
        end {recursive step}
end;  {FINDMIN}
```

Section 9.4

2.
```
function LENGTH (var INSTRING : STRING; NEXT : INTEGER) : INTEGER;
{Returns the length of its character string argument.}

const
    DOLLAR = '$';                               {string terminator}

begin  {LENGTH}
    if INSTRING[NEXT] = DOLLAR then
        LENGTH := 0
    else
        LENGTH := 1 + LENGTH(INSTRING, NEXT + 1)
end; {LENGTH}
```

Section 9.5

1. for 'SAL', HASH := 32 mod 10 + 1 or 3; stored at subscript [3]
   for 'BIL', HASH := 23 mod 10 + 1 or 4; stored at subscript [4]
   for 'JIL', HASH := 31 mod 10 + 1 or 2; stored at subscript [2]
   for 'LIB', HASH := 23 mod 10 + 1 or 4; stored at subscript [5]
   for 'HAL', HASH := 21 mod 10 + 1 or 2; stored at subscript [6]
   for 'ROB', HASH := 35 mod 10 + 1 or 6; stored at subscript [7]

2. Change the statement in the for loop to:

```
    HASHINDEX := HASHINDEX + I * ORD(KEY[I]);
```

Now 'LIB' and 'BIL' may not hash to the same value.

3. Change the statement in the while loop to

```
    INDEX := (INDEX + SQR(PROBE-1)) mod CLASSIZE
```

Section 9.6

2. Trace of SELECTSORT:
   End of pass 1: −5, 5, 7, −3, 4, 9, 7, −3, 10
   End of pass 2: −5, 5, 7, −3, 4, −3, 7, 9, 10
   End of pass 3: −5, 5, 7, −3, 4, −3, 7, 9, 10

End of pass 4: -5, 5, -3, -3, 4, 7, 7, 9, 10
End of pass 5: -5, 4, -3, -3, 5, 7, 7, 9, 10
End of pass 6: -5, -3, -3, 4, 5, 7, 7, 9, 10   unchanged in 7 and 8

Trace of INSERTSORT
End of pass 1: 5, 10, 7, -3, 4, 9, 7, -3, -5
End of pass 2: 5, 7, 10, -3, 4, 9, 7, -3, -5
End of pass 3: -3, 5, 7, 10, 4, 9, 7, -3, -5
End of pass 4: -3, 4, 5, 7, 10, 9, 7, -3, -5
End of pass 5: -3, 4, 5, 7, 9, 10, 7, -3, -5
End of pass 6: -3, 4, 5, 7, 7, 9, 10, -3, -5
End of pass 7: -3, -3, 4, 5, 7, 7, 9, 10, -5
End of pass 8: -5, -3, -3, 4, 5, 7, 7, 9, 10

Section 9.7

1. For Subarray 12, 33, 23, 43, the pivot value is the smallest value.
New Subarray to sort is 33, 23, 43. When pivot value is placed in the middle, two single element arrays are left.
for subarray 55, 64, 77, 75, the pivot value is the smallest value.
New subarray to sort is 64, 77, 75. Pivot value is smallest.
New subarray to sort is 77, 75—it becomes 75, 77

2. In the left subarray.

Chapter 10

Section 10.1

1. a) The string 'CAT' is stored in the world field of the record pointed to by R.
b) The record pointed to by R is copied into the record pointed to by P.
c) Illegal, P.WORD should be written as P^.WORD.
d) Illegal, P cannot be assigned an integer value.
e) The integer 0 is stored in the PLACE field of the record pointed to by P.
f) Pointer P is reset to point to the same record as pointer R.
g) Illegal, -10 is not a string.
h) The PLACE field of the record pointed to by R is copied into the PLACE field of the record pointed to by Q.

2. Exchanges the WORD fields of the records pointed to by P and Q.

Section 10.4

1.
```
procedure PRINTLIST (HEAD {input} : LISTPOINTER);
{Prints the contents of the list pointed to by HEAD.}

begin {PRINTLIST}
   if HEAD <> NIL then
      begin
         WRITELN (HEAD^.WORD);        {print current node}
         PRINTLIST (HEAD^.LINK)       {print rest of list}
      end  {if}
end;  {PRINTLIST}
```

2. The body of iterative function SEARCH shown below assumes FOUND is a local BOOLEAN variable.

```
begin  {SEARCH}
    FOUND := FALSE;                      {TARGET not found yet}
    while (HEAD <> NIL) and not FOUND do
        if HEAD^.WORD = TARGET then
            FOUND := TRUE                {HEAD points to TARGET}
        else
            HEAD := HEAD^.LINK;      {advance down the list}

    {assert:  HEAD is NIL or HEAD points to TARGET}
    SEARCH := HEAD                       {define result}
end;  {SEARCH}
```

3.
```
function LENGTH (HEAD : LISTPOINTER) : INTEGER;
{Finds the length of the list pointed to by HEAD.}

begin  {LENGTH}
  if HEAD = NIL then
    LENGTH := 0
  else
    LENGTH := 1 + LENGTH (HEAD^.LINK)   {1 + length of rest of list}
end;  {LENGTH}
```

Section 10.5

1. Procedures READ1PASS and PRINT1PASS read and print a record of type PASSENGER, respectively.

```
procedure PRINT1PASS (ONEPASS {input} : PASSENGER);
{Prints the contents of record ONEPASS.}

begin  {PRINT1PASS}
    with ONEPASS do
        begin
            WRITE (NAME :10);
            WRITE (NUMSEATS :10);
            case CLASS of
                ECONOMY    : WRITE ('Economy' :13);
                FIRSTCLASS : WRITE ('First class' :13)
            end;  {case}
            WRITELN
        end {with}
end;  {PRINT1PASS}

procedure PRINTPASSLIST (HEAD {input} : PASSPOINTER);
{Prints the passenger list. Uses PRINT1PASS.}

begin  {PRINTPASSLIST}
    while HEAD <> NIL do
        begin
            PRINT1PASS (HEAD^.PASSINFO);
            HEAD := HEAD^.LINK
        end  {while}
end;  {PRINTPASSLIST}
```

Section 10.6

1.

TOP

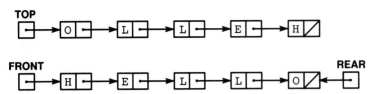

2. Introduce a local pointer TEMP and set TEMP to point to the original top of the stack or front of the queue. After removing the node, execute

    DISPOSE (TEMP)

3. Use an integer variable as a pointer to the last element in the array which will be considered the top of the stack. Initialize the pointer to 0. To push an item, increment the pointer by 1 and insert the new item in the array element selected by the pointer. To pop an item, access the element at the top of the stack (subscript is the pointer value) and decrement the pointer value by 1. The stack is empty if the pointer value is 0.

Section 10.7

1. Inserting parentheses according to the algebraic rules for expression evaluation gives us the two expressions and trees below.

$$((X * Y) / (A + B)) * C \qquad ((X * Y) / A) + (B * C)$$

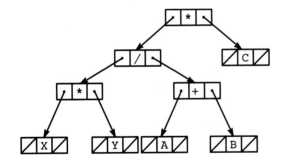

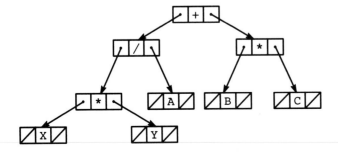

2. Inorder: BDCA−X+Y, Preorder: ABCD−+XY, Postorder: DCBXY+−A

Section 10.8

1. Change the WRITELN statement in INORDER to

WRITELN (ROOT^.WORD, ROOT^.COUNT :5);

2.

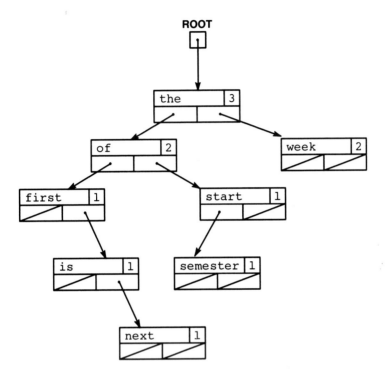

Index

Abacus, 2
ABS, 170
Accumulating a sum, 76-78
Activation frame, 428-429
Actual parameter; *see* Parameter
Address, 3
Address of actual parameter, 123
Algorithm, 47-48
Algorithm decision, 59-66
Allocating memory, 480-481
Analogy, 70
Ancestor, 507
and, 176
ANSI/IEEE Pascal standard, 11, Ap-5
ARCTAN, 170
Argument, 170
Arithmetic logic unit, 4
Arithmetic operations, 4
Arithmetic operator result, 162
array, 263-314
    character, 288-294
    conformant, Ap-8
    copy, 276
    definition, 263
    element, 264, 266
    element as parameter, 280
    general subscripts, 283-288
    implementing list, 482-483
    implementing queue, 506
    implementing stack, 506
    index, 266
    integer subscripts, 266-275
    multidimensional, 295-301
    multidimensional syntax display, 296
    nonlocal reference, 299
    packed, 289-294
    parallel, 334-335
    random access, 275
    of records, 334-335
    reading partial contents, 283
    reference syntax display, 267
    search, 342-344, 449-456
    sequential access, 275
    sort, 456-467
    string, 288-294
    of strings, 294
    subscript, 264
    type compatibility, 281-282
    type declaration, 264
    type syntax display, 266
    variable parameter, 280
    parameter, 276-282
ASCII code, 184-185, Ap-29
Assembly language, 7, 8
Assertion, 205
Assignment compatible, 192
Assignment operator, 18
Assignment statement, 17-19, 40
    syntax display, 18
Atanasoff, Dr. John, 2

Bar graph, 309-312
Base type of set, 372
BASIC, 8

Batch
    data file, 27, 197-100
    mode, 26
    program, 27
`begin`, 23-24, 58, 151
Binary
    file, 396-397
    number, 161
    search, 449-453
    string, 8, 161
    tree; *see* Tree
Blank, 30, 35
Blank padding, 291
Block, 132
Body of a program, 24-26
Bookstore inventory file, 398-400
Boole, George, 36
BOOLEAN, 36, 175-180, 195; *see also*
    Flag
    assignment, 178-189, 409-411
    complement, 177, 227-228
    constant, 175, 183, 195
    data type, 36, 175-180
    expression, 36, 60, 175-180
    flag, 179-180, 345-346
    function, 238
    operator, 176-177
    printing value, 195
Boot up a computer, 28
Boundary values, 172
Branch, 507
Breaking an expression up, 206
Bubble sort, 344-347
Buffer variable, 411-416
Bug, 6, 36

Calling a procedure, 55-58
Calling expression, 236
Cancellation error, 174
Card reader, 4
`case` statement, 218-222
`case` statement syntax display, 220
Case study; *see* Program example
`case` value out of range, 220, 251
`case` versus nested `if`, 221
Central processor, 3, 11
CHAR, 15, 35, 180-188
Character codes, 183-184, Ap-29
Character data type, 180-188
Character string; *see* String
Checking special cases, 236
Child, 507

CHR, 185-186
COBOL, 8
Collating sequence, 186
Collision, 455
Column subscript, 296
Comment, 51-52, 58, 83, 88
Common divisor, 446
Comparison of `for` and `while` loop,
    105
Comparison of iteration and recursion,
    439, 433-434
Comparison of sorts, 461, 467, 469
Compatible type, 192, 281-282
Compiler, 8-10, 36
Compiler listing, 36-37
Complement, 177, 227-228
Compound statement, 82
Computer
    components, 3
    definition, 2
    memory, 3
    terminal, 4
Concatenation, 360-361
Concordance, 285, 511-517
Condition, 59-60
Conditional loop, 105
Conformant array, Ap-8
`const`, 15-16
Constant
    BOOLEAN, 175
    declaration, 15-16, 40, 160
    enumerated type, 190
    identifier, 160, 190
    parameter; *see* Parameter
Contents of memory, 3
Control Data Corporation, 161
Control flow, 58-59
Control language, 28
Control unit, 3
Copy, 19
Copying
    array, 276
    file, 382
    record, 331
    string, 359
Correspondence of parameters, 116,
    125-126, 130, 277-278
COS, 170
Counter, 74
Counting loop, 74-75, 228-229
Creating a file of records, 398-400
Creating a list, 483-485, 492-493

Cryptogram, 286
Cursor, 20, 31

Dangling `else`, 64, 99
Data area for procedure, 123
Data base, 405-410
Data file, 5, 15, 27, 197-200
Data flow, 128
Data structure, 159, 263
Data type, 34-36
Data type of arithmetic operation, 162
Debugging
    list, 518
    procedure, 87
    program, 36
    recursive procedure, 468
    techniques, 87, 97, 132, 150-151
Decision step, 59-66
Decision table, 102
Declaration part, 24-26, 86, 133
Declaration statements, 15
Declaring arrays, 266, 298
Declaring records, 327
Defensive programming, 81
Deleting list node, 496-498
Descendant, 507
Designator; *see* Function designator
Desk check, 6, 39, 67-68
Diagnostic WRITELN, 87, 151
Difference set, 375
Digit characters, 183
Dimensions of an array, 296
Discriminant, 171
Disk, 379
Disk drive, 5
DISPOSE, 497-498
`div`, 34, 162-164
Divide and conquer, 46-47
Division by zero, 36, 99
`do`, 75, 105, 223
Documentation, 51-52; *see also*
    Comment
Doubly linked list, 506
`downto`, 224
Driver program, 123
Dynamic allocation, 480-481
Dynamic data structure, 475-517

EBCDIC code, 287-288, Ap-30
Echo print, 27
Edit a program, 28
Editing a TEXT file, 381

Editing text, 368
Editor, 28, 381
Efficiency of search, 450, 454, 468
Efficiency of sort, 461, 467, 469
Element; *see* Array and List
`else`, 64
`else` dangling, 64
Empty list, 486-487
Empty set, 373
`end`, 23-24, 58, 151
End of file; *see* EOF
End of line; *see* EOLN
End-of-line mark, 197-199, 381-385
ENIAC, 2
Enter key, 20
Enumerated type, 188-190, 193-194
EOF, 197-199, 233, 382-385, 405
EOLN, 195-199, 233, 382-385
Error
    `and`/`or`, 207
    assigning real to integer, 162
    binary files, 417
    cancellation, 174
    `case` expression out of range, 222
    code number, 37, Ap-31
    in comment, 88
    dangling `else`, 99
    `div`/`mod`, 162, 207
    division by zero, 99
    EOF reached before READ, 384
    files in program statement, 416
    formal parameter type, 277
    identifier not declared, 135
    `if` statement, 88
    incompatible index type, 267
    infinite loop, 105, 151, 251, 383
    invalid operand type, 177
    message, 37, Ap-31
    missing `begin` or `end`, 151
    missing `case end`, 251
    missing parenthesis, 206
    mixing types, 207
    negative argument for LN, 207
    negative argument for SQRT, 207
    omitting READLN, 383
    out of bounds subscript, 267, 275
    out of bounds value, 192
    out of range `case` value, 251
    out of range value, 207
    overflow, 174
    parameter type, 194
    parameter usage, 127, 151

Error (*Continued*)
    pointer, 518
    PUT or GET, 417
    reading character data, 199
    representational, 174
    RESET before READ, 384
    RESET with INPUT, 380
    REWRITE before WRITE, 384
    REWRITE with OUTPUT, 381
    stack overflow, 467, 518
    string as case label, 219
    subrange, 207
    subscript range, 312
    subscript type, 313
    syntax, 127
    underflow, 174
    unit set, 416
    using parameters, 127
    with statement, 330, 363
    variant part, 354, 363
Euclid's algorithm, 446
Evaluating expressions, 165
Examples; *see* Program example
Executing a program, 9-11, 25, 36
EXP, 170
Exponent, 34, 161
Expression
    BOOLEAN, 175-178
    evaluation rules, 165
    with functions, 169-174
    operators, 164
    parameter; *see* Parameter
    parentheses, 167, 177
    simple, 18
    simplifying, 206
    in tree, 507-508

FALSE, 36, 183
Field of record, 326-330
Field selector, 327-328, 349-350
Field width, 32
file
    buffer variable, 411-416
    data, 5, 27, 197-200, 371-372
    merge, 401-405
    object, 9
    position pointer, 379-382, 412-413
    of records, 398-400
    source, 9
    TEXT, 197-198, 381-385
    type, 396-397
    update, 401, 404-405

First in first out, 503
Fixed part, 354
Flag, 179-180, 194, 201, 345-346
for statement, 73-75, 223-224
    with arrays, 268-270
    comparison with while and
      repeat, 228
    comparison with while
      statement, 105
    nested, 230-232
Formal parameter; *see* Parameter
Formatting
    integers, 29-30, 74
    output, 29-33
    reals, 31-32
    strings, 33
FORTRAN, 8
FORWARD, Ap-5
function
    argument, 170
    arithmetic, 169
    declaration syntax display, 235
    designator, 236-237
    inverse, 185
    mathematical, 169-170
    nested, 185
    recursive, 439-449
    table of, 170, Ap-1
    user-defined, 234-240

Game of life, 321-322
Games, 295-299, 320-322
Generalizing a solution, 79
GET, 412-416
Global variable, 134-135
goto, Ap-6
Graphics, 5
Graphing, 309-312
Greatest common divisor, 446

Hard-copy output, 4
Hardware, 5
Hash function, 453
Hash index, 453
Hashing, 453-456
Head of a list, 482
Hexadecimal, 219, 221
High-level languages, 7
Host type, 191

Identifier, 15
    category, 15-16
    enumerated type, 190

length, 16
local, 120, 135, 140
multiple declaration, 135
procedure names, 136
scope, 132-136
standard, 14, Ap-1
syntax diagram, 96
syntax rules, 15
if statement, 63-66, 97-103
    indentation, 99
    multiple alternatives, 100-103
    nesting, 100-103
    one alternative syntax display, 66
    syntax diagram, 97
    two alternative syntax display, 66
    versus case statement, 221
Implementing queue in array, 506
Implementing stack in array, 506
in, 222
Income tax table, 320
Incrementing a loop control variable, 107
Indentation in if statement, 88, 99
Index, 266
Infinite loop, 105, 151, 383, 518
Infix, 510
Initializing a variable, 77
Inorder traversal, 509
INPUT, 15, 197, 381-385
Input; see also Reading
    data file, 15, 197-200
    device, 3
    list, 21, 182
    parameter; see Parameter
    to a procedure, 111
Input/output
    BOOLEAN values, 195
    enumerated types, 193
    parameter; see Parameter
Inserting list node, 498-500
Insertion sort, 459-461
INTEGER, 161
Integer
    format, 29-30, 161
    range, 162
    value, 29
Interactive mode, 26
Intersection, 374-375
Intialization counters, 148
Invariant, 205
Inventory file, 398-410
Inverse of a function, 185

ISO International Standard, 11, Ap-8
Iteration versus recursion, 439, 443-444

Joystick, 4

Key to a record, 453
Key to an array, 342
Keyboard, 4
Keypunch, 4

label, Ap-6
Labels for case, 218
Last in first out, 500
Leaf, 507
Linked list; see List
Left associative rule, 165
Length of a string, 290-291, 358-359
Letter characters, 183
Library of procedures, 69
List, 481-500
    creation, 483-485, 492-493
    deletion, 496-498
    dummy element, 489
    element, 482
    head, 482
    insertion, 498-500
    linked, 481
    maintenance, 487-500
    multiply linked, 506
    node, 481
    printing, 485
    stored in array, 482-483
    traversal, 485
LN, 170
Loader, 8-10
Local
    array, 277-278
    identifier, 57, 75, 120, 135, 140
    variable, 75; see also Local identifier
    variable stack, 430-432
Log onto a computer, 28
Logical complement, 177
Loop
    body, 82
    control variable, 74, 105, 223, 268
    counting, 74, 228-229
    for statement, 73-75, 223-224
    infinite, 105, 151
    invariant, 205

Loop (*Continued*)
    nested, 229-233
    `repeat` statement, 225-226
    termination condition, 226
    `while` statement, 104-110
Lowercase, 14
    to uppercase, 186, 240

Machine language, 7-8
Magnetic tape, 5
Main program, 55, 58-59, 133
Mantissa, 161
Matching a data base, 401-410
Mathematical formulas, 166-168
MAXINT, 34, 183
Memory, 3, 11, 25
    for procedure, 123
Menu, 225, 311
Mergesort, 472
Merging files, 401-405
`mod`, 34, 162-164
Monitor, 4
Mouse, 4
Multidimensional array, 295-301
Multiple alternative decisions, 100-103, 153
Multiple declaration, 135
Multiple linked list, 506
Multiple operators, 162, 164-166
Mutually exclusive conditions, 101

Naming identifiers, 17
Naming procedures, 131
Negate, 19
Nested functions, 185
Nested
    `if` statements, 100-103, 221
    loops, 229-233
    procedures, 132
    `with` statements, 350-351
NEW, 476-479
NIL, 485
Node, 475-476
Non-terminating loop; *see* Infinite loop
`not`, 176-177
Number of parameters, 125

Object file, 9-10
ODD, 174
`of`, 266, 296, 372, 397
Operating system, 28
Operator
    arithmetic, 162

BOOLEAN, 175-176
    precedence, 165, 177
    relational, 177
    set, 174-175
`or`, 176
ORD, 183-185
Order of procedures, 58, 136
Ordinal, 183-184
OUTPUT, 15, 381-385
Output; *see also* Printing
    of BOOLEAN value, 195
    data file, 15
    device, 3
    of enumerated type, 193
    list, 22, 31
    parameter; *see* Parameter
    from a procedure, 111
    as a table, 108
Overflow error, 174

PACK, Ap-7
Packed array, 289-294
    assignment, 289, 294
    comparison, 292-294
    printing, 290, 294
    reading, 290-291
Padding a string, 291
PAGE, 108, 292, 389
Parallel arrays, 334-335
Parameter, 111-127
    actual, 114, 123-124
    array, 276-280, Ap-8
    array element, 280
    constant as, 118, 121, 125-126
    correspondence, 116, 125-127
    correpondence for arrays, 277-278, 281
    error in type, 194
    error in usage, 127, 151
    expression as, 118, 121, 125-126
    file, 390
    formal, 114-115, 124-126
    of function, 170
    input, 121
    input/output, 121
    list, 111
    output, 121
    syntax diagram, 124
    record, 331
    stack, 430-432
    syntax rules, 123-127

transposition of, 127
value, 117-118, 120, 125
variable, 117-118, 120-121, 125
variable versus value, 280
Parsing expressions, 473-474
Partition, 462-464
Pascal, 8, 11
Percentage as a fraction, 71
Personal computer, 2
Pivot value, 462
Pointer, 464, 476-480
  assignment, 478-480
  variable, 476-480
Popping a stack, 500, 502
Portable programs, 7
Position pointer, 379-382, 412-413
Postfix, 510
Postorder traversal, 510
PRED, 183-185
Prefix, 510
Preorder traversal, 510
Prime number, 201
Printer, 4
Printing; *see also* Writing
  array, 268
  BOOLEAN value, 194
  check, 246-251
  enumerated type, 195
  list, 485
  packed array, 290
  record, 328-329, 332
  scientific notation, 13, 32
  set, 378
  table, 108
Problem inputs, 49
Problem outputs, 49
Problem solving, 6, 45-90
  divide and conquer, 48
  extending a solution, 69-70
  generalizing a solution, 69
  solution by analogy, 70
  understanding the problem, 49
procedure, 52-59, 86-87, 111-136
  block, 133
  body, 54
  call statement, 55-58, 86, 124, 153
  call syntax display, 58, 124
  data area, 123
  debugging, 150-151
  declaration, 54-55, 58, 124, 133, 153
  declaration syntax display, 57, 124
  heading, 54

input, 111, 121
nesting of, 132-136
order of, 58, 136
output, 111, 121
parameter, 111-136; *see* Parameter
recursive, 427-439
similarity to program, 86-87
testing, 123
tracing, 150-151
program
  block, 133
  body, 24-26, 86
  definition of, 2, 6
  driver, 123
  statement, 15-16, 40
  syntax display, 16
Program example
  adding arrays, 277-278
  addition table, 232
  area and perimeter, 356
  arithmetic functions, 169
  average speed and cost of trip, 31
  balancing a checkbook, 137-143
  binary search, 450-453
  building a tree, 514-515
  changing case, 239
  check amount in words, 246-251
  concordance of text, 511-517
  converting to uppercase letter, 239
  copying a file, 382
  copying a string, 359
  counting blanks, 181
  counting letters, 285
  creating a file of records, 398-400
  data base inquiry, 406-411
  differences between array values
    and average, 268
  distance from point to origin, 330
  echo a file, 233, 397
  echo print a batch file, 198
  entering a move, 298
  exchanging two array values, 280
  Fibonacci numbers, 445
  finding the first letter, 64
  general sum and average, 80
  generating cryptogram, 286
  grading an exam, 144-150
  greatest common divisor, 446
  hash index computation, 454
  home budget computation, 270-274
  inches to centimeters, 13
  income tax computation, 121-122

Program Example (*Continued*)
    inserting in a hash table, 456
    insertion sort, 460-461
    insurance dividends, 70
    list deletion, 496
    maintaining a list, 487-500
    merging files, 401-405
    mother's day message, 52
    multiple employee payroll, 83-86
    ordering three numbers, 111-115
    overtime pay, 69
    payroll with conditional deduction, 61
    plot a sine curve, 173
    prime numbers, 201-205
    printing a letter, 291-292
    printing a list, 485
    printing a message, 12
    printing a row of asterisks, 119
    printing a set, 378
    printing a triangle, 119
    printing array backwards, 432-434
    printing collating sequence, 186
    printing digits in a number, 164
    printing exam statistics, 332
    printing form letter, 385-389
    printing isosceles triangle, 231
    printing day string, 218
    printing powers of a number, 106
    printing tic-tac-toe board, 297
    product of nonzero data, 109-110
    queue deletion, 505
    queue insertion, 504
    quicksort, 462-467
    raising variable to a power, 234
    reading a number as characters, 187
    reading a packed array, 290-291
    reading a positive integer, 180
    reading a set, 378
    reading an enumerated type, 195
    reading menu choice, 226
    reading next non-blank, 226-227
    reading next non-letter, 239
    reading part of array, 283
    reading record, 351
    reading string, 358-359
    recursive array comparison, 442-443
    recursive array search, 440-442
    recursive factorial computation, 444
    recursive palindrome generator, 428
    recursive summation, 440-441
    recursively printing array, 434-436
    returning uppercase letter, 239
    returning days in a month, 237
    returning type DAY result, 237
    sales analysis, 302-312
    searching a list, 486
    selection sort, 458
    simple payroll, 23, 27
    size of a blob, 447-449
    stack pop, 502
    stack push, 501
    stack use, 502
    string concatenation, 360-361
    student grading, 335-342
    sum and average of integers, 80
    sum and average of two numbers, 49
    sum and average using a procedure, 128-130
    table of temperatures, 108
    testing for equal arrays, 279
    testing for filled array, 298
    text analyzer, 240-245
    Towers of Hanoi, 436-439
    tree insertion, 515-517
    tree traversal, 509
    updating time of day, 333
    value of coins, 29
    wheel of fortune, 390-395
Program file, 5
Program flag, 179-180, 194, 201, 345-346
Program input, 10
Program output, 10
Program style
    allowing for array expansion, 275
    analysis of merge, 405
    array parameters in recursive procedures, 436
    avoiding out of bounds error, 275
    caution using the with statement, 330
    checking boundary values, 170
    checking special cases, 236
    choosing formal parameter names, 131
    choosing identifier names, 17
    comment after end, 83
    defensive programming, 81
    files as variable parameters, 390
    list insertion, 498-500
    loop control variables as local variables, 75

multiple alternative decisions, 101
printing a table, 108
program flags as procedure results, 194
referencing a nonlocal array, 299
separately testing a program system, 132
structuring the if statement, 67
testing for an empty list, 487
top down design, 143
use of blank space, 24
use of comments and color, 58
use of constants, 63
use of scratch file, 395
use of semicolon, 82
use of uppercase, lowercase, and computer type, 14
using assertions as comments, 205
using comments, 51
validating the value of variables, 104
variable versus value parameters, 280
when to use function or procedure, 239
Writing driver programs, 123
Writing formal parameter lists, 122-123
Writing if statements, 99
Programmer, 7
Programmer-defined data type; see Enumerated type
Programming language, 7
Prompt, 22, 35
Proper subset, 376
Proper superset, 377
Protection of value parameters, 280
Pseudo code, 60, 72
Punch card, 5, 26
Pushing onto a stack, 500-501
PUT, 413-416

Quadratic equation, 170
Quadratic hashing, 456
Queue, 503-506
Quicksort, 462-467

Radians, 171-172
Random access to array, 275
READ, 182, 384, 398
Reading
    binary file, 398

BOOLEAN value, 195
    character data, 35, 181-183, 193-200
    enumerated type, 193-194
    packed array, 290-291
    part of array, 282-283
    record, 332, 351
    set, 378
    string, 358
    text file, 193-200, 381-385
READLN, 14, 19-21, 35, 40, 182, 196-197, 233, 383-384
REAL, 15, 35, 161
Real
    format, 32, 161
    number, 34, 71
    number range, 161
record, 325-341, 348-362
    component, 326
    definition, 325
    of dynamic data structure, 476-480
    field, 326-330
    key, 342, 453
    parameter, 331-332
    printing, 328-329
    of records, 348-351
    reading, 332, 351
    for storing string, 357-362
    syntax display, 327, 354
    variable, 326-329, 349
    variants, 352-357
Recursion, 426-449
    function, 439-449
    procedure, 427-439
    versus iteration, 439, 443-444
Recursive descent parser, 473-474
Refinement of algorithm, 47-48, 50
Relational operator, 59-60, 177, 182
Relational operator with strings, 292-294
repeat statement, 225-228
    comparison with for and while, 228
    syntax display, 225
repeat-until; see repeat statement
Repeating a program body, 83-86
Repetition; see Loop
Representational error, 174
Reserved words, 13
RESET, 379-380, 412-413
Retrieve from memory, 3
Retrieving records from data base, 406-410

Return from procedure call, 58-59
Return key, 20
REWRITE, 379-381, 414-415
Right justified, 30
Root of function, 471
Root of an equation, 170
ROUND, 170-171
Row-major order, 297
Row subscript, 296
RUN, 28
Run-time error, 36, 38-39

Scientific notation, 21, 32
Scope of identifier, 132-136
Scope rule, 134
Scratch file, 391, 395
Search time comparison, 450, 454, 468
Searching
    array, 342-344, 449-456
    data base, 405-410
    list, 486
    string, 361-362
    tree, 508, 515-517
Secondary memory, 5
Secondary storage, 379
Secondary storage device, 3
Selector, 218-220
Selection sort, 369, 456-458
Semicolon, 23-24, 64, 82
Semicolon use with if statement, 64
Sentinel record, 401
Sentinel value, 109-110, 195
Separate testing, 132, 150-151
Sequential access to array, 275
set, 221-223, 371-395
    assignment, 373-374
    with case, 223
    in decision, 221-223
    difference, 373-375
    empty, 373
    equality, 376-377
    intersection, 374-375
    membership, 222
    operator, 375
    printing, 378
    reading, 378
    relational operator, 376-377
    type, 372
    union, 374-375
    universal, 373
    value, 221-223
Sibling, 507

Side effect, 134
Simple data type, 159
SIN, 170
Software, 5
Solid-state electronics, 2
Sorting an array, 344-347, 456-467
Sorting three numbers, 111-115
Sorting time comparison, 461, 467, 469
Source file, 9-10
Special symbol, 13, Ap-1
SQR, 170
SQRT, 170
Stack, 430-432, 500-502
stack overflow, 467
Stack overflow error, 518
Standard data type, 34-36
Standard deviation, 339-342
Standard for programming language, 8
Standard identifier, 13
Standard Pascal, 8
Statistics, 332, 335-342
Stepwise refinement, 47
Stopping case, 426
Stored program, 2
String
    binary, 161
    case label error, 219
    concatenation, 360-361
    copy, 289, 359-360
    delimiter, 38
    formats, 33
    length, 290-291, 358-359
    manipulation, 323-324, 358-362
    printing, 21, 35, 38
    prompt, 35
    read, 358
    search, 361-362
    stored in array, 288-294
    stored in record, 357-362
Structure chart, 52-54, 128
Structured programming, 6, 11
Stub, 130
Subproblem, 46-47, 52-54, 57
Subrange type, 191-192
Subrecord, 349
Subscript, 264, 267
Subscript range error, 312
Subscripted variable, 264
Subset, 376
Substring, 359, 361
Subtree, 507, 509
SUCC, 183-185

Summing a list, 76-78
Superset, 377
Syntax, 6
Syntax diagram, 96-97, Ap-19
Syntax diagram formal parameter list, 124
Syntax display
  assignment statement, 18
  `array`, 266, 296
  `case`, 220
  CHR, 186
  constant, 16, 160
  comment, 51
  counting loop, 77
  DISPOSE, 498
  `div` and `mod`, 163
  enumerated type declaration, 190
  EOF, 199, 385
  EOLN, 196, 199, 385
  `file`, 397
  `for` statement, 223
  `function`, 235-236
  GET, 413
  `if` statement, 66
  NEW, 479
  ODD, 174
  ORD, 185
  pointer, 479, 480
  PRED, 185
  `procedure` call, 58, 124
  `procedure` declaration, 57, 124
  `program` statement, 16
  PUT, 413
  READ/READLN, 21, 182, 197, 384, 398
  `record` type, 327, 354
  referencing field with pointer, 479
  `repeat` statement, 225
  RESET, 380, 413
  REWRITE, 381, 415
  set assignment, 374
  set membership operator, 222
  set operator, 375
  set relational operator, 377
  set type, 372
  set value, 222
  subrange type, 191
  SUCC, 185
  variable declaration, 16
  `while`, 105
  `with` statement, 329
  WRITE/WRITELN, 22, 30, 384, 398
  PUT, 415

Syntax error, 9, 36-38, 97; see also Error
Syntax for parameter list, 123-127

Tabular output, 108
Tag field, 352, 363
Tape, 5
Target of search, 342
Temporary variable, 206
Terminal, 4
Terminating condition, 226, 428
Test data, 87-88
Testing a program, 87-88
Testing a program system, 132
Testing procedures, 123
TEXT, 381-385
Text editor, 368
Text file, 197-198, 381-385
`then`; see `if` statement
Tic-tac-toe, 295-299, 320-321
Timesharing, 26
`to`, 223
Top down design, 128-130, 143
Towers of Hanoi, 426-427, 436-439
Tracing algorithm, 67-68
Tracing procedure, 150-151
Tracing recursive procedure, 427-430
Translating a program, 9, 36
Traversing a list, 485
Traversing a tree, 508-510
Tree, 506-518
  expression, 507-508
  maintenance, 511-517
  root, 507
  search, 508, 515-517
  terminology, 507
  traversal, 508-510
TRUE, 36, 183
TRUNC, 170-171
Turbo Pascal, Ap-15
`type`, 189, 191
Type compatible, 192, 281-282

UCSD Pascal, Ap-9
Undefined variable, 25, 39
Underflow error, 174
Underscore, 16
Understanding the problem, 49
Union, 374-375
Universal set, 373
UNPACK, Ap-7
`until`, 225
Updating a file, 401, 404-405

Uppercase, 14
Uppercase from lowercase, 186
Uppercase to lowercase, 240

Validating variable values, 104
Value parameter; *see* Parameter
var, 15-16
Variable declaration, 15-16, 40
Variable parameter; *see* Parameter
Variant part, 354
Video screen, 4
von Neumann, Dr. John, 2

What if question, 79
Wheel of fortune, 390-395

while statement, 104-110, 153
    comparison with for and
        repeat, 228
    comparison with for statement,
        105
    nested, 233
Wirth, Dr. Nicklaus, 11
with statement, 328-330
    error, 330, 363
    nested, 350-351
WRITE, 30, 40, 384, 398
WRITELN, 12, 21-22, 33, 40, 383-384
WRITELN for diagnostic, 87
Writing; *see* Printing
Writing a binary file, 398

Reference Guide to Pascal Statements *(continued from first page)*

Statement	Example of Use

procedure declaration	`procedure PRINTSET (INSET : GRADESET);`
	
	`{Prints the elements of set INSET.}`

local variable *declaration*	`var` `    NEXTCH : CHAR;`

for statement
if statement with
function designator
WRITE/WRITELN
procedure
	`begin  {PRINTSET}`
	`    for NEXTCH := 'A' to 'Z' do`
	`        if MEMBER(NEXTCH, INSET) then`
	`            WRITE (NEXTCH);`
	`    WRITELN                        {terminate output line}`
	`end; {PRINTSET}`

program body
WRITELN procedure
 	
assignment (integer)
	`begin {GUIDE}`
	`    WRITELN ('Registration data for ', SCHOOL);`
	`    WRITELN;                            {skip a line}`
	`    I := 0; COUNTPROBATION := 0;     {initialize counts}`

with statement
compound statement
assignment (string)
prompt
READLN procedure
assignment (enumerated)
assignment (pointer)
	`with CURSTU do`
	`    begin                      {define fields of CURSTU}`
	`        NAME := 'Jackson, Michael B. ';`
	`        WRITE ('Enter GPA for ', NAME, ': ');`
	`        READLN (GPA);`
	`        INCOLLEGE := ARTS;`
	`        NEXTSTU := NIL`
	`    end; {with}`

case statement with
record field as
case selector
	`case CURSTU.INCOLLEGE of`
	`    ARTS      : WRITELN ('Arts Major')`
	`    BUSINESS  : WRITELN ('Business Major');`
	`    EDUCATION : WRITELN ('Education Major');`
	`    GENERAL   : {empty statement}`
	`end; {case}`

if statement
(with else if
and else)
 	
incrementing
a counter
	`if CURSTU.GPA >= DEANSLIST then`
	`    WRITELN (CURSTU.NAME, ' is on the Deans List')`
	`else if CURSTU.GPA < PROBATION then`
	`    begin`
	`        WRITELN (CURSTU.NAME, ' is on probation');`
	`        COUNTPROBATION := COUNTPROBATION + 1`
	`    end`
	`else`
	`    WRITELN (CURSTU.NAME);`

Statement	Example of Use
increment subscript	`I := I + 1;` {increment I}
assignment (array element)	`MAJOR[I] := CURSTU.INCOLLEGE;` {save in array}
assignment (set)	`GRADES := ['A'..'F', 'I', 'W'];` {initialize set}
set union	`GRADES := GRADES + ['P'];` {add 'P' to set}
procedure call	`PRINTSET (GRADES);` {print the set}
RESET procedure	`RESET (INFILE);`
access file buffer	`NEXTCH := INFILE^;` {save first character}
GET procedure	`GET (INFILE);` {advance file pointer}
if (with else)	`if NEXTCH = BLANK then`
READLN procedure	`   READLN (INFILE)` {skip line starting with blank}
with file INFILE	`else`
	`   WRITE (NEXTCH);`
while statement	`while not EOF(INFILE) do`
	`   begin`
READ from INFILE	`      READ (INFILE, NEXTCH);`
WRITE procedure	`      WRITE (NEXTCH)`
	`   end; {while}` {echo each character}
REWRITE procedure	`REWRITE (OUTFILE);`
define file buffer	`OUTFILE^ := CURSTU;` {save CURSTU in file buffer}
PUT procedure	`PUT (OUTFILE);` {copy CURSTU to OUTFILE}
WRITE to OUTFILE	`WRITE (OUTFILE, CURSTU);` {second copy of CURSTU}
NEW statement	`NEW (CLASSLIST);` {allocate new list node}
assignment (record)	`CLASSLIST^ := CURSTU;` {save CURSTU in new node}
repeat statement	`repeat`
	`   WRITELN (CLASSLIST^.NAME, CLASSLIST^.GPA :5:1);`
assignment (pointer)	`   CLASSLIST := CLASSLIST^.NEXTSTU` {to next node}
	`until CLASSLIST = NIL` {at end of list}
program end	`end. {GUIDE}`